Cook Book

Stella Standard

BONANZA BOOKS
NEW YORK

Other Books by Stella Standard

More Than Cooking

Whole Grain Cookery

Stella Standard's Cook Book

Complete American Cook Book

Stella Standard's Menus and Recipes for All Occasions

Kitchen Garden Book

The Art of Fruit Cookery

PREFACE

STELLA STANDARD does not tell us how the first egg was cooked, the egg that was laid by the first hen. She does not know. It was long before her time. But what she does know and tell us is of far greater gastronomical importance: she has used her feminine charm and powers of persuasion to get from some of the greatest chefs of today the recipes of their famous creations which are not to be found in any modern cookbooks. This is, of course, a very valuable feature of her book, but it is by no means the only one. She covers the whole field of preparing for the table every kind of food that is available today, both fresh from the land and scientifically preserved, so that our meals may do us good and be a real joy at the same time.

Everything has already been said, and time after time, that was worth saying; everything has already been written time after time about the cooking of our food; in spite of which new books and new cookbooks are being printed, bound, sold, and read year after year. It is as it should be. Old truths may be as old as the world, but there will always be a new way of presenting them in a dress that will appeal to us. Heaven may be overcrowded with good people, but there never will be too many good people on earth, nor will there ever be too many good cookery books: this latest book of Stella Standard is one of the good, of the very good cookbooks, which is why I welcome its publication and wish it a great success.

ANDRÉ L. SIMON
President, The Wine and Food Society

AUTHOR'S NOTE

On rereading the introductions to the chapters and the "chatter" indulged in occasionally between recipes, I feel the reader may agree that I have written enough. I hope, however, that in addition to my recipes and those of others, my comments upon food and upon travel may stimulate many to find real pleasure in sampling both.

S.S.

Contents

PREFACE by André L. Simon   5

AUTHOR'S NOTE   7

HORS D'OEUVRE & ENTRÉES   13

    Cocktail Accessories & Sandwiches   14

    Pâtés & Terrines   19

    Salad, Vegetable & Fish Entrées   28

    Quiches & Crêpes   40

    Egg Dishes   49

    Pastas   61

    Cheese Dishes   78

    Rice Dishes   83

SOUPS   89

    Vegetable & Meat Soups   90

    Fish Soups   107

FISH & SHELLFISH   119

MEATS   149

    Beef   150

    Veal   172

    Lamb   196

    Pork   213

    Poultry & Game   230

    Special Dishes   265

VEGETABLES 275

SALADS 331

SAUCES 339

BREADS—DAILY & FANCY 357

DESSERTS 371
    Les Soufflés 372
    Puddings, Molds & Crêpes 379
    Fruit Desserts 406
    Pastry, Pies & Tarts 415
    Cakes & Cookies 427
    Frozen Desserts 445

MENUS 452

KITCHEN EQUIPMENT & PANTRY SHELF 460

WEIGHTS & MEASURES 464

INDEX 467

NOTE: *Recipe titles appearing in italics may be found by consulting the index.*

Hors d'Oeuvre & Entrées

Cocktail Accessories & Sandwiches · Pâtés & Terrines · Salad, Vegetable & Fish Entrées · Quiches & Crêpes · Egg, Pasta, Cheese & Rice Dishes ·

ACCORDING to the Oxford French dictionary the word entrée means, beginning, enter, debut, etc. One wonders when and how the custom of calling the main dish the entrée began. It reminds me of the answer I got when I asked a taxi driver in Naples why he pronounced Capri—Capree. He replied "on account of the Americans"—a tribute to the power of tourism and the popular song! In this book entrée is a preliminary.

This large section gathers everything together that might be served with cocktails and as a first course. Many of these dishes can also be served for lunch, dinner, supper or a buffet. Pastas, for instance, may be served for lunch or supper as a main dish, or for the first course of lunch or dinner as in Italy. Rather than scatter them throughout the book, I have included all such dishes in this section in the hope that this will be a helpful arrangement. The spreads, dips and hot or cold appetizers suitable for serving at cocktail parties should be dispensed with before a dinner because they dull the appetite. A quiche is a lovely first course for dinner, an excellent main dish for lunch or supper. Oeufs Bourgignons,* delicious to begin an important dinner, also make a fine luncheon dish with a green salad. Meat, game and liver pâtés and terrines are the greatest of all hors d'œuvre—perhaps the gourmet's favorite. Serve one with crusty French or Italian bread, sweet butter and a bottle of good wine, and it will be a promise of what is to come from the imaginative cook. A molded salmon mousse is a most useful first course; it is beautiful to look at, harmonizes with almost anything that may follow and settles the question of the fish course. A vegetable entrée, such as Artichokes or Mushrooms à la Grècque, is a good choice to precede a main-dish fish soup when there are no vegetable accompaniments. Stuffed crêpes or Friandises are very good to serve first when a light main course follows such as scaloppine or fish. Try Salade Niçoise when the main dish is a rich pasta casserole.

* Recipe titles appearing in italics may be found by consulting the index.

Fortunately our large country provides an endless variety of foods to make into dishes which will suit hundreds of differing tastes, for we are from every land on earth.

Cocktail Accessories & Sandwiches

COCKTAIL CHEESE BALL

2 tablespoons soft butter
½ pound cream cheese
¼ pound Roquefort cheese
2 cloves garlic, crushed
½ green pepper, ground
¼ to ⅓ cup chopped red pimento
½ cup chopped browned pecans or walnuts

Have the butter and cheeses at room temperature. Blend them together, then mix in the other ingredients, except the nuts. Form the cheese mixture into a ball and chill. When the ball is firm roll it in the nuts so they cover it entirely. Serve surrounded by crackers. Roquefort is usually salty enough, but taste the mixture and add a little salt if it needs it. Blue cheese or Gorgonzola may be used instead of Roquefort.

ANCHOVY GARLIC SPREAD

4 ounces cream cheese
3 tablespoons anchovy paste
2 tablespoons grated onion
1 teaspoon Worcestershire sauce
4 cloves garlic, crushed
Sour cream

Have the cheese softened at room temperature for easy mixing. Blend everything together and mix it with some sour cream so that it is light and fluffy. Store in a stone jar in the refrigerator. This keeps well. Serve on small squares of dark bread or crackers.

SALMON OR TUNA FISH DIP WITH RED CAVIAR

1 7-ounce can salmon or tuna fish
½ cup fresh breadcrumbs
2 or 3 tablespoons lemon juice
2 or 3 tablespoons oil
½ cup red caviar
Garnish:
Lettuce
Greek or Italian olives in oil

At 60 rue Lafayette in Paris there is a restaurant of the people called Diamantaires. The food is a blend of Greek and Turkish. A captain let me come and watch him make Tarama, a wonderful hors d'œuvre made of puréed fish, bland oil, French breadcrumbs, and lemon juice. The fish was some sort of salmon mixture that came in kegs—quite unavailable in America. I made a very good approximation, using either salmon or tuna puréed in a blender with fresh breadcrumbs, lemon juice, and oil to a thick creamy texture. It is served on small plates with a garnish of lettuce and olives. Tarama has a little extra oil sprinkled over it when it is served. For a cocktail party a fine way to serve this is to put it in a bowl and empty ½ cup of caviar over it, gently mixing it a little to avoid breaking the eggs. Serve with thin buttered hot toast fingers.

CAVIAR CANAPÉS

Red or black caviar
Sour cream
Tomato paste (optional)

Minced green onions
Few drops of lemon juice

There is nothing new about caviar canapés but what is better for whetting the appetite or to serve with any kind of a drink, be it wine or spirits? There are very good domestic caviars which are not as expensive as the imported. Mix sour cream with minced onions and spread it on squares of toast or dark bread or on crackers. Put a teaspoon of red or black caviar on top and sprinkle with lemon juice. For a decorative variation, add tomato paste to the sour cream, and top with red caviar.

PIMENTO CANAPÉS

1 or 2 canned pimentos
4 or 5 tablespoons soft Roquefort
  or Gorgonzola cheese

1 tablespoon soft sweet butter
2 or 3 tablespoons sour cream
2 or 3 tablespoons grated onion

Mash the pimento coarsely with a fork. Blend all the other ingredients to a smooth paste, then work in the pimento. Spread on toast rounds or crackers.

RAW VEGETABLES WITH AIOLI DIP

1 cup *Blender Aioli Sauce*
1 cup sour cream
  Tender raw cauliflowerets
  Carrot sticks
  Cucumber sticks

Cherry tomatoes
Pascal celery
Endive
Radishes

Make the *Aioli Sauce* (omitting the hot water) with 5 or 6 crushed cloves of garlic. This sauce thickens in the blender so do not cook it as you would to serve with hot vegetables. Add the sour cream. Pour the dip into a serving bowl and arrange the vegetables carefully on small platters.

MEATBALLS WITH DIP

½ pound ground beef
½ pound calf's or yearling liver,
    ground
½ cup fresh fine breadcrumbs
    Salt and pepper
1 egg, beaten
4 tablespoons Parmesan cheese
    Butter for frying

Dip:
1 cup tomato sauce or catsup
1 tablespoon lemon juice
1 tablespoon chopped parsley,
    tarragon or chervil
¼ cup sherry or Madeira or
    ⅓ cup sour cream
Garnish:
    Watercress or parsley
    Toothpicks

Mix the ground meats with all the other ingredients, form into tiny balls, and chill. Just before serving, brown quickly in very hot butter 3 or 4 minutes. Keep warm if necessary in a 300° oven with the door open. Serve on a platter garnished with watercress or parsley, and have toothpicks handy to dip the balls in the sauce. For the dip mix the ingredients together, using either wine or sour cream. Serve it in a bowl. Serves 8, or more if other snacks are provided.

CHEESE POPOVERS

1 cup boiling water
½ cup butter
½ cup flour

½ cup grated Parmesan cheese
Dash nutmeg
2 eggs

Put the boiling water and butter in a saucepan over a low flame and when the butter is melted add the flour and stir vigorously until the mixture is smooth. Add the cheese and nutmeg and when it is well blended let the mixture cool. Before baking beat in the eggs, one at a time. Drop small teaspoonfuls onto a greased cookie sheet and put in a 375° oven for 20 to 25 minutes. Serve immediately. Makes 30 little puffs.

CHEESE AND WINE PASTE

2 cups grated Swiss or Gruyère
    cheese, or 6 ounces sliced Brie
2 tablespoons sweet butter

Dash nutmeg
1 clove garlic, crushed
⅓ cup dry white wine

Warm the seasonings, butter, and wine in a saucepan over a gentle flame, then stir in the cheese until it melts and the mixture is smooth. Put it in a stone jar and allow it to cool. Serve from the jar with dark bread squares or crackers. A Moselle or Neufchâtel is a good wine for this.

CHEDDAR CHEESE WAFERS

½ pound grated Cheddar cheese
½ cup softened sweet butter
1 cup sifted flour

1 tablespoon curry powder (or
  Worcestershire Sauce)

If the cheese is brought to room temperature it will mix easily with the softened butter. Sift the flour and curry powder together and blend with the butter and cheese. Worcestershire Sauce may replace the curry if preferred. Roll the mixture into a sausage 1½ inches in diameter and chill several hours. Just before serving cut into slices ¼-inch thick and bake on a cookie sheet about 12 minutes in a 350° oven, or until light brown.

PAILLETTES PARMESAN
(Cheese Straws)

6½ tablespoons Parmesan cheese
¼ cup sweet butter

½ cup sifted flour
¼ teaspoon mustard

Soften the butter to room temperature and mix with the cheese. Mix the flour and mustard and cut it in as you would for pie crust. Chill several hours. Roll out to ⅓-inch thickness and cut straws ⅓-inch wide and 4 inches long. Bake at 375° to a light brown, about 12 minutes. Serve with soup or with cocktails.

MUSHROOM SANDWICHES

½ pound fresh mushrooms
2 tablespoons minced onions
3 tablespoons butter
  Salt and freshly ground pepper

3 tablespoons lemon juice or
  Madeira or sherry
3 tablespoons cream
  Good buttered bread

Remove ⅟₁₆ inch from the stems of fine white mushrooms. Brush the mushrooms to clean them. Slice them very thin and sauté them with the onion 3 minutes (no more) in the butter. Add the seasonings and lemon juice (if used) while they are cooking, then add the cream. Put them in a wooden chopping bowl and chop them fine to make a spread. If wine is used, add the wine and cream after the mushrooms are chopped to make the mixture spreadable. Butter squares of homemade or very good firm bread, light or dark, and spread with the mushroom mixture. They may be covered with thin buttered bread or left open. These are delicious sandwiches for cocktails or for serving with lunch.

STRIPED SANDWICH

1 loaf bread
Fish butters:
   ½ cup sweet butter
   ½ cup cooked ground salmon,
      shrimp, crabmeat, or
      lobster
Meat butters:
   ½ cup butter
   ½ cup cooked ground ham,
      poultry, or sausage

Cheese butters:
   ½ cup sweet butter
   ½ cup Brie, Liederkranz,
      Gruyère, or Blue cheese
Frosting:
   1 cup sour cream
   ½ cup cream cheese
   3 hard-boiled eggs, sieved
   2 teaspoons curry powder
Garnish:
   Chopped nuts or parsley

Get good homemade-type bread and remove the crusts. Cut through the loaf horizontally so you have 4 or 5 long slices. Have the butter at room temperature so that it may be mixed with the ground ingredients to a smooth paste. Use any two or three different pastes. Put the first slice on a damp towel and spread it with one of the pastes, then add another slice of bread, and another paste. Continue until all is used, the top being bread. Press the slices together gently, wrap the whole in the damp towel, and refrigerate (do not freeze) for 24 hours. Before serving blend the frosting ingredients to a smooth paste and spread the top and sides. If you want to be really fancy use a pastry tube to decorate the top. Sprinkle with just 2 or 3 tablespoons of ground nuts or parsley. Serve the loaf from a platter, cutting it in half-inch slices like a loaf cake. Its size depends on the size of the original loaf of bread. It also may be made with a round loaf of good rye bread. Remove the crust and cut in thin slices. Any left may be refrigerated and used the next day. This is nice either for a cocktail party or for the tea table.

COCKTAIL OR SUPPER LOAF

Loaf of French or Italian bread
Soft butter
Sesame seeds or poppy seeds
1 tablespoon mustard or curry
   powder

2 tablespoons anchovy paste or
   3 cloves crushed garlic
Bermuda onion
Bel Paese cheese

Use French or Italian bread with fine crisp crust. Cut the loaf diagonally to the base in slices ¾ inch thick. Have plenty of butter softened to mix with the seeds and any of the seasonings you choose. Spread both sides of each slice. Fit a thin slice of onion and a slice of cheese between each two slices—the more filling the better. Wrap the loaf well in aluminum foil, set it on a baking pan, and heat in a 375° oven 20 minutes before serving. Bring the loaf whole to the table and break or cut it apart to serve. It is good with cold meats and a salad.

BAKED SANDWICHES

Hamburger or frankfurter buns
Butter, or olive oil and crushed
  garlic
Filling No. 1:
  1 cup cubed ham or bologna
  1 cup cubed Cheddar cheese
  ¼ cup mayonnaise
  1 teaspoon curry powder
  Thin sliced onions or pickle
    relish

Filling No. 2:
  Sliced Bel Paese or Mozzarella
    cheese
  Sliced tomatoes
  Anchovy fillets
  Red canned pimentos
Accompaniments:
  Ale or beer
  Black olives in oil

Get good buns and cut them in half. Butter the cut sides, or sauté them a moment in olive oil with some crushed garlic. For filling No. 1, toss the ham, cheese, and the mayonnaise and curry powder together. Put a thin slice of onion or a tablespoon of relish on the bottom half of each bun, spread with the ham mixture, and cover with the top. Put a skewer in each bun to hold on the top, put in a pan, cover tightly with foil, and bake 15 to 18 minutes in a 375° oven. Filling for 6 buns. For filling No. 2, which is Italian, sauté the cut sides of the buns in olive oil and garlic. Cover the bottom half with cheese, then a thick slice of skinned tomato, 2 or 3 anchovy fillets, and a layer of pimento. Skewer on the top and bake the same as the ham and cheese buns. These baked sandwiches may also be made with dark rye bread or Italian or French bread.

Pâtés & Terrines

LA TERRINE DE LAPIN LORRAINE
Capucin Gourmand, Nancy

Driving through the peaceful countryside of Champagne and Lorraine one finds few reminders that this has been a battleground for centuries, including the last two world wars. Our party arrived in Nancy near dinner time and discovered that our hotel conveniently backed up against "the best restaurant in Lorraine," the Capucin Gourmand, where we spent most of our happy dining hours. The owner, M. Georges Romain, is one of the great chefs of France, and certainly a generous one, for he gave me over a dozen recipes for his favorite dishes; this is one of them. The word terrine is used both for a pâté and for the dish in which it is cooked. Pâtés or terrines are served for a first-course entrée with crusty French bread and butter and a good red wine. They are served out of the dish they were baked in.

⅔ pound lean pork
⅔ pound veal
⅔ pound fresh bacon
½ pound sliced smoked bacon
2 rabbit thighs and legs, boned
1 rabbit liver

2 sprigs fresh thyme or 1 teaspoon dried thyme
2 teaspoons salt
½ teaspoon freshly ground pepper
¼ cup cognac
1 cup white wine
¼ cup Madeira

Take two receptacles for the meat, one for the sliced pieces and one for the farce or ground meats. Cut veal and pork in ⅓-inch strips, 2 or 3 inches long. Put them in bowl No. 1. Put 2 or 3 strips of sliced fresh bacon in bowl No. 1, the rest in bowl No. 2. Cut the big pieces of boned rabbit in ⅓-inch strips and put them in bowl No. 1, and put the rest of the rabbit meat and the liver in bowl No. 2. Divide all the seasonings and liquors and put half in each bowl to marinate 24 hours. Then grind all the farce meats in bowl No. 2. Line the terrine or pâté mold with strips of bacon, keeping one for the top. First put in a layer of farce, then cover with a layer of strips of meat. Alternate the layers, ending with farce, and top with a strip of bacon. Set the mold in a pan of hot water and bake 1¾ hours at 325°, covered until the last 20 minutes. Let cool. Well-covered, it will keep in the refrigerator for 10 days. Additions may be sliced truffles and 3 or 4 sliced chicken livers. Duck may be used instead of rabbit in this dish. Serves 12.

PÂTÉ DE CAMPAGNE
Nicolas Flamel, Paris

Few houses in Paris are as old as the one at 51 rue de Montmorency which is occupied by this restaurant. It was built in the fifteenth century by Nicolas Flamel, celebrated alchemist and public scribe, whose renown continued into the seventeenth century. He became rich for those days, and his will, leaving numerous gifts to the city of Paris and her churches, is still to be seen at the Bibliothèque Nationale. On the façade of this ancient house, keen eyes may read a legend which in English would say: "We men and women who inhabit this dwelling built in the year of grace 1407 have vowed to say daily a Pater Noster and an Ave Maria and to pray God to have mercy and to pardon all poor departed sinners. Amen." Today this interesting restaurant is run by a man who loves the old house and has furnished it in keeping with its antiquity. The menu is a huge piece of parchment; and if you sample all the dishes listed, you will have dined amply and well. As soon as you are seated you are brought a pewter jug of wine, three pots of delicious pâtés, and wonderful coarse bread and butter. If you indulge in all this you may find it hard to cope with the omelette, a chicken from the spit or a huge piece of beef, and dessert. This is one of the pâtés:

1 pound pork liver
1 cup onions, chopped
3 shallots, minced
¼ cup cognac
⅔ cup port wine
4 ounces veal
4 ounces fresh pork

1½ teaspoons salt
½ teaspoon pepper
1 bay leaf
1 teaspoon tarragon
1 teaspoon thyme
2 eggs, beaten
Bacon strips

Coarsely chop the liver and marinate it 24 hours with the onions, shallots, cognac, and wine. Grind the veal and pork and mix with the liver and marinade and all the rest of the ingredients. Put the mixture in a terrine or loaf pan which has been lined with strips of bacon. Set it in a pan of water and bake 1 hour at 350°, then turn the heat to 300° and bake 30 minutes longer. Let cool thoroughly, then refrigerate. This makes a good-sized loaf which will serve 12. It will keep a week well covered in the refrigerator.

VARIATIONS. For a game pâté, raw duck may be used instead of the veal. Or you may marinate ½ pound of venison with the liver, omitting the veal. One may experiment, as pâtés are flexible.

PORK LIVER PÂTÉ

1 pound pork liver
1 thick pork chop
1 good sized onion
½ cup dry breadcrumbs
3 tablespoons anchovy paste
⅓ cup Madeira
1¼ teaspoons salt
½ teaspoon freshly ground pepper

1 cup heavy cream
3 eggs, beaten
1 teaspoon thyme
¼ cup pistachio nuts
5 thin strips salt pork
8 chicken livers
Can of madrilene (for aspic)

Cut the liver in strips, cut the meat from the chop, slice the onion, and put all through the meat grinder. Add all the other ingredients except the chicken livers. Grease a good sized breadpan and line the bottom and sides with the salt-pork strips. Put half the liver mixture in the pan. Sauté the chicken livers in a little oil or butter for a minute, then arrange them whole down the center of the pan and cover with the rest of the liver mixture. Tie foil over the pan, set it in a pan of water, and bake at 300° for 1½ hours. Remove the foil and bake 15 minutes more. When the pâté is thoroughly cooled, pour the madrilene over it and refrigerate for 24 hours. Unmold on a platter by turning the pan upside down and holding a hot towel over it for a moment. Decorate with any aspic left in the pan.

FOIE GRAS FRAIS TRUFFÉE ET POCHE AU PORTO
La Mère Guy, Lyon

The visitor to Lyon who sees the fine collection of the Musée des Beaux-Arts, and the Musée Historique des Tissus, with its exhibits presenting the history of the fabric industry, will quickly discover that this is much more than just an industrial city. The list of things to see seemed overwhelming, so we decided on a sightseeing bus. We might have missed Vieux Lyon with its houses dating back to the Middle Ages and the Renaissance and the two Roman amphitheaters unearthed as recently as 1946! We crossed the Saône and climbed the mountain to the Basilica of Fourvière where the view over Lyon is magnificent. A funicular took us down to the eleventh-century Roman Church of St. Paul and through narrow streets past the house where Madame la Marquise de Sevigné lived briefly. Suddenly the bus stopped and we were led through a door and seated at long tables where we were served Burgundy and biscuits. This innovation is highly recommended for all 3½-hour-long bus trips. Not long after the trip ended we were ready to dine in the lovely garden of the Châlet du Parc of Mère Guy, where M. Roger Roucou, the owner-chef, gave us this best of foie gras dishes.

2½ pounds goose livers
Salt and pepper
Truffles cut in sticks

Half bottle of good port
Clear aspic

Freshen the livers by soaking them in very cold water 2 hours. Drain and dry them. Lard each liver with a stick of truffle, salt and pepper them. Put them in a buttered oval baking dish just the size to hold them and cover with port. Put the dish in a pan of water and bake at 350° about 30 minutes. Cool and refrigerate. Several hours before serving pour clear aspic over it. Before serving unmold and decorate with chopped aspic. This may be made with fine chicken livers, which need not be soaked first. Serves 8 to 12.

LIVER PÂTÉ

1 pound chicken livers
½ pound calf's liver
1 fat pork chop
Butter
1 egg, beaten
¾ cup heavy cream
2 tablespoons anchovy paste
⅓ cup flour

1 teaspoon salt
Freshly ground pepper
1 teaspoon thyme
1 teaspoon basil
2 tablespoons Madeira or sherry
1 canned truffle and juices (optional)
3 slices bacon

Put the chicken livers through the meat grinder or slice them and purée in an electric blender. Sear the calf's liver in a little butter to facilitate grinding it. Cut the fat and meat off the chop and grind both, fat and meat. Put all the ground meats in a large mixing bowl and mix in the other ingredients, including the herbs. Add the wine; if the truffle is used, slice it and soak it in the wine an hour, then add both. Line a pâté mold or big loaf pan with bacon. Add any truffle juice and wine marinade to the mixture and put half of it in the pan. Stick the truffle slices along the center of the pâté in the pan, then cover with the rest of the mixture. Cover the pâté mold with its lid (or fasten foil over the loaf pan) and set in a pan of hot water. Bake 15 minutes at 375°, then turn down the heat to 325° and bake 45 minutes more, removing the cover for the last 15 minutes. If it is baking too fast, turn the heat down to 300°. Cool thoroughly, then cover and refrigerate 24 hours before serving. (It will keep in the refrigerator for a week.) The French pâté molds of iron covered with porcelain are most attractive to serve the pâté in; they may also be used for any meat loaf, served hot or cold. For a buffet, this will serve 12 or 16.

ROSE'S ITALIAN PÂTÉ OF COOKED MEATS

½ pound chicken livers
¼ pound salt pork
2 tablespoons butter
¼ pound cooked duck, goose, or
    game
2 large sliced mushrooms
    or 1 small truffle

1 tablespoon heavy cream (more if
    needed)
½ glass Marsala
Salt and pepper
1 teaspoon basil
⅛ teaspoon sage
4 slices prosciutto

Cut the livers in half. Cube the pork and fry it until its is crisp. Scoop out the pieces of pork and sauté the livers in 2 tablespoons of the fat and 2 of butter, until just tender. They should be a little pink inside. Sauté the sliced mushrooms or the truffle (which should be cut in sticks). Put the livers, pork pieces, and duck (or goose or game) through the meat grinder. Add 1 tablespoon of cream, the mushrooms or truffle, the Marsala, and the seasonings. Moisten with a little more cream if the mixture seems too dry to mold and keep its shape. Line an oiled mold with the prosciutto, pack in the mixture, put a weight on top and refrigerate until thoroughly chilled. Unmold and serve with a good red Italian wine and bread and butter. This may be served as part of an antipasto.

LA CROÛTE LANDAISE
Le Coq Hardi, Bougival

This first-course entrée is a good opener when you are entertaining fastidious friends who love good food.

6 slices of brioche ⅓-inch thick
Mushroom sauce:
    ½ pound fresh white mushrooms
    ⅔ cup heavy cream
    1 tablespoon cornstarch
    Salt and pepper
    ¼ teaspoon nutmeg
    1 tablespoon Madeira

6 slices foie gras
Cream sauce:
    ¾ cup heavy cream
    1 tablespoon cornstarch
    Salt and pepper
    1 egg yolk
6 tablespoons Parmesan cheese
6 tablespoons brioche crumbs

Toast the brioche on both sides and put the slices in a shallow fireproof pan. Do not wash the mushrooms but brush them clean. (Washed, they dilute the sauce.) Hash them very fine, almost to a purée. Mix the cream with the cornstarch, add the salt, pepper, and nutmeg, and cook until thickened, then add the mushrooms and Madeira. Divide this mushroom sauce over the brioche toast and put a slice of foie gras on top of the mushroom purée. For the second sauce, blend the cornstarch with the cream, add salt and pepper and cook until it thickens, then add the egg yolk. Mix the cheese and crumbs. Pour the cream sauce over the foie gras, sprinkle with the mixed crumbs and cheese, and put the dish under a hot flame until it browns. Serve on hot plates.

L'OREILLER DE LA BELLE AURORE
(Fair Aurora's Pillow)
La Mère Guy, Lyon

Mère Guy was one of the celebrated "mères" who made Lyonnaise cooking famous. M. Roger Roucou, now owner-chef, happily kept the lady's name for the restaurant. The cooking in Mère Guy's time could not have been better than it is now, for M. Roucou is one of the finest chefs in France. The Foie Gras des Landes en Brioche is ceremoniously brought in on a pedestal; all the dishes are elegantly served, and all merit a careful presentation. Beside a comprehensive list, four complete menus with appropriate wines are suggested. One drives across the Saône to reach this Châlet du Parc where it is sheer delight to dine under the plane trees on a summer night. This is one of the first-course entrées.

2 boned pheasants
Farce:
    Pheasant meat
    8 ounces veal
    10 ounces fresh lean pork
    8 ounces pork fat
    Livers of pheasants
    Salt and pepper
    Jigger cognac
    Truffle essence
Puff Pastry (4 cups flour)
4 ounces foie gras

1 large truffle, cut in sticks
1 egg yolk
Sauce Perigourdine:
    2 tablespoons minced shallots
    2 tablespoons minced onion
    5 tablespoons butter
    1 cup beef broth
    ½ teaspoon beef extract
    1 tablespoon flour
    1 cup Madeira
    1 truffle, cut in sticks
    1 tablespoon cognac

Make *Puff Pastry* * in advance. Skin and bone the pheasants. Cut the breasts in *suprêmes* (skinned, boned half-breasts) and reserve them. Grind the veal and lean pork, spread in a buttered pan, and cook 12 minutes in a 375° oven; this insures its being done. Grind the rest of the pheasant meat, the pork fat, and livers, then mix with the cooked meats, seasoning, cognac, and truffle essence (juice). Roll out the *Puff Pastry* in two strips; one 12 inches long, 4½ inches wide, and ¼ inch thick; the other the same thickness and length but 7½ inches wide. On the narrow strip spread one half of the farce in a mound, and on this lay small cubes of foie gras and the truffle sliced in sticks. Now arrange the pheasant breasts on this and cover with the rest of the farce. Remember this is a pillow. Cover with the wider strip of pastry, moistening the edges a little and pressing them together. Make incisions for the steam to escape. Fancy small cut-outs of pastry may be used to decorate the top. Mix the egg yolk with 2 tablespoons of water and paint the top of the pastry. Put it on a baking sheet and bake it 10 minutes in a 400° oven, then at 350° for 30 minutes more. Meanwhile make the *Sauce Perigourdine*. Sauté the shallots and onion in 2 tablespoons of butter until a little soft, then add the broth and beef extract and simmer 5 minutes. Mix the flour with the Madeira and add it. Cook the sauce in the top of a double boiler for 30 minutes, uncovered. Put the sauce through a sieve, add the truffle sticks, and cook 4 minutes more. Just before serving, beat in 3 tablespoons of butter, a little bit at a time, and add the cognac. Serve in a tureen. This elegant "pillow" and its sauce should be served hot. This will serve 12. If pheasants are not available, small ducks may be used.

* Recipe titles appearing in italics may be found by consulting the index.

JAMBON PERSILLÉ À LA BOURGUIGNONNE
Hotel de la Poste, Beaune

M. Marc Chevillot inherited this charming hotel from his father, a noted hotel man and wine merchant of Beaune. Young Marc supervises the food and wines that are served from its celebrated kitchen and cellars. How fortunate the chef who has such a cellar to draw on for making the dishes which serve the famous who pass through Beaune! A gifted local printer produces lovely menus and wine lists for the banquets for all occasions. Particularly good are the first-course dishes, and this is one of the best.

2½–3 pound sugar-cured ham
Court bouillon:
    2 cups chicken broth
    2 cups dry white wine
    1 teaspoon tarragon
    1 teaspoon thyme
    Veal knuckle (for jelly)
    ¼ cup minced shallots (or green onions)
    ¼ cup minced onions
    Freshly ground pepper

Handful finely chopped parsley
1 clove garlic, crushed
3 tablespoons thick cream
1 tablespoon wine vinegar

Obtain a fine small ham, or part of one, with fat and bone. Cover with the court bouillon, adding a little more broth and wine if necessary to cover the ham completely. Simmer very gently until the ham becomes tender and pulpy (about 1 to 1¼ hours). Let cool and skim off the congealed fat. Bone the ham. Cube meat (with its fat) in ½-inch pieces and pack it in an attractive glass or earthenware bowl. Put the bouillon through a sieve and reduce it over high heat to 2½ to 3 cups. Cool and add plenty of finely chopped parsley, crushed garlic, cream, and vinegar. Mix well, pour over the ham, and chill to obtain a good parsley jelly. This first-course entrée is a popular Burgundian dish and is served with crusty French bread and butter and a chilled white Burgundy.

GÂTEAU DE FOIES DE VOLAILLE À LA BRESSANE
Chapon Fin, Thoissey

½ pound chicken livers
¼ cup sifted flour
3 eggs
3 egg yolks
2 tablespoons thick cream
1¼ cups milk
1 teaspoon salt

Freshly ground pepper
¼ teaspoon nutmeg
1½ tablespoons minced parsley
1 clove garlic, crushed
Garnish:
    Shrimp, crab, or lobster sauce

This chicken-liver cake from Bresse calls for "6 beautiful white Bresse chicken livers." We don't have beautiful white livers from Bresse, so I made this of fresh chicken livers, cut in pieces and puréed in an electric blender, then mixed with the flour, eggs, cream, milk, and all the seasonings. The mixture is quite liquid. Grease an 8-inch baking dish, pour in the mixture, set the dish in a pan of hot water and bake at 375° for 10 minutes, then at 325° for about 25 or 30 minutes more. After taking it out of the oven, let it stand 3 or 4 minutes, then turn it out onto a platter. Serve warm, 10 to 15 minutes later, with a hot seafood sauce in a sauceboat. This is an old Burgundian dish, and when cold, it is of the most delicate texture. Serves 6 or 8.

LA BALLOTINE DE CANARD TRUFFÉE ET PISTACHÉE
M. Paul Blanc, Chapon Fin, Thoissey

This "bundle" of duck, truffled and pistachioed is one of the elegant pâtés served at this Burgundian inn, famous for its food.

4 pound duck
Farce:
    1 pound neck of pork
    Duck meat
    2 eggs
    Salt and pepper
    ¼ teaspoon nutmeg
    ¼ teaspoon mace
    ⅓ cup halved pistachio nuts
    Truffle essence
    1 teaspoon thyme
    1 shallot, minced
    Butter

Fillets of duck breast
¼ cup cognac
1 truffle, sliced
Jelly:
    1½ cups broth (duck bones)
    ½ cup port wine
    1 tablespoon gelatin
    1 egg white, half-beaten

Choose a fine fresh duck (not frozen) and have the butcher cut it from neck to tail and remove the backbone, without breaking any of the rest of the skin. Lay it out flat and with the point of a sharp knife cut out the breast bones and breast meat. Cut the breast meat in fillets and marinate 2 hours with salt, pepper, and cognac. Remove the wing tips but leave the wing and leg bones intact. Make a broth with 3 cups of water, wing tips, neck, bones, gizzard, 1 chopped onion, salt, pepper, and 1 teaspoon of thyme. Simmer 30 minutes. Strain the broth and reserve; this is for basting. Cut the rest of the duck meat from the carcass and grind it with the pork and the liver. Mix the meat with the eggs, seasonings, nuts, and shallot tossed 1 minute in a little butter. To stuff, arrange half of the farce along the duck from neck to tail in a mound; lay the fillets of duck breast along the top of the mound; on top of the fillets put a row of truffle slices, then top with the rest of the farce. Bring the skin together, reshape the duck, and sew it together securely. With string, tie the whole duck into shape and put it in a roasting pan. Roast 1 hour at 350°, then turn the heat down to 300° and roast another hour. Baste frequently with the hot duck broth. When it is done, let it cool completely, then refrigerate overnight. If possible put it into a receptacle in which it just fits. Make a jelly to pour over it, the next day. Degrease the pan juices and measure 1¾ cups. Put the stock with 1 half-beaten egg white in a saucepan and simmer 5 minutes. Line a sieve with a cloth wrung out in cold water and strain the broth; it will be clear. Soak the gelatin in the port wine 3 minutes, then melt it in the hot broth. Let cool. Remove the strings from the duck, put it back in its receptacle, pour the broth over it and again refrigerate. When ready to serve, unmold on a platter and garnish with chopped jelly. This will serve 12 to 16. Cut in slices and serve with French bread and sweet butter, and a fine Burgundy.

Salad, Vegetable & Fish Entrées

AUBERGINES POUR HORS D'ŒUVRE FROID
Chapeau Rouge, Dijon

1 medium eggplant
   or 2 small ones
Salt
Olive oil
Pepper
4 tablespoons minced shallots
   or green onions

1 tablespoon minced onion
7 tablespoons white wine
3 tablespoons wine vinegar
Minced fresh parsley
Minced fresh thyme

This dish is prettier if small eggplants are used. When I specify shallots or green onions, I always intend that shallots be used if they are available. Peel the eggplant, cut in ½-inch thick slices, salt each side, and let the slices "weep." Wipe dry, sprinkle with a little olive oil and salt and pepper, and bake until just tender. Remove the slices to a platter. Use the same pan to sauté the shallots or green onions and the onion, adding a very little more oil if necessary, until they color a little. Add the wine and vinegar and cook down until there is only ⅓ cup of liquid. Pour this over the eggplant and sprinkle with minced fresh parsley and thyme. If fresh thyme is not available, almost any other fresh herb will do: tarragon, chervil, or basil. Serve cold.

ANTIPASTO "PASSETTO"
Passetto's, Rome

Passetto's on via Zanardelli is famous for the beautiful display of antipasto, fish, fruit, and pastries that greets you as you enter the first of two long narrow dining rooms, lined with handsome pictures. It is a formidable task to choose from such an inviting display, so the host, Tonino de Giammarco, may suggest peppers, zucchini, or eggplant, all stuffed and baked. These are always served cold at the restaurant, but they can be served hot as a vegetable accompaniment to meat.

Zucchini stuffing:
- 8 small zucchini
- 5 ounces ground veal
- Butter
- Salt and pepper
- 1 large egg
- ⅓ cup Parmesan cheese
- 3 tablespoons Madeira
- Olive oil
- Tomato sauce

Eggplant stuffing:
- Small eggplant
- Mozzarella cheese
- Tomatoes
- Olive oil
- Salt and pepper

Pepper stuffing:
- Large green pepper
- Dry bread cubes
- Tuna fish
- Black olives in oil
- Olive oil

ZUCCHINI. Choose zucchini 5 inches long, 1 to a serving. Remove some of the flesh by making a tunnel with a small round corer. Simmer the zucchini in boiling water 5 minutes and drain. Toss the veal in a little butter about 3 minutes, season it, then mix it with the egg, cheese, and Madeira. Stuff the zucchini. Pour a little oil in a baking pan and lay the zucchini on the bottom. Moisten the tops with about ½ cup of tomato sauce. Bake them at 375° for 10 or 12 minutes. They are also good stuffed with cubed Mozzarella cheese which has been tossed with Parmesan cheese.

EGGPLANT. Choose small eggplant so that half of one will be sufficient for each serving. Boil them 10 or 15 minutes and drain. Cut them in half lengthwise and scoop out a little of the flesh. Cut the Mozzarella cheese in cubes. Skin, seed, and coarsely chop the tomatoes, combine with the cheese, moisten with a little olive oil, and season with salt and pepper. Stuff the eggplant halves, lay them in a baking pan with a little additional olive oil, and bake them 15 to 18 minutes at 350°.

PEPPERS. Cut the peppers in half lengthwise and seed them. Cover them with hot water and boil about 5 minutes. Drain upside down. Mix equal quantities of small dried fresh bread cubes with flaked tuna fish. Use Italian or Greek black olives; pit and cut them in half. Allow 4 halves for each half pepper. Mix them with the bread cubes and fish and stuff the peppers. Put the peppers in a baking pan, pour a little olive oil on the stuffing and in the pan, and bake 15 to 18 minutes at 350°. Use a half-pepper for each serving.

ANTIPASTO
Da Vasco, Bologna

This fine restaurant is one of the best in Bologna, which means in all the province of Emilia. It is not in the center of town but I advise walking there; after one of their meals I guarantee you will want to walk back anyway. Da Vasco does a humming business because the quality of the food is fine and the prices are reasonable. There is no menu; the carts of inviting food are wheeled to your table. The following list is typical of the antipasto.

Sweet Italian onion rings
Shredded carrots
Peppers in oil
Mushrooms in oil
Pearl onions
Cold yellow-rice salad
Sliced tomatoes
Sliced cucumbers

Russian Salad of cooked vegetables:
Peas
White beans
Cubed potatoes
Cubed carrots
Capers
Fluted mayonnaise
Chicken Salad:
Cubed chicken
Cubed ham cooked in milk
Mayonnaise

The chicken salad is molded and decorated with mayonnaise; it has a hint of nutmeg flavor. Vasco calls it pâté. All Vasco dishes are arranged with care, imagination, and taste. He urges you to try his Capriccio, which is a sampling of three rich pastas: green tortellini, cooked in broth, drained, and tossed in heavy cream and Parmesan cheese, the most delicious I have ever tasted: lasagne; and green fettuccini served with a little tomato sauce. Then comes a cart with a variety of roasted meats and poultry. Last, one is overwhelmed by the pastry cart. Next to our table sat an elderly couple, who had gone through all this and were finishing with *Dolce Vasco*, a very rich cake with zabaione sauce. They gave us a guilty glance, so we clapped and called, "Bravi."

PROSCIUTTO WITH MELON, FIGS, OR PERSIMMONS

Paper-thin Italian ham

Slices of melon, rind removed,
or whole fresh figs
or persimmons, halved

One of the first-course dishes most popular in Italy, and becoming so in America, is very thinly sliced ham draped over melon, served on individual plates or on a platter. In season ripe figs are also a favorite to serve with prosciutto. In winter when melon is a gamble and the figs are not available, try very ripe, translucent persimmons—they are wonderful with prosciutto.

SALADE NIÇOISE

This is one of the best salads and has become so popular that it is served not only in Nice but all over France. It is not usually mixed; instead the ingredients are arranged separately on each plate. It is served as a first course, or for a main dish at lunch or supper, when the quantities of the various ingredients may be more generous. A little lettuce is put on each plate first; everything is cold.

For each plate:

Fresh cooked string beans	1 canned red pimento
Skinned sliced tomato	1 hard boiled egg, quartered
2 or 3 black olives in oil	Fine strips of chicken
Tuna fish	Fine strips of ham
2 or 3 fillets of anchovies	Cubed boiled potatoes (optional)
3 or 4 capers	

Serve with a bowl of French herb dressing with 2 tablespoons of oil mayonnaise per cup of dressing mixed in.

SWEDISH SALAD

½ cup minced chives	1 small can anchovies
1 cup minced green onions	⅓ cup red caviar
1½ to 2 cups tiny cubed boiled potatoes	3 tablespoons capers
3 raw egg yolks	Freshly ground pepper

This is a time to be decorative. Make a design on a platter of rows and nests of the ingredients. Drop an egg yolk in each of 3 nests. Sprinkle with the caviar and capers. Do not add salt but put a sprinkle of pepper over the vegetables. The first to serve himself mixes the yolks with the rest of the ingredients. The Danes and Swedes, famous for their smörgåsbord, frequently use raw egg yolks for an unctuous sauce.

ASPARAGUS AS AN ENTRÉE

In Lorraine and Burgundy plump white asparagus is plentiful in June and is very often served as a first course. Sometimes it comes on individual plates but at Capucin Gourmand in Nancy it was piled high on a platter. It is delicious with very oily French dressing, chopped hard-boiled eggs, capers, and a dash of nutmeg. Our green asparagus has as much flavor, maybe more, and also deserves to be treated as a separate course to show to its greatest advantage.

CHINESE SALAD PLATTER
Lotus d'Or, Paris

We are very fond of Chinese food and we were curious to know what a Paris location would do to Chinese cuisine. Nothing. There, as everywhere else, it is up to the individual Chinese restaurateur or cook what he does with food. The Lotus is a very pretty little restaurant on the Left Bank at 50 rue St. André des Arts. The cold salad platter is a study in culinary aesthetics. The thinly sliced chicken gizzards and raw mushrooms are laid in rows with their edges overlapping to form a beautiful geometric design.

Skinned tomatoes, thinly sliced
Cucumbers, thinly sliced
Raw mushrooms, thinly sliced
Cooked chicken gizzards, thinly sliced
Chicken meat cut in julienne strips
Paper-thin slices of beef
Bean sprouts, cooked

Green beans, cooked
Shredded lettuce
Sauce:
    ½ cup peanut or soybean oil
    2 teaspoons soy sauce
    3 teaspoons sherry
    1 teaspoon vinegar

The sauce is served in a bowl.

ELIE'S CHEF SALAD

This is the way a French friend interprets Chef Salad. It is assembled the same way as *Salade Niçoise;* that is, everything is put in little bunches on the individual plates. Use either salad plates or shallow soup plates. Elie serves it as a main course for lunch or supper.

Coarsely shredded lettuce
Narrow strips of cold turkey, chicken, or leftover game
Narrow strips of ham or tongue
Narrow strips of Gruyère or Swiss cheese
Skinned tomatoes, sliced (optional)

Chopped nuts
Fresh tarragon, chives, chervil, basil or parsley, minced
or aromatic dried herbs put through a fine sieve
French dressing
Mayonnaise dressing

Put some lettuce around the plate to hold the bunches of poultry, meat, and cheese, and put some chopped nuts in the center, then sprinkle the salad with herbs. The two dressings are passed in separate bowls, so that each person may mix his own salad the way he likes. A slice or two of skinned tomatoes may be added to each plate.

ARTICHOKES OR ENDIVE À LA GRÈCQUE

6 medium-sized artichokes
   or 6 big whole endive
6 green onions, minced
   Salt and pepper

18 coriander berries
   or cardamom seeds, crushed
½ cup white wine
½ cup chicken stock
⅓ cup olive oil

Trim the artichokes of coarse outer leaves and soak them an hour in cold salted water, then rinse and drain upside down. Put the artichokes upright in a heavy pot that just fits. Spread the leaves and put a minced onion, salt, pepper, and 3 crushed berries or seeds in each. Pour the liquids over them so that some enters each artichoke. Cover tightly and simmer 30 to 35 minutes (according to their size) over a low flame. The endive need no soaking; just wash, trim, and dry. Lay them on the bottom of a heavy pot, put the other ingredients over them, cover tightly, and simmer 30 minutes over a low flame. Serve either vegetable cold with the liquids poured over as a sauce. This makes a fine first-course entrée. Serves 6.

CHAMPIGNONS À LA GRÈCQUE
Auberge de l'Empereur, Chailly-en-Bière

In the "proximity of the Forêt de Fontainebleau," a comfortable drive from Paris on Route No. 7, you will find a lovely restaurant with a garden for warm-weather dining and excellent food. I suggest your beginning your dinner with these delicious Champignons à la Grècque, a Beaujolais, and French bread and butter. Then you might have *Chicken in Cream with Chives*, a specialty of Chef Mondange, for which he also gave me the recipe.

2 pounds fresh button mushrooms
2 green peppers
1 large onion, minced
3 cloves garlic, crushed
¼ cup olive oil
1 branch thyme
2 bay leaves

2 tablespoons coriander seeds,
   pounded in a mortar
Juice of ½ lemon
1 wineglass dry white wine
½ teaspoon salt
¼ teaspoon freshly ground pepper
   Dash cayenne

Brush the mushrooms clean; perfect white ones need not be washed. They must be dry. Seed the green peppers and cut them in thin rings. Blanch them in boiling water for 3 minutes and drain them. In a heavy saucepan put the peppers, onion, garlic, olive oil, thyme, bay leaves, and coriander seeds and cook 5 minutes over a low flame. Add the rest of the seasonings, the lemon juice, and the wine and bring to a boil; add the mushrooms and cook 10 minutes, gently. The juices should not quite cover the mushrooms. Put the mushrooms and sauce into a pottery jar and when they are cold, cover and store in the refrigerator. Serve chilled from the jar.

STUFFED MUSHROOMS

Small white mushrooms, fresh or
    canned
Olive oil
Salt and pepper

Stuffings:
1. Half Roquefort cheese, half
    sweet butter
2. Liver pâté or foie gras
3. Red or black caviar and
    sour cream
4. Ground ham and
    mayonnaise
    Ground mushroom stems
    (optional)

If fresh mushrooms are used, clean them and take out the stems, which
may be reserved. Sauté the caps in a little olive oil 3 minutes and add salt
and pepper. When they are cool, stuff them with any of the stuffings you
choose. The Roquefort cheese is blended with sweet butter. The caviar is
carefully mixed with a little sour cream. The ham is moistened with mayonnaise. (If you like, the mushroom stems may be sautéed a minute, ground,
and mixed with the ham.) One pound of fresh mushrooms will serve 6 or
8. If canned mushrooms are used, drain them, cut out the stems, and stuff.
They need no cooking. These are one of the most attractive cocktail
accessories.

EGGPLANT "CAVIAR"

1 eggplant, medium to small
Salt
Freshly ground pepper
¼ cup grated onion
2 cloves garlic, crushed

1 tablespoon lemon juice
1 teaspoon cardamom
½ teaspoon powdered fennel
Olive oil

Wipe off the eggplant. Put it on a dry pan in a 350° oven and bake for
about 45 minutes. Test with a cake tester and when soft remove it. Skin
the eggplant, mash the pulp and add the seasonings to taste. Stir in 3 or 4
tablespoons of olive oil. Chill and serve as a spread on dark bread or toast.
This is Russian and Near Eastern. The serving dish may be garnished with
Greek olives.

CARROT SALAD

8 sweet young carrots
3 teaspoons grated orange rind

¼ cup French dressing
2 tablespoons mayonnaise

Grate the orange rind, marinate with the French dressing 1 hour. Shred the
raw carrots. Mix ¼ cup of the dressing with the mayonnaise and toss
lightly with the carrots. It must just moisten them, not make them wet.

CÈLERI-RAVE

½ pound celeriac or celery root
Juice of ½ lemon
1½ teaspoons salt
1 cup boiling water

1 tablespoon red wine vinegar
3 tablespoons olive oil
2 tablespoons Bahamian mustard
Salt and freshly ground pepper

This is a fine and very French hors d'œuvre. It goes well with an assortment of others—sardines, pimentoes, etc.; with others, this amount will serve 6. Wash two good-sized knobs well in cold water and peel them. Cut them into very thin slices, then into fine sticks; there will be almost 3 cups. Put the sticks in a bowl and mix well with the lemon juice, salt, and boiling water. Let stand 3 minutes, then wash in cold water and drain. Shake well in a clean tea towel to dry. Mix the vinegar, olive oil, and mustard with just a dash of salt and pepper. Bahamian mustard, which is prepared with a little sugar and spices, is very good for this. If it is unobtainable, use a mild mustard, adding a pinch of brown sugar. Mix this dressing with the celery sticks and refrigerate for several hours, the first hour uncovered. Empty into a small fancy bowl to serve.

OKRA À LA TURC

1 pound small fresh okra
¼ cup olive oil and
    2 cloves garlic, crushed

(or ¼ cup bland oil, soy or peanut,
and 15 cardamom seeds, crushed)

Trim the ends of the okra. Wash it well in 1 tablespoon of soda and warm water. Rinse in cold water. Boil 3 minutes in boiling salted water and drain. Put the olive oil and garlic in a saucepan and add the okra. Swish it around in the oil for 30 or 40 seconds over a low flame. If the bland oil is used, put it in a saucepan with the crushed cardamom seeds and mix the okra the same way. This is good hot as a vegetable with a curry, serving 5 or 6; or chilled as an appetizer, serving 8.

STUFFED GREEN OR RED PEPPERS

4 fine bell peppers
32 1-inch croutons
⅓ cup olive oil

3 or 4 cloves garlic, crushed
16 black olives in oil
24 Mushrooms à la Grècque

Cut the peppers in half, seed them, and cook them 6 or 8 minutes in boiling water. Drain upside down. Sauté the croutons in the olive oil with the garlic until golden brown. Pit and halve the olives. You may make the Mushrooms à la Grècque, or use mushrooms canned in olive oil. Divide the ingredients and fill the pepper halves. Bake 10 minutes at 375°. Serve cold. Serves 8.

AVOCADO OR ARTICHOKE EGG HORS D'ŒUVRE

Small avocado halves or artichoke bottoms
6-minute boiled eggs

Mayonnaise
Anchovy fillets
Lettuce

These appetizers are made with skinned avocado halves or cooked artichoke bottoms which form cups to receive the eggs. Put eggs in hot water and time them after they come to a boil, and cook them 6 minutes. A medium-sized egg should be hard enough to peel but with the yolk still soft. Cool the eggs and put 1 in each avocado half or artichoke bottom. Add oil mayonnaise to the top and put 2 anchovy fillets crisscross on the top. Garnish with lettuce.

TOMATO-CHEESE-EGG HORS D'ŒUVRE

Fine ripe tomatoes
Hard-boiled eggs, sliced
Gruyère cheese, sliced
Anchovy fillets

Capers
Plain or garlic mayonnaise
Lettuce

Skin good-sized tomatoes and slice them rather thin to the base so that the slices fan out. Between the slices alternate thin slices of egg and cheese. Put 3 anchovy fillets and a few capers in each tomato. Top with a big blob of either mayonnaise and serve on lettuce, 1 tomato to each serving.

CHICKEN LIVER APPETIZERS

1 pound chicken livers
3-inch lengths of bacon
Cooking oil

Batter:
2 eggs, beaten
4 tablespoons flour
Salt and pepper
1 teaspoon sugar

If the livers are large, cut each half in two slices so they may cook quickly. Wrap each piece of liver in bacon and fasten with a toothpick. For the batter, beat all the ingredients together. The sugar facilitates browning. Dip the bacon-wrapped livers in the batter and fry in deep oil at 370° until a golden brown. Serve them on a lettuce leaf or pass them in a shallow dish.

VARIATION. Peel and slice water chestnuts and put 1 slice next to each piece of chicken liver, wrap in bacon, and broil 5 inches from the flame until the bacon is crisp. Turn them once.

SALMON RICE SALAD

1 cup patna rice
1 cup beet juice
1 cup water
Salt
1 cup flaked salmon, fresh or
   canned
6 green stuffed olives, sliced

1 red pimento, sliced
1 cup fresh peas, cooked with
   1 teaspoon basil
Chopped parsley
3 tablespoons French dressing
3 tablespoons mayonnaise

Cook the rice in the beet juice and water until all the liquid is absorbed and the rice is fluffy. Let cool. Add salt. Lightly mix with all the other ingredients. Mix the French dressing, and the mayonnaise. Use only enough dressing to moisten the salad; it doesn't need much. The result looks like a Matisse. Serves 6 or 8 as a first course.

SARDINE HORS D'ŒUVRE

For each plate:
   2 or 3 fine fat sardines in
      olive oil
   Lettuce leaves
   1 red pimento

   2 or 3 small artichoke hearts
      in olive oil
   Black olives
   2 herb butter balls

Arrange the sardines and other ingredients on lettuce. Soften sweet butter to room temperature, mix with minced fresh herbs or season with powdered fennel, chill, and make into balls. Serve with French bread.

BUTTERFLY SHRIMP

1 pound medium-sized fresh shrimp
   Oil for frying
Batter:
   2 eggs, beaten
   Salt and pepper
   1 teaspoon sugar
   4 tablespoons flour

Dipping sauce:
   ¾ cup tomato sauce
   1 teaspoon grated orange rind
   ¼ cup orange juice

Clean the shrimp, removing the shells except for those on the tails. Make a slit on the convex side of each shrimp and flatten them a little. Make the batter by beating all the ingredients together. Dip the shrimp in the batter and fry them in deep oil at 380° a few seconds to a golden brown. Drain on brown paper. Mix all the ingredients for the sauce. Canned tomato sauce may be used. Simmer the sauce 2 minutes, and serve in a bowl. This is a very interesting Chinese sauce. Hold the shrimp by their tails and dip them in the sauce, or they may be dipped in soy sauce. Serves 6 to 8.

SALMON MOUSSE
(OR LOBSTER OR CRAB MOUSSE)

1 1-pound slice fresh salmon	¼ teaspoon nutmeg or mace
3 tablespoons water	1 tablespoon tomato paste
2 tablespoons butter	½ cup light cream
1 teaspoon gelatin	1 tablespoon capers
⅓ cup dry vermouth	½ cup heavy cream, whipped
Salt and freshly ground pepper	Garnish: Sprigs of parsley

Wash the fish and put it in a heavy saucepan with the water and butter. Cover tightly and simmer gently for 10 to 12 minutes on each side. The length of time depends on the thickness of the piece. Meanwhile measure the wine, and use 2 tablespoons of it to soak the gelatin. When the fish is done, lift it out, being careful to remove any skin sticking to the bottom of the saucepan. Add the gelatin-wine mixture to the butter and fish juices in the pan; when the gelatin is melted add the rest of the wine. Skin the fish, bone and flake it, and put it in an electric blender. Add the gelatin mixture, the seasonings, and the light cream. Purée until very smooth; the current will have to be turned off several times and the mixture stirred from the bottom of the blender. Add the capers to the purée and let it become thoroughly cooled. Whip the cream until stiff and fold into the fish mixture. Oil a quart mold, or a fish mold, and pour in the mixture. Let it chill until set. This may take close to 3 hours. Do not add any more gelatin; the bones in the fish contribute a great deal of gelatin, and the mousse must have a delicate texture. Unmold on a platter and decorate with parsley. This is a very fine first-course fish dish and will serve 8 to 10. Serve it with crusty bread, sweet butter, and a good white wine.

LOBSTER OR CRAB MOUSSE. Use 1 pound of cooked fish, flaked fine. Cook 1 minute in 2 tablespoons butter. Remove fish and butter to the blender. Heat the wine a little and melt the gelatin in it before putting it into the blender. Canned fish may be used if fresh is not available.

SALMONE AFFUMICATO

Sliced smoked salmon	Olive oil
2 or 3 tablespoons capers	Freshly ground pepper

In Italy salmon as an appetizer is almost as popular as prosciutto. Put the slices on a platter and sprinkle the capers over them. Set out a cruet of olive oil and a pepper mill and let each person dress his own serving. Thinly sliced black bread and sweet butter should accompany this.

SHRIMP, CRABMEAT, OR LOBSTER COCKTAIL

2 pounds medium-sized fresh
   shrimp
1¼ cups oil mayonnaise
½ cup sour cream

⅓ cup finely-minced green onions
Red or black caviar
Lemon juice

There are about 18 to 20 shrimp to a pound; an average serving is 5 shrimp to each person. Mix the mayonnaise with the sour cream and onions. Mix half of the dressing with the cooked, peeled, cold shrimp. When ready to serve put the dressed shrimp in cocktail glasses. Put a tablespoon of dressing on top of each serving and a good generous tablespoon of caviar sprinkled with lemon juice on top of the dressing. Two pounds of shrimp will serve 8. When using fresh crabmeat or lobster, cut the pieces the size of shrimp and dress the same way. One pound of either will serve 5 or 6.

CREVETTES AU PIERRE
Le Beurre Fondu, London

Chef Ross-Muir suggests these broiled shrimp for a first course.

1 pound medium-sized shrimp
Curry powder

Bacon
Chutney

Boil shrimp 1 minute, peel, and cut them in half. Roll each half in curry powder and wrap in a 2-inch slice of bacon. String 5 on a skewer and broil under flame 2½ to 3 minutes on each side. Serve with chutney.

SCAMPI CANEPA
Canepa, Rome

1½ pounds fresh shrimp
   Beaten egg
   Flour, salt, and pepper
3 tablespoons each, butter and oil
5 drops Worcestershire sauce
3 tablespoons white wine
   Juice ½ lemon
⅓ cup ground ham

⅓ cup chopped mushrooms
3 tablespoons chopped truffles
   (optional)
   More butter
Garnish:
   Quartered lemon dipped in
     ground prasley

Clean and peel the shrimp. Dip them in beaten egg and then in seasoned flour. Sauté them lightly 2 or 3 minutes in a mixture of butter and oil. Put the shrimp on a hot platter. Put the Worcestershire sauce, wine, and lemon juice in the pan, stir, and pour evenly over the shrimp. Toss the ham, mushrooms, and truffles (if available) in a little butter then spread over the shrimp. This is a fine entrée or fish course for 5 or 6.

SCAMPI COCKTAIL

1 pound fresh shrimp	3 tablespoons capers
½ cup ground cooked ham	Shredded lettuce
Homemade mayonnaise	Pimento strips (optional)

The Italians use ham a great deal for seasoning and garnishing because they produce such fine ham, especially in the province of Emilia. Cook a pound of fresh shrimp (18 to 20 medium-sized shrimp) in their shells 3 or 4 minutes in water and let them cool in the broth. Before serving remove the shells and toss the shrimp with the ham, mayonnaise, and capers. If preferred, the ham may be cut in very fine julienne sticks. Be sure the mayonnaise is unsweetened (of course the best is homemade) and use plenty of it. Make beds of the lettuce in goblets and add the shrimp mixture. The top may be decorated with 2 or 3 strips of canned pimento.

HERRING IN SOUR CREAM WITH ONIONS

Maatjes herrings from Holland are served by Jews and Gentiles alike with sour cream and thinly sliced Spanish onions. But if these are not available to you, use a good brand of marinated herring. Add more thick sour cream and thinly sliced Bermuda or Spanish onions, pack in an earthen jar, and keep well covered in a cold place. Serve these as an appetizer with black bread and butter and you will please your guests, especially the men. A good ale or a very dry wine is served with these.

Quiches & Crêpes

QUICHE LORRAINE
Chez Pauline, Paris

Pâté Brisée:
- 1½ cups sifted flour
- ½ teaspoon salt
- ⅓ cup butter
- ¼ cup vegetable shortening
- 1 teaspoon sugar
- ¼ cup ice water or more

Filling:
- 15 slices lean bacon
- 2 tablespoons butter
- 2 cups heavy cream
- ½ teaspoon salt
- ¼ teaspoon nutmeg
- 3 large eggs, beaten

This recipe, given to me by M. Genin of Chez Pauline, is the traditional quiche of Lorraine. We have added so many things to quiches, we might like a simple one for a change. Make the pâté brisée according to the directions for *Pie Pastry*. This quantity will line a 10-inch pie plate. Line a pie plate with the pastry and bake in a 400° oven for 7 minutes while you make the filling. Sauté the bacon in the butter until crisp; remove the bacon from the pan and set aside. Boil up the cream, add the salt and nutmeg, and pour it over the eggs. After the pastry has baked 7 minutes, remove it from the oven. Crumble the bacon over the bottom of the pastry, then pour in the cream-egg mixture. Return the quiche to the oven and bake about 25 or 30 minutes more at 350°, until the filling is set and the top a nice brown. Serve hot. Serves 8.

VARIATION. Add ½ cup tiny cubes of Gruyère cheese to the filling before baking. Sprinkle 2 or 3 tablespoons of Parmesan cheese over the top 3 minutes before the quiche is done.

MUSHROOM AND CHEESE QUICHE

1 10-inch *Pie Pastry* shell
1 cup sliced fresh mushrooms
3 tablespoons butter
⅓ cup sliced green onions
  Salt and pepper
2 strips bacon
1 tablespoon parsley

2 eggs
2 egg yolks
½ teaspoon nutmeg
1 cup heavy cream
1 cup light cream
½ cup shredded Gruyère cheese

Bake the pie shell 8 minutes at 400° while you sauté the mushrooms in half the butter for 2 minutes. Sauté the onions in the rest of the butter 2 minutes, separately. Salt and pepper the mushrooms and the onions. Fry the bacon until crisp and crumble it. Sprinkle these ingredients evenly over the partially baked shell and add the parsley. Beat the eggs and egg yolks and add the nutmeg. Scald the heavy and light cream and pour it over the eggs. Add the cheese and pour this over the ingredients in the pie shell. Bake at 350° about 25 minutes or until set. Serves 8.

HAM QUICHE. Use 1 cup of ham cut in tiny cubes instead of the mushrooms. The ham does not need sautéing.

CRAB OR LOBSTER QUICHE

1½ cups fresh crabmeat or lobster
    or 1 12-ounce can
½ cup chopped green onions
2 tablespoons butter
  Salt and pepper
2 eggs
2 egg yolks
1 tablespoon tomato paste

1 cup heavy cream
1 cup light cream
¼ teaspoon nutmeg
2 tablespoons sherry or Madeira
4 tablespoons shredded Gruyère
  cheese
1 10-inch *Pie Pastry* shell

Flake the fish and bone it. Sauté the onions 2 minutes in the butter and add salt and pepper. Mix the onions with the fish. Beat the eggs and egg yolks together and mix in the tomato paste. Scald the heavy and light cream, add the nutmeg, and pour it over the eggs. Add the wine and cheese. Bake the pastry shell 8 minutes at 400°, then arrange the lobster or crab-meat on the bottom of the shell and pour the cream mixture over it. Bake at 350° about 30 minutes or until the filling is set. Serves 8. This was given to us by our great friend Mme. Fernande Blanc in her Paris days when she had the restaurant Le Bossu back of Nôtre Dame on Quai Bourbon. When we had a reunion in Lyon on the Saône, where she has another Le Bossu, we had it again and, mixed with nostalgia and champagne, it seemed better than ever.

FRESH SALMON QUICHE

1 ½-pound slice salmon
3 tablespoons dry vermouth
3 tablespoons butter
3 tablespoons grated onion
  Salt and freshly ground pepper
1 teaspoon cornstarch

1 cup scalded cream
1 tablespoon tomato paste
¼ teaspoon mace or nutmeg
3 eggs, beaten
1 9-inch *Pie Pastry* shell
¼ cup Parmesan cheese

Wash and dry the salmon. Put it in a pot with the vermouth, butter, onion, salt, and pepper. Cover tightly and simmer 6 minutes; turn the fish over and simmer another 6 minutes. Make a 9-inch *Pie Pastry* shell and bake it at 400° for 10 minutes. Remove the salmon from the liquid, bone, skin, and flake it. Mix the salmon liquid with the cornstarch, add the scalded cream, tomato paste, spice, and beaten eggs. Stir in the flaked salmon and pour the mixture into the pastry shell. Sprinkle with cheese, then bake at 350° 25 minutes, or until the quiche has thickened and browned. Serves 6.

PISSALADIÈRE PROVENÇAL

3 cups sliced onions
4 tablespoons olive oil
1 clove garlic, crushed
1 teaspoon thyme
  Salt and pepper

8 anchovy fillets
8 strips red pimento
16 black olives
3 tablespoons olive oil
  Yeast Dough or *Pie Pastry*

Sauté the onions in the olive oil over a slow fire until they are very soft and tender. When they are done mix in the garlic, thyme, a little salt, and pepper. Use either *Yeast Pizza Dough* or *Pie Pastry* to line a 10-inch pastry shell. Put the onions in the bottom. Make a design like the spokes of a wheel with the anchovy fillets and in between them put strips of pimento. Cut the olives in half, pit them, and arrange them over the pie. Sprinkle the top with olive oil. Bake at 375° about 15 or 20 minutes. Serves 8.

CAPRICE
"Al Teatro" Pizza Palace, Campo San Fantin, Venice

There are so many treasures in Venice, one should spend more time there than is usually given to this amazing city. After visiting the Chiesa di Santa Maria Gloriosa dei Frari and, just behind it, the Scuola San Rocco with its glorious Tintorettos, you have had enough to absorb for one day. You are tired and want to sit and watch the people, perhaps with a glass of wine and a snack of some kind, for it is hours before dinner. The most popular square for refreshment in the city is the Campo around the church of San Fantin, 40 feet from the front door of the Teatro Fenice. Boys in black trousers and cummerbunds, black ties and white shirts, wait on the crowds that come here for a pizza lunch or an afternoon or after-theater snack. Quite a number of pretty girls come here to banter with these dashing youths. If you want something lighter than their unctuous, dripping pizzas, have a Caprice.

Big slice of bread	Egg
Butter and crushed garlic	Strips of prosciutto
Shredded Gruyère cheese	Tomato sauce

Fry a good-sized slice of bread in butter with crushed garlic. Put it on a fireproof dish and make a nest of the shredded cheese to hold a raw egg. Over the egg put three strips of prosciutto or other thin cooked ham and moisten the top with 2 teaspoonfuls of tomato sauce. This is put in a very hot oven for 5 to 7 minutes until the cheese melts and the egg is set but still soft.

ONION TART

2½ to 3 cups sliced onions	Dough:
3 tablespoons butter	1¼ cups sifted flour
Salt and pepper	2 teaspoons baking powder
¼ teaspoon nutmeg	½ teaspoon salt
2 eggs, beaten	6 tablespoons shortening
⅞ cup sour cream	Milk
⅓ cup shredded Swiss or Gruyère cheese	

For the dough, sift the dry ingredients and cut in the shortening with a pastry cutter. Add just enough milk so the dough may be handled and rolled. Line a 9-inch pie plate, and bake 7 minutes at 375°. Sauté the onions in the butter until they are yellow and tender. Add salt and pepper. Combine the nutmeg, beaten eggs, and sour cream. Put the onions on top of the crust, cover with the cream mixture, and sprinkle the cheese over the top. Bake at 325° for 20 minutes or until set and lightly browned. This may be served for lunch with a green salad or as a vegetable accompaniment with poultry or pork. Serves 6 or 8.

PIZZA NAPOLI

Dough:
- 1 envelope yeast
- ½ cup lukewarm water
- 1 tablespoon brown sugar
- ¾ teaspoon salt
- 2 cups flour
- 2 tablespoons olive oil

Filling:
- 2 tablespoons olive oil
- 2 Mozzarella cheeses, sliced ⅛-inch thick
- 2 skinned tomatoes, sliced
- Salt and pepper
- 2 teaspoons powdered fennel or orégano
- 1 can anchovy fillets
- 6 black Italian olives

Let the yeast become foamy with the water and sugar. Sift the salt and flour. Make a hole in the center of the flour and add the yeast mixture and 2 tablespoons olive oil. Stir hard with a wooden spoon. If it needs more lukewarm water to make a soft ball, add a little at a time. Toss onto a floured board and knead a little, then let rise in a warm place until it doubles in bulk. Roll out to ⅛-inch thickness and spread on a 12-inch pie plate. Brush with olive oil, then arrange the slices of Mozzarella cheese over the dough. Lay the sliced tomatoes on top of the cheese, and sprinkle with a very little salt, some pepper, and the fennel or orégano. Arrange the anchovies over the top in a fan-shaped design and between the anchovies put halves of pitted black olives. Sprinkle the top with olive oil. Bake in a 375° oven for 20 minutes. Serve with a good red wine and a green salad. Pimento strips may be added to the pizza if desired. Makes 8 slices, but 4 good appetites can finish it.

ROLL DOUGH FOR PIZZAS, BALLOTINES, MEAT PASTRIES, ETC.

Puff pastry, pie pastry, and roll dough are all used for French or Russian meat- or game-filled pastries. This yeast roll dough is a little simpler to make than *Puff Pastry*. This is a fine light dough for this purpose. For 1 10-inch pizza, only half the recipe would be needed, but use all the yeast.

- 1 envelope yeast
- 1 tablespoon sugar
- 2 tablespoons lukewarm water
- ½ cup butter
- 1½ tablespoons sugar
- 1 cup scalded milk
- 2 eggs, beaten
- 4 cups sifted flour
- 1 teaspoon salt
- 1 egg yolk

Put the yeast in a small bowl, sprinkle it with sugar, add the water and set it in a saucepan of hot water, almost cover it, and let it become frothy. Cream the butter with the sugar. Add the scalded milk to the butter-sugar mixture and cool to lukewarm. The eggs must be at room temperature and well beaten. Sift the flour with the salt and put it in a large mixing bowl. Combine the yeast with the milk mixture and add it to the flour. Beat hard with a wooden spoon. This does not require kneading. Set the bowl in a dishpan of quite warm water, cover with a tea towel, and let rise for 2 to 2½ hours or until double in size. Punch down well and roll to form a rectangle 16 by 12 inches. Make a pillow of the filling the long way of the rectangle, then fold the ends and the sides over to enclose the filling. Lay the loaf on a greased cookie sheet with the lapped dough underneath, make incisions on the top for the steam to escape, and paint the top with egg yolk. Put it in a 400° oven, bake 10 minutes, then turn down the heat to 350° and bake 15 or 20 minutes more.

PARMESAN PIE

Pie Pastry for 10-inch pan
1 tablespoon flour
1 tablespoon butter
1 cup milk
1 cup heavy cream
1 cup Parmesan cheese
3 large eggs, beaten
Salt and pepper
¼ teaspoon nutmeg

Line a pie pan with pastry and bake it 7 minutes at 400°. Meanwhile mix the flour and butter in a saucepan over a low flame and when smooth slowly add the milk and cream and let it come to a boil. Add the cheese and then pour it over the eggs, add a little salt, pepper, and the nutmeg. Remove the pie crust from the oven and add the filling. Return it to the oven, turn the heat to 350°, and bake it until it is set, about 25 minutes. This may be made of finely grated Swiss or Gruyère cheese instead of the Parmesan. Serves 6 or 8.

CHEESE PASTRIES

2 cups very thick *Cream Sauce*
3 egg yolks, beaten
1 cup finely diced ham
1 cup finely diced Swiss cheese
¼ teaspoon salt
1 teaspoon prepared mustard
Rich *Pie Pastry* (2 cups flour)

Make the *Cream Sauce*, pour it over the egg yolks and cook a moment. Cool a little, then add the ham and cheese and stir in the seasoning. Let cool. Make the pastry, roll it out, and cut it in 5- or 6-inch squares. Put 2 or 3 tablespoons of filling on each; fold over opposite points and press the edges together. Pierce the top 3 times and bake at 400° for 10 minutes and at 350° 5 or 10 minutes more. Serve hot. Makes 8. Serve for lunch or supper with a salad. Smaller tarts (2 to 3 inches square) may be served as appetizers.

CRÊPES FOR ENTRÉES

These crêpes, made with beer, mixed and allowed to stand 2 or 3 hours to develop, are extremely light and tender. A little Béchamel sauce is put along the top of each rolled crêpe and a good sprinkle of Parmesan cheese. When ready to serve, put the baking dish in a hot oven for 10 minutes, then under the flame for a minute so the crêpes brown nicely. They may be assembled ahead of time, and should be if you are the cook.

1 cup sifted flour	¼ cup butter
⅛ teaspoon salt	½ cup milk
4 eggs, unbeaten	1 cup beer
2 tablespoons oil	

Put the flour and salt in a mixing bowl and break the eggs into it. Beat together with a rotary beater until smooth, add the oil and beat again. Put the butter and milk in a saucepan and heat until the butter melts. Add this to the batter, then add the beer. Blend well and let stand 2 or 3 hours or longer. Take a stick of butter and rub the crêpe pan a little before each crêpe is fried. The pan should be quite hot. Put 2 or 3 tablespoonfuls of batter in the pan and time it 1 minute before turning, otherwise it will be fragile and break. Turn with a narrow spatula and cook about 20 or 30 seconds on the other side. Turn onto a plate so the first side, the nicer one, is against the plate. I find it easier to fill and roll each crêpe as it is made. A cup and a half of very thick *Cream Sauce* with plenty of cheese and chopped ham added is a good filling. Other fine fillings are creamed crab, lobster, shrimp, chicken livers, or mushrooms. Put a generous tablespoonful of filling on one side of each crêpe, roll it, and lay it on the bottom of a greased shallow baking dish. A lasagne pan, one you can bring to the table, is perfect for these. This recipe makes 18 crêpes, which would serve 8 or 9 as an entrée, or 4 or 5 as a main-course luncheon or supper dish.

LA FRIANDISE DU PETIT COLOMBIER
Le Petit Colombier, rue des Acacias, Paris

This is one of those small Paris restaurants, mostly frequented by the French, where every dish is always cooked and served to perfection. The Salade Niçoise fairly shines, and these friandises are so delicate that they are suitable for an entrée before the main course. The friend who took me there always takes one order of crêpes after another and skips the main dish.

2 7-inch crêpes for each serving	For each crêpe:
	2 tablespoons thick cream (or more)
	1 paper-thin slice cooked ham
	Grated Gruyère cheese

The French matured cream is so thick it stays where it is put. I use *Crème Fraîche* (see sauces). Make the crêpes and fry them. On one half of each crêpe put a big spoon of thick cream, then the ham, then another spoon of cream, then a sprinkle of cheese. Roll the crêpes and put them close together on the bottom of a shallow baking pan. (A lasagne pan would be ideal for this.) These may be prepared an hour before serving. When ready to serve, run the crêpes under a hot flame to brown quickly. Serve hot.

PANZEROTTI ALLA ROMANA
Sabatini, Florence

Crêpes:
- 2 cups flour
- 2 cups milk
- 4 egg yolks
- 1 whole egg
- ½ teaspoon salt
- 2 cups tomato sauce
- Mozzarella cheese, sliced
- Parmesan cheese

Béchamel Sauce:
- ¾ cup flour
- ¾ cup butter
- 2 cups milk
- ⅓ cup cubed Mozzarella cheese
- ⅓ cup cubed Gruyère cheese
- 2 strips prosciutto, sliced
- 2 eggs, beaten
- Salt and pepper
- ¼ teaspoon nutmeg

Mix the batter for the crêpes and fry them 5 or 6 inches in diameter. They may be made ahead of time and allowed to cool. Make a very thick Béchamel sauce. Melt the butter in a saucepan, stir in the flour, and when smooth add the milk. Cook until it thickens, then add all the rest of the ingredients. Spread on a platter and let cool. Cut in strips, fill the crêpes, and roll them. Butter a shallow baking dish and put a little tomato sauce on the bottom, then put in the crêpes and add more tomato sauce to the top. Cover with thin slices of Mozzarella cheese and sprinkle the top with Parmesan cheese. Bake 15 minutes in a hot oven until there is a golden crust. This will serve 8 or 10; cut in half to serve 4 to 6.

CRÊPES PARMENTIER
Restaurant du Chapon Fin, Thoissey

Never was there such a sight as the crowd of eaters which descends on the Chapon Fin for midday Sunday dinner. The courtyard is filled with cars from near and far. We wouldn't have missed it. The diners may begin with a Ballotine de Canard Truffée et Pistachée, or a Salade Niçoise; proceed to some Escargots de Bourgogne or frogs' legs; then settle down to the serious business of a game bird or an entrecôte accompanied by 8 or 10 of these delicious pancakes. We planned to eat "light" for a change but could hardly keep our eyes and minds off the greatest of all fish, a poached salmon trout with the most elegant golden Hollandaise. Finally we broke down and had our share of Crêpes Parmentier. I really think the crowd comes chiefly for these crêpes, which keep the rushing staff busy for 2 hours. A cheese platter came next, then beautiful desserts: Les Poires Belle-Hélène, L'Ananas au Kirsch, Glace Parfum au Choix, among others. As though this wasn't enough, huge plates of Patisseries Maison were passed to the still-enthusiastic patrons.

3 good-sized potatoes	6 eggs, beaten
Warm milk	2 large tablespoons heavy cream
¼ cup flour	Clarified butter
A little salt	Garnish: Powdered sugar

Peel the potatoes and boil them in salted water. Drain and mash through a sieve with a little warm milk to make a smooth purée. Let cool. Blend the flour into the potatoes, then mix in the eggs and cream. Begin with 3 eggs as the batter must be quite rich and thick. Clarified butter is melted butter poured off the white residue. Put plenty of butter in a big pancake pan and when it is very hot add batter by small soup spoonfuls. The crêpes form themselves; they should be rather small. Turn once, and serve hot, 6 or 8 cakes to a person. Pass the powdered sugar shaker for those who want it.

BUCKWHEAT PANCAKES TO SERVE WITH CAVIAR

¾ cup buckwheat flour	¼ cup melted butter or oil
¾ cup rye flour	2 cups buttermilk and more
¾ cup wholewheat flour	Garnish:
3 teaspoons baking powder	Caviar
2 teaspoons salt	Melted butter
3 teaspoons brown sugar	Sour cream
3 eggs, beaten	

This makes 24 pancakes. If you allow 3 apiece—and they are hearty—they are a nice thing to serve for a New Year's Eve supper party for 8. Make them in an electric frying pan which can be set up wherever you are, so there is no disappearing into the kitchen. Serve bowls of caviar, and bowls of sour cream, and plenty of melted butter in pitchers. Mix the 3 flours with the dry ingredients. Beat the eggs until light, then mix with the butter or oil, and 2 cups of the buttermilk. Combine the dry ingredients with the egg mixture and add enough buttermilk to make a rather stiff batter, so the cakes won't spread. Fry in butter, turning once.

Egg Dishes

ŒUFS COCOTTE PERIGOURDINE
Hotel de la Côte d'Or, Saulieu

NOT long after the great Alexandre Dumaine retired from his famous palace of gastronomy, the Hotel de la Côte d'Or lost its Michelin stars. The outcry from everywhere was so loud and long and brought so much loyalty and affection toward the restaurant that the loss may have been a boon after all. Not that Dumaine's young protegé, François Minot, needed all this publicity to bolster his budding fame; he has already proved a worthy successor to his master. We ordered lunch the day before we drove over from Beaune to Saulieu, this rather austere-looking country town in Burgundy. We were warmly greeted by the hostess and by M. Minot who had chosen our lunch. The dining room was already filled with concentrated diners. Our lunch began with little delicate pastries filled with lobster. The main dish was Poularde Vapeur á la Lucien Tendret. This beautiful bird with truffles tucked under its skin was brought in in a huge deep earthenware pot with a towel wrapped around the lid to prevent any juices from escaping. When the waiter unwrapped this long towel every eye in the dining room was directed our way. The chicken was sliced and served with a tureen of creamed morel mushrooms. After that, two of us could deal only with fresh fruit but our third let us taste his Gâteau aux Amandes. M. Minot chose a Montrachet and a Maconnais for our lunch. After lunch he sat with us in the reception room to visit over a liqueur, and gave me two lovely recipes of which I am very proud. This is one.

Foie gras	Truffles
Salt and pepper	Heavy cream
Eggs	

Butter ramekins and put a slice of fresh foie gras on the bottom of each. Put a thin slice of truffle on each slice of foie gras. Break an egg into each ramekin. Add salt and freshly ground pepper and 3 tablespoons thick cream. Put on top a pinch of minced truffles. Set the ramekins in a pan of hot water and bake, covered, for 4 minutes at 375°. (These could be cooked in an egg poacher, in which case they would have to be slid off onto hot small dishes.) When done, complete each with a médaillon (slice) of fresh foie gras on the top. This is an entrée to precede the main course.

SOUFFLÉ SURPRISE

8 eggs (for 4)
⅔ to ¾ cup light cream
1 teaspoon cornstarch
Salt and pepper
¼ teaspoon nutmeg
½ cup shredded Cheddar cheese

1 tablespoon tomato paste
4 fresh mushrooms
¼ cup chopped ham
Butter
Parmesan cheese

A certain lovely soufflé is a secret of a very fine London hotel. That one had to be figured out, but this is also a lovely soufflé and a great deal like the secret one. Butter four 4½-inch individual soufflé dishes and sprinkle sides and bottoms with Parmesan cheese. Make a custard by blending the cornstarch with the light cream. Add the seasonings and cook until it thickens; then stir in the cheese and tomato paste. Separate 4 of the eggs. Stir the yolks into the custard and cook a second or so until it thickens. Sauté the mushrooms 2 minutes in butter and toss with the ham. Beat the 4 egg whites until stiff, stir one fourth of them into the custard, then lightly fold in the rest. Put a big spoonful of the soufflé mixture in each soufflé dish and divide the mushrooms and ham over it. Break an egg into each dish, then cover equally with the rest of the soufflé mixture. Sprinkle the top liberally with Parmesan cheese. Put the soufflés in a 375° oven for 10 or 11 minutes. They will be puffed and golden and the egg inside will be cooked but still soft, forming a liquid dressing.

ŒUFS MAYONNAISE

10-minute eggs
Sour cream
Mayonnaise
Salt and pepper
Minced fresh herbs: parsley, chervil,
  tarragon, chives, or watercress

Garnish:
Anchovy fillets or capers or
  red or black caviar or *Mushrooms à la Grècque*
Lettuce

Prepare 1 egg for each serving. When the eggs have boiled 10 minutes replace the hot water with cold. Remove the shells and cut the eggs in half lengthwise, carefully removing the yolks without breaking the white shells. Mash the yolks and mix to a fluffy paste with sour cream, mayonnaise, salt, pepper, and at least 1 tablespoon of minced herbs for every 2 or 3 eggs. Refill the shells with the paste. Make a bed of lettuce on each small serving plate to hold 2 egg halves. Add a little mayonnaise to the top of each and decorate with any of the garnishes.

ŒUFS JANINE

6 slices of foie gras
6 poached eggs
Aspic:
   2 cups white wine
   1 tablespoon gelatin

Garnish:
   Truffle slices soaked in Madeira,
   or sliced mushrooms cooked
   in butter

Butter 6 ramekins and put a slice of foie gras in the bottom of each. Lay a cold poached egg on each slice of foie gras. An egg poacher cooks a very neat egg which needs no trimming. Soak the gelatin in ¼ cup of the wine and then heat it over hot water to melt. Add it to the rest of the wine and dip the wine over the eggs. Chill. Before serving garnish each with either a thin slice of truffle which has soaked 2 or 3 hours in a little Madeira, or a fine big thin slice of mushroom which has been tossed in hot butter a few seconds and cooled.

ŒUFS BOURGUIGNONS
Hotel de la Poste, Beaune

Sauce to serve 4 or 6:
   1 large onion, thinly sliced
   2 tablespoons butter
   1 sprig fresh thyme or 1 tea-
      spoon thyme
   1 bay leaf
   Salt and freshly ground
      pepper
   3 tablespoons flour
   1 clove garlic, crushed

3 cups "rather young Burgundy"
2 green onions, sliced
4 fresh mushrooms, sliced
4 to 6 slices French bread
2 cloves garlic, crushed
3 tablespoons butter
8 to 12 poached eggs
2 strips bacon, fried crisp

Sauté the onion with the butter, thyme and bay leaf until the onion colors a little. Sprinkle with salt and pepper and stir in the flour. Add 1 crushed clove of garlic then stir in the wine, gradually at first. A Beaujolais would be good for this. Cook this sauce, uncovered, over gently simmering water 1¼ hours. Stir it 2 or 3 times. Strain the sauce through a sieve. This sauce may be made in advance and kept warm over warm water. Cook the onions and mushrooms in a little butter 1½ to 2 minutes over a low flame and add them to the sauce. Sauté the bread in the crushed garlic and butter and put them in sauce dishes. Poach the eggs (use 1 egg for each serving if this dish precedes a full course dinner) and put the eggs on the bread. Sauté the bacon until crisp. Have the sauce hot and add the bacon just before spooning the sauce over the eggs. We appreciated these eggs so much we had them nearly every night when we were in Beaune.

The beautiful and ancient town of Beaune is right in the middle of the great Burgundy vineyards. Leaving Dijon and motoring south six miles, one comes first to the village of Gevrey-Chambertin; a little further, Morey Saint-Denis; and nestling in a slope, the great Chambolle-Musigny. Next comes the smallest wine-producing village of Vougeot, but one of the greatest, originally owned and operated with devoted care by the Cîteau monks who built the imposing manor in the thirteenth century. The manor is now the headquarters of the Brotherhood of the Knights of the Tastevin. We were shown the beautiful rooms where the members meet. The most interesting display is the huge old wine presses, as old as the manor itself. The next town is Vosne-Romanée, which produces various great wines: Romanée-Conti and Richebourg. Just before entering Beaune one arrives at the great vineyards of Nuits St. George. In Beaune one of the most architecturally interesting buildings is the Hôtel Dieu, built in the Middle Ages and still housing a hospital. A view of its amazing sloping roof, especially in the moonlight, is unforgettable. The holy order is at least partly supported from the revenues of the vineyards it owns, the wine being auctioned annually on the third Sunday in November. South of Beaune is one enchanting village after another, through one of the most beautiful countrysides in the world. Succeeding one another are the vineyards of Pommard, Volnay, Monthelie, Meursault, Montrachet, Chassagne, and Puligny—magic names for all wine lovers. When we visit Beaune, our friends take us to the caves in the late afternoon for refreshment. This Burgundian hospitality is the pleasantest way of entertaining thirsty pilgrims.

ŒUFS PÔCHES BOURGUIGNONNE
Capucin Gourmand, Nancy

2 poached eggs per person	1 teaspoon meat extract
1 quart young red wine	Salt and pepper
¼ cup grated carrot	2 cloves garlic, crushed
¼ cup grated onion	Pinch of sugar
2 tablespoons shallots or green onions, chopped	1 tablespoon butter
Bouquet garni:	1 tablespoon flour
parsley, thyme, bay leaf	Butter
¼ cup breadcrumbs	Sliced French bread
	2 tablespoons vinegar

This is a little different from the Beaune Burgundy eggs but both are among the best first-course entrées in any repertoire. Prepare only 1 egg to a serving if these precede a full course dinner. Put the wine in a heavy saucepan with the vegetables, herbs, breadcrumbs, meat extract, salt, pepper, and garlic and cook, almost covered, over simmering water for 40 minutes. Add the sugar and strain the sauce. Make a roux by blending the butter and flour over a low flame. Add a little strained sauce and when smooth, add to the rest of the sauce. Cook a few minutes longer until the sauce thickens. This may be made in advance and kept warm over warm water. Slice French bread ¾-inch thick, toast it lightly, and fry it in butter. Put 1 slice in each shallow sauce dish. Poach the eggs in water with the vinegar added (no salt) until the white is set and the yolk soft. Lift the eggs carefully to the toast and spoon the hot sauce over each. This is enough sauce to serve 6 or 8.

FRITTATA AL VERDE

4 or 5 eggs, beaten
Salt and pepper
2 tablespoons cream
1 teaspoon lemon juice or ½ teaspoon grated lemon rind
2 or 3 tablespoons ground spinach
1 tablespoon Parmesan cheese
2 or 3 tablespoons ground parsley

2 sprigs fresh basil, minced
2 sprigs fresh chervil, minced
2 sprigs fresh tarragon, minced
4 tablespoons butter
Garnish:
    Parmesan cheese
    Pimento (optional)

Beat the eggs until very light, about 3 or 4 minutes. Add all the ingredients except the butter and mix lightly. The more fresh herbs you add to this omelette the more fragrant it will be. Melt the butter in an omelette pan, tipping it so that the sides are buttered. Cook the omelette over a brisk flame, lifting the edges so the uncooked egg runs into the pan. When it is set but not dry, turn it out onto a round plate. The Italians serve this as a round cake, but you may fold it once if you like. Pass Parmesan cheese to sprinkle over the top. Serves 3 or 4. A few short strips of red pimento may be added if desired.

EGGS ANDALUSIA
The Canepa, Rome

Tomatoes, sliced 1 inch thick
Gruyère cheese, cubed
Capers
Mayonnaise

Poached eggs
Prosciutto
Chopped Gelatin

Skin fine firm tomatoes and use a 1-inch slice for each serving. (The Italians never serve overripe tomatoes; they are used in their huge tomato canning industry, or for sauces and paste.) Scoop out the tomato seeds and fill the interstices with little cubes of cheese and capers moistened with a little mayonnaise. On top of each tomato slice place a trimmed cold poached egg. Wrap a slice of prosciutto around egg and tomato and fasten with a toothpick. Cover the egg with a big spoonful of rich oil mayonnaise and top with a little Chopped Gelatin. This handsome and delicious hors d'œuvre may be served also for a light luncheon. The Canepa is a fine restaurant with a separate entrance leading to a little snack bar.

PURÉED SPINACH OR GREEN PEA ROULADE

2 pounds fresh peas or
    1 pound spinach
2 tablespoons butter
4 tablespoons flour
1 cup milk
    Salt and pepper
½ teaspoon nutmeg
3 egg yolks
3 egg whites, beaten

Filling:
    1½ cups ground ham or 1 cup
        sautéed mushrooms
        mixed with ½ cup
        sour cream
Garnish:
    4 tablespoons melted butter
    4 tablespoons Parmesan
        cheese

Cook the peas in very little water and drain them. Purée the peas in a sieve or blender, making 1 cup of quite dry purée. If you use spinach, cook it with only the water clinging to the leaves, then press it against a sieve. Purée the spinach and use 1 cup. Make a thick cream sauce by melting the butter in a saucepan, blending in the flour, and slowly adding the milk. Cook until it thickens, then add the seasonings and egg yolks; remove from the heat and stir in the puréed vegetable. Beat the egg whites until stiff and stir one fourth of them into the sauce, then lightly fold in the rest. Grease a cookie sheet and cover it with greased wax paper, then dust the paper with flour. Spread the batter on the paper 12 inches by 15 or 16 inches and bake 15 to 18 minutes at 375°. For the filling, mix the sour cream with either the ham or the mushrooms. When the roulade is done spread it with the filling and roll it the long way onto a hot platter. Pour the melted butter over it and sprinkle it with the cheese. Serves 4 or 5.

STUFFED EGGS

Stuffed eggs make delicious appetizers and first-course lunch or supper dishes. The eggs are boiled 10 minutes, peeled, cut in half lengthwise, and the yolks carefully removed. The yolks are mashed and any of the additions blended in, then the white shells are stuffed. A mixture of mayonnaise and sour cream makes the yolks creamy and is usually added along with other ingredients. Allow 2 or 3 halves to a serving.

1. Yolks blended with sour cream, minced green or white onions, salt, pepper. Topped with a teaspoonful of black or red caviar.
2. Yolks blended with sour cream and mayonnaise, fresh chopped herbs (chervil, tarragon, or dill), and a dash of mustard.
3. Yolks blended with sour cream and mayonnaise and seasoned with curry or cumin powder. Top with caviar or a piece of chutney.
4. Yolks blended with a little sour cream and nut butter. Top with a tiny pickle slice or ground nuts.
5. Yolks blended with sour cream and mayonnaise, chopped olives or pimentos.

6. Yolks blended with Roquefort or creamy Gorgonzola cheese, or any kind of shredded or grated cheese, and sour cream or mayonnaise.
7. Yolks blended with sour cream, minced green or white onions, and chopped sautéed mushrooms. A tiny button mushroom may top each egg.
8. Yolks blended with sour cream and mayonnaise. Add finely ground fresh shrimp (½ pound for 12 eggs) or flaked crab or lobster meat.
9. Yolks blended with sour cream, mayonnaise, and ground ham.
10. Yolks blended with mashed sardines or fish paste and mayonnaise. Anchovy paste is good with a little crushed garlic and soft cream cheese or sour cream.

Stuffed eggs surrounding a molded fish, meat, or salad dish make an attractive buffet platter.

CODDLED EGGS

Put the required number of eggs in a pot, cover with actively boiling water, cover the pot, and let stand for 5 minutes. This is said to be the most digestible way of cooking eggs. They are of the right consistency to break over a bowl of salad greens to make the French dressing more interesting.

BOILED EGGS

Eggs boiled in boiling water 3½ minutes are soft, 5 minutes medium, and 10 minutes hard. If the eggs are put in cold water, they are boiled 2½ minutes for soft, 3½ minutes for medium, and 9 or 10 minutes for hard. If eggs are boiled too long for hard they will be rubbery, so time them. All eggs are dashed into cold water when they are done to make peeling easy. When possible, eggs should be at room temperature before boiling.

POACHED EGGS

Boil plenty of water, 1½ inches deep, in a shallow pan, adding a little salt and a tablespoon of wine or vinegar. The acid prevents the eggs from spreading. Slide the eggs from a saucer into the boiling water and baste with the water. When they are of the right doneness to your taste, ladle them out with a perforated spoon. Poaching is the best way of cooking eggs for serving on toast, for *Eggs Benedict*, for dressing with various sauces, and for trimming to use in aspics for *Eggs Surprise* and *Oeufs Bourgignons*.

ŒUFS MOLLETS

Hold the eggs under the hot water tap to warm the shells if they are cold. Put them in hot water and after they come to a boil, time them. Large eggs take a full 6 minutes, medium-sized eggs take from 5 to 5½ minutes to cook so the white is set and the yolk is liquid. Dash them in cold water and carefully remove the shells. They are suitable for aspics, for filling artichoke bottoms and avocado halves, and for other hors d'œuvre. They are good to mash over salad to make the dressing richer.

AVOCADO OR ARTICHOKE AND EGG HORS D'ŒUVRE

Small avocado halves or artichoke bottoms
Oeufs Mollets (6-minute eggs)

Anchovy fillets
Oil mayonnaise
Lettuce

These appetizers are made with either skinned avocado halves or artichoke bottoms of sufficient size to hold the egg and dressing. Prepare the required number of eggs by consulting the directions for *Oeufs Mollets*. Put an avocado half (or artichoke bottom) on each small serving plate and garnish with lettuce. Put a cold egg in each and crisscross on each egg 2 fillets of anchovy. Top with plain or garlic mayonnaise.

EVE'S SPANISH EGGS

⅓ to ½ cup bread crumbs
1½ cups light cream
1½ cups milk
3 cloves garlic, crushed
3 tablespoons butter
3 tablespoons olive oil

¼ cup toasted almond slivers
Salt and pepper
2 teaspoons cumin powder
6 to 8 eggs
3 or 4 slices of toast or toasted English muffins

This is a dish for 3 or 4 persons; serve 2 eggs apiece. Soak the crumbs in the cream and milk 10 minutes. Lightly brown the garlic a moment in a large saucepan with the butter and olive oil, then add the almonds and cook a little. Then add the seasonings and the crumbs and liquid. Cook, stirring with a wooden spoon, until the sauce is well blended, then slide in the eggs from a saucer and poach them until they are set but soft. Have toast ready in shallow soup plates and dip out the eggs, putting 2 in each plate. Divide the sauce over the eggs. This is a Spanish peasant dish—a typical use of crumbs instead of flour as thickening.

EGGS POACHED IN POTATO SOUP

1½ cups potato soup or 1 cup
    mashed potatoes and ⅔ to
    1 cup of milk
4 eggs

2 slices of homemade bread or
    toast, buttered
2 tablespoons Parmesan cheese

Put the soup in a good-sized sauté pan. If you have well-seasoned leftover mashed potatoes, blend them with the milk to make a sauce like heavy cream, and use this instead of the soup. Let the potato mixture come to a simmer and slip the eggs into it from a saucer. Cover and let cook slowly until the eggs are set. Put the bread or toast in wide soup dishes, lift 2 eggs onto each slice of bread, and cover with the sauce. Sprinkle with cheese. This makes a fine lunch or supper dish for children or adults. It may be soupy enough to eat with a spoon. Any leftover cream soup may be used for this, including tomato soup. The top may be sprinkled with parsley instead of cheese.

FRIED STUFFED EGGS

10 hard-boiled eggs
1 tablespoon dried fresh bread
    crumbs
2 tablespoons sour cream
2 tablespoons red or black caviar

1 teaspoon chopped parsley
Melted butter
Parmesan cheese
Oil

Boil the eggs 10 minutes. Dash them in cold water, peel them, and cut in half lengthwise, being careful not to break the whites. Scoop out the yolks and mash them with the crumbs, sour cream, caviar, and parsley. You may use 1 tablespoon of anchovy paste instead of the caviar. Stuff the whites and put them together. Roll the eggs in melted butter, then in cheese, and fry to a golden brown in an inch of boiling oil. These may accompany fish or be part of an hors d'œuvre tray.

HOT EGG MOUSSE

6 ounces cream cheese
¾ cup sour cream
½ teaspoon salt

Grated rind 1 lemon
2 teaspoons honey
5 eggs, beaten

Let the cheese soften to room temperature and beat in the sour cream; add the salt, lemon rind, and honey. When it is fluffy and smooth, gradually pour in the eggs which have been beaten a good 3 minutes until thick. Grease a 7½-inch soufflé dish, pour in the mixture, set in a pan of hot water, and bake 15 minutes at 375° and 15 minutes more at 350°. If it is baking too fast turn the oven down to 325°. This has a velvety texture and is very delicate. Serves 4 or 5, as a main dish or as an accompaniment.

EGGS SURPRISE

6 eggs, poached
Aspic:
    3 cups clear chicken consommé
    3 teaspoons gelatin
    2 tablespoons minced fresh
      herb: tarragon, chervil, or
      basil

6 slices pâté or 12 tablespoons
red or black caviar

Poach the eggs, being careful to have the yolks soft. With a cookie cutter trim them slightly smaller than the ramekins you are using. Let them cool. Use ¼ cup of the consommé to soak the gelatin. Bring the rest of the consommé to a simmer with the herb. Melt the soaked gelatin in the hot consommé and let it thoroughly cool. Put 3 tablespoons of gelatin in the bottom of each of 6 ramekins and put in the refrigerator to set. Add a slice of pâté or 2 tablespoons of caviar to the set gelatin, put a poached egg on top, then fill with more gelatin. Refrigerate until set. This is a first-course entrée or a luncheon dish. Serves 6.

OMELETTE MOUSSELINE
Hotel de la Côte d'Or, Saulieu

This is M. François Minot's lovely sweet omelette for two.

4 eggs
1½ tablespoons vanilla sugar
3 tablespoons sweet butter

¼ cup apricot marmalade
Garnish: More vanilla sugar

Vanilla sugar is made by breaking up 2 or 3 vanilla beans and keeping them in a cannister of powdered sugar. Separate the eggs and beat the yolks with the sugar. Fold in the stiffly beaten whites. Melt the butter in an omelette pan, tipping it in all directions to coat the sides of the pan. When it is quite hot, cook the omelette being careful that it does not stick on account of the sugar in it. The jam may be thinned with a little orange juice. When the omelette has set but is still moist, put the jam over half of the omelette and fold over the other half and slide it onto a hot platter. Sprinkle the top with more vanilla sugar and serve immediately. It would not be out of order to blaze this with 2 tablespoons of dark rum.

OMELETTE AU CITRON

4 egg yolks, beaten
3 tablespoons sugar
1 teaspoon grated lemon rind

4 egg whites, beaten
¼ cup butter
Powdered sugar

Beat the egg yolks until thick; add the sugar and beat again. Stir in the lemon rind. Beat the whites until stiff and fold in. Melt the butter in an omelette pan and when it is quite hot add the egg mixture. Stir a little. When the omelette is done, fold it over, sprinkle the top liberally with powdered sugar, and glaze it a moment under a hot flame. Serves 2. For 3, use 6 eggs and add 1 more tablespoon of sugar and ½ teaspoon more lemon rind. These sweet omelettes aren't too sweet for a main dish for lunch.

BUTTER OMELETTE

4 eggs, beaten
¼ teaspoon salt
6 tablespoons sweet butter
  Powdered sugar

Powdered anise
Garnish:
  Whole baked bananas or other
  fruit or berries blazed in rum
  (optional)

All the directions are important in making this omelette. Beat the eggs with the salt 5 minutes. They must be very light and thick. Use 1 tablespoon of butter for each egg and 2 for the pan (6 eggs, 8 tablespoons butter). Melt the butter in the omelette pan, pour in the eggs, and cook over quite high heat, tipping the eggs onto bottom of pan only once. Cook about 50 seconds, then turn off the heat and let the omelette stand on stove for a minute. Sprinkle the top with powdered sugar, then put the omelette under a flame for a few seconds until the top is set but not dried out. Then fold the omelette in half and slide it onto a hot platter. Sprinkle the top with a mixture of powdered sugar and anise. Serve immediately. This may be garnished with 2 baked bananas or other fruit sprinkled with the sugar mixture and blazed with rum. Serves 2. If 8 eggs are used to serve 4, use a 10-inch sauté pan.

SCRAMBLED EGGS WITH FRESH HERBS

6 or 8 eggs
6 or 8 tablespoons heavy cream
  Salt and pepper
4 or 5 tablespoons minced tarragon, basil, watercress, chervil,
  parsley, or chives

4 or 5 tablespoons butter
4 tablespoons grated Swiss or
  Gruyère cheese

Beat the eggs for 3 minutes until light and thick, add the cream, salt, and pepper, and beat again. Stir in the herbs. Use two or three different herbs if available. Melt the butter in the top of the double boiler and tip so the sides are covered. Put in the eggs and stir over simmering water until the eggs thicken but are still creamy. Empty them into a hot shallow baking dish, sprinkle with cheese, and put under the flame a moment, just to melt the cheese a little. Serve 2 eggs per person, with hot bread or popovers.

CREAMED STUFFED EGGS

12 hard-boiled eggs
½ pound fresh shrimp or canned
    lobster or crabmeat
    Sour cream and mayonnaise
    Salt and pepper
1 teaspoon curry powder

Sauce:
¾ cup shrimp broth
¼ cup heavy cream
1½ cups light cream
2½ tablespoons cornstarch
    Salt and pepper
1 tablespoon tomato paste
⅓ cup grated Parmesan cheese

Peel the hard-boiled eggs, cut them in half lengthwise, and remove the yolks. Put the yolks into a mixing bowl. If shrimp are used, wash them and boil 3 minutes in ⅔ cup of water, a slice of onion, and 1 teaspoon of thyme. Let them cool in the broth, then remove them, reserving the broth, shell, and grind them. Put the ground shrimp with the egg yolks. If crab or lobster meat is used, shred it fine and add it to the yolks. Since there won't be fish broth for the sauce, use ¾ cup either light cream or chicken consommé instead. Mash the egg yolks, blend with the fish, and mix with enough sour cream and mayonnaise to make a fluffy paste. Season with salt, pepper, and curry powder. Stuff the egg whites and arrange in the bottom of a large shallow baking dish, one that may be brought to the table. Blend the broth and the heavy and light cream with the cornstarch, salt, pepper, and tomato paste. Any leftover stuffing may be added to the sauce. Cook until it thickens. Pour the sauce over the stuffed eggs, sprinkle the top with the cheese, and put the dish under the flame until the sauce bubbles and browns a little. Use 3 halves to a serving.

MUSHROOM SOUFFLÉ

1 pound fresh mushrooms
1 medium white onion, sliced
2½ tablespoons butter
3 tablespoons flour
½ cup chicken consommé

½ cup cream
    Salt and pepper
¼ teaspoon nutmeg
4 egg yolks, beaten
6 egg whites, beaten

Brush the mushrooms. If they are white and well packed, which they should be, they need not be washed. It is better that they be dry. Put them through a meat grinder with the onion, then sauté 2 or 3 minutes in a little butter. Melt 2 tablespoons butter and blend in the flour, stirring until smooth. Slowly stir in the consommé and cream and cook until the sauce thickens. Add salt, pepper, nutmeg and beaten egg yolks. Cook a moment until it thickens and let cool a little. Mix in the mushrooms, stir in one-fourth of the stiffly beaten egg whites, then lightly fold in the rest of the whites. Bake in a buttered soufflé dish 25 minutes at 350°. This soufflé followed the *Baked Lobster* at the Hanstown Club luncheon in London, which was planned by M. André Simon.

EGGS AND FRESH HERBS

8 or 9 eggs
⅔ cup fresh herbs, coarsely ground
    (watercress, parsley, 3 sorrel
    leaves, tarragon, chervil)

Salt and pepper
⅓ cup whipped sweet butter
⅓ to ½ cup heavy cream, whipped

This should be made in a chafing dish. Beat the eggs very well and add the herbs, salt, and pepper. Put the butter in the chafing dish and when it is melted add the eggs and stir with a wooden spoon until they thicken but are still moist. Fold in the whipped cream and divide on 4 warm plates. With fragrant herbs this is a fine dish for brunch or supper.

Pastas

CANNELLONI ALLA SAN RUFILLO
Buca di San Rufillo, Florence

Stuffing:
    1 pound veal, ground
    1 cup celery, ground
    ½ cup onions, ground
    ½ cup mushrooms, ground
    ⅓ to ½ cup butter
    Salt and pepper
    ½ cup breadcrumbs
    2 egg yolks
    1 tablespoon tomato paste
    White wine

5-inch squares of pasta
Meat Sauce or Mushroom Sauce
Cream Sauce
Parmesan cheese

One morning before lunch time I had the good fortune to be allowed to watch Aldo put these together. This is a great specialty of the Buca di San Rufillo. For the stuffing, the ground veal, vegetables, and mushrooms are sautéed together in the butter for 20 minutes. Stir occasionally so it is well mixed. This is cooked slowly. Add the salt and pepper and when it is done stir in lightly the crumbs, egg yolks, and tomato paste. Moisten with just enough wine to hold the mixture together and form it into rolls the size of one's index finger. The pasta squares are boiled about 3 minutes in salted water, drained, and moistened with cold water so they won't stick together. Wrap each meat roll in a pasta square and let cool. Before serving, butter a shallow baking dish and for each roll put 1 tablespoon of cream sauce and 1 of meat sauce or mushroom sauce in the bottom. Lay the rolls on the sauces; do not pile them. Bake in a 400° oven for 5 minutes. Sprinkle the top with Parmesan cheese and serve. This amount of stuffing will serve about 8 people; allow 4 rolls for a serving. Serve a light red wine.

CANNELLONI ALLA NIZZARDA
Sabatini, Florence

This restaurant, one of the very best in Florence, takes great pride in its pastas and the secret of their goodness is the lavish use of fine sauces.

5-inch squares of homemade pasta
Filling:
  1 pound of lean veal or a
      mixture of veal and
      chicken
  ½ cup thin ham, cubed
  ½ cup Parmesan cheese
  ½ cup shredded Gruyère
      cheese
  3 eggs, beaten
      Pinch salt, pepper
  ¼ teaspoon nutmeg

Béchamel sauce:
  2¼ cups milk
  3 tablespoons butter
  3 tablespoons flour
  3 tablespoons Parmesan
      cheese
      Salt and pepper
  ¼ teaspoon nutmeg
Ragout Sauce Pappagallo
Parmesan cheese

For making pasta, see *Tortellini*. Cook the pasta in plenty of boiling salted water, drain, and rinse in cold water so it won't stick together. Serve 2 or 3 to each person. For the filling grind the meat and chicken and toss it in butter in a saucepan until it is cooked, about 4 or 5 minutes. If cooked chicken is used, do not cook it again but grind it and mix it with the cooked veal. Mix in all the rest of the filling ingredients. Spread 2 or 3 tablespoons of filling on each pasta square and roll them. To make the Béchamel sauce, blend the butter and flour, warm the milk and add it slowly, then add the rest of the ingredients, and cook until it thickens. For the ragout sauce, see *Lasagne Verdi al Forno*. This sauce may be made in a very reduced quantity. Butter a shallow baking dish and put a little of both sauces on the bottom, then lay the cannelloni on top. Cover with ragout sauce and top with Béchamel sauce. Sprinkle liberally with Parmesan cheese. Bake in a 375° oven for 15 minutes or until the crust is golden. This amount of filling and sauces serves 8.

"MAESTOSISSIME FETTUCCINE ALL'ALFREDO"

Quarter-inch egg noodles
The finest butter

The sweetest youngest Parmesan

Alas, the maestro no longer wields the golden spoon with his magic touch, though the restaurant still carries on in Rome, now at the Piazza Augusto Imperatore. However, he once assured us that the secret of the fettuccine is the quality of the three ingredients. Every hotel and restaurant of any consequence in Italy makes its own pasta. It is boiled in salted water to just the right doneness, drained, and then swirled with plenty of butter and cheese. To be at its best, Parmesan must be freshly grated.

FETTUCCINE, PARIS STYLE

12 ounces egg noodles
½ cup soft sweet butter
⅔ to 1 cup heavy cream
⅓ cup Parmesan cheese

¾ cup sliced mushrooms or 1
    truffle, cut in sticks
2 tablespoons butter
Garnish: Bowl of grated French
    Gruyère cheese

Use ½-inch wide egg noodles. Boil them in plenty of salted water and when they are tender, drain them. Have the sweet butter, cream, and cheese in a large skillet, empty the noodles into it, and stir them until they have absorbed a little of the sauce. Sauté the mushrooms or truffle sticks a moment in 2 tablespoons butter then stir them into the noodles. Empty into a hot serving dish and pass the bowl of cheese. Serves 8. If cooking a pound of noodles, increase the amount of dressing because the beauty of this is the lavish use of sauce. Oil mayonnaise instead of the cream makes a good dressing too.

FETTUCCINE, BIANCHE E VERDI
Piccolo Mondo, Rome

There is a gay and crowded restaurant on via Aurora, just off via Veneto, which has five little dining rooms, down a few steps from the street; when there are too many customers they spill out onto the sidewalk. In a "best dish" competition among 2,000 restaurants Marino Camponeschi, owner-chef of Piccolo Mondo, won the prize, a golden fork and spoon. They gave me the honor of eating this prize dish with the golden treasures.

6 ounces green fettuccine
6 ounces white fettuccine
⅓ cup butter
⅓ cup Parmesan cheese

1 cup sliced mushrooms
1 cup fresh peas, cooked with basil
2 or 3 slices prosciutto
Garnish: Bowl of Parmesan cheese

Boil the two kinds of fettuccine in plenty of boiling salted water and drain. Have the butter at room temperature; sauté the mushrooms 3 minutes in butter; cook the peas in butter with basil; cut the ham in small pieces and frizzle a moment in butter. Toss all the ingredients together. Pass a bowl of cheese. Serves 6.

LASAGNE VERDI AL FORNO
Al Pappagallo, Bologna

For some unknown reason, beautiful Bologna, with its miles of arcades, its houses and buildings of all differing shades of yellow to brown and pink to rusty red, does not draw as many tourists as some cities in Italy, but everyone everywhere seems to have heard of Pappagallo as one of the great dining places. Perhaps the sound of the name is partly responsible. Anyway, everyone who visits Bologna dines there extremely well. Signore Zurla gave me this recipe for his famous lasagne, one of the best I have ever eaten. It will serve 12 to 16, so cut the recipe in half if you wish. However, the ragout sauce can be kept tightly covered for a week in the refrigerator, and may be used for other Italian dishes—stuffing zucchini, for instance, or for *Tortellini*—so you may want to make the full amount.

Ragout Sauce Pappagallo:
- 1 cup bacon, cubed
- ½ cup butter
- 2 pounds beef, ground
- 2 cups celery, minced
- 2 cups carrots, minced
- 1 cup onions, minced
- 1 teaspoon salt
- ½ teaspoon pepper
- ½ teaspoon nutmeg
- 1 cup white wine
- 1 cup chicken or beef broth
- ½ cup tomato paste

Cream Sauce:
- ½ cup butter
- ¾ cup flour
- 5 cups milk
- Salt
- Freshly ground pepper
- ½ teaspoon nutmeg
- 1 pound broad spinach pasta
- Parmesan cheese

The ragout sauce may be made the day before serving the lasagne. Fry out the bacon until it is crisp, drain it, and reserve it to add to the ragout sauce when the lasagne is put together. Add the butter to the fat from the bacon and cook the meat and vegetables in it for 15 minutes, stirring often. Mix the seasonings, wine, broth, and tomato paste together and add to the meat mixture. Cover and simmer gently for 2 hours. When ready to make the dish make the cream sauce. Melt the butter, blend in the flour until smooth, gradually stir in the milk and seasonings, and cook until it thickens. Boil the pasta in plenty of boiling salted water for 5 or 6 minutes, drain, and moisten with cold water so that it will not stick together. Butter liberally a long dripping pan or lasagne pan and put in a layer of pasta, then a layer of ragout sauce (with the bacon added), then a layer of cream sauce, then sprinkle thickly with Parmesan cheese. Repeat this until all the ingredients are used, the top layer being cream sauce generously spread with Parmesan cheese. Bake 30 minutes at 350°—uncovered of course, so that the top will be a golden color.

PASTA WITH CLAM SAUCE

12 ounces egg fettuccine
Sauce:
  ¼ cup olive oil
  3 or 4 cloves garlic, crushed
  ¼ cup minced parsley
  1 teaspoon thyme

2 cups drained canned tomatoes
2 dozen fresh clams with juice or
  2 cans whole clams
Salt and pepper

Make the sauce first. Put the olive oil, garlic, parsley, thyme, and tomatoes in a heavy saucepan. If fresh clams are used, scrub them and steam over ½ cup of water until they open. Open them over the pot, remove the clams, and set them aside. Strain the pot juices through a cloth into the tomato sauce. If canned clams are used, strain the juice into the sauce. Never simmer the clams in the sauce or they will become tough. Simmer the sauce until it thickens and add salt and pepper. Boil the fettuccine in plenty of salted water. When it is tender, drain and pile in the center of the serving dish. Heat the sauce, add the clams, and empty the sauce over the pasta. Serves 6. Cheese is not served with clam sauce.

LASAGNE WITH RICOTTA

Ragout Sauce Pappagallo
  1 pound lasagne pasta
1½ pounds ricotta cheese

2 Mozzarella cheeses, sliced thin
½ cup Parmesan cheese

Cook the pasta in boiling salted water until *al dente*, about 8 or 10 minutes, and drain. Put a layer of *Ragout Sauce* in a long shallow pan or baking dish, then layers of pasta, ricotta, ragout sauce, and Mozzarella cheese; then pasta, and repeat until all ingredients are used, ending with Mozzarella cheese with a good sprinkle of Parmesan on top. Cover with foil and bake 30 minutes at 350°; uncover and bake 10 minutes more at 375° to brown. Serves 8.

NOODLES WITH GRATED CHICKEN LIVERS
Hotel Della Rocca, Bazzano

This is another old recipe from this eighteenth-century inn.

12 ounces egg noodles or green
  fettuccine
3 or 4 cups chicken broth

½ cup butter
½ pound chicken livers
Salt and pepper

Sauté the chicken livers lightly in half of the butter—they should be still pink—and add seasoning. Put them in a wooden bowl and chop them fine. Cook the pasta in chicken broth, drain, mix with the rest of the butter, and put in a serving dish. Add the chopped livers to the top. Serves 8.

NOODLES DANIELI
Royal Danieli Roof, Venice

There are many palazzi in Venice but three particular ones come to mind for a morning's diversion. First take a vaporetto to Rezzonico and visit this wonderful palace, then take another boat to Ca' d'Oro, where you will be fascinated by the beautiful rust-colored rooms and splendid works of art. When you reach the third palace, the Royal Danieli, it will be lunchtime, so you go to the restaurant on the roof and sit and ponder why one city has so much, while the little town in Michigan or Iowa, where you may have come from, has comparatively so little. But make the most of the moment and have these delicious noodles which they make for you at your table.

12 ounces egg noodles
3 or 4 sprigs fresh rosemary
⅓ cup butter
1 cup sliced fresh mushrooms

Sauceboat of *Meat Sauce*
Sauceboat of *Tomato Sauce*
Parmesan cheese

The noodles are boiled 10 minutes in salted water and drained. The other ingredients are assembled around a chafing dish. While the noodles are boiling, put the rosemary and butter in the chafing dish over a low fire and stir and bruise the herb 3 minutes; remove the herb and add the mushrooms to the butter and stir for 3 or 4 minutes. Then bring in the drained noodles and add them to the mushrooms. Stir in 1 cup meat sauce and 1 cup tomato sauce. When hot and well mixed, divide on plates, and pass the cheese. This precedes a fish or meat course. Serves 6.

CHINESE NOODLES

1 pound potato noodles or rice
   noodles
Salt and pepper
3 cloves garlic, crushed

3 or 4 tablespoons olive oil
3 or 4 tablespoons butter
Garnish: ½ cup chopped scallions

These thin, delicate noodles may be bought in any Chinese or Oriental grocery store. They are very good served with fish. Cook them in boiling salted water about 2 minutes, drain, and mix with a little salt and pepper. Heat the crushed garlic in the oil and butter until it is lightly colored, and mix this garlic sauce with the noodles. Empty into a hot serving dish and sprinkle the top with the chopped scallions. Serves 6 or 8.

DAD'S BEST NOODLES

1 pound egg noodles
4 cloves garlic, crushed
½ pound sweet butter
Salt and Pepper

1 cup shredded French Gruyère
cheese
⅓ cup Parmesan cheese

My father was as proud of his noodles as Alfredo and he had a right to be. Choose any fancy egg noodles—they come in attractive shapes—or fettuccine, white or green. Let the butter become soft at room temperature then mix it with the crushed garlic and let it "perfume" 1 hour. Boil the noodles in plenty of salted water, drain when done, and toss with the garlic butter; add salt, pepper, and the Gruyère cheese. Then put all the Parmesan cheese on top. Bring to the table, mix in the cheese. Serves 8.

NOODLES WITH HAM AND SOUR CREAM

8 ounces fine egg noodles or shells
2 cups ground ham

1 pint sour cream
1 cup Parmesan cheese

Boil the noodles in salted water until tender and drain. Have the sour cream at room temperature. Mix the ham, sour cream, and ½ cup of the cheese; then add immediately to the hot noodles and stir in. Put the mixture in a baking dish, cover with the rest of the cheese, and brown in a hot oven for 5 or 6 minutes. Serves 6.

FRANK'S SCIUÉ SCIUÉ

6 or 7 large red Italian onions
½ cup olive oil (or more)
Large can Italian plum tomatoes
Salt and pepper
1 tablespoon basil
1 tablespoon powdered fennel

½ cup grated Locatello cheese
1 pound noodle shells
⅓ cup Parmesan cheese
Garnish:
Bowl of Parmesan or Locatello
cheese

Frank is from Genoa and is a great pasta cook. He insists that the dish is like the Italian song, hence its name. The success of this dish depends on the quantity of onions. Frank, with his customary understatement, says you can't cook enough. Bermudas or yellow onions may also be used. Peel the onions, slice very thin, and cook until soft in the olive oil, adding more oil if necessary. Add the tomatoes, mash, and cook over high heat to reduce the liquid in the tomatoes. When the sauce is a good thick consistency, add the seasonings and ½ cup Locatello cheese. Meanwhile cook the noodles in boiling salted water until tender, about 12 minutes, and drain. Mix some of the sauce with the noodles, cover with Parmesan cheese, and serve the rest of the sauce in a bowl. Serves 8.

JACK'S CHICKEN LIVER NOODLES

1 pound chicken livers, sautéed
Butter for sautéing
½ pound fresh button mushrooms
½ cup finely chopped onions
4 cloves garlic, crushed
¼ cup olive oil

4 tablespoons butter
Salt and pepper
⅓ cup Marsala or Madeira
12 ounces egg noodles
Garnish: Parmesan cheese

Sauté the chicken livers in butter until they are lightly browned but still pink inside. If they are large, cut them in half. Cook the mushrooms in a little butter 3 or 4 minutes. Set aside and keep warm. Cook the onions in a little butter until they color. Then add them to the mushrooms. Season livers, mushrooms, and onions with a little salt and pepper. Put the olive oil in the pan, add the garlic and let it just color, then add 4 tablespoons butter. Cook the noodles and drain them. Toss with all the ingredients, then rinse out the frying pan with the wine, let it heat and pour it over the noodles. Serve immediately and pass a bowl of Parmesan cheese. This is the specialty of an old friend and a fine dish to precede a main course. Serves 8.

SPAGHETTI ALLA TONNARA
Licia Grego, Rome

I have a handsome friend in Rome who cooks as well as she looks—an achievement in any language.

12 ounces spaghetti
Sauce:
   1 8-ounce can tuna fish
   4 or 5 anchovy fillets
   3 cloves garlic
   2 cups canned tomatoes
   Freshly ground pepper

Garnish:
   Bowl of Parmesan cheese

Fifteen minutes before you begin to cook the spaghetti, begin simmering the sauce. Flake a can of good tuna fish, cut the anchovies in pieces, crush the garlic, and drain the tomatoes so they won't be too watery. Add pepper. No salt in this. Simmer the sauce very slowly for 30 minutes. Cook the spaghetti in plenty of boiling salted water 15 to 20 minutes and drain. Add the sauce just before serving. Pass the cheese. Serves 6 or 8.

SPAGHETTI NAPOLITANA
Licia Grego, Rome

12 ounces spaghetti
Sauce:
  ¾ cup olive oil
  6 cloves garlic, crushed
  2 tablespoons capers
  12 black olives in oil, pitted
      and halved
  2-ounce can of anchovies
  ¼ cup water
  1 shredded green pepper
  ½ pound mushrooms

⅓ cup finely chopped parsley
Garnish: Parmesan cheese

Start the sauce before you boil the spaghetti. Put the olive oil in a pan with the garlic, capers, olives, anchovies, and water. Cook, stirring, 5 minutes over a low flame, then add the green pepper, very finely shredded, and the mushrooms. Cover and cook 8 minutes. Meanwhile cook the spaghetti in boiling salted water about 15 to 20 minutes, and drain it. Add the parsley to the sauce and pour it over the spaghetti. Pass a bowl of cheese. Serves 8.

TORTELLONI
Sampieri, Bologna

Tortellini Pasta
Chicken broth
Butter and Parmesan cheese
Light tomato sauce

Filling:
  1¾ cups ricotta cheese
  ¾ cup Parmesan cheese
  Salt and pepper
  ¼ teaspoon nutmeg
  2 eggs, beaten
  3 tablespoons chopped
      parsley

Sampieri serves tortelloni as tender and light as can be. They are made the same way as *Tortellini* but are about twice the size and have a cheese filling instead of meat. Mix the filling and put a tablespoon of it on each square of pasta dough. The tortelloni are cooked in broth, drained, and tossed in butter and cheese, and served with a little tomato sauce. A bowl of Parmesan cheese may be passed to sprinkle on top. This amount of filling will be enough to fill a batch of pasta dough.

TORTELLINI ALLA BOLOGNESE
Hotel Majestic, Bologna

Stuffing:
- ⅓ cup fat ham, ground
- ⅓ cup mortadella sausage, ground
- ⅔ cup marrow, chopped
- 1 egg, beaten
- 1 cup Parmesan cheese
- ¼ teaspoon nutmeg

Tomato sauce

Parmesan cheese

Plain Pasta:
- 4 cups flour
- 1 teaspoon salt
- 3 eggs
- Water

Spinach Pasta:
- 3 cups flour
- 3 eggs
- ¾ teaspoon salt
- ½ cup ground spinach

When I was visiting Bologna a few years ago, Mr. Sereno, then manager of the Majestic Hotel, invited me down to the kitchen to watch Signora Ancilla Fangarzi, a handsome woman from the Campagna, make tortellini. Mr. Sereno explained that no man had the patience to make the pasta; the men chefs preferred the new electric machines for rolling and cutting. First the stuffing is made of the ground meats, mixed with the chopped, unmelted marrow, beaten egg, cheese, and nutmeg. Emilia, the province of which Bologna is the capital, produces the finest pork in Italy. The hams are noted, and the fresh pork goes into sausages of many kinds: mortadella, zampone di Modena, salami, culatelli of Parma, salame di Ferrara, cotechini, coppe, salsaiccie, and salamini de Montagna. The fine Italian grocers in this country import or carry many of these sausages.

For the pasta, mix the flour with the salt and put it in a mixing bowl. Break 1 egg at a time into the center of the flour adding 2 tablespoons of water. Mix with the fingers until the dough is firm and stiff. Add 2 more tablespoons of water if necessary. The dough is tossed, kneaded, slapped, and rolled on a board for 10 minutes. Mr. Sereno remarked, "You can see why it takes the patience of a woman." The dough is then rolled paper-thin. If your space is limited, one-third of the dough may be rolled at a time. The spinach pasta is made the same way. The spinach is ground and pressed hard against a fine sieve to extract the juice. The dry spinach is mixed in with the eggs. This dough is used for making noodles of any desired shape. For tortellini the dough is cut in 1½-inch squares. Each square is filled with a small spoonful of stuffing, two opposite corners are pressed together, the other two points meet around your index finger, and the top points are pressed back so the result looks like a tiny padded scarf. The tortellini are spread out to dry for an hour or more. They are boiled in salted water for 15 minutes, drained, and dressed with tomato sauce and Parmesan cheese or with butter and cheese. Tortellini may be boiled in consommé, the soup served with the tortellini floating in it. Another way of serving them is to toss the tortellini (after they are boiled and drained) in heavy cream and Parmesan cheese. One batch of pasta dough will serve 8 people twice. When thoroughly dried the pasta may be kept in a cellophane bag in the refrigerator for a few days.

TORTELLINI ALLA PANNA
Nerina, Bologna

Turning off the Piazza Maggiore you come upon the Piazza Franco Delano Roosevelt and straight ahead is Piazza Galileo and there is the Ristorante Nerina. Signora Nerina is not there now but the cooking still maintains her high standards. The dining rooms are rustic and look rather like a grotto with heavy beams and arches.

¾ pound tortellini
3 cups chicken broth
1 cup heavy cream

½ cup Parmesan cheese
Garnish: Bowl of Parmesan cheese

See recipe for making *Tortellini* stuffed with meat. At Nerina they are cooked in boiling broth, drained, and tossed in a sauté pan with the cream and cheese. Very rich and very good. More cheese is passed in a bowl. Serves 8.

FRANK'S MACARONI GENOVESE

3½-inch strips salt pork, cubed
2 tablespoons butter
3 to 3½ cups thinly sliced onions

½ cup Parmesan cheese
12 ounces macaroni
Garnish: Bowl of Parmesan cheese

Fry the cubes of pork in the butter until crisp, then scoop them out. Fry the onions in the pork fat and butter over a slow flame until very soft and yellow; they must not burn. Add a little water and cook until the onions melt, adding more by tablespoonfuls when necessary. Cook the macaroni until tender in boiling salted water and drain. Add the pork cubes and cheese to the sauce and mix it with the macaroni. Pass a bowl of cheese. Serves 6.

GREEN SAUCE FOR EGG NOODLES

4 cloves garlic, crushed
⅓ cup olive oil
½ cup finely chopped parsley
   (not ground)
1 cup small croutons, sautéed

1 teaspoon fennel
¼ cup more olive oil
6 sliced anchovies
2 tablespoons capers
Garnish: Bowl of Parmesan cheese

Marinate the crushed garlic in ⅓ cup olive oil 2 hours. Sauté the croutons with the fennel in ¼ cup olive oil. Mix the parsley with the hot drained pasta, the garlic and olive oil, the croutons, anchovies, and capers. Serve in a hot bowl and pass the cheese. This is enough sauce for 12 ounces of noodles.

SICILIAN SAUCE FOR EGG NOODLES

2 thick slices salt pork, cubed
4 strips bacon
1 onion, sliced
3 or 4 cloves garlic, crushed

Salt and pepper
⅔ cup Romano cheese
2 eggs
Garnish: Bowl of Romano cheese

Fry out the salt-pork cubes, scoop them out, and reserve. Fry the bacon until crisp and crumble it. Sauté the onion and garlic in the pork fat over a low fire until the onion is tender. Salt and pepper it. Bring the eggs to a boil and remove from the water; they must be hot but still raw. Mix into the pasta the pork pieces, crumbled bacon, onion and garlic and all the fat the pasta will take, and the cheese. Break the eggs over the pasta and toss well. Serve in a hot bowl or the bowl you mix it in. Pass the cheese. This is a rugged dish, good for a cold winter day. The sauce is enough for 12 ounces of noodles.

PESTO ALLA GENOVESE

10 or 12 ounces fine egg noodle
    shells
¼ cup butter
Grated Parmesan cheese

Pesto Sauce:
    6 cloves garlic
    2 teaspoons dry basil
    Large handful fresh basil or
        parsley
    ⅓ cup pine nuts or walnuts
    ⅓ cup mixed Romano and
        Parmesan cheese, ground
    Olive oil
    Salt and pepper

The pesto sauce must be prepared ahead of time. I've often had cooking-minded gentlemen guests mix it and it always seems to amuse them. Put the garlic into a mortar, and crush it with a pestle to almost a liquid, then add all the rest of the ingredients a little at a time, so that the result is an unctuous mass. To facilitate the operation, the garlic can be crushed before it is put in the mortar. I've also found that the stemmed basil or parsley is better if it is ground first. When the sauce is almost ready to serve, the noodles are boiled about 8 minutes in salted water, drained, mixed with the butter, and brought to the table where the pesto sauce is stirred in. The steaming noodles mixed with the garlic, cheese, and herbs make this a very fragrant dish. Parmesan cheese is passed for each person to add to the top of his serving. This serves 8. A slightly more elaborate dish is made by adding a pound of hot cooked fresh peas to the hot noodles.

PESTO SAUCE FOR NOODLES
Taverna la Fenice, Venice

Signor Alfredo Zoppi has definite directions for making this greatest of all pasta sauces. It is served from a large bowl and you help yourself, spooning it over a steaming plate of tender pasta. It calls for basilica, but as we can't always get this fragrant herb, you may substitute watercress.

Big bunch of stemmed parsley	Salt
Big bunch of stemmed watercress	1 cup Parmesan cheese
6 or 8 large cloves of garlic	2 cups olive oil

It is a strange thing but you never notice the garlic in this dish. It never fails to please everybody—men especially never can get enough of it. Wash and drain the greens in a salad basket, then hand-chop them in a wooden bowl. They must be fine and it takes no more than 6 to 8 minutes. Signor Zoppi claims that hand chopping is important, and he is right. Crush the garlic in a mortar to a cream, adding drops of olive oil. To facilitate this you may use a garlic press first, then a pestle. Then add the greens, cheese, and olive oil to the garlic, mixing it to a rather loose mass. It is more liquid than the *Genovese Sauce*. This is served over 1 pound of boiled, drained egg noodles; this amount will serve 8. Pass more cheese in a bowl.

CHICKEN LIVER PASTA SAUCE

1 pound chicken livers	1 cup chicken broth
⅓ cup butter	1 cup vegetable juice
3 strips bacon	1 teaspoon basil
½ pound fresh mushrooms	¼ cup minced ham or salami
⅓ cup minced green onions	1 tablespoon tomato paste
2 cloves garlic, crushed	⅓ cup dry vermouth or Marsala
Salt and pepper	

Cut the chicken livers in half if they are large. Cut the bacon into 1-inch lengths. Put the livers and the bacon in a pan with 2 tablespoons of the butter. Salt and pepper them. Put them in a 375° oven and cook 12 minutes, turning them once. Melt the rest of the butter in another pan and put in the mushrooms, green onions, and crushed garlic. The mushrooms should be the size of the livers. They may be left whole if small or sliced if large. Salt and pepper them and bake in the oven about 8 minutes. Simmer the broth, vegetable juice, basil, ham or salami, and tomato paste about 15 minutes over a gentle fire. When the sauce is done add the wine. Add the livers and the mushrooms to the sauce, scraping all the pan juices from both into it. This is poured over a bowl of steaming hot pasta and Parmesan cheese is passed. Enough for 12 ounces of pasta, which serves 8.

MEAT SAUCE FOR PASTAS

3 strips bacon
¼ cup butter
¾ pound ground beef
1 slice calf's liver, ground
½ cup chopped onions
½ cup chopped carrots
½ cup chopped celery
   Salt and pepper

½ teaspoon nutmeg
½ teaspoon orégano or thyme
½ teaspoon rosemary
1 teaspoon tomato paste
½ cup red wine
½ cup beef broth
1 clove garlic, crushed (optional)

Fry out the bacon in a heavy pot and drain it. Add the butter and cook the beef, liver, onions, carrots, and celery for 15 minutes over a low flame, stirring a little. Add the seasonings, tomato paste, wine, and broth, and simmer gently 1 hour. More wine or broth may be added if needed. A crushed clove of garlic may be added with the wine and broth.

NOODLE SOUFFLE

4 ounces fine noodles
Cream sauce:
   1 stick butter
   2 tablespoons flour
1½ cups milk
1½ cups cream
   Salt and pepper
¼ teaspoon nutmeg
3 egg yolks, beaten
⅓ cup Parmesan cheese

6 or 7 egg whites, beaten

Boil the noodles in plenty of salted water 8 minutes and drain them. Chinese fine noodles or Goodman's 2x double-egg hair-fine noodles are excellent for this. Do not use more than 4 ounces. Make a cream sauce by melting the butter then stirring in the flour and liquids. Cook until it thickens and then add the seasonings, beaten egg yolks, and cheese. Stir in the noodles. Beat the eggs whites until stiff, using 7 if the eggs are small. Grease an 8½- to 9-inch casserole and sprinkle the bottom and sides with Parmesan cheese. Mix one-fourth of the egg whites into the noodle mixture, then lightly fold in the rest of the whites. Put the mixture into the baking dish and sprinkle the top with a little more Parmesan cheese. Bake 10 minutes in an oven preheated to 375°, and 10 minutes more at 325°. Serves 6 with a salad for lunch or 8 as an accompaniment to a meat dish for dinner.

MACARONI DE LUXE, VAUCRESSON

8 ounces macaroni
¼ pound fresh mushrooms, puréed
¼ pound Roquefort or Blue cheese
½ cup milk
⅓ cup heavy cream

10 stuffed green olives, sliced
Freshly ground pepper (no salt)
2 cups shredded Edam or
Cheddar cheese
Butter

This fine dish is the creation of an old friend who now lives in France with his French wife and four beautiful children in the enchanting villa Èclaircie, at Vaucresson, two miles from Versailles. Some of the happiest times I have in France are my visits to this delightful family. George loves to cook for his family and friends for relaxation. He cooks the macaroni in boiling salted water to just al dente, drains it, and mixes it with the rest of the ingredients in a large mixing bowl. He uses an electric blender to purée the mushrooms and the Roquefort or Blue cheese, empties these into the hot macaroni, then rinses the blender with the milk and adds it and the cream, sliced green olives, and pepper. Then toss in 1½ cups of the shredded cheese, empty the mixture into a baking dish, and cover the top with the reserved ½ cup of cheese. Put bits of butter over the top, cover, and bake 45 minutes at 300°. Uncover for the last 10 minutes to brown. This is a fine Sunday night supper dish served with a huge mixed green salad. Serves 10.

EGG NOODLE RING

6 ounces ½-inch egg noodles
2 cloves garlic, crushed
3 tablespoons olive oil or butter
1 tablespoon flour
1½ cups milk or light cream

4 tablespoons Parmesan cheese
4 egg yolks
2 tablespoons chopped parsley
4 egg whites, beaten

Boil and drain the noodles. Warm the garlic in the olive oil; add the flour, blend until smooth, and add the milk and cheese. When it begins to thicken—which will be instantly—remove from the fire, stir in the egg yolks, and mix with the pasta and parsley. Fold in the beaten egg whites last. Grease an 8-inch ring mold and empty in the mixture. Put the mold into a pan of hot water and bake 30 minutes at 350°. Let stand 3 minutes, then loosen the sides. Invert a round chop plate over the mold, turn it upside down, and shake so the noodle ring will drop onto the plate. Fill the ring with creamed vegetables, seafood, chicken, sweetbreads, or any other filling you prefer.

NOODLE CASSEROLE FOR TWELVE

This is a great dish for a party. It is flexible and may be increased or reduced as the occasion requires. Fresh mushrooms may replace unavailable ingredients in either filling.

12 ounces fettuccine or egg noodles
Cream sauce for either filling:
 ¼ cup butter
 ⅓ cup flour
 2 cups light cream
 2 cups milk
 Salt and pepper
 ½ teaspoon nutmeg
 1 teaspoon thyme
Seafood filling:
 1 pound scallops
 Butter, salt and pepper
 1 pound fresh shrimp
 1 can lobster or crabmeat
 ½ cup diced green onions
 3 tablespoons minced parsley

Meat filling:
 1 pair sweetbreads
 Butter, salt, and pepper
 1 pound chicken livers
 4 pork sausages
 ½ cup diced green onions
 1 cup diced cooked ham
½ cup Parmesan cheese

Cook the pasta in plenty of boiling salted water and when it is done, drain it. To make the cream sauce, melt the butter in a saucepan and stir in the flour. When it is smooth, slowly add the liquids and seasonings. Cook until it thickens. For the seafood filling, sauté the scallops in a little butter a scant 2 minutes, salt and pepper them. The ingredients are not cooked done as they are cooked again when the dish is put together. Wash the shrimp and cook them in a cup of salted water for 2 minutes. Strain. You may use the broth to replace some of the milk in the cream sauce. Shell the shrimp. Flake and bone the canned seafood. Combine all the ingredients for the filling and lightly mix with three-fourths of the pasta and 1½ cups of the cream sauce. Empty into a large casserole, add the rest of the pasta and spread the cream sauce over it. Sprinkle the top with the cheese. This may be done ahead of time. Before serving, bake it at 375° for 25 minutes until it is hot and brown. For the meat filling, soak the sweetbreads 1 hour in salted cold water, then remove the membranes and cut the sweetbreads in walnut-sized pieces. Sauté them in butter about 3 minutes and add salt and pepper. Cut the chicken livers in half and sauté separately about 2 minutes in a little butter and season them. Cut the pork sausages in 1-inch lengths, sauté them 10 minutes, and drain from their fat. Lightly mix with all the other ingredients and assemble the dish as directed for the seafood filling. For a buffet supper this substantial dish may be served with *Spinach Salad;* serve white wine if it is made with seafood and red wine if the meat filling is used.

GNOCCHI

4 cups milk
1 cup semolina or cream of wheat
1 teaspoon salt
⅓ cup butter
4 eggs, beaten
½ cup Parmesan cheese
¼ teaspoon nutmeg or ½ teaspoon
    powdered fennel

Soft butter
Parmesan and Gruyère cheese
Garnish (optional):
    Thin tomato sauce seasoned
      with 1 teaspoon powdered
      fennel

Put the milk in the top of the double boiler and stir in the semolina or cream of wheat. Pale yellow semolina is obtainable in Italian grocery stores but if it is not available, cream of wheat gives about the same result. Stir over simmering water until it thickens, about 10 minutes. Stir in the salt, butter, eggs, ½ cup Parmesan cheese, and seasoning. Spread the mixture ½-inch thick on a buttered platter to cool and stiffen. When it is cool, spread it with soft butter and sprinkle liberally with a mixture of grated Parmesan and Gruyère cheese; or Parmesan alone will do. Cut in small disks or 2-inch squares and put them either in a long buttered baking dish (lasagne pan) overlapping a little, or in two layers in a round or square baking dish. Bake 12 minutes at 375° to reheat and to melt the cheese. Serves 6 without sauce or with a tomato sauce seasoned with fennel.

MY POLENTA

1⅔ cups waterground yellow corn-
    meal
1 cup cold water
2 or 3 cups boiling water
2 teaspoons salt

4 Italian sausages, 2 sweet, 2 hot, or
    6 pork sausages
1 cup tomato sauce
1 teaspoon powdered fennel
Butter
Parmesan cheese

Put the cornmeal in the top of the double boiler and blend with 1 cup of cold water to prevent lumping. Add the salt and 2 cups of boiling water, stir well, cover, and let cook over boiling water for 30 minutes. Add more boiling water if needed, as the mush must be thick but soft. Fry the sausages until brown, then cook them slowly 15 minutes. Cut them in 1-inch lengths. Mix the tomato sauce with the fennel and add the sausages. Butter an oblong shallow baking dish and fill it with half the cooked mush, spread all the sausages and sauce over it, and cover with the rest of the mush. Dot the top with butter and sprinkle liberally with Parmesan cheese. Bake in a 400° oven 10 minutes. If possible, make this at the last minute; it takes only a short time to put together with everything ready, and if it has to stand it is likely to stiffen. If it must be made ahead of time, add more water to keep it soft. This is a good accompaniment for poultry or pork, and also a good luncheon or supper dish. Serves 7 or 8.

POLENTA
Trattoria alla Madonna, Venice

Venice is fascinating to visitors who are curious about the back streets, who know there must be adventures away from the crowded Piazza San Marco and the lagoon. One is easily lost, but that too is a pleasure for every little street, alley, or sudden square is rewarding. Some morning walk to the Rialto Bridge, look at everything on the way, examine the markets, cross the bridge, and when you are hungry, walk three minutes to the left to Calle della Madonna (Madonna Alley). Turn down the alley and you come upon this restaurant of the people, where the food is very well cooked and the helpful host, Signore Rado, will suggest the specialty of the day. I had an excellent meat dish with polenta.

2 cups fine cornmeal	¾ cup grated cheese: Fontina,
1½ teaspoons salt	Gruyère, or Parmesan
1 cup cold water	⅓ cup butter
6 cups boiling water	Garnish:
	Parmesan cheese and butter

Using a double boiler, mix the cornmeal and salt with the cold water, which prevents its lumping. Add the boiling water and cook, covered, for 30 minutes over simmering water. Stir occasionally and if it becomes too thick, add a little more boiling water. When it is done, stir in the cheese and butter. Pour into a greased shallow pan so the polenta is an inch thick. Before serving, slice the polenta, sprinkle with a little Parmesan cheese, dot with butter, and warm a moment under the flame. Serve instead of potatoes. At Madonna this accompanies a meat dish. Serves 6.

Cheese Dishes

EGG-WHITE CHEESE SOUFFLÉ

7 egg whites	Dash of salt
1 cup light cream	Freshly ground pepper
1⅓ cups shredded pungent cheese	¼ teaspoon nutmeg
2 tablespoons butter	4 tablespoons Parmesan cheese
3 tablespoons flour	

Beat the egg whites until stiff. Scald the cream and stir in the cheese. Liederkranz or Appenzeller or Gruyère or a mixture of these would be good. Melt the butter in a saucepan, stir in the flour, and add the seasonings. Grease a 7-inch soufflé dish and sprinkle sides and bottom with 2 tablespoons of the Parmesan cheese which makes a fine crust. Stir the cream and cheese mixture into the butter and flour, cooking a few seconds only as it will become quite thick, stir in one-fourth of the egg whites, then fold in the rest. Be sure to mix in this order. Empty into the soufflé dish and sprinkle the top with the rest of the Parmesan cheese. Put into a 375° oven and bake for 15 minutes, then turn down the heat to 325° for another 10 minutes. Serves 4. This is one good way to use collected egg whites. They keep very well refrigerated in a glass jar with a tight screw top. Eight egg whites make 1 cup.

CHEESE PIE WITH POTATO CRUST

Crust:
- 1 cup mashed potatoes
- ¾ cup sifted flour
- ½ teaspoon salt
- ¼ cup melted butter
- 1 egg, beaten

Filling:
- 2 cups shredded Swiss or Gruyère cheese
- 2 eggs, beaten
- ¼ teaspoon nutmeg
- ⅔ cup sour cream

For the crust blend all the ingredients together and fill a 9-inch greased pie plate. Press the dough against the bottom and sides of the plate and over the edge a little. Add the shredded cheese to the crust. Beat the eggs until light, add the nutmeg, and stir in the sour cream. Spread over the cheese and bake at 350° about 25 minutes, until the top is light brown. Do not bake too fast or too long. Serves 5 or 6.

CHEESE SOUFFLÉ FOR THREE OR FOUR

- 2 tablespoons butter
- 2 tablespoons flour
- ⅛ teaspoon salt
- Freshly ground pepper
- ¼ teaspoon nutmeg
- 1 tablespoon tomato paste
- 1 cup milk

- ¾ cup shredded Cheddar or Gruyère cheese
- ¼ cup Brie or Liederkranz cheese
- 4 large egg yolks
- 4 large egg whites
- Parmesan cheese

Preheat the oven to 400°. Melt the butter in a saucepan and blend in the flour with a rubber spatula. Stir in the seasonings and slowly add the milk. When blended add the two cheeses and stir until they melt. Use large eggs or 5 medium-sized eggs. Beat the yolks and add them to the thick sauce. Cook but a moment, stirring continuously. Beat the egg whites until stiff. Grease a 7-inch soufflé dish and sprinkle the sides and bottom with Parmesan cheese. Mix one-fourth of the egg whites into the cream sauce and then fold in the rest of the whites. Pour it into the soufflé dish and bake 5 minutes at 400°, then turn down the heat to 350° and bake 15 to 18 minutes more. It should rise 3 or 4 inches above the top of the dish.

LAZETTE'S FAMOUS CHEESE SOUFFLÉ

4 tablespoons butter
4 tablespoons flour
¾ teaspoon salt
Dash of cayenne or ¼ teaspoon
    nutmeg

1½ cups hot milk
½ pound Cheddar cheese,
    shredded
6 egg yolks, beaten
6 egg whites, beaten

There were always murmurs of approval when Lazette produced this handsome soufflé, which is special and which runs counter to tradition as to time of baking. Put the butter and flour in the top of the double boiler over simmering water and add the seasonings. Blend well, then stir in the hot milk a little at a time, and cook until the sauce thickens, then add the cheese and stir with a rubber spatula until it melts. Pour a little sauce over the beaten egg yolks and then add all the yolk mixture to the cheese mixture and cook only a moment more. Beat the egg whites until stiff and stir one-fourth of them into the custard and then lightly fold in the rest. Put this in an ungreased soufflé dish and run the back of a teaspoon around the soufflé an inch from the rim. This will make a large shiny mushroom top when it is baked. Put into a preheated 300° oven and bake for 1 hour and 10 minutes without opening the oven door. This will serve 5 or 6, or more if served as an accompaniment to boiled salmon or other fish. It makes a nice change from potatoes.

CHEESE FONDUE

1 clove garlic
1 cup light dry wine, such as
    Neufchâtel
½ pound shredded Emmenthaler
    and French Gruyère cheese,
    mixed

¼ teaspoon each salt, pepper, and
    nutmeg
1½ tablespoons cornstarch
1 jigger Kirsch
Cubes of French bread

Cut the garlic in half and rub the chafing dish or fondue pot all over the surface. Put in the wine and when it bubbles a little throw in the cheese a handful at a time and keep stirring with a wooden spoon. Add the seasonings. Blend the cornstarch with the Kirsch; stir in when the cheese is melted. The fondue is kept hot over a low flame. If it becomes too thick add a little warmed wine. The guests are equipped with little dunking forks to spear the cubes of bread and dip them into the fondue. A fine Alsatian wine would go well with this fondue. Serves 4 to 6. To serve 8 use a pound of mixed cheese and 1½ to 1¾ cups of wine.

CHEESE GARLIC TOAST

French or Italian bread
Garlic
Olive oil

Bel Paese or Mozzarella cheese,
sliced ½-inch thick

Cut the bread ¾-inch thick and top each slice with a slice of cheese. For 8 slices, put 3 cloves of crushed garlic in a frying pan with 5 or 6 tablespoons of olive oil and when it begins to heat put in the bread topped with cheese. Cover, turn the heat low, and cook until the cheese melts. This may be done over the flame or in the oven. These may be served as an appetizer or with a green salad. Both types of cheese are good for melting.

FREDDY'S CHEESE TOAST

Large rounds of homemade-type
  bread
Butter

Thick *Mornay Sauce*
Anchovy fillets
Pimento strips

Fry the bread in butter on one side and put the slices on a baking sheet, butter side down. Make the Mornay Sauce with 1 cup of light cream, 2 tablespoons of flour, seasoning, and ⅓ cup of grated Gruyère or Swiss cheese. Let it cool so it is quite thick. Spread the bread with a thick layer of the sauce and crisscross the top with fillets of anchovy and strips of pimento. These may be prepared ahead of time. Before serving run the baking sheet under a hot flame until the top browns but does not burn. These are good with ale or beer.

CHEESE CHARLOTTE

6 slices homemade-type bread
1¾ cups milk
  Butter
3 egg yolks
½ cup light cream
¼ teaspoon nutmeg

¼ teaspoon salt
¼ teaspoon pepper
½ pound Swiss or Gruyère cheese,
  grated
3 egg whites, beaten

Cut 4 of the slices of bread in half, dip them in the milk, and line the sides, but not the bottom of a large greased baking dish. Butter the other 2 slices of bread, cut them in tiny cubes, and soak them in the rest of the milk. (Or you may fry half of the cubes with 1 crushed clove of garlic in 2 or 3 tablespoons of olive oil.) Beat the egg yolks with the cream and add the seasonings. Mix this with the cubes of bread, the milk, and the cheese. Beat the egg whites until stiff and fold them into the mixture, then pour it into the baking dish. Bake at 350° for 28 to 30 minutes or until a silver knife comes out clean. Serves 6.

FONDUTA LOMBARDY

2 cups milk
4 egg yolks, beaten
Dash of salt and nutmeg

1 pound Taleggio cheese
1 truffle or 3 mushrooms
Butter

Scald the milk, pour it over the beaten egg yolks, and add the seasonings. Put the mixture into the top of a chafing dish over simmering water and slice in the cheese. Taleggio is made in Lombardy and is a delicious and delicate pungent cheese. If the truffle is available, cut it into sticks and sauté them a moment in butter. Or cut the mushrooms in slices and the slices in half and sauté 2 or 3 minutes in butter. When the cheese is melted, scatter the truffle sticks or mushrooms over the top. Dunk with Italian bread cubes or serve over thin crisp buttered toast. Serves 6.

FROMAGE À LA CRÈME

2 cups heavy cream
½ teaspoon salt
Few grains cayenne
¼ teaspoon nutmeg

1 cup cheese—Gruyère or Swiss, grated; or Liederkranz, Brie, or Taleggio, sliced
4 egg yolks, beaten

Put the cream with the seasonings into the top of a double boiler over hot water and when it is hot add the cheese. When the cheese is melted pour the mixture over the beaten egg yolks and return it to the fire a moment. When it is hot, pour it into eight ¼-cup-size ramekins to cool and set. Serve with the salad course or with a fruit dessert.

CHEESE PUDDING

8 slices homemade-type bread
1 scant cup melted butter
½ pound sharp Cheddar cheese, shredded
4 large eggs

2 cups milk
Dash of salt
Freshly ground pepper
¼ teaspoon nutmeg

Use only fine bread for this or it will not be a success. If there are hard crusts, trim off a little. Grease a large baking dish. Dice or crumble the bread, 2 slices at a time, into the dish and over each 2 slices put one-fourth of the melted butter and one-fourth of the shredded cheese for even distribution. Beat the eggs and beat in the milk and seasonings. Pour this over the bread. It should almost cover the bread; if necessary, add a little more milk. Let this stand 6 hours or all day. Cover and bake 1 hour; 30 minutes at 350° and 30 minutes at 325°. Uncover the last 15 minutes to brown. The bread texture disappears. It is a fine luncheon dish or an accompaniment to fish, chicken, or pork. Serves 8 or 10.

Rice Dishes

RISOTTO WITH PATNA RICE

1 cup patna rice	3 cups chicken broth
4 tablespoons butter	¼ cup sherry or Madeira
3 tablespoons olive oil	1 teaspoon turmeric
1 good sized onion, chopped	½ cup Parmesan cheese
4 cloves garlic, crushed	

Shake the rice in a cloth to clean it; do not wash, for it must be dry. Put it into a heavy pot with the olive oil and 3 tablespoons butter and cook slowly for about 10 minutes, stirring it with a wooden spoon. Every grain should glisten and absorb the butter and oil a little. Bring the broth to a boil. Stir the onion and garlic and 1 cup of boiling broth into the rice. Cover tightly and cook over a very low flame until the broth is absorbed. Then add the other 2 cups of boiling broth, the wine and the turmeric. Cover and continue cooking until all the liquid is absorbed—about 45 minutes. When it is done stir in the remaining tablespoon of butter and the cheese and serve immediately. Serves 6.

RISOTTO ALLA PRINCIPE DA NAPOLI
Sabatini, Florence

Risotto with Patna Rice	3 tablespoons black truffle sticks
2 tablespoons butter	¼ cup cubed Gruyère cheese
2 fresh tomatoes	¼ cup cubed Mozzarella cheese
1 teaspoon orégano	

Make a risotto according to directions for *Risotto with Patna Rice*, skimping on the Parmesan cheese. Skin, seed, and chop the tomatoes, sauté them in the butter in a separate pan, sprinkle with orégano, and toss with the cooked rice. Cook the truffles in a little butter a moment, add the truffles and cheeses to the risotto, and toss lightly. This fragrant dish is fit for any prince.

SHRIMP RISOTTO

Risotto with Patna Rice
1 pound fresh shrimp
2 cups water
⅓ cup chopped onion
Salt and pepper

1 teaspoon thyme
Chicken broth
Garnish:
Chopped parsley

Wash the shrimp and put them in a pan with the water, onion, salt, pepper, and thyme. Bring to a simmer and cook 3 minutes. Drain out the shrimp, peel them, and set aside. Measure the water and add enough chicken broth to make 3 cups of liquid. Use this liquid in making the *Risotto with Patna Rice.* When it is done, empty the rice into a hot serving bowl, garnish with the shrimp and chopped parsley. Serves 8.

FRIED RICE BALLS
The Canepa, Rome

1¼ cups patna rice
½ cup chopped onions
3 tablespoons butter
2½ cups consommé
2 eggs, beaten

⅓ cup Parmesan cheese
Beaten egg
Fine crumbs
Oil

Cook the onions in the butter for 2 minutes, stir in the dry rice, and cook for 5 minutes over a low flame, stirring continuously. Bring the consommé to a boil and stir it into the rice. Cover tightly and cook over a very low flame until the liquid is absorbed. Stir in the beaten eggs and cheese and let it become cold. Form the rice into balls the size of golf balls. Roll them in beaten egg, then in crumbs and fry at 370° in deep oil. Drain on brown paper. They may be made ahead of time and reheated a few minutes in a hot oven. Serves 6 or 8.

PATNA RICE WITH SAUSAGES

1¼ cups patna rice
2½ cups chicken broth or 1½ cups
    broth and 1 cup tomato juice
¼ cup finely sliced onions
    Butter
1 teaspoon turmeric
1 teaspoon each basil, chervil,
    and tarragon

Salt and pepper
½ pound pork or Italian sausages
Garnish:
    Parmesan cheese or chopped
    parsley

Wash the rice. Have the onions sliced very fine and sauté them a minute in butter. Cook the rice in the liquid with the onions, turmeric, and seasonings, covered tightly, until all the liquid is absorbed, about 30 minutes.

Brown rice may be used and, if so, cook it 45 minutes. Let the cover remain on for 5 minutes after the heat is turned off and the rice will become fluffy. Meanwhile sauté the sausages or bake them in an open skillet at 350° for 20 minutes, turning them once after 10 minutes cooking. Cut them in 1-inch lengths and toss with the cooked rice. If the sausage skins are coarse, skin them first. This is a delicious luncheon dish and may be part of a buffet supper. The rice is fragrant and lends itself to mixing with many cooked things: cooked shrimp, sautéed mushrooms, sautéed chicken livers, etc. It is particularly good served with *Apricot Mustard Sauce*. Serves 6.

ORIENTAL PILAU

1½ cups Indian or patna rice
½ cup sultanas or dark raisins
¼ cup Madeira or sherry
3 cups coconut milk (2 cups dessicated coconut and 2½ cups milk and 1 cup water)
⅓ cup butter
1 large onion, chopped
3 cloves garlic, crushed

½ teaspoon cinnamon
1 teaspoon turmeric
1 teaspoon cumin
1 teaspoon cardamom
1 teaspoon coriander
½ teaspoon allspice or mace
Salt and pepper
⅓ cup pistachio or pignolia nuts

Soak the rice 3 hours in water to cover, before making the pilau. Soak the raisins an hour in the wine. To make the coconut milk, boil up the coconut in half the milk and half the water. Let it cool, then mash it through a sieve. Repeat this with the same coconut and the rest of the milk and water. Discard the coconut. Measure the liquid and add milk if necessary to make 3 cups of liquid. Before making the pilau drain the rice 10 minutes through a sieve. Put the butter in a heavy pot and cook the onion and garlic 4 or 5 minutes over a gentle flame. Add the rice and the seasonings (except the raisins and nuts) and stir for 2 or 3 minutes. Boil up the coconut milk and pour it over the rice. Cover tightly and cook it over a very low flame until the liquid is absorbed and the rice is fluffy. When it is done toss it lightly with the raisins, wine, and nuts and empty it into a hot serving dish. This may be served with pork, poultry, and curries. Serves 8. See Pantry Shelf for suppliers of Indian and patna rice.

BOILED BROWN RICE

1 cup brown rice
2 cups chicken or beef broth
1 teaspoon mixed herbs

3 tablespoons butter
Salt and pepper
Garnish:
½ cup chopped green onions

Wash the rice and put it in a heavy pot equipped with a tight-fitting lid. Add the broth and herbs. Bring to a fast boil, then turn down the flame to pilot-light strength, cover tightly, and let cook for 45 minutes. Turn off the heat and let stand, covered, for 5 minutes. Mix in the butter, add salt and pepper, empty into a hot serving dish and add the chopped onions to the top. This will serve 4. This is excellent served with *Apricot Mustard Sauce.*

BAKED WILD RICE

1 cup wild rice	Bouquet:
5 tablespoons butter	2 celery branches
⅓ cup chopped onions	1 celery root, peeled
1½ cups chicken broth	3 sprigs thyme
Salt and pepper	4 carrot sticks
1 teaspoon each basil and thyme	Garnish: Chopped parsley

Wash the rice in several waters until it is very clean. Let it drain in a sieve for an hour. Melt 3 tablespoons of the butter in a skillet and sauté the onion in it for 3 minutes over a low flame, then stir in the rice. Bring the broth to a boil and season it with salt, pepper, basil, and thyme. When the rice is very hot and a little fragrant, add the broth. Put the rice in a baking dish. Tie the bouquet with a string and bury it in the middle of the rice. Cover tightly and bake an hour at 350°. Remove the bouquet and stir in the other 2 tablespoons of butter with a fork. The rice should be fluffy. Serves 6. This is fine with game or any poultry, and can be used as a stuffing for turkey with chestnuts or sautéed sausages added.

RICE RING

2 cups fluffy cooked rice, patna or brown	Cream sauce:
	3 tablespoons butter
3 eggs	3 teaspoons cornstarch
1 tablespoon curry powder	1½ cups milk
1 tablespoon lemon juice	Salt and pepper
	2 tablespoons grated cheese

The rice can be cooked in water, but if you season a cup of raw rice with herbs and cook it in chicken broth, the ring will be much better. Beat the eggs and mix them and the curry powder and lemon juice with the cooked rice. For the cream sauce, melt the butter, stir in the cornstarch until smooth, then add the milk and cook until the sauce thickens. Add the salt, pepper, and cheese. Mix the sauce with the rice and put in a well-greased ring mold, set in a pan of hot water, and bake at 350° 25 minutes or until set. Remove from the oven, let stand 3 minutes, then turn the ring upside down on a chop plate. Fill with creamed vegetables, sweetbreads, chicken livers, mushrooms, or whatever you choose. Serves 6 to 8.

RICE AND LENTIL CASSEROLE

1½ cups cooked patna or brown
    rice
1 cup washed lentils
2 cups water
½ cup chopped onions
2 tablespoons butter

Tomato sauce:
    ⅔ cup chopped onions
    1 green pepper, sliced
    4 tablespoons butter
    Salt and pepper
    1 teaspoon each basil and
      orégano
    1 small can tomato purée or
      sauce
Parmesan cheese

Soak the lentils in 2 cups water for 6 hours. Sauté the onions in 2 tablespoons butter until almost tender, mix with the soaked lentils, and add ½ cup more water. Simmer until the lentils are tender and the water absorbed so they need not be drained. Toss the lentils with the cooked rice. For the tomato sauce, sauté the onions and green pepper in 4 tablespoons butter until they are tender, then mix with the rest of the ingredients. Mix the sauce with the lentils and rice, put into a baking dish, and cover with cheese. Bake at 350° for 20 minutes or until the cheese is browned. Serves 6.

RICE WITH CHICKEN LIVERS AND MUSHROOMS

1 cup brown or patna rice
1 teaspoon turmeric
2 cups chicken broth
1 pound chicken livers
½ pound fresh small mushrooms
    Butter
⅓ cup chopped onions
    Salt and pepper

⅓ cup red wine
⅓ cup chicken broth
1 teaspoon cornstarch
1 tablespoon brandy
1 tablespoon Madeira
Garnish:
    Chopped parsley (optional)

Put the rice in a heavy pot, add the turmeric and broth, cover tightly, and cook on a low flame until the liquid is absorbed—45 minutes for brown rice, 30 for patna. Let stand covered with the heat turned off for 10 minutes. Sauté the chicken livers in butter until tender. Salt and pepper them. Bake the mushrooms and onions in butter 10 minutes at 350°. Blend the red wine, broth, and cornstarch together and cook until thickened, then mix with the livers, mushrooms, and pan juices. Add the brandy and Madeira, mix with the rice, and serve immediately. Serves 10. Chopped parsley may decorate the top of the rice.

RICE SOUFFLÉ

1 cup cooked rice
1 cup milk
3 tablespoons butter
½ cup grated cheese: Cheddar,
    Swiss or Gruyère

¼ teaspoon nutmeg
4 egg yolks, beaten
5 egg whites, beaten

Any leftover rice can be used for this; a well-seasoned risotto would be especially good. Boil up the milk and add the butter and cheese, and when the cheese is melted stir in the rice, nutmeg, and egg yolks. Beat the egg whites until stiff and stir in one-fourth of them and then lightly fold in the rest. Bake in a greased 7½-inch soufflé dish at 375° 10 minutes and at 350° 15 minutes more, or until it is set. Serves 4.

VARIATION FOR A SWEET RICE SOUFFLÉ. If the leftover rice is unseasoned, omit the cheese and add ⅓ cup of light brown sugar and ⅓ cup of raisins.

Soups

THERE are superb soups made from scratch and there are soups just as superb made from leftovers. Steak and roast bones and carcasses from birds should not be thrown away but treasured for making soup. If there is an abundance of broth, cook rice in it. Leftover cooked vegetables may be puréed with broth or milk. Soups begin a banquet, soups fill out a meal, elaborate soups may be the meal itself. Bean soups are sustaining in winter; new tender vegetables make soups for spring; cold soups are refreshing in the summer.

The French, as everyone knows, have brought soup-making to perfection and I was fortunate in receiving rules for making several fish soups from some of the greatest chefs in France. To your other good habits, add that of making soup.

Wine usually waits until after the soup course. However, a good sherry or Madeira may accompany a clear soup or bouillon, especially when it is turtle. With a great fish soup which is the meal in itself, a fine dry white wine is served; a Pouilly Fuissé, a Chablis, or a white Burgundy.

Vegetable & Meat Soups

KIDNEY BEAN SOUP

1 large can kidney beans
1 large onion, chopped
½ green pepper, chopped
3 tablespoons butter

Salt and pepper
½ teaspoon thyme
Milk or chicken consommé

Reserve ⅔ cup of the beans. Sauté the onion and green pepper in the butter until tender and add salt, pepper, and thyme. Add the rest of the beans to the vegetables and purée through a sieve or in an electric blender with either milk or chicken consommé, using enough so the consistency is like that of heavy cream. A satisfactory consommé may be made with 2 teaspoons of powdered chicken concentrate to every cup of water. Add the reserved beans to the soup and heat before serving. This is a good quick soup. Serves 6.

BEAN SOUP MADE WITH ROAST BEEF BONES

1½ cups dried beans: kidney,
  northern, black, or lima
1 large onion, diced
1 thick slice salt pork, cubed
1 teaspoon mustard
2 tablespoons molasses
2 tablespoons tomato paste
1 tablespoon vinegar

Broth:
  Roast beef bones
4 stalks celery, sliced
2 carrots, sliced
2 big onions, sliced
2 teaspoons mixed herbs:
    thyme, basil and
    marjoram
  Salt and pepper
Leftover gravy
1 teaspoon beef extract

Wash the beans and soak them at least 6 hours in 3 cups of water, adding a little more water if necessary. Meanwhile make the broth with the bones, vegetables, herbs, salt, and pepper, 4½ cups of water if you are using a pressure cooker, or 5 cups of water, if a soup kettle is used. Cover and cook 30 minutes in the pressure cooker, or simmer gently 1½ hours in the kettle. Strain, pressing the vegetables a little against the sieve. Add any leftover gravy and the beef extract. Cook the beans separately in their water and 1½ cups of the strained broth, with the onion, diced fine, the salt pork, and all the seasonings. They may cook 1 hour in the pressure cooker and longer in a covered pot. Limas take much less time than white beans. When the beans are tender scoop out a good cup of them and purée them. Return the purée to the rest of the beans. This gives the soup body. Combine the beans with the broth. This soup has overtones of baked beans. The pork cubes spread on crackers is very good. This makes 10 or 12 cups of soup.

BEET AND FRUIT SOUP

8 new beets
2 cups water
1 teaspoon powdered clove
Salt and pepper
Juice of 2 limes or lemons
Frozen grape juice concentrate

Grapefruit juice
1 tablespoon honey
1 cup red wine
Garnish:
  Fresh or canned Bing cherries
  and juice

Scrub the beets well, as the water they cook in is used in the soup. Cut off the stems 1 inch from the beets. Boil them in 2 cups of water until they are tender. Remove the beets, skin them, and slice them into the beet water. Purée them in the electric blender. Add salt, pepper, lime or lemon juice, and 1 cup of grape juice made by diluting the concentrate with 1½ cans of water instead of 3. Add a little grapefruit juice, the honey, and the wine. Add more grapefruit juice if needed to thin to the consistency of heavy cream. When ready to serve add fresh pitted cherries or canned Bing cherries. This is truly a delicious and beautiful soup, which is served hot in winter and cold in summer. It keeps well in the refrigerator in glass jars. This makes over 2 quarts. You may experiment with other juices and fruit if you desire. A very good soup may be made in a jiffy by using a good brand of canned whole beets instead of fresh beets.

BORSCHT

2 bunches new beets
2 cups water
2 cups beef consommé
1½ cups tomato purée
½ cup red wine
Salt and pepper

1 onion, chopped
Juice and grated rind of 1 orange
1 tablespoon honey
½ teaspoon caraway seed
¼ teaspoon clove
Garnish: Sour cream

Scrub the beets very well, as the water they cook in is used in the soup. Cut off the stems 1 inch from the beets. Cook them in 2 cups of water until they are tender enough to slip off the skins. Strain the beet water into the consommé, add the whole beets and the rest of the ingredients, and simmer for half an hour. Remove 2 beets; dice and reserve them. Strain the rest of the beets and the soup through a sieve or purée it in the blender. Add the diced beets. Taste for seasoning; it may need a little more sweetening or a little lemon juice. Pass a bowl of sour cream so a spoonful may be added to the top of each plate of soup. Serves 8.

CANTALOUPE SOUP

3 or 4 cups cubed cantaloupe
2 tablespoons sweet butter
Salt and pepper
¼ teaspoon nutmeg
1½ cups grapefruit juice
Juice of 2 limes

2 tablespoons honey
¼ cup heavy cream
1 jigger Curaçao or Cointreau
Garnish:
    18 cantaloupe or avocado balls
    Light rum

Sauté the melon in the butter 2 or 3 minutes and season with salt, pepper and nutmeg. Purée the melon in a blender with the juices, add the honey and cream. Chill. Marinate the melon or avocado balls in a little rum. Before serving add the liqueur to the soup. Put 3 balls in each of 6 soup plates and pour the soup over them.

CARROT SOUP

1 bunch new carrots
1 medium-sized onion, minced
3 tablespoons butter
⅓ cup water
1½ cups milk
1 cup light cream

Salt and freshly ground pepper
1 teaspoon tomato paste
1 teaspoon powdered chicken
    concentrate
1½ jiggers Cointreau
Chopped parsley

Scrub the carrots but do not scrape them. Slice them thinly. Cook the onion 2 or 3 minutes in the butter in a heavy pot, then add the carrots and water. Cover and simmer until the vegetables are tender. Remove ¼ cup of the carrots and reserve. Purée the rest of the vegetables and their liquid through a sieve or an electric blender. Add the rest of the ingredients to the soup. Dice the reserved carrots and add them. This may be served hot or cold. If the soup is too thick, add a little more milk or cream. This makes about 5 cups of soup.

CARROT AND TOMATO JUICE SOUP

1 yellow onion, sliced
1 green pepper, sliced
3 tablespoons butter
Salt and pepper
2⅔ cups tomato juice

1 can carrot juice
½ cup grapefruit juice or juice of
    1 lemon
1 teaspoon powdered fennel
Garnish: slices of avocado

This is an excellent soup that may be made in no time. Sauté the sliced onion and green pepper in the butter until tender, then purée with salt, pepper, and some of the tomato juice. Add the rest of the ingredients. This may be served hot or cold. Garnish with 2 or 3 slices of avocado in each soup plate. This makes about 5½ or 6 cups.

CARROT AND ORANGE SOUP

2 bunches new carrots
⅓ cup diced onions
3 tablespoons butter
Salt and pepper
1 cup orange juice

¼ teaspoon nutmeg
1 cup light cream
Garnish:
Chopped mint or chives
Sour cream

Scrub the carrots and if they are perfect do not scrape them. Slice them thin. Sauté the onions in butter 2 minutes, then add the sliced carrots, 1 cup of water, salt, and pepper. Cover and cook until carrots are tender. Put them through a sieve or purée in an electric blender with their liquor and the orange juice. Add the nutmeg and the light cream. Heat. If this is too sweet for your taste add a little lemon juice. This makes over 6 cups of soup. Add a spoonful of sour cream and a sprinkle of mint or chives to the top of each plate of soup.

CARROT AND TOMATO SOUP. To *Carrot and Orange Soup*, add 2 or 3 cups of tomato purée after the carrots are cooked, and the juice of 1 lemon with the orange juice. These are wonderfully refreshing soups and children love them. They are good hot or cold. If too thick they may be thinned with tomato juice or orange juice.

CARROT CONSOMMÉ OR DRINK

1 can carrot juice
1½ cups orange juice or grapefruit
juice

1½ cups tomato juice
½ teaspoon salt
Juice of 2 limes

Mix all the juices together and store them in the refrigerator in a glass jar. This is a very fine drink for breakfast, and can also be served as a soup, either hot or cold, with a little chopped parsley added to the top of each soup cup. Since it is quite sweet, you may prefer to use grapefruit juice instead of orange juice.

POTAGE MARRON SUPRÈME, GREBANIER

1 pound chestnuts
3 cups clear chicken broth
¼ pound salt pork, diced
2 large potatoes, peeled and diced
3 new carrots, sliced
3 bay leaves, crumbled

1 teaspoon salt
2 cups milk
1 cup heavy cream
½ cup good sherry
Garnish: Croutons

Boil the chestnuts in salted boiling water for 1 minute, drain, and while they are hot remove the shells and skins. Put the chestnuts in a large pot with the chicken broth, finely diced salt pork, potatoes, carrots, bay leaves, and salt. Simmer 1 hour or until the chestnuts are soft—the longer the better to improve the flavor. Sieve or purée in the electric blender. The mixture will be thick so a little hot water may be added. Return the mixture to the pot. This may be made ahead of time. A half-hour before serving stir in the milk and cream and heat over the lowest possible flame; do not let boil. Add a little salt to taste. Just before serving stir in the wine. This makes about 10 or 11 cups of very elegant and rich soup for a great occasion. It is the specialty of a Shakespeare scholar and gentleman cook.

CORN AND CHICKEN CHOWDER

⅓ cup diced bacon or salt pork
1½ cups cubed raw potatoes
1 cup finely diced onions
Salt and pepper
½ green pepper, diced

2 cups fresh corn
6 cups chicken consommé
2 tablespoons cornstarch
1 cup light cream

Fry out the bacon or salt pork until crisp, remove the pieces from the pan, and reserve. Sauté the potatoes and onions in the grease until almost tender, add salt and pepper and the green pepper, and cook 3 or 4 minutes more. Score the corn kernels with a sharp pointed knife, cut from the ears, and add to the vegetables. Good canned kernel corn may be used. Heat the consommé and combine with the vegetables. Blend the cornstarch with the cream and stir it into the soup. This may stand several hours before serving; it improves with standing. Reheat to serve, which will be all the cooking the fresh corn needs. This makes about 10 cups of soup.

LEEK AND POTATO SOUP

1 large bunch of leeks
3 good-sized potatoes
⅓ cup sweet butter
Salt and freshly ground pepper
3 cups boiling water

2 cups milk
1 cup light cream
Garnish:
Sour cream
Chopped chives

Quarter the leeks and wash them well. Only the coarsest green ends are discarded. Slice them very thin, less than ¼ inch. There should be 3 overflowing cups. Peel the potatoes and cut in small cubes; there should be 4 cups. Melt the butter in a heavy pot and add the vegetables; cover and cook gently for 5 minutes. Add salt and pepper and the boiling water. Cover and simmer for 20 minutes. Mash the contents of the pot through a coarse sieve, adding any purée that does not go through. An electric blender is not good for this soup, as it makes the texture too smooth. Heat the milk and cream and add to the purée. This makes about 11 cups of soup. It keeps well in covered glass jars in the refrigerator for several days. It may be served hot, or cold with a blob of sour cream and minced chives.

LENTIL SOUP

2 cups dried lentils
4 cups water
　Ham bone, or roast bones (beef
　　or lamb)
2 large onions, chopped
2 carrots, chopped
2 stalks celery, chopped
2 teaspoons orégano
2 teaspoons salt

¼ teaspoon powdered clove
2 bay leaves
　Freshly ground pepper
2 or 3 tablespoons lemon juice oı
　¼ cup sherry
Garnish:
　2 knackwurst
　Bahamian mustard

The night before making the soup, wash the lentils and put them to soak in 4 cups of water. Do not drain them. Put them in a big pot with the bones, vegetables, seasonings, and 4 more cups of water. Let the soup simmer 2 hours (25 minutes in a pressure cooker). When it is done, remove the bones and bay leaves and reserve 1 cup of lentils. Put the rest of the soup through a sieve or purée in a blender. This makes a creamy-textured soup instead of a watery one. Return the lentils to the soup and flavor to taste with the lemon juice or sherry. For garnishing, boil the knackwurst 10 minutes in water, skin, and cut in ½-inch slices. Spread with a little Bahamian or other prepared mustard and put 2 or 3 slices in each plate of soup. As lentils are a Near East staple and so is lamb, lamb bones are very good for this soup. This makes more than 2 quarts of soup.

FRESH MUSHROOM SOUP

1 pound fresh white mushrooms
⅓ cup finely sliced onions
4 tablespoons butter
7 cups rich chicken consommé
1 teaspoon powdered beef con-
　　centrate

Salt and pepper
¼ teaspoon nutmeg
3 tablespoons cornstarch
1 cup heavy cream
3 tablespoons Madeira or 2 of port
3 tablespoons chopped parsley

Brush the mushrooms, remove ¹⁄₁₆-inch of the stem, and slice tops and stems. Melt the butter in a shallow pan, add the mushrooms and onions and bake at 375° for 10 minutes. Put the contents of the pan through a meat grinder, or in an electric blender at its lowest speed, so they aren't puréed but are finely chopped. If the blender is used, add 1 cup of the chicken consommé to the blender. Combine the rest of the consommé with the mushrooms, beef powder, salt and pepper (to taste), and nutmeg. Blend the cornstarch with the cream and let it thicken over the fire, then add to the soup. This may be made hours before serving. Let it stand in a porcelain bowl, not in aluminum. When ready to serve, reheat the soup in a saucepan and add the wine and the chopped parsley. Serves 8 or 10. A small tin of tiny mushrooms may be used for a garnish if desired. They add little in flavor but are attractive.

FRESH PEA SOUP

3 pounds fresh peas
5 white onions, sliced
¼ cup butter
  Salt and pepper
2 teaspoons dried basil

2 cups milk (more as needed)
1 cup light cream
¼ teaspoon nutmeg
Garnish:
  Chopped mint or parsley

Shell the peas. Three pounds makes 3 cups of peas. Sauté the sliced onions in the butter for a minute, then add the peas, salt, pepper, basil, and ¼ cup of water. Cover tightly and simmer about 8 or 10 minutes, or until the peas are just tender. Add 2 cups milk and purée the peas, then add the light cream and nutmeg. Add enough more milk to make 8 cups. This may be served hot or cold. Mint also gives a nice flavor to peas, and may be used instead of basil.

SPLIT-PEA SOUP

2 cups dried peas
2 tablespoons butter
1 large onion, sliced
1 cup chopped carrots
1 ham bone or roast bone
2 bay leaves

Salt and pepper
Milk
Garnish:
  1 pound fresh peas
  Butter
  1 teaspoon basil

Wash the peas and soak them overnight in 2 cups of water. Do not drain them but add 2½ cups of water when ready to cook. Sauté the finely sliced onion in the butter for 2 minutes, then add to the peas, with the carrots, ham or roast bone, bay leaves, and a little salt and pepper. Simmer the soup, covered, until done, 1¼ hours (about 25 minutes in the pressure cooker). Remove the bay leaves and bones and purée the soup through a sieve or in a blender. Thin to the right consistency with milk. For a special touch cook a pound of fresh peas with 1 teaspoon basil in some butter until just tender and add them to the soup. This makes about 8 cups of soup.

SPINACH SOUP

1½ pounds fresh spinach
1 green pepper, sliced
1 large onion, sliced
  Salt and pepper

½ teaspoon rosemary or thyme
Butter
Milk

Wash and stem the spinach, discarding any imperfect leaves. Fill a dish-pan with quite warm water for the first washing and the dirt will sink quickly to the bottom of the pan. Two more rinsings should remove all remaining grit. Drain well. Sauté the sliced pepper and onion in a little butter in the bottom of the cooker, with salt, pepper, and the herb. Put the spinach on top of the vegetables, cover tightly, and cook until the spinach is wilted, about 5 minutes (30 seconds in a pressure cooker). Purée all the vegetables with the liquid in the electric blender. Thin the purée with enough milk to give it the consistency of heavy cream. For a special occasion this lovely soup may be garnished with a few chopped onions and 2 or 3 slices of avocado in each soup plate. Serve hot or cold. Serves 6 or 8.

POTAGE GERMINY
Maxim's, Paris

2½ cups sorrel leaves
  3 tablespoons sweet butter
10 egg yolks, beaten
  2 cups heavy cream

4½ cups very best veal or chicken
  consommé
Salt and pepper

Don't worry about using so many egg yolks for this elegant soup—there are many good uses for egg whites: soufflés, cake, etc. Maxim's called for 15 yolks but I cut the recipe in proportion. They thicken the liquids with the egg yolks instead of with flour. Chop the sorrel leaves very fine in a wooden chopping bowl, then soften in the butter very gently for 3 or 4 minutes. Beat the egg yolks until thick, scald the cream, and slowly pour it over them. Heat the consommé, season well with salt and pepper, and whisk the egg-yolk-cream mixture into it. If it is not cream-smooth put it through a sieve. Heat again—do not let it boil—and add the leaves and butter. Serve immediately, accompanied with cheese straws. Makes 8 cups. This may also be made with watercress.

VICHYSSOISE

4 large yellow onions or 1 pound
  leeks
3 good-sized potatoes
⅓ cup sweet butter
  Salt and freshly ground pepper

3 cups boiling rich chicken stock
2 cups hot milk
1 cup light cream
Garnish: Chopped chives

Follow the directions for *Leek and Potato Soup* but use boiling chicken stock instead of water. Serve hot or cold.

WATERCRESS OR SORREL SOUP

4 large yellow onions or 1 pound
   leeks
⅓ cup sweet butter
3 good-sized potatoes
   Salt and freshly ground pepper
3 cups boiling water
2 teaspoons powdered chicken
   concentrate

1 cup closely packed watercress or
   sorrel leaves
2 cups hot milk
1 cup heavy cream
Garnish: Sprigs of watercress

Mince the onions or leeks into a heavy pot and sauté 2 or 3 minutes with the butter over a low flame. Peel the potatoes and cut in small cubes. Add them to the pot and after a minute add the seasonings, boiling water, and chicken concentrate. Cover and cook until the vegetables are tender. Stem the watercress or sorrel, using some of the tender stems. Finely hand-chop the leaves and add them to the soup 5 minutes before the vegetables are done. Sieve the contents of the pot and add the hot milk and heavy cream. The consistency should be like light cream. This may be served hot or cold. Add a sprig of watercress to each soup plate. Serves 10 or 12.

CLEAR BOUILLON

2 pounds beef knuckle and
   marrow bones
2 pounds chopped beef
1 chicken
2 cups chopped onions
2 cups chopped celery
2 cups sliced carrots
2 sprigs parsley
1 white turnip, sliced
1 parsnip, sliced
2 bay leaves

1 large can tomato purée
1 cup red wine
1 teaspoon basil
1 teaspoon thyme
2 whole cloves
   Salt and pepper
2 egg whites, half beaten
Garnish:
   Croutons
   Parmesan or shredded Gruyère
   cheese

Have the beef knuckle split. Put it, the bones, chopped beef, and chicken in a large soup kettle and add water to just cover. The chicken may be whole or in parts. Bring to a simmer, skim, and gently cook for 1 hour. Remove the chicken, to serve as is, to use for salad, or to be creamed. Add all the vegetables and seasonings to the soup kettle except the salt, pepper, and egg whites. Add a little hot water to just cover, if necessary. Almost cover with the lid and gently simmer for 3½ hours. Never let it boil hard. After 1 hour add salt and pepper. When it is done, strain the broth without pressing the meat or vegetables against the sieve, otherwise it will not be clear. When the broth is cool, refrigerate it until a cake of fat is formed; this you remove. To clarify, put the broth back in the kettle with the half-beaten egg whites and simmer for 5 minutes. Line a fine sieve with a cloth wrung out in cold water and strain the broth through it. It will be clear. Store in the refrigerator in screw-top glass jars. It is the base for sauces and a variety of soups: *Tagliarini al Consommé*, onion, bean, and mushroom soups. *Cheese Balls for Consommé* make a fine garnish for this. For a Sunday night supper in Thoissey, Burgundy, we were served a rich bouillon of this type accompanied by separate bowls of croutons and cheese.

ONION SOUP

1½ to 2 pounds onions: yellow, Bermuda, or Italian red
¼ cup butter
2 tablespoons olive oil
Salt and pepper
¼ teaspoon nutmeg
1 clove garlic, crushed
2 tablespoons flour

2 quarts rich beef broth
½ cup dry white wine
3 tablespoons brandy or Madeira
Garnish:
  Toasted French bread
  Shredded Gruyère or Swiss cheese
  Bowl of Parmesan cheese

Slice the onions very thin and sauté them in the butter and oil very slowly about 20 minutes, until they are softened but not the least burned. Season with salt, pepper, and nutmeg, add the garlic, and stir in the flour. Boil up the broth with the wine, pour over the onions, and simmer gently for 45 minutes. This may be done several hours in advance. When reheating for serving, bring to a simmer and add the brandy or Madeira. Cut French bread in 1-inch slices and dry out in the oven, then cover them thickly with shredded cheese and bake in the oven until the cheese is melted. Place a cheese toast on top of each bowl of soup. Pass a bowl of Parmesan cheese to sprinkle over the top. Serves 8.

VARIATION No. 1. Use one can of V8 and enough beef broth to make 2 quarts.

VARIATION No. 2. Use rich chicken broth instead of beef broth, either alone or with the V8.

GARNISH VARIATION. Sprinkle top of soup with Oignons Frits (Morvandelles). These ready-to-eat fried onions packaged in envelopes are imported.

TAGLIARINI AL CONSOMMÉ

Rich beef, veal, or chicken consommé

Finest egg noodles
Freshly grated Parmesan cheese

This is one of the finest soups to precede a well-planned dinner. Boil the noodles in salted water 8 minutes. Have consommé boiling hot. Put a small helping of hot drained noodles in each soup plate and pour the consommé over them. Pass the cheese for each guest to help himself. The success of the dish depends on the quality of all the ingredients. See index for consommé recipes.

ITALIAN CHEESE BALLS FOR CONSOMME

½ cup ground raw spinach
½ cup cottage cheese, sieved, or
   ½ cup ricotta
1 tablespoon Parmesan cheese
Salt and freshly ground pepper

Rind 1 small lemon, grated
½ teaspoon nutmeg
1 large egg yolk
4 tablespoons sifted flour
Mixed flour and cheese

Press the juice out of the spinach so the result will be a little over ⅓ cup. Italian ricotta or sieved cottage cheese may be used. Mix the spinach, cheese, seasonings, egg yolk, and flour together and roll into small balls. Roll these in a light mixture of flour and Parmesan cheese. Try boiling one ball in a little of the soup to see if it holds together. If it disintegrates, add a very little more flour. The less flour used, the more delicate the balls. Drop the balls into boiling consommé and cook for 2 or 3 minutes. Serve in the consommé, allowing 4 or 5 balls to a serving. They are delicate and delicious. This makes about 20 balls.

SCOTCH BROTH WITH NECK OF LAMB OR MUTTON

3 pounds neck of lamb or mutton
Soup bones
½ cup dried split peas
½ cup barley
1 large onion, minced
Salt and pepper
1 cup finely diced carrots
3 leeks, finely sliced
1 bunch green onions, finely
   sliced
1 cup finely diced white turnip
1 cup celery hearts, finely diced

2 tablespoons chopped parsley
Caper Sauce:
   1 tablespoon cornstarch
   1 cup light cream
   Salt and finely ground
      pepper
   1 tablespoon lemon juice
   ½ teaspoon grated lemon rind
   3 tablespoons capers
   2 tablespoons butter
   1 egg yolk, beaten

Soak the peas in water just to cover, overnight. When ready to make the broth, put the meat and bones in a large soup kettle and add 3 quarts of boiling water. Simmer for 30 minutes, skimming well. Add the peas, barley, onion, salt, and pepper and simmer very gently 1 hour, almost covered. Then add all the vegetables except the parsley and simmer 1 hour more. This makes 2½ hours of cooking and the meat should be tender. Remove the bones and discard. Stir in the parsley. The soup and meat may be served together, or the soup may be served, and the meat left in the kettle to keep warm for serving later. It is excellent with Caper Sauce. Make the sauce while the broth is cooking. Blend the cornstarch with the cream and cook in a saucepan until it thickens, add the seasonings and capers. Reheat before serving and beat in the butter and egg yolk. Do not boil again. Serve in a sauceboat. The meat and broth will serve 8.

GRAVY SOUP

Chicken or Turkey:
  1 cup chicken or turkey gravy
  ½ to ⅔ cup boiled potatoes
  Milk
  1 small can tiny peas
  Chopped parsley
  Salt and pepper

Beef:
  1 cup roast beef gravy
  ½ to ⅔ cup boiled potatoes
  Beef broth (made with
    powdered beef concen-
    trate and water)
  1 small can whole white corn
  Chopped parsley
  Salt and pepper

I've often been asked by friends to write a "leftovers" cookbook. I don't feel that such books are needed; at least they shouldn't be if cooks learn how to make the most of good ingredients and master the arts of roasting and making sauces, soups, etc. Put the gravy in a saucepan to melt. Put the potatoes through a sieve or put them in a blender with milk or broth. Add the purée to the gravy. Add enough milk or broth to make the soup the consistency of heavy cream. The potato purée makes a rich appearing soup without using fat or flour. The addition of peas or corn extends the soup. This quantity will serve 3 or 4. These are as fine soups as could be required for any occasion.

SCOTCH BROTH

3 pounds shoulder and neck of
  lamb
Beef bones
1 large onion, sliced
1 large carrot, sliced
½ cup celery, sliced
Salt and pepper
2 bay leaves

¾ cup dried peas, soaked
½ cup tiny carrot cubes
½ cup tiny onion cubes
1 tablespoon chopped parsley
1 cup barley
Salt and pepper
1 teaspoon thyme
2 tablespoons dried currants

Have the butcher bone the lamb and take the bones. Soak the peas 6 hours in water to cover. In one kettle put the lamb bones and beef bones, the onion, carrot, celery, salt, pepper, and bay leaves. Add 2 quarts of water to the bones and vegetables and simmer, covered, for 3 hours. After 1½ hours, cut the lamb in 1-inch cubes and put it in another kettle with the peas. Simmer very gently in 1½ quarts of water for 1 hour, then add the carrot cubes, onion cubes, parsley, barley, salt, pepper, thyme, and currants, and cook 30 minutes longer. Strain the first kettle of broth into the meat kettle and taste for seasoning. This is a main-dish soup and may be served with hot cornbread or scones and a green salad.

FRESH TOMATO SOUP

4 or 5 large ripe tomatoes
1 green pepper, diced
1 large onion, diced
2 tablespoons olive oil
2 tablespoons butter
Salt and pepper

1 tablespoon honey or brown sugar
1 quart chicken, beef, or veal broth
2 whole cloves
1 teaspoon powdered fennel or
    fresh dill
Garnish: Sour cream

Skin the tomatoes and cut them up. Sauté the pepper and onion in the olive oil and butter for 8 or 10 minutes over a low fire. Put all the ingredients in the broth, add the cloves and fennel, and simmer 15 minutes. Remove the cloves. Mash through a sieve or purée in a blender. If fresh tomatoes are not available, this may be made of 3 cups of canned tomatoes or tomato purée. If fresh dill is obtainable it gives a fine flavor to tomato soup. Cut a handful of stemmed dill very fine with scissors and put it in the soup after it has simmered. Serves 8.

CELERY AND TOMATO SOUP

1 bunch of celery
3 onions
2 carrots
Beef bones
1 teaspoon beef extract
3 whole cloves
1 teaspoon thyme

1 teaspoon basil
Salt and pepper
1 15-ounce can tomato purée
1 teaspoon honey or brown sugar
¼ cup red wine
2 or 3 tablespoons cornstarch
Garnish: Sour cream

Cut the vegetables up very fine and put them in a heavy pot or a pressure cooker with cooked steak bones or roast beef bones, or fresh bones with a little meat on them. Add the extract, cloves, herbs, salt, and pepper. Add enough water so that it covers the bones and vegetables when they are pressed down with a spoon. Cover tightly and simmer 1¾ hours, or cook 45 minutes in the pressure cooker. Add a little more water if cooked in a pot. Strain the soup through a coarse sieve. Add the tomato purée, honey or sugar, and the wine and simmer for 5 minutes. Blend the cornstarch with a little of the soup, then add it and cook until the soup thickens. This makes 2 quarts of rich vegetable soup. Serve with a blob of sour cream added to each soup plate.

EGG SOUP

1 quart chicken or turkey soup
½ cup stuffing
2 tablespoons tomato paste
1 teaspoon cumin powder

¼ teaspoon anise powder
Salt and pepper
6 eggs

This is a soup to serve during the holidays or any time that you make soup from a turkey carcass. If you are serving 6, use 5 or 6 cups of the soup. Add the crumbled dressing, blend the tomato paste and seasonings with a little of the soup, add, and let simmer 10 minutes. Slide each egg from a saucer into the simmering soup and when they are poached lift them out onto soup plates and add soup.

CHICKEN SOUP

2 pounds chicken giblets and parts
Beef marrow bones
1½ cups sliced celery and leaves
3 large onions, sliced
2 carrots, sliced
1 parsnip, sliced
Salt and pepper

1 teaspoon thyme
2 bay leaves
2 whole cloves or ¼ teaspoon ginger
½ cup white wine or dry vermouth
2 teaspoons powdered chicken concentrate

This is a rich consommé made with chicken hearts, gizzards, necks, and backs. If good boiled chicken is required, add the legs and breasts, removing them after they have very gently simmered 45 minutes. To make the soup rich, beef bones are necessary. Put all the ingredients in a large soup kettle and add 2 quarts of water. Simmer gently 2 hours, then strain. This makes a good soup in its own right and a base for many other soups: mushroom, onion, potato, vichyssoise, etc. To clarify for aspic, after it has been strained, simmer it 5 minutes with a half-beaten egg white. Line a sieve with a cloth wrung out of cold water and strain the soup.

TURKEY WING SOUP AS A MAIN DISH

6 or 8 turkey wings
1½ cups celery, sliced
1 carrot, sliced
1 large potato, cubed
1 large Bermuda onion, cubed
2 parsnips, sliced
1 teaspoon basil
1 teaspoon thyme
1 teaspoon turmeric

8 cups water
2 teaspoons powdered chicken concentrate
Salt and pepper
Optional additions:
    1 cup thin cream
    1 tablespoon tomato paste
    3 tablespoons sherry or Madeira

Now that turkey wings are sold as parts in the markets, they can be cooked in soup with vegetables to make a one-dish meal. Put the wings on to cook in 8 cups of water, with all the ingredients except the salt and pepper which is added halfway through the cooking. Simmer, covered, for 1 hour and 15 minutes or until the wings are very tender. This is the only time a wing has a chance to cook tender instead of being dried out in the roasting. If a cream soup is desired the additions may be used. The soup may be thickened with a tablespoon of cornstarch blended with the cream and added just before reheating to serve. Serve a wing in each plate of soup.

GAZPACHO

1 green pepper
3 large tomatoes
4 green onions, minced
1 cucumber, peeled
4 sprigs parsley
1 clove garlic, crushed
Salt and pepper
1 teaspoon cumin powder
Dash cayenne pepper

1 tablespoon vinegar
1 cup tomato juice
¼ cup olive oil
Garnish:
Croutons fried in garlic and
olive oil
Cubes of cucumber
Scallions
Frozen cubes of tomato juice

Boil the green pepper 6 minutes, seed, and cut it up. Skin and slice the tomatoes, mince the onions, slice the peeled cucumber. Put the vegetables in the blender with the parsley, crushed garlic, seasonings, vinegar, tomato juice, and olive oil. When the soup is puréed, chill it. Sauté 1½ cups of ½-inch cubes of dry bread in crushed garlic and olive oil and serve them in a bowl to sprinkle over each soup plate at the table. Peel and cube the cucumber and cut the scallions in ¼-inch lengths and pass them in bowls. Freeze a tray of tomato juice and put 2 cubes in each soup plate. Serves 6. This is a delicious summer soup when tomatoes are at their prime. If you lack a blender a perfectly fine soup may be made the way the Spanish do it. Chop the vegetables very fine. Beat the seasonings and liquids together with a rotary beater, and mix them with the vegetables.

MINESTRONE

¾ cup dried chick peas or kidney
beans
2 cloves garlic, crushed
3 strips bacon, or ham fat
2 big onions, chopped
1½ cups chopped spinach or
cabbage
2 potatoes, cubed
1 carrot, chopped
1 small zucchini, sliced

Salt and pepper
6 cups beef stock
2 cups tomatoes
1 teaspoon marjoram
1 teaspoon thyme
⅓ cup red wine
½ cup small egg noodle shells
1 tablespoon grated lemon rind
¼ cup chopped parsley
Garnish: Parmesan cheese

Wash the chick peas or kidney beans and soak them with 3 cups of water for 8 hours. Add the garlic and simmer them 1¼ hours or until they are tender. Add a little more water if necessary. Fry out the bacon or ham fat a little and sauté the finely chopped onions in it until they are almost tender. Add the spinach or cabbage and the potatoes and cook another 2 or 3 minutes over a low flame. Add this to the soup, with the carrot, zucchini, salt, pepper, beef stock, tomatoes, herbs, and wine. Simmer for ½ hour, then add the noodle shells and cook 12 minutes more. The soup should be thick with vegetables. Stir in the lemon rind and parsley when the soup is done. Pass a bowl of Parmesan cheese. Serves 8 or 10.

TURTLE AND PEA SOUP

1 large can green turtle soup
⅓ cup minced green onions, or 1
    white onion, minced
2 tablespoons butter
1 pound fresh peas

Salt and pepper
1 teaspoon basil
½ cup heavy cream (optional)
¼ cup Madeira or sherry
1 tablespoon chopped parsley

Put the onions in a pot with the butter and cook 1 minute, then add the peas, salt, pepper, basil, and ⅓ cup water. Cook until the peas are tender. Put 1 cup of the turtle soup and the cooked peas through a sieve or blender. Combine with the rest of the turtle soup. Add cream if desired. Just before serving, reheat and add the wine and chopped parsley. Serves 6.

HUNGARIAN MUSHROOM SOUP

¼ cup pearl barley
8 cups veal or chicken broth
1 pound fresh mushrooms
2 tablespoons butter

2 tablespoons flour
Salt and pepper
1 teaspoon sweet paprika
2 tablespoons chopped parsley

Cook the barley in the broth for 30 minutes at a very low simmer. Choose white mushrooms with stems; they must be fresh and not dry. Chop half the mushroom tops and all the stems quite fine and slice the rest of the tops very thin. Simmer them in the broth for 12 minutes. Brown the butter and flour together, then blend in some of the broth, and add the mixture to the soup to thicken it a little. Simmer 5 minutes. Season with salt and pepper to taste; add the paprika and the parsley. Serves 8.

CREAM VEGETABLE SOUP

1 pound fresh peas
1 pound fresh lima beans
½ pound fresh string beans
1 cup water
1 teaspoon basil

Salt and pepper
3 cups chicken broth
1 cup heavy cream
Handful fresh dill
1 or 2 teaspoons wine vinegar

Shell the peas and lima beans and cut the string beans in ½-inch lengths. Put all the vegetables, basil, salt, and pepper in a pot with 1 cup water, cover, and cook about 12 minutes or until the vegetables are tender. Add the chicken broth to the vegetables and their liquid and let stand until ready to reheat and serve. Stem the dill, squeeze, and cut fine with kitchen scissors. Add to the cream and bring to a boil. This may stand so the dill makes the cream fragrant. Add the cream to the soup and reheat, adding vinegar to taste. If the vegetables are fresh this is a very fine soup. Serves 8. To serve 9 or 10, add 1 good-sized potato cut in very small cubes, to cook with the other vegetables, and use a little more broth.

SOUPE AU PISTOU

½ cup dried lima or white beans
4 or 5 cups chicken broth
1½ pounds fresh peas
2 teaspoons basil
   Salt and pepper
   Butter
½ pound fresh string beans
½ teaspoon rosemary
2 small fresh zucchini
½ large green pepper
6 good-sized white onions, sliced

⅔ cup skinned fresh or canned
   tomatoes
1 12-ounce can white kernel corn
1 clove garlic, crushed
½ cup shell egg noodles
Pistou Sauce:
   6 large cloves garlic, crushed
   Large handful parsley
   ½ cup olive oil
   ⅓ cup soup broth
Parmesan cheese

One might say that this soup is a Provençal version of Minestrone, and this recipe is my own version. The traditional soup calls for water instead of broth and for boiling all the vegetables together. Cooking the vegetables separately and adding them and their liquids to the broth as they are cooked assures against overcooking and preserves their individual flavors. This is a very great soup and is always received with delight. As the liquids are added to the soup, use a minimum of water when cooking the vegetables. Soak the beans overnight and in the morning simmer them until they are tender. Put the chicken broth in a 4-quart kettle and add the beans. Cook the peas with the basil, salt, pepper, and a pat of butter, adding as little water as possible. Cut the string beans into ½-inch lengths and cook them with the rosemary, a pat of butter, salt, pepper, and a minimum of water. (In a pressure cooker peas take only 1 minute and string beans 3 minutes.) Slice the zucchini quite thin, put it in a small pot with 3 tablespoons of water, and add the cubed green pepper to the top. Cover tightly and simmer 5 minutes. Slice the onions thin and cook them with salt, pepper, a pat of butter, and very little water. When the vegetables are tender, add them to the soup. Add the sliced tomatoes, the corn, and the garlic. Cook the noodles in salted water, drain, and add them. This makes about 4 quarts of soup and will serve 12; it is good reheated and will keep for several days. It is best made ahead of time and reheated before serving. For the pistou sauce, crush the garlic in a press and then put it in a mortar. Chop the parsley very fine and add it to the garlic. Mash with a pestle, adding the olive oil gradually. Then add the broth. Bring the mortar to the table and let each person stir a big spoonful of sauce into the steaming soup. What a fragrance! Pass a bowl of Parmesan cheese. Other green vegetables in season may be added, such as fresh lima beans. It is difficult to make less than 4 quarts because many vegetables go into the soup and not a great deal of each. Cubed cooked potato may be added when the soup is served as a main dish for a large family.

SQUASH, PUMPKIN, OR SWEET POTATO SOUP

2 cups (1 pound mashed Hubbard
    or acorn squash, pumpkin, or
    sweet potatoes
3 cups chicken broth
2 tablespoons butter
    Salt and freshly ground pepper

3 tablespoons honey
½ teaspoon mace or nutmeg
⅔ cup heavy cream
    Light rum
Garnish: Chestnuts (optional)

Cook the vegetable, mash, and thin with the broth. Add the seasonings. When ready to serve add the cream and bring to a simmer. Put a tablespoon of rum in each soup plate and add the soup. This makes about 6 cups and will serve 7 or 8. For a holiday dinner add to each plate some sliced boiled chestnuts, or chestnuts packed in syrup, drained.

Fish Soups

BURGUNDY FISH STEW

3 or 4 pounds fresh-water fish,
    filleted (pike, pickerel, trout, bass,
    etc.)
Broth:
    Fish trimmings
   1 quart water
   1 sliced lemon
    Pinch sage
   2 cloves garlic, crushed
   1 carrot, sliced
   1 onion, sliced
  ½ teaspoon cloves
   1 teaspoon thyme
   1 teaspoon sugar
   2 bay leaves
    Salt and pepper

¼ pound salt pork, diced
2 cups sliced onions
3 cups diced potatoes
2 cups canned tomatoes
    Dash cayenne
2 cups Burgundy
    Salt and pepper
Garnish: Garlic toast

This will serve 8 if 4 pounds of fish are used. Reserve the fillets. Put the fish trimmings (bones, skin, heads) and other broth ingredients in 1 quart water, simmer for 20 minutes, and strain. Fry out the pork and put the crisp pieces of pork in the fish kettle. Sauté the onions in the pork fat for 6 minutes without browning them. Put alternate layers of vegetables and fish in the kettle, adding a little salt and pepper and cayenne to the fish broth if it needs it. Cover with the broth and add the wine. Cook slowly for 30 minutes. Slice French bread 1-inch thick and sauté it in olive oil with the crushed garlic. Put a slice in each soup plate and add the soup.

BOUILLABAISSE À LA MARSEILLAISES
Le Drouant, Place Gaillon, Paris

One evening during an after-dinner stroll we turned off busy Avenue de l'Opèra for a little relief from the din of rushing cars and motor scooters. We found it at Place Gaillon, a lovely quiet circle surrounded by old houses, with two restaurants opposite each other. It seemed like another world, this sudden quiet; the muted lighting was like moonlight. We came back the following night to the Drouant, a restaurant some eighty years old, still in the Drouant family and keeping up its tradition of entertaining and periodically banqueting the world of arts and letters. It is known for its fine seafood dishes, so I was happy to receive this recipe from M. Jules Petit, Chef de Cuisine. The recipe calls for 5 pounds of fish to serve 10 persons. The specified fish are Rascasse, Chapon, St. Pierre, Merlan de Palangre (whiting), Ficlas, Boudreuil, Rouquier, Rouget (red mullet or gurnet), Langouste, and Langoustines. Even in France, Mediterranean fish aren't always available away from the sea, and here we have to make do with the fish the market affords, preferably sea fish. Those that most nearly approximate the French varieties are fresh cod, sea bass, sole, red snapper, bluefish, eel, lobsters and shrimp.

Fish broth:
  Fish trimmings, shrimp shells
  1 onion, chopped
  1 teaspoon thyme
  Little salt and pepper
  2 quarts of water
5 pounds mixed fish
¼ pounds onions, chopped
  White part of 1 large leek, minced
2 large tomatoes, peeled, seeded, crushed
2 cloves garlic, crushed
2 tablespoons parsley, minced
½ cup olive oil

1 big pinch saffron
1 bay leaf
1 branch fennel
2 teaspoons salt
½ teaspoon pepper
  Slices of French bread
Rouille:
  2 cloves garlic, crushed
  2 red pimentos, mashed
  Lobster coral
  2 tablespoons breadcrumbs
  ⅓ cup olive oil
  ½ cup fish broth
  French bread, sliced

The fish are cleaned, skinned, and boned and the shrimp are shelled. Put the fish trimmings and the shrimp shells in a kettle with a chopped onion, 1 teaspoon of thyme, a little salt and pepper, and 2 quarts of water. Almost cover the kettle and simmer gently for 30 minutes, then strain the broth. A half hour before you are ready to serve the bouillabaisse, put all the vegetables, the olive oil, and the seasonings in the bottom of the fish kettle and lay the firmest fish on top. Have the lobster split and put it on the fish, shell down so that it steams tender. Add the strained fish broth and if necessary a little water to cover. Cover the kettle and simmer gently for 15 minutes; add the more delicate fish and simmer 8 minutes; then add the shrimp and simmer 3 minutes longer. Mash all the ingredients of the rouille into a thick sauce. Carefully strain the fish from the kettle and put it on a hot platter. Ladle the broth into soup plates and add to each plate a slice of crisp French bread, not toasted, but sliced 2 hours before serving. A big soupspoon of rouille is added to each plate. If you prefer, serve 2 or 3 pieces of fish in each soup plate with the broth, instead of separately on a platter. Serve the lobster at the table, each receiving a piece.

LA BOURRIDE
Le Petit Navire, Paris

M. Marcel Gilot has developed a devoted clientele for this wonderful soup, which he says is also called "Bouillabaisse Blanche" in Provence. Rock fish is a necessary ingredient; only white-fleshed fish go into this soup. All the cooking in this lovely restaurant is of superior quality but La Bourride is perhaps its most popular dish.

5 pounds assorted fish
Fish broth:
    Fish trimmings
    1 large onion, minced
    1 tomato skinned and seeded
    ½ cup olive oil
    2 tablespoons minced parsley
    2 bay leaves
    2 teaspoons savory
    1 teaspoon powdered fennel
    1 teaspoon orégano
    2 cloves garlic, crushed
    Salt and pepper

Fish fillets
    Good pinch saffron
10 slices French bread rubbed with
    garlic
Rouille:
    1 tomato or 1 tablespoon
      tomato paste
    4 or 5 cloves garlic, crushed
    2 red pimentos, mashed
    3 tablespoons olive oil
    ½ cup fish broth

Have the fish man skin and fillet the fish and give you all the bones and trimmings. Put the vegetables and olive oil in the fish kettle and cook 2 or 3 minutes, then add the fish trimmings and all the seasonings, including the salt and pepper. Cover with boiling water and simmer for 20 minutes. This may be made ahead of time and let stand to ripen. When ready to make the soup, strain the broth; do not press the trimmings through the sieve. Add the saffron to the broth, and then the fish fillets and gently poach them for 10 minutes. The Marseillaise do not toast the bread. Slice it an hour before serving so it will dry a little and then rub each slice with cut garlic. For the rouille, skin, seed, and mash the tomato or use tomato paste. Add the garlic, mashed pimentos, olive oil, and fish broth, and mix well. Serve the mixture in a bowl. Put a slice of bread in each wide soup plate. Serve the fillets and broth from a tureen, adding a spoonful of rouille to each plate of soup. The soup serves 10.

SOUPE AU POISSON À LA ROUILLE
Capucin Gourmand, Nancy

4 pounds fish: perch, bass, sole,
    pike, etc.
1 tablespoon tomato paste
2 teaspoons salt
2 leeks
2 onions, minced
6 cloves garlic, crushed
1 teaspoon basil
¾ cup olive oil
1 pinch saffron
¾ pound fresh tomatoes

1 pound fresh mussels
3 ounces macaroni, cooked
Rouille:
   3 cloves garlic, crushed
   2 egg yolks, beaten
1¼ cups olive oil
   2 canned red pimentos,
     mashed
   ¼ cup boiling fish soup
Grilled croutons

M. Georges Romain says of this: "We are distant from the Mediterranean and we wish to eat a fish soup; we must be content with the fish we find in our rivers and it will not be less good." This is true for us too, even if we are obliged to change the types of fish and use a variety of those at hand. Wash the fish, clean, and cut in pieces. Put it in a kettle with 2½ quarts of water, tomato paste, salt, the green part of the leeks, minced, 1 minced onion, 1 crushed clove of garlic, and the basil. Let this simmer, partially covered, very gently for 1 hour to obtain a fish fumet (broth). In another kettle put the olive oil, the minced white part of the leeks and 1 minced onion, and cook until the vegetables are soft, without coloring. After the fish have simmered 1 hour, strain it through a sieve into the kettle with the onion and leek. Add the other 5 cloves of crushed garlic, the saffron and the skinned, seeded, coarsely chopped tomatoes and let it simmer gently 1 more hour. At the last moment, add the well-scrubbed mussels and the cooked macaroni. Meanwhile make the rouille. Crush 3 cloves garlic in a mortar to a paste and stir in the well-beaten egg yolks. Add the olive oil drop by drop to make a sauce like mayonnaise. Add the mashed pimentos and the strained soup. Pour the boiling soup in wide hot plates, stir a big spoon of rouille into each plate of soup and serve with buttered grilled croutons. Serves 8.

TOAST FOR FISH SOUP
Mont Blanc, Paris

Small thin rounds of toasted
    French bread
2 cloves garlic, crushed

2 red pimentos, mashed
½ cup oil mayonnaise

Mix the garlic and mashed pimentos with mayonnaise to a smooth paste. Spread this on the rounds of toast and serve with or in the fish soup. They go like popcorn, so if you are serving more than 6, double the recipe.

SEAFOOD BISQUE

1 pound fresh shrimp
1 cup water
½ cup diced onion
1 teaspoon thyme
Salt and pepper
Tomato soup

1½ pounds fresh peas
1 teaspoon basil
2 tablespoons butter
Salt and pepper
¾ cup light cream
2 tablespoons dark rum

Put the washed shrimp in a saucepan with 1 cup of water, the onion and seasonings. Cover and simmer a scant 3 minutes. Let the shrimp cool in the liquor, then remove and peel them. Return the shells to the liquor, partially cover, and simmer for 10 minutes. Strain out the shells and add the broth to the shrimp. Use unsweetened canned tomato soup and add it to the shrimp. Cook the peas with the basil, butter, salt, pepper, and very little water until tender. Purée the peas and their juice through a sieve or in a blender. If the blender is used rinse it out with some of the cream. Add the purée to the shrimp and the cream. This may stand several hours, which improves it. When ready to serve, reheat and stir in the rum. Serves 6 or 8.

VARIATION. 1¼ cups of either cooked crab or lobster meat may replace the shrimp. There won't be shrimp broth so add ¾ cup of chicken consommé.

CLAM CHOWDER

⅓ cup minced green or white
   onions
3 tablespoons butter
2 cans Snow's New England style
   condensed clam chowder
1½ cups milk
1 tablespoon cornstarch
1 cup light cream

1 cup clam broth
1 small can minced clams
1 teaspoon turmeric
1 teaspoon thyme
Freshly ground pepper
1 can whole clams
1 pound fresh shrimp (optional)

This is a fine soup for 8 or 10 people. It may be cut in half for the family. Sauté the onions 2 minutes in the butter. Put the onions in a large glass or pottery mixing bowl (not metal) and add the contents of the chowder cans rinsed out with the milk. Blend the cornstarch with the cream, let it boil up, and add it. Add the clam broth, minced clams, and seasonings. Let it stand 6 hours to ripen. Just before serving, heat the soup and add the whole clams and their juice. They must not cook or they will become tough. The shrimp are a good addition. Wash them and boil them 3 minutes. Drain, shell, and add them and their broth to the soup.

ITALIAN CLAM AND MUSSEL SOUP

2½ dozen fresh mussels
2½ dozen fresh Littleneck clams
1 cup dry white wine or dry
   vermouth
1½ cups water
3 cloves garlic, crushed
1 green pepper, chopped

¾ cup chopped onions
4 tablespoons olive oil
3 cups tomato purée
1 teaspoon fennel powder
Salt and pepper
Chopped parsley

Scrub the mussels and clams. Put the wine, water, and garlic in the bottom of a steamer and put the clams and mussels in the top. Cover and steam over the simmering liquid until the shells open. Remove the shellfish to a shallow pan, emptying their juices into the steaming-liquid. Do not shell the fish. Keep them warm in a 300° oven with the door open. Chop the vegetables very fine and sauté them in the olive oil until they are just tender, then add the tomato purée and fennel powder. Simmer gently 5 minutes. Wring out a cloth in cold water and line a sieve and strain the steaming-liquid into the tomato mixture. Add salt and pepper to taste. Put 5 mussels in their shells and 5 clams in theirs in each of 6 wide soup plates and pour the boiling soup over them. Sprinkle with chopped parsley.

MYRON'S CLAM CHOWDER

25 round hardshell clams
2 ounces diced salt pork
1½ cups diced onions
6 potatoes, diced
½ teaspoon salt

1 pint clam juice
Freshly ground pepper
1 cup milk
1 cup heavy cream

If you have the clams opened at the fish market, take along a glass container to catch all the clam juice. Fry the salt pork until it is crisp, then scoop out the pieces and reserve. Sauté the onions and potatoes in the pork fat until they are tender. Add the salt, clam juice, and pepper and simmer 10 minutes. Cut up the clams with scissors, add them to the stew and cook for 15 minutes on a very low fire. Heat the milk and cream and add it to the stew. Serves 4 to 6. This New England classic can be made with bottled clam juice if fresh is not obtainable. Serve with pilot crackers.

FISH STEW

4 pounds fish fillets (cod, bass, sole)
   Fish trimmings
1 carrot, minced
1 onion, minced
1 clove garlic, crushed
2 cups water

Salt and pepper
3 cups sliced onions
½ cup butter
2 cups dry white wine
Garnish: Cheese toast

Have the butcher fillet the fish, removing all skin and bones. Take all the trimmings and make the fish stock with the carrot, onion, garlic, salt, and pepper, and 2 cups water. Simmer this 20 minutes very slowly, then strain out the trimmings through a sieve. You should have 1½ cups of broth. Sauté the onions in the butter for 6 or 8 minutes. Put them on the bottom of a casserole, then lay the fish fillets on top of the onions, and add the broth and wine. Cook slowly, uncovered, 25 minutes. Serve the fish and soup from the casserole, trying not to break up the fish. Serve with cheese toast. Dry out thickly sliced French bread, cover with shredded Swiss cheese or sliced Mozzarella, and bake in the oven until the cheese melts. The toast is dipped into the broth. Serves 6.

CREOLE OYSTER GUMBO

1 4-pound young chicken	1 small can tomatoes
1 ¾-inch slice of ham	1 teaspoon curry powder
6 tablespoons butter	Salt and freshly ground pepper
3 tablespoons flour	⅛ teaspoon, red pepper
2 cups chopped onions	2 teaspoons each thyme and basil
1 large green pepper, sliced	1 pound fresh shrimp
2 cloves garlic, crushed	1 pound okra
1 cup sliced celery and leaves	2 dozen oysters
2 quarts chicken stock	1 tablespoon gumbo filé

Be sure to get a young chicken. Quarter the chicken and cut the ham into ½-inch cubes. Melt 3 tablespoons of the butter in a heavy pan and heat the flour in it to a dark brown without burning it. Put the browned flour in a large pot, rinsing out the browning pan with a little stock. Put in the chicken and ham. Sauté the onions and pepper in the other 3 tablespoons of butter for 5 minutes, and add them to the pot with the garlic, celery and leaves, sliced very thin, the chicken stock, tomatoes, curry powder, salt, pepper, thyme, and basil. Simmer 1½ hours. Meanwhile wash the shrimp and cook 4 minutes in 1 cup of water. Let cool, peel, and set aside. Return the shells to the shrimp broth and simmer 15 minutes, then strain the broth into the stewing kettle. When the chicken is tender, remove it, cut all the meat from the bones, and return the meat to the pot. Clean okra, removing the ends, add it to the pot, and simmer another half-hour. When ready to serve, reheat, and when hot add the shrimp and oysters and stir in the filé powder. Do not cook further but serve immediately. The filé is crushed dried sassafras, a thickening agent, and is not to be cooked. Serve with bowls of steaming rice. Serves 10 or 12.

LOBSTER STEW

2 1½- to 2-pound raw lobsters
½ cup butter
2 cups water
1 teaspoon thyme
¼ teaspoon nutmeg
Salt and pepper
1½ tablespoons cornstarch

1 cup chicken broth
1 teaspoon turmeric
1 tablespoon tomato paste
1 quart light cream
¼ cup light rum, brandy, Madeira, or sherry

Boil the lobsters about 20 minutes. Remove from the water and open them in a large pan so as to retain all the juices. Remove all the meat, any roe or coral and tomalley, and put it in the top of a double boiler with the butter. When the butter is melted remove from heat and let stand several hours. This is best made in the morning. Put all the juices with the lobster meat, squeezing in the juice from the little claws. Pound all the shells and put them through the meat grinder. Boil them in 2 cups water, with the thyme, nutmeg, salt, and pepper for 30 minutes over a low flame. This broth will make the stew rich in flavor. Let it cool and strain it through a very fine sieve into the lobster meat. Blend the cornstarch, the turmeric and tomato paste (for color and flavor), with the chicken broth; add the cream, and bring to a boil. Pour this into the lobster mixture and taste for seasoning. When ready to serve, reheat and add the liquor. Serves 8.

MUSSELS SOUP

2 quarts fresh mussels
1 cup dry vermouth
12-ounce jar clam juice
⅓ cup shredded onion
1 teaspoon thyme
1 clove garlic, crushed

Freshly ground pepper
3 tablespoons butter
3 tablespoons flour
¼ teaspoon nutmeg
1 tablespoon tomato paste
1 cup heavy cream

Choose large mussels. The small ones are tender and of good flavor but won't provide enough fish for the soup. There are about 30 large mussels to a quart (1 pound). Soak the mussels several hours in cold water. Cut off any moss clinging to the shells, scrub them hard with a rough brush, then rinse them very well, and let them stand again in the cold water 1 hour before steaming them. Put them in a large kettle, add the wine, cover, and cook until they open, shaking them twice. This will take about 5 minutes. When the mussels cool, shell them over the kettle so that all the juices will mix with the wine broth. Line a sieve with a fine cloth wrung out in cold water and strain the broth. Meanwhile simmer the clam juice with the onion, thyme, garlic, and pepper for 5 minutes, then add the wine broth. Melt the butter in a saucepan, blend in the flour, nutmeg, tomato paste, and stir in the cream. Thin this with a little broth and then combine the two mixtures. When ready to serve, bring to a simmer, and add the mussels. Serves 7 or 8.

OYSTER STEW

Fish stock:

4 ounces cod
Fish heads, bones, trimmings
1 cup chopped onion
1 cup chopped celery
Salt and pepper
1 teaspoon thyme
½ teaspoon mace
1 cup white wine or dry vermouth
2½ cups water

Chicken broth
1 tablespoon cornstarch
1¼ cups heavy cream
Paprika
2½ dozen oysters, with their liquor

Make the stock with the fish trimmings and cod. Boil the fish trimmings with the onion, celery, seasonings, wine, and 2½ cups water over a gentle flame for 30 minutes. Strain the broth through a sieve; measure it and add enough chicken broth to make 5½ cups liquid. Blend the cornstarch with the cream and cook until it thickens, then add it to the broth. Just before serving, put the oysters and their liquor in the top of a double boiler over hot water just long enough to warm them. Add the oyster liquor to the soup and reheat. Put 5 oysters in each soup plate, and pour the hot soup over them. Sprinkle the top of each plate with paprika. Serve with pilot crackers. Serves 6.

ROSE'S TUNA FISH SOUP

1 carrot, chopped fine
1 onion, chopped fine
1 stalk celery, chopped fine
1 medium-sized potato, cubed
1 green pepper, chopped fine
1½ cups water
1½ cups chicken broth
¼ pound fresh mushrooms

Butter
1 8-ounce can tuna fish
1 tablespoon curry powder
Salt and pepper
Garnish:
Thin lemon slices
Chopped parsley
Fried croutons

Make the soup by simmering the carrot, onion, celery, potato, and green pepper, in the water and broth for 25 minutes over a low flame. Slice the mushrooms thin, sauté them in a little butter for 5 minutes, and add them when the broth is done. Flake the tuna fish very fine, sauté it in its own oil and a little butter for a minute, and add it to the soup. Season to taste with the curry powder, salt, and pepper. Garnish each soup plate with a slice of lemon, chopped parsley, and 4 croutons fried in oil or butter. Serves 6.

SHRIMP AND SALMON SOUP

1 pound fresh shrimp	1 thick slice fresh salmon
1 onion, minced	2 tablespoons tomato paste
½ cup minced celery	1 tablespoon cornstarch
½ cup dry white wine	Milk
2 cups water	1 cup heavy cream
1 teaspoon thyme	2 egg yolks, beaten
¼ teaspoon nutmeg	¼ cup Madeira or sherry
Salt and pepper	

Wash the shrimp but do not peel them. Simmer them 4 minutes in 2 cups water with the onion, celery, wine, thyme, nutmeg, salt, and pepper. Let them cool, then peel them. Put the shells back in the broth and simmer for 15 minutes very slowly, thus giving the broth a rich fish flavor. Wash the salmon and poach it gently in the broth for 15 or 18 minutes, until it begins to flake. Strain the broth and reserve. Flake the fish very fine, discarding skin and bones. Blend the tomato paste and cornstarch with 1 cup of milk, add to the broth, and cook until it thickens. Add the shrimp and salmon, with a little milk if the broth is too thick. Remember the cream and wine are yet to be added. Let stand until ready to serve. Scald the cream, pour it over the beaten yolks. Reheat the soup and add the cream, egg yolks, and the wine. Do not let the soup boil again or it may curdle. Serve immediately. Serves 8. This soup may be extended by adding a cup of flaked canned or fresh cooked crabmeat at the time the salmon and shrimp are added. More milk and cream would be needed.

RED SNAPPER OR SEA BASS CHOWDER

2½ pounds fish, filleted	2 strips, fat salt pork, cubed
Broth:	2 cups diced onions
Fish trimmings	2 cups diced potatoes
3 cups water	Salt and pepper
1 cup dry white wine or dry	½ cup cracker crumbs
vermouth	1 cup heavy cream
1 onion, sliced	2 egg yolks, beaten
1 carrot, sliced	
1 teaspoon thyme	
1 stalk celery, sliced	
1 leek, sliced	
Salt and pepper	
1 clove garlic, crushed	

Have the fish filleted, reserving the skin, bones, and heads, which you use for the broth. Put the trimmings and all the other broth ingredients in a kettle and simmer for 20 minutes, then strain. A porcelain-covered iron casserole is good for serving this at the table. Put the pork fat cubes in the bottom of the casserole and fry out a little then put in alternate layers of fish fillets, onions, potatoes, salt, freshly ground pepper, and crumbs. Pour in the strained broth, cover, and simmer very gently for 40 minutes. Gentle cooking prevents the fish from breaking into pieces. When the soup is done, scald the cream and pour it over the egg yolks and add it to the soup. Reheat without boiling. Lift a piece of fish onto each wide soup plate and cover with the soup. This will serve 8 as a fish course or 4 or 5 as a main dish.

TURTLE CONSOMMÉ WITH MADEIRA

1 quart canned turtle consommé
1 can turtle meat

Madeira or imported dry sherry
Chopped parsley

Mix the consommé with the turtle meat, bring to a simmer, and add the wine (⅓ cup to every 4 cups of soup). Sprinkle the top of each plate with chopped parsley, and serve immediately. This is a fine soup to serve at an important dinner. If canned turtle consommé is not available, the turtle meat may be added to a rich beef consommé. Serves 6. Cheese straws are a good accompaniment.

ANGUILLES AU VERT
Cuisine Specifiquement Belge, Grand Hotel, Brussels

3 pounds eel
½ cup minced shallots
½ cup minced onions
⅓ cup butter
1 wineglass dry white wine
Consommé
1½ cups finely chopped fresh herbs:
sorrel, chervil, burnet, sage,
tarragon, cress

2 tablespoons cornstarch
1 cup heavy cream
6 egg yolks, beaten
Salt and pepper
Juice of 1 lemon

Cut the eel in 3-inch lengths and cook it in the butter with the shallots and onions for 5 minutes. Add the wine and enough hot consommé just to cover the eel, put in the finely chopped herbs, and simmer the eel for 10 minutes. It must not be cooked until it falls apart. Blend the cornstarch with the cream and bring it to a boil, then blend with the beaten egg yolks. Season with salt and pepper. Remove a little broth, blend it with the cream mixture, and add this to the eel and sauce. Add the juice of 1 lemon. Do not boil after the cream and egg yolks are added. Serve in deep wide plates. Serves 7 or 8. This is one of the great Belgian dishes. The recipe for it was given me by M. M. G. Gablin, Directeur of the Grand Hotel in Brussels.

Fish & Shellfish

BRILLAT-SAVARIN once entertained a friend who had complained of never having had his fill of oysters. The great epicure quit after his third dozen but his guest went on to thirty-two dozen, and while he was in "full career" his host, tired of being inactive, stopped him, and said, "My friend, it is not your fate to eat your fill of oysters today. Let us dine." They dined, and the friend acquitted himself with the vigor and address of a man who had been fasting. While this story suggests that fish does not have the satisfying qualities of flesh, it nevertheless has plenty of nourishment and certainly is valued highly by the gourmet. A light fish course does not interfere with the enjoyment of the meat that follows; an elaborate fish dish is suitable for the main course, especially if it is preceded by a good entrée such as *Oeufs Bourgignons* or a meat pâté; then the meal is complete indeed.

Rules for serving wine are made to be broken. When we think of fish we think of white wine. A sole sauced with cream calls for a white wine; but fish such as brill and eel are cooked in red wine; then a red wine is served. There are very accommodating white wines from the Rhine, Moselle, and Palatinate; some are full-bodied and not sweet and go with almost everything. For lobster and other shellfish choose, among French wines, a Pouilly Fuissé, a Montrachet, or Champagne.

FISH FOR BAKING

Fish for baking include whitefish, salmon, shad, pike, pompano, red snapper, trout, striped bass, sea bass, butterfish, perch, weakfish, halibut, mackerel, and fresh cod, to mention the most typical. Fish for baking are usually selected for size, weighing 1½ pounds or more. The fish man prepares them by scaling them well, slitting, and cleaning. Fish look better when the head is left on. There is nothing handsomer than a well-baked and dressed whole fish. It is important to have a long narrow baking dish especially for fish, as when the fish is cooked, it can easily break when it is lifted from one dish to another. About ¾ pound is allowed for each serving of delicate fleshed fish. Less than ½ pound is sufficient for a serving of firmly fleshed fish, such as salmon.

119

FISH FOR FRYING OR BROILING

Small and lean fish are suitable for frying or broiling: smelts, herring, sole, flounder, trout, bass, crappie, halibut, haddock, pickerel, yellow perch, yellow pike, red snapper, swordfish, spotted trout, sea trout, kingfish, whiting, etc. The fish are scaled, cleaned, and left whole, or are skinned and filleted. They may be soaked in milk for ½ hour, wiped dry, rolled in cornmeal, and fried a golden brown in a mixture of butter and oil. Broiled fish are spread and basted with plenty of butter.

FISH FOR POACHING IN BROTH AND WINE

Fish for poaching in fish stock and wine are always filleted and the stock made of the trimmings. The poaching liquid usually goes into the sauce. Salmon is boned and skinned after poaching.

MOUSSELINES DE SAUMON, ADAM
The Connaught Hotel, London

This grand dish was given me by M. Henri J. Rusconi, chef of fish cuisine at the Connaught, who created it. I have cut down the quantities but left the proportions.

1½ pounds raw salmon
2 unbeaten egg whites
1 whole egg
Salt and pepper
1 cup heavy cream
Garnish:
   1 cup sliced fresh mushrooms, sautéed
   ½ pound fresh shrimp, boiled and sliced

Sauce Cardinal (recipe follows)
Sauce Bercy:
   ¼ cup chopped shallots
   ⅓ cup Chablis
   1 cup heavy cream
   1 tablespoon chopped parsley
   Salt and pepper
   1½ cups sweet butter

You will probably want to make the Sauce Cardinal the day before serving Mousselines. The recipe follows this one.

Remove the skin and bones from the raw salmon and put it through the meat grinder, using the finest blade. Beat it very hard with a single-wire whisk to a smooth purée. There should be 2 full cups of fish purée. Then beat in the egg whites, one at a time. Season the purée well with salt and pepper. Put the purée in a cold part of the refrigerator so that the natural gelatin in the fish will stiffen it. Two hours before poaching the mousselines (quenelles), beat in the cold heavy cream. Return it to the refrigerator to chill again.

Now begin the Sauce Bercy. Cook the shallots and wine over a good flame until it is reduced to half. Add the cream and reduce the quantity to ½ cup. Add the parsley and season with salt and pepper. Set aside and have the butter softened to room temperature.

To cook the mousselines, grease a long shallow pan and form the mousselines with 2 good-sized serving spoons into egg-shaped spoonfuls. Put them an inch apart in the pan. There should be 16 mousselines. Pour boiling water into the pan to the depth of 2 inches, cover loosely with a buttered parchment paper, put the pan into a 350° oven, and cook 15 minutes. The water must never boil but must be maintained at a very gentle simmer. Lower the heat if necessary. Have the sautéed mushrooms ready and the sliced cooked shrimp. Grease a large shallow baking dish, one that may be brought to the table, and put the mushrooms and shrimp on the bottom. Spread with *Sauce Cardinal*. With a slotted spoon carefully drain out the mousselines onto a dry napkin to drain a little. Then arrange them over the dressing in the dish.

Finish the Sauce Bercy. Beat the butter, bit by bit, into the reduced wine-cream sauce and spread it over the mousselines. Run the dish under a hot flame until the sauce bubbles and is golden. This takes but a little over a minute and it must be watched; otherwise the sauce will separate because of the large quantity of butter.

This serves 8 and deserves a fine white Burgundy.

SAUCE CARDINAL

1 2-pound lobster	2 tablespoons butter
¼ cup diced carrots	2 tablespoons minced shallots
¼ cup diced onions	(or green onions)
1 teaspoon mixed herbs	1½ tablespoons flour
1½ cups water	1 teaspoon tomato paste
Lobster butter:	½ cup heavy cream
Ground shells	1 tablespoon cognac
½ cup butter	Salt and freshly ground pepper
⅓ cup boiling water	

Have the fish man split the live lobster in half for you. Make a bed of the carrots and onions in a long pan and lay the lobster on it, shell down. Sprinkle with the herbs and add 1½ cups water. Bake in the oven at 350° about 18 minutes or until the lobster is done. Remove the meat, liver and coral, and the broth, and reserve. For the lobster butter, dry out the shells in the oven, pound them, and put them through the meat grinder. Put them in a heavy pot with ½ cup butter and 2 or 3 tablespoons of boiling water, cover, and simmer gently for 10 minutes. Line a sieve with a cloth wrung out in warm water and strain the lobster shells and butter. Sprinkle the boiling water over them to extract any butter clinging to the shells. Refrigerate this and when chilled remove the cake of butter and add any liquid residue to the reserved broth. This may be done the day before. When ready to make the sauce put the butter in a heavy pot and sauté the shallots (or green onions) until tender but not colored. Add the lobster broth and reduce over high heat to ¾ cup, then strain. Blend the flour and tomato paste with the cream, add to the broth and cook until thickened. When ready to serve, heat with the liver, coral, lobster butter, salt, pepper, and cognac. This is *Sauce Cardinal* as specified in the recipe for *Mousselines de Saumon, Adam.*

To serve as creamed lobster, add the sliced lobster meat to the sauce. Serve as a main fish course in a vol-au-vent shell or on crisp toast. The sauce may be increased with a little thickened dry white wine or dry vermouth and cream.

CREAMED SALMON

Thick slice boiled fresh salmon
    or 1 8-ounce can of salmon
¼ cup milk
1 tablespoon cornstarch
1 cup light cream
1 tablespoon tomato paste

2 teaspoons powdered chicken
    concentrate
¼ teaspoon nutmeg or mace
Salt and pepper
3 tablespoons Parmesan cheese
1 hard-boiled egg
8 capers

If fresh salmon is used, boil it and remove the skin. If canned is used, remove it from the can and put it whole in a saucepan. In another pan make the sauce. Blend the milk and cornstarch until smooth and add the cream, tomato paste, chicken concentrate, seasonings, and cheese. Cook and stir until it thickens. Pour the sauce over the fish and when it is hot, lift it to a serving dish with a large spatula, being careful not to break the fish. Sieve the egg over the top and add the capers. Serves 4.

COLD BOILED SALMON IN ASPIC

2½ to 3 pounds fresh salmon
2 cups dry white wine
2 cups water
1 sliced onion
3 bay leaves
Salt and pepper
1 egg white, half-beaten

3 teaspoons gelatin
¼ cup white wine
Garnish:
    Slices of hard-boiled eggs
    Sliced cucumbers
    Oil mayonnaise with capers
        and chopped tarragon

Wash the salmon and simmer it with onions, bay leaves, salt, and pepper in the wine and water for 15 minutes on one side; turn it carefully with two spatulas and simmer it 10 or 15 minutes more on the other side. Let it cool in the liquid. Remove and skin it, put it on a deep serving platter to cool, then chill in the refrigerator. Strain the broth and let it come to a boil for 2 minutes with the half-beaten egg white, then strain it through a fine sieve lined with a fine cloth wrung out in cold water. Meanwhile soak the gelatin in the wine and then melt it in 3 cups of the hot broth. Let it cool thoroughly, then take 1 cup of the liquid and stir it over ice water until it becomes syrupy. Pour this over the salmon 1 tablespoon at a time, letting it set. Repeat with a second cup of the broth so that the salmon will be covered with aspic. Grease a cup and pour in the third cup of broth, chill and set. When ready to serve, unmold the cup of aspic, chop it with a knife, and decorate the edge of the fish with it. Put slices of egg and thin slices of cucumber around the platter. Serve with a sauceboat of mayonnaise. This will serve 8 or 10 for a buffet supper with other dishes, or 7 or 8 for a main-course summer dinner.

BOILED SALMON WITH SHRIMP SAUCE

2½ pounds fresh salmon (tail end)	¼ teaspoon cumin
3 thin slices of onion	¼ teaspoon mace or nutmeg
3 bay leaves	½ teaspoon turmeric
Salt and freshly ground pepper	2 tablespoons cornstarch
1½ cups dry white wine	2 tablespoons sherry
½ pound fresh shrimp	Garnish:
⅓ cup heavy cream	2 hard-boiled eggs, sieved

See that the salmon is washed well with cold water as the broth it cooks in is used for the sauce. Lay the salmon in an enamel pan and add the onion, bay leaves, salt, pepper, wine, and enough water almost to cover the fish. Simmer for 15 minutes, then carefully turn the fish with two spatulas and simmer another 10 minutes. Let the fish cool in the broth. Remove it and skin it. Wash the shrimp, cook them in the salmon broth for 3 minutes, remove and shell them. Return the shells to the broth and boil for 10 minutes. Strain the broth and reserve 1 cup of it for the sauce. Put the salmon back into the rest of the broth to reheat before serving. Blend the cream with the seasonings and cornstarch, add the fish broth, and cook until it thickens, then add the shrimp and the sherry. Reheat the salmon, drain it well, and remove it to a hot platter. Cover it with the hot sauce. If the sauce is too thick add a spoonful or two of the fish broth. Sieve the eggs over the fish. This is a handsome dish and deserves an excellent white wine—a Meursault, for instance. Serves 7 or 8.

BOILED SALMON WITH LOBSTER SAUCE

2½ pounds fresh salmon (tail end)   Sauce:

    1 cup cooked sliced lobster
    3 tablespoons butter
    2 tablespoons cognac
    ¼ teaspoon nutmeg
    Salt and pepper
    1 tablespoon tomato paste
    1 teaspoon powdered chicken
        concentrate
    1½ teaspoons cornstarch
    1 cup light cream

Wash the salmon and cover it with lukewarm water to which 1 teaspoon salt has been added. Let it simmer for 15 minutes, turn it carefully, and simmer for 10 minutes more. Let it cool in the water, skin it and return it to the water to be reheated just before serving. Cut the lobster in quite small pieces and cook a minute in butter, then blaze with cognac. Add the seasonings and cornstarch to the cream, blending so there are no lumps. Cook until it thickens; if it is thicker than cream thin with a little dry vermouth. Pour this over the lobster and let it stand for 2 hours. When ready to serve, reheat the salmon and drain it carefully to avoid diluting the sauce. Reheat the sauce. Put the salmon on a hot platter and cover with the sauce. Serves 7 or 8.

QUENELLES DE BROCHET LYONNAISE

These exquisitely light quenelles are offered on every menu at most restaurants in Lyon, as typical a dish as tripe in Caen. Brochet is pike which is easily obtained in New York fish markets and from middle-western lakes; when it is not available, fresh cod or halibut may be used.

1¼ pounds fish fillets, ground   ¼ teaspoon nutmeg
Pâté à choux: ½ teaspoon salt
    ½ cup milk   ½ teaspoon freshly ground pepper
    ½ cup water   2 eggs
    ¼ cup butter   2 egg whites, unbeaten
    1 cup sifted flour   ½ cup soft butter
    1 teaspoon salt   Garnish:
    2 eggs   Shrimp, Lobster, or Crab Sauce

Put the fish through the meat grinder, using the finest blade, then mash with a hard rubber spatula until it is smooth. Make the paste by heating the milk and water in a saucepan with the butter. Dump in the flour and the salt and stir vigorously until the mixture leaves the sides of the pan.

Remove from the heat and beat in the eggs, 1 at a time. Mix the fish with the nutmeg, salt and pepper, then beat it into the paste, a little at a time. Beat in the eggs, 1 at a time, then the egg whites. The butter has softened at room temperature. Beat it in, a little at a time. The mixture should be fluffy and smooth. Cover tightly and chill at least 6 hours. When ready to poach, put 3 inches of boiling salted water in a wide pan. Form the paste into egg-shaped quenelles with two large serving spoons and scrape them into the water. Have the flame very low. They should cook uncovered at the barest simmer for about 18 to 20 minutes. They will double in size, so cook no more than 6 at a time. Drain onto a tea towel. When they are all cooked they may stand an hour. To reheat before serving, put them on the bottom of a buttered pan, cover with a medium seafood sauce, and let them heat at 375° for 5 minutes. Run under the flame a moment to brown lightly. This makes an elegant fish course for 8. If the quenelles are served for a main course, a generous hors d'œuvre may be served first.

TUNA FISH, CRAB, LOBSTER, OR SALMON CASSEROLE

1 7-ounce can of fish, flaked
2 medium-sized onions, sliced
3 tablespoons butter
1 cup cooked rice, or 1 cup little noodles, cooked, or 1 can of kernel corn
2 red pimentos, cut in strips
5 stuffed olives, sliced

Cream sauce:
1 cup milk
¾ cup (1 small can) evaporated milk
1½ tablespoons cornstarch
½ teaspoon salt
Freshly ground pepper
1 tablespoon tomato paste
1 teaspoon curry powder
2 eggs, beaten
¼ cup Parmesan cheese

Canned fish casseroles need not be tasteless affairs that you feed to the family when you can't think of anything else. (I shouldn't say that: no imaginative cook is ever at a loss!) Flake the chosen fish. Sauté the sliced onions in the butter until tender. Use leftover rice, or cook a cup of noodle shells in salted boiling water until they are tender, or use a can of whole kernel corn. Any of these gives the dish body. Mix the fish with the other ingredients, and put it in an 8-inch baking dish. Make the sauce by blending the milk and evaporated milk with the cornstarch and cook until it thickens then add seasonings. Beat eggs lightly, add them, and pour the sauce over the mixture in the baking dish. Sprinkle the top with cheese and bake at 350° for 20 minutes. This will serve 4. Double, it makes a good side dish for a buffet supper. Obviously it is flexible as to ingredients and additions. A half pound of fresh mushrooms may be sautéed 2 minutes and added. Drained canned artichoke hearts are also good in this.

BAKED STUFFED FILLETS OF WHITEFISH OR POMPANO

2 thick fish fillets
Butter
Salt and pepper
⅓ cup dry vermouth or white wine
1½ tablespoons cornstarch
½ cup heavy cream
Garnish: Sieved hard-boiled egg

Stuffing No. 1:
6 or 8 sautéed shrimp or 6 or 8 sautéed fresh mushrooms
¼ cup minced green onions
Butter
Salt and pepper
2 tablespoons heavy cream
2 tablespoons sherry

Stuffing No. 2:
4 tablespoons red or black caviar
1 teaspoon lemon juice
½ cup sour cream
¼ cup minced green onions
Freshly ground pepper

Choose good-sized fillets to serve 4. Wipe the fish and put 1 fillet on the bottom of a well-buttered fish baking dish. Sprinkle lightly with salt and pepper. For Stuffing No. 1, peel the shrimp (if used) and toss it a minute with the onions and butter. Season with salt and pepper. Mix in the cream and sherry. If mushrooms are used, slice them, sauté them with the onions in the butter, and add the other ingredients. Spread the mixture on the fillet in the baking dish, top with the other fillet, and put 3 skewers along the top fillet to keep it in place. Pour the vermouth or wine over the top and sprinkle lightly with salt and pepper. Bake at 350° for 10 minutes, then turn down the heat to 325° and bake about 10 or 15 minutes more, depending on the thickness of the fish. When the fish becomes white, it is done. Blend the cornstarch with the cream and mix this with some of the wine broth the fish baked in, then stir it into the dish, blending it with the rest of the liquid. Heat until the sauce thickens. Sieve the hard-boiled egg over the top and serve.

Stuffing No. 2 needs no previous cooking but is just mixed and spread between the fillets before baking.

FISH FILLETS WITH ANCHOVY BUTTER

6 or 8 fillets of sole or flounder
⅓ cup soft sweet butter
3 tablespoons anchovy paste
¼ cup dry white wine

Fine cracker crumbs
Chopped parsley
Garnish: Slices of lemon

Clean and wipe dry the fillets. Mix the butter with the anchovy paste, spread it on the fillets, roll them, and fasten with toothpicks. Set them on one end in a well-buttered baking dish. Pour the wine over them and bake for 9 minutes in a 350° oven; remove, sprinkle lightly with crumbs, then bake another 9 minutes. When done sprinkle with chopped parsley. Garnish with slices of lemon. Serves 6 or 8 as a fish course.

TRUITES FARCIES BASQUAISE
Maurice Cazalis, Chartres

This is an example of fine French fish cookery, three recipes in one: how to cook fish in parchment paper; how to make a creamy velouté; how to make a Basque sauce with vegetables. Use small fish weighing a scant half-pound, 1 or 2 to each serving.

8 or 10 small trout
Fish stock:
    Fish bones, trimmings, and shrimp shells
    Bouquet garni: thyme, parsley, bay leaf
    1 sliced onion
    Salt and pepper
Farce:
    ½-pound fish fillet, ground
    Salt and pepper
    1 pound small fresh shrimp
¾ cup chopped onions

3 tablespoons butter
Salt and pepper
1¼ cups dry white wine or dry vermouth
3 tablespoons sweet butter
Vegetables:
    ½ cup shredded lettuce
    ½ cup sliced fresh mushrooms
    ¼ cup minced shallots or green onions
    2 tomatoes, skinned, seeded, and sliced
    1 green pepper, thinly sliced

Have the trout scaled, cleaned, and the back bones removed. Get an extra fish fillet for the farce—this may be trout, sole, or flounder. Shell the shrimp and make the fish stock first. Put the bones, trimmings, shrimp shells, bouquet garni, sliced onion, salt and pepper in a kettle, add 2 cups of water and simmer almost covered 25 minutes. Strain through a sieve. Meanwhile prepare the vegetables and set aside. Prepare the farce by grinding the fillet and adding salt and pepper. Stuff each trout with a little ground fish and 2 or 3 shrimp. Sauté the ¾ cup of chopped onions until almost tender in the 3 tablespoons of butter. Butter parchment papers, each large enough to hold 3 fish. Spread with onions and lay the fish on top of the onions. Salt and pepper the fish. Wrap the paper around the fish and lay the packages of fish flat on the bottom of a large shallow pan. Mix 1½ cups of the strained fish stock with the wine and pour it into the pan. Bake the fish at 375° for 15 minutes. Now arrange the vegetables in a steamer or vapeuse, making a bed of the lettuce and putting the mushrooms and vegetables on top. Cover and steam over boiling water for 7 or 8 minutes. Lightly steamed vegetables make a wonderful fresh-tasting sauce. When the fish is done, unwrap it and let the juices drain into the fish pan. Put the fish on a hot platter and keep it warm in the oven with the door open. Put the liquid in which the fish cooked through a fine sieve and reduce over a hot flame until it has body and is a creamy velouté. Whisk in the sweet butter, add the steamed vegetables, and pour the sauce over the fish. Serve with French bread, sweet butter, and a good dry white wine.

FISH FILLETS IN WINE AND CREAM
(POMPANO, SOLE, WHITEFISH)

2 to 2½ pounds fillets
4 tablespoons butter
2 tablespoons grated onion
2 tablespoons grated carrot

Salt and pepper
2 tablespoons flour
¾ cup heavy cream
¾ cup dry white wine

Dry the fillets. The vegetables must be grated to blend with the sauce. Put the butter in a saucepan with the onion and carrot and cook gently until they begin to soften, add salt and pepper, and stir in the flour. Add the cream gradually to make a smooth sauce, then the wine. Butter a fish baking dish that you can bring to the table. Put a little sauce in the bottom, lay in the fillets, and cover with the rest of the sauce. Put in a 350° oven for 5 minutes. When the sauce begins to bubble, turn the oven down to 300° and cook until the fish turns white and begins to flake. Baste if the sauce does not cover the fish. Boned fillets are so delicate that it is dangerous to turn them. Serve with parsley or rissolée potatoes. Serves 4.

CREAMED TERRAPIN

2 cups cooked, prepared terrapin meat
Yolks of 3 hard-boiled eggs
½ cup terrapin broth or chicken broth
¼ cup butter
1½ cups heavy cream, scalded

Salt and freshly ground pepper
¼ teaspoon mace
¼ teaspoon nutmeg
3 egg yolks, beaten
⅓ cup imported sherry
Garnish: buttered toast

Sieve the hard-boiled egg yolks into the broth, add the butter, and heat. Scald the cream, add the seasonings, and pour it slowly over the beaten egg yolks. Combine with the broth mixture and add the terrapin meat. Heat, add the sherry, and serve on buttered toast. Serves 6. The tradition is to cook terrapin stew with either Madeira or sherry and to drink Madeira with it. As this is a rich dish, champagne should also go with it very well.

SOLE LUCULLUS
Valentin-Sorg, Strasbourg

This restaurant, the most elegant in this ancient city, is on the top floor of Strasbourg's new skyscraper. The restaurant itself is not new but its sumptuous new quarters seem very modern until you get the breathtaking view of the many-colored gabled roofs of the old city from a window table. Mme. Gaby Sorg is understandably proud of the food her chef produces and she kindly gave me this fine dish, and another which she whispered had been a secret until now.

4 fillets of sole, boned and
    skinned
2 tablespoons butter
2 tablespoons Riesling
1½ teaspoons cornstarch
½ cup heavy cream

Salt and pepper
3 tablespoons hashed mushrooms
2 tablespoons more wine
Garnish:
    Minced fresh tarragon or parsley

Steam the fish tender in the butter and wine. Remove to a hot platter and keep it warm. Blend the cornstarch with the cream, add salt and pepper, and mix with the pan juices. Stir in the finely hashed mushrooms (the sauce must be flecked, not lumpy); then add 2 more tablespoons of wine and boil up. Pour over fish and garnish top with minced herb. Serves 4.

SOLE NORMANDE

2 large soles, filleted
½ pound (1 pint) large mussels
½ pound shrimp
½ teaspoon thyme
½ cup dry vermouth
4 shallots or green onions, minced
2 tablespoons butter

4 large mushrooms, sliced, or
    2 tablespoons truffle sticks
1 tablespoon cornstarch
⅓ cup heavy cream, scalded
1 egg yolk
Freshly ground pepper

Have the fish man fillet the soles and give you the trimmings. Make a broth with the trimmings and 1 cup of water. Simmer for 15 minutes and strain into a big kettle. Add the mussels, very well washed, and the shrimp, thyme, and vermouth. Cover and steam for 4 minutes, shaking the pot several times. Remove the shrimp and mussels; peel the shrimp and take the mussels out of their shells. Reserve both. Strain the broth through a fine sieve lined with a cloth wrung out of cold water. Reduce over a good flame until there is 1 cup of broth. Butter a fish baking dish which may be brought to the table. Cover the bottom with the shallots or green onions, very finely minced. Wipe the soles dry, lay them on the shallots or onions, and pour the broth over them. Bake at 350° about 8 or 10 minutes or until the soles are milky white and have lost their translucence. They must not cook long enough to fall apart or flake. Drain off all the liquid, else the sauce will be diluted. Keep the fish warm in an open over. Sauté the sliced mushrooms or truffle sticks in butter about 3 minutes, then add them to the reserved shrimp and mussels. Scald the cream and mix it with the egg yolk. Blend the cup of fish broth with 1 tablespoon of cornstarch and cook until it thickens. Add the shellfish to the broth, and when it is hot add the cream and egg. Do not cook again or the egg will curdle. Add pepper and taste for salt, adding a little if it needs it. Pour the sauce over the sole and serve immediately. This classic French dish calls for fine sole. If English sole is not available, grey or lemon sole will be satisfactory. Many filleted fish may be prepared this way with a less elaborate sauce— that is, cooked in wine and a broth made of trimmings, and enriched with cream and egg yolks. Serves 4, or 6 if fillets weigh 3 or more pounds.

SOLE ALBERT
Maxim's, Paris

Firm, fresh sole
Salt and freshly ground pepper
Melted butter
Fresh breadcrumbs
3 shallots, finely minced

3 tablespoons minced fresh herbs:
  parsley, chervil, tarragon
1 wineglass Noilly Prat dry
  vermouth
3 tablespoons sweet butter

Choose a fine sole, remove the skin, and make a light incision along the bone. Season the fish with salt and pepper and dip it in melted butter. Sprinkle the side to be presented with fine fresh crumbs. Put the shallots and herbs on the bottom of a buttered baking pan and put the fish on the herbs, crumb side up. Add the vermouth. Put the fish in a 375° oven until the crumbs are browned. When it is done remove it to a serving dish and keep it warm. Put the baking pan over a brisk fire to reduce the sauce and when it has attained a good body stir in the sweet butter. Spread some sauce on the sole and pass the rest. One 1½-pound sole will serve 2.

TURBAN OF SOLE

1½ pounds fillets of sole
Filling:
  1 fish fillet, ground
  4 or 5 potatoes
  ½ cup heavy cream
  ¼ teaspoon nutmeg
  Salt and pepper
  2 tablespoons butter
  ½ cup minced green onions
  3 egg yolks

Seafood sauce:
  Shrimp, crab, mussels, scal-
  laps, or lobster (see index)
Garnish:
  2 pounds fresh cooked peas
  (optional)

Lavishly butter a 9½- to 10-inch savarin mold and line it with fish fillets which you lightly sprinkle with salt and very little flour. Reserve 1 fillet for the filling. The fish must line the outer side of the mold to the top. Boil the potatoes, skin and mash them with all the other ingredients of the filling, including the ground fish. Pack this filling in the fish-lined mold. Set the mold in a pan with a little hot water and bake 25 minutes, half the time at 375° and half at 350°. Meanwhile make a good seafood sauce to accompany the turban. You may want to use 1½ pounds of shrimp, creaming the shrimp with 1 cup of chicken consommé and 1 cup of heavy cream. Pile the shrimp inside the turban ring and serve the rest of the sauce in a sauceboat. Or the sauce may all be served separately and the center of the ring filled with fresh peas. This dish may be as simple or elaborate as required. When the turban is done, remove it from the oven and let it stand 1 minute, then cover it with a round serving plate and quickly turn it upside down. If it is well buttered it will come out perfectly. This will serve 8 as a fish course or 6 as a main course.

CHINESE SEA BASS WITH MARINADE

Whole bass, skinned but not boned
Marinade:
    4 tablespoons soy sauce
    1 clove garlic, crushed
    1 tablespoon brown sugar
    1 tablespoon minced preserved
        ginger, or fresh ginger root,
        minced

Garnish:
    3 tablespoons peanut oil
    ¼ cup minced green onions

Soak the fish in the marinade an hour or more, turning occasionally. Bake or broil in a 375° oven, basting continuously with the marinade. When the fish is done, lift it to a hot platter. Put the oil in a skillet over a hot flame, add the onions for a second, and then pour it over the fish.

BROILED SWORDFISH WITH CUCUMBER SAUCE

¾- to 1-inch swordfish steaks
    (½-pound fish per serving)
2 tablespoons olive oil and 2 table-
    spoons lemon juice for each
    steak
3 tablespoons grated onion

Butter and oil
Salt and freshly ground pepper
Lemon juice
Chopped parsley
Garnish: *Cucumber Sauce*

You will need 3 pounds of fish for 6 people. Mix the olive oil, lemon juice, and grated onion together and marinate the steaks 2 hours, spreading the mixture on both sides of the steaks and turning them several times. When ready to cook the fish, scrape off the marinade and discard it. Spread the steaks with soft butter and oil, sprinkle with salt and pepper and broil 5 inches below the flame for 8 or 10 minutes on each side, basting several times with the juices. The fish will be white when it is done. Cover the steaks with the basting juices and sprinkle with lemon and a little chopped parsley. Serve *Cucumber Sauce* as an accompaniment.

CUCUMBER SAUCE

2 cucumbers, sliced and chilled
1¼ cups sour cream
1 teaspoon salt
¼ teaspoon freshly ground pepper
2 tablespoons lemon juice

3 tablespoons chopped chives, or
    chopped fresh dill, or grated
    white onion
1 canned pimento, sliced

Peel the cucumbers, slice them rather thin, and chill. Mix all the other ingredients and chill. Stir into the cucumbers just before serving. Serve in a bowl. This is served in side dishes with hot fish or on the fish plate with cold fish, such as cold boiled salmon. Good with almost any fish.

SHAD ROE À L'OSEILLE
Chateaubriand, New York

2 large pairs roe, or 4 small pairs
6 shallots or green onions, minced
4 tablespoons butter
1 cup dry white wine or dry vermouth

Salt and pepper
½ pound sorrel leaves
1½ cups heavy cream

Clean the roe and wipe them dry. If the roes are small, 4 pairs will be needed for 4. Put the shallots or green onions in a sauté pan with the butter and lay the roes on top. Cook gently 1 minute, then add the wine, salt and pepper. Stem the sorrel leaves and chop well; do not grind them. Add them to the roes, and cook gently, uncovered, for 10 minutes, then turn the roes and cook another 10 minutes. Using two spatulas, lift the roes onto a hot platter and keep them warm. Add the cream to the pan and cook about 4 minutes to reduce the sauce, then pour it over the roes and serve immediately. Serves 4.

BRANDADE AVEC POMMES DE TERRE, PROVENÇAL

1 pound lightly smoked cod
½ cup butter
1 tablespoon lemon juice
1 pound potatoes
¼ cup olive oil

2 cloves garlic, crushed
Pinch of salt
Freshly ground pepper
¾ cup heavy cream

Choose a fine, fat, lightly smoked piece of cod, cover it with water, cook 20 minutes, and drain. Flake the fish and mash it with the butter and lemon juice. Peel the potatoes and boil until tender, then mash them with the oil, garlic, pinch of salt, pepper, and cream. Lightly mix the potatoes with the cod, put in a buttered baking dish, and reheat. This is a variation of the brandade which is made with fish only. Serves 4 to 6.

DORADE GRILLÉE AU FENOUIL
Restaurant Voltaire, Paris

This strategically located little restaurant right across the Seine from the Louvre does a flourishing business not only at lunch and dinner but all afternoon, when both natives and tourists crowd the sidewalk tables to sip aperitifs and gaze at one of the loveliest vistas of Paris. We lived nearby and whenever we passed this restaurant we glanced at the menu to see if Dorade was on it. This fragrant fish with dried fennel sticks sticking out of it and over the top looks as though it were fished from a haystack. Either red snapper or sea bass is a good substitute for dorade.

1 plump fish for each serving	Dried fennel sticks
½ teaspoon fennel powder or seeds for each fish	Salt and pepper
	Olive oil

Clean and scale the fish and leave it whole. Rub the fish well with olive oil, salt and pepper. Sprinkle the inside of each fish with fennel powder or seeds and stick a few dried fennel sticks inside and on top. Add salt and pepper. Snap the sticks as they give off fragrance. The fish are grilled 15 minutes without turning them and are served immediately.

BAKED FRESH COD

2 thick fillets of cod	2 tablespoons butter
Butter	⅓ cup heavy cream
½ cup dry vermouth	½ teaspoon turmeric
Salt and pepper	1 hard-boiled egg, sieved
2 tablespoons flour	3 tablespoons Parmesan cheese

Lavishly butter a long fish baking dish. Wipe the fish, lay it in the dish, and pour the wine over it. Add bits of butter and salt and pepper. Bake at 350° about 18 minutes or until the fish firms and whitens; the time depends on the thickness. Drain off the broth to use in the sauce. Put the flour and butter in a saucepan over a low flame, blend, and when it is smooth stir in the broth and cream. Add the turmeric and season with salt and pepper if it needs it. Pour the sauce over the fish. Mix the sieved egg with the cheese and sprinkle it over the top of the fish. Run the baking dish under a hot flame a moment. Serves 4 to 6.

VARIATION. Add ½ pound of fresh, peeled, raw shrimp to the fish 5 minutes before it is done.

FINNAN HADDIE

Lightly smoked fillet	1 teaspoon lemon juice
Butter	Freshly ground pepper
1 cup light cream	Parmesan cheese

Choose a fine fat fillet. Soak it 1 hour in cold water, drain and wipe dry. Sauté the fish in a little sweet butter 1 or 2 minutes on each side. It may be cooked over a low flame or removed to a baking dish and cooked in the oven. Heat the cream, pour it over the fish, and cook about 20 minutes or until the fish is tender. Add the lemon juice and pepper. Taste before adding any salt. Sprinkle the top with a little cheese and serve with mashed or boiled potatoes. If the fillet is large, it will serve 4.

SUPRÈME DE BARBUE BORDELAISE
L'Escargot Montorgueil, Paris

One of the great restaurants of Paris is to be found at 38 rue Montorgueil, in a little street in back of Les Halles. An enormous golden snail is perched over the entrance as if to signify that Escargots de Bourgogne are cooked better here than anywhere else. The décor is of the 1890s, nostalgic and charming. A narrow winding stair leads up to a private salon where important people have little private dinners. It is never easy to write convincingly about one's favorite persons, places, and things; however, this restaurant with its every dish cooked to perfection and its quiet elegance is for me one of the greatest dining establishments I've ever been in. The onion soup is the best I have ever tasted; their specialty may be fish but the entrecôte is one of the best in Paris. The dark-red sauce on the barbue resembles the black sauce served on lamprey in Bordeaux and is one of the great fish sauces. M. L. Pacaud, the director, gave me this specialty.

4 fillets of brill, or any fine firm
    fish
Fish stock:
    Fish trimmings
    ⅓ cup shredded onion
    ⅓ cup shredded carrot
    3 shallots or green onions,
      minced
    1 tablespoon minced parsley
    Mushroom stems, chopped
    Salt and pepper
    2 cups water

1 cup fine red wine
12 mushroom caps
Beurre manie:
    1 tablespoon butter mixed with
      1½ tablespoons flour
    3 tablespoons fresh butter
    Salt and pepper
Garnish: Croutons fried in butter

Make a fish fumet (stock) with the trimmings, vegetables, seasonings and 2 cups water. Boil 10 minutes and strain it over the fish through a coarse sieve. Add the wine and mushroom caps and poach very gently until the fish is done, 8 to 10 minutes, according to the thickness of the fillets. Remove the fish and mushroom caps. Make the beurre manie and add it a little bit at a time. When the sauce has thickened to the consistency of heavy cream, pass it through a sieve. Whisk in 3 tablespoons butter and pour the sauce over the fish. Decorate each serving with 3 mushroom caps and some croutons. Serves 4.

FILETS DE BROCHETS À LA CRÈME
Chapon Fin, Thoissey

4 fillets of pike (or other river fish,
    or sea bass)
Salt and freshly ground pepper
Flour
Butter

2 tablespoons minced shallots or
    green onions
⅓ cup dry white wine
⅓ cup heavy cream

Add to the French mastery of fish cookery the excellence of the fish, fresh from nearby rivers. We have good fish too, and if river fish aren't available we may use those from the sea. Sea bass would be very good for this dish. Dry the fillets, flatten a little, and sprinkle with seasoned flour. Shake off the excess, for they must be very lightly floured. Cook them in butter lightly on both sides, without letting them brown. Remove to a baking pan and make the sauce. Cook finely minced shallots or green onions in butter a minute without coloring, add the wine, and reduce to almost a glaze, then add the cream. Cook slowly, stirring, until the mixture is smooth and thick, season with salt and pepper, and put through a sieve. Spread the sauce over the fish and put it under the flame until it glazes. Don't heat it too long or the sauce will separate. Serves 4.

SEAFOOD PIE

2 lobster tails
2 cups clam juice
1 teaspoon thyme
½ pound fresh shrimp
1 slice salmon
6 scallops
6 oysters
6 white onions

3 tablespoons butter
3 tablespoons flour
Salt and pepper
¼ teaspoon nutmeg or mace
1 cup heavy cream
3 tablespoons Madeira or dry
   sherry
Top crust (*Pie Pastry*)

A good fish broth for the pie is obtained by poaching the lobster tails 5 minutes in the clam juice with the thyme. Drain them out and shell them. Poach the shrimp 2 minutes in the same broth, drain them out, and shell them. Poach the salmon 8 or 10 minutes in the broth; remove it; skin and bone it. Cut the lobster tails in 1-inch-thick slices and the salmon in pieces the same size. The scallops and oysters need no poaching. Arrange all the fish in a 9-inch baking dish. Boil the onions in very little water and when they are tender drain them out and add them to the fish. Measure the broth and add enough onion water to make 2 cups. Make a roux of the butter and flour in a saucepan over low heat and when it is smooth add the broth and then the seasonings. Taste before adding salt. Add the cream and cook until it thickens, then add the Madeira or dry sherry. Pour the sauce over the fish and cover with a rich top crust. One and one-fourth cups of flour will make the right amount of crust. Make a thick edge and flute it. Make 5 or 6 incisions for the steam to escape. Put in a 400° oven for 8 minutes, then reduce the heat to 350° and bake 12 to 15 minutes more until the crust is a golden brown. Crab may also be used in this. Serves 6.

DRIED CODFISH CAKES

10 ounces dried codfish
¼ cup grated onion
1 tablespoon chopped parsley
1½ cups fluffy mashed potatoes
Freshly ground pepper
2 tablespoons butter

2 tablespoons cream
1 egg, beaten
Cornmeal, or Parmesan cheese
and cracker crumbs
Butter and oil for frying

Soak the codfish 6 or 8 hours, changing the water several times. Rinse it and boil it slowly in fresh water for 25 minutes. Drain and flake it very fine or put it through the meat grinder. Mix it lightly with the other ingredients including the beaten egg. Add salt if needed. Form into cakes and roll either in fine cornmeal or in a mixture of cracker crumbs and Parmesan cheese. Fry until brown on both sides in a mixture of oil and butter. Ten ounces of fish make 1½ cups cooked flaked fish. This will make 8 cakes. Serve with hot tomato sauce if desired. For good cocktail snacks make tiny codfish balls and serve hot with toothpicks.

FISH SOUFFLÉ

1¼ cups cooked, ground fish or
seafood
2 tablespoons grated onion
Salt and pepper
¼ teaspoon mace or nutmeg
1 tablespoon chopped parsley

¾ cup heavy cream
1 tablespoon tomato paste
1 tablespoon cornstarch
4 egg yolks, beaten
5 egg whites, beaten
3 tablespoons Parmesan cheese

Any freshly cooked or leftover fish or other seafood may be used. Put the fish through the meat grinder and follow it with the onion. It must be a smooth paste. Add the seasonings and parsley. Blend the cream with the tomato paste and cornstarch and cook until it thickens, add the beaten egg yolks, and blend with the fish mixture. Mix one-fourth of the beaten egg whites with the fish mixture, then fold in the rest of the whites very lightly. Grease a baking dish and sprinkle the sides and bottom with the cheese. Put in the fish mixture and bake at 400° for 8 minutes; then turn down the oven to 325° for 18 or 20 minutes more. The soufflé should be moist inside. Serves 4. This may be served with a fresh shrimp or lobster sauce and makes an elegant fish course or entrée for lunch. Serve with a good white wine.

VARIATION. For a lighter soufflé to serve 6 or 8, increase the fish to 1½ cups, the cream to 1¼ cups, use 5 egg yolks and 8 whites. Bake 12 minutes at 400° and 20 minutes at 325°.

GRATIN DE CRABES, SAUCE CREVETTES
Capucin Gourmand, Nancy

2 cups cooked fresh crabmeat or
  2 cans Japanese crabmeat
10 fresh shrimp
4 cups milk
2 tablespoons butter
4 tablespoons flour

1 tablespoon tomato paste
1 cup heavy cream
2 egg yolks
Salt and pepper
8 ounces fine egg noodles

Pick over the crabmeat, bone it, and leave it in good-sized pieces. Wash and peel the shrimp and cook the shells in 2 cups of the milk over simmering water for 20 minutes. Grind the raw shrimp or purée them in an electric blender with 1 more cup of the milk. Drain the shells from the milk and mix the milk with the shrimp purée. Make a roux with the butter and flour and when it is smooth, stir in the fourth cup of milk. Add this to the shrimp mixture and the tomato paste and cook this sauce 15 minutes over simmering water, uncovered. Stir occasionally. Scald the cream and pour it over the egg yolks. Add this to the sauce, season well, and let it stand off heat. Boil the noodles in salted water until tender, drain, and put them in a buttered, shallow, oven-proof serving dish. Heat the crabmeat in a little hot sauce and lay it over the top of the noodles, then pour all the sauce over the top. Run under a flame until the sauce browns a little. Serves 8 as a fish course or 6 as a main dish. M. Romain recommends a Muscadet or Sauvignon to drink with this.

CRAB FOO YONG

1 cup flaked crabmeat, fresh or
  canned
½ cup thinly sliced celery
3 tablespoons peanut oil
½ cup thinly sliced onions
½ cup sliced water chestnuts
½ cup bean sprouts
¾ teaspoon salt
6 eggs

Sauce:
1 cup chicken broth
1 to 2 tablespoons soy sauce
½ teaspoon brown sugar
1 tablespoon cornstarch
1 tablespoon tomato paste

Flake the crabmeat quite fine and remove the bones. Sauté the celery and onions in the oil for 4 minutes. Peel and slice the water chestnuts, wash and drain the sprouts, and mix both lightly with the crabmeat and sautéed vegetables. Add the salt to the eggs, beat them well, and mix with the crab mixture. Blend all the sauce ingredients together and cook until it thickens. Make thick pancakes of the crab mixture and brown on both sides in peanut oil. Serve hot with the broth sauce. If fresh water chestnuts and soy bean sprouts are not available use more celery and onions. Makes 6 cakes.

FRESH CRAB CAKES

1 pound cooked fresh crabmeat
1 egg, beaten
1 cup soft fresh breadcrumbs
2 tablespoons fresh onion juice
   Salt and pepper

1 teaspoon prepared mustard
4 drops Worcestershire sauce
1 tablespoon lemon juice
¼ cup heavy cream
   Bacon fat and butter for frying

Pick over the crabmeat and remove the bones. Mix the egg with the crumbs, add the rest of the ingredients, and when well mixed add the crabmeat. Heat a mixture of bacon fat and butter and when it is hot drop spoonfuls of the crab mixture into the fat, flatten them a little, and fry brown on both sides. Remove when they are brown as they do not need much cooking. Serves 4.

CRABMEAT CAKES

1 large can crabmeat
1 red pimento, sliced
1 cup fluffy mashed potatoes
2 green onions, minced
1 egg
   Salt and pepper

¼ teaspoon nutmeg or mace
2 tablespoons melted butter
2 or 3 tablespoons cream
   Dry crumbs and Parmesan
     cheese
   Oil and butter for frying

Flake the crabmeat and mix it lightly with the pimento, mashed potatoes, and onion. Beat the egg and add to the mixture with the seasonings, melted butter, and cream. The mixture should be light and fluffy. Form into cakes and roll them in a mixture of crumbs and cheese. Fry a delicate brown in hot oil and butter. Fried in tiny balls and served with toothpicks they make a good hors d'œuvre.

CREAMED CRABMEAT

1 pound fresh crabmeat, cooked
4 mushrooms, sliced
4 green onions, diced
1 medium-sized fresh tomato
1 teaspoon basil or chervil
4 tablespoons butter
2 tablespoons flour

   Salt and freshly ground pepper
¼ teaspoon nutmeg
1¼ cups heavy cream
¼ cup good sherry
   Buttered toast or pastry shells
Garnish: Strips canned pimento

Pick over the crabmeat to remove bones but leave it in good-sized pieces. Sauté the fresh mushrooms and onions in 2 tablespoons of the butter for 3 minutes over a low flame. Skin the tomato, seed it, and cut the pulp in

1-inch chunks. Melt the remaining butter in a saucepan, blend in the flour until it is smooth, add the seasonings and cream, and cook until it thickens. Add the mushrooms and onions, the tomato and chervil. This sauce may be made ahead of time. When ready to serve, reheat the sauce and add the crabmeat and sherry. If the mixture is too thick, thin with a little sherry and cream. Serve over toast or in pastry shells and decorate each serving with 2 strips of pimento. Serves 6.

BUTTERED FRESH COOKED CRABMEAT

Crabmeat is good served hot with melted butter the way fresh lobster is, the favorite way for many people. Season plenty of melted butter with salt, pepper, nutmeg, and 1 tablespoon (or 2 or 3) of brandy.

LOBSTER AMÉRICAINE
Henri's, New York

3 1½- to 2-pound lobsters (for 6)
3 tablespoons olive oil
3 tablespoons butter
¼ cup grated carrot
¼ cup grated onion
Salt and pepper
⅓ cup cognac
2 cloves garlic, crushed
⅓ cup tomato purée

1 cup dry vermouth
½ cup clam juice or fish stock
1 tablespoon tomato paste
1 tablespoon chopped parsley
2 sprigs fresh tarragon
Dash of cayenne
Lobster liver and coral
½ cup soft butter

Have the fish man split the lobsters in half, remove the claws and crack them, and cut the lobster bodies in half across. Remove the liver and coral and reserve. Put 3 tablespoons each olive oil and butter in the bottom of a big kettle. When the butter is melted, add the carrot and onion and sauté 1 minute, then add the lobster and cook over a gentle flame. Add salt and pepper and stir the pieces until the shells are red. Pour the cognac over the lobster and ignite. Shake it until the flames die down. Now add all the rest of the ingredients except the liver, coral, and soft butter. Cover and simmer very gently 18 or 20 minutes, tossing the lobster twice so that it is all moistened with the sauce. Mash the coral, liver, and ½ cup soft butter together. When the lobster is done, remove all the pieces to a large serving casserole. Reduce the sauce a little over a hot flame, then beat in the butter-coral mixture. Pour this sauce over the lobster and serve, providing your guests with bibs. At the restaurant the meat is removed from the shells but it is more fun to suck the legs and dip the meat in this wonderful sauce at home. Serve with buttered noodles or rice.

CREAMED LOBSTER

2 cups cooked fresh lobster meat
3 tablespoons sweet butter
Salt and pepper
1 jigger brandy or cognac

Sauce:
2 tablespoons cornstarch
1⅔ cups heavy cream
1 teaspoon powdered chicken concentrate
Salt and pepper
1 tablespoon tomato paste
¼ teaspoon nutmeg
¼ cup dry vermouth
1 tablespoon onion juice
2 egg yolks, beaten

Garnish:
Fine crumbs and Parmesan cheese
Buttered toast or pastry shells

Cut the lobster in good-sized pieces and put them with the butter in the top of a double boiler (or in a chafing dish if this is made at the table). Let it stand over boiling water with the heat turned off, to keep it warm. Sprinkle with salt and freshly ground pepper. Pour the liquor over it and blaze. Just before you serve it, make the sauce. Blend the cornstarch with the cream and cook until it is hot and begins to thicken then add all the other ingredients except the egg yolks. When it is the right consistency (like heavy cream) and is bubbling, pour it gradually over the egg yolks, then add the sauce to the lobster. If the lobster is cooked at the table, bring the hot sauce in from the kitchen and pour it over the lobster. This may be served on buttered toast or in prebaked pastry shells which have been baked in muffin tins. Or it may be put in large scallop shells, sprinkled with a mixture of crumbs and cheese, and put under the flame a moment until it becomes hot and pale yellow. Serves 6. To serve 8, add ½ pound of sautéed little white fresh mushrooms. This makes a fine fish course or a main luncheon dish.

BAKED LOBSTER
Hanstown Club, London

1½-pound lobsters (1 per person)
Anchovy butter
Heavy cream
Fine crumbs

Freshly ground pepper
Parmesan cheese
Garnish: Melted butter

When André Simon took us to the Hanstown Club in London for lunch we had this delicious lobster. The fish man splits live lobster for you. Mix anchovy paste in equal amounts with sweet butter and spread thinly over the lobster meat. Bake 10 minutes at 375°, remove and add 2 tablespoons of cream and some fine fresh crumbs to the top of each half. Sprinkle lightly with pepper and return to the oven for 10 more minutes at 325°. Sprinkle with a little Parmesan cheese, run the lobster halves under the flame a few seconds until the cheese melts, and serve immediately. Pass a tureen of melted butter.

CHAUSSONS AUX QUEUES DE HOMARD
Grand Hotel, Brussels

These exquisite "lobster puffs" are the chef's specialty. The manager is proud of the hotel's restaurant and planned a wonderful dinner for us, including this delicacy.

6 8- by 3-inch ovals of *Puff Paste*
1 1¾-pound lobster or 1 pound
    fresh lobster meat
Mushroom cream:
  6 fresh mushrooms, minced
  2 tablespoons butter
  1 tablespoon cornstarch
  ½ cup heavy cream
   Salt and pepper
  ¼ teaspoon nutmeg
  2 tablespoons sherry

Lobster sauce:
  1¼ cups light cream
  3 teaspoons cornstarch
  1 cup cubed lobster meat
   Salt and pepper
  ¼ cup Madeira

Prepare *Puff Paste* well ahead of time so it will be ready to fill and bake, just before serving. Roll the ovals ¼-inch thick. If you use a whole lobster, have it split, moisten the meat with melted butter and bake it 18 minutes at 375°. The sauce will be better, because you put the liver and coral into it. Or you may use prepared fresh lobster meat. Make the mushroom cream. Toss the minced mushrooms in the butter 2 minutes over a low flame. Blend the cornstarch with the cream and cook until it thickens, then add the mushrooms, seasonings, and sherry. It should be quite thick. Spread a big spoonful of this sauce on one half of each of the puff paste ovals, lay a slice of lobster meat on the sauce, fold over the other half, and press the edges together. Make 3 incisions in the top for the steam to escape. Put the puffs on a baking sheet and bake 7 minutes at 400°, then turn the heat to 375° and bake 9 to 12 minutes more, until they are puffed and golden. Meanwhile, make the lobster sauce. Blend the cream with the cornstarch and cook until it thickens, then add the cubed lobster, salt, pepper, and Madeira. Put 2 big spoonfuls of sauce over each puff and serve hot. This may be served as the main dish for an important lunch or an entrée for dinner. Serves 6.

GRATIN AUX FRUITS DE MER

1 pound scallops
1 pound fresh shrimp
1 onion, sliced
1 cup fresh or canned lobster meat
  or crabmeat
4 shallots or green onions, minced
2 tablespoons butter

3 teaspoons cornstarch
1 cup heavy cream
Salt and pepper
3 tablespoons sherry
⅔ cup shredded Swiss or Cheddar
  cheese, or Bel Paese

Sauté the scallops 2 minutes in a little butter. Cook the shrimp in their shells in ½ cup water with the salt, pepper, and sliced onion 3 minutes. Let the shrimp cool in the broth, then strain it to use for the sauce. Shell the shrimp. Pick over the cooked lobster meat or crabmeat and cut it into pieces the size of the scallops and shrimp. Sauté the minced shallots or onions in a little butter until tender and mix with the fish. Blend the cornstarch with the shrimp broth and cream and cook until it thickens. Season to taste with salt and pepper. Add the sherry. Butter a large shallow deep pie dish or baking dish and distribute the seafood over the bottom. When ready to heat and serve, cover it with the cream sauce and put the cheese on top. Put in a hot oven for 7 or 8 minutes, then under the flame until the cheese is lightly browned. This may be made in large scallop shells instead of in a baking dish. Bel Paese is a good melting cheese and is mild. If it is used, 2 or 3 tablespoons of Parmesan may be added to the top of the cheese before the dish goes under the flame. This may be served as a fish course, or as a main course to follow a rather hearty soup, *Soupe au Pistou* for instance. Serves 8.

CLAM PIE

1 can whole clams (10½–11½
  ounces)
1 can minced clams (7½ ounces)
½ cup heavy cream
2 tablespoons cornstarch
¼ teaspoon mace or nutmeg
  Freshly ground pepper

3 tablespoons grated onion
2 tablespoons butter
Prebaked 9-inch pie shell
Top:
  ⅓ cup Parmesan cheese
  ¼ cup fine cracker crumbs

Drain the whole clams and the minced clams and use 1 cup of the juice. Make a sauce by blending the juice and cream with the cornstarch, nutmeg or mace, and the pepper. Cook until it thickens. Sauté the onion in the butter for a minute, add it to the sauce, stir in the clams. Put the prebaked crust in a pie pan and heat it a moment in the oven. Add the clam mixture, cover it with the mixed cheese and crumbs, and run the dish under the flame until the top is browned. This will serve 6 or 8 as a fish course.

CREAMED CLAMS

1 10½-ounce can whole clams
1 7½-ounce can minced clams
⅓ cup minced green or white onion
2 tablespoons butter
Dash of salt
Freshly ground pepper
¼ teaspoon mace

½ teaspoon thyme
Heavy cream
2 tablespoons cornstarch
6 pastry shells or slices of buttered toast
Chopped parsley

Drain both cans of clams and set them aside. Measure the broth and add enough heavy cream to make 2 cups. Sauté the onions in the butter until tender and add them, the salt (taste first), pepper, mace, and thyme. Blend the cornstarch with a little of the liquid mixture then add the rest of it and simmer until it thickens. This may be made ahead of time. When ready to serve, reheat and add the minced and whole clams. Put the clams and sauce in pastry shells (baked in muffin tins and reheated), or over crisp buttered toast. Sprinkle with chopped parsley. The mixture may also be put in ramekins, covered with mixed Parmesan cheese and crumbs, and run under the flame. Doxee and Snows produce very good clams and fish soups. Serves 6.

OYSTERS POULETTE

32 fresh oysters
8 tablespoons butter
Oyster liquor, plus dry vermouth to make 1 cup liquid
¼ pound fresh mushrooms, sliced
1 small onion, grated
1 cup chicken broth
4 tablespoons flour

1 cup heavy cream
Salt and freshly ground pepper
¼ teaspoon nutmeg
8 small prebaked pastry shells or patty shells or 8 slices buttered toast
Chopped parsley

Have the fish man open the oysters and give you all their liquor. Strain the oysters and liquor through a sieve lined with a damp cloth to strain out the grit. Put 2 tablespoons of the butter in the top of a double boiler over hot water and add the oysters to keep warm. Do not cook them. Add enough dry vermouth to the oyster liquor to make 1 cup. Sauté the mushrooms and onion in 3 tablespoons butter for 3 minutes and add them to the oysters with the chicken broth. Melt 3 tablespoons butter in a saucepan, blend in the flour, and when smooth add the cream and seasonings. Cook until it thickens, then add the oyster liquor and vermouth. When it bubbles add the oyster mixture. Serve immediately in patty or pastry shells which have been baked in muffin tins. Put 4 oysters in each shell with the sauce. Sprinkle the tops with chopped parsley. The oysters may also be served on slices of buttered toast. Serves 8. Pouilly Fuissé, Chablis, or a white Burgundy may be served with oysters.

OYSTERS WITH SAUCE MORNAY

30 oysters on the half shell
2½ cups light cream
3 tablespoons cornstarch
Salt and freshly ground pepper

¼ cup Parmesan cheese
½ cup grated Gruyère cheese
Garnish: Parmesan cheese

Put the opened oysters on the bottom of a large baking pan. Put the cream in a saucepan, blend in the cornstarch and cook until it is hot, then add the salt, pepper, and cheese. Stir until it is thick. Put 2 tablespoons of sauce on each oyster, sprinkle with a little Parmesan, run the pan under the flame until the sauce bubbles, then serve at once. Use 5 oysters to a serving.

COQUILLES ST. JACQUES

1½ pounds fresh scallops
Juice ½ lime
½ cup dry vermouth
Salt and freshly ground pepper
½ pound fresh mushrooms
3 tablespoons butter
¼ cup minced green onions or
shallots

2 tablespoons cornstarch
1 cup heavy cream, scalded
1 egg yolk
6 scallop shells
6 tablespoons Parmesan cheese

Bay scallops are small and are left whole; large sea scallops are cut in 1-inch cubes. Clean and dry the scallops and marinate 1 hour in the lime juice, vermouth, salt, and pepper. When preparing the dish, bring them to a gentle simmer in the liquid and cook 5 minutes. Drain them and reserve the broth. Bake the mushrooms (whole if very small, or sliced if large) with the green onions or shallots in the butter in a 350° oven for 7 or 8 minutes. Blend the scallop-wine broth with the cornstarch and add the scalded cream. When the sauce thickens, stir in the egg yolk. Butter the scallop shells, put in the scallops and mushrooms, and cover with the sauce. This may be done ahead of time. Just before serving sprinkle 1 tablespoon of cheese over the top of each and run the shells under the flame until the mixture is hot and the cheese browns. Serves 6.

BROILED SCALLOPS AND MUSHROOMS

2 pounds scallops
1 pound mushrooms
Bacon
Skewers

Marinade:
½ cup olive oil
Juice 1 lemon or 2 limes
Salt and pepper
1 clove garlic, crushed
1 teaspoon thyme

Get scallops of quite good size and mushrooms the same size if possible. Use only the mushroom caps. Mix the marinade and marinate the scallops and mushrooms in it an hour or more. Before broiling remove them from the marinade and reserve it. Cut bacon in 1½-inch pieces. Thread 5 scallops and 5 mushrooms alternately on each skewer with pieces of bacon between them. Preheat the broiler and lay the skewers across a shallow pan 5 inches below the flame. Broil, basting with the marinade, for 3 minutes, when the scallops will be cooked through and the bacon crisp. Serves 6.

LES MOULES FARCIES DE TANTE ANNETTE
Le Petit Colombier, rue des Acacias, Paris

The food in this restaurant makes up for the fact that there is not even one tree in front of this "dovecot." M. Jean Delouvrier, the owner-chef, has run this establishment for thirty-four years and has given dining pleasure to countless people. His secret is his pride and continued lively interest in cooking.

2 quarts fresh mussels	½ cup heavy cream
⅓ cup butter	½ cup *Hollandaise Sauce*
2 onions, finely chopped	

Wash and scrub the mussels very well. Put the butter and very finely chopped onions in the bottom of a pot and put the mussels on top. Cover and cook until the mussels open. Remove the top shells. Put the mussels on the half shell on the bottom of a long pan. Put the broth through a sieve, whip in ½ cup heavy cream, and add ½ cup thick *Hollandaise*. The sauce must have a good body. Dress each mussel copiously with the sauce, glaze to a golden color under a hot flame, and serve immediately on hot plates. Serves 6.

MOULES NORMANDE

1 to 1½ quarts mussels	1 teaspoon thyme
½ cup Calvados (Applejack)	Pinch salt
½ cup water	Freshly ground pepper
1 small shredded white onion	¼ cup sweet butter
¼ cup shredded carrot	1 cup heavy cream

Soak the mussels an hour in cold water, then scrub them well with a rough brush and remove all the moss. Put the liquor, water, vegetables, and thyme in a big pot, add the mussels, cover, and steam for 5 minutes. Remove the mussels to wide soup plates. Mash the sauce through a coarse sieve; add salt to taste, and the pepper, butter, and cream. Let come to a boil and divide over the mussels. Use 1½ quarts of mussels to serve 3.

CREAMED MUSSELS

2 quarts fresh mussels
1 cup dry vermouth
¼ cup shredded onion
1 teaspoon thyme
1 clove garlic, crushed

Cream sauce:
3 tablespoons butter
2 tablespoons cornstarch
¼ teaspoon nutmeg
1 tablespoon tomato paste
Dash of salt
Freshly ground pepper
1 cup heavy cream
Garnish:
Crumbs and Parmesan cheese

Scrub the mussels with a coarse kitchen brush, removing the moss clinging to them. Wash and rinse well. Put them in a kettle with the vermouth, cover tightly, and simmer until the shells open. This takes only a minute or two. Open the mussels over the kettle so their juices may be added to the wine. Put the mussels in the top of a double boiler over hot water to keep warm. Line a sieve with a cloth wrung out in cold water and strain the juices. Add the onion, thyme, and garlic to the juices and simmer gently, almost covered with the lid, 5 minutes. There should be 1 cup of liquid. Make the sauce by melting the butter, blending in the cornstarch, and stirring in all the rest of the ingredients. When it begins to thicken, add the mussel liquid, and cook until it is the consistency of heavy cream. Pour the sauce over the mussels and serve on toast; or they may be put in scallop shells, sprinkled with a mixture of crumbs and cheese, and run under the flame a moment, until a pale yellow. Serves 4 or 5.

MOULES MARINIERE

5 or 6 quarts large mussels
½ cup ground onions
2 cloves garlic, crushed
1 teaspoon thyme
Freshly ground pepper
4 tablespoons butter

2 tablespoons chopped parsley
2 cups dry vermouth, or 1 cup dry
vermouth and 1 cup clam juice
Garnish:
⅓ cup chopped parsley

Scrub the mussels, remove all the moss, and soak them several hours in cold water. They must be completely free from sand and grit, as the broth is served without being strained. Put all the other ingredients together in a big kettle and bring to a simmer, then put the mussels in, cover, and cook until they open, about 4 or 5 minutes. Shake the pot several times. Scoop out the mussels with a big spoon and divide them (unshelled) in 6 wide soup plates. Pour the broth over them and sprinkle with parsley.

VARIATION. Omit the garlic. When the mussels are done add a cup of hot cream which has been blended with a tablespoon of tomato paste.

SHRIMP FLAMINGO
Hotel Danieli, Venice

Pilau:
1½ cups patna rice
⅓ cup butter
½ cup chopped onions
1 clove garlic, crushed
1 teaspoon turmeric
3 cups chicken broth

2 pounds fresh unshelled shrimp
½ cup each onions, celery, and
carrots, minced
1 teaspoon dried thyme, or sprig
of fresh thyme
¾ cup butter
Salt and freshly ground pepper
Jigger of cognac
3 teaspoons flour
1½ cups heavy cream
Jigger sherry
2 tablespoons lemon juice

Start the pilau first, as it takes longer to cook. The rice must be dry so rub and shake it in a clean towel. Melt ⅓ cup butter in a heavy pot, add the onions and garlic, and cook until the onions soften a little. Add the rice and stir it for 5 minutes over a low flame. Sprinkle the top with the turmeric. Bring the broth to a boil and add it gradually. Cover tightly and cook over a low flame until the liquid is absorbed, about 25 to 30 minutes. Wash the shrimp but do not shell them. Mince the vegetables very fine, add the thyme, and cook in ½ cup of the butter until tender but not colored. Lay the shrimp on top, cover, and cook slowly about 3½ minutes or until the shrimp are done. Add salt and pepper, stir, and then blaze with the cognac. Take out the shrimp, peel them, and keep them warm. Melt the remaining ¼ cup butter in another pot, stir in the flour, and when smooth, stir in the cream and cook until it thickens, then add the sherry. Combine with the vegetables and cook 1 minute. Either purée the mixture in a blender or mash it through a sieve, then add the lemon juice. When the rice is done, empty it onto a hot platter and cover with the shrimp. Heat the sauce and serve it separately in a tureen. Serves 8.

BROILED SHRIMP

2 pounds fresh shrimp
3 cloves garlic, crushed
½ cup olive oil

Salt and pepper
Juice of 1 small lemon
¼ cup ground parsley

Wash, peel, and dry the shrimp. Marinate the shrimp for 2 hours in a mixture of all the other ingredients. Put the shrimps and the marinade in the bottom of a big pan and broil 4 inches below the flame 1 minute on each side. They may be emptied into a hot serving dish and served with rye bread and butter and beer. Or they may be served over 12 ounces of hot noodles or steaming rice. Serves 6.

INDIAN SHRIMP CURRY

1 pound fresh shrimp
2 tablespoons minced onion
1 teaspoon thyme
Salt and pepper
1 cup water
1 cup packaged coconut
1¼ cups milk
¼ cup chopped onion
2 cloves garlic, crushed
¼ cup butter
1 teaspoon cardamom
1 teaspoon turmeric

1 teaspoon cumin powder
1 teaspoon coriander powder or
   2 tablespoons crushed coriander seeds
½ teaspoon cinnamon
½ teaspoon cloves
2 tablespoons cornstarch
Light cream or dry vermouth
Accompaniments:
   Boiled patna rice
   Fried bananas
   Chutney

Wash the shrimp and cook them 3 minutes with the minced onion, thyme, salt, pepper, in 1 cup water. When they are cool, strain and reserve the broth. Peel the shrimp and cook the shells in the broth 10 minutes, covered, at a low simmer. This makes a rich broth for the sauce. Strain out the shells and discard. Boil up the coconut in the milk and let it cool, then press out the milk through a fine sieve and reserve the milk. Sauté the onion and garlic in the butter for 2 minutes, then add the condiments and cook 2 minutes more. Remove from heat. Stir in the shrimp and let it marinate in this mixture 1 hour or more. For the sauce blend the cornstarch with the shrimp broth and when smooth add the coconut milk. Cook until it thickens. If too thick add a little light cream or dry vermouth. Mix the sauce with the shrimp, reheat, and serve with rice. Serves 4.

SHRIMPS ALLA FREDDY
(Bologna)

When Freddy Martini gave me the recipe for these delicious shrimps he had a gay and lively restaurant in Bologna. Now he is managing a hotel in the south of Italy, but I know that wherever he is the food will be good.

4 or 5 large shrimp for each skewer
   Olive oil
   Fine crumbs
   Salt and pepper

Parmesan cheese
Lemon juice
Handful of chopped parsley

Shell and clean the shrimp. Dip them in olive oil, then in a mixture of fine crumbs, salt, pepper, and Parmesan cheese. On each skewer thread 4 or 5, packed close together so they will slide off like a cutlet. Cook over an outdoor grill or lay them across a skillet 4 inches below a medium-hot flame, turning often for 4 or 5 minutes until they are a golden brown. Slide them off on hot plates. For 5 or 6 skewers put the juice of 1 lemon and plenty of chopped parsley in the skillet with the juices and scrape the contents over the shrimp.

Meats, Poultry & Game

FIVE or six days a week, as a rule, dinner is planned around the choice of meat or poultry. Meat, then, is an important part of a book on food. It is good sense to seek out the best meat market, because the best quality of meat or poultry provide the maximum of nourishment; it is economy, for there is a minimum of waste; and then of course there is the great enjoyment of a fine roast, chop, stew or bird.

To cook meat well takes care and thought. Actually it takes more time to ruin a good piece of meat than to cook it properly, because unfortunately a great many cooks overcook meat. The temperatures and time of cooking I have given with each recipe are for meats of first quality and for young poultry. Nowadays most perceptive cooks buy roasting chickens for steaming and stewing. The cooking time is cut in half, the texture of the meat is fine, and the few more cents a pound are well worth it. Gentle roasting and gentle simmering prevent shrinkage and the fine texture of the meat is preserved. Don't be afraid of buying too much meat for any occasion. If meat is cooked and prepared correctly, any leftover is very often as good as, if not better than, the first presentation.

When we serve a fine piece of meat, such as a tournedos, a fillet or a roast, we may like to match it with a good wine—of course a red wine. The great Bordeaux region gives us Haut Brion or Château Mouton Rothschild and many others; and there are many great Burgundies to choose from. One could keep on name-dropping indefinitely, the names are so musical; Chambertin, Nuits St. Georges, and Clos Vougeot. For simpler cuts of meat one does not need to be so lavish, for there are countless lesser but excellent wines. There are good American red wines. For duck, goose, venison, and feathered game the wine should also be red. Turkey and chicken call for white wine, unless a coq au vin is cooked in red wine. Drink the same wine with the bird.

Veal calls for lighter wines than beef; either red or white wines may be served with it. If veal is cooked with cream and mushrooms for instance, then choose a white Moselle wine. For a garlicked roast of veal serve a

149

Beaujolais, a St. Emilien, or an Italian Frascati. Always serve red wine with lamb or mutton. For pork choose an Alsatian or a full-bodied Rhine wine. The same goes for ham unless an important occasion demands Champagne.

Beef

ROAST RIBS OF BEEF

3-rib roast
  Caramel or molasses and Kitchen
    Bouquet
  Flour

1 teaspoon powdered beef concentrate mixed in 1 cup water
1 tablespoon cornstarch
Salt and pepper

For maximum flavor the bones should always be left in a roast. The first cut is preferable; there is less fat than on the second cut. The meat must be aged and marbled with fat to be of fine quality. Never roast in an oven hotter than 300°, and if the meat seems to be cooking too fast, turn it lower. This makes for even red meat all the way through, rare but not dark red, and for less shrinkage and greater tenderness. Remove the meat from the refrigerator several hours before roasting, so that it will be at room temperature when it goes into the oven. Mix ¼ to ⅓ cup of molasses or caramel with Kitchen Bouquet and paint the meat all over, then catch the syrup with a light sprinkling of flour. Paint it again when it is half through roasting. The meat attains a rich dark glaze and the gravy is flavored but not sweet. Set the roast on the bones in an open pan with no water and roast 20 minutes to the pound, or about 1 hour a rib, for rare. For the gravy, mix a teaspoon of powdered beef concentrate with 1 cup of water, then blend in the cornstarch and season with salt and pepper. When the meat is done lift it onto a hot platter. Pour off some of the fat from the pan. Pour in the broth, scrape all dark crumbs from the bottom, and cook the gravy until it thickens. If it gets too thick add a little more hot water. Serve separately in a sauceboat. Three ribs will serve 10 or 12.

TOURNEDOS AUX CHAMPIGNONS

1½-inch fillets of beef tenderloin
  Butter and oil
  Salt and freshly ground pepper
  Large mushroom caps, 1 to a
    fillet
3 tablespoons olive oil
1 clove garlic, crushed
¼ cup chopped shallots or green
  onions

¼ cup Madeira or dry sherry
⅓ cup heavy cream
  Slices of French bread, 1 inch
    thick
  Sweet butter
Garnish:
  Parsley or watercress
  New potatoes
  Buttered new peas

Allow 1 fillet for each serving and as it is cooked at the last minute prepare the vegetables first. Everything must be ready at the same time. Brush fine large white mushrooms and remove the stems. Put the olive oil, garlic, and shallots or green onions in the bottom of a baking pan, lay the mushroom caps on top, and sprinkle with the wine, salt, and pepper. Remove the crusts from 1-inch thick slices of bread and fry both sides in sweet butter. Put the mushrooms in a 375° oven and cook 10 minutes; 4 minutes before they are done put in the bread to become a little crisp. Sauté the meat in half oil and half butter about 4 minutes on each side until nicely browned but still rare. Put the toast on hot serving plates; place a fillet of beef on top of each and a mushroom cap on the beef. Add the cream to the mushroom juices, boil up, and divide the sauce (serves 6) over the meat. Garnish with parsley or watercress and a serving of each vegetable.

TOURNEDOS BELLE HÉLÈNE
Capucin Gourmand, Nancy

6 1½-inch slices fillet of beef
  Julienne French fried potatoes
6 artichoke bottoms
  Sprigs of watercress

Sauce Béarnaise for 6:
  2 tablespoons chopped
    shallots
  2 tablespoons minced chervil
  2 tablespoons minced tarragon
  2 tablespoons tarragon vinegar
  2 egg yolks
  3 tablespoons cold water
  ½ cup sweet butter
  Salt and pepper

M. Romain remarks that this is a very simple cuisine but at the same time greatly appreciated for a grand dinner. The beef is broiled rare at the last minute. Peel the potatoes and slice very thin, then cut the slices in thin julienne sticks. Put them in a wire basket and fry them at 375° in deep oil until light brown and crisp. This takes very little time. Drain, lightly salt and pepper them, and keep them warm. The artichoke bottoms are steamed tender in butter over a low flame. This takes about 15 minutes. They form cups to hold the Béarnaise Sauce which may be made ahead of time and stand over warm water an hour. For the sauce, put all the shallots, half the chervil and half the tarragon, with the vinegar and a pinch of pepper, in a heavy saucepan and cook until the vinegar is almost evaporated. Let it cool a little, then add the egg yolks and water and whisk over simmering water until the consistency of mayonnaise; add the butter, bit by bit, whisking continuously until thick and smooth, then add the rest of the herbs, salt, and another pinch of pepper. Broil the fillets quickly. Put the meat on each of six hot plates and garnish with watercress. Add to each plate a serving of the potatoes and an artichoke cup filled with Béarnaise Sauce, and serve immediately with a fine red Burgundy.

STEAK AU POIVRE FLAMBÉ À LA NORMANDE
Maurice Cazalis, Chartres

When M. Cazalis uses Armagnac instead of Calvados to flame a steak he calls it Steak au Poivre Flambé à la Armagnac.

Thick fine steak, sirloin or porter-house	1½ tablespoons butter
	¼ cup Calvados or applejack
Salt	½ teaspoon beef extract
Butter or goose fat	¼ cup hot beef broth
Crushed aromatic pepper (see	¼ cup thick cream
Pantry Shelf)	2 tablespoons butter

Rub a fine steak on both sides with salt and either butter or goose fat, then rub in crushed aromatic pepper on both sides. Pan-fry in butter to your taste; it ought to be rare. Pour the liquor over the steak, set it ablaze, and remove it to a hot platter. Melt the beef extract in the broth, put it in the pan, add the cream and cook to reduce it a little, then whisk in the butter, and pour the sauce over the steak.

FILET AU POIVRE À MA FAÇON
Maurice Cazalis, Chartres

Ma façon (my way) is certainly an entirely new idea of slicing a whole fillet of beef. M. Cazalis has learned in his long experience that many consider the tenderloin or fillet too soft in texture and prefer heavier cuts of beef. So he slices a fillet lengthwise, as thick as one pleases, and cuts it across in individual servings. He says, "It gives more resistance to chewing and has a more agreeable taste."

Fillets of beef, cut "ma façon"	Sauce for 4:
Salt	½ teaspoon beef extract
Soft butter	¼ cup beef broth
Crushed aromatic pepper	¼ cup white wine
Minced shallots	4 tablespoons butter
Butter for sautéing	

Rub salt and soft butter on the meat, then rub in the pepper and minced shallots. This may be prepared a little ahead of time. When ready to serve, sauté the slices of meat in butter until nicely browned but rare. Put the meat on a hot serving dish. Melt the extract in the broth, put it with the wine in the sauté pan, and let it reduce a little, over a high flame, then whisk in the butter. Divide evenly over the meat.

BROILED PORTERHOUSE, SIRLOIN, OR CLUB STEAK

Steak 1½- to 2-inches thick (6½
  ounces per serving)
Olive oil and melted butter
Salt and freshly ground pepper

Marrow from 3 beef bones
1 tablespoon lemon juice
3 tablespoons butter
Chopped parsley

When you get a fine steak have the butcher give you 3 marrow bones. Pre-heat the oven. Rub the steak with a mixture of seasoned olive oil and melted butter. An aluminum grill with a removable, perforated top is worth getting for steaks and chops. Put the steak on the grill, 6 inches be-low the flame. Turn it several times and baste with oil and butter. Most steak lovers want it rare. I sometimes put a 2-inch thick steak in a 325° oven for 15 minutes before broiling it; then there is no danger of overcook-ing or burning the surface of the meat. (Thin steaks are better pan-fried. Put a little fat in the pan, sear the steak on both sides, lower the heat, and cook it as you like it.) Meanwhile extract the marrow from the bones with a sharp-pointed knife. Cut it in thin slices. Mix the lemon juice with the 3 tablespoons of butter. When the steak is done, remove it to a hot platter. Put the slices of marrow in the hot broiling pan with the juices and when it is hot and almost melted, pour it over the steak. Put bits of lemon butter over the steak and a little chopped parsley.

WINE SAUCE FOR STEAK

½ cup red wine
1 tablespoon minced shallots or
  onion
1 tablespoon lemon juice
  Salt and pepper

2 teaspoons minced parsley
1 teaspoon meat glaze
½ teaspoon prepared mustard
3 tablespoons sweet butter

Put the wine, shallots or onion, lemon juice, salt, and pepper in a saucepan and reduce it to half its quantity over a good flame, then stir in the other ingredients. When the steak is on the platter, boil up the sauce and pour it over the steak.

STEAK MARINADE

2 cloves garlic, crushed
3 tablespoons olive oil
  Dash Worcestershire sauce

⅓ cup red wine
1 teaspoon curry powder

Crush the garlic and mix all the ingredients together. Marinate the steak for 3 hours in this mixture, 1½ hours on each side. Remove the steak, and after it is cooked, scrape the remaining marinade into the grill or pan juices, add salt and freshly ground pepper, and pour over the steak.

FILET MIGNON

2-inch thick fillets from the tender-
  loin
Olive oil and butter
Salt and pepper
Parsley

Mushroom sauce:
  ½ pound mushrooms
  3 tablespoons butter
  2 tablespoons cognac
  ¼ cup Madeira
  1 tablespoon cornstarch
  ¼ cup cream
  1 tablespoon Bahamian mus-
    tard or prepared mustard

Prepare 1 fillet for each person. Make the sauce before you cook them. Cook the sliced mushrooms in the butter for 4 or 5 minutes, then blaze with the cognac. Blend the cornstarch with the wine and cream and mustard, and stir it into the mushrooms until the sauce thickens. Keep hot. Sauté the fillets in hot oil and butter, half and half, until they are nicely browned on both sides but rare inside. Put the meat on hot plates or platters, decorate with sprigs of parsley, and pour the sauce over the meat. This amount of sauce will serve 6. Serve with new potatoes cooked slowly in butter and broth; and a green vegetable.

CHATEAUBRIAND MAISON

2 3-inch slices fillet of beef (to
  serve 4)
4 shallots or green onions, minced
2 tablespoons butter

⅓ cup red wine
½ cup *Brown Sauce*
2 or 3 marrow bones
Parchment paper bags

Cut the 3-inch-thick slices of beef three-fourths through across the grain, as they are to be stuffed with marrow later. Make the sauce first. Cook the shallots or green onions in the butter until they are soft, add the wine, and cook down to a rather sticky residue. Add the *Brown Sauce* and simmer gently 10 minutes. Broil the meat 5 inches below a medium flame 25 minutes, 12½ minutes on each side. Extract the marrow from the bones with a sharp-pointed knife and when the meat is done, stuff them with slices or cubes of marrow. Put 2 tablespoons of *Brown Sauce* on each piece of meat and put them in paper bags, fastened securely. Put them in a 400° oven for 4 or 5 minutes or until the bags puff up. Bring the bags to the table, open them, and slide the meat and sauce off onto a hot platter. Slice the meat down. These are served with *Pommes Soufflés* and are a specialty of the Brussels Restaurant, New York.

BRAISED FRESH BRISKET

5½- to 6-pound fresh brisket of beef
3 or 4 tablespoons caramel and
Kitchen Bouquet, mixed

Flour
Freshly ground pepper

If possible get a very thick cut of brisket. Your butcher may have to order it for you, as the thick cuts usually are reserved for corning. Paint the meat all over with the mixture of caramel and Kitchen Bouquet. This makes a wonderful glaze when the meat is done. Lightly sprinkle with flour and freshly ground pepper. Put it in a heavy iron roaster or Dutch oven with no water. Cover tightly and cook 3 hours at a scant 300°. Do not open the lid during roasting. This meat is so juicy and rich you may dispense with gravy. Serve with mashed potatoes generously mixed with minced onion and sour cream. Serves 8 or 10. Pour off the fat and scrape the roaster. The next day remove the heavy cake of fat and there will be a jellied essence of beef which may be used in *Goulash Sauce*. Leftover brisket is excellent.

BRAISED STUFFED FILLET OF BEEF

1 4- or 5-pound whole fillet of beef
6 ounces liver pâté, or ½ pound
chicken livers
½ cup sliced fresh mushrooms, or
1 large truffle, sliced
Soft butter
Salt and pepper

¼ cup chopped onions
¼ cup chopped carrots
¼ cup beef broth
⅔ cup red wine or dry vermouth
¼ cup heavy cream
1 teaspoon tomato paste
Garnish: Parsley or watercress

The fillet may be left in one piece or it may be sliced in the required number of 1¾-inch thick slices. The whole fillet is slit along its length to within 1 inch from either end. The slices are slit three-fourths through. A good brand of pâté may be used or ½ pound of chicken livers may be sautéed and puréed. The mushrooms (or truffle) are sliced thin and tossed in butter a minute, then mixed with the pâté. Stuff the whole fillet or the slices with the mixture and tie securely with string. Rub the meat with soft butter and sprinkle with salt and pepper. Make a bed of the onions and carrots in a baking pan and put the meat on it. Pour the broth over it and half the wine. Roast uncovered at 350° about 50 or 55 minutes, turning the meat once. If necessary add a little hot broth; the vegetables should not burn. When it is done, remove the meat to a hot platter, remove the strings, and keep the meat warm. Sieve the contents of the roasting pan or put it in an electric blender. Add the rest of the wine and if the mixture seems too thin blend a teaspoon of cornstarch with the cream and tomato paste before adding them. Blend the sauce in a saucepan and heat until it thickens. Mask the meat with a little of this sauce and serve the rest in a sauceboat. Garnish the platter with parsley or watercress. A 4-pound fillet serves 10. This dish deserves a fine red Burgundy or Bordeaux.

SWISS STEAK FONDUE

Thin strips of the finest tenderloin
  or sirloin of beef
Hot butter and oil mixed
Equipment:
    A chafing dish
    A pepper mill
    Spearing forks

Dipping sauces:
  Béarnaise Sauce
  Curry Sauce
  Tartar Sauce
  Mustard Sauce
  Chili Sauce with Sour Cream
  Horseradish Sauce

This is a delightful thing to have in a good Swiss restaurant, and there is
no reason why it can't be done just as well at home. The more bowls of
sauces there are, the better; the Béarnaise is the most important. Only the
tenderest aged steak is suitable for this. A mixture of oil and butter is
brought to the bubbling point in the chafing dish; each guest is given a
4-inch fine-pronged wooden-handled fork with which he spears a strip of
beef, cooks it in the oil and butter to the doneness he likes, then dips it in
one of the sauces. Have a pepper mill handy for anyone who likes just a
grind of aromatic pepper on his meat. Allow 6 ounces of steak for each
person.

SAUERBRATEN

5 to 6 pounds bottom round of beef
4 cloves garlic
Marinade:
    1½ cups vinegar
    1½ cups water
    1 large onion, sliced
    3 bay leaves
    1 sliced lemon
    Freshly ground pepper
    1 teaspoon salt
    ½ teaspoon powdered clove
    ½ teaspoon cinnamon

Flour
Beef fat, oil, or butter
1 cup chopped onions
⅓ cup chopped carrots
⅓ cup chopped celery
1½ cups strained marinade
1 teaspoon ginger, or 3 gingersnaps, crumbled
⅔ cup red wine
1 cup tomato juice
Salt and pepper

Select fine seasoned beef. Cut the garlic into slivers and insert them in the
beef with a sharp pointed knife or icepick. Boil up the ingredients for the
marinade and let cool. Put the beef in a large crock and cover with the
marinade, cover and put in the refrigerator, or, in winter, in a cool place,
for 4 or 5 days. Turn the meat 2 times a day. When ready to cook, remove
the beef and reserve the marinade. Wipe the meat dry, sprinkle with
flour, and sear all over in a little hot beef fat. Remove the meat. Sauté the
onions in the beef fat until a little yellow, adding a little oil or butter if

necessary. Put the onions in a casserole and lay the beef on them. Add the carrots, celery, and 1½ cups of warmed strained marinade. Add the ginger or the crumbled gingersnaps. Put the wine and tomato juice into the skillet the onions cooked in, heat, and pour over the meat. Cover tightly and cook very slowly for 3½ hours at 300°, turning when it is half cooked. Remove the meat to a hot platter and strain the sauce through a fine sieve or put it in an electric blender. The sauce must have a tart flavor. If it is thin, add a little flour or cornstarch so it has the consistency of cream. Taste it for salt and pepper. Put a little sauce over the meat and serve the rest in a sauceboat. Serve with potato dumplings, noodles, or potato pancakes (see index for *Potato Parsley Dumplings*).

CHIPOLATA

1 pound tender fillet of beef
Butter
12 tiny cocktail sausages
2 veal kidneys, cubed
Salt and freshly ground pepper
1 pound small fresh mushrooms
8 roasted chestnuts
12 small white onions
Honey or brown sugar

Bordelaise Sauce:
  4 shallots or green onions,
    minced
¼ cup diced bacon
3 tablespoons grated carrots
1 cup red wine
3 tablespoons cornstarch
2 cups strong beef stock
Cubes of poached beef
  marrow
Accompaniment: Rice

This most elegant of mixtures could never be called stew—blanquette perhaps. This is the way Richard T. Clark makes it at the Voisin. All the ingredients are cooked separately and blended at the last. It is suggested that the Bordelaise Sauce be made ahead of time. Cook the minced shallots or green onions and carrot in the diced bacon for a few minutes over a low flame, then add the wine and cook until it is reduced by one-third. Blend the cornstarch with the beef stock. When smooth add it to the wine mixture and let it simmer slowly for 10 minutes. Extract marrow from 2 beef bones, cut it in cubes and add to the sauce just before reheating. Prepare the meat by cutting it in 1-inch cubes and sautéing it in a little butter for a moment to sear it; it must be rare. Set aside. Sauté the cocktail sausages in butter. Cut the veal kidneys in 1-inch pieces and sauté them in a little butter. Salt and pepper the meats. If possible get small mushrooms, and use them whole; if not slice medium-sized ones. Sauté the mushrooms 5 minutes in butter. Roast 8 chestnuts until tender and cut them in half. Cook the onions until just tender, then glaze them in brown sugar or honey. Keep the foods warm in an open oven. Reheat the sauce. If it is thicker than cream add a little red wine. Put all the foods into the sauce, heat a moment and serve immediately with rice. Serves 6.

BOEUF BOURGUIGNONNE

This glorified beef stew from Burgundy is never called stew, because the dish is important for special occasions. It takes some time to prepare and is made of only the finest beef and other ingredients. While one hardly chooses a La Tâche for the wine to go into it, a good Burgundy or Bordeaux is essential. For the beef, 2½-inch cubes of rump, chuck, or sirloin are used. I prefer rump or chuck for long cooking because the cuts are juicier. For 9 or 10, use 2½ pounds of meat; 3 pounds will serve 12. The rest of the quantities are the same except the onions; for 12 prepare 24 white onions.

2½ to 3 pounds beef, cubed
1 large beef kidney
¼ cup sweet vermouth
1 cup red Burgundy or Bordeaux wine
2 teaspoons thyme
¼ cup diced lean bacon
¾ cup cubed salt pork
2 tablespoons olive oil
1 large onion, diced
3 tablespoons brown sugar
18 to 24 white onions

4 or 5 young carrots
3½ tablespoons flour
Salt and pepper
2 cloves garlic, crushed
1 tablespoon tomato paste
1 cup rich beef broth
1 more cup wine
2 bay leaves
½ pound fresh small mushrooms
2 tablespoons butter
¼ cup chopped parsley

Put the beef in a crock. Cut the fat from the kidney and cut it in pieces the size of a mushroom. Combine the meats and add the vermouth, 1 cup of the wine, and thyme. Cover and let it marinate all day. Allow 45 minutes to put the stew together. When ready empty the meat into a colander, keeping the marinade. Fry the bacon with the olive oil in a large skillet until it is crisp, then drain it out and reserve. Do the same with the cubes of pork fat, adding them to the bacon. These are sprinkled over the top of the stew when it is done. Pour off some of the grease to use later. Put half the diced onion in the pan with a few grains of the sugar and sear half of the meat. When it is browned well, remove it to a large 12-inch casserole. Add the rest of the onion and more fat, sear the rest of the meat, and remove to the casserole. Add more of the reserved fat to the pan with the rest of the sugar and glaze the white onions. Put them on top of the meat. Cut the carrots in 1-inch lengths and glaze them; remove to the casserole. Put the rest of the grease in the pan, blend in the flour, and when smooth stir in a little of the marinade. Add salt, pepper, crushed garlic, and tomato paste. Slowly blend in the rest of the marinade and cook until it thickens, then add the broth, another cup of wine, and the bay leaves. When this is hot pour it over the meat and vegetables. Cover tightly and cook in the oven at 300°, keeping it at a slow simmer. Sauté the mushrooms in the butter 2 or 3 minutes. Add them to the top of the dish after it has cooked 2½ hours and cook ½ hour longer. When it is done and the meat is tender, remove the lid and sprinkle the crisp bacon and pork and the parsley over the top. Take to the table bubbling. This is a fine dish for a dinner of 8 or for a large party. Serve a fine Burgundy with it. This dish is even better when warmed up, so it may be made ahead of time. With it you may serve buttered noodles, mashed potatoes, or just good *homemade* bread without any other vegetable.

BEEF À LA MODE

5 pounds rump of beef
18 strips fat pork for larding
  Tarragon, thyme, nutmeg, and
    chervil
1 jigger brandy
3 cups red wine
  Beef fat and oil
  Salt, pepper, nutmeg, and
    cinnamon
1 large onion, shredded
1 carrot, shredded

2 cloves garlic, crushed
⅓ cup chopped celery and leaves
2 calf's feet, split, blanched and
    drained
2 teaspoons basil
  Salt and pepper
1 teaspoon thyme
12 small white onions
6 young carrots, cut in thirds
⅓ cup Madeira
½ pound fresh mushrooms

The beef is marinated 24 hours before cooking. First marinate the fat salt pork strips in the herbs, nutmeg, and brandy for 1 hour, then make deep incisions along the grain of the beef, and insert the lardings. Pour the brandy mixture and 1 cup of the red wine over the beef, put it in a covered crock, and let it stand 24 hours, turning it several times. Melt some beef fat and oil in a skillet. Remove the beef, reserving the marinade. Wipe the meat and rub it with salt, pepper, and a little cinnamon and nutmeg and brown it quickly on all sides in the fat. Make a bed of the shredded onion, carrot, and crushed garlic in a big casserole and lay the meat on it. Let the calf's feet boil up in water to cover for 5 minutes, then drain them. Put them beside the meat. Add the basil, thyme, some salt and pepper, the marinade from the beef, and 2 cups of red wine. Cover tightly and braise 3½ hours at 275°. Remove the meat and calf's feet. Strain the sauce. Remove the meat from the calf's feet and put it and the beef back in the casserole. Boil up the white onions and small carrots, drain them, and arrange them around the meat. Pour the strained sauce over them and the Madeira over the meat. Cover and cook for another hour at 300° or until the vegetables are tender. Sauté the mushrooms lightly in a little butter and add them to the dish. Put the meat and vegetables on a big platter and serve the sauce separately. No flour is used in this dish, because it is served cold as often as it is served hot. When serving it cold, put the meat in a large oiled bowl and strain the sauce over it. And when it has stiffened, arrange the vegetables around it and if more aspic is needed add a small can of jellied Madrilene. When it is turned out on a big chop plate, the meat and vegetables are covered with aspic. This is one of the great beef dishes and appropriate for a large dinner or buffet. A creamed mustard sauce is good to serve with it, and a green salad. Serves 10 or 12.

BEEFSTEAK AND KIDNEY PIE

2 pounds chuck or round of beef
4 tablespoons flour
Salt and pepper
1 teaspoon thyme
½ teaspoon clove
Fat
3 onions, chopped fine
3 carrots, chopped fine
1 tablespoon Worcestershire Sauce
½ cup red wine
3 cups rich beef broth (or 2 cups broth and 1 cup vegetable juice)

3 veal kidneys
Butter
Rich *Pie Pastry* (1 cup flour), or
Top crust:
  ⅓ cup white flour
  ⅓ cup wholewheat flour
  ⅓ cup cornmeal
  2 teaspoons baking powder
  ¾ teaspoon salt
  2 teaspoons brown sugar
  ¼ cup corn oil
  ½ cup buttermilk or more

Cut the beef in 1¼-inch cubes and shake in a bag with the flour, salt, pepper, thyme, and clove. Melt 3 or 4 tablespoons of fat or butter in the bottom of a heavy stewing kettle and brown the meat in it for 1 or 2 minutes, then add the onions and carrots and cook 2 minutes. Warm the wine and broth and add, with the Worcestershire sauce. Cover and simmer gently for 1½ hours or until the meat is tender. Cut the kidneys in pieces the size of the meat pieces. Sauté them in a little butter until lightly browned, then add them 10 minutes before the meat is done. Remove the meats to a greased baking dish and add a little over 2 cups of the sauce. The sauce should be creamy. Cover with a rich *Pie Pastry* crust and bake 10 minutes at 400°, then 15 minutes more at 350°, until the crust is nicely browned. The alternate crust is very easy, and is delicious if you want to stray from tradition. Mix all the dry ingredients. Mix the oil with ½ cup of buttermilk and stir it in very lightly. Add more buttermilk if needed to make a light dough. Spread on top of the stew with a spoon leaving a few air vents for steam to escape. Bake at 375° for 10 minutes, and 12 minutes more at 325°.

BRACIOLINE ALLA FIORENTINA
Sabatini, Florence

Bracioline is another way of saying scaloppine, only this time it is beef instead of veal.

2 pounds lean beef
2 tablespoons flour
Salt and pepper
¼ cup olive oil
½ cup each finely chopped onions, carrots, celery

1 cup red wine
1 large fresh tomato
3 or 4 fresh or dried mushrooms
¼ cup beef broth

The beef is sliced thin and pounded with a *batticarne* (mallet). Put the flour and seasonings in a bag and shake the meat in it until it is lightly covered. Put the olive oil in a pot and cook the vegetables until they color a little, then add the meat and cook gently for 12 or 15 minutes, stirring a couple of times. Warm the wine, add it, and cook gently until the wine is somewhat reduced. Skin, seed and chop the tomato and slice the mushrooms; either fresh, or dried ones that were previously soaked and rinsed. Add these and the broth, almost cover the pot, and simmer until the meat is tender. It should cook slowly for 1½ hours altogether. Serve with buttered noodles or boiled potatoes. Serves 6.

STUFATINO DE MANZO CON PEPERONI ALLA ROMANA
Hosteria Romano, 70 Dean Street, London

Mario Carboni and Angelo Mansi, two very attractive young men, run the liveliest restaurant in Soho, always filled, with plenty of customers waiting in line, and for good reason: the food is excellent, the atmosphere Italian, friendly, and gay, and the prices are reasonable. They gave me one of their popular dishes.

2½ to 3 pounds cubed beef	2 bay leaves
Salt and pepper	4 dried mushrooms, soaked and
3 tablespoons flour	drained
⅓ cup olive oil	Red wine
1 cup chopped onions	1 large tomato, peeled and sliced
¾ cup chopped carrots	1 cup consommé
½ cup chopped celery	2 green peppers
2 cloves garlic, crushed	Garnish: Boiled potatoes
1 teaspoon rosemary	

Choose rump or chuck and cut it in 1½-inch cubes. Put 3 tablespoons of flour with salt and pepper, in a paper bag and shake the meat in it until it is well covered. Put the olive oil in a heavy pot and brown the meat in the hot oil, then remove the meat. Add more oil if necessary, put in the vegetables and cook 3 minutes, then lay the meat on top of them. Add garlic, the seasonings, drained mushrooms, and enough wine to almost cover the meat. Put the casserole in the oven half-covered in order to reduce the wine somewhat, and bake 1 hour. Add the tomato and consommé and cook 1 hour more. Test the meat with a fork and if necessary cook 45 more minutes. Remove the seeds from the peppers and slice them coarsely. Twenty minutes before the stew is done, lay the peppers on top. They must have a fresh taste. Three pounds of meat will serve 8. Serve with boiled potatoes and good red wine.

BEEF STROGANOFF, RUSSIAN STYLE

2 pounds prime sirloin steak
   (1½ inches thick)
1½ cups thinly sliced onions
1½ cups thinly sliced mushrooms
Butter
Salt and pepper

¼ cup sherry or Madeira
1 cup heavy sour cream
1½ teaspoons prepared mustard
1 teaspoon tomato paste
Chopped parsley

Many years ago an enchanting vaudeville show called the Chauve Souris came to New York and after the company disbanded the performers stayed here. Several men and women of the troupe became our friends. One singing actor taught me what I consider the only way to make Beef Stroganoff. He insisted that each main ingredient be cooked separately and all blended together at the last minute, each thereby retaining its own flavor. The steak must be of absolutely top quality, as it is sliced in thin strips and seared about 30 seconds in butter, just to remove the raw taste; this is done after the vegetables are cooked. Put the thinly sliced onions in a pan with melted butter and bake them in a 325° oven about 18 minutes, stirring once. Put the mushrooms in another pan with melted butter and put in the oven 6 minutes before the onions are done. Salt and pepper both onions and mushrooms. "Frying" this way insures even cooking with little chance of burning. Cut the steak in paper-thin strips and sear quickly in hot butter. Salt and pepper the meat, pour the wine over it, and mix quickly with the mushrooms and onions. Have the cream at room temperature and blend with the mustard and tomato paste. Stir the cream into the meat and vegetables and reheat without boiling. Empty into a large serving dish and sprinkle the top with chopped parsley. Serves 6. Steaming wild rice or patna rice is a good accompaniment.

CASSEROLE OF BEEF AND BEANS

1 pound dried kidney beans
1 teaspoon salt
1 clove garlic, crushed
2 cups chopped onions
1 cup chopped carrots
3 tablespoons fat
3 tablespoons molasses

3-pound chuck steak
Salt and freshly ground pepper
1 tablespoon chili powder
1 cup red wine
Broth and tomato juice
Parsley and breadcrumbs

Wash the beans and soak them overnight in 4 cups of water. Do not drain them but add enough fresh water to cover them and simmer 1 hour with the salt and garlic. Drain off the water and reserve. Make a bed of half the onions and half the carrots in the bottom of a big casserole which has a tight lid. Put half the beans on the vegetables. Melt the fat in a skillet, add the molasses, and glaze the meat in this until it is a rich brown on both sides. Add the meat to the casserole and spread the rest of the vegetables on it and then the rest of the beans. Add some salt and pepper, the chili powder, and the wine to the sauté pan and rinse it over the beans. Cover with the bean water, cover tightly, and bake at 300° or less from 4½ to 5½ hours, the longer the better. When necessary add hot broth or tomato juice to keep the beans moist. Before serving sprinkle the top with a mixture of chopped parsley and fine breadcrumbs. This is a fine buffet supper dish for 10 or 12.

ROGNONS DE BOEUF, VIGNERONNE
Capucin Gourmand, Nancy

1 beef kidney
2 tablespoons butter
1 onion, minced
3 shallots, minced
2 tablespoons flour
1 cup red wine
1 cup beef broth
1 pinch thyme

1 pinch basil
1 teaspoon minced parsley
Salt and pepper
4 ounces fresh mushrooms
2 tablespoons butter
1 tablespoon oil
Garnish: Boiled rice or potatoes

Skin a fine beef kidney and cut it in not too thin scallops. Put the butter and onion in a heavy saucepan and cook a little, then add the shallots and stir in the flour. Cook over a low flame for 5 minutes, then add the wine, broth, herbs, salt, and pepper. Let this simmer over boiling water 30 minutes, then add the sliced or button mushrooms. In another pan heat the butter and oil and sauté the kidney scallops until they are brown on both sides, turn low, and cook 2 or 3 minutes more. Drain them into the sauce. Empty into a hot serving dish and sprinkle a little minced parsley over the top. Serves 4. This is another recipe from Georges Romain.

POLPETTINE
(Italian Meatballs)

⅓ pound ground beef
⅓ pound ground veal
1 egg, beaten
Salt and pepper
1 teaspoon basil

1 teaspoon fennel powder
¼ cup Parmesan cheese
Fine crumbs
Olive oil and butter for frying

Mix all the ingredients together and make into tiny balls. Roll them in fine crumbs and sauté in a mixture of oil and butter until brown all over. Larger meat cakes (polpette) may also be made if desired. The little ones may be served with a tomato sauce over a pasta.

FINE MEAT LOAF FOR TEN OR TWELVE

2 pounds top round of beef, ground
1 thick slice yearling steer liver, ground
1 cup shredded raw potato
1 cup shredded raw carrot
¾ cup chopped onion
½ pound fresh mushrooms, sliced
Butter
2 egg yolks, beaten

1 teaspoon each thyme, basil, and marjoram
½ cup tomato sauce or catsup
1 teaspoon Worcestershire sauce
2 tablespoons sweet vermouth
1 tablespoon lemon juice
⅓ cup milk
½ teaspoon clove
2 egg whites, beaten
6 slices Canadian bacon or lean bacon

Mix the ground meats with the vegetables. Sauté the mushrooms in a little butter for 2 or 3 minutes. Add all the ingredients except the bacon to the meats, folding in the beaten egg whites last. Grease a large baking dish and line it with the bacon. Fill the dish with the mixture, set it in a pan of hot water, and bake at 300° for 2 hours. When it is done, empty it out onto a large chop plate. Brown the bacon and return it to the top of the meat. There will be some liquid, which may be made into sauce. It may be thickened with cornstarch, extended with a cup of sour cream, and flavored with prepared mustard. Heat and serve in a sauceboat. See Sauces in the index for other sauces appropriate to serve with meat loaf.

CORNED BEEF WITH VEGETABLES

Corned brisket of beef
4 cloves garlic, sliced
8 whole cloves
2 onions, finely sliced
1 teaspoon ground pepper
4 bay leaves

White onions
Carrots
White turnips
Potatoes
New cabbage
Garnish: *Mustard Sauce* or *Horseradish Sauce*

Soak the meat in cold water for 20 minutes, drain, and wipe dry. Make 1-inch incisions in the brisket and insert the slices of garlic. Stick with the cloves. Tie it with string and put it in a kettle of water to cover, with the sliced onions, pepper, and bay leaves. Cover and simmer slowly for 3½ to 5 hours so that it is very tender. You may wish to serve the brisket hot with vegetables to make a fine boiled dinner. Taste the broth and if it is too salty to cook the vegetables in, remove 1 cup of it, and add 3 cups of fresh water. Put all the vegetables in a large kettle and cook them together in the liquid. Put in the onions and carrots first, then the turnips and potatoes, and last the cabbage cut in sixths. When they are done, drain them. Put the meat on a large platter and surround it with the vegetables. This broth may also be used in soups and gravies.

BEEF STEW

3 pounds of beef, round, chuck,
    or brisket
3 tablespoons flour
1 teaspoon thyme
    Salt and pepper
3 tablespoons fat
2 tablespoons brown sugar
1 chopped onion

½ cup red wine
1 cup beef broth
½ cup vegetable juice (or more)
8 white onions
4 young carrots, cubed
1 cup small fresh mushrooms
¼ cup minced pickles

Cut the meat in 2-inch cubes. Put the flour, thyme, salt, and pepper in a bag and shake the meat in it so it is well covered. Heat the fat and brown sugar, brown the meat, add the chopped onion, and cook a minute longer. Add the wine, broth, and enough vegetable juice to just cover. Cover the pot and simmer gently for 1½ hours or until tender. After it has cooked almost an hour boil up the white onions and the carrots, drain and add to the meat. Sauté the mushrooms in a little butter and add them and the pickles 10 minutes before the stew is done. If the gravy isn't thick enough, remove ½ cup of liquid, thicken it with a little cornstarch, return it to the stew, and simmer uncovered 1 minute. This may be served with white or sweet potatoes, baked or mashed. Serves 6 to 8.

STEW OF COOKED MEAT WITH DUMPLINGS

    Leftover beef, lamb, or fowl
8 white onions
2 carrots, sliced
1 white turnip, sliced
2 parsnips, sliced
    Salt and pepper
2½ cups gravy, broth, and vege-
    table water
    Flour

Dumplings:
    2 cups flour
    ¾ teaspoon salt
    4 teaspoons baking powder
    2 teaspoons butter or lard
    ¾ cup milk
    1 tablespoon minced parsley
        or dill (optional)

This is a fine way to use leftover meat. Cut it in good-sized pieces or cubes. Cook the vegetables separately in very little water until almost done. Season them. Use the vegetable water and mix with any leftover gravy or broth to make 2½ cups of liquid. If it is thin, thicken it with a little flour to make it the consistency of light cream. Put the liquid, vegetables, and meat in a heavy pot and 12 minutes before you are ready to serve the stew, bring it to a simmer and drop the dumplings on top from a spoon, cover tight and simmer 12 minutes without lifting the lid. Serves 4 to 6, of course depending on how much meat is used. For the dumplings, sift the dry ingredients and cut in the fat with a fork. If an herb is used it may be stirred in with the milk. Use no more milk than is necessary to make a light soft dough.

BEEF KIDNEY STEW WITH RED WINE

3 beef yearling kidneys
3 tablespoons butter and oil,
   mixed
½ cup finely chopped onions
½ cup finely chopped green pepper
2 tablespoons flour
1 teaspoon thyme
   Salt and pepper

2 tablespoons tomato paste
½ cup beef consommé
½ cup red wine
8 white onions or ½ pound fresh
   mushrooms
Garnish:
   Mashed potatoes or boiled rice

Like yearling beef liver, yearling kidneys are very good. Soak them 10 minutes in salt water and remove all skin and membrane. Cut them in good-sized pieces. Mix 3 tablespoons of butter and oil and sauté the onions and green pepper 2 minutes. Put the flour, thyme, and a good sprinkle of salt and freshly ground pepper in a bag and shake the kidneys in it until well covered. Sauté them for 5 minutes with the onions and pepper. Remove the meat and vegetables to a casserole. Mix the tomato paste with the consommé, heat it in the skillet that the meat cooked in, and scrape it over the meat. Add the wine. Meanwhile boil the white onions for 5 minutes and drain. Put them with the meat, cover tightly, and bake 25 minutes in a 350° oven. If they cook too fast turn the heat down to 325°. If the sauce is too thin, blend a little flour or cornstarch with 3 tablespoons of either dry or sweet vermouth, and stir it into the stew. Cook until the liquid thickens to the consistency of heavy cream. This is good served over mashed potatoes or rice. If mushrooms are used instead of, or in addition to onions, sauté them in a little butter and add them to the stew 10 minutes before it is done. Try to get small ones and leave them whole. Serves 6.

BOILED BEEF WITH HORSERADISH SAUCE

4 pounds brisket, rump, or round
   of beef
   Juice of 1 lemon
2 onions, quartered
2 carrots, thickly sliced
2 white turnips, quartered

2 stalks celery and tops, chopped
2 bay leaves
6 cups beef stock
   Salt and pepper
Garnish: 10 white onions
   Horseradish Sauce

Put all the ingredients except the salt and pepper in a large pot. See that the meat is covered with stock. Canned beef consommé mixed with chicken consommé can be used. Bring to a simmer in a covered kettle and skim several times. Cook the meat very slowly for 3 hours or longer until tender. An hour before it is done, boil up the white onions, drain, and add to the meat. Put the meat on a hot platter surrounded by white onions. Serve the broth separately in soup plates or cups along with the meat. Choose one of the Horseradish sauces to serve with it. A fine summer dish is cold boiled beef;

the consommé jellies when it is refrigerated. Serve the sliced beef in a shallow soup dish garnished with the jelly, chopped parsley, and quartered lemons, and accompanied with horseradish. Serves 8.

BRAISED OXTAILS

2 oxtails, cut in 4-inch lengths
3 tablespoons flour
Salt and pepper
1 teaspoon marjoram
1 teaspoon basil
3 tablespoons fat or butter

1 large onion, chopped
⅓ cup chopped celery
1 cup Madeira or red wine
1 cup beef broth
10 white onions

Wash the oxtails, cut them in 4-inch lengths, and shake them in a bag with the flour, salt, pepper, and herbs. Sauté them with the chopped onions in a heavy pot in the fat or butter until nicely browned. Add the celery, wine, and broth. Cover tightly and cook 1 hour very slowly, over a low flame or in a 300° oven. Boil the white onions for 4 or 5 minutes, drain, and add to the oxtails and cook another hour, or until the onions are done. Lift out the oxtails and white onions. Strain the sauce through a sieve or put it through a blender. If it seems thin, add a little flour and cook it in a saucepan for a few minutes. You may add 2 or 3 tablespoons more wine. Reheat the oxtails and onions in the sauce and serve in a deep platter. Mashed potatoes, rice, or noodles may be served with it. Serves 4.

BRAISED SHORT RIBS OF BEEF

3½ to 4 pounds short ribs of beef,
   cut in 2½-inch lengths
1 cup chopped onions
½ cup chopped carrots
½ cup chopped celery
½ cup chopped green pepper
1 teaspoon each thyme and
   tarragon

Salt and pepper
2 tablespoons brown sugar
½ cup tomato catsup
1 cup beef consommé
½ cup red wine
1 tablespoon flour

Short ribs are very fat, so to keep the sauce from being too greasy, braise the short ribs at 325° 50 minutes in an open pan with no water. Remove from the oven and drain off all the fat. In a casserole, make a bed of the vegetables mixed with the herbs. Put the short ribs on top and sprinkle with salt and pepper. Mix the sugar, catsup, consommé, and wine together, boil up, and pour over the meat. Braise covered at 300° for 1 hour or until the meat is tender. Remove the meat. Sieve the sauce with the flour or put it in an electric blender. Cook in a saucepan until thickened. If it is too thick add a little broth. This sauce is excellent over mashed potatoes.

BRAISED VENISON OR RUMP ROAST OF BEEF

5½ pounds of meat
1 cup red wine
1 cup chopped onions
1 teaspoon thyme
2 tablespoons brown sugar

2 tablespoons fat
Salt and pepper
⅓ cup caramel
1 cup sour cream
Flour

Marinate the meat in the wine, onions, and thyme for 24 hours, turning every 5 or 6 hours. When ready to braise, remove the meat and wipe it with a paper towel. Reserve the marinade. Melt the fat and brown sugar in a Dutch oven or iron casserole, and sear the meat all over. Strain out ½ cup of the marinade and reserve. Add the rest of the marinade and the onions to the pot. Braise, covered for 1½ hours at 300°, turn the meat, salt and pepper it, and cook another 1 to 1½ hours or until it is tender. Remove the meat and keep it warm. Strain the sauce, add the strained marinade, and put it in a saucepan. Put the meat back in the roaster, cover with the caramel, and cook for 10 minutes, turning the meat in the caramel so that it is covered. Lift the meat onto a hot platter. Pour the sauce into the caramel and thicken with a little flour if necessary. Stir in the sour cream. Taste and add salt and pepper if necessary. Cover the meat with the sauce. Serve with baked potatoes. This recipe comes from a wonderful game cook in Banff, Alberta. Serves 8 or 10.

DEER OR VENISON STEAK

Steak, 1½-inch thick
Marinade:
    ¼ cup olive oil
    ¼ cup dry vermouth
    Salt and pepper
    1 teaspoon thyme
1 strip bacon

Sauce:
    1 teaspoon crushed juniper
      berries
    3 tablespoons gin
    3 tablespoons heavy cream

The steak of young deer is tender so that it is cooked only a few minutes. If you are using venison steak, put it in a receptacle that just fits so the marinade will keep it moist. Marinate it 3 or 4 hours outside the refrigerator, turning it several times. Before cooking, make a slit almost to the bone on both sides and slip ½ strip of bacon into each slit. This is instead of larding. Return the meat to the marinade. Preheat the oven to 400°, put the meat and the marinade in the oven and cook for 10 minutes, turn the meat, then turn off the heat; it will continue cooking for 5 more minutes. Put the juniper, gin, and cream in a small frying pan over high heat and let it reduce a little. Remove the meat to a hot platter, stir the sauce into the pan juices, and pour it over the meat. An 8- or 9-inch steak, 1½ inches thick, will serve 4. *Potatoes Baked with Bacon* are good with this; so is a bottle of very good red wine—Burgundy or Bordeaux.

HASH OF COOKED MEAT

2 cups ground or finely cubed meat, boiled or roast beef, or corned beef
1 cup sliced onions
1 small can kernel corn, or fresh corn
1 small green pepper, finely sliced

1 cup cubed boiled potatoes
Oil or butter
¼ cup tomato sauce or purée
½ teaspoon chili or curry powder
Salt and pepper
Garnish: Chopped parsley

One may stretch hash in several ways. One way is by adding all these vegetables, mixing them with the meat at the end, as cooked meat is not cooked again. Sauté the onions in oil or butter, add the corn, sauté the finely sliced green pepper and add, then toss together with the potatoes and meat. Mix the tomato sauce with the chili or curry powder, salt and pepper, and add to the hash. Heat well. Empty the hash into a hot serving dish and sprinkle the top with chopped parsley. This will serve 4 well. This hash may also be made with 1 pound of raw ground beef which is sautéed in a little oil or butter before it is combined with the other ingredients.

BRAISED CHUCK STEAK

3½ to 4 pounds thick chuck steak
1 large onion, sliced thin
1 young carrot, sliced
1½ cups red wine
1 teaspoon each basil and thyme
2 tablespoons brown sugar
3 tablespoons beef fat or bacon fat

2 cloves garlic, crushed
Salt and pepper
2 tablespoons flour
1 tablespoon tomato paste or chili sauce
¼ cup dry vermouth
Chopped parsley

A chuck steak 2 inches thick is best for this. Put it in a crock with the onion, carrot, red wine, and herbs to marinate overnight. When ready to cook, remove the meat and wipe it off, reserving the marinade. Melt the sugar and fat in a heavy skillet, and sear the meat on all sides. Lay it in a casserole, put the marinade in the skillet, heat up, and scrape over the meat. Add the crushed garlic, salt, and pepper. Cover very tightly and cook at 325° for ½ hour, then turn down to 300° for 1 hour. Turn the meat and cook for 1½ hours longer. Remove the meat from the casserole, put the sauce through a sieve or the blender with the flour and tomato paste or chili sauce. Let it thicken in a saucepan to the right consistency, adding the vermouth. Put a little of the sauce over the meat and keep it warm until ready to serve. Sprinkle the top of the meat with chopped parsley. Serve the rest of the sauce separately. White or sweet potatoes are good with this. They may be put in the oven an hour before the meat is done. This will serve 7 or 8.

HUNGARIAN GOULASH

2½ pounds round of beef
3 tablespoons butter
1½ cups onions, chopped
1 teaspoon caraway seeds or powder
2 cloves garlic, crushed
3 tablespoons sweet Hungarian paprika
Salt and pepper

2 tablespoons flour
1 cup tomato purée
⅔ cup claret or Burgundy
1 cup beef or chicken broth
1 cup heavy sour cream
Garnish:
    Boiled noodles or *Tarhonya* (egg barley)

Because goulash is a rich dish, lean beef, such as round, is preferable to the fat cuts, such as brisket or chuck; otherwise the sauce is too greasy. Cut the meat in 1-inch cubes and sauté it in the butter with the onions, caraway, and garlic for 5 minutes, then add the paprika and cook and stir it until it is all colored red. Sprinkle the meat with salt, pepper, and flour. Put it in a casserole. Rinse the sauté pan with the tomato purée, wine, and broth and scrape over the meat. Cover and cook at 300° for 1½ hours or until the meat is tender. The sauce should be about as thick as light cream. If necessary blend in a little cornstarch or flour. When ready to serve stir in the cream. Serves 6. Serve with 12 ounces of buttered noodles or *Tarhonya* which is egg barley.

To make Tarhonya, sauté ⅓ cup chopped onions until a little soft, then add 1½ cups of egg barley and stir it in the onions 2 minutes over a gentle flame. Season with salt and pepper and add 3 cups of boiling chicken or beef broth. Cover and cook over a very low flame 25 minutes. The broth will be absorbed and the barley will be fluffy. This is excellent with goulash and may be served with other meats and poultry instead of potatoes or rice. Serves 6.

GYPSY GOULASH

1½ to 2 pounds chuck
3 medium-sized onions, chopped
1 tablespoon sweet Hungarian paprika
1 teaspoon caraway seeds or powder
Salt and pepper

1 cup boiling broth or water
1 cup red wine
2 medium-sized potatoes, cubed
1 cup large egg noodle shells
¼ cup shredded green pepper
½ cup heavy sour cream

Cut the chuck in 1½-inch cubes. Chop the onions quite fine and stir them with the meat in a heavy pot, then stir in the paprika, caraway, salt and pepper. Cover tightly and simmer 1 hour. No liquid is added but the dish won't burn, as there will be some meat and onion juice soon after it begins to cook. After 1 hour add the boiling broth or water and the wine and cook covered 45 minutes or until the meat begins to be tender. Add the cubed potatoes; 15 minutes later add the noodle shells, and 10 minutes later add the green pepper. Cook 5 minutes more. This gives the potatoes 30 minutes cooking, and the noodles 15 minutes. Stir in the sour cream and empty into a large warmed serving dish. This will serve 4, if 2 pounds of meat are cooked.

BOILED FRESH TONGUE

1 large tongue	1 teaspoon thyme
2 cups tomato juice	1 teaspoon basil
2 cups V8	Salt and pepper
2 cups grapefruit juice	2 tablespoons prepared mustard
½ cup carrots, diced	¾ cup sour cream (optional)
½ cup onions, chopped	

Lightly pickled tongues are juicier and have a more delicate flavor and texture than smoked tongues, but either may be cooked this way. Wash the tongue, cover with water and put it on to cook very gently for 2 hours. Remove the tongue and skin it. Put it back in the kettle with the juices, vegetables, herbs, salt, and pepper. Let it simmer, almost covered with the lid, 2 more hours or until it is very tender. The liquid may be used for soup. The tongue may be served hot or cold. To make a mustard sauce, strain out ¾ cup of liquid and mix it with the mustard. This liquid may be added to sour cream. A large tongue serves 8.

CHILI BEEF

3½ to 4½ pounds brisket or chuck	1 teaspoon thyme or orégano
⅓ cup flour	¼ cup butter and oil, mixed
1 teaspoon cumin powder	1 large onion, chopped fine
3 tablespoons chili powder	4 cloves garlic, crushed
1 tablespoon curry powder	2 cups chicken or beef broth
1½ teaspoons salt	1 cup red wine
Freshly ground pepper	3 red pimentos

Have the meat cut in 2-inch cubes. Put the flour and all the dry ingredients in a bag and shake the meat in it until it is well coated. Sauté each piece in the butter and oil so that it is browned on all sides. Remove the pieces to a casserole as they are browned. Chop the onion very fine and add it and the crushed garlic to the broth. Put it in the sauté pan, let it boil up, and scrape it over the meat. Add the wine. Cover tightly and bake very slowly at 300° for 3 hours. If it seems to be cooking too fast, turn the oven lower. This may be made the day before serving, as the longer it stands the better. Reheat to serve. When ready to serve cut the canned pimentos in strips and put them over the top. If you like chili hot, a little more powder may be added. Serve with *Mexican Beans* or kidney beans. Three and a half pounds will serve 8.

BARRY'S POT ROAST

4 pounds rump, chuck, or brisket
    of beef
3 tablespoons butter or good fat
1 tablespoon brown sugar
1 cup finely chopped onion
½ cup finely chopped carrot
1 cup beef stock
1 cup milk
2 tablespoons anchovy paste
1 teaspoon thyme

3 anchovy fillets, sliced
½ teaspoon mace or allspice
½ teaspoon freshly ground pepper
1 teaspoon salt
2 whole cloves
3 tablespoons vinegar
3 tablespoons whisky
2 tablespoons simple syrup
2 or 3 tablespoons flour

Tie the meat in shape. Put the butter or fat in a Dutch oven or iron casserole with the sugar and brown the meat on all sides over a medium flame. Add the onion and carrot and cook a minute more. Put the stock and milk in a saucepan and heat it. Add all the rest of the ingredients except the flour to the hot liquid and pour it over the meat. The anchovy, milk, and whisky do something very special to the flavor of this dish. Put the meat, covered tightly, in a 300° oven and cook for 3 hours. Turn the meat once or twice during the cooking. When the meat is tender, remove it from the casserole, put it on a hot platter, and keep it warm. Strain the sauce through a sieve and blend in 2 tablespoons of flour. Cook until it thickens. Blend in more flour if it needs it. It should be the consistency of heavy cream. Put a little sauce over the meat and serve the rest in a sauceboat. Potato pancakes are the traditional dish with this. Serves 8.

Veal

FILET DE VEAU À LA MOUTARDE
Hôtel du Chapeau Rouge, Dijon

There are many beautiful things to see in Dijon and time should be allowed to see them. Francis I thought so, for in 1515, riding through upper Burgundy toward Italy and the battle of Marignan, he stopped before Dijon on the vast plain extending to the Jura and exclaimed, "What a beautiful city—a city of a hundred steeples." In Roman times its name was Divio and the city was quite prosperous in the second century A.D. A barbarian invasion about 272 ruined the city and it was rebuilt within fortifications which now form the heart of the city. The Abbey of St. Bénigne, named for the martyr, was founded in the sixth century and its church is one to see. The rule of the great dukes of Burgundy began in the eleventh century. Philippe le Hardi (bold), Jean Sans Peur (fearless), Philippe le Bon (good), and Charles le Téméraire (reckless) all ruled over a great deal of eastern France and the lands which now are Belgium, Luxembourg, and Holland. These dukes were patrons of the arts and were responsible for enriching their capital city, Dijon, with its treasures of architecture. The 156-foot tower of Philippe le Bon still dominates the city. Every wine lover knows that Burgundy produces the world's greatest red wine. Sumptuous receptions of the Brotherhood of the Chevaliers du Tastevin take place in Dijon and every year the Gastronomic Fair occurs the first two weeks in November. Among Dijon's gastronomic specialties are gingerbread, black currant liqueur (cassis), and mustard—the last being one of the important ingredients of this fine veal dish.

4½ pound fillet of veal
Sliced bacon
Veal or chicken broth
Purée soubise moutarde:
  ½ pound onions, thinly sliced
  2 tablespoons butter
  2 tablespoons flour
  Salt and pepper
  1 cup light cream, or half
    cream, half broth
  Salt and pepper
  2 tablespoons flour
  ¼ teaspoon nutmeg
  2 tablespoons strong Dijon
    mustard

Mornay sauce:
  1 cup light cream
  1 tablespoon flour
  Salt and pepper
  3 tablespoons grated Gruyère
    cheese
  3 tablespoons Parmesan cheese

Tie strips of bacon over a fillet of veal and roast it 1¾ hours at 300°, basting with a little broth, perhaps ½ cup. Meanwhile make the sauces. Put the very thinly sliced onions in a heavy pot with the butter, cover, and cook to a mush over a slow fire. Stir in the flour. Mash the onions through a sieve and add salt and pepper. Mix the cream (or half cream and half veal or chicken broth) with the salt, pepper, flour, and nutmeg and when it is smooth, cook until it thickens, then add the mustard. Mix this with the onion purée. Cook over gently simmering water, uncovered, for 30 minutes. To make the Mornay sauce, mix the cream and flour until smooth, heat, and stir in a few grains of salt and pepper and the cheeses. Cook until it thickens. When the veal is done, slice it not quite through in ½-inch thick slices. Spread the soubise mustard sauce between the slices and reshape it. Mask the entire roast with this sauce. Cover the top with the Mornay sauce and glaze quickly in a 450° oven. Lift to a hot platter and serve immediately. Serves 8. String beans would be a good accompaniment.

ROAST VEAL WITH ROSEMARY

4 pounds boned fillet of veal
Marinade:
    4 cloves garlic, crushed
    2 teaspoons rosemary
    ¾ cup dry white wine or
        dry vermouth
4 strips bacon
2 tablespoons butter

¾ cup chopped onions
½ cup chopped carrots
1 tablespoon tomato paste
1 teaspoon rosemary
Salt and pepper
1 tablespoon cornstarch
3 tablespoons wine
Chopped parsley

Do not have the meat tied. Marinate it in the garlic, rosemary, and wine for 24 hours, turning it occasionally. When ready to cook the veal, remove it from the marinade, wipe, and tie it into shape. Strain the marinade and reserve the liquid. Put the strips of bacon and butter in the bottom of the roasting pan and brown over a medium flame, then make a bed of the vegetables on the bacon. Lay the meat on the vegetables. Mix the tomato paste with the liquid, add the rosemary, salt, and pepper. Pour it over the meat, cover and roast it 30 minutes at 350°, turn down the heat to 300° and roast 1 hour more. Remove the meat, strain the pan juices, and add the cornstarch blended with the wine. Cook until it thickens. Put the meat on a hot platter, spread the top with a little of the sauce, and sprinkle with chopped parsley. Serve the rest of the sauce in a sauceboat. Serves 6.

CAVIAR SAUCE FOR SLICED ROAST VEAL

¾ cup veal broth or liquid from
    roast
¼ cup dry vermouth
1 tablespoon cornstarch

1 teaspoon lemon juice
1 tablespoon butter
4 to 6 tablespoons red or black
    caviar

This sauce may be added to hot or cold roast sliced veal (preferably a fillet). Put the broth in a saucepan, blend the vermouth with the cornstarch, and add. Cook until it thickens. Add the lemon juice, and salt and pepper if it needs more seasoning. Skimp the salt because the caviar may be salty. Add the butter and lightly add the caviar last, trying not to break the eggs. Cover the sliced meat with the sauce or serve it in a sauceboat.

ROAST VEAL WITH CHEESE AND PORT

4 or 5 pounds rump or boned leg
    of veal
½ cup chopped onions
1 cup port wine
⅓ to ½ pound Gruyère or
    Cheddar cheese
Salt and pepper

1 teaspoon basil
½ teaspoon rosemary
2 tablespoons port
2 tablespoons cornstarch
⅓ cup heavy cream
Chopped parsley

The meat should not be tied. Put it into a large bowl with the onions and wine and let it marinate overnight. When ready to roast the meat lay it open and cut any muscles which prevent its lying out rather flat. Reserve the marinade. Cut the cheese in slices and cover the meat, roll it, tucking in the ends, and tie it securely into a loaf shape. Add salt and pepper to the marinade, put it in a roasting pan, lay the meat on it, and roast at 300° for 1¾ hours. Remove the meat and sieve the sauce or purée it in a blender. Put the meat back in the roaster and roast it 10 more minutes. Put the sauce in a saucepan, mix the port with the cornstarch, and stir it in. Cook until it thickens, then add the cream. Pour the sauce over the meat and when ready to serve, put the meat on a hot platter, mask with a little sauce and sprinkle the top with chopped parsley. Serve the rest of the sauce in a sauceboat. Serves 8. Serve with a fine white Burgundy. Mashed potatoes with chopped green onions may accompany this.

OSSO BUCO

Calf's shinbones and knuckle
bones, with meat and marrow
½ cup chopped onions
⅓ cup chopped carrots
⅓ cup chopped celery
Butter and olive oil
Salt and pepper
Flour
½ teaspoon rosemary
½ teaspoon sage
1 teaspoon thyme

2 tablespoons tomato paste
1 clove garlic, crushed
1 tablespoon anchovy paste
1 cup chicken or veal broth
1¼ cups dry white wine or dry
vermouth
Gremolata:
⅓ cup chopped parsley
2 cloves garlic, crushed
Grated rind of 1 lemon

Have the butcher saw the bones 2½ to 3 inches long so that there is marrow in each bone and meat enough on each to serve 1 to a person. This sauce is enough for 7 or 8 bones. Sauté the onions, carrots, and celery in butter and olive oil so they are colored a little. Make a bed of them in a casserole. Put salt, pepper, and several tablespoons of flour in a bag and shake the veal bones in it until they are lightly covered. Brown them in more butter and oil and lay them on the vegetables. Put the herbs, tomato paste, crushed garlic, and anchovy paste in the chicken or veal broth and when well mixed add the wine. Heat in the pan the vegetables and meat browned in and pour over the meat. Cover tightly and cook at 300° 1½ hours. Lift the meat and bones carefully onto a platter so as not to disturb the marrow. Sieve the sauce, return the meat to the casserole, and pour the sauce over it. To serve, reheat, mix the ingredients of the gremolata, and spread it over the meat. Serve with noodles or a risotto.

JARRETS DE VEAU À L'ORANGE
Capucin Gourmand, Nancy

6 to 8 shins of veal
Salt, pepper, and flour
Oil and butter
1 tablespoon sugar
1 tablespoon vinegar
1 cup white wine
2 carrots, minced
1 onion, minced

4 shallots or green onions, minced
4 cloves garlic, crushed
Julienne rind of 3 or 4 oranges
1 teaspoon tomato paste
8 orange slices
Accompaniment:
    Nouilles aux Pommes Gratinées

Have the butcher saw veal shins (meat and bone) into lengths of ½ pound each. Allow one for each serving. Roll them in seasoned flour and sauté until golden in a mixture of oil and butter. Remove from the sauté pan and put them in a large casserole. Put the sugar in the sauté pan and let it caramelize a moment over a gentle flame, then add the vinegar, wine, carrots, onion, shallots, garlic, orange rind (the yellow skin cut in julienne sticks, previously blanched in water and drained), and tomato paste. Scrape this mixture of vegetables and wine over the meat, cover and cook gently 1½ hours. Remove the pith from the oranges and add 8 generous slices to the top of the meat 10 minutes before it is done. Accompany with *Nouilles aux Pommes Gratinées* (recipe follows).

NOUILLES AUX POMMES GRATINÉES

4 potatoes, finely diced
8 tablespoons butter
2 tablespoons oil

Salt and freshly ground pepper
6 ounces egg noodles
⅓ cup buttered crumbs

Sauté the potatoes in 4 tablespoons of the butter and the oil until tender. Salt and pepper them. Boil the noodles in salted water until tender, drain, and mix them with the rest of the butter. Grease a baking dish, put half the potatoes in the bottom of the dish, cover with half the noodles, then add the rest of the potatoes and cover with the rest of the noodles. Sprinkle the crumbs over the top and bake 20 minutes at 350°. This may be prepared ahead of time and baked before serving.

ITALIAN ROAST VEAL

5 to 6½ pounds boned fillet, rump,
    or leg of veal
5 large cloves garlic, crushed
Anchovy paste or fillets
1 cup dry vermouth or dry white
    wine

2 tablespoons cornstarch
1 cup light cream
Salt and pepper
3 tablespoons capers

Italian butchers seem to know all about the cuts of veal for boning and roasting. The boned fillet is not as expensive as the leg but it is very good. Spread out the meat and generously spread with the crushed garlic and plenty of anchovy paste or fillets. Roll it, reshape, and tie securely. Marinate the meat 24 hours in the wine, turning it occasionally. Roast it in the marinade, covered, at 300°, 1¾ hours for 5 pounds and 2 hours for 6½ pounds. If it is roasting too fast, turn the heat lower. Measure the pan juices and use 1 cup for the sauce. Reserve the rest for future sauces. Blend the cornstarch with the cream in a saucepan, add the cup of pan juice, and cook until it thickens. Taste before adding salt. Add pepper and the capers. Put the meat on a hot platter, remove the string and spread with a little sauce and serve the rest in a sauceboat. Five pounds serves 6 or 8. This veal, sliced, served hot or cold, is excellent for *Vitello Tonnato*. The pan juices and the leftover gravy may go into making a fine curry.

VITELLO TONNATO

Sliced cold roast veal
Tuna sauce:
    1 cup broth drained from roast
    1 small can of tuna fish
    2 tablespoons lemon juice
    Light cream or milk

Garnish: 3 tablespoons capers

A good time to make this popular North Italian summer dish is a day or two after having *Roast Veal* (larded boned rump or fillet marinated in wine). A cup of broth may be drained off from the roast; this jellies and is excellent for making this sauce. Mix it with the flaked tuna fish, lemon juice, and enough milk or cream to make the sauce the consistency of heavy cream. Mix it in an electric blender or mash it through a sieve. Slice the veal and arrange it on a platter, cover with the sauce, and sprinkle the capers over the top.

VEAL CUTLETS PAPPAGALLO
Pappagallo, Bologna

Cutlets, pounded flat
Beaten egg
Fine crumbs
Butter

Sour cream
Tomato sauce
Grated Parmesan or Gruyère
    cheese

Prepare 1 cutlet per person. Pound them flat, dip them in beaten egg, then in crumbs, and fry in butter until done. Mix 2 tablespoons of sour cream and 2 tablespoons of tomato sauce for each cutlet and spread over the top of the cutlets. Sprinkle with plenty of cheese, then run them under the flame until the cheese melts. Serve immediately.

BLANQUETTE DE VEAU

3 to 4 pounds boned breast or
    shoulder of veal
3 tablespoons butter
1 tablespoon oil
⅔ cup chopped onions
¼ cup flour, plus 2 tablespoons
    Salt and pepper
1 teaspoon rosemary
1 teaspoon thyme
1⅓ cups good broth, beef, veal,
    or chicken

¾ cup dry vermouth (or more)
1 celery root, minced
2 small carrots, minced
1 stalk celery, minced
1 parsnip, minced
1 tablespoon syrup
12 or 14 white onions
2 carrots, cut lengthwise
½ cup heavy cream
    Chopped parsley

This elegant stew makes a fine party dish. Have the meat cut in 2-inch cubes. Put the butter and oil in a heavy stewing pot and add the onions. Sauté very gently while you shake the cubes of meat in a bag containing the flour, salt, pepper, rosemary, and thyme. Put the meat into the pot with the onions and stir it around in the onions until well covered and browned a little. Heat the broth and add it, the vermouth, the minced vegetables, and the syrup. Cover and simmer on the gentlest flame so that it just faintly bubbles for 30 minutes. Boil up and drain the whole white onions and the carrots, cut in inch lengths, and lay them on top of the stew. Let simmer 1 to 1½ hours longer, until the meat is tender and the vegetables are done. Drain out the meat, onions, and carrots. Put the sauce through a sieve; or, better, purée it in a blender with 2 tablespoons flour. Return the sauce to the pot and cook until it thickens. If it is too thick add a little more vermouth. Then return the vegetables and meat to the sauce and cover the top with the heavy cream. Leave uncovered on the back of the stove until ready to reheat and serve. If it can ripen for several hours, the flavor will be improved. Empty into a deep platter and sprinkle the top with chopped parsley. Serves 6 to 8.

VEAL MARENGO

3 pounds boned breast or shoulder
    of veal
2 teaspoons basil
1 teaspoon thyme
    Salt and pepper
3 tablespoons flour
2 or 3 tablespoons butter
2 or 3 tablespoons oil
1 cup finely chopped onions

1 cup veal or chicken broth
1 cup dry vermouth
½ cup tomato juice or purée
4 tablespoons orange juice
1 tablespoon grated orange rind
2 cloves garlic, crushed
½ pound small fresh mushrooms
3 soft poached eggs (optional)
3 tablespoons chopped parsley

Cut the veal in 2-inch cubes and toss the pieces in a bag containing the herbs, seasonings, and flour. Put the butter and oil in a heavy skillet and sauté the onions about 3 minutes, then add the veal. Sauté the meat, part of it at a time, until it has colored a little. Put it in a casserole with the heated broth, vermouth, tomato juice or purée, orange juice and rind, and the garlic. Almost cover and simmer 1½ to 2 hours. I specify whole mushrooms because the dish looks better, but sliced large mushrooms may be used. Sauté them in a little butter for 5 minutes. When the meat is tender, remove it from the casserole, and sieve the sauce. If it is thinner than heavy cream, add a little flour or cornstarch. Replace the meat and sauce and add the mushrooms. Before serving, reheat. The traditional Marengo calls for soft fried eggs. You may either fry or poach them very soft, place them on top of the stew, and sprinkle with the parsley. When the stew is served the eggs break and mix with the sauce. Serve with noodles or mashed potatoes or steaming rice. Serves 6.

VEAL STEW WITH DUMPLINGS

2½ pounds boned breast or
    shoulder of veal
¼ cup flour
    Salt and pepper
¼ teaspoon nutmeg
1 teaspoon rosemary or basil
2 tablespoons butter
2 tablespoons oil
⅓ cup finely chopped celery
⅔ cup finely chopped onions
⅓ cup finely chopped carrots
1 tablespoon tomato paste
1 cup dry white wine or dry
    vermouth
1 cup broth, chicken or veal

Cornmeal Dumplings:
¾ cup cornmeal
1 cup flour
4 teaspoons baking powder
1 teaspoon salt
1 tablespoon chopped onions,
    or 1 tablespoon chopped
    parsley, or 3 tablespoons
    chopped fresh dill
3 tablespoons sour cream
1 beaten egg
    Buttermilk

The meat is cut in 2-inch cubes and shaken in a bag with the flour, salt, pepper, nutmeg, and herbs. Put the butter and oil in the bottom of a heavy pot and when it is bubbling add the chopped vegetables, then the meat, let cook for 10 minutes, stirring it well. Do not let the vegetables burn. Make the tomato paste smooth with the wine and broth, heat, and add it to the meat and vegetables. Cover tightly and let simmer for 1½ hours or until the meat is tender. Make the dumplings by sifting the dry ingredients, lightly tossing in the onions or parsley or dill. Beat the sour cream and egg together and add to the flour mixture. Add just enough buttermilk to make a soft dough that may be dropped from a spoon. Put these on top of the stew, cover tightly, and gently boil for 12 to 15 minutes; do not remove the cover for 12 minutes. Lift out the dumplings and put them on the edge of a big platter; put the stew in the center. Chopped parsley may be added to the top of the meat and vegetables. Serves 4.

VEAL AND LIVER MEATBALLS AND SAUCE

1 pound veal, ground
½ pound calf's liver or yearling
   liver, ground
4 strips bacon, ground
2 onions, ground
2 tablespoons carrots, ground
   Salt and pepper
1 tablespoon basil
1 egg, beaten

Butter and oil
Sauce:
   2 tablespoons chopped olives
   ¾ cup tomato sauce
   1 tablespoon mustard
   2 cups sour cream
12 ounces egg noodles
   Parmesan cheese

Mix all the ingredients for the meatballs together. Roll into balls the size of a marble and brown them all over in hot oil and butter. Mix the ingredients for the sauce and heat it. Boil the noodles in salt water until tender, drain, and empty onto a large platter. Put the meatballs in the sauce, bring to the boil, and pour over the noodles. Sprinkle the top with Parmesan cheese and pass more with the dish. Serves 8.

BREAST OF VEAL WITH MUSHROOMS AND CREAM

4 pounds boned breast of veal, in
   one piece
Broth:
   3 or 4 cups cubed vegetables:
      white turnip, carrot,
      parsnip, celery, and leeks
   3 sprigs parsley
   1 large onion, sliced
   3 bay leaves
   1 teaspoon rosemary
   Salt and pepper
   Veal bones
   5 cups water
   2 teaspoons powdered chicken
      concentrate

½ cup minced leeks
1 teaspoon turmeric
3 tablespoons cornstarch
1 cup heavy cream
½ to 1 pound fresh small white
   mushrooms
Chopped parsley

A whole veal breast weighs 8 or 9 pounds. Have the butcher cut about half of the heavier part, bone it, and give you the meat and bones. To make the task of preparing this lovely dish easier, get the vegetables for the broth ready the day before serving and store them, covered, in the refrigerator. Begin the broth well before serving so the meat may stand in the sauce 1 hour or more. Put all the vegetables, seasonings, veal bones, and water in a kettle, almost cover, and let it simmer gently a good hour. Remove and discard the bones and put in the veal and the chicken concentrate, almost cover, and simmer the veal 1½ hours, turning it once after 45 minutes. Remove the meat and strain the broth, pressing the vegetables against the sieve a little. Put the meat back in the kettle with 2¼ cups of the strained broth and the minced leeks. Simmer very gently ½ hour, turning the meat after 15 minutes. Mix the turmeric and cornstarch with the cream, and when the meat is done, remove it and stir the cream into the broth. Cook until it thickens, then add the mushrooms. Return the meat to the sauce and let it stand at room temperature, uncovered, until just before serving. Bring it to a slow simmer for 5 minutes to cook the mushrooms. Lift the veal onto a hot platter and pour the sauce and mushrooms over and around it. Sprinkle with a little chopped parsley. Serves 8 generously. This is good served with a risotto or an Indian rice. A Rhine or Moselle wine would be fine with this.

VARIATION. ½ cup of dry vermouth may be part of the 2¼ cups of strained broth, thus giving the sauce a more piquant flavor.

STUFFED BREAST OF VEAL OR SHOULDER OF LAMB

4 pounds boned breast of veal, or
   3½ to 4 pounds boned shoulder
   of lamb
Stuffing:
   2½ ounces ground lean pork
   2½ ounces ground veal
   4 ounces chicken livers or
      pork liver, ground
   ⅓ cup fresh breadcrumbs
   Salt and pepper
   ½ teaspoon basil or rosemary
   ¼ cup Marsala or Madeira
   1 sliced truffle or 4 diced
      mushrooms (optional)
Butter and oil for basting

Sauce:
   1 cup veal or chicken broth
   1 tablespoon cornstarch
   1 tablespoon lemon juice

Have the chosen meat boned; it will flatten out nicely for stuffing. If veal is used trim it to make a better rectangle. Grind the trimmings and add them to the stuffing. Mix all the ingredients for the stuffing and spread it on the meat within an inch of the edges. Roll and tie neatly. Put the meat in a roasting dish and spread it with the butter and oil, 3 or 4 tablespoons of each. Cover and roast at 300° for 1½ to 2 hours, turning the meat several times. It ought to be tender in 1½ hours. Small peeled potatoes may be added to the meat after it has been in the oven ½ hour. When the meat is done lift it onto a large hot platter, remove the strings, and surround it with the potatoes. Blend the cornstarch with the broth, add the lemon juice, and stir it into the roasting pan. Boil up until it thickens and scrape it over the meat. Makes 8 or 10 slices. Serves 6 or 8. Creamed onions are a good accompaniment.

VEAL SCALOPPINE PASSETTO
Passetto's, Rome

Signore Eleuterio Guerini, the director of Passetto's, has one of the loveliest restaurants in Rome. It is near the Tiber, almost across from St. Peter's, near the Piazza Navona and 30 paces from the Napoleonic Museum on via Zanardelli. Best of all the outdoor summer dining terrace is in the rear of the restaurant, opposite a church and pin-drop quiet. This is a boon in any busy Italian city. Signore Tonino Di Giammarco, the host, is helpful in suggesting your menu and generously gave me some Passetto specialties. The carefully trained staff makes the service unsurpassed anywhere; this attention is a compliment to every diner.

Veal scallops	Parmesan cheese
Prosciutto	Butter
Mozzarella or Bel Paese	Garnish: Fresh peas or asparagus

A good-sized piece of veal, cut from the leg, is pounded very thin. On half of it lay a piece of prosciutto and on that a slice of a good melting cheese (Bel Paese is good if you can't get Mozzarella). Fold the other half of the scallop over to encase the stuffing. Dip both sides in Parmesan cheese and sauté in butter to a golden brown on both sides. If the veal is thin, this takes 3½ to 4 minutes on each side, no longer. No salt on this. Unless they are very small, one of these scallops makes a serving.

VITELLO CASTELLANA
Hotel Della Rocca, Bazzano

The road passing Bazzano is a short cut for travelers from Rome to Milan, avoiding Bologna. I suspect many plan their time so they may stop at this charming eighteenth-century inn where the food is superb and the cave well stocked with good wines. You may dine out-of-doors or in an indoor dining room with the charm of an old manor house.

Cutlets from a leg of veal	Prosciutto
Beaten egg	Parmesan cheese
Fine crumbs	Gruyère or Emmenthaler cheese
Butter	Broth
Fresh mushrooms	Garnish: French-fried zucchini
No salt	

Pound the veal a little. This veal is not paper-thin but about ⅓-inch thick. Dip each slice in beaten egg, then in fine crumbs. Sauté the cutlets in butter about 2 minutes on each side and remove from pan. Add a little more butter and 3 sliced mushrooms for each cutlet. Cook 3 minutes slowly. Cover each cutlet with a slice of prosciutto to fit, then sprinkle lightly with Parmesan cheese. Lay on a slice of Gruyère or Emmenthaler, then sprinkle again with Parmesan. Put the cutlets back in the pan with the mushrooms. Add a few drops of broth, cover, and sauté over a good flame until the cheese melts. Serve on hot plates, garnished with the mushrooms and sauce. This is accompanied with zucchini cut in julienne sticks and deep-fried at 375° a few seconds. This vegetable is so tender when raw that it takes but little time to cook. Serve 1 cutlet per person.

POJARSKY AUX POMMES AMANDINES
Capucin Gourmand, Nancy

¾ pound veal
⅓ cup softened butter
1 cup fresh grated breadcrumbs
Milk
Salt and pepper

Sauce:
  1 tablespoon minced onion
  3 tablespoons Madeira
  ½ cup heavy cream
  1 tablespoon tomato paste
  Salt and pepper
Garnish: *Pommes Amandines*

These cutlets were named after the famous Russian chef Pojarsky and have become a specialty of Georges Romain. Make the *Pommes Armandines* in advance (recipe follows). Grind the veal very fine and mix it with the softened butter. Soak the breadcrumbs in milk a few minutes then squeeze out the crumbs and discard the milk. Mix the veal with the crumbs, salt, and pepper. Form into small cutlets, flattening them a little with the hand. Dip both sides of the cutlets in a little flour and sauté in butter and oil. Remove them from the pan and keep them warm. Put the ingredients for the sauce in a saucepan. Heap the cutlets in the center of a hot platter, boil up the sauce, and pour it over them. Put *Pommes Amandines* around the cutlets. Serve 4.

POMMES AMANDINES

1 pound potatoes
3 egg yolks

Anglaise:
  2 eggs
  2 tablespoons water
  2 tablespoons oil
  ¼ teaspoon salt
Finely chopped almonds

Peel the potatoes and boil them in salted water until tender. Drain them, put them through a sieve, and mix with the egg yolks to a smooth paste. Roll the paste on a floured board, cut in pieces, and roll between the palms of your hands into balls the size of a walnut. Make an anglaise, so called, by beating the eggs with the water, oil, and salt. Dip the potato balls in this, then in the finely chopped almonds. Toss the balls in butter over a gentle flame until a light golden color. Serves 4.

VEAL CUTLET ALLA CANEPA
The Canepa, Rome

Cutlets, pounded flat
Sage
Salt and pepper
Flour
Prosciutto

Beaten egg
Butter
White wine
Large mushroom caps, sautéed

Allow 1 cutlet to a person. Pound the cutlets flat. Mix sage, a little salt, and freshly ground pepper with the flour. Add a piece of prosciutto to each cutlet, dip them in beaten egg, then in the seasoned flour, and sauté in butter until the meat is tender. Put the cutlets on warm plates, put a jigger or so of wine in the pan, boil up, and scrape over the cutlets. Sauté 1 or 2 mushroom caps for each cutlet, and put them on top.

SCALOPPINE SAN GIORGIO
Danieli, Venice

6 thick slices of veal
6 slices Gruyère cheese
6 slices prosciutto
  Butter
1 wine glass of Marsala

1 teaspoon meat glaze
Accompaniments:
  Tiny potato balls cooked in
  butter
Puréed spinach

Have the veal cut thick enough so that the slices may be cut almost through like the pages of a book. Pound them to break some of the fibers. Stuff each with a slice of cheese and a slice of prosciutto to fit. Cook them in butter on both sides over a medium fire until they are done. Put on warm plates, boil up wine and meat glaze in pan, and scrape over the scaloppines.

ESCALOPE DE VEAU À LA CREME
Le Café Procope, Paris

4 veal scallops
¼ cup butter
¼ cup minced shallots or green
  onions

Salt and freshly ground pepper
⅓ cup white wine
⅓ cup sliced mushrooms
⅓ cup heavy cream

Pound the scallops quite thin. Melt the butter in a sauté pan and cook them 1 minute on each side, then add the shallots or green onions, salt and pepper, and cook 2 minutes more on each side. Remove to a hot platter and keep them warm. Add the wine and reduce a little over a good flame, then add the mushrooms and cook a minute, then add the cream. When the sauce is hot pour it over the scallops. Serves 4.

PICCATA ALLA PIZZAIOLA
Taverna La Fenice, Venice

The best restaurant in Venice is just behind the Teatro Fenice, the most enchanting theater in the world. The ceiling decoration of angels floating on pink and blue clouds around circles of tiny ceiling lights is like tinkling laughter. The auditorium has five wedding-cake balconies. Altogether, the theater alone is worth a trip to Venice. Getting back to the restaurant, it is a perfect place to dine before a performance of *La Bohème* or *La Traviata*; you can sip your last drop of espresso at curtain time and still make it. My old friend Alfredo Zoppi gave me several of his specialties. See his green *Pesto Sauce for Noodles*, a perfect choice to precede this piccata.

1¼ pounds veal
Flour, salt, and pepper
¼ cup olive oil
1 pimento, sliced thin
¼ cup diced mushrooms (in oil)
8 capers
3 cloves garlic, crushed

4 skinned, halved, plum tomatoes
¼ cup butter
¼ cup dry white wine or dry vermouth
8 small, pitted, halved, green or black olives
Chopped parsley

Piccata means pieces of veal 2 inches square, cut from the leg and pounded paper-thin. It is tender and must be cooked very quickly. Prepare the vegetables for the sauce first as they must be ready; and have the olives prepared and the parsley chopped. Sprinkle the veal very lightly with a little flour, salt, and pepper. Brown the veal in very hot olive oil but 2 or 3 seconds. Remove the veal and put the vegetables in the sauté pan, and cook slowly. In another pan put the butter and wine and over high heat quickly glaze the meat in it. Add the olives to the cooked vegetables and when the sauce is very hot add the meat and parsley. Divide on 4 hot plates and serve immediately. If everything is prepared in advance, this dish takes very little time to do.

VEAL WITH HAM AND MOZZARELLA

4 to 6 slices leg or fillet of veal
4 to 6 slices thin ham or prosciutto
4 to 6 slices Mozzarella
2 eggs, beaten

⅔ cup fine crumbs
⅓ cup Parmesan cheese
Chopped parsley
Olive oil and butter

Pound the veal slices very flat. On one half of each put a slice of ham and a slice of Mozzarella, fold over, and fasten with a toothpick. Dip the meat in beaten egg, then in crumbs mixed with the cheese and a little chopped parsley. Brown the meat on both sides in a mixture of oil and butter about 5 minutes, then cover and steam 2 minutes. Serve immediately, 1 to a person.

VEAL WITH SOUR CREAM AND MUSHROOMS

1½ to 2 pounds veal scaloppine
  Butter
½ cup finely sliced onions
½ cup finely sliced mushrooms
  Salt and pepper
¼ cup dry white wine or dry
  vermouth

1 tablespoon flour
¼ cup veal or chicken consomme
1 cup sour cream
Garnish:
  Buttered noodles and
    Parmesan cheese

Have the meat sliced from the leg and pound it very flat. Cut each slice in ¾-inch-wide strips. Toss the meat 4 or 5 minutes in butter until it is tender. Remove it from the pan. Put 3 tablespoons of butter in the sauté pan and sauté the onions gently until they begin to soften, then add the mushrooms and cook 3 minutes. Sprinkle with salt and pepper. Return the meat to the pan, add the wine, and cook 1 minute. Blend the flour with the broth and stir it in. When it begins to thicken, stir in the cream and when hot serve immediately. Serves 6. Noodles are good accompaniments.

ROSE'S SCALOPPINES

4 to 6 slices from fillet of veal
  Celery leaves
4 to 6 slices prosciutto

Juice of 1 lemon
¼ cup olive oil

Flatten the veal, allowing 1 slice for each serving. Put 2 celery leaves and a slice of prosciutto on each slice, roll, and fasten with toothpicks. Beat the lemon juice and oil together and marinate the veal rolls in the mixture for 1 hour before cooking. Brown the rolls quickly in the marinade.

WIENER SCHNITZEL

2 pounds veal fillet, leg, or rump,
  sliced
Lemon juice
Salt and pepper
Flour
Beaten egg

Crumbs
⅓ cup butter
⅓ cup oil
Garnish:
  Fried egg or lemon slices or
    anchovy fillets

Pound the slices of veal to a scant ½-inch thickness and rub them with a little lemon juice. Sprinkle a little salt and pepper on them, dip in flour, then in beaten egg, and then in fine crumbs. Pat the breading in well. Melt the butter and oil in a large sauté pan and when it is hot brown the veal 2 minutes on each side. Then turn down the heat and let cook about 4 more minutes, until the slices are just cooked through and tender. Each cutlet may be topped with a fried egg or garnished with lemon slices or 2 anchovy fillets. Serves 6.

VEAL CUTLETS WITH CHEESE AND HAM SAUCE

4 cutlets, ¾-inch thick
Butter
4 large mushroom caps
Salt and pepper

Sauce:
⅓ cup heavy cream, scalded
2 egg yolks
⅓ cup cubed Bel Paese or
  Gruyère
⅓ cup cubed ham
2 tablespoons sweet vermouth
Parmesan cheese

Brown the cutlets on both sides in butter. Put them in a baking pan with a mushroom cap on top of each, add a little salt and pepper, and bake in a 375° oven for 15 minutes. Scald the cream and put it in the top of the double boiler; stir in the egg yolks, cheese, and ham. When it thickens a little stir in the vermouth. When the meat is done, remove the mushroom caps, spread the sauce on the chops, cover with a sprinkle of Parmesan cheese, and run the pan under the flame until the sauce browns on top. Return the mushroom caps to the top of each chop and serve immediately, 1 cutlet per person.

STUFFED ROLLED VEAL CUTLET

1 large veal cutlet
Butter
Salt and pepper
½ cup Marsala, plus 2 or 3
  tablespoons
¼ cup tomato sauce
¼ cup sour cream
½ cup sliced mushrooms

Filling No. 1:
4 tablespoons anchovy paste
1 slice of dark bread, cubed
4 cloves garlic, crushed
3 tablespoons olive oil
Filling No. 2:
3 slices prosciutto
4 slices Mozzarella or Bel
  Paese cheese

Have the meat pounded to flatten it a little. For Filling No. 1, spread the meat with the anchovy paste. Toss the small bread cubes and garlic in the olive oil over a low flame 1 minute, then sprinkle over the meat. Roll the meat and tie securely with string. For Filling No. 2, put the slices of ham on top of the meat and cover the ham with slices of cheese. If the cutlet is very large you may need more ham and cheese. Roll and tie securely. Put the roll in a heavy skillet or baking pan and brown in butter. Sprinkle with salt and pepper and pour ½ cup of the Marsala over it. Roast 45 minutes; 15 minutes at 350°, and 30 minutes at 300°, turning it twice. If the pan becomes at all dry add a little boiling water. When the meat is done, mix 2 or 3 tablespoons of Marsala with the tomato sauce and sour cream. Lift the meat to a hot platter and keep it warm. Stir the cream mixture and the thinly sliced mushrooms into the baking pan and when it is hot pour it over the meat. Serves 4.

VEAL CHOP SURPRISE, ALSACIENNE
Maison Kammerzell, Strasbourg

4 veal chops, ¾-inch thick	Thick Béchamel Sauce:
3 tablespoons butter	2 tablespoons butter
¼ cup Madeira	1 tablespoon flour
2 tablespoons cognac	¾ cup light cream
	Salt and pepper
	2 egg yolks
	Parmesan cheese

Brown the chops on both sides in the butter over a hot flame. Add the Madeira, cover, and cook slowly until tender, turning once. This should take about 12 to 15 minutes. Blaze with cognac. To make the thick Béchamel sauce, melt the butter, blend in the flour until smooth, then add the cream, season, and stir in the egg yolks. Mask the chops with the Béchamel, top and sides, sprinkle well with the cheese, and run the pan under a flame until the top browns. Serve on hot plates, scraping the pan juices over the chops. Serves 4.

VEAL OR PORK CHOPS

¾-inch-thick chops	Salt and pepper
Oil or melted butter	Mustard or curry powder
Fine cracker crumbs or bread-	Thyme, basil, or parsley
crumbs	Cream
Parmesan cheese	Port, Madeira, or sweet vermouth

Dip the chops in either oil or melted butter. Mix crumbs, cheese, salt and pepper, mustard or curry powder and one of the herbs. Basil is good with veal, thyme with pork, parsley with either. Dip the chops in the mixture and lay them in very hot oil or butter on the bottom of a heavy skillet. Bake them uncovered in a 350° oven for 15 minutes, then turn them, and bake another 10 minutes for veal and 15 minutes for pork. If they are baking too fast turn the heat to 325°. Lift them onto hot plates or platter. Put 1 tablespoon cream and 1 tablespoon wine for each chop in the pan and heat. Scrape all the crumbs into the sauce and pour it over the chops. More cream and wine may be used if desired. Allow 1 chop for each serving.

CALF'S LIVER, FRENCH STYLE

4 slices of liver, ½ to ¾ inch thick	3 or 4 tablespoons butter
Pinches of sage	3 tablespoons dry vermouth or port
Salt and pepper	3 tablespoons heavy cream
Flour	1 tablespoon chopped parsley
2 tablespoons caramel	

The butcher who carries the finest beef usually has the best calf's liver. The liver should be a rich red—on the light side rather than dark. If the liver is not cooked too long, this can be a great dish, fine enough for an important dinner. Put a pinch of sage on each slice of liver and sprinkle both sides with a little salt and pepper and a light sifting of flour. Heat the caramel and butter in a large pan. Put in the liver and brown well on one side, turn it, cover, and cook on a low flame for 4 minutes. Lift the liver onto a hot platter. Put the wine and cream into the pan and boil up. Scrape the contents of the pan over the liver and sprinkle with a very little parsley for appearance. Serves 4.

BAKED WHOLE CALF'S LIVER

1 2½- to 3-pound calf's liver
10 1½-inch strips salt pork
3 tablespoons brandy
½ teaspoon mace or nutmeg
3 tablespoons butter
2 tablespoons oil
2 tablespoons caramel or honey
  Salt and freshly ground pepper
½ cup finely chopped onions

¼ cup finely chopped celery
¼ cup finely chopped carrots
⅔ cup dry vermouth or dry white
  wine
⅔ cup veal or chicken broth
12 or 14 white onions
1 tablespoon cornstarch
2 tablespoons chopped parsley

Do not wash the liver. Soak the salt pork in the brandy and spice for half hour, then make incisions in the liver with an icepick and push the strips in all sides with your little finger. Put the butter and oil in a skillet with the caramel or honey and sear the liver quickly so it has a fine glaze. Salt and pepper it. Make a bed of the vegetables in a roasting pan and lay the liver on top. Pour the wine and broth over it. Glaze the onions in the skillet, adding a little more butter and sweetening if necessary. Put them around the liver, cover, and roast at 300° for 45 minutes. Remove the liver and onions from the pan and empty all the sauce through a sieve, or add the cornstarch and put it in an electric blender. Meanwhile return the liver and onions to the pan and roast 15 minutes uncovered. Heat the sauce in a saucepan. When the liver is done, put it on a hot platter with the onions surrounding it. Mask with a little of the sauce and serve the rest in a sauceboat. Sprinkle the liver and onions with the parsley. Slice the liver thin. This will serve 7 or 8. Serve with a fine white wine and *Gratin Dauphinois* (potatoes baked in cream).

LIVER AND ONIONS

4 slices calf's liver
2 tablespoons flour
1 teaspoon sugar
Salt and freshly ground pepper
4 tablespoons butter (or more)

1 jigger cognac
1 cup thinly sliced Bermuda
onions
Chopped parsley

The liver is sliced ½-inch thick and cut in 1½-inch squares. Put the flour, sugar, salt, and pepper in a bag and shake the liver in it until it is lightly covered. Melt 3 tablespoons of the butter in a sauté pan and put in the onions; they take somewhat longer to cook than the liver does. Sauté them until they soften, salt and pepper them. In another pan cook the liver in butter until it is nicely glazed and still pink inside. Blaze with cognac. Mix the liver and onions and sprinkle with chopped parsley. Serves 4.

VEAL AND LIVER LOAF

1 pound veal, ground
¾ pound calf's liver or yearling
liver, ground
1 medium onion, ground
2 egg yolks, beaten
Salt and pepper
2 tablespoons pistachio nuts
⅓ cup sherry or Madeira

4 tablespoons heavy cream
2 tablespoons flour
1 teaspoon thyme
½ teaspoon nutmeg
2 egg whites, beaten
5 strips bacon
6 halved chicken livers or 3 hard-
boiled eggs

Put the veal, liver, and onion through the meat grinder. Mix the other ingredients together with the meat mixture, folding in the egg whites last. Grease a loaf pan or long pâté dish and lay 3 strips of bacon on the bottom. Put half the meat mixture into the pan and spread either the chicken livers or the peeled hard-boiled eggs, laid end to end along the mixture. Cover with the rest of the liver mixture. When the loaf is sliced each piece will contain either a slice of egg or a slice of chicken liver. Cover with 2 strips of bacon. Put the loaf pan in a pan of hot water and bake at 300° for 1 hour and 10 minutes. This is served either hot or cold as a pâté.

SWEETBREADS WITH MADEIRA SAUCE

3 pairs sweetbreads
3 tablespoons lemon juice
¼ cup butter
Salt and pepper
¼ cup chopped shallots or green
onions
⅓ cup chopped mushrooms

¾ cup Madeira
⅓ cup beef consommé
1 tablespoon cornstarch
1 tablespoon tomato paste
Chopped parsley
Crisp toast or fried bread

Soak the sweetbreads in salted cold water for 2 hours, then remove the membranes. Soak them with the lemon juice in cold water just to cover for half hour, then bring to a boil and drain. Firm them in cold water. Slice the sweetbreads and sauté them in quite hot butter until a golden brown on both sides, then remove to a baking dish. In the sauté pan cook the shallots or onions and the mushrooms a moment in the remaining butter and scrape them over the sweetbreads. Add ½ cup of the Madeira and the consommé and bake at 325° for 20 minutes. Blend the cornstarch and tomato paste with the rest of the wine and when the sweetbreads are done stir it into the juices in the baking dish and let it thicken. The sweetbreads may be served out of the baking dish or put in a rice or noodle ring. Serves 6.

SWEETBREADS IN CREAM

3 pairs sweetbreads
3 tablespoons lemon juice
⅓ cup butter
Salt and pepper
1 jigger cognac
¼ cup chopped green onions
½ cup sliced fresh mushrooms
3 tablespoons butter

1¼ cups heavy cream
1 tablespoon cornstarch
1 teaspoon powdered chicken
concentrate
1 tablespoon tomato paste
Salt and pepper
3 tablespoons sherry or Madeira
Pastry shells or crisp toast

Soak the sweetbreads 2 hours in salted cold water, then remove the membranes. Put them with the lemon juice in cold water just to cover for ½ hour, then bring to a boil and drain. Cover with cold water to firm them. Cut them in slices ¾-inch thick. Put the butter in a large sauté pan and when it bubbles, brown the sweetbreads, then blaze them with the cognac. Salt and pepper them and remove to a baking dish. In the sauté pan cook the onions and mushrooms 3 minutes, then scrape them onto the sweetbreads. Put the sweetbreads in the oven and bake at 300° for 20 minutes while you are making the sauce. This method obviates the old way of blanching sweetbreads for 15 to 20 minutes, which destroys some of the flavor. Blend the cream with the cornstarch, chicken concentrate, and tomato paste. Cook until it thickens and add salt and pepper to taste. When ready to serve, add the sweetbreads and juices to the sauce and stir in the sherry. Serve in rich pastry shells or on crisp toast. Serves 6.

SWEETBREADS TETRAZZINI

Sweetbreads in Cream

12 ounces fine egg noodles
Butter and Parmesan cheese

Prepare *Sweetbreads in Cream,* using 1 more teaspoon cornstarch and ⅓ cup more cream. Cook the noodles in boiling salted water and drain them. Make a bed of the noodles mixed with a little butter, cover with the sweetbreads, and sprinkle with cheese.

SWEETBREADS CREOLE

2 or 3 pairs sweetbreads
Juice of ½ lemon
Butter
Salt and pepper

Sauce:
⅓ cup chopped onions
⅓ cup chopped green pepper
Butter
1⅓ cups tomato purée
Salt and pepper
2 tablespoons chopped green olives
2 tablespoons dark rum

Soak the sweetbreads in salted water for 2 hours. Drain and remove the membranes. Soak ½ hour in the lemon juice and just enough water to cover, then bring to a boil and drain. Put cold water over them and then wipe them dry. Slice them ½-inch thick and sauté them in butter over a low flame until they are tender, about 6 or 7 minutes on each side. Salt and pepper them. For the sauce, sauté the onion and green pepper in butter until tender, then add the tomato purée and cook slowly 4 or 5 minutes. Add salt and pepper and the green olives. Just before serving heat the sauce and add the rum and the sweetbreads. Serve on crisp toast or noodles or rice. Serves 4 or 6.

SAUTÉED SWEETBREADS

1 pair sweetbreads (1 pound)
2 tablespoons vinegar
2 tablespoons brown sugar
½ cup water
Salt and freshly ground pepper
Flour
¼ cup butter

1 tablespoon honey or simple syrup
1 green onion, chopped
3 mushrooms, sliced
2 tablespoons dry vermouth, or 1 tablespoon lemon juice
2 tablespoons cream
Garnish: Chopped parsley

Put the sweetbreads in an enameled saucepan with the vinegar, sugar, water. Simmer slowly 10 minutes, turning the sweetbreads once after 5 minutes. Dip the sweetbreads in cold water to firm them, then remove all the membranes and cut them in slices 1 inch thick. Lay them on a plate and sprinkle them on both sides with salt and freshly ground pepper and a very light sprinkle of flour. Smooth the flour over them with your fingers. Have the butter quite hot in a big sauté pan and add the honey or syrup. Brown the sweetbreads on both sides to a golden color, then add the onions and mushrooms, cover, and cook over a very low flame for 6 or 8 minutes. Remove the cover, stir in the vermouth and cream, and then empty onto a hot platter and sprinkle with a little parsley. One tablespoon of lemon juice may be used instead of the vermouth. Serves 2 or 3.

CERVELLE DE VEAU AUX PISTACHES
Maurice Cazalis, Chartres

M. Cazalis elevates calf's brains to a company dish. Serve them with an elaborate casserole of potatoes and you have a fine main course.

2 pairs brains
Salt and pepper
Flour
6 tablespoons clarified butter

¼ to ⅓ cup sliced pistachio nuts
Thin slices of lemon
Ground parsley

Soak the brains in cold salted water for ½ hour, drain, and remove the membranes. Put them in fresh water, bring to a boil, drain, and cool. When ready to cook them, slice through to make 2 flat slices of each half, season with salt and pepper, and very lightly sprinkle with flour. To clarify butter, melt it, pour off the clear butter, and discard the white residue. Use 4 tablespoons to sauté the brains a delicate golden on both sides. Lift to a hot platter. Put 2 tablespoons of clarified butter in the pan and cook the nuts a few seconds. Scrape them over the brains. Garnish the platter with slices of lemon dipped in ground parsley. Serves 4.

SWEETBREADS OR CALF'S BRAINS WITH HAM

2 pairs sweetbreads or calf's brains
Butter
Salt and pepper
¼ cup minced green onions or shallots
¼ cup chicken broth

¼ cup dry vermouth or dry white wine
4 thin slices of ham
1 teaspoon cornstarch
2 tablespoons more wine
Chopped parsley

Soak the sweetbreads or brains in cold salted water an hour, then remove the membranes, and dry on paper towels. Brown on both sides in quite hot butter, add salt and pepper them, and lay them on a bed of the onions or shallots in a baking pan. Pour the broth and wine over them and bake 15 to 18 minutes at 325°. Frizzle the ham an instant in hot butter and put it on 4 hot plates. When the meat is done divide it on the ham. Mix the cornstarch with 2 tablespoons of wine and stir it into the pan juices. Boil up and pour it over the meat and sprinkle the top with chopped parsley. Serves 4.

CALF'S BRAINS, BEURRE NOIR

2 pairs calf's brains
Butter and oil for sautéing
Salt and pepper
2 tablespoons lemon juice

Chopped parsley or chives
5 tablespoons butter
2 tablespoons capers

Soak the brains in strongly salted cold water for 1 hour. Then strain from the water, remove all the membrane, rinse, and wipe dry. Have the butter and oil quite hot in a large skillet and sauté the brains a light brown on both sides, then turn down the flame and continue cooking for about 18 minutes. Add salt and pepper while they are cooking. When they are done, remove to a hot platter, sprinkle with lemon juice and parsley or chives. Brown butter in a skillet, add capers, and scrape over brains. Serves 4.

BROILED VEAL KIDNEYS OR LAMB KIDNEYS

3 veal kidneys or 18 lamb kidneys
Butter
Salt and pepper

4 shallots or green onions, minced
5 tablespoons heavy cream
5 tablespoons Madeira

Remove the fat and skin from the kidneys, rub them well with plenty of butter, and broil them 5 inches from the flame, 3 or 4 minutes on each side. Salt and pepper them. Slice the veal kidneys lengthwise in two; leave the lamb kidneys whole. Sauté the shallots or green onions a minute in butter. Scrape them into the broiling pan, add the cream and wine, boil up, and pour over the kidneys. Depending on the size, should serve 6.

KIDNEYS FLAMBÉE

3 veal kidneys
6 tablespoons butter
Salt and pepper
1 jigger cognac
6 mushrooms, sliced
5 shallots or green onions, minced

¼ cup chicken broth
1 tablespoon cornstarch
¾ cup heavy cream
3 tablespoons sherry or Madeira
Chopped parsley

Remove the fat and skin from the kidneys. Sauté them whole in 5 table-spoons foaming butter. Salt and pepper them. Blaze with cognac and sim-mer for 7 or 8 minutes very slowly. Sauté the mushrooms and the shallots or green onions in the remaining butter for 2 minutes, then add the broth and cook for 3 minutes. Blend the cornstarch with the cream and cook until it thickens, then add it to the mushrooms and onions. When the kidneys are done, cut them in half lengthwise and add them to the sauce, then stir in the sherry or Madeira and the kidney pan juices. Serve on crisp toast or just on hot plates with mashed potatoes. Serve a Beaujolais or any light red wine with kidneys. Serves 6.

ROGNONS DE VEAU, BERCY
L'Escargot Montorgueil, Paris

3 veal kidneys
3 tablespoons salted butter
Salt and pepper
3 shallots, minced fine
½ cup dry white wine

¼ cup veal broth
2 tablespoons sweet butter
Chopped parsley
Garnish: French-fried potatoes or
Rissolée Potatoes

Slice the kidneys through the long way to make 2 flat slices; one or two slices for each serving. Sauté gently in butter on each side until done but still rosy inside. Season and set aside to keep warm. Put the shallots in the sauté pan and cook a moment, then add the wine and broth and cook 2 or 3 minutes to reduce to ½ cup. Beat in the sweet butter with a whisk. (The French call this "mounting" the sauce with the butter.) Pour the sauce over the kidneys and sprinkle with finely chopped parsley. Serves 6.

Rissolée Potatoes are potatoes cut in small balls or olive shapes, cooked 4 or 5 minutes in boiling water, drained, and browned in butter.

ROGNON DE VEAU GRILLÉ EN PAUPIETTE AVEC SAUCE BÉARNAISE
Maurice Cazalis, Chartres

This gourmet dish is for special occasions. M. Cazalis is one of the most inventive and imaginative of cooks. He demonstrated this recipe for L'Academie Culinaire de France in 1959. For each individual serving:

½ veal kidney
Butter
1 good-sized veal scallop
Farce:
    Small slice raw chicken
  2 tablespoons diced mush-
      rooms
    Salt and pepper
  2 tablespoons butter
  1 tablespoon minced shallots
  1 tablespoon heavy cream

Garnish:
  Béarnaise Sauce
  Pommes Soufflés

Remove the fat and skin from the kidney and cut it into 2 flat slices. Sauté the kidney slice in a little butter until done but still rosy inside. Pound the scallop very flat. For the farce grind the chicken and mushrooms and season with salt and pepper. Toss in the butter with the shallots a minute or two over a good flame, then moisten with the cream. Spread this on the scallop, put half a kidney in the center, fold over the sides of the scallop, and tie with fine thread. Sauté 3 or 4 minutes on each side. Sprinkle with parsley. Serve with Pommes Soufflés and Béarnaise Sauce from a tureen.

Lamb

LAMB COOKING NOTE

Lamb must be aged to be tender. Its delicate flavor is preserved if it is cooked gently and served when the meat is still pink. A boned leg or shoulder roast takes from 20 to 30 minutes longer to cook than one which has the bone left in. For those who like lamb well done, I suggest roasting it at 275° for an hour to an hour and a half longer than the time specified in these recipes.

BABY SPRING LAMB

3-pound leg of baby lamb, boned
Olive oil
Lemon juice
Fresh tarragon or chervil
Salt and pepper
Flour
Butter

⅓ cup hot chicken consommé
⅓ cup dry white wine or vermouth
1 tablespoon cornstarch
3 tablespoons cream
Accompaniments:
    Mint sauce
    Creamed new peas
    Parsleyed new potatoes

Baby spring lamb is marketed when it is less than 3 months old. No garlic for baby lamb; it must be treated gently. Spread out the boned leg and rub it all over with oil, crushed herbs, and lemon juice. Spread minced herbs on the inside, reshape, and tie securely with string. If fresh herbs are not available, use dried tarragon or rosemary. Sprinkle the lamb with salt, pepper and flour. Melt butter in a pan and glaze it on all sides until it is a golden color. Put it in a roasting pan, mix the hot consommé with the wine, and pour it over the meat. Roast 15 minutes at 375°, then turn the heat to 300° and roast about 45 minutes more. Lift the meat to a hot platter. Blend the cornstarch with the cream and add it to the pan juices. Stir over a low flame until it thickens; serve in a sauceboat. Serves 6.

ROAST LAMB WITH SHERRY

5- or 6-pound leg or shoulder of
    lamb, boned
1 tablespoon curry powder
1½ tablespoons honey
    Salt and pepper
2 tablespoons chopped onion

2 tablespoons chopped carrot
2 tablespoons melted butter
1 cup good sherry
1½ tablespoons cornstarch
⅓ cup heavy cream

Have the lamb boned. Remove most of the fat. Mix the curry powder with the honey and rub it all over the lamb, inside and out. Shape and tie the meat. Sprinkle with a little salt and pepper. Mix the onion, carrot, and melted butter, and put in the bottom of a roaster, and lay the lamb on top. Roast for an hour, uncovered at 350°, then pour the warmed sherry over it, cover, and continue roasting at 300°. Cook 18 minutes to the pound including the first hour. When it is done, remove to a hot platter. Sieve the sauce. Blend the cornstarch with the cream and use it to thicken the sauce. Serve the sauce in a tureen. Mashed potatoes and new peas would be good accompaniments. Serves 8 to 10.

ROAST RACK OF LAMB

2 8-rib racks of lamb
3 tablespoons honey
    Salt and pepper
¼ cup flour
2 teaspoons rosemary
¼ cup shredded white turnip

½ cup shredded carrots
½ cup shredded onions
½ cup dry vermouth or dry white
    wine
1 tablespoon cornstarch
    Chopped parsley

Choose the small ribs. Have the butcher saw through the rib joints, leaving the racks intact. This will facilitate carving. Remove the outer skin and some of the fat from the racks, leaving a thin layer of fat. Rock the ribs back and forth over a very hot skillet to sear off more of the fat, otherwise the sauce will be too greasy. Discard this fat. Rub the racks well with honey on the meat side. Mix the salt, pepper, flour, and rosemary and sprinkle the meat side of the racks. Make a bed of the mixed vegetables in a roaster and lay the racks on it, fat side up. Add ⅓ cup of the wine, cover, and roast for 1 hour and 10 minutes at 300°. Remove the racks, then pour out the sauce and return the racks to the roaster to keep warm. Sieve the sauce or put it through the electric blender and put it in a saucepan. Blend the cornstarch with the rest of the wine; add it a little at a time, cooking it slowly until it has the consistency of heavy cream. Serve in a tureen. Put the racks on a platter and sprinkle with the parsley. Serves 10 or 12.

ROAST LAMB WITH DRY VERMOUTH

5- or 6-pound leg of lamb, boned
1½ tablespoons cornstarch
½ cup light cream

Marinade:
¼ cup olive oil
1 cup dry vermouth
½ cup chopped onions
⅓ cup chopped carrots
1 tablespoon chopped parsley
¼ cup chopped celery
1 clove garlic, crushed
Salt and pepper

Mix the marinade ingredients together. Soak the lamb in the marinade 24 hours, turning it 6 times. Remove the lamb, wipe it dry, and tie it into an oblong loaf. Sear it all over in a little fat. Put it in a roasting pan, boil up the marinade, and pour it over the lamb. Roast, covered, 1½ to 1¾ hours; the first hour at 325°, then the rest of the time at 300°. Turn it once. When it is done, remove it to a hot platter. Sieve the pan juices and use 1½ cups for the sauce. Blend the cornstarch with the cream, combine with the sieved juices, and heat until it thickens. If the sauce is too thick add a little wine. Serve in a sauceboat with the lamb. Serves 8 or 10.

AGNELLO DELL'ACCADEMICO
3 G Rosticceria-Ristorante, Bologna

Cavalière Renato Gualandi, Commandeur des Cordons Bleus de France, presides over the open kitchen at the entrance of this restaurant with its decidedly *cucina internazionale*. Signore Gualandi, a personable man and cooking enthusiast, has won fame not only in his own country but in Belgium and France. "3 G" stands for the first letter of his own name and of the names of his two former partners. Signore Gualandi, with the help of his handsome wife, has made this one of the great restaurants. An enormous pheasant with flowing tail on one wall is meant to signify that the restaurant specializes in game cookery in season. The wines served here are excellent, especially one that could be taken for a very fine Burgundy, which was selected by Signore Gualandi and bottled under his name. The following lamb recipe was on the menu of the banquet given here for the Accademia Italiana della Cucina in Bologna, March 1964.

Leg of lamb
Butter

Grand Veneur Sauce:
1¼ cups *Brown Sauce*
6 crushed peppercorns

Roast the lamb on a spit until it is half done; or if you have no spit or rotisserie, brown it all over in butter over a hot flame. Put the lamb in a roasting pan three-fourths covered with the lid, and baste with the *Brown Sauce* mixed with the crushed peppercorns. Lamb is roasted 15 minutes a pound, the first 15 minutes at 375°, then the rest of the time at 325°. Allow for the cooking on the spit, and reduce the cooking time in the oven. Signore Gualandi suggests Lyonnaise potatoes and cooked chestnuts as accompaniments. A 6-pound leg will serve 8.

BLANQUETTE D'AGNEAU

3 pounds shoulder or neck of
  lamb
1 teaspoon thyme or orégano
1 teaspoon rosemary
¼ cup flour
  Salt and pepper
1 tablespoon honey or brown
  sugar
3 tablespoons good fat or oil
1 large onion, diced

1½ cups chicken broth
1 tablespoon tomato paste
3 cloves garlic, crushed
½ cup red wine
12 white onions
6 white turnips
2 young carrots
1 pound new peas
  Chopped parsley

This stew should be begun in the morning to allow time to drain off the fat. Unlike veal, lamb does have fat which spoils the sauce if not skimmed. Have the meat cut in 2½-inch cubes and shake them in a bag with the flour, herbs, salt, and pepper. Melt the fat or oil in a heavy pan with the sugar or honey and finely diced onion. Sauté the onion while you are preparing the lamb. Add the meat, brown well, and as it is browned remove each piece to a casserole. Put the broth, tomato paste, and garlic in the sauté pan, bring to a boil, then scrape it over the meat. Add the wine to the pan and rinse it over the meat. Cover the casserole and cook for 1 hour at 300°. Remove from the oven and carefully remove all the meat. Let the sauce stand in a bowl until the fat collects; it may stand in the refrigerator. Remove the cake of fat, then purée the sauce either in a blender or through a sieve. Return the sauce and meat to the casserole. Boil up the onions, small white turnips, and carrots cut in 1-inch lengths, drain them, and put them around the meat. Cover and cook slowly 45 minutes or until all the meat and all the vegetables are done. Cook a pound of peas with a little basil and when the meat is done garnish the top with the peas. Add the chopped parsley. Mashed potatoes or rice may be served with this fine stew. Serves 6.

CROWN ROAST OF LAMB

Crown roast of ribs
2 teaspoons rosemary
Salt and pepper
2 tablespoons flour
2 tablespoons oil
⅓ cup chopped onions
⅓ cup chopped carrots
1 cup chicken broth
3 teaspoons lemon juice

Stuffing:
1 cup patna rice
2 cups chicken broth
Salt and pepper
1 teaspoon turmeric
2 lamb kidneys, sliced
4 chicken livers, sliced
¼ cup butter
Chopped parsley
Accompaniment:
New peas in butter

This may be an old-fashioned dish, but it is festive and one of the best ways to compliment your guests. Any good butcher knows how to prepare 14 to 16 ribs of lamb, sawing the joint bones for easy carving, tying the ribs into a circle, and frenching the tips of the ribs so that when it is ready to be brought to the table, paper frills are put on each tip. Wash the rice for the stuffing and cook it in the broth, with some salt and pepper and the turmeric, until the liquid is absorbed. Sauté the sliced kidneys and livers in the butter 2 minutes, then toss them with the rice. Mix the rosemary, salt, pepper, and flour. Rub the lamb with oil, then sprinkle with the flour mixture. Put the vegetables and broth in the roasting pan, set the crown on top, and fill it with the rice mixture. Roast at 300° for 1 hour and 10 minutes. Remove from the oven and put the crown on a platter. Sprinkle the top of the lamb and stuffing with chopped parsley. Strain the sauce, add the lemon juice, boil up, and serve in a tureen. Have 3 pounds of peas cooked and put them around the crown on the platter. This should serve 10. Serve a white Burgundy with this.

ROAST LAMB WITH BEANS, FRENCH STYLE

5-pound boned leg or shoulder of
  lamb
Filling:
  ⅓ cup diced onions
  2 tablespoons butter
  1 cup dry bread cubes
  Salt and pepper
  1 teaspoon rosemary
Butter
½ cup veal or chicken broth

½ cup dry vermouth or dry
  white wine
1½ cups dried white beans or
  flageolets
3 slices bacon
⅓ cup diced onions
2 cloves garlic, crushed
Salt and pepper
Chopped parsley

Have the leg or shoulder of lamb boned. First soak the beans 6 hours or overnight with 3 cups of water. Then add water to make 2 cups and simmer the beans 2 hours or until they are tender. Make the filling by cooking the onion in the butter until soft; then mix in the small bread cubes, salt, pepper, and rosemary. Spread out the lamb and put the filling on top. Roll and reshape the meat and tie it securely with string. Brown it all over in a little butter, then put it in a roasting pan and pour the broth and wine over it. Roast the lamb 45 minutes at 350°. Meanwhile the beans have cooked tender. Fry the bacon until crisp, remove it from the pan, and crumble it in the beans. Cook the onion in the bacon grease until tender and add to the beans. Add garlic, salt, and pepper. Remove the meat from the oven and pour off the liquid. Put the beans around the lamb, cover, and roast 45 minutes more at 325°. Degrease the liquid from the lamb and baste the meat and beans with the liquid to keep them moist. When the meat is done, lift it to a hot platter and put the beans around the meat. Sprinkle the beans with chopped parsley. Serves 8.

CÔTES DE MOUTON CHAMPVALLON
Capucin Gourmand, Nancy

6 fine mutton cutlets
  Butter
  Salt and pepper
2 pounds potatoes
2 large onions

2 cloves garlic, crushed
2 teaspoons mixed herbs: chervil,
  thyme, and basil
  Veal or chicken broth

Choose 5-ounce cutlets, 1 to a serving. Brown both sides in hot butter. Salt and pepper them. Peel the potatoes and onions and slice very thin. Sauté them 5 minutes in a little butter. Season them and mix with the garlic and herbs. Make a bed of half the potatoes and onions in the bottom of a large greased baking dish, lay the chops over them, and cover with the rest of the potatoes and onions. Add broth to just the height of the potatoes and bake uncovered for about ¾ hour. The top will be golden. Serve very hot. This is another recipe from Georges Romain.

BAKED BONED LAMB CHOPS

6 1½-inch boned rib lamb chops
6 strips lean bacon

Paste:
  2 tablespoons tomato paste
    Salt and pepper
  1 teaspoon lemon juice
  2 tablespoons prepared
    mustard
  1 teaspoon Worcestershire
    sauce

Preheat the oven to 400°. Blend the paste ingredients. Wrap the bacon around the chops and fasten with a toothpick. Spread paste on both sides of the chop. Put them in the oven for 10 minutes, turn them, and bake 10 minutes more. Serves 6.

BRAISED LAMB SHANKS

4 or 6 lamb shanks, 1 to a
   serving
½ cup flour
1 teaspoon rosemary
   Salt and pepper
3 or 4 tablespoons ham fat, oil,
   or butter
½ cup chopped onions

½ cup chopped celery
½ cup chopped carrots
⅔ cup red wine
⅔ cup chicken broth
6 potatoes
12 white onions
1 green pepper, sliced
1 eggplant, cubed (optional)

Choose meaty shanks. These are so good, we should cook them more frequently. Mix ¼ cup flour (or more) with the rosemary, salt, and pepper. Put the mixture in a paper bag with the shanks, and shake until the mixture covers them. Brown the shanks well in the fat, oil, or butter. In a roasting pan, make a bed of chopped onions, celery, and carrots, put the shanks on top, and cover. Rinse out the browning pan with the wine and broth and empty the liquid onto the meat. Cover tightly and braise 1½ hours at 300°. Peel medium-sized potatoes and boil them up with the white onions, and green pepper, drain, and add them to the roasting pan. Cover and cook another 30 or 40 minutes or until the vegetables are done. If eggplant is added, cut a thin slice from each end, cut the rest into 2-inch cubes and lay them on the top of the vegetables and meat 25 minutes before the stew is done. When done, remove the vegetables and meat from the pan and put the sauce from the pan through a sieve or blender. If it is too thick, skim off a little fat, add 2 tablespoons each of broth and wine, reheat, and serve in a sauceboat. Serves 4 to 6.

MINCED LAMB PATTIES

1 pound lean lamb, ground
1 medium onion, ground
1 teaspoon grated lime rind
1 teaspoon lime juice
¼ teaspoon nutmeg
1 teaspoon cumin powder
   Salt
   Freshly ground pepper

1 egg, beaten
2 tablespoons sherry
Garnish:
   Boiled rice
   Sautéed green peppers and
     onions

Mix the lamb with all the other ingredients and form into patties, flattening them a little. Make 4 or 8 patties. Moisten with oil and broil or fry to a nice brown on both sides. They take about 6 minutes. A good way to cook "fried" green peppers and onions is to cut a big Bermuda onion in thin rings, cut a big pepper or two medium peppers in ½-inch strips, and put them in an iron skillet with 2 tablespoons each of butter and oil mixed, and cook them in a 350° oven for 20 minutes. Add salt and pepper. They cook evenly and do not burn. Stir them a couple of times. Add more butter if necessary. One pound of lamb serves 4.

TURKISH KEBABS

1½ pounds rump of lamb cut in
   strips
1½ cups yogurt
3 tablespoons grated onion

1 teaspoon cumin powder
Salt
Cayenne pepper
1½ cups yogurt, heated
Garnish: Boiled rice

For kebabs, rump of lamb is used, cut in strips so it may be quickly broiled. Marinate the lamb all day with 1½ cups yogurt, the onion, cumin, salt, and a dash of cayenne pepper. Discard the marinade. Broil the lamb. Put it and the pan juices on top of a mound of cooked rice (*Patna* or *Indian Rice with Indian Spices*). Heat 1½ cups yogurt well but do not let it boil. Pour it over the meat and rice. Serves 4.

LAMB STEW WITH DILL OR MINT DUMPLINGS

2 pounds lamb from leg
2 tablespoons oil or butter
¾ cup chopped onions
3 tablespoons flour
Salt and pepper
1 teaspoon mixed spices or curry
   powder
1½ cups chicken consommé
2 parsnips
2 carrots

6 white onions
Dumplings:
   1½ cups flour
   2 teaspoons baking powder
   ¾ teaspoon salt
   1 tablespoon butter
   3 tablespoons chopped dill or
      2 tablespoons chopped
      mint
   Milk for soft dough

Have the lamb boned and cut the meat in 1½-inch cubes. Save the bones for the stew. Put the oil in a heavy pot, add the onions and sauté a minute. Shake the lamb in a bag with the flour, salt, pepper, and spices or curry powder, then empty all into the onions, add the bones, and stir well, simmering over a low fire, for 5 minutes. Bring the consommé to a boil, and add. Cover the pot tightly and simmer on a low flame for ½ hour. Cut the parsnips and carrots in 1-inch lengths, boil them up with the whole white onions. Drain, add to the meat, and simmer until meat and vegetables are tender, about 45 minutes to 1 hour. Remove and discard the bones. There should be at least 2 cups of liquid with the meat. For the dumplings—mix the dry ingredients, cut in the butter with a wire pastry cutter, stir in the dill or mint, and just enough milk to make a light soft dough. Drop by tablespoonfuls on top of the simmering stew, cover tightly, and cook gently for 12 minutes without lifting the lid. Line the edge of a large platter with the dumplings and put the stew in the center. This will serve 4 or 5.

CURRIED LAMB OR PORK, WESTERN STYLE

1½ to 2 pounds rump or shoulder
    of lamb or pork, cut in
    1½-inch cubes
1½ cups peeled tart apples cut in
    ½-inch cubes
1 cup cubed onions
2 cloves garlic, crushed
3 tablespoons oil or butter
2 tablespoons curry powder

Salt and pepper
½ cup drained canned tomatoes
    or tomato purée
½ cup red wine
⅓ cup raisins
1 tablespoon cornstarch (optional)
Garnish:
    Boiled rice
    Curry accompaniments

Wipe the meat and cut it in 1½-inch cubes. Shoulder of pork is a good cut for this. Sauté the apples, onions, and garlic in oil or butter for 6 or 8 minutes over a low fire, then stir in the curry powder and cook 2 minutes more. Stir in the meat and cook for 5 minutes. Add salt and pepper, tomatoes or purée, and wine. Cover and simmer very slowly for an hour or until the meat is tender. Ten minutes before the meat is done add the raisins. If there is too much liquid to serve over rice, a little may be removed, blended with the cornstarch, returned to the stew, and cooked until it thickens. Serve with toasted coconut, chutney, radishes, browned almonds, fried bananas, etc., and of course rice.

COOKED LAMB OR VEAL WITH CUMIN SAUCE

Slices of roast lamb or veal
Sauce:
    1 cup chicken broth or
        broth and gravy
    1 tablespoon cumin powder
    3 teaspoons cornstarch
    ⅓ cup light cream

1 tablespoon capers
4 stuffed green olives, sliced
2 tablespoons Madeira or sherry

This is a fine sauce for leftover roast lamb or veal and will serve 4 to 6; of course the ingredients may be increased to serve 6 or 8. Leftover gravy makes the sauce richer; use any you have and add enough broth to make 1 cup. Blend the cumin, cornstarch, and cream, add to the broth, and cook until it thickens. Add the capers and green olives. The slices of meat may marinate in the sauce for an hour or more. When ready to serve, add the wine and reheat. If the sauce is too thick add a little more cream or broth. This may be served with a green vegetable and rice or noodles.

CURRY SAUCE FOR COOKED LAMB OR VEAL

1 cup packaged coconut
1 cup milk
1 cup water
2 teaspoons powdered chicken concentrate
1 tablespoon cornstarch
2 tablespoons butter
⅔ cup chopped onions
2 cloves garlic, crushed

1 teaspoon cumin powder
1 teaspoon coriander
1 teaspoon cardamom
½ teaspoon each clove and cinnamon
1 teaspoon turmeric
Salt and pepper
¼ cup raisins
¼ cup Madeira or sherry

Put the coconut in a saucepan with the milk and bring it to a boil. Let it cool, then mash it through a sieve. Put the coconut back in the saucepan with 1 cup water, bring to a boil, let cool, and mash through a sieve. Discard the coconut. Blend the chicken concentrate with the coconut water, then with the cornstarch, stir until smooth, add the coconut milk, and cook until it thickens. Put the butter, onions, and garlic in a skillet and cook until tender without burning, then add all the condiments and cook 2 minutes longer. Add the thickened coconut mixture. Let stand several hours to "ripen." The meat may marinate in it. Marinate the raisins in the wine for 1 hour. When ready to serve, reheat the sauce with the meat and add the raisins and wine. This makes about 2 cups of sauce. This sauce is also suitable for currying seafood and hard-boiled eggs.

LOIN OF LAMB WITH JUNIPER

Loin ribs of lamb
Crushed juniper berries
Oil
Salt and pepper
1 chopped onion
½ cup chicken broth

½ cup dry white wine or dry vermouth
1½ teaspoons cornstarch
Accompaniment: *Puréed White Turnips and Potatoes*

Have the butcher saw the chop joints without cutting the meat. Tuck ½ teaspoon crushed juniper berries between each two chops. Rub the meat with oil and sprinkle with salt and pepper. Put the onion on the bottom of the roasting pan and lay the meat on top, meat side up. Add the broth and wine to the pan and roast at 300° for 1 hour. Remove the meat. Strain the sauce. Blend the cornstarch mixed with a little more wine, and use to thicken the sauce. Reheat and serve in a tureen.

ROAST LAMB WITH BUTTERMILK MARINADE
(or Venison or Veal)

6-pound leg of lamb, boned
Marinade:
    1 quart buttermilk
    1½ cups chopped onions
    3 teaspoons thyme
    1 teaspoon marjoram
    Salt and pepper
3 strips salt pork or bacon
2 tablespoons oil
2 tablespoons lemon juice
    Salt and pepper

1 tablespoon flour (or more)
1 cup sour cream
Stuffing:
    1 cup ground ham
    ½ cup onions, chopped
    1 teaspoon basil
    1 teaspoon thyme
    ½ cup breadcrumbs
    1 tablespoon chopped parsley
    2 cloves garlic, crushed

Mix the marinade and soak the meat in it for 2 days, turning it every 6 hours. When ready to roast, wipe it dry and discard the marinade. Mix the stuffing, fill the leg, and tie it into shape. Lay the salt pork or bacon in the bottom of a roaster. Rub the meat with oil, lemon juice, salt, pepper, and a little flour. Lay the meat on the pork or bacon, pour ½ cup sour cream over it, cover, and roast at 300° 1½ to 2 hours for lamb, 20 minutes to the pound for veal or venison. Turn the meat twice while it is roasting. Remove the meat. Blend 1 tablespoon flour, or more, with the rest of the sour cream and thicken the sauce in the roaster, cooking it 2 or 3 minutes. Coat the meat with a little of the sauce and serve the rest in a tureen. Serve with mashed potatoes. Serves 8 or 10.

BOILED LEG OF LAMB OR MUTTON

Leg of lamb or mutton
3 bay leaves
1½ tablespoons pepper
1 tablespoon salt

Boiling water to cover
Garnish: *Soubise Sauce* or *Caper Sauce*

If the leg is not boned, have the butcher saw through the end of the leg, so the meat may be put in a kettle. Cover with boiling water, add the seasonings, and lower the heat to a simmer. Cook the leg 15 minutes per pound. Remove from water and let it stand a few minutes before carving. Either *Soubise* or *Caper Sauce* is good with boiled lamb. Leftover lamb has many good uses: cold with chutney and creamed potatoes; in the party dish *Moussaka*; warmed in a prepared curry sauce. If it is cut in slices or cubes and added to freshly cooked, slightly thickened vegetables, you have a lamb stew already made. Serves 8 or 10.

CASSEROLE OF BREAST OF LAMB

2½ to 3 pounds of breast of lamb
  Salt and pepper
2 teaspoons tarragon or basil
  Flour
  Oil
1 cup tomato juice or tomato
  purée

1 cup broth, chicken or beef
12 white onions
6 small potatoes, halved
4 carrots, cut in 1-inch lengths
1 green pepper, sliced
1 pound fresh peas

Cut the lamb into servings and roll these in the seasonings and flour. Brown each piece in oil and put them in a casserole. Heat the tomato juice or purée and the broth in the pan the meat browned in and scrape it over the lamb. Cover tightly and bake at 300° for 50 minutes. Boil up the onions, potatoes, and carrots for 4 minutes, drain, add to the casserole, and cook until the vegetables are done. Cook the pepper with the peas until tender. When the meat is done add the peas and pepper to the top and serve. Buttered noodles or rice are good accompaniments. Serves 5 or 6.

BRAISED LAMB WITH EGGPLANT

2½ to 3 pounds neck and breast
  of lamb
½ cup olive oil (or more)
  Salt and pepper
1 clove garlic, crushed
2 onions, chopped

2 teaspoons orégano
1 cup chicken consommé
½ cup sliced or canned tomatoes
1 tablespoon tomato paste
1 medium eggplant
8 fresh mushrooms

Have the lamb cut in servings. Put ¼ cup olive oil or more in a skillet, add the salt and pepper and garlic, and brown the pieces of lamb. As they are browned put them in a casserole. Cook the onions a moment in the browning pan and add them to the lamb. Sprinkle with orégano. Heat the consommé, tomatoes, and tomato paste in the browning pan and pour over the lamb. Cover the casserole tightly and bake in a 300° oven for 1 hour. Cut the eggplant in 2-inch cubes, boil up, drain, and lay on top of the stew with the mushrooms to steam tender. Cook 40 minutes more very slowly, when the meat should be done. Serve with steamed patna or Indian rice flavored lightly with curry. Serves 5 or 6.

LAMB KIDNEY STEW

6 lamb kidneys
Salt and pepper
Butter
1 jigger brandy
½ pound fresh mushrooms
12 tiny cocktail sausages
1 cup chicken broth

1 tablespoon prepared mustard
1 tablespoon tomato paste
½ cup Madeira
1 tablespoon cornstarch
Garnish: Steamed rice (patna or Indian)

Slice the kidneys in half, salt and pepper them, and sauté in butter 3 minutes on each side over a very low flame, then blaze them with brandy. Remove to a serving casserole or baking dish. Select fresh mushrooms of medium size if possible so they may be left whole. Sauté them in the same pan with a little more butter for 5 or 6 minutes, add salt and pepper, then remove to the dish with the kidneys. Brown the sausages lightly on both sides and add them to the dish. Mix the broth with the mustard and tomato paste and pour into the baking dish. Mix the wine and cornstarch until smooth and add. Bake in the oven uncovered for about 8 minutes or until well heated and thickened. Serve with rice. This will serve 4, or may be expanded to use as one of the dishes for a buffet supper.

LAMB KIDNEYS AND CHICKEN LIVERS

12 lamb kidneys
Butter
1 pound chicken livers
½ pound small fresh mushrooms
Salt and pepper
1 cup finely sliced onions
2 teaspoons mustard

2 tablespoons tomato paste
1½ tablespoons cornstarch
⅓ cup chicken consommé
1½ cups sour cream
¼ cup sherry or Madeira
Garnish: *Indian Pilau*

This is a useful dish for a few people or for quite a number. This will serve 6 or 8, but it can be served for a buffet supper for 20 by increasing the ingredients. To prepare the kidneys, remove the fat, and skin and cut them in half. Sauté them in butter 2 or 3 minutes on each side. Season with salt and pepper. Put the livers in a baking pan with butter, season with salt and pepper, and bake them 12 minutes at 375°. Do the same with the mushrooms, in a separate pan, and bake them 10 minutes. As with Beef Stroganoff, the secret of preserving the flavors and the success of the dish is cooking everything separately. Sauté the onions in butter in a good-sized heavy pot until they are yellow and just tender. Do not overcook any of the ingredients. Scrape the livers and mushrooms and their juices into the onions and add the kidneys. Blend the mustard, tomato paste, cornstarch, and consommé in a saucepan until smooth, then stir in the sour cream. Cook over a low flame until the sauce thickens, then add it to the meats. Stir in the wine. This is served with a hot *Indian Pilau*.

ROGNONS FRICADELLES

5 lamb kidneys or 1 veal kidney
¼ cup chopped onions
2 tablespoons butter
  Salt and pepper

2 eggs
⅓ cup fresh breadcrumbs
  Butter
  Goose-liver sausage (optional)

Slice the kidneys or kidney and sauté in the butter with the onions for 10 minutes over a very low fire, covered. Chop fine and season with salt and pepper. Mix with the eggs and crumbs and form into patties. Before serving, brown on both sides a minute in hot butter. Makes 4 patties; the quantities may easily be increased.

VARIATION. To serve to guests make 8 small patties and brown them on one side. Lay a slice of fine goose-liver sausage on half the patties, then cover each patty with another, browned side up; cover the pan and cook two minutes to thoroughly warm the goose liver. Serve with a good potato dish; creamed potatoes with cubes of Gruyère, for instance. Serves 4.

NOISETTE D'AGNEAU DE BEHAGUE, EDWARD VII
Maxim's, Paris

"Nut" or tenderloin of lamb, cut from saddle chops (2 to a serving)
Thin slices of truffle (fresh or canned)
3 tablespoons cognac
Butter
Salt and freshly ground pepper

Slices of foie gras
Jigger of port
½ teaspoon veal or beef extract
Garnish:
  Artichoke bottoms filled with creamed minced mushrooms
  Rissolée or Parisienne potatoes

The butcher will prepare these tenderloins, ¾-inch thick. The truffles are sliced and marinated an hour before the meat is cooked. Use 3 tablespoons of cognac for every truffle; add the truffle juice if canned truffles are used. The artichoke and potato garnishes are prepared before the meat is cooked. Have butter medium hot and sauté the meat on both sides; it should be pink inside. Salt and pepper the meat, remove to the edge of a large chop plate, and keep warm. Meanwhile heat the slices of foie gras a moment on each side in butter and lift 1 slice to the top of each piece of meat. Toss the slices of truffle and their juices in butter and put 1 slice on each slice of foie gras. Put the port and meat extract in the truffle pan, boil up, and scrape this sauce over the meat. Put the artichoke bottoms filled with creamed mushrooms under the flame a moment to heat and glaze. Put them around the edge of the chop plate, alternating with the meat, and pile the potatoes in the center. This Lucullan dish is served to Maxim's most important guests.

LAMB OR VEAL PIE

1½ pounds boned neck, shoulder,
    or breast of lamb or veal
2 cups veal or chicken broth
⅓ cup shredded onions
⅓ cup shredded carrots
1 teaspoon basil or thyme
    Salt and pepper
1 pair sweetbreads
1 pair calf's brains

Butter
8 fresh mushrooms
½ pound chicken livers
8 white onions, boiled
⅓ cup Madeira
⅓ cup heavy cream
2 tablespoons cornstarch
Top: Crust (see *Beef and Kidney Pie*)

This is a delicious party dish to serve 8 or 10. Cut the lamb or veal in 1-inch cubes and simmer it in the broth with the onions, carrots, and seasonings until the meat is tender. Strain; reserve the broth for the sauce. Soak the sweetbreads and brains in cold salted water 1 hour, then remove the membranes and cut them in 1½-inch cubes. Sauté in butter until they are half done. Sauté the mushrooms 1 or 2 minutes; do the same with the livers. Boil the onions in very little water until almost done and add the onion water to the reserved broth. Arrange all the meats and mushrooms in a large casserole or baking dish. Blend the wine, cream, and cornstarch together with the broth and add a little more broth if necessary to make 2½ cups of sauce. Cook until it thickens and pour it over the meats. Make a rich pastry to cover the dish with double fluted dough around the edge. Make incisions in the top for the steam to escape. Bake at 400° for 10 minutes, then at 325° about 15 to 18 minutes more, or until the crust is a rich medium brown.

BROILED LAMB CHOPS OR
MUTTON CHOPS WITH KIDNEYS

1 2-inch chop per person
1 kidney for each chop
½ cup sherry or Madeira
2 tablespoons chopped green
    onions

Salt and pepper
Oil or butter
Chopped parsley

Marinate the chops and kidneys 1 hour in the wine with the green onions. Scrape them off and rub the chops and kidneys with salt, pepper, and oil or melted butter. Reserve the marinade. Broil the chops for 8 minutes on each side 5 inches below the flame. For the last 5 minutes broil the kidneys 2½ minutes on each side. Put both into the oven to finish cooking while you make the sauce. Cook the marinade over a low flame 2 minutes, add the parsley, and pour over the meat. Tuck a kidney into each chop, curving the end of the chop around the kidney. Serve with baked potatoes stuffed with cheese, which may be made ahead of time and reheated with the meat.

LAMB OR VEAL STEW WITH LEEKS

1½ pounds of neck of lamb or veal
3 tablespoons oil or butter
Flour
1 or 2 tablespoons brown sugar
   or honey

½ cup chopped onions
Salt and pepper
6 large leeks
½ cup tomato purée
⅓ cup water

Have the meat cut in 2-inch pieces. Sprinkle it well with flour. Put the oil or butter in a frying pan with the sugar or honey and brown the meat. Add the onions and cook a little longer. Add salt and pepper. Put the meat in a heavy pot or casserole. Quarter the leeks, wash them well, cut them in ½-inch lengths, and sprinkle them over the meat. Put the tomato purée and water in the browning pan, heat, and scrape over the meat. Cover tightly. Simmer in the pot on top of the stove, or cook in the oven, if a casserole is used, for 1¼ hours or until the meat is tender. Instead of water dry white wine or dry vermouth may be used. This is a fine stew to serve with mashed potatoes. Serves 4 to 6.

SHISH KEBAB

Boned rump of lamb, in 1½-inch
   cubes
Fresh mushrooms
Blanched cubes of peeled eggplant
Sweet red onions, thickly sliced
Tomatoes, quartered
Green peppers, blanched

Marinade:
1 jigger brandy
2 teaspoons orégano
3 cloves garlic, crushed
⅓ cup olive oil
¼ cup chopped onions
2 tablespoons chopped
   parsley
Salt and pepper
Red wine

Prepare 3 or 4 cubes of lamb for each skewer. Mix the ingredients for the marinade and add enough red wine to cover the lamb. Let it marinate all day. An hour before cooking add the prepared vegetables to the marinade. Have the mushrooms and vegetables the same size as the meat. Peel the eggplant, cut into cubes, cover with boiling water, and drain immediately. Slice the green peppers 1½-inches thick, cook for 5 minutes, and drain. Thread on a skewer a cube of lamb, a mushroom, lamb, eggplant, lamb, an onion slice, a tomato quarter, ending with lamb. Broil over charcoal, turning continuously, or lay the skewers over an iron skillet and broil 5 inches below a hot flame, turning often.

SHOULDER LAMB CHOPS AND LENTILS

4 to 6 chops
1½ cups dried lentils
2 cups water
1 cup chicken broth
1 good-sized minced onion
¼ cup minced carrot

¼ cup minced green pepper
1½ teaspoons salt
½ teaspoon pepper
2 teaspoons thyme
Butter
⅔ cup tomato sauce

Choose thick chops, 1 to a serving. Soak the washed lentils in 2 cups of water 6 hours or overnight. Do not drain them but add the broth, vegetables, and seasonings, cover tightly, and simmer until they are tender, about 35 to 40 minutes. Add a little hot broth or water if necessary. Brown the chops in a little butter. When the lentils are done put half of them in a casserole, put the chops on top, cover with the rest of the lentils, and pour the tomato sauce over the top. Bake 40 minutes at 325°, adding a little broth if they become dry. Serve 1 chop per person.

LAMB CURRY, INDIAN STYLE

2 pounds boned rump, leg, or
    shoulder of lamb
1 large onion, diced
3 cloves garlic, crushed
⅓ cup bland oil
1 teaspoon coriander, crushed
    seeds or powder
1 teaspoon cardamom powder
½ teaspoon cinnamon
1 teaspoon turmeric

½ teaspoon powdered ginger or 3
    tablespoons minced green
    ginger root
1 teaspoon cumin powder
¼ teaspoon chili powder
Salt and pepper
1 small green pepper, sliced
1 cup water
⅔ cup coconut
Garnish: Steamed rice and chutney

Have the lamb cut in 1½-inch cubes. Put the onion, garlic, and oil in a heavy pot and cook slowly for 4 or 5 minutes without browning, then add all the condiments, and stir for a minute, then add the meat. Turn off the fire and let the curry marinate an hour, stirring it often. Boil ½ cup water and the coconut together, mashing the coconut well, then let it cool. Mash through a sieve. Then repeat with the rest of the water and the same coconut. Combine the two infusions. There will be about ¾ cup of coconut milk. Add the green pepper and ½ cup of the coconut milk to the lamb. Cover and simmer very slowly until the lamb is tender, about 1¼ hours. If necessary scoop out the lamb and boil the sauce down until it thickens somewhat. Or you may wish to serve a quantity of sauce over rice. Flour is not added to this sauce. If this is made ahead of time, and the sauce is boiled down, return the lamb to the pot and reheat before serving. Indian cooks generally add their ingredients separately instead of using curry powder. See Pantry Shelf for sources of fine curry as well as the ingredients. This serves 6.

ROAST LOIN OF PORK

6- to 10-rib roast of pork
3 or 4 tablespoons caramel or
   molasses
2 tablespoons Maggi or Kitchen
   Bouquet

Flour
Salt and pepper
2 cups vegetable juice
1 tablespoon cornstarch

Have the butcher saw through the bone of each rib for easy carving. Mix
3 or 4 tablespoons of caramel or molasses with 2 tablespoons Maggi liquid
seasoning or Kitchen Bouquet and paint the meat all over, catching the
syrup with a light sprinkle of flour. Put the meat in an open pan with no
water and roast at 300° for 2 hours. Twenty minutes before the meat is
done, if there are more than 3 tablespoons of fat in the pan, pour some off
and add 1 cup of the vegetable juice and let it roast with the meat. Blend
in the cornstarch with the other cup of juice. When the meat is done, remove it to a warm platter. Add the cornstarch-juice mixture to the pan,
cooking it until it thickens. Cooked slowly, the meat is tender and juicy
with a rich glaze and the gravy is delicious, especially when served over
baked sweet potatoes. Allow 1 thick chop for a serving. Good cold.

ROAST LOIN OF PORK WITH NUT BUTTER

6- or 8-rib roast of pork
½ cup nut butter: peanut, almond,
   or cashew
Flour
6 or 8 slices of onion

Salt and pepper
1 cup hot milk
1 tablespoon cornstarch
12 to 16 white onions

The end opposite from the tenderloin is the juicier cut. (Have the butcher
saw through the bone of each rib for easier carving.) Spread the nut butter
on the meat side of the ribs and sprinkle very lightly with flour. Cover with
the onion slices and fasten with toothpicks. Add salt and pepper. Put the
ribs down in the pan and roast in a 375° oven for 15 minutes, uncovered,
then baste with a little of the milk. Cover and roast at 300° for 1¼ hours,
or 25 minutes per pound. An hour before the roast is done, boil up the
whole white onions for 3 minutes, drain, and put around the roast. Remove
the toothpicks. Blend the cornstarch with the rest of the milk. When the
meat is done lift it to a hot platter and surround it with the onions. Put
the milk into the roasting pan and cook until it is thickened. Thin with
a little more hot milk if it is too thick. Add salt and pepper to taste.

ROAST MARINATED FRESH HAM

5- to 8-pound fresh ham
Marinade:
    2 cups dry white wine
    1 good-sized chopped onion
    ½ cup chopped carrot
    1 stalk of celery, with leaves
    1½ teaspoons salt
    Freshly ground pepper
    8 crushed juniper berries
    1 teaspoon ginger

Salt and pepper
½ teaspoon clove
3 tablespoons honey
¾ cup chopped onions
½ cup chopped carrot
½ cup sour cream
1 tablespoon cornstarch

Have the butcher remove the rind from the ham but leave most of the fat. Boning facilitates carving. The bone may cook with the meat. Mix the marinade and soak the ham in it for 2 days, turning it several times a day. When ready to roast the ham, remove it from the marinade and wipe it dry. Reserve the marinade. Tie if the ham is boned. Make a mixture of salt, pepper, clove, and honey and rub it all over the ham. Put the ham in a 375° oven and cook 15 minutes uncovered, then lift it so you can make a bed for it with the chopped vegetables. Lay the ham on them and pour over 1 cup of hot strained marinade. Cover tightly, turn the heat to 300°, and roast 30 minutes to the pound. When done remove the ham and strain the pan juices through a sieve. Mix the sour cream with the cornstarch and add. Cook until it thickens, then thin with some strained marinade so that it is the consistency of cream. Serve in a gravy boat. Mashed potatoes and brussels sprouts with chestnuts, and a fine white Burgundy, would be good accompaniments.

ROAST BONED SHOULDER OF PORK

5- or 6-pound boned shoulder of
    pork
2 or 3 tablespoons each
    molasses or honey and
    Kitchen Bouquet
1 small onion, chopped
2 tablespoons cornstarch
1½ cups milk

½ cup dry vermouth
Salt and pepper
Garnish:
    12 big sweet prunes
    ½ cup red wine
    ¼ cup white corn syrup
    ¼ teaspoon clove

Tie the meat and rub well with a mixture of the molasses or honey and Kitchen Bouquet. Put the meat in a roasting pan, cover it, and roast 2½ hours at less than 300°. Never let the heat become higher than 300°. Fifteen minutes before it is done, pour off half the fat and put the chopped onion in the pan. Return to the oven. Blend the cornstarch with the milk and cook until it thickens, then add the vermouth and salt and pepper. When the meat is done, remove it to a hot platter. Put the milk-wine mixture in the roasting pan and stir until the juices are blended. Add a little more milk and wine if the sauce is too thick. This is a great sauce for mashed white potatoes or mashed sweet potatoes. Steam the prunes in the wine, with syrup and clove, until tender and plump, and use as a garnish. Serve the sauce in a sauceboat. Serves 8.

ROAST PORK WITH VEGETABLES. Vegetables are very good cooked with roast shoulder or loin of pork. Onions, potatoes, cabbage, white turnips, or sweet potatoes are brought to the boil, drained, and arranged around the roast after it has roasted 1 hour. Before adding the vegetables, pour off all but 3 tablespoons of fat. After the meat is done, remove it to a platter and the vegetables to serving dishes, make the gravy with milk, cream, broth, or wine, thickened with cornstarch.

PORK LIVER LOAF WITH VEGETABLES

1 pound pork liver	1 small can evaporated milk
2 tablespoons butter	1 egg, beaten
1½ cups raw potato, shredded	2 teaspoons salt
1 cup raw carrots, shredded	1 teaspoon pepper
1 large onion, shredded	1 teaspoon each thyme and tarragon
4 tablespoons anchovy paste	2 tablespoons sherry
4 tablespoons fine cornmeal	3 strips bacon

Slice the liver and sear it in the butter a moment, then grind it. Shred all the vegetables on a fine disk shredder, then thoroughly blend all the ingredients (except the bacon). Line a pâté mold or breadpan with the bacon and fill with the mixture. Cover the mold, set it in a pan of hot water, and bake 45 minutes at 325° and another 25 minutes at 300°, uncovering it for the last 15 minutes. This may be served hot or chilled, and as a pâté.

KOLOZSVARI KAPOSZTA
(Pork Goulash, Sauerkraut, and Sour Cream)

2½ pounds boned shoulder of pork	Salt
2 large onions, chopped fine	⅓ cup boiling water
3 tablespoons oil or pork fat	2 cups sauerkraut
2 tablespoons sweet Hungarian paprika	1¼ cups heavy sour cream
	Garnish: Bowl of sour cream

Cut the meat in 2-inch cubes. Sauté the onions in the oil until they are yellow. Add the paprika and salt, mix well, then stir in the meat and cook for 10 minutes. Add ⅓ cup of boiling water, cover tightly, and cook over low heat until the meat is tender, about 1½ hours. Cover the sauerkraut with lukewarm water and drain well; this is important, for the dish must have a delicate flavor. Add the kraut to the meat and cook for 10 minutes, then add the sour cream and cook for 1 minute longer. Serves 6.

PORK CUTLETS WITH PORT AND CREAM

4 to 6 cutlets from boned
  shoulder of pork
  Pork fat or oil
1 tablespoon caramel or honey
  Salt and pepper
1½ teaspoons tarragon

⅓ cup port wine
⅓ cup heavy cream
1½ teaspoons cornstarch
Accompaniments:
  Fried apples
  Mashed sweet potatoes

Boned shoulder of pork is very tender, juicy meat and may be sliced and cooked the same way as pork chops. Glaze the cutlets in fat or oil with the caramel or honey until they are a rich brown. Season with salt, pepper, and tarragon. Cover tightly and simmer very gently 15 minutes; then turn the meat and add 2 or 3 tablespoons of the wine. Cover and cook 10 to 15 minutes more, according to the thickness of the meat. If the cutlets are over ½-inch thick, they will need a total of 30 minutes of very slow cooking. Blend the rest of the wine and the cream with the cornstarch. Lift the meat to hot plates or a hot platter and put the wine mixture in the cooking pan. Scrape the juices and mix with the sauce and when it thickens pour it over the meat. The cutlets may be baked in the oven or cooked over a flame. Tart sliced apples seasoned with plenty of cinnamon and brown sugar and covered with bits of butter may be baked 20 minutes in the oven along with the meat. Allow 1 or 2 cutlets for each serving.

PORK CHOPS ITALIAN STYLE

6 1-inch-thick chops from loin or
  boned shoulder
  Pork fat or butter
2 tablespoons brown sugar
  Salt and pepper
2 teaspoons thyme
1½ cups small noodle shells

Sauce:
1 cup tomato purée
1 small can tomato sauce
3 cloves garlic, crushed
  Salt and pepper
1 cup chopped onions
1 green pepper, chopped
½ cup dry white wine
1 teaspoon fennel
Garnish: Chopped parsley

Glaze the chops in a skillet in the fat or butter and the brown sugar. Salt and pepper them and sprinkle with thyme. Put the chops in a casserole and add the uncooked noodles around them. Mix all the ingredients for the sauce and simmer for 10 minutes, then pour it over the chops. Cover and bake 40 minutes at 325°. Sprinkle parsley over the top. Serve out of the casserole if desired. Serves 6.

BAKED PORK CHOPS AND CABBAGE

4 or 6 thick chops
Oil
Caramel or honey
Salt and pepper
1 small new cabbage

1 teaspoon caraway powder or 1
    tablespoon anise seeds
½ cup thin onion rings
1 cup light cream
½ cup shredded Gruyère or Swiss
    cheese

Glaze the chops on both sides in a little oil and caramel or honey. Salt and pepper them. Wash the cabbage and cut it in eighths. Steam it with only the water that clings to it about 8 minutes, covered, so it is half tender. Arrange it in a casserole, sprinkle with the caraway powder or anise seeds and a little salt and pepper, and the onions. Lay the chops on top. Heat the cream, melt the cheese in it, and pour over all. Bake in a 325° oven for 35 or 40 minutes, uncovered. Serves 4 or 6.

PORK CHOPS WITH APPLES AND ONIONS

6 pork chops, 1 inch thick, from
    loin or boned shoulder
Pork fat or oil
3 tablespoons honey
Salt and pepper
Tarragon

6 tart apples
6 red sweet onions
½ cup light brown sugar
1 cup dry white wine
2 teaspoons cinnamon
½ cup buttered crumbs

Glaze the chops in fat or oil, and the honey. Sprinkle them with salt, pepper, and tarragon. Peel the apples and onions and cut them in very thin slices. Mix them and put half on the bottom of a casserole, lay the glazed chops on next, and cover with the rest of the apples and onions. Boil up the sugar, wine, and cinnamon and pour over the top. Cover and bake for 1 hour at 300°. Sprinkle the top with the buttered crumbs and let the casserole stand in the oven uncovered for 5 minutes. Serves 6.

SHOULDER CHOPS WITH CARAMEL

4 ¾-inch-thick boned shoulder
    chops
Salt, pepper, and thyme
Oil

4 tablespoons *Caramel Syrup*
3 tablespoons sherry
⅓ to ½ cup sour cream

Rub the chops with salt, pepper, and thyme. Put them in a heavy skillet with a little oil and the caramel, sauté until they have a good glaze. Cover and bake them at 350° for 15 minutes, then turn them over and bake at 300° for 10 minutes more. Lift the chops onto hot plates. Add the sherry and sour cream to the pan and stir with the juices. Heat and pour over the chops. Serves 4.

BAKED PORK CHOPS WITH BROWN OR PATNA RICE

6 thick chops from loin or
  boned shoulder
Pork fat or oil
Honey or brown sugar
Salt and pepper
1 cup chopped onions
1¼ cups patna or brown rice,
  washed

3 cups chicken broth
1 teaspoon turmeric
½ teaspoon cinnamon
½ teaspoon clove
1 teaspoon cumin
1 teaspoon curry powder

Glaze the chops in the fat or oil and the honey or sugar. Salt and pepper them. Sauté the onions. Cook the washed rice in 2 cups of the chicken broth, over very low heat, tightly covered, patna for 30 minutes or brown rice for 45. Mix the rice and onions. Put half of the rice and onions in a casserole, lay the chops on it, and cover them with the rest of the rice and onions. Mix all the condiments with the rest of the broth, bring to a boil, then pour over the dish. Cover tightly and bake at 300° for 40 minutes. If the rice becomes at all dry add a little more broth. Serves 6.

BAKED PORK CHOPS OR SPARERIBS

6 thick chops, or enough meaty
  spareribs for 6
Molasses or caramel
Kitchen Bouquet
⅓ cup shredded green pepper

½ cup shredded onion
Salt and pepper
1 tablespoon cornstarch
1¼ cups milk

Paint the chops (or spareribs cut in servings) with a mixture of molasses or caramel and Kitchen Bouquet. Put the meat in the bottom of a baking pan and bake uncovered 10 minutes at 350°; turn it and bake 10 minutes more on the other side. Salt and pepper it. Mix the pepper and onion with their juices and sprinkle over the meat. Turn down to 325°. Bake 10 minutes, then turn the meat so the vegetables are on the bottom of the pan. Bake 5 minutes more. Mix the cornstarch with the milk and cook until it thickens, add a little salt and pepper. Remove the meat to a hot platter and keep warm. Stir the milk into the pan juices and cook until it is thoroughly blended with the vegetables. Thin a little with milk if the sauce seems too thick. If the vegetables have been shredded fine the sauce will not have to be sieved. This is fine gravy to serve over mashed potatoes. Serves 6.

FEGATELLO CON RETE
da Vasco, Bologna

Via Santo Stefano is a very important street in Bologna because just before you turn into it from via Rizzoli you come to Pappagallo, just to the right of it is Sampieri, and down it is the magnificent ancient Church of Santo Stefano, "a sacred edifice of diverse epochs," begun in the eleventh century. Along via Santo Stefano there are several good restaurants and shops. To reach da Vasco you walk until you come to the end of the street, and I advise you to walk for two reasons: to work up an appetite, and to be able to stop and gaze at the fascinating old houses and examine the courtyards as you go along. Bologna is a walking city and it would take years of strolling to see it all. Even in the rain you may walk miles under arcades. I have described the service of da Vasco under *Antipasto da Vasco.*

Pork liver	Thin pork fat
Salt and pepper	Bread

Season the chunks of liver and wrap them in a thin layer of pounded pork fat. String them on long skewers, alternating with 1-inch-thick slices of French or Italian bread, and cook on a spit. The bread catches some of the burning fat and is as good, almost, as the liver. The fat burns off. This takes about 15 minutes of turning on the spit. It could be done over a skillet under the flame. This wonderful dish is one of the meats on the meat cart that comes to the table at da Vasco. The other meats are roast chicken from the spit, roast beef, pork, lamb, veal, and turkey; also browned potatoes and French fried zucchini sticks. Allow 1 good-sized piece of liver to a serving.

PORK SAUSAGE

1½ pounds lean pork, ground	2 teaspoons marjoram
½ pound fat and lean pork, ground	1 teaspoon chervil
	1 teaspoon thyme
1 clove garlic, crushed	2 teaspoons fennel
1 medium-sized onion, ground	½ teaspoon sage
1 tablespoon salt	1 teaspoon cumin powder
1 teaspoon freshly ground pepper	2 teaspoons basil
2 teaspoons grated lemon rind	1 teaspoon chili powder

Have the butcher grind the meat. Fat and lean pork means pork with a marbling of fat. Grind the meats again at home with the garlic and onion then mix it with the rest of the ingredients. Use as many of the herbs as you wish, as they are all mild except the chili and 2 pounds of meat needs that zest. Make into patties and fry quickly until brown on both sides in a little oil or butter, then put them in a 325° oven for 15 minutes to finish cooking. You can keep any uncooked sausage wrapped in foil in a cold part of the refrigerator for several days. Serve with hot applesauce or fried apples.

BARBECUED SPARERIBS

Meaty fresh spareribs
Marinade:
  1 tablespoon chili powder
  Brown sugar
  1 tablespoon orégano
  1 tablespoon paprika
  2 cloves garlic, crushed
  ½ cup olive oil

Basting sauce:
  1 cup chopped onions
  ¼ cup olive oil
  Salt and pepper
  1⅔ cups tomato sauce
  ¼ cup vinegar
  2 tablespoons Worcester-
    shire sauce
  ¼ cup honey

Have the spareribs cut in serving lengths. Mix the marinade, rub it into the ribs, and let them stand all day. This is enough marinade for 4 servings. For the basting sauce, sauté the onions in the oil until tender, then add all the rest of the ingredients. Let the marinade cling to the spareribs and add any that remains to the sauce. If the ribs are grilled outdoors, baste them with the sauce as they cook. If they are done indoors, put them in a long baking pan and cover each rib with some of the sauce, using half of it. Bake them at 350° for 30 minutes, turning once after 15 minutes. See that they are well moistened. When the ribs are done, remove them to a hot platter and put the remaining sauce in the baking pan, scraping all the residue into the sauce. Serve the sauce separately. If more sauce is required, increase the tomato sauce.

CHINESE SWEET-AND-SOUR SPARERIBS

Meaty spareribs
Oil for deep frying
Batter:
  2 eggs, beaten
  4 tablespoons cornstarch
  1 teaspoon salt
  1 tablespoon sugar

Sauce:
  1¼ cups chicken broth
  ⅓ cup Madeira or sherry
  1 tablespoon vinegar
  2 tablespoons cornstarch
  ¼ cup minced sweet pickles
  1 teaspoon sugar
  ½ cup pineapple chunks,
    drained
  2 tablespoons minced pre-
    served ginger
  ½ cup canned pineapple
    syrup (if needed)
  8 raw carrot curls

Have the spareribs cut with a cleaver into 1½-inch lengths, allowing 4 or 5 to a serving. Beat the ingredients for the batter together, dip the spareribs in it, and deep-fry at 365° measured by a deep-oil thermometer 7 or 8 minutes till golden brown. Drain them on brown paper and keep warm in the oven with the door ajar until all are fried. This batter ought to be sufficient for enough spareribs to serve 5. More batter may be made quickly for a larger quantity of ribs. For the sauce, blend the liquids with the cornstarch and cook until thickened. Stir in the other ingredients (except the carrot curls). If the sauce is too thick stir in the pineapple syrup drained from the chunks. Add the carrot curls just before serving. This sauce may accompany *Chinese Glazed Spareribs*, which are simpler to prepare and also very good.

CHINESE GLAZED SPARERIBS

Meaty fresh spareribs
Soy sauce
Salt

Honey or molasses
Peanut oil or soy oil

Have the spareribs cut in 5-inch lengths with the ribs cut apart. Rub with a mixture of soy sauce, a very little salt, and honey or a mixture of honey and molasses, and let the ribs marinate 1 hour. Put oil in a long pan, lay the spareribs on the bottom, and scrape the marinade over them. Bake uncovered in a 375° oven for 15 minutes, turn the ribs over, and continue baking another 15 minutes at 325°. The spareribs should have a fine glaze and be juicy and tender; I find dried up spareribs very discouraging. If they are baking too fast at 325° turn the heat to 300°. They may be served with the sauce for *Chinese Sweet-and-Sour Spareribs*, or accompanied with sauerkraut, applesauce, rye bread, and beer.

BAKED PORK CHOPS WITH DRIED SPLIT PEAS OR LENTILS

5 or 6 1-inch chops from loin or
    boned shoulder
2 cups dried peas or lentils
    Pork fat or oil
2 tablespoons brown sugar

Salt and pepper
2 teaspoons basil
1 cup chopped onions
2 tablespoons tomato paste
1 teaspoon prepared mustard

Soak the dried peas or lentils 6 hours in 4 cups of water, then cook them in the water they soaked in for 15 minutes. Add a little more water if necessary. Drain and reserve the water for basting. Brown the chops on both sides in the fat or oil and the sugar until they have a rich glaze. Add salt, pepper, and basil. Sauté the onions in fat or oil until they are tender and mix them with the peas or lentils. Put half of the mixture on the bottom of a casserole, lay the chops on this and cover with the rest of the peas or lentils and onions. Mix the tomato paste and mustard with 1 cup of the reserved water, season with salt and pepper, and pour it over the top. Add another ½ cup of the liquid, cover, and bake 1 hour at 325°. If it is cooking too fast, turn down to 300°. Add more liquid if necessary to keep moist. Serves 5 or 6.

BOILED HAM WITH BING CHERRIES

10- to 12-pound ham
2 quarts cider
1 teaspoon powdered clove
1 tablespoon cinnamon
3 bay leaves
⅔ cup brown sugar

1 teaspoon powdered clove
½ cup port
1 can Bing cherries
3 teaspoons cornstarch
2 teaspoons prepared mustard

If the ham is sugar-cured, ready-to-cook ham, it needs no preliminary soaking. Hickory-smoked Virginia hams need from 12 to 24 hours soaking and are then scrubbed and rinsed. Put the ham in a large kettle and pour the cider over it, adding enough water to cover it. Add the clove, cinnamon, and bay leaves. Cover and simmer gently 3 or 4 hours, according to the type of ham—15 minutes a pound for sugar-cured hams and 20 minutes a pound for Virginia hams. When the bone loosens from the meat, the ham is done. Take it from the kettle and remove the skin with a sharp-pointed knife, leaving all the fat on the ham. Score the fat with a sharp knife, making 1½-inch squares. Make a paste of the brown sugar, clove, and ¼ cup of the port. Spread and pat this over the surface of the ham. Drain the cherries from the syrup. Pit the cherries and fasten 1 cherry with a toothpick in each square over the ham. Boil down the cherry syrup to 1 cup, add the rest of the wine, and use this to baste the ham. Put the ham in an open baking pan, put it in a 325° oven and bake for 45 minutes, basting occasionally with the cherry liquid. Remove the ham to a platter. Pour the pan juices into a cup and add enough wine to make 1¼ cups. Blend the cornstarch with the juices and cook until thickened; add the rest of the pitted cherries and the mustard. Serve in a sauceboat to accompany the ham. Serves 12, or more. Virginia ham is carved in paper-thin slices.

NEW ENGLAND BOILED DINNER

Small ham, or 6- to 7-pound
    shank end of ham
8 white turnips
8 young carrots
8 white onions

8 medium-sized potatoes
1 new cabbage cut in eighths
Freshly ground pepper
Garnish: *Mustard Sauce*

Soak the ham overnight in cold water. Three hours before dinner put the ham in a very large kettle, cover with fresh water, bring it to a simmer for 10 minutes, and drain. Cover with fresh hot water and simmer 2 hours very gently. Boil up the turnips, drain, and add them to the ham. Ten minutes later boil up the carrots and onions, drain, and add them. Ten minutes later boil up and drain the potatoes and cabbage. Add them and cook until the potatoes are tender. Lift the ham on to a platter and arrange all the drained vegetables around it. Serve with the *Mustard Sauce* made with sour cream. Serves 4 to 8.

CHOUCROUTE
Maison Kammerzell, Strasbourg

Lovely Alsace is a paradise for gourmets. Its fertile countryside produces fine vegetables—especially asparagus—poultry, geese for foie gras, and grapes for its flowery wines: Riesling, Tokay, Gewurtztraminer, Muscat, Pinot, and Sylvaner. Its excellent beer goes very well with Choucroute and Baeckenofe, two Alsatian specialties. Strasbourg has many interesting things to see besides its famous cathedral: the Fine Arts Museum, the eighteenth-century Château des Rohan, canals, and picturesque old houses. It was the home of Gutenberg, and it was here that Rouget de Lisle composed the Marseillaise in 1792. The Rhine and the Marne meet here and there are delightful Rhine-Vosges excursions by boat. One should not get as far as Strasbourg without visiting Colmar, a few miles to the south, to see one of the world's great masterpieces, the Isenheim altarpiece by Matthias Grünewald. Back to Strasbourg, and across from the cathedral, the Maison Kammerzell occupies a wonderful 5-story fifteenth-century Mother Goose house, with three dining floors all decorated and furnished in antique style. Its food is among the best in Alsace; specialties include Vosge Mountain trout, foie gras in various ways, chicken and venison pies, Alsatian ham and bacon, wild game, Metz strawberries and many more. Here is their famous Choucroute.

3½ to 4 pounds sauerkraut	10 coriander berries, crushed
½ cup goose fat	2 cups Riesling
1 pound onions, thinly sliced	2 pounds fresh bacon
2 cloves garlic, crushed	2½ pounds fresh pork belly
1 crushed bay leaf	2 pounds smoked uncooked loin
1 whole clove	of pork
3 juniper berries, crushed	1 wineglass Riesling, warmed

Melt the goose fat in a heavy pot and sauté the onions until tender without browning them. Add the seasonings. Wash the sauerkraut in warm water and drain it. Mix half the sauerkraut with the onions, put this in the bottom of a big casserole, arrange the meats on it, and cover with the rest of the sauerkraut. Pour 2 cups wine over it and cook slowly at 300° for 2 hours. Pour the small glass of warm wine over it just before serving. The dish may be served from the casserole or the meat put on a large platter surrounded by the sauerkraut. Each person is given a slice of each kind of meat. Serve with boiled or mashed potatoes and a choice of beer and Riesling, black bread and butter. Serves 10.

The meats specified are not always available except in good pork stores. In New York City, I recommend Schaller & Weber, 86th Street and 2nd Avenue, where they have them all and were very helpful in translating the cuts peculiar to Alsace. When we left Nancy, Georges Romain of the Capucin Gourmand expressed regret that we would not be there in the winter when he could serve us his really great dishes, too heavy for summer.

Alsace has none of these restrictions; its residents consume Choucroute and other "winter" dishes all summer long.

MAYA'S ROAST SUCKLING PIG

10- to 12-pound pig
   Salt and freshly ground pepper
   Flour
   Fat from the pig
   Broth
Garnish:
   Red apple
   Wreath of parsley
   Baked sweet potatoes
   Applesauce

Stuffing No. 1:
   2½ cups coarse rye-bread crumbs
   ¼ cup sherry
   ½ pound calf's liver
   3 pork sausages
   Salt and pepper
   1 teaspoon each sage and thyme
   2 eggs, beaten
Stuffing No. 2:
   1 pound cooked chestnuts
   3 tart apples
   Salt and pepper
   Cinnamon or anise
   3 pork sausages
   2½ cups coarse rye-bread crumbs
   ½ teaspoon mace
   1 teaspoon tarragon
   ¼ cup sherry

Have the piglet well cleaned by the butcher. Wash it well inside and dry it. Remove some of the fat and reserve. For the first stuffing, put the crumbs in a large mixing bowl and sprinkle with the sherry. Sear the sliced liver a moment on both sides in a little fat, then grind it. Brown the sausages and cut them in 1-inch lengths. Mix all the ingredients together, stuff the pig, and sew it up. Rub it well with salt, pepper, and flour. It has a block of wood in the mouth to keep it open. Tie pieces of foil over the snout and ears to prevent their burning. Tie all the legs forward under the pig. Put it in a large uncovered roaster in a 400° oven for ½ hour, then turn down the heat to 325°. Roast it 15 minutes to the pound—2½ hours for a 10-pound pig. Baste often with the reserved pig fat, melted and mixed with chicken or veal broth. When the pig is done rub it well with melted fat. Remove the wood from its mouth and put in a red apple. Make a wreath of parsley to hang over one ear so it will look like Bacchus. Bring it to the table on a long platter and carve it across. This is a most wonderful and delicate meat, and this stuffing is like a pâté. If you prefer Stuffing No. 2, boil the chestnuts 1½ minutes, skin while warm, cook them 10 minutes, and drain. Peel and slice 3 large apples and fry them in a little butter. Season with salt, pepper, and a little cinnamon or anise powder. Mix all the ingredients together and stuff the pig. This serves 8. Serve with a fine Moselle or a light red wine such as Beaujolais.

HAM, KRAUT, AND KNACKWURST CASSEROLE

Slice of ham 1¾-inch thick
1 cup white wine
3 cups sauerkraut
3 teaspoons crushed juniper berries
   or 1½ teaspoons caraway
   powder
Freshly ground pepper

8 fat knackwurst
Accompaniments:
   Boiled or mashed potatoes
   Mustard Sauce with cream
   Dill pickles
   Beer
   Black bread

Select a fine tender piece of ham. Simmer it in the wine, covered, for 15 minutes then cut it into 8 servings. Cover the sauerkraut with lukewarm water and drain it through a sieve. Mix it with the juniper or caraway and some freshly ground pepper, no salt. Put half of it in a big baking dish, cover with all the ham, then the rest of the sauerkraut, then pour over it the wine that the ham cooked in. Bake 20 minutes at 350°. After 10 minutes, cover the knackwurst with water, boil 10 minutes, drain, lay on top of the sauerkraut, and serve immediately. This serves 8. It makes a very good Sunday night supper.

CASSEROLE OF HAM AND KIDNEY BEANS

2 slices of cooked ham, ½-inch
   thick
Butter
1 cup sliced onions
1 green pepper, cut in strips

1 teaspoon tarragon or powdered
   fennel
1 small can tomato sauce
1 large can kidney beans
4 strips crisply fried bacon

Dip the ham in hot butter and cut each slice into 4 serving pieces. Sauté the onions and green pepper until tender. Mix the herb with the tomato sauce. Mix the onions, pepper, tomato sauce, and beans together. Put half the beans in a casserole or baking dish, add the ham, and cover with the rest of the beans. Bake, covered, at 350° for 20 minutes, then uncover, put the crisp bacon on top, and bake 15 minutes more at 325°. This will serve 8 as a buffet supper dish or 6 as a main dish.

HAM TETRAZZINI

2½ cups finely cubed ham
½ pound fresh button mushrooms
¼ cup butter
½ cup finely sliced green onions
2 cloves garlic, crushed
8 sliced Greek or Italian black
   olives (in oil)

Sauce:
   1⅔ cups light cream
   3 teaspoons cornstarch
   2 tablespoons tomato paste
   ¼ teaspoon nutmeg
   Salt and pepper
12 ounces small noodle shells
Garnish: Parmesan cheese

Cut the ham in ¼-inch cubes. Put the mushrooms, butter, onions, and garlic in a pan and bake 12 minutes at 375°, then mix lightly with the ham. Add the olives to the mixture. Make the cream sauce. Blend the cream with the cornstarch and cook over a low flame until it thickens, then stir in the tomato paste, nutmeg, salt, and pepper. Stir the sauce into the ham mixture. Boil the noodle shells in plenty of salted boiling water about 12 minutes or until they are tender, then drain. Put the noodles on a deep platter or serving dish and put the heated sauce on top. Sprinkle with cheese and serve immediately. Pass a bowl of Parmesan cheese. Serve with a green salad and red wine. Serves 4 to 6.

CRÊPES FILLED WITH HAM

Crêpes:
- 4 eggs, beaten
- 1⅞ cups sifted flour
- ½ teaspoon salt
- 2 cups milk
- ¼ cup melted butter
- Butter for frying

Filling:
- 2½ cups ground ham
- ½ cup medium cream sauce
- ¼ cup minced shallots or green onions
- 2 tablespoons butter
- 4 fresh mushrooms, chopped

Sauce:
- 2 cups light cream
- 2 tablespoons cornstarch
- 1½ tablespoons tomato paste
- Salt and pepper

Parmesan cheese

Mix all the ingredients for the crêpes in an electric blender or with a rotary beater and let the batter stand 2 hours before frying the crêpes. Have the filling and sauce ready. For the filling, grind the ham and moisten it with the cream sauce. Sauté the shallots or green onions in the butter 2 minutes; add the mushrooms and cook 1 minute more. Mix with the ham. For the sauce, blend the cream, cornstarch, and tomato paste until smooth and cook until it thickens. When ready to make the crêpes, lightly butter a crêpe pan or 7-inch skillet and let it become quite hot. Put in 2 soupspoons of batter and after timing it 1 minute turn the crêpe and fry a few seconds more. Turn out, fill it with a large kitchen spoon of ham filling, roll it, and put it on the bottom of a well-buttered shallow baking pan. A lasagne pan is ideal for this. Make and fill 12 crêpes and moisten the top of each with the sauce. Sprinkle well with cheese and run the pan under the flame to reheat and brown the sauce and melt the cheese. The crêpes may be prepared 1 hour ahead of time and run under the flame just before serving. Serves 6.

HAM LOAF

1¼ pounds smoked ham, ground
1½ pounds lean fresh pork, ground
4 ounces fat bacon, ground
1 green pepper, ground
1 medium sized onion, ground
1 cup soft breadcrumbs
3 eggs, beaten

1 teaspoon clove
1 teaspoon thyme
¼ teaspoon nutmeg
1 teaspoon tarragon
½ cup milk
½ cup light brown sugar
3 tablespoons sweet vermouth

Grind all the meats and vegetables and mix them well. Add the crumbs, beaten eggs, and seasonings. When well blended together stir in the milk. Grease a good-sized breadpan and pack the brown sugar on the sides and bottom, then put in the mixture. Set the pan in a pan of hot water and bake at 300° 1½ hours. When the loaf is done, turn it upside down onto a platter. Put the vermouth into the pan and let it boil up over a flame, then scrape it over the loaf. Serve with Mustard Sauce made with sour cream. This is a fine loaf, suitable for guests, or for a buffet supper. Serves 8 to 10.

COLD HAM MOUSSE

2¼ cups ground ham
1 cup sliced fresh mushrooms
2 tablespoons butter
2 tablespoons grated onion
1½ cups canned madrilene
2 tablespoons gelatin
¼ cup Madeira or sherry

¾ cup chicken broth
⅓ cup mayonnaise
½ teaspoon mustard
1 cup heavy cream, whipped
1 tablespoon tomato paste
Garnish: Stuffed hard-boiled eggs

Chill a metal charlotte mold; also chill the canned madrilene. Put the madrilene in the mold. If the aspic is too stiff let it stand at room temperature until it is runny, then tip the mold in all directions so that the aspic covers bottom and sides. Refrigerate for a few minutes, then remove it and again tip in all directions. Repeat this until the mold is covered with aspic which clings to it. Keep refrigerated until ready to fill with the cold ham mixture. Grind the ham very fine. Sauté the mushrooms in the butter, add the onion, then put through the grinder and mix with the ham. Soak the gelatin in the wine. Heat the broth, melt the gelatin in it and let cool thoroughly. Whip the cream until stiff, mix it with the tomato paste, and add the ham mixture, mayonnaise, and mustard. Pack into the mold and refrigerate several hours. To unmold invert on a round serving plate and hold around the mold a moment a towel which has been wrung out of hot water. Decorate with stuffed hard-boiled eggs and salad greens. This is a fine buffet dish or a summer dinner entrée. Serves 8 or 10.

HAM AND SWEET POTATOES

Slice of ham, ¾-inch thick
4 or 5 sweet potatoes
½ cup light corn syrup
½ cup orange juice
3 tablespoons butter

½ cup heavy cream
Salt and pepper
2 jiggers Cointreau or Curaçao
¼ teaspoon nutmeg

Choose tender ham. Boil the potatoes until just tender, skin, and mash them. Add to the potatoes all the ingredients except 1 jigger of liqueur. Put half the potatoes in a well-greased shallow oblong baking dish, lay on the ham, then cover with the rest of the potatoes. Cover with a lid or foil and bake at 325° for 40 minutes. Pour the other jigger of liqueur over and serve. Serves 6. For a holiday-season touch, the top may be covered with halved fresh chestnuts. Or use chestnuts packed in syrup, which are drained first. The syrup may be used in the sweet potatoes instead of the corn syrup, but it will be quite sweet.

HAM AND POTATO HASH

2 cups cubed ham
½ green pepper, cut in strips
1 medium-sized onion, sliced thin
3 tablespoons ham fat or butter
A little salt and freshly ground pepper

1 egg
3 boiled potatoes, cubed
1 tablespoon sweet vermouth or Madeira
Garnish: Chopped parsley

Leftover baked ham is used for this and the hash is well flavored if the sweet encrusted fat is retained. Sauté the pepper and onion in the ham fat or butter until tender. Add the salt and pepper. Stir in the raw egg, and let it scramble a little, then add the potatoes and toss all the ingredients together. Garnish with the parsley. Serves 4.

JAMBON À LA CRÈME

Slice of fine sugar-cured ham, ¾-inch thick
1 tablespoon honey
½ teaspoon powdered clove
3 tablespoons butter
⅓ cup chopped green onions or shallots
½ cup diced fresh mushrooms

⅓ cup dry vermouth
⅓ cup chicken or veal broth
Freshly ground pepper
3 teaspoons cornstarch
¾ cup heavy cream
Garnish: Chopped parsley

This is a fine dish for 4; double the recipe for 8. Rub the ham on both sides with the honey and clove. Be sure to leave the fat on the ham. Melt the butter in a skillet and when it is quite hot heat the ham in it on both sides, just to glaze a second, not to stiffen it. Scrape the butter into a shallow baking pan and make a bed of the onions or shallots and the mushrooms. Lay the ham on it and pour the vermouth and broth over it with a sprinkle of pepper. Bake uncovered for 20 minutes at 350°. Blend the cornstarch with the cream. Pour off some of the ham juices and add to the cream. Pour the cream mixture over the ham to blend with all the juices and let it thicken in the oven. Serve in its baking dish or lift onto a hot platter and cover with the sauce. Sprinkle with parsley. Serve with a buttered green vegetable and parsley potatoes, and a bottle of white Burgundy.

HAM SOUFFLÉ

2 cups ground ham
3 egg yolks
Freshly ground pepper
1 tablespoon tomato paste

1 teaspoon powdered chicken concentrate
1 cup heavy cream, scalded
3 tablespoons Madeira or sherry
4 egg whites, beaten

Grind the ham with its fat. Mix the egg yolks with pepper, tomato paste, and chicken concentrate, then pour the scalded cream slowly over the mixture. Cook a moment until it thickens a little. Add the wine and ham, fold in ¼ of the stiffly beaten egg whites, mix well, then lightly fold in the rest. Put the mixture into a greased soufflé dish and bake at 350° for 25 minutes or until set but still moist inside. This may be served with *Fresh Mushroom Sauce*. Serves 4 to 6 depending on the size of the menu. A larger soufflé may be made by increasing the ingredients, using 2½ cups of ground ham and 1¼ cups heavy cream, 5 egg yolks, and 7 whites.

HAM WITH ORANGE RAISIN SAUCE

Slice of ham, ¾-inch thick
2 tablespoons butter
¼ cup brown sugar
1 tablespoon grated orange rind
½ cup tomato purée

Freshly ground pepper
¼ teaspoon clove or nutmeg
½ cup orange juice
⅓ cup raisins

Melt the butter in a skillet and add the brown sugar. Over a very low flame glaze the ham in this on both sides. Add the rind, purée, pepper, and spice. Put into a 325° oven. Marinate the raisins in the orange juice, and add after 15 minutes' baking, then bake another 15 minutes. The sauce should be syrupy. Serve with sweet potatoes or mashed white potatoes. Serves 4.

HAM BAKED WITH LIMA BEANS

1½ cups dried lima beans
1¾-inch-thick slice sugar-cured ham
    Butter
1 cup milk

1 small can evaporated milk
2 tablespoons tomato paste
1 teaspoon mustard
½ cup thinly sliced onions

Soak the beans overnight or all day, well covered with water. Put the ham in a buttered baking dish. Drain the beans, mix them with all the rest of the ingredients, and put on top of the ham. Cover and bake at 300° 1¾ hours, then uncover and bake 15 minutes more—2 hours in all. During the baking add a little boiling milk if the beans become at all dry. A good idea is to put a pan of cornbread in the oven 25 minutes before the ham and beans are done. Serves 4 to 6.

Poultry & Game

ROAST CHICKEN, TURKEY, OR GOOSE

The bird
Caramel
Flour
Salt and pepper
Stuffings (see end of this section)
  2 tablespoons cornstarch
¼ cup dry vermouth (port for
    goose)

Broth:
    Giblets and wing tips
    Salt and pepper
⅓ cup chopped onions
1 teaspoon thyme
2½ cups water

The bird is wiped dry, trussed, and brought to room temperature. Paint the surface all over with Caramel which makes a rich glaze. Sprinkle lightly with seasoned flour. Stuff or not as you choose. Make the broth by simmering all the ingredients for 25 minutes. Strain it and baste the bird frequently. After roasting a goose 1 hour, remove it and pour off all the grease, return it to the pan and continue roasting, then its basting begins. Chicken and turkey do not need this degreasing. A thick slice of pork fat, split to the rind, may be fastened over the breast of chicken and turkey. After they are browned 10 minutes in an open roaster, the pan is covered. When the bird is done it is removed to a platter and kept warm. Blend the cornstarch with the wine and add it to the pan juices, a little at a time. Two tablespoons of cornstarch will thicken 2¼ cups of liquid. The sauce is served in a sauceboat. The roasting time table is for young poultry of prime quality. One pound of meat is allowed for each serving. The 10 minutes of browning is included in the roasting time.

Time Table for Roasting Poultry

The bird is browned for 10 minutes in a 400° oven, then the heat is reduced to 325° for the first hour, then is reduced to 300° for the remainder of the roasting.

	WEIGHT (POUNDS)	TIME (MINUTES PER POUND)	TOTAL
Chickens	2	20	40 to 45 minutes
	4	18	1¼ hours
	5	17	1 hour 25 minutes
	6	15	1 hour 30 to 45 minutes
Turkeys	10 to 12	15	2½ hours
	16	13	3 hours 18 minutes
	20	12	4 hours
Geese	10 to 12	15	2½ hours

POULET À L'ANGEVINE

2 2½- to 3-pound chickens
½ cup butter
8 or 10 shallots or green onions, chopped
Salt and pepper
1 pound fresh button mushrooms

½ to ¾ cup dry white wine or dry vermouth
2 tablespoons flour
2 cups heavy cream
3 tablespoons brandy or applejack
3 tablespoons sweet butter

This dish was created by Alphonse Denis at the fair at Angers in 1926 and since has become one of the specialties of the region. We don't have to go to Angers or even to Henri's in New York for it; we can make it at home by choosing fine chickens and other ingredients of the best quality. Have the chickens disjointed. Melt the butter in a large pan or casserole and add the finely chopped shallots or green onions. Stir the chicken in this for about 15 minutes over a low flame. Season with salt and pepper. The chicken will be about half done. Add the mushrooms and the wine to the chicken, cover, and cook slowly for 15 to 25 minutes more, or until the chicken is just done. This may be done in a 325° oven. Remove the chicken and mushrooms to a hot platter and keep them warm. Add the flour to the pan juices and blend until smooth; when it has thickened add the cream and let it bubble about 8 minutes to reduce. Add the liquor and beat in the butter, a little at a time. Pour the sauce over the chicken and serve. A flowery Anjou wine would be nice with this. Serves 6.

FRICASSEE DE VOLAILLE AUX MORILLES
Chapon Fin, Thoissey (Ain)

About 260 miles from Paris, between Mâcon and Lyon, there is a country inn with some of the very best cooking in France. It is owned and run by the well-known chef Paul Blanc and his attractive and hospitable wife. When all Paris is shut down for the month of August, or in fact at any other time, there isn't a better vacation spot than this well-appointed hotel-restaurant where one may enjoy outdoor dining and lovely walks and drives over the countryside. A look at the guestbook will inform you that a prince of Sweden and other important gastronomes pay frequent visits to Chapon Fin. M. Blanc gave me a half-dozen favorite dishes which have made his cooking famous. La Cave du Chapon Fin shelters every good vintage wine the connoisseur might ask for.

A fine 2½-pound chicken
Bouquet garni:
   Thyme, bay leaf, parsley
6 white onions
6 cloves
1 pound fresh mushrooms or 2 ounces dried mushrooms
⅓ cup butter

Salt and freshly ground pepper
Paprika
Beurre manié:
   2 tablespoons flour mixed with 2 tablespoons butter
2 cups heavy cream

Cut up the chicken as for frying. Tie the bouquet garni with a string. Put a clove in each of the onions, leaving the onions whole. If dried mushrooms are used, they must be previously soaked and washed. Melt the butter in a big casserole. Season the chicken with salt, pepper, and paprika, and put it in. Add the bouquet garni and the onions and cook uncovered until the chicken is about half done. Add the mushrooms, cover, and cook about 20 minutes. The mushrooms will render a little juice. Remove the chicken, mushrooms, bouquet garni, and onions. Thicken the sauce with the beurre manié, and when it is smooth, add the heavy cream. Heat and pour the sauce over the chicken, which should be very "unctuous."

COQ AU RIESLING
Maison Kammerzell, Strasbourg

1 fine 2½-pound chicken
3 tablespoons butter
2 tablespoons oil
⅓ cup chopped shallots or green
    onions
6 ounces fresh mushrooms, sliced

1½ cups Alsatian Riesling
1½ cups fresh heavy cream
    Salt and freshly ground pepper
Beurre manié:
    2 tablespoons flour mixed
      with 2 tablespoons butter

Cut the chicken in quarters and brown it on both sides in the butter and oil until it is golden. Meanwhile soak the shallots and sliced mushrooms in the wine. Put the chicken in a shallow baking dish, rinse the sauté pan with the wine and vegetables, and pour it over the chicken. Cook the chicken 20 to 25 minutes, until it is tender, add the cream, and cook 10 minutes more. This may be done in a 350° oven or on top of the stove in an almost-covered pan. Add the salt and pepper and bind the sauce with the beurre manié by stirring in bits of the mixed flour and butter. There is sauce to serve over rice or mashed potatoes. The blend of Alsatian wine, shallots, and mushrooms produces a delicious flavor. Serves 4.

LA VOLAILLE À LA CRÈME
Chapon Fin, Thoissey

This is another chicken dish of M. Paul Blanc, who seems to be a specialist in every kind of cooking. His gift turns either humble or great dishes into masterpieces.

1 2½-pound chicken
    Salt and freshly ground pepper
    Paprika
¼ cup butter
4 onions, minced
Bouquet garni:
    Parsley, thyme, bay leaf

1 cup dry white wine
½ pound button mushrooms
Beurre manié:
    1 tablespoon butter mixed
      with 2½ tablespoons flour
½ cup heavy cream

Quarter the chicken or, if you prefer, disjoint it as for frying. Sprinkle it with salt, pepper, and paprika. Put the butter in a sauté pan and add the chicken, minced onions, and the bouquet garni, tied with a string. Brown the chicken, turn it over, and when it has cooked 15 minutes slowly, add the wine and the whole mushrooms. Cover and cook gently until the chicken is tender—20 to 30 minutes. Remove the chicken and mushrooms to a serving dish and keep warm. Remove bouquet garni. Thicken the sauce with the beurre manié. When smooth, add the cream and taste for seasoning. Bring to the boil and pour it over the chicken and mushrooms. Serves 4.

CHICKEN DEMI-DEUIL

1 fine young 5½-pound chicken
1 black truffle, thinly sliced
½ cup finely diced carrots
1 cup finely diced onions
¼ cup finely diced celery
3 cups rich chicken broth

Sauce:
1¼ cups chicken broth
1 cup light cream
2 tablespoons cornstarch
¼ teaspoon nutmeg
Salt and pepper
½ pound fresh mushrooms
3 tablespoons butter
3 tablespoons Madeira or
sherry

We had this Burgundian specialty both in Lyon and Saulieu. "Demi-Deuil" (half mourning) is the quaint name inspired by the black truffle spots over the white chicken. A fine, unfrozen, well-fed bird has slices of truffle tucked under its skin over the breast and 1 or 2 under the skin of each leg. It is steamed tender in a daubière, a deep earthen pot, covered and hermetically sealed with a towel wrapped around the lid. The vegetables are chopped very fine and, with the broth, are put in with the chicken. The pot is put in a preheated 300° oven and steamed 1½ to 2 hours, or until the chicken is tender. It is brought to the table, the pot ceremoniously unwrapped and the chicken lifted from this fragrant brew, put on a platter and carved. The mushroom sauce is served over the chicken and is passed in a large sauceboat. For the sauce, steal 1¼ cups of broth from the pot before it leaves the kitchen. Blend it and the cream with the cornstarch, add the seasonings, and cook in a saucepan until it thickens. Slice the mushrooms and sauté them 3 or 4 minutes in the butter. Add them to the sauce, reheat, and just before serving stir in the wine. Serves 6.

PAUPIETTES DE POULET AUX MORILLES À LA CRÈME
Le Drouant, Place Gaillon, Paris

Paupiettes are flattened meat; filled, rolled, tied, and cooked. The French call them "birds without heads" or paupiettes (veal birds?).

2½-pound fine chicken, boned and
quarter
Farce:
1 extra chicken breast, boned
and ground
¼ cup heavy cream
Salt and pepper
4 slices truffle
4 slices foie gras
4 tablespoons butter

½ pound fresh button mushrooms
3 tablespoons butter
⅓ cup port
1¾ cups heavy cream
½ cup rich chicken broth
Salt and pepper
Dash cayenne
Garnish:
4 paper frills
4 truffle sticks

When the chicken is boned and quartered have a little knob of bone left on, so when it has been cooked the knob may be covered with a frill to look like a chop. Spread out each piece of chicken and flatten a little. For the farce, mix the boned, ground breast with the cream, salt, and pepper. Divide the farce in 4 parts and roll each part into a ball and flatten them a little. Put a cake of farce on each piece of chicken and on each cake a slice of truffle and a slice of foie gras. The restaurant folds each chicken over the filling and wraps them in crêpines (flattened pork-fat membranes). We may omit this and simply fold over, tuck in the edge, and tie securely with string. Put them in a sauté pan with the butter, cover, and cook very gently for 15 minutes, turning them once. Meanwhile sauté the mushrooms 3 or 4 minutes in butter. Remove the paupiettes from the pan. Glaze the pan with the port and reduce a little, then add the cream and broth, cayenne and a little salt and pepper. Return the paupiettes to the pan and very gently simmer for 15 minutes. Remove the paupiettes and reduce the sauce over high heat until it is "unctuous but not very thick." Put the paupiettes on 4 hot plates, put a paper frill on each knob bone, and force a truffle stick into the top of each. Add the mushrooms to the sauce and divide the sauce over the paupiettes. This elegant dish is from the chef of Le Drouant, M. Jules Petit.

CHICKEN IN CREAM WITH CHIVES
Auberge de l'Empéreur, Chailly-en-Bière

1 2½-pound chicken, disjointed
4 tablespoons butter
2 tablespoons minced shallots or
　green onions
¼ cup dry white wine

Salt and pepper
½ cup minced chives
1¼ cups light cream
3 teaspoons cornstarch

Wipe the chicken pieces and sauté in the butter until lightly colored, add the shallots or green onions and cook a few seconds more. Add the wine, salt and pepper. Cover and simmer until the chicken is tender. Meanwhile mince a generous half cup of chives and let them marinate in 1 cup of the cream. Blend the cornstarch with the ¼ cup of cream. When the chicken is done remove it to a serving dish and reduce the sauce in the pan to ½ cup, then add the cornstarch and cream and the chives and cream. Cook the sauce until it thickens and pour it over the chicken. Serve with either string beans or mashed potatoes. Serves 4.

POULET SAUTÉ AU DUC DE BOURGOGNE
Chez Pauline, Paris

If you walk past the Comédie Française down rue Richelieu you will come upon a large statue of Molière who seems to be looking toward a house in which, an inscription states, he once lived. Look to your left and there is rue Villedo. Walk down this street to the middle of the block, turn in to Chez Pauline, and you will dine extremely well. Perhaps you had better make a reservation as it is always full. M. Genin, owner-chef, gave me several of his specialties.

1 fine 2½-pound chicken, disjointed	¼ cup whisky
Salt and pepper	¼ glass *fine Champagne* (brandy)
Butter	¼ glass Kirsch
¼ cup port	2 cups heavy cream
	2 egg yolks

If the sauce seems a bit recherché, remember this was for a duke of Burgundy. Make it sometime for somebody's birthday or anniversary. Shake the pieces of chicken in a bag with salt, pepper, and 2 tablespoons flour. Put the chicken in a big sauté pan with 3 or 4 tablespoons of butter and brown it lightly over a gentle flame. Cover and let it cook slowly until tender, from 45 to 55 minutes. Remove it to a casserole and keep it warm. In the sauté pan add all the liquors and reduce to half over a brisk flame. Boil up the cream and pour it slowly over the egg yolks. Put the chicken in a "large timbale, worthy of this dish," combine the cream with the sauce, heat a moment (do not boil again), and strain the sauce over the chicken. Serve with a light potato purée. Serves 4.

CHICKEN IN ONIONS AND CREAM

1 fine young chicken, disjointed	1½ tablespoons cornstarch
2 cups chopped onions	¼ cup white wine
⅓ cup butter	¼ teaspoon nutmeg
Salt and pepper	1 tablespoon tomato paste
1½ cups heavy cream	Garnish: Rice or mashed potatoes

Cut the chicken in serving pieces. Cook the onions in the butter in a big sauté pan until they begin to color, then put in the chicken, cooking it over a low flame for 10 minutes on each side. Season with salt and pepper. Cover and cook 10 minutes. Warm the cream, add, and cook 10 minutes more, or until the chicken is tender. Blend the cornstarch with the wine and add the nutmeg and tomato paste. Remove the chicken to a hot serving dish or platter. Either sieve the sauce or not, as you choose. Sieve it for guests. Add the cornstarch mixture and cook until it thickens. Pour it over the chicken. The sauce is to serve over rice or mashed potatoes. A 2½-pound chicken serves 4.

CAPON STEAMED IN WINE
(to serve hot or cold)

5½- to 6-pound capon
1 cup water
1 cup white wine or dry
   vermouth
2 bay leaves
½ cup finely cubed carrots
½ cup finely chopped onions

3 mushrooms, chopped
1 tablespoon tarragon
Salt and pepper
1½ tablespoons cornstarch
½ cup heavy cream
3 tablespoons more wine
¼ cup almonds (optional)

Choose a fine bird; this is not just stewed chicken. Put the bird on its back in a big granite kettle with the water, wine, bay leaves, carrots, onions, mushrooms (for flavor), and tarragon. Cover tightly and let it take a full half hour to come to a simmer. Turn it on one side for 15 minutes, then on the other side for 15 minutes, then return it to its back for 30 to 40 minutes more of gentle simmering. If cooked slowly the breast meat is like satin. Half an hour before it is done add salt and pepper. When it is tender the legs move easily. Do not overcook it. Blend the cornstarch with the cream and add to the sauce and when ready to serve add the extra wine for a fresh wine flavor. Mashed potatoes with plenty of chopped onions and sour cream added are very good to serve with this chicken and sauce. Serve the chicken whole with a little sauce poured over it and the rest in a tureen. If you desire an added rich flavor, grind ¼ cup of almonds and add them to the sauce. If the vegetables are chopped very fine the sauce will not have to be strained. Serves 6 to 8.

SMOTHERED CHICKEN WITH HAM

2 2½-pound chickens, cut up for
   frying, or 8 chicken parts,
   breasts and legs
Salt and pepper
Flour
1 cup finely chopped onions
¼ cup butter
2 tablespoons oil

1 teaspoon basil or tarragon
8 slices very thin ham or
   prosciutto
⅔ cup chicken broth
⅔ cup dry vermouth
2 tablespoons cornstarch
1 cup heavy cream
Chopped parsley

Wipe the chicken and shake it in a bag with salt, pepper, and flour. Sauté it for 15 minutes with the onion in the butter and oil over a low flame, turn the pieces occasionally. Then sprinkle the chicken with tarragon or basil. Lay the slices of ham in a baking pan and top each with a piece of chicken. Heat the broth and vermouth in the sauté pan and scrape it over the chicken, cover tightly, and bake at 325° until the chicken is tender, about 45 or 50 minutes. Blend the cornstarch with the cream and warm a little, then pour it over the chicken, mixing it well with the pan juices. Sprinkle the top with parsley or with Parmesan cheese and let it heat uncovered a moment, then serve from the casserole. Serves 8.

CHICKEN PIES, COQ HARDI
Le Coq Hardi, Bougival (Paris)

These lovely little pies, served with sauce, are a specialty of Coq Hardi.

1 2½-pound chicken
1½ cups chicken broth
Salt and pepper
1 cup heavy cream
2 tablespoons minced parsley
Puff Pastry
Thin slices cooked ham
Egg yolk

Sauce:
1¼ cups chicken broth
1 tablespoon tomato paste
1½ tablespoons cornstarch
⅓ cup sliced mushrooms
2 tablespoons butter
¼ cup Madeira
¼ cup heavy cream

Put the chicken in a roasting pan with the broth, cover, and roast at 325° until it is tender, about 1¼ hours. Save the broth for the sauce. Remove the skin and bones from the chicken and cut 6 or 8 nice thick slices for 6 or 8 individual pies. Grind the rest of the chicken to make a farce, mixing it with the salt, pepper, ⅓ cup of the cream, and parsley. Roll Puff Pastry thin and cut in 4-inch squares, 12 or 16 of them. On the bottom of each of 6 or 8 squares of pastry, put a thin slice of ham, then a slice of chicken, then a spoonful of the farce. Lay a slice of truffle on the farce, and cover with another layer of pastry. Pinch the edges together and make incisions in the top for the steam to escape. Make a round hole in the center of each to receive cream later. Paint the tops with an egg yolk mixed with 2 tablespoons of water. Put the pies on a cookie sheet and bake in a 400° oven for 10 minutes. Reduce the heat to 350° and bake about 15 minutes more. Heat the remaining ⅔ cup of cream, and pour a big spoonful of hot cream into the hole in the top of each pie. For the sauce, blend the broth with the tomato paste and cornstarch and cook until thickened. Sauté the mushrooms 3 minutes in the butter and add to the sauce. Add the Madeira and cream and when hot serve the sauce in a sauceboat with the pies. One pie to a serving.

BREAST OF CHICKEN, FLORIDA
Louise Junior, New York

Mr. Aldo Mercandetti, head chef of this popular restaurant on East 53rd Street, makes a very fine dish of chicken breasts to serve 6.

6 good-sized half-breasts of chicken
6 slices of foie gras
  Melted butter
  Dry fine fresh breadcrumbs
  Salt and pepper

½ cup butter
6 rings fresh pineapple
  More melted butter
  Brown sugar

Make a slit in each chicken breast and fill with a slice of foie gras. Enclose the filling by sewing up the edge with thread. Dip the pieces of chicken in plenty of melted butter, then dip lightly in the crumbs seasoned with salt and pepper. Melt the ½ cup of butter in a baking pan and lay the chicken on the bottom. In another pan put the pineapple which you have dipped in melted butter and then in brown sugar. Bake both at the same time. Preheat the oven to 400° and bake the chicken (and pineapple) 5 minutes, then turn the chicken and bake both for another 5 minutes. The chicken is done when firm to the touch. The secret of this dish is not to overcook the chicken. Put the pineapple rings on 6 hot plates and put a chicken breast on each slice of pineapple. A white Alsatian wine is good with this.

CHICKEN MARENGO

1 2½-pound broiler, quartered
3 tablespoons oil
3 tablespoons butter
8 fresh mushrooms
  Salt and pepper
½ cup dry white wine or dry
  vermouth
1½ teaspoons cornstarch

1 cup chicken broth
2 tablespoons tomato paste or ¼
  cup tomato sauce
Garnish:
  Bread fried in butter
4 eggs
  Chopped parsley

Wipe the chicken dry and brown it in the oil and butter. Lift to a casserole. Cook the mushrooms 2 minutes in the browning pan and add to the chicken. Sprinkle both with salt and pepper. Pour the wine over the chicken and mushrooms. Blend the cornstarch with the broth, add the tomato paste or sauce, and heat. Pour this over the chicken, cover and bake at 325° about 50 minutes or until the chicken is tender. Fry 4 pieces of bread in butter, put 1 on each of 4 hot plates, and cover with a piece of chicken and the mushrooms. Slip 4 eggs from a saucer into the pan juices and poach them at 400° until they are just set but still soft. Lift 1 to the top of each piece of chicken and divide the sauce around it. Top with parsley. The egg mixed in makes this an unctuous sauce. Serves 4.

POULARDE AU CHAMPAGNE

1 fine 3½- to 5-pound chicken,
    whole
4 tablespoons butter
¼ cup grated carrot
¼ cup grated onion
4 mushrooms, minced

Salt and pepper
1½ cups Champagne
1 tablespoon cornstarch
1 cup heavy cream
⅓ cup more Champagne

This elegant dish is for very special occasions when you want to give dear friends a real treat. Only the finest chicken should be used for this. There are shops specializing in corn-fed varieties. Wipe the chicken dry and brown it a little in 2 tablespoons butter in a large skillet. In a casserole make a bed of 2 more tablespoons butter, the carrot, onion, and mushrooms, and lay the chicken on it. Add salt and pepper to the vegetables and chicken. Put 1½ cups Champagne in the skillet and rinse over the chicken. Roast covered at 325° 15 minutes on each side, then turn it on its back and continue roasting until it is tender, about 30 minutes to 1 hour more, depending on the weight. If it is cooking too fast turn the heat to 300°. It must not be overcooked. A 3½-pound bird of quality should take 1 hour altogether. Remove the chicken and bring the sauce to a fast boil to reduce it a third. Blend the cornstarch with the cream, add it to the sauce, and when it has thickened add ⅓ cup more Champagne. The chicken is put on a hot platter and the sauce poured over it. A 3½-pound chicken will serve 4, a 5-pound one 6 or 7.

COQ AU VIN, BOURGUIGNON

2 3-pound young chickens,
    disjointed
½ cup butter
Salt and freshly ground pepper
18 white onions
18 fresh white mushrooms
½ cup flour
3 cups good Burgundy

⅓ cup chicken broth
Bouquet garni:
    Celery, parsley, thyme, bay leaf
2 strips salt pork, cubed
Garnish:
    20 fried croutons
    3 tablespoons chopped parsley

Salt and pepper the chicken pieces and brown them well in the butter. Remove them to a casserole which may be brought to the table. Glaze the onions in the butter the chicken browned in and add them to the casserole; do the same with the mushrooms, which should be of medium size so they may be left whole. Add the flour to the browning pan and smooth with a little of the wine, then add the rest of the wine and the broth and pour over the chicken. Tie the bouquet garni together with string and add it. Fry out the pork cubes, scoop from the pan, and sprinkle over the top of the casserole. Cover and cook in the oven at 325° about 45 minutes, or until the chicken is done. The sauce should be like heavy cream. Remove top and sprinkle with croutons and parsley. Serves 8 or 10.

FRIED CHICKEN

2 2½-pound broilers, disjointed
⅓ cup flour
1 teaspoon salt
½ teaspoon pepper
¾ cup lard
¼ cup butter
⅓ cup water

Gravy:
3 tablespoons flour
1 cup milk or chicken broth
1 cup light cream
Salt and pepper
1 tablespoon caramel

Wipe the chicken dry. Put the flour in a bag with the salt and pepper and shake the pieces of chicken in the bag until all are covered. Heat the lard, butter, and water in a large iron skillet until quite hot, brown the chicken, and then turn down the heat and cook until it is tender, turning occasionally. Pour off some of the grease, leaving all the crumbs and ¼ cup of grease in the pan. To make the gravy, put in the flour and stir until it is smooth and lightly browned. Add the milk or broth slowly, then the cream, and cook a minute or two. Add the salt and pepper, and the caramel for flavor and color. Serves 5 or 6. Serve this gravy over mashed potatoes.

CASSEROLE OF CHICKEN WITH VEGETABLES

4 legs and 4 breasts of young
    chicken
16 white onions, glazed
    Butter
    Honey
1 large green pepper, sliced
2 tomatoes, skinned and seeded

Salt and pepper
Flour
8 strips of bacon
1¼ cups dry white wine or dry
    vermouth
¾ cup heavy cream, scalded
2 egg yolks, beaten

This quantity of chicken will serve 6 or 8. The legs are attached to the second joints and the breasts are halved. Glaze the onions in butter with the honey and transfer the onions to the bottom of a large casserole. To insure tenderness of green peppers, it is well to boil them 6 or 8 minutes in water. Slice them, remove the seeds, and add to the onions. Skin the tomatoes, seed, and cut in pieces and add them to the other vegetables. Salt and pepper the vegetables. Mix salt, pepper, and flour in a bag and shake the pieces of chicken in it until covered, then glaze them in the butter and honey and arrange the pieces over the vegetables. Add a strip of bacon to each piece of chicken, pour 1 cup of wine or dry vermouth over the chicken, cover tightly, and bake 1 hour at no more than 300°. Scald the cream, pour it over the egg yolks, and add it with the rest of the wine. Serve the chicken and vegetables from the casserole. A simple rice or noodle dish to dress with the chicken sauce may accompany this.

BROILERS OR VEAL CHOPS
BAKED WITH CHEDDAR CHEESE

2 small broilers, halved
⅓ cup butter
Salt and pepper
¼ cup chopped shallots or ½ cup
    chopped green onions
⅓ cup dry vermouth

4 strips bacon
½ cup hot heavy cream
8 slices Cheddar cheese
Garnish:
    4 slices bread fried in butter

Brown the chicken in the butter in a sauté pan and salt and pepper it. Lift the chicken to a baking pan, bone-side down. Sauté the shallots or green onions a moment, add the wine and when it is hot, scrape it over the chicken. Lay a strip of bacon over the top of each half-broiler and bake in a 325° oven until the chicken is done, about 20 minutes. Pour the cream over the chicken, turn it, and put 2 slices of cheese on top of each half. Cover tightly and let the chicken remain in the oven until the cheese melts. Have the fried bread ready on 4 hot plates and put a half chicken on each piece of bread. Pour this delicious sauce over the chicken. Veal chops may be cooked exactly this way.

CHICKEN INDIAN CURRY

6 chicken legs or second joints
¼ cup butter
1 good-sized onion, chopped
2 cloves garlic, crushed
Salt and pepper
¼ teaspoon clove
1 teaspoon cardamom

2 tablespoons coriander seeds,
    crushed
1 teaspoon turmeric
1 teaspoon cumin
1 cup flaked coconut
1 cup milk

To think that all Indian food is hot with curry is as much a mistake as thinking that all Spanish food is as hot as Mexican food can be. Indian cooks season their curried dishes to suit their own tastes just as we do. This chicken dish is mild and fragrant. I specify these cuts of chicken as they cook quickly and are easily covered with the sauce. Put the butter in a big skillet or pot with the onion and garlic and sauté 4 or 5 minutes over a very low fire. Add all the condiments, and after stirring a minute add the chicken and cook 3 minutes. Make an infusion of the milk and coconut by boiling it, then letting it cool. Mash it through a sieve, discard the coconut, and add the hot milk to the chicken. Cover and simmer about 40 minutes or until the chicken is tender. Remove the chicken to a hot platter. Boil the sauce furiously until it reduces a little and thickens, then pour it over the chicken. There is no flour in Indian sauces. How many this will serve depends on the size of the pieces of chicken, if they are small it will serve only 3. This may be served with fried bananas and rice, or with mashed potatoes if it is not part of a whole curry meal.

STUFFED STEAMED CHICKEN

3-pound chicken
¾ cup water or broth
¾ cup white wine
⅓ cup chopped carrots
⅓ cup chopped onions
    Juice of ½ lemon
2 tablespoons cornstarch
½ cup light or heavy cream

Stuffing:
¼ pound mushrooms, sliced
⅓ cup onions, chopped
    Butter
1 slice bread, cubed and
    toasted
    Giblets, sliced and sautéed
1 egg, beaten
½ teaspoon tarragon
    Salt and pepper

Sauté the mushrooms and onions 2 minutes in a little butter, then mix with the rest of the stuffing ingredients. Stuff the chicken and sew it up. Put the water or broth (which may be made with powdered chicken concentrate), the wine, carrot, onion, and lemon juice in a pot, lay the chicken in on one side, and let the liquid come to a slow simmer over a flame so low that this should take nearly ½ hour. Then turn the chicken onto the other side and simmer 20 minutes, then onto its back to simmer until it is done. The whole simmering for a young chicken should take 1¼ to 1½ hours. Mix the cornstarch with the cream and add it to the liquid in the pot. Stir until it thickens. Put the chicken on a platter and surround it with sauce. Serve with mashed potatoes, rice, or noodles. Serves 4. Large chickens are also fine cooked this way. A 6-pound roasting chicken or capon takes an hour longer to cook.

CHICKEN OR SMALL TURKEY STEAMED IN WINE

5½-pound chicken, or 6- to 7-pound
    turkey
Stuffing:
    2 cups mashed potatoes
    3 tablespoons butter
    ½ cup sour cream
    ⅓ cup minced green onions
    1 slice dark bread, cubed and
        toasted
    2 teaspoons mixed herbs:
        tarragon, thyme, basil
    Salt and pepper

1 cup chicken broth
1 cup dry vermouth or white
    wine
1 carrot, sliced
1 onion, sliced
¼ cup celery, sliced
    Giblets
    Salt and pepper
2½ tablespoons cornstarch
1 or 2 teaspoons tarragon
    Cream (optional)

Now that turkeys come in small sizes they are fine steamed, as chicken is. Turkey is a drier bird so it lends itself perfectly to this treatment. For the stuffing, mix all the ingredients together. Stuff the bird and tie it securely. Put the bird on one side in a good-sized heavy pot and add the broth, wine, vegetables, and giblets. Cover and begin on such a low fire that it takes 25 minutes to come to a simmer, then turn the bird over on its other side and simmer gently 25 minutes more. Turn it onto its back for 25 minutes more, adding salt and pepper. From now on young birds must be watched carefully so that they do not overcook. When the legs move back and forth easily, the bird is done. A 7-pound turkey may take 2 hours. When the bird is tender, remove it from the kettle and strain the sauce. Blend the cornstarch with a little sauce and mix it with the rest of the sauce and cook until it thickens. If it needs thinning add either cream or a little more wine. Return the bird and sauce to the kettle and reheat (but not cook) just before serving. Do not cover again, as the steam will thin the sauce. Serve the bird on a hot platter, covered with a little sauce, and the rest of the sauce in a sauceboat. Serves 6 or 8.

CHICKEN OR TURKEY PIE

3½-pound chicken or 2½ cups
    cooked turkey meat
1 cup peas, cooked with basil
8 fresh white mushrooms
8 small white onions, cooked
2 cups broth
2½ tablespoons cornstarch
1 cup heavy cream
3 tablespoons sherry

Top crust:
1¼ cups sifted flour
½ teaspoon salt
½ teaspoon baking powder
⅓ cup mixed butter and lard
Ice water
2 tablespoons soft butter

Cook the chicken as instructed in *Jellied Chicken*. When it is tender remove all the meat from the bones and leave it in good-sized slices. Or if you have leftover turkey, this is a good way to use it. Now you might like to mix your top crust and chill it before rolling and covering the pie. Sift the flour with the salt and baking powder. Cut in the butter and lard and add just enough ice water to make the dough hold together and chill it. Cook the peas in very little water and season with salt, pepper, and basil.

Use the water to add to the broth. Cook the onions until almost done and add their water to the broth. Measure 2 cups of broth and blend it with the cornstarch, add the cream and sherry, and cook until it thickens. Arrange the meat, mushrooms, and vegetables in a good-sized baking dish and pour the sauce over them. Roll out the crust, spread with the soft butter, fold over and roll out to a circle a little larger than the top of the dish, fold it in half, lay it over half the dish, unfold, and make a rim around the edge with the dough. Make several incisions for the steam to escape. Bake 10 minutes at 400° then turn down the heat to 350° and bake 15 or 20 minutes more, until the crust is golden. Serve immediately. Serves 6.

VARIATION. See bread section for other crusts using wholewheat and corn-meal flours.

CREAMED CHICKEN OR TURKEY

2½ cups sliced chicken or turkey
1 cup leftover gravy or rich broth
1¼ cups light cream
2 tablespoons cornstarch
¼ cup sherry, port or Madeira

1 tablespoon Kirsch or brandy
Garnish:
Chopped parsley, or pistachio nuts, browned slivered almonds, or macadamia nuts

This a grand dish for guests even if it is made from the holiday bird. This will serve 4 to 6; if you wish a greater quantity, use more sliced meat and increase the sauce. Always cut the meat in good-sized slices. Put the gravy or rich broth in a large saucepan with the cream and heat. Blend the cornstarch with the wine and add it to the sauce, cooking until it thickens. Add the meat. Letting the meat marinate in the sauce adds to its flavor. When ready to serve, reheat, add the Kirsch or brandy and empty into a large hot serving dish. Sprinkle the top with parsley or any of the nuts. Noodles or rice make a good accompaniment, and a bottle of white Burgundy, a Montrachet.

VARIATION. To extend this dish 1 cup of cooked fresh peas or small white mushrooms or chicken livers—sautéed—may be added after the sauce is made. Allow about 1 cup of sauce to every cup of meat.

CHICKEN PAPRIKA

2 2- to 2½-pound young chickens
Broth:
    Chicken trimmings
  2⅔ cups water
    1 cup finely chopped onions
    ½ cup shredded carrot
    Salt and pepper
    1 teaspoon thyme
1 teaspoon powdered chicken
  concentrate
3 tablespoons butter

3 tablespoons oil
1¼ cups chopped onions
2½ tablespoons sweet Hungarian
  paprika
2 tablespoons tomato paste
2½ tablespoons flour
1 cup sour cream
Garnish:
  Bowl of sour cream
  Buttered noodles

Have the butcher disjoint the chicken, removing the wing tips, necks, and back bones with a cleaver. Make the broth with these trimmings and the giblets, water, onion, carrot, salt, pepper, and thyme. Let the broth simmer 30 minutes, then strain out the chicken bones and mash the vegetables through the sieve. Add the chicken concentrate for extra richness. Measure the broth and if necessary add water to make 2 cups. Put the butter and oil in a large heavy pot with the finely chopped onions and cook the chicken in this for 15 minutes, stirring and turning it frequently over a gentle fire. Add the paprika and stir it for 5 minutes so all the pieces color pink. Reheat the broth and add it, cover tightly, and simmer until the chicken is tender, about 25 or 30 minutes. Mix the tomato paste with the flour. Remove ½ cup of liquid from the chicken, blend with the flour, and add. Tip the pot so that the juices will mix with the blended flour, then stir a little, and cook until the sauce thickens. Stir in the sour cream just before serving. Put the chicken on a hot deep platter and pour the sauce over it. This is a grand dish for a party of 8. Pass a bowl of sour cream to add to the top of each serving of chicken, sauce, and hot noodles.

JELLIED CHICKEN

1 5-pound young chicken
2 cups chicken broth
1 cup dry white wine or dry
  vermouth
1 carrot, sliced
1 onion, sliced
1 tablespoon tarragon
  Salt and pepper
  Juice of 1 lemon
½ pound small fresh mushrooms

¼ cup olive oil
1 egg white, half-beaten
½ cup more wine or dry vermouth
2 tablespoons gelatin
Garnish:
  Stuffed eggs
  Sliced stuffed olives
  Red pimento strips
  Lettuce
  Mayonnaise

Have the chicken disjointed and put it on to simmer very slowly with the broth, 1 cup wine, carrot, onion, tarragon, salt, pepper, and lemon juice. It should take ½ hour to come to a bubble. This slow cooking makes the flesh silky, even that of the breast. Continue cooking about 1 hour or until it is tender. Let the chicken cool in the broth. When it is cool, take it out and remove all the meat from the bones, leaving it in good-sized pieces. Strain the broth but do not mash the vegetables through the sieve. Meanwhile cook the mushrooms about 8 minutes in the olive oil and drain. Measure the broth and if it is less than 3½ cups add chicken broth or water. Add the half-beaten egg white and let the broth simmer 2 minutes, then pour it through a cloth-lined sieve. This will make it clear. Have the gelatin soaking in ½ cup wine or vermouth and pour the hot strained broth over it. Let it cool. Oil a mold, arrange the chicken and mushrooms in it, and pour the cooled gelatin broth over them. Let chill and set. Unmold and decorate with any gelatin left in the mold, chopping it with a fork. Decorate the edge of the platter with stuffed eggs, olives, pimento strips, and shredded lettuce. Pass the mayonnaise. Serves 10.

GLAZED BAKED CHICKEN

1 2½- to 3-pound young chicken, quartered
1 tablespoon tarragon
1 teaspoon basil
3 tablespoons olive oil
Salt and pepper
¼ cup butter
2 tablespoons caramel or honey
¼ cup dry vermouth
¾ cup heavy cream
1 teaspoon cornstarch
1 egg yolk

Marinate the chicken with the herbs and olive oil in the refrigerator all day. An hour before cooking it remove it so it may attain room temperature. Remove it from marinade, reserving this, salt and pepper it, and glaze it all over in the butter and caramel or honey in a large skillet. Scrape the marinade over it, add the vermouth, and ¼ cup of cream, and bake in the oven at 325° about 30 minutes or until the chicken is tender. Lift the chicken onto hot plates or a platter and keep it warm. Mix the cornstarch with ½ cup of cream, heat, pour over the egg yolk, and mix with the hot pan juices. Do not boil after the egg is added. Pour this sauce over the chicken. Serves 4.

BREAST OF CHICKEN
Buca di San Rufillo, Florence

4 slices raw chicken breast, ½-
    inch thick
2 tablespoons flour
    Salt and pepper
⅓ cup butter

Jigger cognac
½ pound fresh mushrooms
1 teaspoon meat glaze
⅓ cup heavy cream

Put 2 tablespoons flour in a bag with salt and pepper. Shake the slices of breast in the bag so they are lightly covered. Sauté them in the butter very gently to a golden color, so they are just cooked through. Blaze with cognac. Separately sauté the mushrooms 3 or 4 minutes in butter and season them with salt and pepper. Put the meat glaze in the pan with the chicken and when it is melted stir in the cream. Put a piece of breast on each of 4 hot plates, divide the mushrooms, and pour the sauce over the meat. Serves 4.

TURKEY PANCAKES RICHELIEU
Pappagallo, Bologna

Important people from all over the world visit Bologna, and of course Pappagallo's. This elegant dish was served to the Maharajah of Petiala.

1 pound raw turkey breast
½ cup Parmesan cheese
⅓ cup warm cream
2 eggs, beaten
¼ teaspoon salt
2 tablespoons flour
    Butter

Garnish:
2 pounds fresh peas
    Butter
    Parmesan cheese
1 cup *Hollandaise Sauce*
    Sliced white truffles or
    mushrooms

Cut the turkey in very small pieces and mix with the cheese, cream, beaten eggs, salt, and flour. Put the mixture through a meat grinder, then stir until it is very smooth. Divide it into 6 oval cakes. Flatten them a little, sprinkle with a very little dusting of flour, and sauté in butter, about 4 minutes on each side over a low fire. Meanwhile cook the peas in butter and 3 tablespoons of water, until they are just done. Make a mound on each of 6 hot plates and sprinkle the peas with a little Parmesan cheese, then lay a turkey pancake on top. Top the pancake with a thick layer of *Hollandaise Sauce* and sprinkle the top with a few sticks of truffles or mushrooms sautéed a moment in butter. This deserves a chilled fine white wine.

PETTI DE POLLO ALLA SABATINI
Sabatini, Florence

4 half-breasts of chicken, boned
Beaten egg
Salt and pepper
Flour
Oil and butter
Sliced Gruyère cheese

Tongue or Ham sauce:
½ cup tiny cubes of tongue
or ham
½ cup tomato sauce
1 teaspoon basil or fennel
powder
¼ cup meat broth

Good-sized chicken breasts are cut in two, each half for 1 serving. The chicken breasts are flattened a little, dipped in beaten egg and then in seasoned flour. Put ⅓ cup of mixed oil and butter in a sauté pan and when it is quite hot put in the chicken breasts. After a few seconds, turn them and turn down the heat immediately. Cook gently about 3 minutes on each side. For the sauce, mix the meat, tomato sauce, and herb; heat it. Put a good slice of cheese on each piece of chicken and a big spoonful of tongue or ham sauce. Add the broth to the pan. Cover and cook over a very low flame until the cheese melts. Put the chicken on 4 hot plates and divide the sauce over it. Serve with a garnish of fresh peas or asparagus and a couple of grilled mushrooms.

BRAISED GOOSE LYONNAISE

10- to 12-pound goose
3 tablespoons caramel
Flour
Salt and pepper
1 cup dry white wine or dry
vermouth

16 white onions
16 chestnuts, shelled
16 whole fresh mushrooms
2 tablespoons cornstarch
¼ cup more wine

Choose a fine young goose and remove the fat from its inside. Wipe it dry and paint it all over with the caramel, catching it with a light sprinkle of flour seasoned with salt and pepper. Put it in a 400° oven for 10 minutes, then cover and reduce the heat to 325°. After 45 minutes, remove the goose, pour off all the grease, return it to the roaster, pour the wine over it and roast another 1½ hours. Forty minutes before it is done, boil up the onions, drain them, and put them around the goose. In another 20 minutes add the chestnuts, and 10 minutes later add the mushrooms. When it is done, remove the goose to a hot platter and drain out the onions, chestnuts, and mushrooms and put them around the goose. Blend the cornstarch and the wine and thicken the pan juices, adding a little cornstarch mixture at a time. Serve the sauce in a sauceboat. Mashed potatoes is a good accompaniment. Serves 8. Render the fat you removed from the goose; there is nothing better for frying.

BUONGUSTAIA NERINA
Nerina, Bologna

6 strips baked *Pie Pastry*
6 slices chicken or turkey breast
Butter

½ pound fresh mushrooms, sliced
6 slices Gruyère cheese

Make pie pastry with 2 cups of flour. Roll the dough ¼-inch thick and cut it in strips 5½ by 3½ inches. Prick them with a fork and bake them on a cookie sheet about 12 minutes at 400° to a light brown. Cut the chicken or turkey meat to fit the pastry strips. If it is raw, sauté the meat in butter over a gentle flame until it is just tender. If it is cooked meat, dip it in cream (and drain) to prevent its drying out. Put a piece of meat on each piece of cooked pastry. Sauté the mushrooms 3 minutes in butter and divide them over the meat, then top with a slice of Gruyère to fit. Run these under the flame until the cheese melts. These are a specialty at Nerina. Serves 6.

FILLETS OF TURKEY
Pappagallo, Bologna

Slices of raw turkey breast
Flour
Salt and pepper
Butter

Prosciutto
Thick *Cream Sauce*
Parmesan or shredded Gruyère
cheese

Cut ½-inch-thick slices from the breast of a turkey and flatten them a little. Dust very lightly with flour, only a few grains of salt, and pepper. Sauté gently in butter to a rich yellow on both sides, 3 or 4 minutes on each side. Lay each slice on a slice of prosciutto, cover with cream sauce, and top with a good layer of cheese. Run the pan under the flame until the cheese melts. This is a favorite at Pappagallo's, where they are apt to put a few slices of truffles or mushroom sticks, previously sautéed a moment in butter, on the turkey before adding the cream sauce. One slice to a serving.

TURKEY FILLETS ALLA FREDDY
Freddy Martini, Bologna

Thick slices of cooked turkey breast
Slices of prosciutto

¼-inch-thick slices of French
Gruyère cheese

This is a good answer to that leftover turkey during the holidays or at any other time of the year. Cover each slice of turkey with a slice of prosciutto, top the ham with a slice of cheese, and run the pan under the flame until the cheese melts. A sautéed breaded veal cutlet may be treated the same way.

ROAST DUCK WITH VEGETABLES

5½- to 6½-pound duck
Stuffing:
    4 tart apples, sautéed
      Butter
    4 white onions, sautéed
    2 teaspoons cinnamon
      Salt and pepper
Glaze: Molasses and Kitchen
    Bouquet

8 white turnips
8 white onions
8 small new potatoes
Broth for basting:
    Giblets
    Neck
    Salt and pepper
    1 teaspoon thyme
1 tablespoon cornstarch

Prepare the duck for stuffing. Sauté the apples in butter, sprinkle with 1 teaspoon of the cinnamon, salt, and pepper. Sauté the sliced onions in butter and season the same way. Mix them together. Stuff and sew up the duck. Paint it all over with a mixture of molasses and Kitchen Bouquet, catching it with a light sifting of flour. Make a broth of the giblets, neck, seasonings, and 1¼ cups of water. Simmer 25 minutes and strain. Roast the duck, uncovered, for 45 minutes at 350°. Drain off the grease. Baste with hot broth, cover, and roast 25 minutes at 325°. Meanwhile prepare the vegetables, boil them 2 or 3 minutes, drain, and put them around the duck. Cover the roasting pan and cook the duck until the vegetables are done, about 30 to 40 minutes more. Lift the duck to a hot platter, surround it with vegetables, and keep warm. Blend the cornstarch with 2 or 3 tablespoons of cold water and add it to the pan juices. Cook until it thickens and serve the gravy in a sauceboat. Serves 4.

CANARD BRAISÉ AUX PÊCHES, MAURICE CAZALIS

3½- to 4-pound duck
⅓ cup butter
1 cup duck broth
½ cup sugar
¼ cup water

1 tablespoon cornstarch
1 wineglass port
¼ cup peach brandy
2 tablespoons more butter
Garnish: 3 fresh peaches, skinned

Make a broth with the neck, wing and leg tips, and giblets of the duck, 1 sliced onion, 2 cups of water, salt and pepper. Simmer 30 minutes and strain. Truss the duck and brown it all over in ⅓ cup butter. Put 1 cup of the broth over the browned duck and roast it about an hour at 350°. Remove the duck, quarter it, and put it in the oven to keep warm. Make a caramel of the sugar and water, boiling it until it is very dark. Degrease the pan juices and add the caramel, scraping the bottom of the pan. Reduce to three-fourths of its volume over a brisk flame. Dissolve the cornstarch in the port wine, add it to the sauce, and after a minute's cooking, pass the sauce through a sieve. Add the brandy, whisk in 2 tablespoons butter, and pour the sauce over the duck. Put the halved skinned peaches around the duck. Serves 4.

CANARD BRAISÉ À L'ORANGE
Maurice Cazalis, Chartres

My last visit to my friend Maurice Cazalis in Chartres was most rewarding, because M. Cazalis, a teacher of chefs, gave me some very interesting recipes which he had used in a demonstration of French cooking at the invitation of The Friends of Chartres at Chichester, England. He was assisted in the demonstration by three famous English chefs, two from the Carlton Towers, London, and the chef of the Duke of Marlborough.

2 4-pound ducks, quartered
Salt and pepper
4 tablespoons butter
2 cups white stock
1 cup white wine
Caramel:
    ½ cup sugar
    3 tablespoons water
    ¼ cup Curaçao
2 oranges
3 tablespoons cornstarch
⅓ cup port or Banyuls
Salt and pepper
¼ teaspoon clove
2 tablespoons more butter

White stock:
    2 or 3 veal bones
    Duck giblets and neck
¼ pound onions
3 whole cloves
2 carrots, sliced
2 sticks celery, sliced
1 leek, sliced
1 parsnip, sliced
Bouquet garni: Bay leaf,
    parsley, thyme
Salt and pepper
7 cups water

If you choose fresh (not frozen), undressed 5-pound ducklings, they will weigh 4 pounds when dressed and are just the right size to serve a quarter for each serving. Make the white stock first, as it must simmer 1½ hours. Put the ingredients in a 4-quart kettle. Stick the cloves in 1 onion and slice the rest very fine. Almost cover, bring to the boil, skim, and simmer 1½ hours. Strain the stock through a sieve; 2 cups of it will be needed. Wipe the duck quarters dry, sprinkle with salt and pepper. Put 2 tablespoons butter in a skillet and brown the duck on both sides over high heat to a rich brown, then put each piece in a long baking pan, skin side up. Add more butter to the pan as you need it. Pour 2 cups of the white stock over the duck, then the wine, and roast 1 hour: 15 minutes at 350° and 45 minutes at 325°. Remove the duck, drain the pan juices into a saucepan, and put the duck back in the pan. Put a tablespoonful of stock over each piece, lay a big piece of parchment paper over all, and keep warm in the oven with the door open. Degrease the broth and reduce it 3 minutes over high heat. Make the Caramel by putting the sugar and water in a skillet and letting it get brown but not black. Take it off the heat and stir in the Curaçao. Pour this Caramel into the reduced sauce and reduce again for 1 minute. While the stock was simmering or the duck was roasting, prepare the oranges. With a sharp knife remove the rind with none of the white, then cut the rind into very fine sticks. Put them in boiling water and cook at a simmer just 2 minutes and drain. These are added to the sauce. Peel the white from the oranges and either quarter them or cut in rings. Mix the cornstarch with the port or Banyuls and add it to the sauce, taste for seasoning and add a dash of clove. Cook the sauce until it thickens. It must be like heavy cream. If it is too thick, thin with a little more white wine or broth. A good 15 minutes before serving reheat the duck. Put it on a large platter and garnish the edge with the oranges. Reheat the sauce, whisk in 2 tablespoons butter, and pour it over the ducks. You will receive compliments from 7 people.

LE CANARD À L'ORANGE
Le Coq Hardi, Bougival

Another dish from this flower-decked restaurant with the terrace setting, quite remarkable for its beauty, and an easy drive of about 15 miles south from Paris. It is a lovely place for lunch on your way south or for dinner on a summer evening.

4-pound duck	1 tablespoon tomato paste
4 tablespoons sugar	Salt and pepper
1 wineglass Curaçao	1 tablespoon flour
1 tablespoon vinegar	¼ cup white wine
2 cups poultry broth	4 oranges

Roast the duck 30 minutes, then remove it from the pan, quarter it, and put it in a casserole. Degrease the pan it cooked in, put in the sugar, and caramelize it over a low flame. Add the liqueur, vinegar, broth, tomato paste, salt, and pepper. Let it gently simmer 10 minutes. Mix the flour with the wine and add it to the sauce. Pour the sauce over the duck and cook it very slowly in a 300° oven for 20 minutes. Cut the peel of the oranges (without any white), in julienne sticks. Blanch them in boiling water and drain. Remove the white from the oranges and slice them. When the duck is done put it on a hot platter. Add the sticks of orange peel to the sauce, scrape it over the duck, and surround with the slices of orange. Serves 4.

ROAST WILD DUCK

Mallard, canvasback, or teal
Lemon juice and oil
Caramel
Butter and oil
Jigger brandy or cognac
Strips of bacon
Madeira
Chicken or beef broth
Cornstarch
¼ cup currant jelly

Wild Rice Stuffing:
1 cup wild rice (for 4 ducks)
½ cup chopped onions
4 fresh mushrooms, sliced
Butter
Salt and pepper
2 cups chicken broth
1 teaspoon thyme
1 teaspoon marjoram
Garnish: Slices of bread fried in
butter

Wild duck are usually served 1 to a person. Teal are small so 1½ to 2 are usually allowed for each serving. Small game birds are cooked at high heat and a short time; just the opposite from their tame counterparts. Ducks are not washed but freshened by wiping them inside and out with a mixture of oil and lemon juice. Make the stuffing first. Wash the wild rice in many waters until it is clean. Sauté the onions in butter until almost soft; add the mushrooms and cook 2 minutes more. Mix the vegetables with the raw wild rice, season with salt and pepper, and add the broth and herbs. Put the rice in a heavy pot, cover tightly, and after it comes to a boil, turn the flame down to pilot-light strength and cook until all the liquid is absorbed. Stuff the ducks and sew them up. Rub them with Caramel and brown them in a skillet in a mixture of oil and butter. Pour brandy or cognac over them and ignite. Tie strips of bacon across their breasts and a half strip around their legs. Put them breast side up in a baking pan in a 400° oven for 15 minutes, basting every 3 or 4 minutes with hot Madeira and hot broth. After 15 minutes turn down the heat to 325°, cover tightly, and cook good-sized ducks 15 minutes more; teal only 6 or 8 minutes more. Have bread fried in butter to go under each duck. Take the ducks out of the oven and put them in another pan to keep warm, while you make the sauce. Use 1 tablespoon cornstarch for each cup of pan liquid. Blend together and cook until it thickens, then add the currant jelly. Serve the sauce in a sauceboat. Put the bread on hot plates or a platter and put a duck on each slice. *Mexican Corn, Puréed Spinach,* or Brussels sprouts are good accompaniments, as well as a dish of jellied apple rings. To most people, nowadays, wild duck is such a treat that it should be treated to only the finest Burgundy.

CANARD AUX CERISES
Le Café Procope, Paris

This old restaurant on rue Ancienne Comédie behind St. Germain des Prés was founded in 1686 by one Procopio, a man of the theater, when "cabaret" meant a wineshop or tavern. It was the meeting place of men of arts, letters, and the theater for two centuries and of revolutionaries in the late 1700s. The plaque before the entrance bears the names of illustrious men from Molière to Anatole France. In 1929 Jean Maura and Paul Louvet published a book called *Le Café Procope*, which reads like a history of Paris. The faded old-rose walls and antique gold lights resemble the décor shown in the old prints which hang on the walls. An old print of the café reproduced in the book shows ten men in deep conversation: among them, Buffon, Diderot, J. B. Rousseau, and Voltaire. Today the café is very well patronized; the food is good and not expensive. If you dine at the popular hour of 8:30 you may wait a while for a table. M. Michel Deroussent takes a lively interest in his attractive restaurant. He gave me recipes for two dishes, of which this is one.

4-pound duck
¼ cup butter
3 tablespoons sugar
2 tablespoons wine vinegar

½ cup white wine
⅓ cup veal stock or giblet stock
1 tablespoon cornstarch
1 cup pitted cherries

Brown the duck in the butter, then roast it 15 minutes to the pound at 350° until it is done. Remove the duck and quarter it. Keep it warm. Degrease the pan juices, add the vinegar, ¼ cup of the wine, and the veal stock or stock made from the duck neck and giblets. Let this reduce a little. Mix the other ¼ cup of wine with the cornstarch and thicken the sauce, scraping the bottom of the pan. If it is too thick, add more stock or wine. Add the cherries and boil up. Put the duck on hot plates and pour the sauce over it. Serves 4.

FAGIANO AL VINO ROSSO
Piccolo Mondo, Rome

2 pheasants
⅓ cup butter
3 tablespoons olive oil
½ cup chopped onions
½ cup chopped carrots
⅓ cup chopped celery

½ teaspoon sage
1 cup good red wine
Salt and pepper
Garnish: 8 slices bread fried in
  butter

The pheasants are dressed and wiped dry. Brown them all over in the butter and oil in a casserole. Remove them, put the vegetables in the butter that is left, and sauté a moment, then lay the birds on the vegetables, cover, and cook gently for 20 minutes in a 350° oven. Warm the wine and add it with the sage, salt, and pepper. Cook slowly another 20 minutes or until the birds are tender, turning down the oven if they cook too fast. Remove the birds and quarter them. If they are a good size a quarter will make 1 serving. Put the sauce through a sieve. Put 8 slices of bread fried in butter on hot plates and top with a quarter of pheasant. Reheat the sauce and pour it over the birds.

DUCK À LA ROBERT
Le Beurre Fondu, London

There is a little hotel near Sloane Square with a very fine restaurant attached. Haute cuisine is practiced here by Chef Robert Ross-Muir, who served his long apprenticeship in some of the best hotels in France. The rooms are furnished with quiet elegance and the food is excellent. The famous Aylesbury ducklings are the finest raised anywhere.

3-pound duck
¾ pound fresh apricots, stoned
½ teaspoon rosemary
1 teaspoon fennel seeds

½ cup apricot wine, or white wine
  with 1 tablespoon apricot
  brandy
1 tablespoon potato starch
Jigger apricot brandy

Stuff the duck with the fresh apricots, rosemary, and fennel seeds. Roast it 30 minutes at 375°, then remove it from the oven. Take out the apricots, and put them in a saucepan. Mix the wine with the potato starch, add it to the apricots, and simmer 10 minutes over low heat. Quarter the duck, put it in a casserole, pour the sauce over it, and reheat. At the moment of serving pour the apricot brandy over it. This is absolutely delicious. Serves 4. There is an apricot wine in England, but I don't think it is available here, so I suggest an alternative. If you can't get a duck as small as 3 pounds, use a 4- or 5-pound duck and roast it 1 to 1¼ hours at 325°. With this duck Mr. Ross-Muir serves only a salad, composed of chopped tart apples, celery, and sliced green stuffed olives, mixed with a dash of sour cream, on a bed of shredded lettuce.

QUAGLIA ALLA DIAVOLA
Piccolo Mondo, Rome

Game seems to be plentiful in Italy and it isn't considered such an expensive specialty as it is in the United States.

6 or 8 quail
4 or 5 tablespoons butter
Salt and pepper
¼ to ⅓ cup cognac

Garnish: Bread fried in butter
Accompaniments:
  Brown rice or wild rice
  Fresh peas

Cut the quail in half and flatten them. Sauté them gently in butter, 5 or 6 minutes on each side, sprinkling with salt and pepper. When they are tender, and cooked through (they don't take long), blaze with cognac. Have the fried bread on hot plates, put the quail on top, and pour the pan juices over the birds. If necessary add a little more fresh butter to the cognac juices. Two quail make 1 serving.

PHEASANTS WITH AGRODOLCE SAUCE

An old waiter with courtly manners, who had been trained in one of the great English houses, used to hand out little booklets containing his philosophical poetry and recipes from Fagiano. Umberto and Fagiano's have vanished, but one of the dishes that made the restaurant famous has remained—it was given to me many years ago. The Italians also use this old recipe for sour-sweet sauce to serve over stewed hare.

6 young pheasants
Salt and pepper
6 strips bacon
⅓ cup butter
½ cup chopped onions
⅓ cup chopped celery
⅓ cup chopped carrots
2 cups dry white wine or dry vermouth
1 teaspoon orégano

Agrodolce Sauce:
½ cup sugar, caramelized
⅓ cup boiling water
1 tablespoon cocoa
2 tablespoons cornstarch
3 tablespoons wine vinegar
1 cup dry white wine or dry vermouth
1½ tablespoons grated orange rind
2 tablespoons butter
Garnish: Bread fried in butter

Salt and pepper the birds and tie a strip of bacon around each. Melt the butter and gently cook the vegetables until they are tender. Quickly brown the birds in the vegetables, then lift them to a large casserole. Add the wine to the vegetables and mash it through a coarse sieve or purée it in a blender. Add the orégano and pour this sauce over the pheasants. Sieving this sauce before roasting the birds facilitates making the sauce at the end. Cover the casserole and roast the birds 45 minutes at 350°. If they are cooking too fast, turn down the heat to 325°. Baste twice. Meanwhile make the *Agrodolce Sauce*. Put the sugar in a skillet and let it become quite dark brown over a hot flame. Turn off the heat and add the water. Cook over low heat until the sugar is melted. Blend the cocoa and cornstarch with the vinegar, mix it with the wine, and add the orange rind. Stir this into the caramel syrup and when blended beat in the butter. Let this stand off heat until the pheasants are done. Have 6 slices of bread fried in butter on a hot platter or on 6 hot serving plates. Lift a bird onto each piece of bread. Add the caramel sauce to the pan juices and cook until it thickens. Pour this sauce over the pheasants and serve immediately. Serves 6 if the birds are the size for individual servings, or more if they are large. Roast tame duck is wonderful with this sauce.

PHEASANT CASSEROLE WITH MUSHROOMS

2 young pheasants
4 tablespoons butter
2 tablespoons caramel
1 jigger cognac
½ pound mushrooms
½ pound chicken livers
8 white onions, half-cooked
½ cup more butter
2 teaspoons crushed juniper
    berries

Salt and pepper
½ cup Madeira
2 teaspoons cornstarch
½ cup heavy cream
¼ cup currant jelly
Garnish:
    4 slices of bread fried in butter
Watercress

This is for young birds, wild or tame. The birds are well plucked, dressed, and wiped dry. Put the butter and caramel in a sauté pan and brown the birds, turning them until they are well glazed on all sides. Pour the cognac over them and blaze. Lift them out of the sauté pan into a casserole. Add more butter to the pan and sauté the mushrooms 2 or 3 minutes, then put 3 in each bird, and put the rest in the casserole. Sauté the livers in more butter 1 minute on each side and put half the livers in each bird. Arrange the onions around the birds. Lift the birds and put the ½ cup of butter under them. Sprinkle the juniper, salt, and pepper over them. Rinse the sauté pan with the Madeira and pour it over the birds. Cover very tightly and cook in a 350° oven for about 25 minutes. Blend the cornstarch with the cream. Remove the birds and cut them in half. Have the fried bread on 4 hot plates and put a half pheasant on each slice. Put 2 onions on each plate. Pour the cream into the casserole and cook until the sauce thickens. Add the jelly and when it is melted, divide the mushrooms and sauce over the birds. Garnish with watercress. Corn or peas may be served with game. Serve a bottle of Burgundy.

GALLINA FARAONA

3-pound guinea hen or 4-pound
    chicken
Stuffing:
    1 cup diced cooked veal
    ½ cup diced cooked ham
    1 small truffle, sliced
    1 tablespoon butter
    ½ teaspoon orégano
    ½ teaspoon sage
    ½ teaspoon basil
    Pepper, dash of salt

2 thin strips salt pork
¼ cup ham, ground
¼ cup onion, ground
¼ cup celery, ground
1 teaspoon thyme
½ teaspoon mace
½ cup Madeira
2 egg yolks, beaten

Gallina Faraona (Pharaoh's hen) is a guinea hen. The old Italian recipe calls for boning, stuffing the spread-out bird, reshaping, and tying securely.

You may leave the bird whole, if you choose. It is such a good dish I suggest using a chicken if guinea hen is not available. Sauté the truffle a moment in the butter. Mix the stuffing ingredients and stuff the bird and sew it up. Put the pork strips on the bottom of a casserole or roaster and make a bed of mixed ham, onion, celery, thyme, and mace. Lay the bird on it, breast up, and pour the wine over it. Cover it with a buttered paper, then with the lid. Roast 15 minutes at 375°, then 1 hour more at 300°. Lift out the bird and keep it warm. Strain the sauce into a saucepan. Let it reheat and pour it over the beaten egg yolks. Heat but do not boil. Serve the sauce in a sauceboat with the bird. The guinea hen serves 3 or 4, the chicken 4.

SQUAB OR CORNISH GAME HEN

4 birds	2½ cups chicken consommé
1 tablespoon honey or caramel	1 teaspoon thyme
3 tablespoons butter, more butter	1 teaspoon basil
Salt and pepper	1 teaspoon cumin powder
Bacon strips	½ cup heavy cream
1¼ cups patna rice	Chopped parsley

Each person is served 1 bird. Put the honey or caramel in an iron skillet with 3 tablespoons of butter and brown the birds quickly on all sides. Put a lump of butter inside each bird, salt and pepper them, put a strip of bacon over each side of the breast, and lay the birds on their backs in a casserole. Boil up the rice in the consommé, add all the seasonings, and pour it around the birds. Cover very tightly and bake in a 350° oven for 45 minutes. After the dish has been in the oven 25 minutes, see if it needs more consommé and if so add a boiling ½ cup. When the birds are tender and the liquid absorbed pour ½ cup of boiling cream over the dish. Sprinkle the top with parsley and serve from the casserole. Fresh new peas may accompany this dish.

GROUSE SMITANE
Louise Junior, New York

Louise Junior (the name inherited from a previous owner) is a very fine and very busy restaurant run by two men from San Marino. Paul Paolini greets the guests and his partner-nephew Alberto Savoretti does an expert and lively business at the bar. A feature here is the hors d'œuvre, which is brought to your table without ado, because it will be asked for anyway. Generous bowls of fresh shrimp in a good pink sauce, fresh mushrooms in oil, fresh crabmeat, prosciutto and melon, fennel, celery, radishes, toast and butter load your table, and you are apt to eat too much.—But excellent main dishes, well and freshly cooked for you, are still to come. When you think you have reached your limit, a huge and beautiful pastry, another specialty of the house, is wheeled to your table. There is a good selection of wines. Mr. Aldo Mercandetti, the head chef, gave me this recipe for grouse, which may be used for any game bird or for squab.

6 grouse, squab, or small game birds	Salt and pepper
3 tablespoons salt-pork cubes	12 strips bacon
6 tablespoons butter	½ cup veal or chicken broth
⅓ cup chopped celery	½ cup dry vermouth
⅓ cup chopped carrots	½ teaspoon powdered bay leaf
⅓ cup chopped onions	1⅓ cups heavy sour cream

There is nothing finer than the delicate dark meat of grouse. Clean and wipe the birds dry. (If you have their livers, sauté them a moment in butter, chop them and mix with a little shredded onion, some fresh breadcrumbs, salt, and pepper, and stuff the birds.) Sauté the pork cubes in the butter and when hot, brown the birds on all sides. Make a bed of the vegetables in the baking pan; season them and the birds with salt and pepper. Tie the bacon strips on the breasts and legs of the birds and lay them breast side up on the vegetables. Rinse the sauté pan with the broth and vermouth and pour it over the birds. Put them in a preheated 400° oven for 15 minutes, baste them, and then reduce the heat to 350° and roast them 20 minutes more. Remove the birds to a hot platter and keep them warm. Strain the vegetables and pan juices through a sieve, add the bay leaf and reduce the sauce a little over a hot flame. Stir in the sour cream and when it is hot, pour the sauce over the birds. This dish may be served with rice and Brussels sprouts or green beans and a bottle of very good red wine. Serves 6.

GROUSE OR GUINEA HEN STEW

2 birds, disjointed	1½ cups boiling game broth or chicken broth
2 strips salt pork fat	
¾ cup chopped onions	2 or 3 tablespoons flour
¼ cup chopped carrots	1 cup heavy cream
Salt and pepper	2 egg yolks, beaten
	Garnish: Hot corn bread or biscuits

When I was young my father brought home specimens of all the feathered game that flew over the western prairies from the Arctic Circle to the Gulf of Mexico. One of our favorites was prairie chicken, now extinct; he always said he had his share in its extermination. The texture of its meat, which resembled grouse or guinea hen, lent itself to this most delicious stew. The dark meat was heaped in the center of a large platter, split-open biscuits were placed around the edge, and golden rich gravy was poured over all.

Cube the salt pork and fry it out in an iron Dutch oven or porcelain-covered iron casserole. Scoop out the pieces. Put the onion and carrot in the grease and add salt and pepper. Brown all the pieces of fowl in this mixture for about 12 to 15 minutes, until the meat is glazed and well seasoned. Pour in the boiling broth, cover tightly, and simmer gently until the meat is tender. Do not overcook. Blend the flour with ¾ cup of the cream, heat, add to the meat and gravy, and cook until it thickens. Heat the rest of the cream, pour it over the beaten egg yolks, and stir it in the last minute before serving. Do not boil again. You will have to decide how many birds you have and how many they will serve. If you cook more than 2 birds you must increase all the other ingredients.

SAUTÉED SQUAB OR QUAIL

This is a fine way of cooking very small birds. They are split in half, two halves to a serving.

4 split birds for 4
4 tablespoons butter
2 tablespoons caramel or brown
   sugar
Salt and pepper
½ cup good port wine
½ cup heavy cream

1 tablespoon flour
Garnish: Bread fried in butter
Accompaniments:
   Rissolée Potatoes
   Baked Halved Tomatoes

Wipe the birds and brown them on both sides over a good flame in a heavy frying pan with the butter and caramel, using more if needed. Salt and pepper them. Put them in a baking dish or pan. Put the wine in the browning pan, boil up, and scrape it over the birds. Cover very tightly, and bake 20 minutes at 350°. When they are done, blend the cream with the flour and thicken the sauce in the pan. Meanwhile you have fried two pieces of bread for each hot plate. Put the bird halves on the bread, divide the sauce over them, and serve immediately.

OYSTER STUFFING FOR SMALL GAME BIRDS

3 or 4 oysters for each bird
   Melted butter
   Fresh fine dry breadcrumbs

Salt and pepper
½ to 1 teaspoon thyme

Mix the seasoning with the crumbs. Dip the oysters in melted butter and then in the seasoned crumbs. Stuff the birds and sew them up. Never keep crumbs. When the words "fresh" and "dry" are both used, fresh bread should be dried in the oven and either rolled, put through a grinder, or put in a blender. Stale bread contributes less than nothing.

CHESTNUT STUFFING FOR TURKEY, GOOSE, OR OTHER BIRDS

1 pound fresh chestnuts
1 medium-sized onion, sliced
½ cup sliced celery
3 tablespoons butter
Salt and pepper
2 cups fresh dry or toasted small cubes of rye bread, or 2 cups cooked brown or patna rice

2 tablespoons chopped parsley
1 teaspoon thyme
1 teaspoon curry or cumin powder
½ pound little pork sausages
6 small fresh mushrooms
½ cup turkey or chicken broth
¼ cup sherry or Madeira

Score each chestnut with a sharp pointed knife, boil them 1½ minutes, and skin while warm. Cut each in 2 or 3 slices. Sauté the onion and celery in the butter until tender and add salt and pepper. Mix the parsley with the bread and seasonings. Sauté the sausages (Jones are good) until lightly browned and cut them in half. Cut the mushrooms in half and sauté them for a minute in 1 tablespoon of the sausage grease. Mix all the ingredients lightly together, fill the bird, and sew it up. For a very large turkey, increase the ingredients a little, but no bird should be stuffed too full.

MASHED POTATO STUFFING FOR TURKEY OR CHICKEN

4 medium-sized potatoes (for 8-pound bird)
1 medium-sized onion, chopped
4 tablespoons good fat or butter
¾ cup tiny dark bread cubes

Salt and pepper
⅞ cup light cream, or small can evaporated milk
1 tablespoon anise seeds
Brazil nuts or other nuts, browned (optional)

Peel the potatoes, quarter them, and cook until just tender in very little water. Meanwhile sauté the onion in half of the fat or butter until tender. Sauté the bread cubes separately in the rest of the fat or butter. Mash the potatoes, add the salt, pepper, cream or milk, and the anise seeds. They make the dressing very fragrant. Mix all the ingredients lightly together, stuff the bird, and sew it up. This will stuff a capon. If you are stuffing a large turkey, double the ingredients. For a holiday, browned brazil nuts or other nuts may be added.

APPLE AND RAISIN STUFFING FOR DUCK OR GOOSE

½ cup chopped onions
½ cup chopped celery
3 tablespoons butter
Salt and pepper
1 to 1½ cups fresh dry breadcrumbs

1 teaspoon powdered anise
1 teaspoon chopped parsley
1 cup chopped green apple
2 tablespoons Madeira
⅓ cup raisins

Sauté the onions and celery in the butter until tender. Add salt and pepper. Mix lightly with all the other ingredients and stuff and sew up the bird. This quantity will stuff a duck; double it for a goose.

FRUIT STUFFING FOR DUCK OR GOOSE

6 or 8 large sweet prunes
½ cup red wine
1 large banana
1 small onion
2 tablespoons butter

1 large tart apple
Salt and pepper
½ teaspoon cinnamon
¼ teaspoon clove
½ teaspoon anise powder or seeds

Wash the prunes and soak them in the wine several hours. Drain and save the wine to baste the bird. Cut the prunes in half and pit them. Cut the banana in 1-inch lengths. Slice 1 small onion and sauté it in butter until it is tender. Peel the apple and cut in eighths. Mix all the ingredients lightly together and season to your taste. Fill and sew up the bird. When stuffing a goose, add 1 to 1½ cups of toasted rye-bread cubes to the fruit.

Special Dishes

DÉSIR DES GOURMETS
Lapérouse, Paris

People who love Paris love it because it doesn't change, and the charm of Lapérouse is that *it* doesn't change. The restaurant is in one of the most fascinating parts of Paris, on the Quai des Grands-Augustins with its windows facing Nôtre Dame, a lady who has changed little since the Middle Ages. The restaurant's rooms are small and intimate and the atmosphere is very friendly, especially if you make it known that you are there for serious dining. M. Roger Topolinski generously gave me a very elegant dish.

8 lamb kidneys	1 jigger brandy
Salt and freshly ground pepper	1 cup heavy cream
Hot oil	Beurre manié:
¾-pound chicken livers	2 tablespoons butter mixed
3 tablespoons sweet butter	with 1 tablespoon flour
2 truffles, finely sliced	Squeeze of a lemon

Remove the skin from the kidneys, cut them through the long way, and remove the tendon from the center of each half. Season them with salt and freshly ground pepper and sauté them in very hot oil until browned to your taste but still rosy pink inside. Sauté the chicken livers in more oil. Remove the meats to a hot dish and keep them warm. Empty the oil from the sauté pan and put in the sweet butter, add the truffles, and simmer very gently for 5 minutes without letting them color. Then add the brandy and blaze. Add the cream and thicken the sauce with the beurre manié, stirring in pea-sized lumps at a time. When the sauce is "sufficiently unctuous," add a squeeze of lemon juice and check the seasoning. Reheat the kidneys and livers in the hot sauce. The livers may be served in the center of a turban of noodles or rice with the kidneys and sauce around it. Or serve in pastry shells, accompanied by steamed potatoes. Serves 4.

CASSOULET WITH DUCK

3 or 4 cups dried white beans
2 cups chopped onions
1 shredded carrot
2 tablespoons chopped parsley
3 cloves garlic, crushed
2 teaspoons mixed herbs
2 whole cloves
Salt and pepper
¾ cup tomato purée
1 5½-pound duck
3 tablespoons caramel

2 pounds boned shoulder of pork
1 onion, chopped
½ cup white wine
3 to 4 cups beef or chicken broth
(or more)
½ pound pork sausage
1 pound Czech, Hungarian, or
Italian garlic sausage
1 cup dry breadcrumbs
1 tablespoon grated lemon rind
2 tablespoons chopped parsley

Wash the beans and soak in plenty of water overnight. In the morning put them to simmer gently with the onions, carrot, parsley, garlic, herbs, and cloves, adding more water to cover. Cook them very slowly 2 hours or more, until tender. Add more water if necessary. When they are tender add salt, pepper, and tomato purée. Meanwhile you have cooked the duck and the pork. Have the butcher quarter the duck and cut each quarter in half. Rub the pieces with caramel, lay them bone-side down in an open dripping pan, and roast them 45 minutes at 350°. Remove from the oven, pour off the grease, and set the pieces aside. Brown the pork shoulder in a little duck fat or oil, pour the wine over it, add salt and pepper, and roast it 1 hour at 325°. When the pork is done add the pan juices to the cooked beans. Slice the pork ¾-inch thick and cut the slices in half. In a large casserole put a third of the beans and half of the duck and half of the pork on top, then add another third of beans, the rest of the duck and pork, then the rest of the beans and all the liquids, adding hot broth to the top. Cover the pot and bake at 325° for 45 minutes. Brown the pork sausages a little and bury them in the casserole. Cut the garlic sausage in 1-inch lengths and bury it. Add more hot broth if necessary, just to the top of the beans. Cover and bake at 350° for 1 hour. Uncover, sprinkle the mixed crumbs, lemon rind, and parsley over the top, and brown 15 minutes at 375°. This serves 12. This must be kept as moist as Boston Baked Beans but must not be too liquid at the end. The French cook their meats first so that when the dish is put together the cooking time is shortened and a fresher bean dish results. If Hungarian Kolbaz or Czech Debrecinky sausage are not available, German or Spanish may be used. This is a flexible dish. The French also use lamb or mutton and preserved goose. Goose legs are sometimes available in German meat markets and they may be used instead of duck.

BRIOCHE DE BRILLAT SAVARIN
Le Coq Hardi, Bougival (Paris)

On a July evening we made a brisk 45-minute drive south of Paris to the village of Bougival to reach this modest-looking inn on a sleepy street. Upon entering, the whole scene changed to the most elegant flower-decked restaurant. Each terrace was packed with hundreds of huge deep-pink hydrangeas. In the dusk the garden in the back seemed to reach up to the sky. It was a ravishing sight, made more so by a Floradora Sextette, each member parading past the tables carrying a large platter of elaborately aspicked lobsters, meats, salads, vegetables, etc. It all may sound like a great production but the quality of the food justified it.

6 good-sized brioches	Sauce:
2 pairs sweetbreads	¾ cup rich chicken broth
Butter	¾ cup rich veal broth
Salt and pepper	¾ cup heavy cream
½ pound fresh button mushrooms	2 tablespoons cornstarch
Tiny veal meatballs	2 egg yolks
1 truffle, sliced thin	1 wineglass port

Obtain the brioches 1 to a serving, from a good French bakery. Remove the knobs and reserve them. Scoop out enough of the crumb so the brioches may be filled with the sauce and meats. Soak the sweetbreads an hour in salted water, then remove the membranes. Cut them in walnut-sized pieces and sauté them in butter until they are done, about 5 minutes. Salt and pepper them. Brush the mushrooms and sauté them in butter 3 minutes and season them. For the meatballs, grind ¾ pound of veal, season with salt, pepper, and ¼ teaspoon nutmeg, and stir in 1 egg yolk and 1 tablespoon of flour. Roll into 18 tiny balls and sauté them about 3 minutes in butter. Put the prepared foods in a bowl with the sliced truffle. For the sauce, put the chicken and veal broths in a saucepan, blend the cornstarch with the cream, add it to the broth, and cook until it thickens. Meanwhile heat the brioches in the oven. Pour a little sauce over the egg yolks, add to the rest of the sauce, and add the port. This may be kept warm over warm water. Empty the meats and truffle into the sauce and reheat if necessary. Fill the brioches, replace the knobs, and serve. This is an elegant dish for luncheon or for a supper after the theater. It may be prepared ahead of time to warm up the last minute. Champagne would be nice with this.

COUSCOUS LIBANAIS
Caverne Ali-Baba, rue Jacob, Paris

When you look in the door of this tiny restaurant and see only three tables, all full, don't walk by, because there are two or three rooms upstairs accommodating forty more people. This is a delightful little restaurant with ceiling and walls covered with red and blue velvet of Oriental design. Riad Karam from Lebanon and Lolita Bell from Paris run this friendly Left Bank café. I was given a demonstration in the kitchen of the wonderful way the couscous is cooked. This especially prepared wheat is available in the United States in packages labeled Couscous. The grain is cooked separately and the lamb stew ladled over it at the table.

2 cups couscous
3 or 4 tablespoons bland oil
1 large can chick peas
  Butter
Stew:

2 pounds neck, breast, or shoulder of lamb, cubed	2 leeks, sliced
1 2-pound chicken, disjointed (optional)	3 bay leaves
Salt, pepper, and flour	1 teaspoon thyme
⅓ cup butter	2 teaspoons salt
2 cups chopped onions	½ teaspoon pepper
2 carrots, chopped	1 teaspoon marjoram
2 white turnips, cubed	1 tablespoon coriander
1 diced green pepper	1 teaspoon cumin powder
½ cup diced celery	1 quart can tomatoes
	Garnish: Chutney

We will make the stew first as it takes longer to cook. Shake the 1½-inch cubes of meat (and the pieces of chicken if used) in a bag with 2 or 3 tablespoons of flour, salt, and pepper until they are lightly coated. Brown the meat on all sides in the butter and remove it to a soup kettle. Cook the onions 1 minute in the sauté pan and add them to the meat with all the other vegetables and seasonings. The tomatoes are used to rinse the sauté pan, then scraped over the meat. Add just enough water to almost cover. Simmer gently for 2 hours or until the meat is tender. Keep the kettle almost covered. This is brought to the table to ladle meat, vegetables and broth over the steaming couscous. The chick peas are warmed in butter and brought to the table in another bowl. Serve chutney with this.

To cook the couscous, put the 2 cups of grain in a bowl and cover with cold water for 2 minutes. Drain it and put it in the top of a steamer and cook it 15 minutes over boiling salted water. The grains are then rubbed between the hands with 3 or 4 tablespoons of bland oil, never olive oil. This may be done ahead of time. Before serving the grains are again put in the steamer and boiled another 15 minutes over boiling salted water. The grains will be fluffy, separate, and tender. Serves 6 to 8.

PAELLA

The chicken:
    6 chicken legs and 6
        second joints
    1 onion, chopped
    1 carrot, chopped
    ½ cup dry white wine
    1 cup water
    1 teaspoon tarragon
    Salt and pepper
The shrimp:
    1 pound shrimp
    1½ cups water
    1 teaspoon thyme
    1 small onion, chopped
    Salt and pepper
The lobster (optional):
    ½ pound fresh cooked
        lobster meat or canned
        lobster

⅓ cup olive oil
    2 large cloves garlic, crushed
    1 large green pepper, sliced
    2 skinned fresh tomatoes, sliced,
        or 2 large canned tomatoes,
        drained
    Salt and pepper
    2 cups patna or bomba (Spanish)
        rice
Garnish:
    4 canned pimentos cup in strips
    1 tin of buttered mussels
        (optional)

The chicken and the seafood are prepared ahead of time and the dish assembled 20 minutes before it is to be served. Cut the legs and second joints of the chicken apart. Put them in a pot with the other ingredients to simmer very gently until they are tender, about 1 hour for young chicken. Remove the chicken and strain and reserve the broth. Wash the shrimp but do not shell them. Simmer them 3 or 4 minutes in the water with the thyme, onion, salt, and pepper. Take out the shrimp, let them cool, shell them, and put the shells back into the broth. Cover and simmer for 10 minutes. Strain and reserve this broth also—this makes a strong broth. Leave the lobster in good-sized pieces. The lobster is optional but adds a great deal to the dish. The Spanish make paella in a large sauté pan 2 or 3 inches deep, cooking all the ingredients with the rice, uncovered. If you do not have such a pan to bring to the table, begin with a large iron skillet. Put the olive oil and crushed garlic in it, add the green pepper, and cook for 6 to 7 minutes, then add the tomatoes and cook for 10 minutes more. Add some salt and pepper and the rice. Stir well and then empty all into a large shallow casserole, 12 inches in diameter. Arrange the chicken, shrimp, and lobster over the rice and add 4 cups of mixed shrimp and chicken broth. Put the uncovered casserole in a 375° oven for 20 minutes, until the rice is cooked and each grain is separate. Across the top arrange the pimento strips and the little buttered mussels, which make the dish look beautiful. This is a Spanish dish of the people; in Spain it includes local seafood, local sausage, and the meat or fowl available. This quantity will serve 6 to 8, but it is evident that it can be a useful dish for big occasions.

LE BAECKENOFE—"UNE SPECIALITÉ ALSACIENNE"
Maison Kammerzell, Strasbourg

2 or 3 pigs' knuckles
2 or 3 pigs' feet
2 pounds boned shoulder of
    mutton
3 pounds round of beef
Marinade:
    2 cups Riesling wine
    3 cloves garlic, crushed
    2 bay leaves, crushed
    2 cloves
    ½ cup minced onions
    Salt and pepper

2 tablespoons lard or goose fat,
    melted
2 pounds onions, sliced
2 pounds potatoes, sliced
3 tablespoons butter
Flour and water paste

Mix the marinade and marinate the meats in it for 24 hours. Drain and reserve the marinade. Grease a very large casserole and put the melted lard or goose fat on the bottom. Put a bed of one-third of the sliced onions on the fat, then half the sliced potatoes. Then come the meats, another third of the onions and the rest of the potatoes. Over the top put the rest of the onions and dot with the butter. Sieve the marinade over the pot. Make a thick paste of flour and water and spread on the rim of the casserole to seal the lid hermetically. Put the dish into an oven preheated to 375° for 20 minutes, then turn down the heat to 300°, and continue baking another 2 hours and 40 minutes—3 hours altogether. When done, remove the lid, turn up the heat to 400°, and let the top become golden—about 6 to 10 minutes. One is directed to serve this with "une bonne salade verte." Don't forget a good Alsatian wine. This will serve 8 or 10.

LIÈVRE EN SAUPIQUET
Capucin Gourmand, Nancy

1 large hare
Pork fat
½ cup sliced carrots
½ cup sliced onions
½ cup chicken or veal broth
Salt and pepper

Saupiquet (Sharp Sauce):
    Hare liver, chopped fine
    Hare blood
    ⅓ cup cognac or Armagnac
    Pork fat
    ½ cup finely chopped ham or
        lean bacon
    ½ cup chopped onions
    2 cloves garlic, crushed
    3 tablespoons red wine
        vinegar
    1 teaspoon thyme
    2 cloves

M. Romain makes this sharp sauce also for roast pork or ham, using 3 or 4 poultry livers. The very finely chopped liver and the hare blood, if any, are marinated an hour in the cognac or Armagnac. Melt some pork fat in a heavy saucepan, add the ham or bacon and the onions, and cook a little. Then add the garlic, red wine vinegar, thyme, and cloves, and cook over simmering water 20 minutes. If it becomes at all dry, add a little red wine, a spoonful or so. Mash through a sieve. Meanwhile the hare has been larded with strips of pork fat. Lay it in a casserole on a bed of sliced carrots and onions and pour the broth over it. Roast at 350° 1½ hours— longer if the hare is very large. If it is roasting too fast turn down to 325°. Lift the hare to a hot platter. Sieve the pan juices and add the marinade, the sieved ingredients and cook for 2 minutes. Pour the sauce over the hare. Serves 6 or 8.

BOLLITI WITH GREEN SAUCE
Rosticceria Giuseppe, Bologna

The Rosticceria Giuseppe on the Piazza Maggiore is a restaurant of the people. It is on the street floor and in the arcade of the twelfth-century palace of Re Renzo. In the summer the arcade is filled with tables, occupied from 12 to 3 when all the shops and museums are closed. One of the most popular dishes is Bolliti—huge steaming platters of whole boiled meats. A tureen of *Green Sauce* accompanies the meats.

Meats:
- 3 pounds fresh brisket or chuck
- 3 pounds fillet of veal
- 1 calf's head
  Bones and giblets
- 4½- to 5-pound roasting chicken
- 1½ cups chopped onions
- 1½ cups chopped carrots
  Parsley and thyme
  Salt and pepper

Green Sauce:
- 1 cup ground parsley and watercress
- 2 tablespoons simple syrup
- ⅔ cup olive oil
- ¼ cup lemon juice
  Salt and pepper
- 1 clove garlic, crushed
- ⅔ cup meat broth
- 12 capers

Put 3 quarts water in a very large kettle, add half the vegetables and seasonings, and bring to a boil. A large can of V8 would be a good addition. Put in the beef and simmer gently for 50 minutes, then add the veal and the calf's head, well trimmed and washed. Skim and simmer gently until the meat is tender. Add salt and pepper after 2 hours' cooking. Marrow bones and giblets add to its flavor. The marrow, meat, and gristle of the head are a great delicacy. The chicken is simmered separately with the rest of the vegetables and seasonings, to keep its own flavor. Cook it 2 hours. Serve it on the platter with the other meats. Mix all the ingredients for the sauce. It is quite thick with herbs. This is a great dish for a party of 12. Serve with a pasta, a green salad, and a vigorous red wine.

FRITTO MISTO

This amusing grab-bag is a popular Roman and Florentine dish. Any or all of the vegetables may be used with either the mixed meat-fry or the mixed fish-fry; and so can the cheese.

Meat:
  Calf's brains, cubed
  Chicken livers
  Calf's liver, cubed
  Sweetbreads, cubed
  Tiny meatballs
Fish:
  Any fish, cubed
  Scallops
  Mussels, shelled
  Clams, shelled
  Oysters, shelled
  Shrimp, shelled

Vegetables:
  Artichoke hearts
  Mushrooms
  Eggplant, cubed
  Zucchini, cubed
  Mozzarella cheese, cubed
Batter:
  2 eggs, beaten
  ¼ cup flour
  Salt and pepper
  ½ teaspoon sugar
  Oil for frying
  Garnish: Lemon slices

All the foods are whole or in 1-inch cubes. The batter is made by beating all the ingredients together. The pieces are dipped in the batter and fried in deep oil at 370° until a golden brown. They are served on a platter garnished with slices of lemon. The deep-fried cubes of cheese are especially good. The little meatballs are made of ground veal or beef, mixed with egg, salt, pepper and a pinch of thyme. A green salad is a good accompaniment. Allow 10 pieces for each serving.

CHINESE RICE-STICK NOODLES
Tom's Shangri-La, New York

Rice sticks   1 cup corn oil (or more)

These noodles of fascinating crisp texture and pure whiteness are a mystery until you see how they are cooked. Imported rice sticks are obtainable in any Chinese grocery store. Put a cup or more of fresh corn oil in a wok and when it is smoking drop in a bundle of the rice sticks. Leave them no more than 2 seconds. They do not separate so are easily scooped out with the big flat wire long-handled sieve that the Chinese use. The wire part is about 5 inches in diameter. The noodles are put in a towel-lined sieve to drain. These, used to garnish almost any Chinese dish, make it very attractive. They retain their crispness for hours if stored in the refrigerator; do not freeze them. Chinese philosophy of cooking—the dish must be pleasant to the eye, fragrant to the nose, and exquisite to the palate.

CHINESE STEAK FLAMBÉ
Tom's Shangri-La, New York

Tenderloin fillet or sirloin of
    beef
1 cup corn oil, plus 2 tablespoons
¼ cup sliced mushrooms
¼ cup sliced onions
2 teaspoons sherry
    Pepper

Sauce:
1 teaspoon oyster sauce
1 teaspoon sugar
1 teaspoon Hai Sen Sauce
    (brown sauce)
1 teaspoon Chinese molasses
    soy sauce
½ teaspoon sesame oil
1 tablespoon water mixed
    with ¼ teaspoon corn-
    starch
5 tablespoons soup stock
¼ teaspoon salt

Garnish:
1 notched lemon cup
3 or 4 tablespoons Cointreau

The beef must be of fine, tender quality. It is cut in 2- by 3-inch pieces, ¾-inch thick and pounded 3 or 4 times for added tenderness. Allow 3 pieces for each person. If more than 6 pieces are cooked the quantities of the sauce ingredients will have to be increased. Put the oil in a wok and when it smokes put in the meat and stir it for a good minute so that it is browned on all sides. Then put it in a sieve. Meanwhile mix all the sauce ingredients in a small bowl and stir it so that it is well mixed. Empty the oil from the wok and put in a little fresh oil, about 2 tablespoons. When it is hot return the steak to the wok with the mushrooms and onions. Stir in the sherry and add a little pepper. Stir in the sauce and when it is very hot empty everything into a shallow serving dish. (This is for rare to medium. If well-done steak is desired, stir it a minute longer.) Scoop out half a lemon to make cup and notch rim. Set this on top of the steak, pour the Cointreau into it, and set ablaze. Bring to the table burning. Empty the liqueur over the meat; it will continue to burn. This sauce is absolutely delicious. Gentlemen cooks can really show off with this dish. *Steak Flambé* is one of many creations of the imaginative and highly dextrous chefs, Sel Ngan Hum and Chi Kit Wong, which you will find nowhere else. Several times in their offhours they kindly gave me lessons in short fast cooking. The Chinese frying pan called a wok is a great invention and anyone interested in cooking Chinese style will surely want to own one. With a dome cover they are ideal for steaming so that the wok may be used for many dishes in Western cookery. The Chinese chef is a busy man; so that he may fill all orders instantly he has at hand jars of oyster sauce, Hai Sen or brown sauce, soup stock, Chinese molasses soy sauce, soy sauce, accent, sugar, liquid cornstarch, etc. All of these are available at any Chinese grocery store, as well as fresh or canned bamboo shoots, water chestnuts, and bean sprouts.

CHICKEN WITH GARDEN GREENS
Tom's Shangri-La, New York

1 boned breast of chicken
2 egg whites
8 snow peas, cut in strips
2 tablespoons bamboo shoots, cut
   in strips
5 water chestnuts, sliced
1 cup corn oil

Sauce:
  4 tablespoons chicken stock
  1 teaspoon sugar
  ¼ teaspoon salt
  ¼ teaspoon cornstarch mixed
    with 1 tablespoon water

A boned breast of raw chicken is cut through in 4 thin slices. These are put together and cut down into fine strips. Beat the egg whites 4 times with a fork to break them down a little and marinate the chicken in them in the refrigerator for 1 hour. The peas and bamboo shoots are cut in the same thickness as the chicken. The chestnuts are sliced. Put the oil in a wok (Chinese frying pan) and when it is smoking hot, put in first the vegetables and then the chicken on top. Stir and cook very fast for a minute, then scoop the chicken and vegetables out into a sieve to drain. Empty the wok of oil and wipe it out. Put all the ingredients for the sauce in a bowl and mix them. Put them in the wok, add the chicken and vegetables, and stir for a minute over heat. Empty into a shallow serving dish and serve immediately. This dish is a complete surprise; the chicken melts in the mouth. This will serve 4 with other dishes, 2 if served alone.

SHRIMP IN EGG WHITE
Tom's Shangri-La, New York

½ pound fresh raw shrimp
2 egg whites
1 cup smoking corn oil
8 snow peas
1 tomato, skinned and seeded
½ green pepper, shredded

Sauce:
  1 teaspoon sugar
  Salt and pepper
  ¼ teaspoon cornstarch mixed
    with 1 tablespoon water
  2 tablespoons soup stock

Peel the shrimp and cut them in half lengthwise. Beat the egg whites 3 or 4 times with a fork, mix with the shrimp, and marinate in the refrigerator an hour. When ready to cook, put the oil in a wok and when it smokes add the shrimp and stir briskly for 10 or 12 *seconds*. The shrimp is white, tender, and delicate and must not cook too long. Cut the tomatoes in 1-inch pieces. Put the vegetables in a sieve, scoop out the shrimp, and let it drain on top of them. The oil is emptied from the wok and it is wiped out. Mix the ingredients of the sauce together and put it in the wok, then add the shrimp and vegetables. Stir and cook 6 or 8 seconds. This may seem a short time but the sauce is already hot and all the cooking is done over quite high heat. Empty onto a shallow serving dish and serve immediately. With other dishes, this serves 4.

Vegetables

THERE are vegetables that should be served as a separate course; and there are those that are always served as an accompaniment or garnish. Artichokes, stuffed and served with a sauce, take so long to eat, dealing as we must with each separate leaf, that they should be served alone. Asparagus, that loveliest of vegetables, certainly makes a wonderful first course, hot or cold, with butter or a vinaigrette or Hollandaise sauce; or it may follow the meat, depending on the menu. I've thought for a long time that corn on the cob deserves a course to itself. If the family loves corn then surely 3 or 4 ears should be allowed for each good appetite when the season is on and the corn is picked nearby. It should be eaten piping hot and that takes some time, so that everything else waits and becomes cold. *Moussaka*, the elaborate eggplant-lamb-rice molded production is certainly a course by itself. *Mushroom Soufflé* may be a separate course or an accompaniment depending on what comes before or after. If lobster is served in its shell and demands full attention, a mushroom soufflé would be fine to follow it. Nothing should accompany broiled lobster, except perhaps potato chips which can be ignored.

Vegetables are not always given the importance they deserve and the art of cooking them is often neglected. Young and tender vegetables take so few minutes to cook that the pressure cooker is ideal for them. No water is added to spinach, just butter, and it takes 30 seconds. Add 4 tablespoons of water and a lump of butter to new peas and cook them a minute or two. String beans take ½ cup of water and some butter and cook in 3 minutes. Don't forget that the liquid is as precious as the vegetable.

ARTICHOKES ALLA CREMA
(Linda Bocconi, Rome)

Artichokes	Salt and pepper
Mozzarella cheese	Ham
Cream cheese	Olive oil
Crushed garlic	

This dish is from the mother of my beautiful friend Licia, and wonderful it is. Remove the coarse outer leaves from fresh artichokes and clip the hard tips of the leaves with kitchen shears. Roll the artichokes on their sides with the palm of your hand to soften them. Soak in cold water 1 hour, then rinse and drain upside down. Spread the leaves and fill with cubes of Mozzarella, some cream cheese, crushed garlic, 1 bud in each, and pieces of cooked ham or Italian prosciutto. Sprinkle the tops with a little salt and pepper and put a good 2 tablespoons of olive oil in each artichoke. The more lavish you are with the filling the better. Put the artichokes in the bottom of a heavy pot with a tight lid and put water in the bottom halfway up the artichokes. Cook until the water is almost absorbed. Forty minutes for small ones and 1¼ hours for the large. Always serve artichokes as a separate course.

BOILED ARTICHOKES WITH VINAIGRETTE SAUCE

6 large globe artichokes	¼ cup olive oil
6 tablespoons finely chopped onions	2 cloves garlic, crushed
6 tablespoons dry vermouth	*Vinaigrette Sauce:*
6 tablespoons olive oil	More wine and olive oil
Salt and pepper	1 tablespoon capers
1 cup white wine or dry vermouth	1 tablespoon prepared mustard

Remove the stems and a few coarse outer leaves of the artichokes. Plunge them in boiling salted water for 5 minutes, keeping the water simmering. Rinse the artichokes with fresh water and turn them upside down to drain a minute or two. Use a large kettle so that the artichokes may stand right side up on the bottom. Separate the leaves and fill each artichoke with onions, 1 tablespoon each of vermouth and olive oil, salt and pepper. Put 1 cup of wine, ¼ cup olive oil, and the garlic in the bottom of the kettle, put in the artichokes, cover tightly, and cook slowly from 25 to 35 minutes, depending on the size. Artichokes are best served as a separate course, as they are slightly messy to eat and take some time. Lift each onto a salad plate. Use the broth to make the sauce. Mix with the broth in the kettle enough more wine and olive oil to make 2 cups, add the capers, and mustard, and salt and pepper if needed. These may be served either hot or cold. Serve the sauce in a bowl so each person may dip the leaves.

ARTICHOKE BOTTOMS WITH MUSHROOM SAUCE

6 very large artichokes or 12
   medium-sized ones
2 cups chicken broth
2 tablespoons lemon juice
½ pound fresh mushrooms
3 tablespoons butter

¼ teaspoon nutmeg
3 teaspoons cornstarch
Salt and pepper
1 cup light cream
Sherry or dry vermouth

If the artichokes are very large, the bottom of one may be large enough for a serving; if not two will be needed. Remove the stems and most of the outer leaves. Put them into salted boiling water for 5 minutes, rinse well, and drain. Put them in a large kettle with the broth and lemon juice, cover tightly, and simmer until tender, from 25 to 35 minutes depending on their size. When they are tender drain them from the broth and reserve it to make the sauce. Remove the rest of the leaves and scoop out the choke with a spoon. Meanwhile slice the mushrooms if they are large; button mushrooms should be left whole. Sauté them in the butter 4 or 5 minutes. Blend the nutmeg, cornstarch, and some salt and pepper with the cream, add ¾ cup of broth from the artichokes, and cook until it thickens. Thin with sherry or dry vermouth to the consistency of cream and add the mushrooms. Put the artichokes on salad-size serving plates and pour the sauce over them. This may be served as a separate course if desired.

ASPARAGUS ON TOAST

1 bunch of asparagus
   (2½ pounds)
6 slices homemade bread, toasted

12 tablespoons asparagus water
Salt and pepper
⅔ cup butter, melted

Asparagus is one of our most treasured vegetables, so we ought to cook it the best way. Don't confuse a fish cooker with something to cook asparagus in. Use a large double boiler. Clean and trim the asparagus, tie it in a bundle, and stand it up in the bottom of the double boiler. Add hot water two-thirds of the way up the stalks. Invert the top of the double boiler over the tips. Cook asparagus of good size 18 minutes. The white part cooks tender and the tips steam and do not fall apart. Spread the toast on a large platter and moisten each slice with 2 tablespoons of the asparagus water. Lift the drained asparagus onto the toast, and cut and remove the string. The asparagus should cover the toast. Add salt and pepper to the butter, melt it, and pour it over the asparagus so that the toast will get some of it. Use more butter if you like. The toast can be as good (almost) as the asparagus, but the bread must be of the very best. Serves 6.

VARIATIONS. Asparagus may be dressed with *Mornay Sauce, Hollandaise Sauce,* crushed garlic in olive oil and Parmesan cheese (Italian style), buttered crumbs and cheese, etc. The Dutch serve a pat of butter, quartered hard-boiled eggs, and nutmeg, which you mix and eat with the vegetable.

ASPARAGUS FRENCH STYLE

3 pounds asparagus
Sauce:
   ⅔ cup heavy cream, whipped
   Salt and pepper
   ¼ teaspoon nutmeg

3 tablespoons melted butter
⅓ cup mixed Parmesan and
   Romano cheese

Trim the asparagus, cut it into 5-inch lengths, and tie it in 4 bundles. Put it tips up in the bottom of a double boiler, with water halfway up the stalks, and the top inverted over it. Boil 18 minutes. Drain the bundles well, put them on a 11- or 12-inch chop plate, and snip the strings. Fan the stalks out so the points are at the edge of the plate and pile the sauce in the center. Have the sauce ingredients at room temperature and mix the sauce the last thing. Whip the cream and add the rest of the ingredients. Serves 6 or 8.

GREEN BEANS WITH CHEESE

1 to 1½ pounds green string
   beans
2 tablespoons butter
⅓ cup water
   Salt and pepper

1 tablespoon cornstarch
½ cup light cream
1 tablespoon tomato paste
⅓ cup shredded Cheddar cheese

Wash the beans in salt water, drain them, and cut them in half, removing the tips. Melt the butter in the cooker, add the beans, the water, and some salt and pepper. Cover tightly and cook slowly until tender, about 15 minutes or so. A pressure cooker takes 3 minutes. Empty the beans into a hot serving dish but reserve the bean water. Before the beans are done, blend the cornstarch with the cream and tomato paste, heat, and add to the bean water, then put in the cheese. Cook until the sauce thickens and the cheese melts, then pour over the beans. One pound of beans serves 4 or 5.

GREEN BEANS, OR YELLOW WAX BEANS

1½ pounds beans
⅓ cup water
3 tablespoons butter
   Salt and pepper

1 tablespoon lemon juice
1 teaspoon cornstarch
   Chopped parsley or fresh dill

Wash the beans and trim both ends. Put them in a heavy pot with the water, butter, salt, and pepper. Cover tightly and simmer 12 minutes or until tender. This takes 2½ minutes in the pressure cooker. Mix the lemon juice and cornstarch in a saucepan and drain the bean liquor into it. Put the beans in a hot serving dish, boil up the sauce, and pour it over the beans. Sprinkle the top with chopped parsley or dill. Serves 6.

VARIATION. Chopped onion may be cooked with the beans. One-fourth cup of heavy cream may be used for the sauce instead of lemon juice.

BIG-PARTY BEANS

1 quart can chick peas
1 quart can baked beans
1 quart can kidney beans
2 cups chopped onions
2 cups cubed ham
Salt and pepper
1 tablespoon chili powder

1 tablespoon curry powder
1 tablespoon mustard
3 tablespoons molasses or brown sugar
1 cup canned tomatoes
4 strips salt pork

Mix together all the ingredients except the pork and empty into a large casserole. Lay the salt pork over the top. Cover and cook slowly at 300° for 3 hours. If the beans become at all dry, baste with a little juice drained from the tomatoes or with V8 juice, heating the juice first. This is an easy dish and will serve 10 or 16; it is great for a picnic because it is good hot or cold. Instead of the ham, browned pork sausages may be mixed in. Brown the sausages first and drain off the grease.

CASSEROLE OF LIMA BEANS, PEAS, AND ONIONS

⅓ cup finely diced onions
¼ cup butter
2 pounds lima beans
Salt and pepper
2 pounds fresh peas

1 teaspoon basil
12 small white onions
1¼ cups light cream
2 tablespoons cornstarch
⅓ cup grated cheese

This casserole for a dinner for 8 may be made ahead of time; it is much better if the vegetables are cooked separately. Put the diced onions and butter in a pot and cook a minute. Add the lima beans, salt, pepper, and ¼ cup of water. Cover tightly and cook slowly until tender, about 10 minutes. Cook the peas in a tightly covered pot in ¼ cup water with salt, pepper, and basil until tender, 5 to 8 minutes. If these vegetables are cooked in the pressure cooker the beans take 1 minute and the peas 30 seconds. Cook the white onions in as little water as possible about 15 minutes, or until tender. Drain the vegetables and put them in a casserole. Add the vegetable liquids to the cream. There should be about 2 cups of liquid. Blend in the cornstarch and cook until it thickens. Add salt and pepper and pour over the vegetables. Cover with the cheese. When ready to serve put in a hot oven for 10 or 12 minutes until the cheese browns.

LIMA BEANS

2 pounds fresh lima beans
3 tablespoons butter
¼ cup minced green onions or
    white onions
¼ teaspoon nutmeg

Salt and pepper
¼ cup water
Chopped parsley
¼ cup heavy cream (optional)
Parmesan cheese (optional)

Lima beans, one of our best vegetables, are fine buttered or dressed with cream. Shell the beans. Melt the butter in a heavy pot and sauté the onions a minute, then add the beans, seasonings, and water. Cover tightly and simmer until tender, about 10 minutes. In the pressure cooker they take 1 minute. Do not drain. Sprinkle with parsley. If the cream is added, sprinkle with parsley or Parmesan cheese. Serves 4 (or 5, if the pods are full).

BAKED BEANS

2½ cups dried beans: northern,
    navy, red, or kidney
3 tablespoons currants
3 tablespoons raisins
2 tablespoons minced sweet
    pickle
3 cloves garlic, crushed
½ cup red wine
4 strips bacon

2 ½-inch thick slices salt pork
1 cup sliced onions
¼ cup honey
1 teaspoon curry powder
1 teaspoon mustard
1 teaspoon chili powder
1½ teaspoons salt
Chicken broth
2 or 3 tablespoons dark rum

Wash the beans and soak them overnight in water 2 inches above the beans. Soak the currants, raisins, pickle, and garlic in the wine overnight in a covered glass jar. In the morning, add just enough water to cover the beans and simmer them slowly for 45 minutes. Fry the bacon until crisp, then remove it, crumble it, and reserve. Fry the salt pork in the bacon fat a light brown on both sides; remove and reserve it. Fry the onions until tender in the pork and bacon fat. Mix the crumbled bacon with the beans. Add the wine marinade and all the other ingredients and seasonings except the pork, broth, and rum. Mix well and put them in a bean pot. Put the slices of pork on top. If necessary add chicken broth. The beans must be kept moistened while baking. Cover and bake at 300° 6 hours at least, the longer the better. Uncover and add a little hot broth when necessary. When the beans are done pour the rum over them. If you wish, the beans may be baked the day before serving. The more they are warmed up the better they are; a little more rum may be added. Serves 10 or 12.

BAKED KIDNEY BEANS WITH BURGUNDY

1 pound kidney beans	1 tablespoon tarragon
4 cups water	2 tablespoons honey or brown sugar
2 cups diced onions	Salt and pepper
3 tablespoons ham fat or bacon fat	1 cup Burgundy wine
1 green pepper, sliced thin	4 strips bacon
1 clove garlic, crushed	8 or 10 small pork sausages

Wash the beans and soak them in 4 cups of water 6 hours or overnight.
Cook the beans for 1 hour in the water they soaked in, adding more water
if necessary. Sauté the onions in the ham fat or bacon fat until tender.
Sauté the green pepper in a little fat for 5 minutes. Put the beans in a
casserole and add the onions, pepper, garlic, and seasonings. Pour the wine
over the beans and lay the bacon on top. Bake at 325° 3 hours. An hour
before the beans are done, sauté the sausages and bury them in the beans.
The beans must be kept moist, so add a little boiling water when needed.
Sour cream may be passed with these. Serves 10.

BEETS WITH ORANGE SAUCE

2 bunches new beets	¼ teaspoon nutmeg
1¼ cups water	½ cup beet water
1 teaspoon vinegar	Salt and pepper
1 tablespoon grated orange rind	1 teaspoon brown sugar
Juice ½ lime or lemon	(if needed)
½ cup orange juice	Garnish: Chopped parsley or
1½ tablespoons cornstarch	chives

Scrub the beets well because some of the beet water is used in the sauce.
Cut the stems within 1 inch of the beets. Cook the beets in the water and
vinegar until tender—about 25 minutes. Skin them. Mix the orange rind,
lime or lemon juice, and orange juice and blend in the cornstarch. Add the
nutmeg and beet water and simmer until the sauce thickens. Season and
add 1 teaspoon of brown sugar if it is needed. Large beets are sliced; small
beets are left whole. Pour the sauce over the beets, warm them a moment
over the fire, and serve. Serves 4 to 6. There are about 5 beets in a bunch.

BEETS AND SOUR CREAM

Boiled new beets are good dressed with sour cream and chopped green
onions. A fine cold beet dish in summer is julienne sticks of beets dressed
with sour cream mixed with onion juice and lemon juice. Season with salt,
pepper, and a dash of brown sugar. Chopped green onions may be added.

MASHED BEETS

8 new beets
Juice of ½ lime
¼ teaspoon clove
Salt and pepper

⅓ cup red wine
Butter
Chopped parsley

Boil the beets and skin them while they are hot. Mash them through a sieve with the seasonings and wine. Add a little butter. Put them in a baking dish. They can be reheated for serving. Sprinkle the top with chopped parsley. Serves 6. If the mixture seems thin add a tablespoon of cornstarch and it will thicken when reheated.

BEET SOUFFLÉ

8 cooked beets (scant 3 cups, diced)
⅓ cup fruit juice: orange, grape, or grapefruit
Juice of 1 lemon
2 tablespoons grated onion
Salt and pepper
½ teaspoon powdered clove
4 egg yolks, beaten

¼ cup cornstarch
5 egg whites, beaten
Sauce:
  1 cup beet water or juice
  Juice of 1 lime
  Salt and pepper
  ⅛ teaspoon clove
  1 tablespoon honey
  1 tablespoon cornstarch

Put the beets through a sieve with all the seasonings, or puree in a blender. Beat the egg yolks with the cornstarch and blend with the beet purée. Beat the egg whites until stiff and stir one-fourth of them into the purée, then lightly fold in the rest. Bake in a greased 8-inch soufflé dish 30 minutes at 350°. The soufflé must be moist inside. For the sauce, blend all the ingredients with the cornstarch and cook until it thickens. Serve in a small tureen. This is a very handsome dish for luncheon or to accompany beef or pork at dinner. Serves 6.

STEAMED BROCCOLI

1 bunch of broccoli
1 cup boiling water
Salt and pepper
1 tablespoon cornstarch

1 teaspoon powdered chicken concentrate
2 tablespoons lemon juice
3 tablespoons butter
Parmesan cheese (optional)

The little French steamers called Cuiseur à la Vapeur are sold everywhere and are very convenient, as they fit into pots of varying sizes. Wash the broccoli well and if necessary cut off the outside of the larger stalks. Cut the stalks in 1-inch lengths and put them in the bottom of the steamer, then add the uncut flower tops. Pour the boiling water over the vegetable and sprinkle salt and pepper on top. Cover tightly and steam for 15 minutes, or until tender. Empty into a hot serving dish. Meanwhile, blend the chicken concentrate, lemon juice, cornstarch, and butter together. Add this to the broccoli water in the kettle. When the sauce is thick pour it over the broccoli and if desired sprinkle the top with cheese. Serve immediately. If the sauce is too thick it may be thinned with a little cream. I like to steam some vegetables, cauliflower for example, this way, because all the vegetable water is used and the dressing is very good. Serves 4 to 6. Broccoli may also be served with *Mornay Sauce* or *Hollandaise Sauce*.

BROCCOLI ITALIAN STYLE

1 bunch broccoli, steamed
2 cloves garlic, crushed
¼ cup olive oil

⅓ cup ground ham
⅓ cup Parmesan cheese

Steam the broccoli as in *Steamed Broccoli*. Cook the garlic in the olive oil a few seconds until it is pale yellow, then mix with the ham and a little broccoli water. Mix with the drained broccoli, empty into a serving dish, and sprinkle with the cheese. Serves 4 to 6.

BRUSSELS SPROUTS, MARIE

1 quart Brussels sprouts
    Salt and pepper
Sauce:
    ⅔ cup heavy cream
    3 or 4 egg yolks, beaten
    Salt and pepper

½ teaspoon turmeric
2 tablespoons lemon juice
¼ cup sweet butter, softened

Trim and wash the Brussels sprouts and put them in a steamer over a cup or so of water. Add a little salt and pepper, cover tightly, and steam until the sprouts are tender but firm—about 10 minutes. Heat the cream in the top of the double boiler and when hot let it come to a boil over the flame, then pour it over the egg yolks (use 4 if the eggs are small). Put over simmering water and stir until the cream thickens. Add salt, pepper, and turmeric. This may be begun ahead of time. When ready to serve reheat the sauce and add the lemon juice and the softened butter. (This is really an easy and very good variation of Hollandaise.) Put the sprouts in a hot serving dish and pour the sauce over them.

Brussels sprouts are very good just served with butter and sprinkled with a little chopped parsley or chives.

BRUSSELS SPROUTS WITH CHESTNUTS

1½ quarts Brussels sprouts	1 cup heavy cream
2 tablespoons butter	2 tablespoons cornstarch
⅓ cup chopped onions	¼ teaspoon nutmeg
1 cup chicken broth	2 or 3 tablespoons sherry
12 or 15 chestnuts, cooked and skinned	Salt and pepper

Wash and trim the sprouts. Put the butter and onions in a heavy pot and cook until the onions are almost tender. Add the sprouts and broth, cover, and cook slowly until the sprouts are tender but still firm. Drain, and add the liquid to the cream. Put the chestnuts and sprouts in a baking dish. Blend the cream mixture with the cornstarch, add the nutmeg, and cook until it thickens. If it is too thick add a little broth. Add salt and pepper and the sherry. Pour over the sprouts and put in the oven a moment to heat. Serves 6 or 8.

BUTTERED CABBAGE

1 new cabbage	Salt and pepper
3 tablespoons butter	1 teaspoon mixed herbs

Soak the cabbage in cold water 15 minutes. The outer leaves may be removed if they are disfigured. Cut a large cabbage in eighths, a small one in quarters. Drain. Put it in a heavy pot with no water added, cover tightly, and cook over low heat until it is tender, 10 minutes or more (3 minutes in a pressure cooker). Add the butter and seasonings and empty into a serving dish. A medium-sized cabbage will serve 4.

CREAMED CABBAGE

Buttered Cabbage	Cornstarch
½ cup light or heavy cream	3 tablespoons grated cheese
Cabbage liquid	

Pour off the liquid from the cabbage after it is tender and add it to the cream. Add 1½ teaspoons of cornstarch for each cup of liquid (there should be only 1 cup with the cream), cook until thickened, and add the cheese. Pour the sauce over the cabbage.

SAUERKRAUT WITH SEEDLESS GRAPES

1½ pounds sauerkraut
⅓ cup diced onions
2 tablespoons butter

½ cup dry vermouth or white wine
1½ cups seedless grapes

Wash the sauerkraut with hot water and drain well. Sauté the onions in the butter until they soften, then mix with the sauerkraut and wine. Cover and simmer 12 minutes. Add the grapes and cook 1 minute more. The grapes must not be allowed to become limp. Empty into a hot serving dish. This is good with game, goose, or pork.

SAUERKRAUT WITH KNACKWURST. Cook the sauerkraut, omitting the grapes. Boil 2 fat knackwurst 10 minutes. Drain and skin them. Cut them in ½-inch slices and toss them with the sauerkraut. Serve with mustard.

RED CABBAGE WITH RED WINE AND APPLES

1 medium-sized red cabbage, thinly sliced
3 tablespoons butter or good fat
⅔ cup finely chopped onions
½ cup red wine
1½ teaspoons anise powder
1½ tablespoons honey or brown sugar

Salt and pepper
4 tart apples
3 tablespoons butter
2 tablespoons lemon juice (if needed)
1 tablespoon cinnamon
Cornstarch

Trim the cabbage of any bruised leaves, slice it thin, and soak it in cold water a few minutes, then drain well. Sauté the onions in the butter or fat until almost tender, then put the cabbage on the onions. Mix the wine with the anise, honey or sugar, salt and pepper. Pour it over the cabbage. Cover tightly and cook slowly until the cabbage is tender, from 30 to 45 minutes, depending on the age of the cabbage. New young cabbage takes 15 to 20 minutes, but it is not always available. I don't go along with the European way of cooking cabbage for hours, to a sodden mass. Meanwhile, peel and slice the apples and sauté them in the butter, adding the lemon juice if they aren't very tart (a little won't hurt), and the cinnamon. Cook until they are tender. When the cabbage is done, pour off the liquid and thicken it with cornstarch, 1 teaspoonful to ½ cup of liquid. When it is thick, pour it over the cabbage, add the apples, and lightly mix together. This is a fragrant dish and delicious with goose, game, or pork. A medium-sized red cabbage serves 5 or 6; a large one will serve 8.

BUTTERED NEW CARROTS

1 or 2 bunches carrots
2 or 3 tablespoons water or
    orange juice
2 or 3 tablespoons butter

Salt and pepper
Choice of fresh herbs: mint, tarragon, parsley, chives, green onions,
basil, or chervil

Trim the carrots and scrub them with a vegetable brush; they do not need scraping. Cut them in sticks, rather than circles; they seem to taste better. Put them in a heavy pot with the water or orange juice, butter, salt, and pepper. Cover tightly and cook slowly until they are tender. Sprinkle with herbs. Chopped fresh herbs give a great lift to this bland vegetable.

CARROTS WITH ORANGE OR LEMON SAUCE

Cook the carrots in ⅓ to ½ cup of orange juice and 2 or 3 tablespoons butter. Add a little chopped parsley while cooking. When they are done thicken the sauce with ½ to 1 teaspoon cornstarch. For lemon sauce, add 2 tablespoons lemon juice to the sauce.

CARROTS CURAÇAO

2 bunches new carrots
    Grated rind 1 orange
½ cup orange juice
¼ cup light corn syrup

3 or 4 tablespoons butter
    Salt and pepper
1 teaspoon cornstarch
1 jigger Curaçao or Cointreau

Shred the carrots on a disk grater and mix with the orange rind and juice and the syrup. Melt 3 tablespoons butter in a heavy pot. Add salt and pepper to the carrot mixture and put it into the butter. Cover tightly and cook slowly until tender. Drain out the carrots. Thicken the sauce with the cornstarch and add a little more butter. Cook until it thickens, add the liqueur, and pour it over the carrots. Serves 6 or 8.

CARROT-ORANGE SOUFFLÉ

2 cups mashed carrots (7 new
    carrots)
2 tablespoons honey
¼ teaspoon mace or nutmeg
    Salt and pepper
1 tablespoon grated orange rind
4 tablespoons finely minced green
    or white onion

½ cup orange juice
4 tablespoons cornstarch
⅓ cup orange juice
    Juice of ½ lemon
4 egg yolks, beaten
4 egg whites, beaten

Trim and scrub the carrots, cut them up fine, and put them in a heavy pot with the honey, spice, salt, pepper, orange rind, onion, and ½ cup orange juice. Cover tightly and cook slowly until they are done. Mash them fine through a sieve or purée in a blender. Blend the cornstarch with ⅓ cup of orange juice and the lemon juice. Cook until it thickens, adding some of the carrot mixture so it won't get too thick. Blend the rest of the carrots with the cornstarch mixture and add the beaten egg yolks. Stir in one-fourth of the stiffly beaten whites, then lightly fold in the rest. Bake in an 8-inch soufflé dish 25 minutes at 350°. Serves 6.

MASHED CARROTS

2 bunches new carrots
⅓ cup orange juice
1 tablespoon lemon juice
2 tablespoons grated onion
Salt and pepper

1 tablespoon grated orange rind
¼ cup butter
½ cup heavy cream
¼ teaspoon mace or nutmeg

Trim and scrub the carrots and cut them up fine. Put them in a heavy pot with the juices, onion, salt, pepper, orange rind, and 1 tablespoon of the butter. Cover tightly and cook until the carrots are tender. Heat the cream. Mash the carrots and add the rest of the butter, the hot cream, and the spice. Serve immediately. Serves 6.

CARROT RING

2½ cups mashed carrots (8 new carrots)
⅓ cup orange juice
1 tablespoon lemon juice
2 tablespoons grated onion
Salt and pepper
1 tablespoon butter
1 tablespoon grated orange rind

1 teaspoon mustard
2 tablespoons chopped parsley
2 tablespoons flour
2 tablespoons melted butter
1 cup soft fresh breadcrumbs
1 cup light cream, scalded
4 egg yolks, beaten
4 egg whites, beaten

Trim and scrub the carrots, and cut them fine. Cook them with the juices, onion, salt, pepper, butter, and orange rind in a heavy covered pot until tender. Mash them and add the other ingredients. Last, stir in one-fourth of the stiffly beaten egg whites and then lightly mix in the rest. Empty the mixture into a well-greased, floured ring mold, set it in a pan of hot water, and bake at 350° 30 to 35 minutes or until the ring is set. Remove from the oven and let it stand 3 minutes, then reverse a round serving plate over the mold and quickly turn it upside down. If any of the contents sticks to the mold, it may be used to build up the ring. Fill with creamed mushrooms, creamed seafood or ham or chicken, or with another creamed vegetable: potatoes, peas, or sprouts. Serves 8 or 10.

SHREDDED CARROTS WITH PEAS

¼ cup butter
¼ cup shredded onion
1½ cups shredded young carrots
2 pounds fresh peas, shelled

4 tablespoons water
Salt and pepper
⅓ cup heavy cream

Shred the onion and carrots on a fine disk grater. Melt the butter in the bottom of a heavy pot, add the onion, and sauté it over a low flame for a minute or two. Make a bed of the carrots on top of the onion and add the shelled peas, the water, salt, and pepper. Cover tightly and cook slowly until the peas are tender. Heat the cream, mix lightly with the vegetables, and serve. Serves 6 or 8.

CAULIFLOWER WITH CURRY SAUCE

1 whole cauliflower
⅔ cup water
¼ cup heavy cream
Salt and pepper
1 teaspoon cornstarch

1 teaspoon powdered chicken
    concentrate
1 teaspoon curry powder
½ teaspoon cumin powder

Cauliflower is so easy to cook whole, and that is the most attractive way to serve it. Trim off all the leaves. Put the cauliflower in a heavy pot, salt the top and pour ⅔ cup of water over it. Cover tightly and cook at high heat until the water boils, then turn down to medium heat and continue cooking until it is just tender. A small to medium cauliflower takes 20 minutes and a large one 30 to 35 minutes. It should be firm and tender and not even on the verge of mushiness. Lift it onto a round shallow dish. Mix the cream with a little salt and pepper, the cornstarch, chicken concentrate, curry, and cumin. Pour the cauliflower water into the cream mixture, little by little, and cook until it thickens. Use all the cauliflower water the sauce will take. Pour the sauce over the cauliflower and you will have a beautiful and delicious dish.

CAULIFLOWER PARMESAN

1 fine large cauliflower
3 cloves garlic
¼ cup olive oil

2 tablespoons butter
⅓ cup Parmesan cheese
Salt and pepper

Steam the cauliflower, either cut into flowerets or whole. While it is cooking add salt and pepper. Slice the garlic cloves very thin and cook them in the olive oil and butter until they color a little. Put the hot cauliflower in a serving dish, pour the sauce over it, and cover with the Parmesan cheese.

VARIATIONS. Steamed cauliflower may be dressed with *Mornay Sauce* or *Hollandaise Sauce* or plenty of buttered crumbs. A whole cauliflower, boiled and chilled and served with *Aioli Sauce,* is a fine summer dish. This may accompany a cold fish dish.

BRAISED CELERY

6 cups celery, cut in 1½-inch
    lengths
¼ cup butter
⅓ cup chopped onion
    Salt and pepper

1 cup vegetable juice
1 tablespoon cornstarch
1 tablespoon prepared mustard
⅓ cup heavy cream
    Chopped parsley

Choose fine crisp pascal celery. Put the butter in a heavy pot, add the onion and cook a few seconds, then stir in the celery and mix it well with the onion. Add salt and pepper and the vegetable juice (V8 is excellent for this). Cover tightly and simmer gently for 1 hour. Mix the cornstarch and mustard (Bahamian mustard is recommended) with the heavy cream, drain off all the liquid from the celery into the cream, and cook until it thickens, then pour it over the celery. Heat a minute, pour into a hot serving dish and add chopped parsley to the top. This is excellent to accompany any meat or poultry. Serves 4 to 6.

BRAISED CELERY IN BROTH. Proceed as in *Braised Celery* but use 1¼ cups of rich chicken or beef broth instead of the vegetable juice, omit the cream and reduce the cornstarch by ½ teaspoon. A tablespoon of Madeira or sherry or 1 tablespoon of tomato paste may be added to the thickened sauce. Add a sprinkle of Parmesan cheese or chopped parsley to the top. This is fine to accompany grilled meats.

CREAMED CELERIAC

2 pounds celeriac (celery root)
¼ cup diced onion
4 tablespoons butter
4 tablespoons chicken broth

Salt and pepper
¾ cup light cream
1 tablespoon cornstarch
¼ cup Parmesan cheese

Peel the celeriac and cut it in ½-inch-thick slices; if desired cut it in sticks. Sauté the onion in the butter in a heavy pot for a minute, then add the celeriac and the broth and some salt and pepper. Cover tightly and cook slowly until it is tender. Blend the cornstarch and cream and cook until it thickens, then add to the celeriac and pot juices. Empty into a hot serving dish and sprinkle with the cheese. A dash of curry powder may be added to the sauce if desired. Serves 4 to 6.

VARIATION. Celeriac is very good mashed with potatoes. Use 1 pound of cooked celeriac to add to 4 medium-sized potatoes. It gives a good flavor.

CORN ON THE COB: THREE WAYS

If corn can't be cooked right after it is picked, keep it unhusked in the refrigerator, as warm temperatures begin immediately to turn the sugar to starch. Husk it just before cooking.

No. 1. Put the husked corn in a large kettle and cover with warm water. Add 1 tablespoon of sugar. When the water boils, wait 30 seconds, then turn off the heat and let the corn cook no more than 2 minutes. Remove and serve with salt and melted butter.

No. 2. Put the husked corn in a big steamer and steam over boiling water for 15 minutes.

No. 3. To roast unhusked corn, turn back the husks, remove the silk, butter the corn, then close the husks and tie the ends with string. Put the ears in the oven ½-inch apart and roast 30 minutes at 350°. Never salt corn before it is cooked.
Three 8-inch closely packed ears yield 2 cups of cut corn.

EARLY DAYS CORNCAKES

6 large ears fresh sweet corn	Salt
3 eggs, beaten	Crisco for frying
1 *teaspoon* flour	

Mr. K. T. Keller of Detroit has been eating these cakes since the 1880s at his grandmother's and his great-grandmother's whose name was Bennett and who lived in Columbia, Pennsylvania. He has every right to insist that these corncakes be made exactly as he directs. "The real corn base comes from the milk and heart of the corn kernel which is extracted by slitting the kernel and scraping out the milk and heart, leaving the skin on the cob." I wish I could find a board equipped with a row of knives and scraper like the one he describes. However, we should take the pains to extract the milk and heart of the kernels as best we can. *Do not use any more flour.* Mix the corn with the beaten eggs, flour, and a teaspoon or so of salt to taste. Drop by tablespoons on a hot griddle greased with a tablespoon of Crisco or any good bland fat. Serves 6.

CORNCAKES NO. 1

1 cup corn
½ cup milk
3 tablespoons fine cornmeal
½ teaspoon salt
½ teaspoon baking powder

1 teaspoon maple syrup or honey
2 egg yolks
2 egg whites, beaten
Butter

Reserve 2 tablespoons of the corn. Grind the rest or put it in an electric blender with the milk. Return the 2 tablespoons of corn to the ground corn and milk. Mix the cornmeal with the salt and baking powder and add. Beat in the syrup or honey and the egg yolks. Fold in the stiffly beaten whites last. Fry on a griddle with plenty of butter. These are light; they may be served with syrup, or plain to accompany chicken. If fresh corn from the cob is not available, use a 7-ounce can of fine white corn—Le Sueur Brand (the dry). This makes 18 rather small cakes or 12 of medium size.

CORNCAKES NO. 2

2 cups raw corn, scored and cut
   from ears
1 tablespoon fresh onion juice
1 tablespoon melted butter
⅓ cup heavy cream

Salt and pepper
3 egg yolks
3 egg whites, beaten
Butter for frying

Score the corn kernels with a sharp pointed knife, then cut them from the ears. Mix all the ingredients, folding in the stiffly beaten egg whites last. Drop the batter from a spoon onto a well-buttered griddle and brown delicately on both sides. These are delicious with meat or poultry or for a lunch dish. Makes 6 or 8 cakes.

CORN PUDDING

1 green pepper, diced
½ cup finely diced onion
4 tablespoons butter
4 cups raw corn, scored and cut
   from ears
1 teaspoon salt
   Freshly ground pepper

¼ teaspoon nutmeg
½ teaspoon turmeric
2 tablespoons light brown sugar
1 cup light cream
½ cup milk
3 eggs, beaten

Sauté the pepper and onion in the butter until tender. Score the kernels and cut the corn from the ears. This will take about 6 ears. Mix all the ingredients together. The eggs should be well beaten; they may be beaten separately if you like. Bake in a casserole at 350° about 25 minutes, until set but moist inside. Serves 6 or 8.

MEXICAN CORN

1 Bermuda onion
1 green pepper
4 tablespoons olive oil
2 tablespoons butter
½ pound fresh okra
2 small zucchini

Salt and pepper
1 clove garlic, crushed
2 cups raw corn
1 cup tomato sauce, or 1 large
tomato skinned and chopped
1 teaspoon chili powder

Slice the onion and green pepper very thin and sauté until half tender in 2 tablespoons of olive oil and 2 of butter. Remove the ends of the okra, boil it up with salt water, and drain. Remove the ends of the zucchini; do not peel it. Cut it in ¾-inch slices. Combine the vegetables and add salt and pepper. Cook the garlic a few seconds in the 2 tablespoons of unused olive oil and mix with the vegetables. Stir in the corn, the tomato or tomato sauce, and the chili powder. Empty into a baking dish and bake at 350° 20 to 25 minutes. Serves 6 or 8.

SAUTÉED CORN WITH ONIONS AND PEPPERS

2 cups raw corn (3 8-inch ears)
1 Bermuda onion, sliced
1 large green pepper, sliced

¼ cup butter
Salt, pepper, paprika

Score the rows of kernels to release the milk and make the corn more tender, then cut the corn from the ears. Slice a good-sized onion very thin. Slice the pepper in thin strips. Sauté them together in the butter until half tender, then add the corn. Add a little salt, pepper, and paprika. Cover tightly and simmer 10 minutes.

BRAISED CUCUMBERS WITH DILL

2 unpeeled cucumbers
2 slices hickory-smoked bacon
Salt and pepper
½ teaspoon cumin or turmeric
2 tablespoons water

1½ teaspoons cornstarch
½ cup light cream
Handful fresh dill, stemmed,
squeezed, and chopped fine

Slice the cucumbers a scant ½-inch thick. Cut the bacon in 1-inch lengths and fry it in a big pan until it begins to brown, add the cucumbers and fry with the bacon until the slices are a delicate brown on both sides. Sprinkle with salt, pepper, and the cumin or turmeric. Add the water, cover, and cook about 2 minutes or until tender. Blend the cornstarch with the cream and add the dill. Pour this over the cucumbers and cook until it thickens. This is very good and it is worth the effort of getting good bacon. Serves 4 or 5.

BAKED WHOLE EGGPLANT WITH BACON AND CHEESE

2 medium-size eggplants or small
    individual eggplants
8 slices hickory-smoked bacon
    Orégano

8 slices Cheddar cheese
Salt and pepper
Olive oil

Remove a thin slice from the ends of the eggplants. Make 4 deep length-wise slits in each, ¾ inch from the ends. Put a strip of bacon in each slit and sprinkle in a little orégano. Fill each slit with a slice of cheese and a very little salt and pepper. Put them in a baking dish and pour some olive oil in the slits. Cover tightly and bake 35 to 45 minutes at 375°. Halfway through the baking, pour more olive oil in. If they are baking too fast, turn down the heat to 325°. They are cut apart at the table. If the eggplants are small, serve 1 to each person. They are delicious cooked this way. Crushed garlic may also be put into the slits, and other cheese, such as Mozzarella.

BAKED FRIED EGGPLANT WITH HERBS

1 eggplant
2 tablespoons olive oil
2 tablespoons butter
    Salt and pepper

2 cloves garlic, crushed
    Choice of herbs: fresh or dried
    basil, chervil, thyme, or parsley,
    minced

Peel the eggplant and remove a slice from each end. Slice it in ½- to ¾-inch thick slices. Salt both sides of each slice and let the slices drain ½ hour, then wipe with paper towels. Put the oil and butter in a heavy pan with the garlic and fry the eggplant slices on both sides, removing them to a cookie sheet as they become lightly browned. Salt them a little and sprinkle with pepper and one of the minced herbs. Bake in a 375° oven about 12 or 15 minutes. Serves 4 to 6, depending on the size of eggplant.

EGGPLANT BAKED WITH CHEESE AND CREAM

1 large eggplant or 2 medium-
    sized ones
    Salt and pepper
1 to 1½ cups shredded cheese:
    Cheddar or Swiss

Fat
½ cup heavy cream
Cracker crumbs

Peel the eggplant and cut it in ½-inch slices. Salt both sides of each slice and let drain 30 minutes. Wipe off with a paper towel and sauté in a mixture of fat: bacon, oil, butter. When sautéing eggplant, each batch may be lightly browned then covered for a minute to soften. As they are done, lightly salt and pepper them and put them in a baking dish. Sprinkle cheese on each layer. Heat the cream and when all are ready pour it over them, cover with crumbs, and bake at 350° 20 minutes. Serves 6 or 8.

MOUSSAKA

4 or 5 small eggplants
   (7 inches long)
Oil

Stuffing:
2½ cups cooked ground lamb
Eggplant pulp
1 cup cooked patna rice
½ pound fresh sliced mushrooms
Salt and pepper
1 teaspoon orégano
2 cloves garlic, crushed
⅔ cup diced onions
2 eggs, beaten
½ cup light cream
⅓ cup grated cheese

Cut the eggplants in quarters. Put them cut side down in a long baking pan with ½ inch of water in the pan and bake them at 375° until they are tender, 25 to 35 minutes. Carefully remove the pulp with a spoon without cutting or tearing the skins. Grease a charlotte mold 7 inches in diameter and 4 inches deep. Put the points of the skins in the center of the mold, lining it with the purple next to the mold, the skins hanging over the outside. Fry the pulp a little in very hot oil to reduce the water in it. Chop and mix it lightly with the lamb. Sauté the mushrooms and onions separately. Toss all the ingredients together. Add the beaten eggs. Heat the cream, mix with the cheese, and add to the stuffing. Carefully fill the mold without disarranging the skins. Bring the overhanging skins over the top. Put the mold in a pan of hot water and bake at 325° for 1 hour. Let stand 4 or 5 minutes before unmolding on a round chop plate. Serve with a light mushroom sauce or tomato sauce. Serves 8.

RATATOUILLE

1 medium-sized eggplant
Olive oil
2 teaspoons basil
2 cups diced onions
2 green peppers, sliced
Salt and pepper

2 cloves garlic, crushed
3 large tomatoes, skinned and
   chopped
2 tablespoons lime or lemon juice
3 canned red pimentos
Chopped parsley

As the vegetables are cooked separately, an easy way to cook the eggplant is to bake it. Peel the eggplant and cut it in slices and then in strips an inch wide. Dip the strips in olive oil and sprinkle with basil. Put them in a long pan and bake at 375° 15 minutes or until tender. Sprinkle with salt and pepper. Cut the green peppers in narrow strips and cook with the diced onion in olive oil until tender. Remove and season them. Put the garlic in the skillet with a tablespoon of oil and cook until it colors. Swish the tomatoes with the garlic and sprinkle with the lime or lemon juice. Cut the pimentos in strips and add to the tomatoes. Cook covered for 5 minutes. Season a little. Put half the tomato mixture in the bottom of a big casserole. Mix the eggplant lightly with the peppers and onions and spread on the tomato mixture, then cover with the rest of the tomato mixture. Cover and bake in a 350° oven for 15 minutes; uncover and bake another 15 minutes. If the mixture seems at all dry put 3 or 4 tablespoons of olive oil over the top. When done sprinkle with chopped parsley. Serve either hot or cold. Serves 8.

EGGPLANT BAKED WITH HAM AND TOMATO SAUCE

2 medium-sized eggplants	3 cloves garlic, crushed
Olive oil	2 cups ground ham
2½ to 3 cups tomato sauce	2 small Mozzarella cheeses
2 teaspoons fennel powder	1 cup Parmesan cheese

Peel the eggplants and cut them in ⅓-inch thick slices. Salt both sides of each slice and let them drain, or soak them in salted water ½ hour. Wipe them dry with paper towels. Sauté the eggplant in olive oil until tender. Mix the tomato sauce with the fennel powder and crushed garlic. As the eggplant is done, put layers of it in a baking dish, covering each layer with tomato sauce, ground ham, thin slices of Mozzarella cheese, and a sprinkle of Parmesan cheese. Cover the top with Parmesan cheese. Bake 20 minutes at 350°. Serves 8 or 10.

CHINESE EGGPLANT

1 large eggplant	Sauce:
¼ cup sesame oil or corn oil	1 teaspoon cornstarch
Salt and pepper	½ cup water
	1 tablespoon light brown sugar
	1 tablespoon soy sauce
	1½ tablespoons minced preserved ginger
	1 tablespoon ginger syrup
	⅓ cup chopped green onions

Cut a thin slice from each end of the egplant, peel it and cut in ¾-inch-thick slices. Lightly brown them in the oil on both sides over a hot flame, lay the slices on an oiled baking sheet, and bake in a 375° oven about 15 minutes or until just tender. Sprinkle with salt and pepper. Put on a hot platter, overlapping the slices a little. Blend the cornstarch with the water, add the sugar and soy sauce, and cook until thickened, then add the rest of the ingredients. Spoon the hot sauce over the eggplant. Serves 6.

EGGPLANT BAKED IN TOMATO SAUCE AND CREAM

1 medium-sized eggplant	1 small can tomato sauce
Olive oil and butter	1 tablespoon cornstarch
Salt and pepper	⅔ cup heavy cream
⅓ cup chopped onions	⅓ cup grated cheese

Peel and cut the eggplant in ⅓-inch slices, soak them in salted water 30 minutes, and wipe dry. Sauté the onions in butter and mix with the tomato sauce. Sauté the eggplant until tender in a mixture of olive oil and butter. Put layers of eggplant in a baking dish covering each layer with tomato sauce and onions. Blend the cornstarch with the cream, pour it over the eggplant, and cover with the cheese. Bake 10 minutes at 375°. Serves 4.

BRAISED ENDIVE

12 medium-sized endives (for 6)	½ cup softened butter
3 tablespoons lemon juice	Salt and pepper
1 teaspoon sugar	Chopped parsley or chives

Get firm, perfect endive, wash and trim it, and dry it. Put it in a steamer and cook it 10 minutes over boiling water. Remove it to a shallow baking dish. Mix the lemon juice, sugar, softened butter, salt, and pepper. Smear it over the endive. Cover the dish with a tight lid or fasten foil over it and bake it for 35 minutes at 300°. Uncover the last 15 minutes. Sprinkle with parsley or chives.

VARIATION. When the endive is braised, cover it with 1½ cups heavy cream thickened with 1 tablespoon of cornstarch and 6 tablespoons of grated cheese. Pour the sauce over the endive and run the dish under the flame until the sauce bubbles and browns. This is a delicious party dish.

BRAISED ENDIVE WITH PROSCIUTTO

12 medium-sized endives	½ cup butter
Salt and pepper	12 slices prosciutto

Prepare the endive as in *Braised Endive*. After it has steamed 10 minutes, add a very little salt and pepper and smear with butter. Wrap each endive in a thin slice of prosciutto and lay them in a shallow baking pan. Cover with a lid or foil and bake 25 minutes at 325°. Serves 6.

LEEKS BRAISED IN BROTH

1 or 2 bunches of fine leeks
2 to 4 tablespoons butter
Salt and pepper
½ to ⅔ cup chicken broth

2 teaspoons cornstarch
1 to 2 tablespoons lemon juice
Garnish: Chopped parsley

One good-sized bunch of leeks will serve 4. If the leeks are more than 1 inch in diameter at the white end, cut them in two. Leave as much of the green ends on the leeks as possible. Trim off all the coarse outer leaves, separating them so they may be washed free of grit. Melt the butter in a heavy pot, put in the leeks, and add a little salt and pepper and the broth. Cover tightly and simmer until tender, from 10 to 15 minutes. Blend the cornstarch with the lemon juice. Drain off the liquid from the leeks into the cornstarch and cook until it thickens. Put the leeks in a hot serving dish, pour the sauce over them, and sprinkle with parsley.

CREAMED LEEKS WITH CHEESE. Increase the cornstarch to 3 teaspoons and add ⅓ cup of heavy cream. Thicken the sauce as directed, pour it over the leeks, cover with ¼ cup of Parmesan cheese, and run under the flame until the cheese melts. Leeks are one of the favorite seasoning vegetables but they deserve to be served on their own.

CREAMED JERUSALEM ARTICHOKES

1½ pounds Jerusalem artichokes
Salted water
1 tablespoon cornstarch
¾ cup light cream
1 tablespoon butter

Salt and pepper
¼ teaspoon nutmeg
⅓ cup grated cheese or chopped parsley

Scrub the artichokes and remove any blemishes. This vegetable resembles the potato but is more moist and delicate. It may be cooked and dressed in ways potatoes are. Boil in ¾ cup of slightly salted water about 20 minutes or until tender. Reserve ⅓ cup of the vegetable water. Remove the skins while they are hot or the delicate flesh will come off with the skins. Blend the cornstarch with the cream, add the butter, salt, pepper, and nutmeg. Add the vegetable water and cook until it thickens. Put the artichokes in the sauce to reheat, empty into a serving dish, and sprinkle with either cheese or parsley. Serves 6.

SALSIFY (OYSTER PLANT) can be cooked the same way.

WILTED LETTUCE

Large bowl of salad greens,
coarsely shredded
3 strips hickory-smoked bacon
¾ cup finely sliced onions
2 tablespoons minced fresh herbs:
basil, tarragon, chives, parsley,
chervil

2 teaspoons light brown sugar
Salt and pepper
1 tablespoon lemon juice
1 tablespoon sweet vermouth
1 tablespoon vinegar
Garnish: 2 hard-boiled eggs, sieved

Mixed salad greens may be used if desired: Simpson lettuce, raw young
spinach leaves, romaine, or any crisp greens. Fry out the bacon until crisp,
remove, and crumble over the lettuce. Sauté the onions in the bacon fat
until tender, then add them to all the other ingredients, pour all over the
greens, and mix well. Sieve the eggs over the top and serve immediately.

LENTIL PURÉE

1½ cups lentils
2 cups water
Water or chicken broth
1 ham bone
1 carrot, shredded
1 onion, shredded
1 stalk celery, minced
1 teaspoon salt

Freshly ground pepper
1 teaspoon thyme
½ teaspoon rosemary
¼ cup heavy cream or ⅓ cup
tomato purée
2 tablespoons lemon juice
¼ cup Parmesan cheese
¼ cup fine crumbs

Wash the lentils and soak them in 2 cups of water 6 hours or overnight.
Drain them and measure the water. Add water or chicken broth to make 2½
cups. Put the lentils in a heavy pot with the liquid, ham bone, vegetables, salt,
pepper, and herbs. Cover and cook until the lentils are cooked to a mush.
Add a very little water or broth if they become dry before they are soft.
Discard the ham bone and mash the lentils through a sieve. Add the cream
or tomato purée and the lemon juice. Put the purée in a baking dish and
sprinkle the mixed cheese and crumbs over the top. Reheat a few minutes
in a hot oven. Serves 6 or 8. This is a fine dish to serve with lamb.

CURRIED LENTILS, INDIAN STYLE

1 cup lentils
2 cups water
1 medium-sized onion, chopped
2 cloves garlic, crushed
¼ cup oil or butter
1 tablespoon Bedekar's Mango
Pickle (see Pantry Shelf)

¼ teaspoon clove
1 teaspoon cumin
1 teaspoon cardamom
1 teaspoon coriander
2 tablespoons lime or lemon juice
Salt and pepper

Wash the lentils and soak them 1 hour, in 2 cups water, then drain. Add 2 more cups water and some salt, and boil them for 40 minutes or until they are tender. Put the onions and garlic in a saucepan with the oil or butter and cook until tender but not brown. Add the pickle. Make a paste of the spices and the lime or lemon juice. Add a little salt and pepper. Add the paste to the onion and garlic and cook 2 or 3 minutes. Add the lentils and their liquor and cook 8 or 10 minutes. Serve with curries or with lamb. Serves 6. For variation, add 2 or 3 tablespoons tomato sauce or 1 tablespoon tomato paste to the cooked lentils. Add a little olive oil. Cold, these are good served as an hors d'œuvre.

BAKED MELON AS A VEGETABLE

Cantaloupe or honeydew
Salt, pepper, nutmeg
Bits of butter

Lime or lemon juice
Dribble of honey or light corn
  syrup

This is a fine way to use a melon that is not good enough to serve raw. It makes a delicious accompaniment to game, curry, or pork. Cut the melon in half, seed it, peel and cut in 1½-inch cubes. Put it in a shallow baking dish, lightly add salt, pepper, nutmeg, bits of butter, and a sprinkle of lime or lemon juice. Dribble a little honey or corn syrup over the top. Bake, uncovered, 20 minutes at 350° and serve hot.

MUSHROOMS

The cultivated mushrooms in our country are delicate and should be cooked only a short time. They do not compare in flavor with the wild mushrooms of Europe. Tasting the porcini mushroom in Italy for the first time is an unbelievable taste experience.

Chinese dried mushrooms, obtainable in 4-ounce cellophane bags, give a fine flavor to meat dishes and pastas. They are washed a little in lukewarm water, then soaked in 1 cup of water for an hour. They may be cooked an hour in their soaking liquid with some chicken broth added and served as a vegetable. Two ounces may be soaked an hour and added to a stew or *Veal Marengo* an hour before it is done. The soaking liquid is strained through a fine sieve and added with the mushrooms. If the stem is hard, it is removed.

TRUFFLES
(Tuber Melanosporum)

Truffles are found in the ground in France, especially around Perigord, and in Italy in Piedmont. The French truffles are black; the Italian truffles mostly white or gray. Pigs have a sensitive nose for these flavoring agents and are used for digging them out of the ground. Truffles are brushed and sliced, and tucked under the skin of poultry, or used in omelettes, sauces, pâtés, foie gras, sweetbreads, kidneys, vegetables, and fish dishes. The fragrance of fresh truffles in cookery is quite fabulous. Fresh ones are flown to this country, canned truffles are also available. A good way to use canned truffles in a pâté is to slice them and soak them 1 hour in Madeira with the truffle juices. They may not be as good as the fresh but they do add a lovely taste to the foods they season.

GRILLED MUSHROOMS, ITALIAN STYLE

Fresh mushrooms
Crushed cloves of garlic
Salt and pepper

Olive oil
Chopped parsley
Lemon juice

In Italy large porcini mushrooms grow wild under the chestnut trees. Some measure 4 inches across so that 1 or 2 are sufficient for a serving. The stems are not served. Our mushrooms may be cooked the way the Italians cook these, but allow 1 pound to serve 4 persons. Crush 4 large cloves of garlic and season with salt, pepper, and ⅓ cup of olive oil. Choose perfect white mushrooms, brush them, and toss them well in the olive-oil mixture. Bake them in a 375° oven for 6 minutes, then put them under the flame for a few seconds. Remove the mushrooms from the pan, add the chopped parsley and 2 or 3 squeezes of lemon juice to the pan juices, and scrape over the mushrooms. This may be an accompaniment for a veal scaloppine or a steak

CREAMED MUSHROOMS FOR FILLING RINGS
(Spinach, Rice, or Noodle Rings)

1½ pounds fresh mushrooms
4 tablespoons butter
⅓ cup chopped green onions
1¼ cups chicken broth
1 cup heavy cream
Salt and pepper

½ teaspoon nutmeg or 1½ teaspoons curry powder
2 tablespoons cornstarch
¼ cup Madeira or port
3 hard-boiled eggs, quartered
Garnish: Chopped parsley or chives

This dish looks better if the mushrooms are small to medium-size so they may be left whole. Trim 1⁄16 inch from the stem. If the mushrooms are white they need only brushing; if they must be washed do it quickly with cold water and hang them up in a lettuce basket to dry. Put the butter in a pan with the onions, add the mushrooms, and sprinkle with salt and pepper. Bake at 350° for 10 minutes. Mix the broth, cream, and seasonings and blend with the cornstarch. Cook until the sauce thickens and add the mushrooms, wine, and eggs. If necessary reheat. Pour into the ring and sprinkle the top with the garnish. This will serve 8 or 10. This dish could be served as a vegetable, omitting the eggs; it will then serve 6.

MUSHROOM PUREE

1 pound fresh mushrooms	1 cup heavy cream
Salt and pepper	1 tablespoon cornstarch
¼ teaspoon nutmeg	1 tablespoon Madeira or port
2 tablespoons fresh onion juice	

Clean and dry the mushrooms. Only perfect, fresh ones may be used for this. Hash them in a wooden bowl until they are very fine. Do not grind them. Spread them out in a good-sized pan and put them in the oven to dry out a little—10 to 15 minutes at 325°—being careful they do not dry out or burn. Meanwhile mix the seasonings with the cream and cornstarch and boil down until the sauce is quite thick. Combine with the mushrooms and wine. This should be thick enough so it does not spread on the plate. This is for an important dinner for 4. Serve with chicken or game—or anything mushrooms are served with.

MUSHROOMS, RUSSIAN STYLE

1 pound fresh mushrooms	2 tablespoons butter
4 tablespoons butter	½ teaspoon mace
1½ tablespoons flour	1 cup sour cream
Salt and pepper	3 tablespoons sherry or Madeira
½ cup chopped onions	Garnish: Chopped parsley

Always get fine white mushrooms when making special mushroom dishes to serve alone. Brush them clean. Bake them 7 minutes in the butter and then sprinkle the flour with the juices until smooth. Add salt and pepper. Chop the onions very fine, sauté them in the butter until tender, and blend with the mushrooms. Have the cream at room temperature, and mix with the mace. Blend the cream with the mushroom mixture, heat, add the wine, and serve immediately. Garnish the top with parsley. Serves 5 as an accompaniment to meat; on toast as a luncheon dish this serves 6. This may be put on top of hot rice or noodles.

MUSHROOMS, PROVENÇAL

1 to 1½ pounds fine white
 mushrooms
Olive oil
¼ to ⅓ cup finely chopped
 parsley

Salt and pepper
¼ to ⅓ cup fine fresh dry crumbs
3 or 4 cloves garlic, crushed
¼ to ⅓ cup Madeira or dry
 vermouth

The mushrooms are to be left whole; they should be of medium size. Wipe them clean. Remove and grind the stems. If 1 pound is prepared you may use the smaller quantity of ingredients. Put 3 tablespoons of oil in the bottom of a baking pan and put the mushroom caps in upside down. Make a farce of the ground stems, moistening well with 3 or 4 tablespoons of olive oil, and adding parsley, salt, pepper, crumbs, and garlic. Sprinkle this over the mushrooms, then sprinkle with the wine. Bake at 375° for 12 to 15 minutes. Empty into a hot serving dish, scraping all the crumbs and pan juices over the mushrooms. One pound will serve 4. This is good served with veal or beef.

STUFFED MUSHROOMS. This farce may be used to fill mushroom caps of good size to serve as a garnish for fish and meats.

CREAMED FRIED OKRA

1 pound okra
⅓ cup water
3 strips hickory-smoked bacon
2 teaspoons cornstarch

1 cup light cream
Salt and pepper
½ teaspoon turmeric
⅓ cup grated Cheddar cheese

Remove the tips of the okra. Try to choose it of medium size. Wash it in salt water with a pinch of soda added to freshen it. Rinse well. Put it in a saucepan with ⅓ cup of water, cover, and cook 5 minutes. The water will be evaporated and the okra tender. Cut the bacon in 1-inch lengths and fry it until crisp, remove it, and reserve. Put the okra in the bacon fat and brown it a little—about 2 minutes over a medium fire. Blend the cream with the cornstarch, add the seasonings and cheese, and cook until it thickens. Pour it over the okra. Serves 4 or 5.

CASSEROLE OF CREAMED OKRA AND WHITE ONIONS

Fried Creamed Okra
12 or 16 small white onions, boiled until tender and drained

Add the drained onions to the creamed okra. Empty into a baking dish, sprinkle with a little more cheese, and have a very attractive dish to serve 6 or 8.

OTHER USES FOR OKRA

Okra adds taste and interest to many dishes: Succotash, fried corn, buttered Brussels sprouts, lamb stews, etc. Stewed okra may also be dressed with a mixture of tomato sauce and sour cream. Sprinkle cheese over top.

GREEN ONION PIE

2 cups diced green onions or 2 or
    3 yellow onions, sliced
3 tablespoons butter
⅛ teaspoon clove
    Salt and pepper
2 large eggs, beaten
1 tablespoon flour
1 tablespoon Parmesan cheese
1 cup sour cream

Dough:
1 cup flour
1 teaspoon baking powder
½ teaspoon salt
¼ cup shortening
    Milk
1 tablespoon soft butter

When new onions come in, they are sometimes of quite good size. Whichever onions are used, sauté them in the butter until tender and season with clove, salt, and pepper. Meanwhile make the dough. Sift the dry ingredients toegther, cut in the shortening, and add just enough milk so the dough may be rolled. Spread it with the butter and roll to the size of an 8- or 9-inch pie plate. Line the pie plate with the dough and put in the onions. Beat the eggs, add the flour and a very little salt and pepper, the cheese, and the sour cream. Spread over the onions. The top may be sprinkled with a little more cheese. Bake at 400° for 10 minutes and at 325° for another 10 to 12 minutes, or until set. Serves 6 or 8.

CREAMED ONIONS

2 to 2½ pounds white onions
1 to 1¼ cups water
    Salt and pepper
    Heavy cream
1 teaspoon powdered chicken
    concentrate

2 teaspoons cornstarch
¼ teaspoon nutmeg, or 1 tablespoon tomato paste
Garnish: Chopped parsley or
    Parmesan cheese

There are 12 to 14 white onions to a pound. To serve 6, 4 onions to a serving, 2 pounds are needed. Peel the onions and put them in a heavy pot. Add 1 cup of water for 2 pounds of onions, add salt and pepper. Cover tightly and simmer until the onions are tender, about 25 minutes. They must not overcook but remain whole. Drain off the precious water, measure it, and add enough heavy cream to make 1½ cups of liquid. Blend in the chicken concentrate, cornstarch, and seasoning. Cook until thickened and pour over the onions. Empty into a hot serving dish and garnish. Serves 6.

GLAZED ONIONS

1½ pounds white onions
1 tablespoon honey or brown
   sugar
3 tablespoons butter

Salt and pepper
⅓ cup chicken or beef broth, or
   Madeira
¼ cup seedless raisins (optional)

Peel the onions, boil them 3 minutes, and drain well. Put the honey or sugar and the butter in a heavy skillet and glaze the onions until they are a medium brown. Keep shaking the skillet until all are glazed. Add the broth or wine, cover tightly, and cook over a low fire or in a 325° oven for 40 to 50 minutes. They must be tender but hold their shape. If the wine is used, add the raisins 15 minutes before the onions are done. If after 20 minutes they become dry, they are cooking too fast; add a little broth or wine. The onions glazed in broth go with any meat. Glazed in wine with raisins, they are good with poultry, pork, and game. Serves 4.

EMILY'S CREAMED ONIONS

1½ pounds small white onions
1 cup heavy cream, heated
Salt and pepper

½ teaspoon turmeric
⅛ teaspoon clove
Garnish: Chopped parsley

Boil the onions in water for 5 minutes, drain well, and put them in the top of the double boiler with the hot cream and seasonings. Cover tightly and cook for 30 minutes or until they are just tender. Boil up twice over the flame while cooking. Empty into a serving dish and sprinkle chopped parsley over the top. These can be made ahead of time and left over hot water, uncovered. Serves 6.

BAKED BERMUDA ONIONS WITH CREAM

4 medium-sized onions (for 8)
⅔ cup water
Salt and pepper
Powdered clove
Light brown sugar

Sauce:
   ½ cup onion water
   Salt and pepper
   1 cup heavy cream
   2 tablespoons cornstarch
Garnish:
   Chopped parsley or Parmesan
   cheese

Peel the onions and cut them across in half. Boil them in ⅔ cup of water for 15 minutes or until they begin to cook tender. Drain them well, reserving the water. Put them in a well-buttered long pan on the bottom, cut side up. Sprinkle the onion halves with salt, pepper, clove, and brown sugar. Salt and pepper the onion water, mix it with the cream, and blend in the cornstarch. Cook until it thickens and divide it over the onions. Bake uncovered in a 325° oven 35 to 40 minutes or until they are tender. If cheese is used for a garnish, sprinkle a little over the top of the onions 5 minutes before they come from the oven. If parsley is used, remove the onions with a spatula to a hot platter and sprinkle with parsley. Serves 8. Choose onions large enough so that half of one is enough for a serving.

CURRIED ONIONS

1½ pounds small white onions
¼ cup dried currants
3 tablespoons Madeira or sweet vermouth
3 tablespoons butter
½ cup water
Salt and pepper

2 or 3 teaspoons curry powder
2 tablespoons butter
Heavy cream
3 teaspoons cornstarch
1 tablespoon lemon juice
1 teaspoon honey or brown sugar

Soak the currants in the wine 1 hour. Cook the onions in a heavy pot, tightly covered, with the butter, water, add salt and pepper. They must not cook to pieces, so watch them. Put the curry powder and butter in the top of the double boiler and cook 10 minutes over simmering water. When the onions are done, drain the liquid into a cup and add enough heavy cream to make 1¼ cups. Blend in the cornstarch and cook until it thickens; add the lemon juice and honey or sugar. Pour this into the top of the boiler with the curry and stir until blended. Taste for salt; it may need a few grains. Add the onions, currants, and wine. These are delicious with seafood, fish, poultry, or pork. Serves 6.

"FRIED" ONIONS

1 or 2 large Bermuda onions, sliced thin
Butter

Salt and pepper
1 teaspoon sugar

One large onion will serve 4. Melt 3 tablespoons butter in a heavy skillet and slice in the onions, seasoning each layer with salt and freshly ground pepper. When they are all in sprinkle the top with salt, pepper, and the sugar. Put dots of butter over the top. Bake uncovered in the oven at 375° for 10 minutes, stir them well, then continue baking at 325° another 10 minutes or until they are tender. To crisp a little they may be run under the flame a moment before serving. This is a very easy way to "fry." Sausage, fried apples, and other dishes may be oven-fried with little attention and less fear of burning.

Onions and Peppers. Include a large sliced green pepper with "Fried" Onions, and bake as directed. This is excellent with steak.

ONION SOUFFLÉ

10 white onions
⅓ cup water
  Salt and pepper
¼ teaspoon powdered clove
2 tablespoons butter

4½ tablespoons flour
½ cup heavy cream
5 egg yolks, beaten
4 egg whites, beaten

Peel the onions and slice very thin. Cook them with the water, seasonings, and butter until very tender. Add the flour and cream and mash through a sieve or purée in a blender. Mix with the beaten egg yolks. Beat the whites until stiff and stir one-fourth of them into the onion mixture, then lightly fold in the rest. Put into a greased 8-inch soufflé dish and bake at 375° 10 minutes, then at 350° 20 minutes more or until the soufflé is set and light brown. It may be served with a light cheese or tomato sauce. Serves 6.

GLAZED PARSNIPS

6 or 8 new parsnips
  Salt and pepper
3 tablespoons butter
⅛ teaspoon mace

3 tablespoons orange juice
1 tablespoon lemon juice
1 tablespoon honey or brown sugar

There is a thoroughly unreasonable indifference to this lovely vegetable. The indifferent are the losers. Trim the parsnips and scrape a little. I know a man who eats the skin. Steam them or boil them in very little water until they are tender. Skin and cut in half lengthwise. Put the butter, mace, juices, and sweetening in a heavy skillet and glaze the parsnips until they are brown and syrupy. Salt and pepper them. They may have a little cream added if you like—2 or 3 tablespoons. This vegetable may be used in stews and chicken pies or mashed or baked with roasts.

BUTTERED PEAS

3 or 4 shallots or green onions
4 tablespoons butter
2 pounds new peas
  Salt and pepper

1 teaspoon basil, tarragon, chervil,
  or fresh mint
¼ cup heavy cream (optional)

Slice the shallots or onions thinly and sauté in the butter in the bottom of a heavy pot until they are a little tender. Put in the peas with all the seasonings and 3 or 4 tablespoons of water. Cover tightly and cook 10 or 12 minutes or until tender. They take 40 seconds in a pressure cooker; reduce the pressure and remove the peas so they don't cook soft. Never drain the juices from peas. Serves 4.

BUTTERED PEAS AND LIMA BEANS WITH CHEESE SAUCE

Buttered Peas
2 pounds fresh lima beans

Sauce:
  2 tablespoons flour
  2 tablespoons butter
  1 cup light cream
  ⅓ cup grated Cheddar, Swiss,
    or Parmesan cheese
  Vegetable water
  Salt and pepper
  2 tablespoons Parmesan cheese

Cook the peas as directed for *Buttered Peas*. Cook the beans the same way, separately. Blend the flour and butter over low heat, stir in the cream and cheese; cook until thickened. Drain any vegetable liquid from the peas and beans into the sauce to thin it. Combine the vegetables and sauce and empty into a serving dish. Sprinkle the top with cheese. Serves 6 or 8.

PURÉE OF FRESH PEAS

3 pounds fresh peas
1 bunch green onions
3 tablespoons butter
1 teaspoon basil

Salt and pepper
3 or 4 tablespoons water
2 tablespoons flour
¼ cup heavy cream

Shell the peas. There should be 3 full cups. If the pods don't all look full, get 3½ pounds. Mince the green onions and put them with the butter in the bottom of a heavy pot or pressure cooker. Sauté a minute, then add the peas, basil, salt, pepper, and water. Cover tightly and steam over a low flame, 10 or 12 minutes, until very tender (1 minute in the pressure cooker). Mash through a sieve or purée in a blender with all the liquid. Blend the flour with the cream, cook a moment, and mix with the purée. Empty into a baking dish and heat in the oven until it is thick enough to serve like soft mashed potatoes. Serves 6 or 7.

COLD PEA SALAD

3 pounds new peas
¾ cup finely sliced green onions
¼ cup mayonnaise
Salt and pepper

1¼ cups sour cream
1 tablespoon lemon juice
2 tablespoons fresh chopped
  mint, chives, or dill

Cook the peas as for *Buttered Peas* and let them get cold. Mix all the other ingredients together and add the peas, draining them a little if necessary. This is good with cold salmon or other fish, or with cold meats for a summer buffet supper. Serves 8.

PEAS-AND-NOODLES PUDDING

1 cup tiny noodle shells
Salt
1½ pounds new peas, cooked as
    for *Buttered Peas*
1 tablespoon cornstarch
1 cup light cream
¼ teaspoon nutmeg

Salt and pepper
¼ cup Parmesan cheese
4 egg yolks, beaten
4 egg whites, beaten
2 tablespoons more Parmesan
    cheese

Cook the noodle shells in boiling salted water for 7 minutes and drain them. Meanwhile cook the peas (with 2 tablespoons water, 2 tablespoons of butter, ¼ cup minced onion, and 1 teaspoon of basil) as for *Buttered Peas*. Make a sauce, blending the cornstarch with the cream, nutmeg, salt, pepper, and cheese. Cook until it thickens and add the beaten egg yolks. Cook a moment and then mix with the peas and noodle shells. Beat the egg whites until stiff and stir one-fourth of them into the pea mixture, then lightly fold in the rest of the whites. Empty into a greased baking dish, sprinkle the top with the cheese, and bake at 375° for 10 minutes, then at 350° for 10 to 15 minutes more, or until the pudding sets and is puffed and brown. Serves 6.

MASHED SPLIT PEAS

2 cups dried split peas
3 cups water
⅔ cup diced onions
½ cup diced carrots
⅓ cup diced celery and leaves
1 teaspoon each basil and thyme
    Salt and pepper
1 tablespoon lemon juice
2 tablespoons butter

1 tablespoon brown sugar or
    honey
⅓ cup light cream
Garnish:
    3 tablespoons chopped
      browned almonds
    2 strips bacon, fried and
      crumbled

Wash the peas and soak 5 or 6 hours in the water. Drain. Measure the water and add enough fresh water to make 2½ cups. Put the peas, water, all the vegetables, basil, thyme, salt, and pepper in a heavy pot, cover, and cook the peas and vegetables to a mush over a low flame. If necessary add a little more water. Mash all through a sieve and season with the lemon juice, butter, and sugar or honey. Add the cream. The mixture should have the consistency of fluffy mashed potatoes. If it is to be reheated later, more cream will have to be added, as it becomes stiff. This is a fine dish to replace potatoes for serving with pork or poultry. Serves 6 or 8.

PEA SOUFFLÉ

Purée of Fresh Peas
3 tablespoons Parmesan cheese (for
   soufflé dish)

¼ cup additional heavy cream
4 egg yolks, beaten
5 egg whites, beaten

Follow the directions for the purée. When blending the flour with the cream use ½ cup instead of ¼ cup. Heat and add to the purée. Beat the egg yolks and add to the purée, stir in one-fourth of the stiffly beaten whites, then fold in lightly the rest of the whites. Grease an 8-inch soufflé dish, sprinkle the sides and bottom with the Parmesan cheese, and put in the purée. Bake at 400° for 7 minutes, turn down to 350°, and bake 20 to 25 minutes more. The soufflé should be moist inside. Serves 8.

ROASTED PEPPERS

4 large sweet bell peppers
4 cloves garlic, crushed

½ cup olive oil
Salt and pepper

Wash the peppers, remove any stem, and set them stem end down on a baking sheet. Roast them at 350° 15 to 25 minutes, depending on how thick the flesh is. Test with a sharp pointed knife. Skin them or not as you choose. Seed and cut in 1-inch strips. Mix the garlic, olive oil, salt, and pepper, and pour over the peppers. They may be eaten hot or warm as an antipasto or be stored in a covered glass jar in the refrigerator and served cold as an appetizer, or tossed with green salads or potato salads, or to accompany fish or meat on a cold buffet. If served hot they may be quartered and will serve 4.

PIPÉRADE

2 large peppers, sliced
2 cups sliced onions
   Ham or bacon fat
   Salt and pepper
1 clove garlic, crushed
3 ripe tomatoes

1 teaspoon basil
6 or 8 eggs, beaten
Accompaniments:
   Prosciutto
   French bread
   Red wine

Slice the peppers thin, also the onions, and put them in a heavy skillet with 3 or 4 tablespoons of ham or bacon fat and sauté, covered, until they are tender. Do not let them burn. Salt and pepper them and stir in the garlic. Skin, seed, and chop the tomatoes and add them when the onions and peppers are tender. Add the basil. Cook 5 or 6 minutes until the mixture is a sauce. Beat the eggs well and add them to the top of the vegetables and stir until they set. This is a dish from the Basque country and is served with ham, French bread, and a good red wine. Serves 4 to 6.

TO PREPARE PEPPERS FOR STUFFING

Select perfect peppers of uniform size. Cut them in half from top to bottom and remove the seeds and pith. Put them in a large pot with plenty of hot water, cover, and boil them from 5 to 7 minutes, or until they seem tender when pierced with the point of a knife. This lessens the baking time, as they are stuffed with precooked food. Allow about ⅓ to ½ cup of stuffing for each pepper half. One or two halves are allowed for each serving, depending on whether they are a main dish or an accompaniment.

RICE STUFFING FOR GREEN PEPPERS

1 cup brown or patna rice
2 cups chicken broth
1 teaspoon basil, tarragon, or
    chervil

Garnish:
    Chopped parsley or Parmesan
    cheese

Cook the rice with the broth and herb in a heavy pot, tightly covered, until all the moisture is absorbed and the rice is fluffy. Brown rice takes 45 minutes, patna 30. Poached peppers may be filled with rice or with rice and one cup of the following additions and baked 15 to 18 minutes at 350°. The tops may be garnished with a sprinkle of either chopped parsley or Parmesan cheese. When you bake the peppers set them close together in an open baking pan so they will hold their shape. Put a little hot water in the bottom of the pan.

ADDITIONS TO RICE STUFFING.

Sliced cooked shrimp, lobster, or
    crabmeat
Tuna fish and sliced black olives
Sautéed sliced mushrooms
Ground corned beef or ham
Sautéed chicken livers

Cooked peas or lima beans
Sautéed sliced sausages
Minced roast lamb, ⅓ cup raisins
    or currants soaked in sherry,
    chopped almonds

OTHER STUFFINGS.

Creamed vegetables
Creamed chicken livers
Creamed seafood
Creamed veal or lamb kidneys
Creamed turkey or chicken

Puréed split peas or stewed lentils,
    topped with a sautéed small
    sausage when done
Corned beef hash or ham hash
Sautéed fresh corn and minced
    green onions
Sautéed coarsely diced calf's brains
    with chopped hard-boiled eggs,
    chopped almonds, curry powder

STUFFED BAKED POTATOES

Choose big round potatoes for baking. This may not be traditional but for texture and flavor they are superior. When they are baked, cut them in half lengthwise and carefully scoop out all the potato, leaving the skins intact. Mash the potato with any of the following fillings (quantities are for 6 large potatoes).

No. 1.
1¼ cups ground ham
½ cup heavy cream, hot
    Salt and pepper
3 tablespoons butter
1 egg, beaten
Top: Grated cheese

No. 2.
1 cup grated Swiss Gruyère
    cheese
½ teaspoon nutmeg
½ cup hot cream
    Salt and pepper
3 tablespoons butter
1 egg, beaten
Top: Chopped parsley

No. 3.
1 cup minced leeks or green
    onions or white onions,
    sautéed in 4 tablespoons
    butter
1 cup light or heavy cream
    Salt and pepper
1 egg, beaten
Top: Grated cheese

No. 4.
1 cup sliced mushrooms sautéed
    in 3 tablespoons butter
¼ cup finely diced onion, sautéed
½ cup cream
    Salt and pepper
1 egg, beaten
Top: Cheese or parsley

Potatoes may be prepared and stuffed ahead of time; the egg is added so that the stuffing won't stiffen. Before serving heat them in a 400° oven for 8 minutes.

POTATOES BAKED WITH BACON

4 large potatoes
    Salt and freshly ground pepper

10 strips hickory-smoked bacon

Peel the potatoes and cut very thin. Put the slices of 1 potato in the bottom of a greased baking dish and sprinkle with salt and freshly ground pepper. Not too much salt. Cut the bacon in ½-inch lengths and fry it so that it begins to crisp a little. Scoop out ⅓ of the bacon and sprinkle it over the potatoes. Repeat, ending with a layer of potato. Pour the grease over the top, sprinkle with very little salt and freshly ground pepper. Cover very tightly and bake 45 minutes, the first 15 minutes at 375°, the next 30 minutes at 350°. These are wonderful with fish, meat which is not too rich, etc. Four very large potatoes serve 6.

POTATO CROQUETTES

1 to 1½ pounds potatoes
Salt and pepper
¼ teaspoon nutmeg
2 egg yolks

Heavy cream
Beaten egg
Fresh fine breadcrumbs
Deep oil for frying

Peel, boil, and rice the potatoes. Add the seasonings and the egg yolks. Beat in just enough cream so that the mixture is smooth but stiff enough to roll into balls the size of walnuts. Cool the mixture first as it stiffens. Before frying roll the balls in beaten egg, then in crumbs, and fry in 3 inches of oil at 375° to a delicate light brown. Drain on brown paper in a warm oven with the door open. One pound of potatoes serves 6. Sweet-potato croquettes are delicious, especially with grated orange rind added to the mixture.

BAKED POTATOES WITH CHEESE

Potatoes baked in their jackets
Slices of imported Swiss or Gruyère
  cheese

Salt and freshly ground pepper
Butter

Scrub and bake good-sized potatoes, preferably Maine potatoes. Have the cheese at room temperature, cut in slices ⅓-inch thick and 2 or 3 inches long. Split the hot potatoes, sprinkle with a little salt and pepper, and tuck in a pat of butter and a slice of cheese. Put them back in the oven to melt the cheese and keep warm about 3 or 4 minutes.

POTATOES DAUPHINOIS

2 pounds potatoes, shredded
1 clove garlic
2 cups milk, scalded
½ cup heavy cream
2 eggs, beaten

Salt and freshly ground pepper
Top:
    3 tablespoons grated cheese,
    Parmesan or Gruyère

Peel the potatoes and shred them on a disk grater, quite fine. Cut the garlic in half and rub over the sides and bottom of a baking dish. Put in the potatoes, mix the other ingredients, and pour over the potatoes. Bake uncovered at 350° about 50 minutes, until set but moist. Ten minutes before they are done sprinkle with the cheese. Serves 6 or 8.

POMMES SOUFFLÉS
Maurice Cazalis, Chartres

When visiting Chartres, visit Chez Cazalis, a restaurant where the food is superb. M. Maurice Cazalis, teacher of chefs, gave me this recipe which he demonstrated for The Friends of Chartres in Chichester, England.

For serving 8:
4½ pounds medium-sized potatoes
  3 quarts cooking oil
  Salt

Peel the potatoes, put them in cold water, wash, and dry between towels. Cut them lengthwise in slices $\frac{1}{10}$-inch thick and square off the corners. Divide the oil, putting 3 pints in each of 2 deep fat fryers, and heat to 400°. Put in the potatoes. Turn up the heat to High, as the potatoes have cooled the oil. Do not crowd the potatoes; put a few in at a time and keep them moving by rocking the fryer back and forth. When they are done they rise to the surface. Scoop them out with a wire skimmer and put them in a wire basket to drain. For the second cooking lower the basket into 400° oil and they will swell. Remove them before they become too brown. Drain on a towel, salt lightly, and serve 5 to a person.

DOUBLE-BOILER CHEESE POTATOES

  1 pound new potatoes
1½ cups milk, scalded
  Salt and pepper

  1 cup Swiss or Gruyère cheese, shredded

Scrape the potatoes as some of the tender skin left on is good. Shred them quite fine on a disk shredder, put them in the top of a double boiler, pour the scalded milk over them, add some salt and pepper. Cover and cook over boiling water 20 minutes. Stir in the cheese and cook 10 minutes more. Serves 4.

PARSLEY POTATOES

Small new potatoes
Butter

Salt and pepper
Finely chopped parsley

Scrub little new potatoes, 3 or 4 to a serving, with a rough vegetable brush. If the skin is thin they need not even be scraped. Boil them until just tender. Drain. Roll them in plenty of butter that has been seasoned with salt and pepper, then in a great deal of finely chopped parsley so that each potato is quite green.

MASHED POTATOES WITH SOUR CREAM

6 or 7 good-sized potatoes
½ cup butter
½ cup finely sliced green onion or white onions

Salt and pepper
2 cups sour cream
1 egg

Boil the potatoes in their jackets and skin them. Put the butter, onions, salt, pepper, and sour cream in a pot over a low fire so that the butter will become warm without melting. Mash the potatoes with a heavy fork rather than with a potato masher; they are fluffier. Mix all the seasonings with them and the egg. This will be very light and moist so that it may be made ahead of time and put in a baking dish to reheat before serving. Keep wax paper over the top. If mashed potatoes do not have enough liquid added they become stiff when made ahead of time. This will serve 8 or 10 and is a very fine dish. If there are any left over, blend with a little chicken broth and milk to make a super vichyssoise.

RISSOLÉE POTATOES
(or Pommes de Terre a la Parisienne)

Potato balls or new potatoes
Sweet butter
Oil

Salt and freshly ground pepper
Chopped parsley or chives

Potatoes may be cut in small olive shapes or into balls, or very small new potatoes may be scraped. Allow 5 or 6 balls to each serving. For 1 pound of potatoes use ⅓ cup of butter and add 2 tablespoons of bland oil to prevent burning. Wipe the prepared potatoes dry and put them in a heavy skillet with the melted butter and the oil over a gentle flame. Shake them occasionally. When they are nicely browned, salt and pepper them. Cover and cook very slowly until they are done, about 12 to 15 minutes. Put the potatoes in a hot serving dish and sprinkle the parsley or chives over top.

SHREDDED FRIED-POTATO CAKE

5 good-sized potatoes, shredded
⅓ cup butter

3 tablespoons olive oil
Salt and freshly ground pepper

Peel the potatoes and shred them on a fine disk shredder. Melt the butter in a big iron skillet and add the oil to prevent burning. When the oil and butter are quite hot, add the potatoes and some salt and freshly ground pepper. Cook the potatoes until a good light brown crust forms, but do not attempt to turn them. Put them, uncovered, in a 350° oven for 15 minutes to bake through. When they are done loosen the potatoes with a spatula, turn upside down on a round serving plate. Serves 5 or 6.

GRUYÈRE CREAMED POTATOES

4 or 6 medium-sized potatoes
1¼ to 1½ cups light cream
1 tablespoon cornstarch
¼ teaspoon nutmeg

Salt and pepper
¾ cup tiny cubes Gruyère or
Swiss cheese

Boil the potatoes in their jackets until tender, then skin them and cut in
¾-inch cubes. Put them in a hot serving dish or in a baking dish to keep
warm. Blend the cream with the cornstarch, add the nutmeg, salt, and
pepper and cook until thickened. Add the cheese cubes, empty the sauce
over the top of the potatoes, and cook until cheese is partly melted. If desired sprinkle the top with a little chopped parsley. Serves 4 to 6.

DILL CREAMED POTATOES. Omit the cheese and add a big handful of
chopped fresh dill to the sauce.

CREAMED POTATOES WITH HAM. A cupful of fluffy ground ham is a good
addition to creamed potatoes.

BAKED GLAZED POTATOES AND ONIONS

8 or 10 white onions
8 or 10 potatoes
6 tablespoons butter

Salt and freshly ground pepper
Garnish: ⅓ cup chopped parsley

Peel good-sized white onions and potatoes of the same size. Roll them
around in the butter in a heavy skillet over a brisk flame until they are a
good yellow. Sprinkle with salt and pepper. Cover tightly and bake in a
325° oven 45 minutes or until they are tender. Empty into a hot serving
dish and sprinkle with plenty of chopped parsley. Serves 4 or 5. They are
good with beef, steak or roast.

Potatoes and onions, boiled up and drained, may be put around a roast
1 hour before it is done, to finish cooking with the meat.

BOILED POTATOES LYONNAISE

6 potatoes
1 cup sliced onions
3 tablespoons butter

Salt and pepper
2 tablespoons dry vermouth
Chopped parsley

Boil the potatoes, skin them, and cut in thick slices. Have the rest of the
ingredients ready. Sauté the onions in the butter until tender and sprinkle
with salt and pepper. Lightly mix the potatoes with the onions and
sprinkle the wine over them. Empty into a hot serving dish and sprinkle
with chopped parsley. Serves 5 or 6.

NEW POTATOES WITH PARSLEY AND SOUR CREAM

12 small or 6 medium-sized new
    potatoes
½ cup ground parsley, or ⅔ cup
    finely chopped parsley

Salt and pepper
⅓ cup butter, melted
½ cup sour cream

Scrub the potatoes with a rough vegetable brush so they need not be peeled nor scraped. Boil them until just tender. Leave the small ones whole but cut those of medium size in half. Prepare plenty of parsley, the more the better. Put it in a saucepan with salt, pepper, the melted butter, and the sour cream. Put the cooked potatoes in the sauce and stir gently or shake them until they are all covered. Serve immediately. These go with *anything*. The more generous you are with the ingredients the better they are. You may want to use more than specified. If you have an herb garden, a handful of chervil, tarragon, or basil added to the parsley will make them even more fragrant.

SWEDISH ANCHOVY POTATOES

5 medium-sized potatoes
2 good-sized onions
4 tablespoons butter

20 Swedish anchovies (canned)
1½ cups light cream
Garnish: Chopped parsley

Peel the potatoes and shred them quite fine on a disk shredder. Sauté the sliced onions in 3 tablespoons butter until tender. Put alternate layers of potatoes, onions, and anchovies in a baking dish, the top layer potatoes. Sprinkle with some anchovy juice and dot with the remaining butter. Bake 10 minutes in a 375° oven, scald ¾ cup of the cream, and pour it over the potatoes. Bake 10 minutes more, then scald the rest of the cream and pour it over the potatoes also. Reduce the heat to 300° and bake 30 minutes. Serves 6. A variation of this may be made by cooking the potatoes and onions without the anchovies 10 minutes, then pouring over ¾ cup hot cream. Bake 10 minutes more. Mix 4 tablespoons anchovy paste with the second ¾ cup cream, heat, and pour over the potatoes. Pepper may be added to this dish but no salt. Bake 30 minutes at 300°.

POTATO PANCAKES

4 medium-sized potatoes, finely
    shredded
Salt and pepper
3 tablespoons flour
1 egg, beaten

¼ cup grated onion
½ cup shredded Swiss or Gruyère
    cheese
Heavy cream
Butter and oil for frying

Peel the potatoes and shred on a fine disk shredder. Add all the other ingredients immediately. If allowed to stand after shredding, potatoes become watery. Add just enough cream to make a moist but not wet batter. Fry to a crusty brown on each side and put the cakes on a baking sheet when done. Bake 5 minutes in a 400° oven to finish the cooking. They may be fried ahead of time and heated before serving. Serves 4.

POTATO CAKES

4 good-sized potatoes
1 cup sour cream
3 tablespoons butter
Salt and pepper
1 cup ground ham

1 cup shredded Swiss or Gruyère
    cheese
2 tablespoons chopped chives or
    parsley
Parmesan cheese and crumbs

Boil the potatoes, skin, rice them or mash through a sieve. Lightly mix with all the other ingredients. Form into thick cakes and dip them in a mixture of cheese and crumbs. Fry them a golden brown on both sides. They may be made ahead of time and fried at the last minute or baked on a cookie sheet 10 minutes in a 400° oven, turning them once. Serves 6.

POTATO DUMPLINGS WITH FRESH DILL OR PARSLEY

5 medium-sized potatoes
Salt and pepper
¼ teaspoon nutmeg
1 egg, beaten
3 tablespoons ground parsley or
    dill

2 tablespoons ground onion
⅓ cup flour
¾ cup dry breadcrumbs
2 tablespoons butter

Peel and quarter the potatoes. Boil them in water until they are tender, drain, and mash through a sieve. Frying the crumbs in the butter a little. Mix all the ingredients lightly together. Form into balls, roll in a light sprinkle of flour, and boil in salted boiling water. When they come to the top they are done. This takes but about 2 minutes. They may be prepared ahead of time and boiled the last minute. Serve with pot roast or sauerbraten. These also may be made into very small balls, dropped into chicken or turkey soup, and served in the soup. Serves 5 or 6 with meat.

POTATO TART

Crust:
- 2 cups soft mashed potatoes
- 1 egg, beaten
- 2 tablespoons flour
- Salt and pepper

Filling:
- 1 cup sour cream
- 2 eggs, beaten
- Salt and pepper
- ¼ teaspoon nutmeg
- ⅔ cup shredded Gruyère or Swiss cheese

Top: 2 or 3 tablespoons Parmesan cheese

If the potatoes are left over, just smooth in the rest of the ingredients. If they are freshly cooked, a little cream will be needed. Press the mixture into an 8-inch greased pie plate, sides and bottom, as though for a rolled crust. Mix the filling ingredients, put the mixture on top, and sprinkle with Parmesan cheese. Bake at 350° about 20 minutes. Serves 4 to 6.

CHINESE BLACK RADISH CAKES

- 2 cups black radish, shredded
- ¼ cup green or white onions, minced
- 1 egg, beaten
- 4 tablespoons cornstarch
- Salt and pepper
- Butter and oil for frying

Black radishes are 2 inches thick and about 8 inches long. Peel them and shred them quite fine. Mix with the other ingredients. Fry in oil and butter until light brown on both sides. The cakes are a little thick and 2 inches in diameter. Put them on a baking sheet and finish cooking in the oven, about 12 minutes at 350°. These are very good and resemble potato pancakes. Makes 6 cakes.

BUTTERED SPINACH

- 1½ pounds fresh spinach
- 1 good-sized onion, sliced
- 1 green pepper, sliced
- 3 tablespoons butter
- Salt and pepper
- ½ teaspoon rosemary, or 1 teaspoon basil

Garnish:
- Fried croutons, or sliced hard-boiled egg, or Parmesan cheese

Stem the spinach and discard any bruised discolored leaves. Wash in quite warm water, letting it stand a few minutes so the grit will go to the bottom of the pan. Wash in 2 or 3 waters until all grit has disappeared. The last water should be cold. Drain well in a basket. Sauté the onion and green pepper in the butter in a heavy pot 2 minutes, then add the spinach and seasonings. Cover very tightly and cook over a low flame until the spinach is tender. Do not add any water. A pressure cooker takes about 40 seconds. Empty the spinach into a serving dish and top with croutons fried in butter and garlic, or cover with thinly sliced egg or grated cheese. One-fourth cup of crumbled Roquefort cheese gives spinach a fine flavor. Serves 4.

VARIATION. The drained liquid from the buttered spinach may be measured and enough chicken broth or heavy cream added to make a cup. Blend in 1 tablespoon of cornstarch, cook until it thickens, and pour over the spinach. Cheese or croutons may be added to the top.

SPINACH SOUFFLÉ

Buttered Spinach
½ cup spinach liquid
3 tablespoons flour

⅓ cup heavy cream
4 egg yolks, beaten
4 egg whites, beaten

Put the well-seasoned cooked spinach, preferably flavored with rosemary, into a sieve and save ½ cup of the liquid. Put the spinach through the blender with the flour, cream, spinach liquid and egg yolks, or sieve the spinach and add the other ingredients. When it is well mixed stir in one-fourth of the stiffly beaten egg whites then lightly fold in rest of the whites. Put in a greased soufflé dish and bake 10 minutes at 375° then another 15 to 20 minutes at 350°. It should be moist inside. Serves 6.

SPINACH PURÉE

1½ pounds fresh spinach
⅓ cup chopped onions
⅓ cup chopped green pepper
2 tablespoons butter
Salt and pepper
1 teaspoon basil, or ½ teaspoon rosemary

1 tablespoon cornstarch
2 egg yolks, beaten
¼ cup heavy cream
Garnish:
½ cup small toasted buttered croutons

Stem and wash the spinach (see Buttered Spinach) and drain it in a wire lettuce basket for ½ hour. Sauté the onions and green pepper in the butter in the bottom of a heavy pot for 2 or 3 minutes. Add the spinach and seasonings. Cover tightly and cook slowly until it is tender. Do not add any water. The pressure cooker takes 40 seconds. Put the spinach and juices through a food mill, sieve, or blender. Add the cornstarch, egg yolks, and cream. When the mixture is smooth put it in a greased baking dish. When ready to serve, heat it for 10 minutes in a hot oven. Sprinkle the top with croutons. The purée should be moist but firm enough not to spread on the plates. Serves 6.

SPINACI BOLOGNESE

Buttered Spinach
1 cup tiny noodle shells
½ pound fresh mushrooms
2 tablespoons butter

Sauce:
Spinach liquid
Heavy cream
3 teaspoons cornstarch
Salt and pepper
¼ teaspoon nutmeg
½ cup grated cheese

Cook the spinach as directed for *Buttered Spinach* and put it in a sieve, do not mash. The liquid goes into the sauce. Cook the noodle shells in boiling salted water 8 minutes and drain. Sauté the sliced mushrooms 5 minutes in the butter. Mix the spinach, noodles, and mushrooms and put them in a baking dish. Measure the spinach liquid and add enough heavy cream to make 1½ cups. Blend the cornstarch with the liquid, add salt, pepper, nutmeg, and half of the cheese. Cook until it thickens, pour it over the top of the spinach mixture, sprinkle with the rest of the cheese, and bake 20 minutes at 325°. Serves 6.

ACORN AND HUBBARD SQUASH

Acorn squash may be boiled whole or baked whole, then cut in half, seeds and pith removed, and dressed at the table; or the squash taken out, mashed and seasoned and reheated in a baking dish. Small or medium-sized acorn squash take about an hour to bake whole. They are tested with a cake tester. They can also be cut in half, seasoned, and baked 45 minutes. Hubbard squash can either be cut in 4-inch squares, seasonings added to each piece, and baked; or it may be peeled, cut in small cubes, and steamed, then mashed and seasoned. The seasonings for baked squash are butter, salt, pepper, mace or nutmeg, honey or brown sugar or molasses. Mashed squash calls for the same. Sherry also is a good addition.

ACORN OR HUBBARD SQUASH PUDDING

2½ to 3 cups mashed squash
2 tablespoons cornstarch
3 egg yolks
1 cup light cream
⅓ cup light molasses or honey
Salt and pepper

½ teaspoon each cinnamon, clove, ginger, nutmeg
3 tablespoons dark rum
3 egg whites, beaten
Pecan halves, browned

Mix all the ingredients, except the nuts, together, folding in the stiffly beaten whites last. Put the mixture in a greased baking dish and bake at 350° until set, 35 minutes or more. It must be moist inside. Arrange the pecans over the top when it is done. Serves 6.

MASHED BUTTERNUT SQUASH

2 or 3 medium-sized butternut
  squash
4 tablespoons butter
½ teaspoon nutmeg

Salt and pepper
⅓ cup sour cream (or more)
2 or 3 tablespoons honey

Cut the squash across in 3-inch lengths. It is much easier to peel off the hard skin if it is in small pieces. Peel the pieces, remove seeds and pith, and cut into very small pieces. Put the squash in a steamer, pour a cup or more of water over it, cover tightly and steam until tender. This takes about 15 minutes. Put all the seasonings in a big bowl, add the squash, and mash it into either a rather lumpy mass or as smooth as a purée if you wish. Add more sour cream if necessary to make it fluffy. Put it in a hot serving dish. This may be made ahead of time, put in a baking dish, and heated 7 or 8 minutes in a hot oven just before serving. Two squashes serve 6.

BUTTERNUT, CROOKNECK, OR BUSH SCALLOP SQUASH

1 large squash
Salt
1 cup hot water
  Freshly ground pepper
2 or 3 tablespoons butter
¼ teaspoon nutmeg or mace

1 tablespoon honey or brown
  sugar
½ cup squash water
2 teaspoons cornstarch
1½ teaspoons powdered chicken
  concentrate

Peel the squash, seed and cut in ½-inch pieces. Put it in a steamer, sprinkle with salt, and pour the hot water over it. Cover tightly and cook about 15 minutes or until it is tender. Reserve the liquid. Mash the squash and add pepper and butter, mace and sweetening. Blend ½ cup of squash liquid with the cornstarch and chicken concentrate, cook until it thickens, and stir into the squash. Serves 4 to 6.

YELLOW SUMMER SQUASH WITH DILL SAUCE

1 cup sour cream
  Large handful fresh dill
1 teaspoon lemon juice
½ teaspoon sugar

3 young yellow squash
⅓ cup diced onions
3 tablespoons butter
Salt and pepper

Stem the dill, squeeze it, and cut it very fine with kitchen scissors. Marinate it in the sour cream 1 hour. If the squash is young and tender it may not need to be peeled but if the skin is tough, scrape it. Cut in ¾-inch thick slices. Sauté the onions in the butter a minute, then add the squash, salt, and pepper. Cover tightly and cook slowly until the squash is tender, about 10 minutes. Heat the cream over hot water, add the lemon juice and sugar, and stir it into the squash. Serves 4 to 6, depending on size of squash.

SUCCOTASH

3 or 4 ears of corn
1½ pounds fresh peas
2 teaspoons basil
Salt and pepper
1½ pounds fresh lima beans

3 tablespoons butter
1 green pepper, thinly sliced
½ cup thinly sliced white onions
Salt and pepper
1 cup heavy cream

Boil the corn 2½ to 3 minutes, score the kernels, and cut from the cobs into a big saucepan. Cook the peas with basil, salt, pepper and 3 table-spoons of water until tender. Add to the corn. Cook the lima beans in the butter with a very little water; add to the other vegetables. Sauté the onions and green pepper in butter until just tender and add them. Add the cream. This may be made ahead of time and warmed up before serving. This is a fine dish when fresh vegetables are at their prime and if one takes care in cooking them separately. This will serve 6 or 8.

SWEET POTATOES
BAKED WITH ROAST MEATS OR POULTRY

This is one of the most delicious ways to cook sweet potatoes. Boil them just long enough so they may be skinned, perhaps 10 or 12 minutes, but do not cook them through. Put them in the roaster with roast pork or roast chicken 30 minutes before the meat is done.

When you bake sweet potatoes in their jackets alone in the oven, boil them first for 5 minutes, then put in the oven to bake. When they are done, break them open and put a big pat of butter and freshly ground pepper and salt in each potato.

MASHED SWEET POTATOES

6 good-sized sweet potatoes
Grated rind and juice 1 orange
(optional)
½ to ⅔ cup cream, light or
heavy
⅓ cup butter
Salt and pepper

¼ teaspoon cinnamon, nutmeg,
or mace
⅓ cup light brown sugar, or ¼
cup honey
¼ to ⅓ cup Madeira, sherry, or
light rum

Seasoning and flavoring sweet potatoes is up to individual taste. They may be as lean or as rich as you like. Boil the sweet potatoes until they are tender, skin them, and mash with the other ingredients. These may be served immediately or put in a buttered baking dish and reheated a few minutes in a hot oven. There are a number of uses for mashed sweet potatoes; some of these follow.

SWEET POTATO CAKES. *Mashed Sweet Potatoes* when cold may be made into cakes, rolled in nuts or crumbs, and fried a golden brown in butter.

SWEET POTATOES IN PIMENTO FORMS. Line little fluted tin molds with whole canned pimentos, fill with *Mashed Sweet Potatoes*, set them in muffin tins, and bake 15 minutes at 350°. Unmold, put a sprig of parsley on top of each, and serve at an important dinner. They are both beautiful and delicious.

SWEET POTATO BISQUE. *Mashed Sweet Potatoes*, puréed with milk, or milk and a little chicken broth, make a marvelous soup. Flavor with a little rum or sherry.

SWEET POTATO SOUFFLÉ. Mix 1½ cups *Mashed Sweet Potatoes* with ¼ cup light or heavy cream, and 4 egg yolks. When smooth stir in one-fourth of 4 stiffly beaten egg whites, then lightly fold in the rest of the whites. Bake in a greased soufflé dish at 375° 10 minutes and another 15 minutes at 350°, until set but still moist inside. Serves 4 to 6.

ORANGE SWEET POTATOES, BLAZED

6 sweet potatoes
⅔ cup white corn syrup
   Grated rind 1 orange
⅔ cup orange juice

⅓ cup butter
Mace or nutmeg
Jigger rum

Boil the sweet potatoes in water to cover until just tender. Skin them and cut them in half lengthwise. Put them on the bottom of a buttered baking dish close together so that the syrup covers them. Boil up the syrup, orange rind, juice, and butter together and pour over the potatoes. Lightly sprinkle the top with powdered mace or nutmeg. Bake at 350° for 20 minutes, then turn them over and bake 25 minutes more. If they become dry add a little more mixed syrup and juice. When they are done blaze with rum. These are very good with duck, goose, ham, or pork.

CARAMEL SWEET POTATOES

6 sweet potatoes
½ cup sugar

⅓ cup boiling water
⅓ cup heavy cream

Choose rather slender sweet potatoes, not too large. Boil them until tender, then skin them. Melt the sugar in a heavy iron skillet and cook it until it is almost black, turn off the heat, and add the boiling water. When it subsides, cook to a heavy syrup. Roll the potatoes around in this syrup until they are well caramelized and remove them to a serving dish. Add cream to the caramel, boil up, and empty over potatoes. Serves 4 to 6.

SWEET POTATO PUDDING

2½ pounds sweet potatoes
¾ cup heavy cream
½ cup butter
1 teaspoon salt
½ teaspoon mace
Freshly ground pepper

Grated rind and juice 1 large
orange
½ cup light brown sugar
6 eggs, beaten
2 teaspoons baking powder

Boil, skin, and mash the sweet potatoes. Heat the cream with the butter, and mix with the potatoes. Add the salt, mace, pepper, orange rind and juice, and sugar and mix well. Beat the eggs until light, add the baking powder and mix with the potatoes. This mixture will be rather thin. Grease a large baking dish and empty in the potato mixture. Bake at 300° for 1 hour. This will serve 10 or 12. Don't worry about its disappearing. If you have any left over, purée it with milk, heat and add a little port or rum and you have a marvelous sweet-potato bisque. The pudding is fine with poultry or pork.

SWEET POTATO COCONUT PUDDING

5 sweet potatoes
2 bananas
⅓ cup butter
Salt and pepper
¼ teaspoon nutmeg

¼ cup honey
Coconut milk:
    1 cup light cream
    1 cup dessicated coconut
2 tablespoons rum

Boil, skin, and mash the sweet potatoes. Mash the bananas and mix with the sweet potatoes, butter, and seasonings. Meanwhile mix the cream with the coconut, scald it, and when it is cool mash through a sieve. Add this milk and the rum to the potato mixture. Pile into a baking dish and reheat before serving, 10 or more minutes in a hot oven. Serves 5 or 6.

SWEET POTATO STUFFED PIMENTOS

Mashed sweet potatoes
Canned whole red pimentos

Sprigs of parsley

These must be made in fluted tin molds. This is one of the most attractive ways to serve a vegetable. Each fluted mold holds ½ cup, minus the thickness of the pimento. Oil each mold, line with a whole red pimento, and carefully stuff with well-seasoned mashed sweet potatoes. Set each mold in a muffin tin. These may be prepared hours ahead of time. Before serving bake them 15 or 20 minutes in a 350° oven to heat them thoroughly. Turn out upside down and stick a small sprig of parsley into the top of each.

They may be put on individual serving plates in the kitchen or they may line a chop plate, garnishing chops; or they may be set around the edge of a platter with heaped riced white potatoes or steaming rice in the center; or whatever your menu requires. One is usually prepared for each serving.

ITALIAN STUFFED TOMATOES

6 fine firm tomatoes
1 cup brown or patna rice
2 cups chicken consommé
8 black Italian olives, sliced
6 anchovy fillets, sliced
1 clove garlic, crushed
2 tablespoons capers

¼ cup olive oil
¼ cup oil mayonnaise
Garnish:
    12 fresh cooked shrimp
    Mayonnaise
    Lettuce

Hold the tomatoes over a flame until they blacken and the skin cracks. Remove the skin and a slice from the top. Scoop out the pulp and seeds and discard, keeping the shell intact for filling. Cook the rice in the consommé over a low flame until tender. Brown rice takes 45 minutes, patna rice about 30. Cool it thoroughly. Lightly toss all the ingredients together and fill the tomatoes. Garnish the top of each with 1 tablespoon of mayonnaise and 2 shrimp. Serve them on a lettuce leaf. This may be served as a first course or a luncheon dish.

BAKED TOMATOES

6 large ripe tomatoes
  Salt and pepper
  Curry powder, or minced fresh
    herbs, or dried powdered
    fennel, tarragon, or basil

3 tablespoons butter
3 tablespoons olive oil
Shredded or sliced cheese: Swiss,
    Gruyère, Bel Paese, or Brie
⅔ cup heavy cream

Skin the tomatoes either by dipping them in boiling water or holding them over a flame until the skin cracks and blackens. The latter is the quicker and better way. Cut them in half across. Put them on the bottom of a well-greased baking pan with the cut side up. Sprinkle liberally with salt, pepper, and curry powder or any of the herbs. Almost any fresh herb is good, cut fine; chervil, tarragon, dill, parsley, chives, or basil. Powdered fennel is particularly good with tomatoes. Melt the butter and mix with the olive oil. Pour over the tomatoes and top each half with a liberal quantity of cheese. Put them in a 375° oven for 12 to 15 minutes or until the cheese melts. Lift them onto a hot platter. Put the cream in the baking pan, let boil up, and pour it over the tomatoes, scraping up every bit of the juices. These may serve 6 or 12 depending on the menu. They are good with almost any meat or fish. They may be served on toast for lunch.

HAM STUFFED TOMATOES

6 large ripe tomatoes
1¼ cups ground ham
1 cup cooked fresh peas or 1
    cup kernel corn
1 teaspoon basil

A little salt
Freshly ground pepper
3 tablespoons heavy cream
Butter
Chopped parsley or grated cheese

Skin the tomatoes and remove a thin slice from the tops. Scoop out the pulp and seeds, being careful not to break the tomatoes. Mix together all the ingredients except the butter and the parsley or cheese. Stuff the tomatoes, sprinkle the parsley or cheese on top, and put them in a lavishly buttered baking dish and bake 20 minutes at 350°.

TOMATOES WITH SOUR CREAM

1 quart of tomatoes, fresh or
    canned
2 tablespoons grated onion

Salt and pepper
2 tablespoons flour
1 cup sour cream

If the tomatoes are fresh, skin and cut them up. Add the onion to either fresh or canned tomatoes, salt, and pepper, and simmer for 15 minutes. This removes the raw taste and should always be done to canned tomatoes. Blend the flour with a little of the juice, then add it to the tomatoes. When the mixture thickens a little stir in the sour cream, heat, and serve in sauce dishes. This is a very fine dish. Serves 4 or 5.

TOMATOES CREOLE

6 or 8 large ripe tomatoes
    Salt and pepper
¾ cup finely minced green or
    white onions

Flour
½ cup light molasses
2 tablespoons butter

Skin the tomatoes and cut them in half across. Put them in layers in a baking dish, sprinkling each layer with a light sifting of flour, salt, pepper, and onions. Boil up the molasses with the butter and pour it over the tomatoes. Bake 50 minutes uncovered at 325°; check after 25 minutes, and if they are baking fast, turn the oven down to 300° for the rest of the time. Serves 6 or 8.

TOMATO PILAU

1 cup brown or patna rice
2 cups chicken broth
½ pound okra
1 large Bermuda onion, sliced
   Salt and pepper
1 green pepper, sliced

4 large ripe tomatoes
4 strips bacon
2 tablespoons butter
1 teaspoon each chili powder
   and curry powder
⅓ cup grated cheese

Cook the rice in the chicken broth until it is tender; 45 minutes for brown rice and 30 minutes for patna. Remove the ends of the okra, wash it in salted water, and rinse. Cook it 5 minutes or until tender and drain it. Slice the onion thin, also the seeded pepper. Skin and slice the tomatoes. Fry out the bacon, remove it, crumble it, and set it aside. Add the butter to the bacon fat and sauté the onion, and green pepper until they are almost tender, then add the tomatoes and cook for 8 to 10 minutes. Add salt, pepper, and the chili and curry. Add the okra to this and stir together 2 minutes, then toss with the rice and add the bacon. Put it in a baking dish and cover with the cheese. Bake for 10 minutes or until the cheese melts. This will serve 8. It is excellent with chicken.

TOMATO SAUCE WITH DILL DUMPLINGS

1 quart fresh or canned tomatoes
1 large onion, chopped
1 teaspoon basil
1 teaspoon brown sugar
1 tablespoon butter
   Salt and pepper

Dumplings:
   1 cup flour
   2 teaspoons baking powder
   ½ teaspoon salt
   1 tablespoon shortening
   ¼ cup finely minced fresh
      stemmed dill
   ½ cup milk
Garnish: Chopped parsley

Mash the tomatoes a little, add all the other ingredients, and simmer 10 minutes in a large pot. For the dumplings, sift the dry ingredients and cut in the shortening with a pastry cutter, add the dill (only fresh dill will do). Stir in the milk so that it is a soft dough. Drop in 6 equal parts off a serving spoon into the simmering tomato sauce, cover tightly and cook for 12 minutes at a steady simmer. Do not lift the lid. In each of 6 sauce dishes put 1 dumpling surrounded by the sauce and sprinkle with chopped parsley.

PURÉED WHITE TURNIPS AND POTATOES

6 or 8 small white turnips
3 or 4 good-sized potatoes
¼ cup butter
Pinch mace

Salt and pepper
¾ cup heavy cream
Chopped parsley

Peel the turnips and boil in a very little salted water. Do the same with the potatoes, separately. Drain. The vegetable water—there should be very little left—may be saved to use in soups or gravies. Mash the vegetables. Boil up the butter, mace, salt, pepper, and cream together, and add. This must be a light, fluffy, moist purée, so add a little more butter and cream if necessary. If this is made ahead of time, put it in a baking dish and cover with wax paper; reheat in the oven before serving. Add chopped parsley to the top. This combination is good with lamb. Serves 8.

WHITE TURNIPS AND CREAM

6 or 8 new white turnips
2 tablespoons chopped parsley
Salt and pepper
¼ cup water

¼ to ⅓ cup heavy cream
1 tablespoon cornstarch
1 teaspoon powdered chicken
  concentrate

Peel the turnips and cut them in half. Add the parsley to the turnips, salt, pepper, and water. Cook them for 5 minutes in a pressure cooker or cook in a heavy pot with a tight lid until just tender. If they are cooked in a pot, watch that they do not burn, and if necessary add 1 or 2 tablespoons of water. Blend the cream with the cornstarch; add the chicken concentrate and all the juice from the turnips. Cook until it thickens and heat with the turnips. If it is too thick add a little cream. This can safely be served at any important dinner.

ZUCCHINI AL FORNO
(Helen di Georgio, Rome)

6 zucchini
⅓ cup olive oil
2 cloves garlic, crushed
Salt and pepper
1 teaspoon marjoram
1 teaspoon basil

1 cup sliced onions
2 shallots or green onions, minced
6 eggs, beaten
⅓ cup Parmesan cheese
Butter

Choose zucchini of medium size. Remove a small slice from each end, but do not peel them. Slice ⅛-inch thick. Put the olive oil in a big sauté pan, add the crushed garlic, and cook a few seconds, then add the zucchini and cook a little. Add the seasonings, onions (very thinly sliced), and shallots or green onions, minced. Sauté a little, then empty into a greased baking dish. Beat the eggs, add the cheese, and pour over the vegetables. Dot with butter and bake at 350° about 20 minutes, until set. This may be served hot or cold.

Artichoke hearts or eggplant may be cooked the same way. Eggplant should be sliced thin and sautéed until almost done; then cut the slices in half. Serves 6.

ZUCCHINI, ITALIAN STYLE

1 to 1½ pounds small zucchini	Salt and pepper
¼ cup olive oil	Parmesan cheese
3 cloves garlic, crushed	

Trim the ends of the zucchini but do not peel it. Slice it very thin. Put the olive oil and crushed garlic in the bottom of a heavy skillet and cook a few seconds. Put in the zucchini and sauté slowly for 5 or 6 minutes, turning it often, so it is all well covered with the oil and garlic. If a greater quantity of zucchini is cooked use more oil and garlic. When it is done (it is tender before it is cooked), empty it into a hot serving dish and sprinkle liberally with Parmesan cheese.

BAKED ZUCCHINI

Zucchini of uniform size	Grated Swiss or Gruyère cheese
Fine crumbs	Bacon

Cut a very thin slice from the stem ends of the zucchini. Do not peel. Parboil the zucchini 5 minutes. Cut in half lengthwise and lay them close together on the bottom of a shallow baking dish or pan. Sprinkle with crumbs and cheese and lay a strip of bacon on top of each half. Bake at 350° 15 minutes, until the bacon is brown. Serve 2 small zucchini or 1 large one to each person. Large ones should not exceed 8 inches in length.

ZUCCHINI STUFFED WITH SAUSAGES

Zucchini	Salt and pepper
Pork sausages	Chopped parsley

Cut the zucchini in half lengthwise and scoop out a little of the seeds to make boats. Parboil 3 or 4 minutes. Sauté the sausage 8 minutes, until browned, or half done. Lay one in each zucchini half. Put the zucchini close together in the bottom of a shallow pan and bake 12 or 15 minutes in a 350° oven. Sprinkle with chopped parsley. They may be served as is or with a light cheese sauce.

salads

SALADS have an important place in our daily fare. The simple green salad is served at dinner, separating the meat course from the dessert. It is served with or without cheese. The important dinner calls for green salad and the *plateau de fromages*, especially if the dessert is a soufflé which may take a little waiting for. The hearty salad has no place in the dinner menu; it is decidedly a first course or the luncheon or supper dish. These are the *Niçoise* and the rice salads. *Potato Salad Provençal* is ideal for a picnic or a Sunday night supper with cold meats. The elaborate turkey and lobster salads are for a buffet or reception. They can be very great dishes indeed. They require homemade oil mayonnaise and should be molded in a bowl and emptied onto a plate, piped with mayonnaise, and decorated with pimento strips, sliced olives, and sieved egg. It is easy to make them look professional. One of the greatest salads is tender raw leaves of spinach dressed with garlic, bacon, and egg. It deserves to be a course by itself. But again for the daily fare there is nothing so good as the tender greens of Bibb lettuce, chicory, field salad, and endive, with French dressing to suit your own taste.

BIBB LETTUCE SALAD

1 Bibb lettuce per serving   French dressing
Mayonnaise

It takes more than just a good dressing to make a good salad; the greens also must be flavorful and interesting of texture. Bibb is delicate and tender and deserves to be served as a separate course. Clean, dry, and crisp it a little. Make a rosette of it on each plate and pass a dressing of mayonnaise thinned with French dressing.

FIELD SALAD

Field salad   French dressing

This tender leaf which comes in the spring is one of the very best salads to serve with dinner. Use dressing with a very light hand, because it must be just a little moist, not soppy. The tender meaty leaves need very little added to them. It is well to serve it as a separate course with a good Brie.

ROMAINE OR CHICORY WITH CROUTONS

Salad bowl of crisp greens for 8   6 anchovy fillets, sliced
12 French bread croutons   French dressing
2 cloves garlic, crushed   2 hard-boiled eggs
¼ cup olive oil

Pick over fine crisp romaine or chicory. Mix equal quantities of the two if desired. Clean, drain, and dry the greens and store in the refrigerator until ready to use. When preparing the salad, tear the greens in 2½-inch lengths and fill the bowl. Croutons should be cut from French bread in 1-inch cubes before the bread becomes too dry to cut. Let the croutons dry out. Heat the crushed garlic in the olive oil, fry the croutons all over, cool a little, then mix with the greens. Cut the anchovy fillets in 1-inch lengths and mix with the greens. Add the French dressing just before serving; don't use too much as the other ingredients give flavor and the salad must be light and not wet. Sieve the hard-boiled eggs over the top, and do not disturb the greens again. This is a handsome and refreshing salad.

SPINACH SALAD

It must be made of fresh young spinach leaves, no frozen or packaged.

Spinach leaves to fill your salad   4 strips hickory-smoked bacon
    bowl   3 cloves garlic, sliced
2 or 3 tablespoons French dressing   2 hard-boiled eggs, sieved

Put the stemmed spinach leaves in warm water, swish up and down, then wait 2 minutes for the soil to sink to the bottom of the pan. Then rinse well in cold water until there is no grit left. Drain in a lettuce basket. Chill the leaves in a cellophane bag an hour or two before serving the salad. Moisten the leaves with a very little French dressing. Cut the bacon in 1-inch lengths and fry it until crisp. Scoop out the bacon and sprinkle it on the leaves. Add the sliced garlic to the bacon grease and let it color over medium heat, then pour the garlic and grease over the leaves. Toss well and sieve the eggs over the top. Do not disturb the leaves again. It must be served immediately, before the bacon grease hardens.

SUMMER VEGETABLE SALAD

1 pound fresh peas
1 teaspoon basil
1 cucumber
¾ cup chopped green onions
½ cup chopped celery hearts
Mayonnaise

French dressing
Sour cream
2 tablespoons capers
Garnish:
   Sliced tomatoes
   Lettuce

This is a main-course luncheon or supper salad. To serve more than 4 or 5, increase the amounts. Cook the peas with the basil in very little water so they need not be drained. Save 2 tablespoons of the liquid. Peel the cucumber, cut it in ½-inch-thick slices, then quarter the slices. Chop the onions rather fine, also the celery hearts. An hour before serving, mix all the vegetables lightly with a mixture of mayonnaise, well-seasoned French dressing, and sour cream. Add the capers. Chill in a small bowl. When ready to serve empty the bowl in the center of a chop plate, and surround the vegetables with skinned sliced tomatoes and lettuce. Tomatoes allowed to stand in a mixed salad tend to make it watery, so they are better as a garnish. This salad served with a hot *Gougère* and followed by a sweet makes a fine lunch, and a complete one.

ENDIVE SALAD

Endive
French dressing

Roquefort cheese

One of the best salads is crisp endive served with French dressing blended to a heavy cream with mashed Roquefort cheese. A good creamy Gorgonzola may be used also. To ½ cup of dressing use 3 or 4 tablespoons of cheese. Serve six or seven endive leaves on each plate.

FRENCH DRESSING

1 part vinegar or lemon juice
3 or 4 parts good olive oil
   Salt and freshly ground pepper
     to taste
   Dash of sugar (optional)

Additions:
   Crushed fresh tarragon, basil,
     chervil
   Fennel powder
   Pinch mustard

There is much leeway and many differing tastes about French dressing. Some like it sharp; I can't stand it sharp. Some fight the sugar war as they fight the mint julep war in the South. I've had these diehards rave about my dressing when it had a pinch of sugar in it or some of the vinegar from pickled fruit, which I always save. You can add a dash of sweet vermouth to dressing and the herb flavor makes it delicious. Suit your taste. I like to dilute vinegar with something, lemon juice or wine, because some of our vinegar is so strong. Sometimes good Burgundy or Bordeaux "turns" in the bottle; this should be saved for the acid part of French dressing.

CABBAGE SALAD

3 or 4 cups shredded new cabbage
Additions:
    1½ cups seedless grapes
    1 sliced large pear (Anjou
      or Comice)
    1 cup shredded carrot

Dressing:
    ½ cup sour cream (or more)
    Salt and pepper
    ½ teaspoon anise
    1 tablespoon honey
    2 tablespoons lemon juice

Shred the cabbage quite fine on a disk shredder. Mix with any of the additions you like; grapes and carrot are good together. Mix the dressing ingredients to taste—a little more of any of them may be used—and toss with the salad.

CHICKEN OR TURKEY SALAD

3 cups chicken or turkey meat
1 cup sour cream
⅓ cup minced green onions or
    chives
8 stuffed green olives or black
    Italian olives, sliced
1 cup cooked peas
⅔ cup sliced celery hearts
¾ cup to 1 cup oil mayonnaise
½ cup sliced browned almonds,
    walnuts, pecans, or macad-
    amia nuts

¼ cup sliced mushrooms, or 1
    truffle
Fresh tarragon leaves
3 tablespoons capers
Garnish:
    Lettuce
    Hard-boiled eggs
    Mayonnaise
    Artichoke hearts
    Tomatoes
    Cucumbers
    Pimentos

With poultry or seafood salads the quantity desired is easily regulated by the addition of more meat or other ingredients. Two cups of chicken or turkey meat should serve 5 or 6 persons, 3 cups 8 or 10, depending on what else is served. The chicken or turkey is cut in good-sized pieces, never minced. Mix it with the sour cream so it is moist and chill it for 2 hours before mixing with the rest of the ingredients. Slice the mushrooms, sautée them 3 minutes in a little butter or oil, and let cool. (The truffle is cut in thin slices or sticks and sautéed a moment in a little butter.) If fresh tarragon leaves are available, they should be squeezed and cut and bruised so they may lend their perfume to the salad. Mix the salad and pack it in a mold or round bowl and chill 1 hour before serving. Empty it onto a big plate, mask with more mayonnaise, and decorate with sliced eggs and strips of pimentos. If the salad is served at a large supper or buffet reception surround it with a garnish of lettuce leaves holding little artichokes in oil, tomatoes, quartered or cut in eighths, or whole plum tomatoes, and sliced cucumbers.

CRABMEAT, LOBSTER, OR SHRIMP SALAD

1 pound cooked crab, lobster, or shrimp
⅓ cup sour cream
⅓ cup unsweetened mayonnaise
1 tablespoon tomato paste
2 pimentos, cut in strips
¾ cup sliced celery hearts
2 tablespoons capers
¼ cup minced chives or green onions

Optional additions:
Artichoke hearts in oil
1 pound peas, cooked
4 green olives, sliced
Avocado pear balls
Chopped hard-boiled eggs
Garnish:
Lettuce
Sliced hard-boiled eggs
Mayonnaise

One pound of any of the seafoods will serve 4 to 6 as a main dish. For a large buffet supper, a mixture of the crab, lobster, and shrimp may be used. Any of the optional additions may be added for both flavor and interest as well as a means of extending the quantity. Leave the crabmeat and lobster in quite good-sized pieces; of course the shrimp are left whole. Mix the sour cream, mayonnaise, and tomato paste together, then mix with the fish, and if necessary, add a little more dressing. Add all the other ingredients to the mixture, put it in a mold or round bowl, and chill. When ready to serve, turn it upside down on a serving plate, mask with mayonnaise and decorate with thinly sliced eggs. Garnish with lettuce around the plate. Never use a sweetened mayonnaise with fish. It is best to make your own oil mayonnaise for this fine dish as most commercial mayonnaise contains sugar. Tomato paste makes the dressing a nice pink; it is recommended instead of catsup or chili sauce because they are somewhat sweet.

GRAPEFRUIT SALAD WITH GREENS

A very refreshing salad is made with fresh grapefruit segments. Free the segments of all skin and membrane. Lay them on a bed of crisp salad greens, endive or chicory, and add *Roquefort French Dressing*.

MICHELINE'S RICE SALAD
Paris

1 cup patna rice
2 cups chicken consommé
2 tomatoes, skinned and seeded
Italian black olives, pitted and halved
¾ cup flaked tuna fish
Salt and freshly ground pepper
2 or 3 tablespoons olive oil
Garnish: Lettuce

Cook the rice in the consommé, covered, until the liquid is absorbed. Let it become cool. Cut the tomatoes in rather small pieces. Lightly mix all the ingredients with the rice and moisten with the olive oil. Line a bowl with crisp lettuce, put the rice salad in and serve cold.

WILD RICE SALAD

1 cup wild rice
2 cups chicken consommé
Salt and pepper
1 pound fresh small mushrooms
½ cup olive oil

1 clove garlic (optional)
2 pimentos, sliced
¼ cup sour cream
¼ cup mayonnaise

Wash the rice in several waters. Cook it in the consommé tightly covered over a slow flame until it is tender. Add more consommé if necessary. Cook the mushrooms 10 minutes in the olive oil, with the garlic (if used) in a 350° oven; save the oil. Slice the pimentos in strips and toss with the rice and mushrooms. Add the oil the mushrooms cooked in to the cream and mayonnaise, and mix all lightly together. This salad may be served hot or cold. If served cold, let the rice cool before mixing it. Serves 8.

RICE AND SEAFOOD SALAD

1 pound fresh shrimp or crabmeat
1 cup patna rice
1 teaspoon turmeric
2 cups broth, chicken or fish
10 Italian black olives
Salt and pepper
2 red pimentos

12 small fresh mushrooms
¼ cup olive oil
1 clove garlic, crushed
¼ cup mayonnaise
¼ cup sour cream
¼ cup French dressing
Garnish: Crisp lettuce

If fresh shrimp are used, cook them in 1 cup of water with some minced onion, salt and pepper 4 minutes. Let them cool in the liquid, then peel them and use the broth as part of the liquid to cook the rice. If crabmeat is used, it may be either fresh cooked or canned. Shred it and remove the bones or tendons. Cook the rice in the broth with the turmeric until the liquid is absorbed so that the rice is light and fluffy. The olives are pitted and sliced, the pimentos are cut in strips, and the mushrooms are cooked in the olive oil with the garlic 10 minutes and then cooled. Mix all the ingredients lightly together, mixing in the oil and garlic the mushrooms cooked in. Mix the mayonnaise, sour cream, and French dressing, and mix with the salad. Chill in a round bowl 1½ hours and then unmold and decorate with crisp lettuce. These elaborate salads are served for first courses or buffets or picnics, never with a soup-meat-vegetable menu. The turmeric gives the rice a yellow color and is especially attractive with shrimp. Serves 6 or 8.

SALADE PROVENÇALE

6 large potatoes
1 small green pepper
12 Italian black olives
6 stuffed green olives
1 red pimento
2 tablespoons tiny sour pickled onions
2 tablespoons capers
½ cup sliced celery hearts
½ cup minced green onions

1 small can anchovies
Salt and pepper
1 cup oil mayonnaise
3 tablespoons breadcrumbs
4 cloves garlic, crushed
¼ cup sour cream
Garnish:
More mayonnaise
3 hard-boiled eggs

This is a great salad for a picnic, a buffet supper, or with cold meats just for the family. These quantities will serve 12; halve them for 6. Boil the potatoes, and when they are cool, skin them, and cut them in good-sized cubes. Boil the green pepper 6 or 8 minutes, then cut it in strips. Pit and slice the black olives. Slice the green stuffed olives. Cut the pimento in strips. Cut the anchovies in 1-inch lengths. Toss all these ingredients lightly together and add a little salt and freshly ground pepper. If you make your own mayonnaise of good olive oil the salad will be seasoned the way it is in Provence. Commercial mayonnaise has sugar in it and that doesn't go with this. Mix the mayonnaise with the fine crumbs, garlic, and sour cream. Mix this through the salad, adding more mayonnaise and sour cream if necessary to make it well moistened. Pack it in a round bowl and chill 1½ hours before serving, then empty it out on a chop plate in a round mound. Coat it with mayonnaise and decorate it all over with sliced hard-boiled eggs. If this is served with ham, several pungent cheeses, and a fragrant white wine, not forgetting French bread, the supper will be greatly appreciated.

HOT EGG AND POTATO SALAD

3 or 4 potatoes
3 or 4 eggs
Salt and freshly ground pepper
¼ cup sour cream

4 strips bacon
Crisp lettuce
French dressing (optional)

As the potatoes are served hot it is well to peel the potatoes and cube them before boiling. Try to have the eggs ready when the potatoes are done. Put the eggs in cold water, bring to a boil, and cook 3½ minutes. The yolks will be half-cooked. Fry the bacon very crisp. Drain the potatoes and empty them into a warmed bowl. Open the eggs and scoop out over the potatoes and add salt and freshly ground pepper and the sour cream. Mix lightly and crumble the bacon over the top. Garnish with lettuce. This is served as a vegetable. A little French dressing may be added if desired. Serves 4 or 5.

BEET ASPIC

1 large can whole beets	Salt and pepper
½ teaspoon clove	Garnish:
Grapefruit juice	Fruits in season
Grape juice	Mayonnaise and French
Juice of 1 or 2 limes	dressing
Gelatin	Lettuce or watercress
Honey	

Purée the beets and the clove with beet juice in the electric blender. Measure and add enough grape juice and grapefruit juice to make 6 cups. Soak 1 teaspoon of gelatin for every cup of liquid in the lime juice. Melt the gelatin over hot water and add it to the beet mixture. Season with honey, salt and pepper to taste. If your ring mold holds more than 6 cups, add more juice and gelatin. Oil the mold and add the mixture and refrigerate until it is set. If frozen grape concentrate is used, add 2 cans of water instead of 3 to dilute it. This aspic, filled with melon balls, strawberries, pitted Bing cherries, or any fruit in season, is delicious for a summer luncheon. Unmold the ring on a round plate and fill the center with fruit. Mix mayonnaise with French dressing and dribble it over the fruit. Garnish the edge of the plate with lettuce or watercress. A good-size ring serves 8.

TOMATO ASPIC RING

2 cups tomato juice	Filling:
1 cup chicken consommé	Lobster, crabmeat, or shrimp
1 cup vegetable juice	salad
2 tablespoons gelatin	Garnish:
Juice of 1 lime	Crisp lettuce
1 tablespoon horseradish	Mayonnaise
	Sieved hard-boiled eggs

Heat 1 cup of the tomato juice. Soak the gelatin 4 minutes in the lime juice, and add to the hot juice to melt. Mix all the juices, consommé, and horseradish together and empty into an oiled ring mold. Chill until set. Unmold and fill with a salad. Serve a bowl of mayonnaise for the aspic. Sieved hard-boiled eggs over the salad gives this a festive touch for a buffet table. If more aspic is required for a larger mold, add 1 teaspoon of gelatin for each additional cup of juice or consommé. Measure your mold first to see how much you need. Add more horseradish to taste. This is a good flavor to serve with a fish salad. Chicken or turkey salad also may be made for this aspic.

Sauces

THERE are good, fine, and great sauces. They are themselves a whole branch of cookery. Far too many cooks make a lumpless Béchamel or a simple and good pan gravy for the roast, and let it go at that. There is a great deal more involved. It raises cookery to something quite different and imaginative to know what sauce is the right one and how to make it—for game, eggs, vegetables, fish, seafood, all kinds of meats, poultry, and pasta. One must be equipped with saucepans, a double boiler, whisks, a rotary beater, and above all rubber spatulas. There are a few important things to know, such as that when a sauce curdles, it may be brought back in a blender or with a rotary beater. There is the fragrant herby Béarnaise; there is the thick, rich Hollandaise for fish, eggs, and vegetables. For a change freeze puréed cranberry sauce for an ice to serve with the Thanksgiving turkey. Can you make a fine pesto sauce with lots of garlic for green noodles? These are the familiar ones. Try Soubise sauce for leftover veal. One should know that the extra boiling of the shells enriches shrimp sauce. Sauces are made, not to conceal a dish, but to embellish it.

In addition to the sauces in this section, many others are given with individual dishes. Dessert sauces are included in the section on Desserts. All sauces are listed in the index.

ALMOND SAUCE FOR FISH OR CHICKEN

½ cup blanched browned almonds
¾ cup chicken or fish broth
1 tablespoon cornstarch

Salt and pepper
¼ cup heavy cream
¼ cup dry vermouth

Blanch the almonds, skin them, and brown them a little in the oven. Coarsely grind them. Blend the broth (chicken broth for chicken and fish broth for fish) with the cornstarch; add salt, pepper and cream. Cook until it thickens, then add the nuts and wine. If it is too thick add more broth and cream. Pour over boiled or broiled chicken or boiled or baked fish.

AIOLI SAUCE
(Garlic Mayonnaise)

3 tablespoons breadcrumbs
2 or 3 tablespoons milk
6 to 8 cloves of garlic, crushed
2 egg yolks

1½ to 2 cups olive oil
Salt and pepper
1 or 2 tablespoons lemon juice

Use fresh breadcrumbs and soak them 5 minutes in the milk. Press the crumbs against a fine sieve to extract the milk. Put the crumbs in a mortar, add the crushed garlic, and with a pestle mash the garlic with the crumbs to a liquid mass. Stir in the egg yolks. With a wire whisk mix in the olive oil drop by drop until the sauce is quite thick, then add the rest of the oil more quickly, as you would for mayonnaise. Add salt, pepper, and lemon juice to taste. In Provençal cookery this is the favorite sauce for boiled fish, cooked vegetables, beans, or cauliflower, and for fish soups. A tablespoon of the sauce may be added to each plate of *Bouillabaisse*.

APRICOT MUSTARD SAUCE

½ pound dried apricots
¼ cup white corn syrup
2 tablespoons brown sugar
½ teaspoon almond extract
1 teaspoon curry powder

1 tablespoon ginger
Salt and pepper
2 tablespoons mustard
Sherry or sweet vermouth

Wash the apricots, add ⅓ cup boiling water, the corn syrup, and the brown sugar, and cook covered until the apricots are soft. Mash through a sieve, or purée in an electric blender. Add all the seasonings and thin with sherry or vermouth until the sauce has the consistency of prepared mustard. This sauce is served with ham but is also particularly good with Chinese dishes and boiled rice. Tightly covered, it keeps indefinitely in the refrigerator.

BEURRE BLANC SAUCE FOR FISH

1 tablespoon minced shallots or
   green onions
3 tablespoons wine vinegar

Salt and pepper
¼ to ½ pound sweet butter, cut
   in pats, chilled

Put the shallots or green onions in a heavy saucepan with the vinegar and cook until the vinegar is reduced to 1½ tablespoons. Add salt, pepper, and the chilled butter, 1 pat at a time, whisking until the sauce is creamy. If more than ¼ pound of butter is needed, just keep on whisking more in. It is advisable to make this just before serving, as it may separate if it stands. It only takes a minute or two to make, and the virtue of it is a light creamy texture. Pour it over cooked fish and serve at once.

BEURRE NOIR

½ cup butter, clarified
1 teaspoon fresh onion juice
1 teaspoon minced parsley

Salt and pepper
1 tablespoon capers
Lemon juice

Put the butter into a shallow saucepan or little skillet and melt it slowly. Pour off the yellow oil and discard the white residue. Heat the butter until it is a light golden color and add the onion juice, parsley, and salt and pepper to taste. Pour over dish and sprinkle with the capers and a squeeze or so of lemon juice. Serve this with boiled fish, calf's brains, or cooked vegetables.

BÉARNAISE SAUCE

3 shallots or green onions, finely
   minced
1 tablespoon chopped parsley
1 tablespoon of fresh tarragon

Salt and pepper
⅔ cup white wine
3 egg yolks, beaten
½ to ⅔ cup butter, softened

Mince the shallots or green onions very fine. There should be 2 tablespoons. Chop the parsley and tarragon. Put the shallots or onion with the herbs, salt, pepper, and wine in a saucepan and boil for 5 minutes, until it is reduced to half. Beat the egg yolks in the top of a double boiler until thick, then strain in the wine mixture. Set over simmering water and beat in the butter, 1 tablespoon at a time, until the sauce is thick. This is for steak or fish.

BÉCHAMEL SAUCES
(White or Cream Sauces)

THIN SAUCE

1 tablespoon butter
1 tablespoon flour
1 cup milk

Salt and pepper
1 egg yolk (optional)

Melt the butter in a heavy saucepan, stir in the flour over a low flame, and cook until the flour loses its raw taste, about 2 minutes. Heat the milk and stir it in very slowly so that the flour will not lump. Season to taste with salt and pepper and stir in an egg yolk if desired, for added richness and smoothness.

MEDIUM SAUCE

1 tablespoon butter	Salt and pepper
1½ tablespoons flour	1 egg yolk (optional)
1 cup milk	

Proceed as directed for *Thin Sauce.*

THICK SAUCE

1 tablespoon butter	Salt and pepper
2 tablespoons flour	1 egg yolk (optional)
1 cup milk	

Proceed as directed for *Thin Sauce.*

RICH SAUCE

Follow the recipe for *Thin, Medium,* or *Thick Sauce,* as desired, using half milk and half heavy cream, all light cream, or all heavy cream.

VELOUTÉ SAUCE

Velouté Sauce is made the way the *Béchamel Sauces* are made, except that a rich broth—fish, chicken, or meat—is used instead of milk or cream.

CRÈME FRAÎCHE

The French have a thick natural cream that they serve over pastries and fresh fruit, especially over the raspberries and strawberries that are abundant all spring and summer. The cream has been matured and has a slight tang. Compared to it, our heavy cream is quite pallid. Here is a quick way to make a good imitation.

3 ounces cream cheese	1 cup heavy cream
⅓ to ½ cup sour cream	

Soften the cheese at room temperature, then whisk in the sour cream until it is very smooth, then slowly whisk in the heavy cream. Make this an hour before serving and let it stand outside the refrigerator. Serve it the traditional French way out of a 6-inch-tall earthen jar with a medium-sized wooden spoon.

CAVIAR SAUCE FOR SLICED ROAST VEAL

¾ cup veal broth or liquid from
    roast
¼ cup dry vermouth
1 tablespoon cornstarch

1 teaspoon lemon juice
1 tablespoon butter
4 to 6 tablespoons red or black
    caviar

This sauce may be added to hot or cold roast sliced veal, preferably a fillet. Put the broth in a saucepan, blend the vermouth with the cornstarch, and add. Cook until it thickens. Add the lemon juice, and salt and pepper if needed. Skimp the salt because the caviar may be salty. Add the butter and lightly add the caviar last, trying not to break the eggs. Cover the sliced meat with the sauce or serve it in a sauceboat.

BROWN SAUCE

3 cups strong beef stock
⅓ cup chopped onions, ground
⅓ cup chopped carrots, ground
¼ cup chopped celery
4 sprigs parsley, minced
½ teaspoon thyme

1 teaspoon basil
½ cup red wine
2 tablespoons flour
1 tablespoon tomato paste
1 teaspoon meat extract
2 tablespoons Madeira

Put the beef stock in a heavy saucepan and add the vegetables, herbs, and wine. Almost cover and simmer for 30 minutes, then mash through a fine sieve. Brown the flour in a heavy saucepan until it is a pale yellow, blend with 3 tablespoons of the hot sauce until it is smooth, then add the rest of the sauce with the tomato paste and meat extract. Simmer 5 minutes, then add the Madeira. This foundation sauce is a simplified version of the French Brown Sauce or Sauce Espagnol which takes days to make. It is the base for Mustard Sauce, Madeira Sauce, Curry Sauce, and Piquante Sauce. It may be added to roasting-pan juices. If more is made than is needed, it may be stored in a glass screw-top jar in the refrigerator for a week.

CAPER SAUCE

2 tablespoons butter
1½ tablespoons flour
⅓ cup chicken or beef broth
⅓ cup heavy cream

⅓ cup dry vermouth
1 egg yolk
Salt and pepper
3 tablespoons capers

Melt the butter in a saucepan, stir in the flour, and let it brown a little, then slowly add the broth, stirring so the sauce does not lump. Add the cream and cook until it thickens. Mix the wine with the egg yolk and stir it in, but cook only a moment more. Season with salt and pepper and add the capers. This is for fish or lamb or mutton.

CARAMEL

1 cup white sugar ⅓ cup boiling water to caramelize a mold, or 1 cup boiling water for caramel syrup

Put the sugar in a heavy iron skillet and over a good flame let it melt and brown to almost black. Turn off the heat and pour ⅓ cup boiling water into the melted sugar. Turn on a medium heat and let the mixture melt and cook down until it is very thick. Pour this into a metal mold and tip the mold so that the bottom and sides are covered with heavy syrup. If it is too thin to stick, put it over the flame a moment. Refrigerate for 2 or 3 minutes; it will become hard and is ready to receive the crème for a renversée or other puddings.

CARAMEL SYRUP. Melt the sugar as instructed for caramelizing. Add 1 cup of boiling water to the melted sugar and let it cook until it is a syrup. Do not let it get too thick, as it thickens more as it cools. This is stored in a glass container and used for flavoring and coloring soups or gravies and glazing meats and poultry. Every pantry shelf should have this syrup.

CRANBERRY RED WINE SAUCE

1 pound cranberries ¼ teaspoon clove
1¾ cups light brown sugar 1 teaspoon cinnamon
1 cup red wine

Wash and pick over the cranberries. Boil the ingredients together until very soft, then first purée in a blender, and then mash through a sieve; there is a residue of skins that the blender doesn't liquefy. This is a delicious sauce with plenty of body.

CRANBERRY JELLY

1 quart cranberries 1 cup light brown sugar
½ cup orange juice or red wine

Wash the cranberries and boil them with the juice or wine until they are soft. Mash them through a sieve or purée in an electric blender. If they are puréed in the blender they must be sieved afterward to remove the skins. Put the purée back on the stove with the sugar and cook down until quite thick, then put it in an oiled mold and chill. Orange juice instead of water gives cranberries a very interesting flavor, as does the red wine. Serve with pork or poultry.

CRANBERRY SAUCE

1 quart cranberries   1 cup light brown sugar
⅔ cup orange juice

Wash the cranberries and put them in a heavy saucepan. Add the orange juice and sugar and simmer almost covered until the cranberries are tender. Drain them out with a skimmer and boil down the juice until quite thick. Pour over the berries and chill.

CHILI SAUCE WITH SOUR CREAM

⅔ cup chili sauce   ⅔ cup heavy sour cream
½ teaspoon chili powder   1 tablespoon lemon juice

Mix all the ingredients together and serve with cold meats or fish.

CREOLE SAUCE FOR FISH OR OMELETTES

¼ cup butter
⅔ cup diced onions
⅓ cup diced carrots
¼ cup chopped celery
1 green pepper, finely sliced
¾ cup sliced fresh mushrooms
1 tablespoon flour

1 tablespoon light brown sugar
Salt and pepper
1 tablespoon chili powder
2 tablespoons lemon juice
2 cups mashed tomatoes
1 teaspoon basil
12 green olives, sliced

Put the butter in a heavy pot, melt it, and sauté the onions, carrots, celery, and green pepper in it 3 or 4 minutes. Add the mushrooms and cook another 2 minutes over a low flame. Stir in the flour and brown sugar and add a little salt and pepper. Add the chili powder gradually, to taste. Add all the other ingredients and cook gently almost covered for 20 minutes.

EGG SAUCE FOR BOILED FISH

Cream Sauce:
     2 tablespoons butter
     1½ tablespoons flour
     ⅔ cup heavy cream
     ⅓ cup fish stock
     ¼ teaspoon nutmeg
     ½ teaspoon paprika

Salt and pepper
1 teaspoon grated lemon rind
2 hard-boiled eggs
1 tablespoon fresh onion juice
3 tablespoons dry vermouth

Make the *Cream Sauce* first. Melt the butter and blend in the flour and cook a minute, then stir in slowly the hot cream and ⅓ cup of the stock the fish cooks in. Cook until it thickens and season with salt, pepper, nutmeg, and paprika. Add the lemon rind and let the sauce stand until ready to serve. Shell the eggs, chop the whites, and add them to the sauce with the onion juice. Reheat the sauce, add the wine, and pour over the well-drained fish. Sieve the egg yolks over the sauce. This is very attractive.

GOULASH SAUCE FOR LEFTOVER MEATS

3 large onions, sliced thin
2 tablespoons butter
1 tablespoon oil
2 tablespoons sweet Hungarian
  paprika
1 clove garlic, crushed
  Leftover meat, cut in cubes

¼ cup leftover gravy or meat
  jelly
⅓ cup tomato sauce or purée
1 tablespoon cornstarch
  Salt and pepper
⅓ to ½ cup red wine
1 cup sour cream

Slice the onions and sauté them in the butter and oil until they are tender, then add the paprika, garlic, and meat. Swish the meat around until it is well covered with the paprika and onions. Heat the gravy or jelly, blend the tomato sauce or purée with the cornstarch, mix, and cook until it thickens. Add seasonings and pour over the meat. Add the wine and let this stand several hours. When ready to serve, heat and stir in the sour cream. Leftover meat should not be cooked again. Boiled beef, steak, roasts, or brisket may be used in this sauce.

CHERRY WINE SAUCE FOR HAM OR GAME

½ cup broth, or meat drippings
  strained of fat
¼ cup orange juice
1 teaspoon grated orange rind
1 tablespoon cornstarch
⅓ cup cherry juice

⅛ teaspoon each cinnamon and
  clove
½ teaspoon almond extract
¼ cup sherry or port
½ cup pitted cherries

Put the broth or drippings in a saucepan and add the juice and rind. Simmer gently for 4 minutes. Blend the cornstarch with the cherry juice and add it and the seasonings to the broth mixture. Cook until it thickens. Add the wine and cherries. This may be made ahead of time and reheated just before serving. Serve in a sauceboat to accompany the ham or game. Canned Bing or sour cherries may be used.

QUICK CURRY SAUCE

⅓ cup heavy cream
3 teaspoons cornstarch
¾ cup beef or chicken broth
1 tablespoon lemon juice
  Salt and pepper

1 tablespoon curry powder (or
  more to taste)
2 tablespoons grated apple
1 teaspoon brown sugar
¼ cup sherry or Madeira

Blend the heavy cream with the cornstarch, add the broth, and cook until it thickens, then add all the other ingredients. This is better if it stands several hours before reheating to serve. This may be used for warming cooked meats, fish, or eggs, and for the *Swiss Steak Fondue*.

HOLLANDAISE SAUCE

½ pound country-fresh sweet
   butter
4 egg yolks
1 tablespoon water

1 tablespoon lemon juice
⅓ cup boiling water
Salt and pepper

Cut the butter in three equal parts and let it stand at room temperature a couple of hours to soften. Take pains to obtain the freshest eggs and the white sweet butter that comes in pound or half-pound chunks. This fine sauce must taste of eggs and butter, delicately seasoned. Put the yolks, a tablespoon of cold water, and the lemon juice in the top of a double boiler over lukewarm water and whisk until the yolks are thick. Turn on the fire under the water, add one-third of the butter, and whisk until it is smooth and melted. Never let the water boil but let it become just hot enough to thicken the mixture. Then add another third of the butter, whisking continuously. When it is blended and smooth, add the rest of the butter and beat until smooth. When it is thick gradually whisk in the boiling water and cook a few more seconds until it again becomes thick, then season with salt and pepper. If you insist, add a few more drops of lemon juice to suit your taste. This may stand an hour over lukewarm (not hot) water until it is served. A classic fish dish is poached turbot, barbue (brill) or salmon with Hollandaise; it is *the* fish sauce as well as for seafood and vegetables when they are served as a separate course: asparagus, cauliflower and artichokes.

VARIATION. A simpler Hollandaise may be made using 1 cup of *Rich Sauce* made with light cream, and stirring in 2 egg yolks and ½ cup of softened sweet butter. Season with salt, pepper, and lemon juice.

BLENDER HOLLANDAISE SAUCE OR AIOLI SAUCE

4 egg yolks
2 tablespoons lemon juice
Salt and freshly ground pepper

½ cup softened butter
¼ cup boiling water

Put the yolks, lemon juice, seasonings, and butter in the blender and when they are well blended slowly add the boiling water. Scrape the contents into the top of the double boiler and cook over hot water until it has thickened. Serve over fish or vegetables. For the aioli sauce crush 2, 3, or 4 cloves of garlic into the blender with the egg yolks, juice, and seasonings, and add ½ cup of olive oil instead of the butter. When well blended, add the boiling water, scrape the sauce into the double boiler and cook until it thickens. These blender sauces are easy, quick, and sure. A few drops more of hot water may be added if they become too thick.

HORSERADISH APPLESAUCE

1½ cups tart applesauce   5 tablespoons horseradish

Make tart applesauce flavored with lemon juice and season to taste with horseradish. This is good to serve with roast goose or duck, or with roast pork.

HOT HORSERADISH SAUCE

1 cup *White Sauce* or
   Velouté Sauce
1 tablespoon fresh onion juice

1 tablespoon lemon juice
3 tablespoons freshly grated horseradish

A medium-rich *White Sauce* may be used, or a *Velouté Sauce*. Make the *Velouté Sauce* with fish stock if the sauce is to be served with fish, or with meat stock for serving with meat. Add the rest of the ingredients to the sauce and serve it hot. A popular way of serving horseradish in the Scandinavian countries with boiled pike or other fish is to serve separate bowls of melted butter and grated fresh horseradish.

HORSERADISH SOUR CREAM SAUCE

1 cup heavy sour cream
3 tablespoons grated fresh horseradish
1 tablespoon fresh onion juice

1 tablespoon lemon juice
Salt and pepper
1 teaspoon tomato paste

Blend all together. This may be used as one of the sauces for *Swiss Steak Fondue* or with fish.

JELLY GAME SAUCE

1 tablespoon butter
1 tablespoon flour
½ cup stock, or ½ cup meat
   drippings strained of fat

1 teaspoon grated orange rind
Salt and pepper
⅓ cup currant jelly
¼ cup Burgundy or Port

Melt the butter in a saucepan and blend in the flour. Add the stock or meat drippings and the orange rind. Simmer for 3 or 4 minutes gently so there will be no evaporation. Season to taste. Add the jelly and wine. Heat and serve in a sauceboat.

LEMON BUTTER SAUCE

⅓ to ½ cup butter, clarified
Salt and freshly ground pepper

Juice of ½ lemon
2 tablespoons fine dry crumbs

Melt the butter slowly in a saucepan, then pour off the yellow oil and discard the white residue. Add salt, pepper, and lemon juice. Bring to a simmer with the crumbs which must be fresh but fine and dry. Pour over brains, asparagus, broccoli, cauliflower, green beans, or thin scaloppine.

MINT SAUCE FOR LAMB

½ cup finely chopped fresh mint
⅔ cup water
¼ cup sugar

Juice of ½ lemon
⅓ cup dry vermouth

Only fresh mint can be used. Boil the sugar and water 5 minutes, add the lemon juice, and pour it over the mint. When it is cool add the wine. Serve at room temperature.

MAYONNAISE

2 egg yolks
1 teaspoon salt
¼ teaspoon mustard
1 tablespoon wine vinegar
1 to 1½ cups olive oil

Freshly ground pepper
½ teaspoon paprika
More vinegar or lemon juice
   to taste

Have the ingredients at room temperature. Put the yolks, salt, mustard, and vinegar in a mixing bowl and beat with a rotary beater until the mixture is thick, or mix in an electric blender. Add olive oil drop by drop until it begins to thicken, beating continuously. The oil may then be added faster until it is very thick. Thin with a little more vinegar or lemon juice to taste. Use a good wine vinegar.

GREEN MAYONNAISE. For meat salads, potato salads, and fish.

1 cup mayonnaise
2 tablespoons each: minced parsley,
   tarragon leaves, chives, onions

2 tablespoons capers
1 teaspoon powdered fennel

SOUR CREAM MAYONNAISE. For fruit salads and aspics.

1 cup mayonnaise
½ cup sour cream
1 tablespoon lemon juice

2 or 3 tablespoons minced
   preserved ginger or chutney
1 teaspoon curry powder

MUSTARD MAYONNAISE. For ham, cold meats, or fish.

1 cup mayonnaise	3 tablespoons prepared mustard
½ cup sour cream	1 or 2 tablespoons sweet vermouth

MAYONNAISE CREAM SAUCE FOR LOBSTER OR CRABMEAT

1 cup oil mayonnaise	¼ cup heavy sour cream
1 teaspoon tomato paste	¼ cup dry vermouth
1 tablespoon minced fresh tarragon or chervil	

Mix all the ingredients together. This is a fine sauce to serve on cold or hot boiled lobster or to cover a molded fish salad. A salad may be decorated with strips of red pimento and sliced green olives.

TARTAR SAUCE

1 cup oil mayonnaise	2 tablespoons chopped pickles
1 tablespoon ground onion	1 teaspoon horseradish
1 tablespoon ground parsley	1 tablespoon chopped green olives
1 tablespoon minced tarragon or chervil	1 tablespoon whole capers
	½ teaspoon paprika

Mix unsweetened oil mayonnaise with all the ingredients. (Do not use a sweetened commercial mayonnaise.) This is served with seafood, especially with softshell crabs and scallops.

MOUSSELINE OR CHANTILLY SAUCE

3 egg yolks	1 tablespoon lemon juice
Salt and pepper	½ to ⅔ cups butter, cut in pats
1 tablespoon butter	¼ cup heavy cream, whipped

Put the yolks, some salt and pepper, 1 tablespoon butter, and the lemon juice in a heavy pot set in a pan of simmering water. Whisk until the mixture is creamy. Turn off the fire and whisk in the rest of the butter, a pat at a time, until it thickens. This may stand over warm water until ready to serve. Stir in the whipped cream just before serving. For fish and vegetables.

MOUSSELINE SAUCE NO. 2

1 cup of *Hollandaise Sauce*   ⅓ cup heavy cream, whipped

Combine the Hollandaise with the whipped cream. Suitable for fish, vegetables, and fish soufflés.

MORNAY SAUCE

1 cup white sauce
2 tablespoons Parmesan cheese
⅛ teaspoon nutmeg

3 tablespoons grated Swiss or
 Gruyère cheese
2 tablespoons dry vermouth
 (optional)

This is the proportion of cheese to cream sauce. If the sauce is used over fish the wine is a nice addition. Mornay Sauce is usually made of *Rich Sauce*.

MUSTARD SAUCE

1 tablespoon butter
2½ tablespoons dry mustard
1 tablespoon brown sugar
1 teaspoon salt
 Freshly ground pepper

2 eggs, beaten
2 tablespoons water
¼ cup wine or tarragon vinegar
1 cup sour cream or heavy sweet
 cream

Melt the butter in the top of the double boiler over simmering water. Add the dry ingredients and the beaten eggs. Add the water and either wine or vinegar. Stir until it thickens. When it is cool add the sour cream or the sweet cream, whipped. This is fine with ham or ham loaf or with *Swiss Steak Fondue*.

MUSTARD WINE SAUCE

1 tablespoon butter
1 tablespoon cornstarch
½ cup beef broth
2 tablespoons prepared mustard

1 teaspoon brown sugar
 Salt and pepper
⅓ cup dry vermouth
2 tablespoons sweet vermouth

Melt the butter in a saucepan and blend in the cornstarch and broth. Add the mustard, brown sugar, salt and pepper and simmer until it thickens. Add the two wines and stir until smooth. This is good with pork and with cold meats.

SOUBISE SAUCE

½ pound white onions
¼ cup butter
1 tablespoon flour
Salt and pepper

Cream Sauce:
2 tablespoons flour
1 tablespoon butter
Salt and pepper
¼ teaspoon nutmeg
1 cup light cream

Slice the onions very fine and put them on to cook in the butter for 15 minutes. Stir in the flour, season, and mash through a sieve or purée in an electric blender. Make the cream sauce in the top of a double boiler. Blend the flour with the melted butter, add seasonings, and slowly stir in the cream. Add the onion purée and cook 30 minutes over simmering water. If it needs thinning, stir in a little cream or broth. Serve with fish, chicken, veal, or vegetables. The cream sauce for Soubise sauce may be made with half chicken broth and half light cream if desired.

LOBSTER SAUCE

1 pound fresh cooked lobster meat
3 tablespoons butter
3 tablespoons cognac
Cream Sauce:
  2 tablespoons butter
  1½ tablespoons flour
  1½ cups light cream, or 1 cup
    light cream and ½ cup
    fish stock

Salt and pepper
¼ teaspoon nutmeg
1 teaspoon tomato paste
½ teaspoon turmeric
3 tablespoons Madeira or sherry

Pick over the lobster meat and remove any tendons or shell. Leave the meat in good-sized pieces and reserve ¼ cup of the more shredded meat to put through the grinder. Put the butter in a saucepan and stir the big pieces of lobster in it over a low flame for a few seconds, then blaze with the cognac. For the sauce, melt the butter, stir in the flour and cook a minute over a low flame. Have the cream or the cream and fish stock hot and stir it in. Cook until it thickens, then season with salt, pepper, nutmeg, tomato paste, and turmeric. This gives the sauce a rich color. Add the ground lobster to the sauce and then the pieces of lobster. This can be made ahead of time. When ready to serve, reheat the sauce and stir in the Madeira or sherry. This may be served in patty shells or as a sauce over boiled salmon or other fish. If you desire more sauce or a thinner sauce, add a little more cream or fish stock with a teaspoon of cornstarch blended into it. Use a scant teaspoon of cornstarch to ½ cup of liquid.

MUSHROOM BROTH SAUCE

½ pound fresh mushrooms
3 tablespoons grated onion
3 tablespoons butter
Salt and pepper
¼ teaspoon nutmeg

1 teaspoon tomato paste
1¼ cups chicken or beef broth
1½ tablespoons cornstarch
3 tablespoons sherry or Madeira
Chopped parsley

Clean the mushrooms. If they are very small, they may be left whole; otherwise slice them. Put them in a pan with the onion and butter, salt and pepper them, and bake them, uncovered, in a 375° oven for 6 or 8 minutes. Blend the nutmeg, tomato paste, broth, and cornstarch together and simmer until it thickens. Empty the mushrooms and their pan juices into the sauce. This may be made ahead of time. When ready to use, reheat and add the wine and a little chopped parsley. This may be served with warmed-up meats or for omelettes or cheese soufflés.

MUSHROOM CREAM SAUCE. This is made the same way as *Mushroom Broth Sauce* except that ¾ cup of heavy cream and ½ cup of broth are used instead of all broth. Baking mushrooms is a fine way to cook them. Sautéing is apt to make them limp.

ORANGE SAUCE FOR COOKED CARROTS

3 egg yolks
¼ cup orange juice
2 or 3 tablespoons carrot water

Grated rind 1 orange
Salt and pepper
⅓ cup butter

Cook enough carrots to serve 6; reserve the liquid. Put the egg yolks, juice, carrot water, orange rind, salt and pepper in a heavy saucepan and whisk over simmering water until the sauce thickens, then add the butter a little at a time. When the sauce is thick and creamy pour it over the hot carrots. Carrots should never be cooked with much water, so the juice left from cooking them shouldn't exceed 2 or 3 tablespoonfuls.

REMOULADE SAUCE

1 cup mayonnaise
1 teaspoon anchovy paste
1 tablespoon minced chives
1 tablespoon minced tarragon and
    chervil

1 tablespoon minced parsley
½ teaspoon mustard
3 tablespoons capers

·The ingredients are mixed with the mayonnaise. It goes without saying that the sauces calling for mayonnaise are most successful when the mayonnaise is made with good olive oil and fresh egg yolks, and made by you. This sauce is served over seafood, fish, potato salads, and vegetables.

SAUCE RAVIGOTE

½ cup French dressing
½ cup mayonnaise
2 tablespoons finely minced
    green onions

1 tablespoon each minced fresh
    chives, tarragon, parsley, and
    chervil
1 hard-boiled egg, sieved

Mix all the ingredients together. Instead of using the mayonnaise, you may make Ravigote Sauce with 1 cup of French dressing. This is served over chicken, meats, artichokes (hot or cold), and mussels, on the half shell.

SHRIMP SAUCE

1 pound fresh shrimp
1¼ cups water
1 small onion, minced
1 teaspoon thyme
Salt and pepper
1 teaspoon lemon juice

1 cup heavy cream, or more
2 tablespoons cornstarch
1 teaspoon tomato paste
¼ teaspoon nutmeg
3 tablespoons sherry or Madeira

Wash the shrimp but do not shell them. Put them in a saucepan with the water, onion, thyme, salt, pepper, and lemon juice, and let simmer for 3 minutes. Let the shrimp cool in the broth, then shell them and set aside. Put the shells into the broth, almost cover the pan, and cook for 15 minutes at a low simmer. Let cool and strain out the shells, pressing them against a sieve to extract all the juice. This is a strong fish broth which goes into the sauce. There should be 1 cup of broth; if not, add enough cream to make 1 cup. Blend the cream with the cornstarch, add the shrimp broth, tomato paste, and nutmeg. Let it cook until it thickens. Chop 3 or 4 shrimp very fine and add these and the whole shrimp to the sauce. This may be made ahead of time. When ready to serve, reheat and add the wine. This may be served over a fine baked or boiled fish or by itself in patty shells or on toast.

FRESH TOMATO SAUCE FOR PASTAS

⅓ cup olive oil
¾ cup finely chopped onions
1 teaspoon powdered fennel
Salt and pepper
¼ cup Marsala

⅓ cup minced fresh herbs: basil,
    watercress, or parsley
5 large ripe tomatoes
Garnish: Parmesan cheese

Put the olive oil in a heavy saucepan and sauté the onion in it until just tender. Sprinkle with the fennel, salt, and pepper and add the wine. Cook a moment. Skin the tomatoes, slice them or cut them in eighths, and add them and the fresh herbs to the sauce. Stir until they are well heated, then empty the sauce over a bowl of hot pasta. Pass the cheese. This fragrant dish should have a fresh taste so the tomatoes are not cooked. Use plenty of herbs.

QUICK TOMATO SAUCE

½ cup chopped onions
⅓ cup olive oil
3 cloves garlic, crushed
1 chopped green pepper
4 or 5 fresh mushrooms and/or
    ¼ cup dried mushrooms
1 teaspoon powdered fennel

1 teaspoon thyme
2 or 3 cups tomato purée
Salt and pepper
3 tablespoons tomato paste
½ teaspoon powdered beef
    concentrate

This is a good tomato sauce which can be made in a short time. It is good for pastas, such as *Noodles Danieli*. Sauté the chopped onions in the olive oil for 2 minutes, then add the garlic, green pepper, and, after 5 minutes, the mushrooms. If the dried mushrooms are used, soak them previously for ½ hour, then drain them. They give a very good flavor. Add all the other ingredients and simmer very slowly for 25 minutes. If 3 cups of tomato purée are used, this makes over 3 cups of sauce.

MEAT TOMATO SAUCE FOR PASTAS

1 cup diced onions
½ cup diced celery
½ cup diced carrots
4 tablespoons butter
½ pound ground beef
2 ounces chopped ham or salami
1 cup Madeira or Marsala
2 teaspoons salt
    Freshly ground pepper
2 cloves garlic, crushed

2 tablespoons tomato paste
2 teaspoons thyme
2 teaspoons basil
1 teaspoon powdered fennel
5 dried mushrooms, soaked and
    drained
1 cup mixed vegetable juice or
    tomato purée
½ cup beef or chicken broth
Garnish: Parmesan cheese

Put the vegetables in a heavy pot and sauté them in the butter over a slow flame for 5 minutes, then add the beef and stir it in the vegetables for another 5 minutes. Add all the other ingredients and simmer for 1½ hours. If the sauce becomes too thick, add a little juice or meat broth. If preferred all tomato purée may be used instead of canned vegetable juice. Pass the cheese.

SOUR CREAM TOMATO SAUCE FOR BAKING FISH

1 small can tomato sauce (¾ cup)
⅔ cup heavy sour cream

1 teaspoon curry powder, or chili
    powder, or powdered fennel
½ teaspoon salt

Mix all the ingredients together and spread the sauce over the top of a big fish fillet, cod, halibut, or salmon. Bake slowly until the fish flakes.

TOMATO CHEESE SAUCE

½ cup chopped onions
⅓ cup chopped green pepper
3 tablespoons butter
Salt and pepper
1½ cups canned tomato purée

1 teaspoon fennel powder
1 teaspoon basil
½ cup grated Cheddar or
Gruyère cheese

This is an excellent quick sauce when you want something to serve over spaghetti or noodles in a hurry. It is also excellent for fish, meat loaf, omelettes, etc. Sauté the onions and green pepper in the butter until they begin to soften—4 or 5 minutes over a low flame. Then add all the other ingredients except the cheese, and simmer for 10 minutes. Stir in the cheese until it melts. Canned tomatoes or tomato purée must be cooked 10 or more minutes to remove the raw taste.

PORT WINE JELLY FOR DUCK AND GOOSE AND GAME

½ cup sugar
1 cup water
Grated rind 1 lemon

Juice of 1 lemon
1 tablespoon gelatin
1 cup fine port

Boil the sugar, water, and lemon rind for 5 minutes. Meanwhile soak the gelatin in the strained lemon juice. Using a very fine sieve to remove the rind, strain the hot syrup onto the gelatin to melt it. Stir until it is melted, let cool a little, then mix with the wine. Empty into a fancy oiled mold and chill. This is served with either hot or cold roast duck, goose, or game.

SIMPLE SYRUP

2 cups sugar

1 cup water

Boil the sugar and water for 3 minutes. Cool and store. This is a convenient quick sweetener for cold drinks, soups, gravies, sauces, salad dressing, etc., when a dash of syrup may rescue a dish from dullness.

PRALINÉ POWDER

1 cup sugar
⅓ cup water

½ cup browned nuts: almonds,
pecans, black walnuts, or
hazelnuts

Boil the sugar and water until the syrup becomes a medium brown. Slice the nuts and brown them a little to improve their flavor. Add them to the syrup and cook second or two longer, then pour onto a greased marble slab or into an iron skillet. When it is cool, break it up with an ice pick, and put it through the grinder or blender. This powder is sprinkled on crèmes, ice cream, biscuit tortoni, custards, etc.

Bread—Daily & Fancy

SOME people aren't allowed as much bread as they like, and some eat too much bread which may take the place of the variety of food everyone needs. Some of us, after a surfeit of meat, vegetables, and fruit, crave bread. It may be good sensible bread of whole grains or it may be a croissant, but certainly there is nothing we can think of that takes the place of something made of flour and yeast.

I have tried to make a selection that will include all tastes, besides many of my own favorites. For a steady diet there is nothing better tasting or better for us, and especially for growing children, than good homemade bread from whole-grain flours, preferably water-ground.

How wonderful to enter a house on a cold winter night and be greeted by the fragrance of hot bread baking. There is the English muffin for tea, and the crusty French bread or rich croissant to serve with the first-course appetizer. Serve a puffy hot gougère with creamed shrimp for lunch or supper; it never fails to give great pleasure. Make a hot skillet bread and serve it as a change with chicken or pork for a small dinner for friends.

Homemade bread should become a habit; fancy breads may remain the occasional treat.

FRENCH OR ITALIAN BREAD

2 cups lukewarm water
2 envelopes yeast
3 teaspoons sugar
2 teaspoons salt

5 to 6 cups flour, all white or half
  wholewheat and half white
Milk
Sesame or poppy seeds

Mix the water, yeast, and sugar in a bowl. Set the bowl in a saucepan of quite warm water to let the mixture become foamy. Sift the salt with 5 cups of flour. Add the water-yeast mixture and beat very hard. Add more flour if necessary to make a light spongy dough. There is a difference in flours. Set the bowl in a dishpan of quite warm water, cover with a tea towel, and let it rise to double its bulk. Punch it down and beat hard with a wooden spoon for 4 or 5 minutes. Divide in 3 parts and make long loaves, not more than 2 inches in diameter, brush them with milk, and put them on a greased sheet in a warm place to rise to double the bulk. Slash slantwise with a sharp knife and sprinkle with either sesame or poppy seeds. Put the bread in a 425° oven for 15 minutes, then turn down to 375° for about 25 minutes more, or until the loaves are a golden color.

PANE MISTO

Make on the day you are going to have an assortment of hors d'œuvre.

2 full cups of unsifted white flour
1 full cup of unsifted wholewheat
  flour
1 envelope of dry yeast
⅓ cup lukewarm water
1 teaspoon honey

½ cup water
1 tablespoon salt
2 tablespoons butter
1 teaspoon powdered fennel
Water and warm milk

Mix the flour in a large mixing bowl and stir in the powdered fennel if you use it. Put the yeast, ⅓ cup lukewarm water, and honey in a small bowl and set it in a saucepan of quite warm water, almost cover, and let it stand until the mixture is frothy. Boil up ½ cup of water with the salt and butter, turn off the heat, and let it become lukewarm. When the yeast is ready, combine the two mixtures, stir into the flour, and add a little more warm water if necessary. Beat hard for 5 minutes. It must be a firm dough, or it won't hold its shape when baked. Set the bowl in a dishpan of quite warm water, cover with a tea towel, and let rise 1½ hours. Grease and flour a 17-inch-long cookie sheet. Punch down the dough, oil your hands and knead it a few minutes in the bowl, then divide the dough in half and roll it between your hands into long, round loaves, the length of your cookie sheet. Brush with warm milk to make a good crust. Set in a warm place and cover lightly with a tea towel. When it is half risen, slash 5 times slantwise with a very sharp knife. The second rising shouldn't take more than 45 minutes. Bake 20 minutes in a 400° oven. Do not cover while it is cooling.

DELICATE BREAD

1 envelope yeast
1 cup flour
¼ cup light brown sugar
½ cup lukewarm water
2¼ cups flour, unsifted

2 whole eggs plus 1 white, beaten
1 teaspoon salt
⅓ cup melted butter
½ cup warm milk
2 tablespoons rum

I don't know whether it is the eggs, butter, or rum, or a combination of all of them, that makes this such a beautiful bread. It is easy to make, is of fine texture, and bakes a beautiful brown. Mix the first four ingredients together, stirring them well in a large bowl, set the bowl in a dishpan of quite warm water, cover it with a tea towel, and let the dough rise 1 hour. Mix in all the other ingredients, first beating the eggs and white together until light. The batter should be both light and with some body. Beat hard for 2 or 3 minutes. Set it again in a dishpan of almost hot water, covered, to rise for 45 minutes to 1 hour. Beat quite hard with a wooden spoon and put the dough in an oiled breadpan, again in a pan of hot water, to rise again for almost an hour. Put the risen bread in a cold oven with the heat turned high for 15 minutes, then turn down to 325° for another 20 to 25 minutes. The breadpan should be of good size or the dough will drip over onto the oven floor.

SWEDISH LIMPA BREAD

1 envelope yeast
¼ cup lukewarm water
2 tablespoons light brown sugar
1½ cups white flour, unsifted
1 teaspoon salt
1 tablespoon anise seed

1 teaspoon powdered fennel
Grated rind 1 orange
⅓ cup molasses
1½ cups beer, ale, or stout
1 tablespoon butter
2 cups rye flour

Combine the yeast, water, and sugar and let stand until frothy. Put the white flour in a large mixing bowl and add the salt, anise seed, fennel, orange rind, and molasses. Heat the beer (or ale or stout) in a saucepan to lukewarm and melt the butter in it, then make a well in the flour and pour it in. Before mixing it add the yeast, then stir all together until well mixed. Set the bowl in a dishpan of quite hot water, cover with a towel, and let it rise for 45 minutes to 1 hour. Add the rye flour and beat very hard. It should be a light, elastic dough; if necessary add a spoon or so of lukewarm water. Beat for 4 or 5 minutes, cover with a towel, and set the bowl in hot water again to rise to double in bulk. Beat it down well and put the dough in a greased loaf pan covered and set in warm water, to rise an hour or more. Put the loaf in a cold oven with the heat turned to 375°, and bake 15 minutes, then reduce the heat to 325° and bake 25 to 30 minutes more. This bread has a fascinating flavor.

PUMPERNICKEL

1 cup rye flour	¼ cup molasses
1 cup buckwheat flour	1¼ cups boiling water
1¾ cups wholewheat flour	1 tablespoon salt
1 envelope dry yeast	3 tablespoons good fat or butter
¼ cup lukewarm water	

Mix the flours together in a large mixing bowl. Put the yeast with the lukewarm water in a small bowl and pour the molasses over it. Sweetening helps develop yeast. Set the bowl in a saucepan of quite warm water, partially cover it, and let it become frothy; this takes 10 minutes or so. Boil up the salt and fat with the boiling water, turn off the heat, and let the water become lukewarm. When the yeast is frothy add it to the lukewarm water-butter mixture, then stir into the flours. With a little practice you learn just how stiff the dough should be. If necessary, add some quite hot water to make a soft but resilient dough. Stir it vigorously 2 minutes or so, then put the bowl in a dishpan of quite warm water and cover the dishpan with a tea towel. The moist warm air that is created promotes rising. When the dough has risen (about 1 hour) and is soft to the touch, beat it 3 minutes with a wooden spoon. If it is too soft it has too much liquid; add about ¼ cup flour. If it hasn't risen well it is too heavy with flour, and a little warm water, perhaps ¼ cup, may be stirred in. Grease a breadpan, put the dough in it, and set the pan in the warm water in the dishpan. The second rising will take less time. When the dough has risen well above the breadpan, put it in a cold oven, turn the heat on high, and let it finish rising. After 15 minutes the heat should be over 375°; if the oven is too hot turn it down to 325°. Continue baking for another 35 minutes, 50 minutes in all. After it has been out of the oven a minute, turn it onto a bread board, cover lightly with a towel to cool.

WHOLEWHEAT AND RYE BREAD

2 cups wholewheat flour	⅓ cup lukewarm water
1 cup rye flour	3 tablespoons brown sugar or honey
½ cup oatmeal flour	
⅔ cup raisins	1 cup hot water
1½ tablespoons anise seeds	4 tablespoons butter
1 teaspoon anise powder	1 tablespoon salt
1 envelope dry yeast	

This is a fine mixture of grains. Follow the procedure specified for *Pumpernickel*. One-half cup of coarse cornmeal may replace some of the other flour in these breads, or all wholewheat may be used. It is interesting to vary the flours almost every time you make bread. These breads make wonderful sandwiches, good to serve with liver pâté, good for hors d'œuvres and everyday eating.

SALLY LUNN

3 to 3½ cups flour
1 envelope dry yeast
¼ cup lukewarm water
3 tablespoons honey
2 eggs, beaten
¾ cup milk, scalded

⅓ cup butter
1 tablespoon salt
4 or 5 tablespoons powdered
  sugar
2 teaspoons cinnamon, anise, or
  cardamom

This is a lovely light fragrant loaf if not too much flour is used. There is a difference in flours so the amount can't be too exact. The dough must be light but not thin. Put the yeast in a little bowl with the lukewarm water and honey and set the bowl in a saucepan of hot water for the yeast to become frothy. Have the eggs at room temperature so as not to chill the yeast. Beat them very light. When the yeast is frothy, mix it with the eggs. Meanwhile the milk has been scalded, the butter and salt added and the milk cooled to lukewarm. Combine the mixtures and stir into the flour. Beat with a wooden spoon until light and elastic—about 5 minutes. Set the mixing bowl in a dishpan of hot water and cover with a tea towel. When the dough has risen to double in bulk, beat again and put the dough in a well-greased loaf pan. Sift the powdered sugar with the spice you choose and sprinkle liberally over the top of the dough. Let it rise again. When it has risen put the loaf in a cold oven with the temperature set at 375°. After 15 minutes turn the heat down to 325° and bake for 25 to 30 minutes more.

MARITOZZI

The Italian pasticceria (pastry shop) windows are a mouth-watering sight; the pastries and ice cream molds are all works of art.

Light roll dough (*Almond
  Coffee Cake*)
¼ *cup sugar*
⅓ cup candied orange peel

⅓ cup raisins
⅓ cup pignoli nuts
Yolk of 1 egg
Powdered sugar

Make a light roll dough and after the first rising mix in the sugar, candied peel, raisins, and nuts, one at a time. Form into little oval buns, brush with yolk of egg, sprinkle with powdered sugar, and let rise to double. Bake in a 375° oven for 12 to 15 minutes.

ALMOND COFFEE CAKE

Dough:

1 envelope dry yeast
¼ cup lukewarm water
1 tablespoon sugar
1 cup milk, scalded
¼ cup butter
2 teaspoons almond extract
1 large egg
½ cup sugar
1½ teaspoons salt
3 to 3½ cups sifted flour

⅓ to ½ cup melted butter
½ cup sugar
2 or 3 tablespoons cinnamon
¾ cup browned ground almonds

Put the yeast, lukewarm water, and 1 tablespoon of sugar in a little bowl, set it in a saucepan of warm water, almost cover it, and let the yeast become foamy. Scald the milk and add the butter; when it is melted and lukewarm add the almond extract. Beat 1 egg, add ½ cup sugar and the salt and beat until thick, then combine with the yeast and milk mixtures. Sift the flour into a large mixing bowl, then stir in the liquid mixture and beat until the dough is elastic. Add the rest of the flour if necessary to make a light, rather firm dough. Set the bowl in a dishpan of rather warm water, cover with a tea towel and let the dough rise. When it has risen, beat it down and let it rise again. When it has risen again pinch off pieces of dough and make balls. Roll them in melted butter, then in mixed sugar and cinnamon. Drop these on the bottom of a greased tube pan. Over each layer sprinkle some ground almonds. If there are 3 layers of balls use one-third of the nuts over each layer. Continue until all the dough is used. You may need more butter and mixed cinnamon and sugar. Let this rise again, setting the pan in the dishpan of warm water and covering with the tea towel. When it is risen and very light put it in a cold oven. Turn the heat to 400° for 12 minutes, then down to 375° and bake 15 minutes, then to 325° for 12 or 15 minutes more. After it has been out of the oven 5 minutes, loosen the cake from the sides and turn it on to a bread board. This dough also makes fine bread or rolls.

BABKA

½ cup butter
½ cup heavy cream
1 envelope of yeast
3 tablespoons lukewarm water
2 tablespoons sugar
½ cup sugar

6 egg yolks, beaten
2 cups flour
1 teaspoon vanilla
6 egg whites, beaten
Garnish: Powdered sugar

Put the butter and cream in a saucepan and heat just enough to melt the butter. Let the yeast stand with the lukewarm water and 2 tablespoons of sugar in an almost covered bowl set in a saucepan of quite warm water, until it is foamy. Stir the sugar and beaten egg yolks into the melted butter and cream. Combine the yeast and cream mixtures and stir into the flour, a little at a time. Add the vanilla and beat the batter hard. Beat the egg whites until stiff and add them to the batter. Grease and sprinkle with sugar the bottom and sides of a tube pan 9 inches across and 4 inches deep. Pour in the mixture, set the pan in a dishpan of warm water, cover with a tea towel and let it rise for 1 hour; it should rise to the top of the pan. Put it in a 375° oven for 15 minutes; turn down the heat to 325° and bake 20 minutes more. Let it stand 3 minutes, then loosen the sides with a slender sharp knife. Turn the pan upside down on a serving plate and the loaf will drop out. Sprinkle the top with powdered sugar. It is served warm or at room temperature.

BRIOCHE

1 envelope yeast
1 teaspoon sugar
3 tablespoons warm water
3 cups flour
¾ cup soft butter

2 tablespoons sugar
¼ cup milk
6 large eggs
Beaten egg yolk and milk

Put the yeast in a bowl, sprinkle with 1 teaspoon sugar, and add the luke-warm water. When the yeast becomes frothy, mix with 1 cup of the flour and put it in a warm place to rise 1 hour. Meanwhile have the butter softening at room temperature. Sift 2 cups flour and 2 tablespoons sugar together and beat in the butter, milk and 1 egg. Beat very hard. Add the rest of the eggs, one at a time, beating very hard after each egg is added. Beat in the yeast mixture very well. Cover the dough with a towel and let it rest 1 hour, then beat down, cover well, and refrigerate overnight. Three hours before using remove it from the refrigerator, let stand 1 hour, and then beat with a wooden spoon. Let rest ½ hour. Put the dough in greased fluted forms or iron popover forms. Some of the dough may be put in greased round fireproof bowls. Brush with egg mixed with a little water or milk. Let rise in a warm place 20 to 30 minutes. Preheat the oven to 400° and bake 10 to 15 minutes for the small forms and a little longer for the larger. This makes 12 to 20 small forms and less if larger ones are baked. As butter and eggs are the main ingredients they must be the best and freshest. The brioche are light as a feather and may be served hot with butter. They are good cold or may be reheated in an open paper bag in a 375° oven 2 or 3 minutes.

CROISSANTS

1 envelope yeast
⅓ cup lukewarm water
1½ tablespoons sugar
2 tablespoons olive oil
1 teaspoon salt

2¼ cups sifted flour
¾ cup lukewarm milk
1¼ cups sweet butter
Beaten egg and milk

Put the yeast, lukewarm water, and sugar in a bowl in a warm place to dissolve. Sift the flour with the salt into a large mixing bowl. Add the olive oil to the yeast mixture, pour it over the flour, and mix well with a wooden spoon, adding a little warm milk. Add more milk to make a smooth dough. Stir with a kneading motion 4 or 5 minutes until it is elastic. Cover and let rise to double its bulk in a warm place. (The bowl may be set in a dishpan of warm (not hot) water, covering all with a tea towel.) Then beat down and roll out, spread with the butter, fold over one-third of the dough, lift the unfolded to the top of the folded third to make 3 layers, roll out, and fold again. Put the dough in the refrigerator, well covered, for 6 hours or overnight. When ready to use remove from the refrigerator and roll out, fold as before, roll out and fold, then let it rest 1 hour in a cold place. Then roll out in 3 parts, each ⅛-inch thick, in strips 4½ inches wide. Cut the strips into triangles, roll from the wide side so that the point is on the outside, and bend the ends into crescents. Brush with beaten egg yolk mixed with a little milk. Bake at 400° 10 minutes, turn the heat down to 350° for 10 minutes more or until the croissants are a light golden brown. They are served hot or may be reheated in an open paper bag in a hot oven 3 or 4 minutes.

FILLED CRESCENT ROLLS

2 envelopes yeast
2 tablespoons sugar
¼ cup lukewarm water
3 eggs, beaten
1¾ cups cold milk
6 cups flour
1½ cups sweet butter

Almond Filling:
 2 tablespoons butter
⅓ cup sugar
 1 teaspoon almond extract
 4 ounces almonds, ground
 1 beaten egg
Vanilla Cream Filling:
 1 egg yolk, beaten
 1 tablespoon flour
 2 tablespoons sugar
¾ cup scalded milk
 1 teaspoon vanilla

Dissolve the yeast with the sugar and water in a little bowl set in a saucepan of hot water, almost covered. Beat the eggs and add to the frothy yeast with the cold milk. Add the flour to make a soft dough. This dough is not kneaded and is handled as little as possible. Roll out the dough and spread with the softened butter. Fold over and roll out gently, repeat 3 more times so that the butter is mixed in well. Cover the dough well and refrigerate 4 or 5 hours or overnight. When ready to make the crescents, let the dough stand at room temperature 20 minutes. Roll out in thin strips 5 inches wide, using only part of the dough at a time. Cut in triangles, add a teaspoon of filling at the wide end, and roll up so the point is outside. Bend slightly into a crescent. Bake at 450° about 10 minutes. While hot brush with melted butter and dip in sugar. These are positively the most melting morsels I have ever eaten. The almond filling is made by creaming the butter and sugar and adding the other ingredients. For the vanilla cream filling beat the egg yolk, flour, and sugar together, then beat in the scalded milk. Cook until it thickens, then cool it and add the vanilla.

ENGLISH MUFFINS

1 envelope yeast	2 tablespoons butter
½ cup lukewarm water	1½ teaspoons salt
2 teaspoons sugar	3 cups flour
¾ cup milk, scalded	Cornmeal

Put the yeast in a small bowl with the lukewarm water and sugar. Set the bowl in a saucepan of quite warm water, partially cover, and let stand until the yeast is frothy. Scald the milk and add the butter; let this cool until lukewarm, then mix with the yeast. Sift the salt with the flour and stir in the liquid. Beat 2 or 3 minutes, then set the bowl in a dishpan of quite warm water, cover with a tea towel, and let rise until it doubles in bulk. Beat down and knead on a floured board 2 or 3 minutes, then roll out ½-inch thick. Cut in 3-inch rounds. Butter a cookie sheet and sprinkle lightly with cornmeal. Put the rounds on the sheet, cover with a towel, and let rise to double. Put them in a 400° oven and bake them 20 minutes, turning them 3 times while they are baking. If they are baking too fast turn the heat down to 375° or 350°. When they cool, split, toast, and butter them. Makes 9 or 10 muffins.

PIMENTO CORNBREAD

2 cups cornmeal	1 cup heavy sour cream
2 teaspoons baking powder	½ cup milk
1 teaspoon salt	½ cup diced red pimentos
1 teaspoon brown sugar	½ cup whole kernel sweet corn
2 eggs, beaten	

Mix the cornmeal with the dry ingredients. Beat the eggs until light, mix with the sour cream and stir into the dry ingredients. Add the milk. Drain the pimentoes and corn thoroughly, and lightly mix them in. Bake in a greased 11-by 9-inch pan 10 minutes at 375° and 15 minutes more at 325°. Serve hot with butter. This may be served with fish, instead of potatoes.

GOUGÈRE

1 cup milk
¼ cup butter
Salt and a dash of pepper
⅞ cup sifted flour
4 eggs

1 tablespoon heavy cream
⅓ cup shredded Swiss or Gruyère
cheese
2 tablespoons diced cheese

Heat the milk with the butter in a saucepan and add the salt and pepper. When the butter has melted, add the flour all at once and beat, over a low flame, until the dough is smooth and leaves the sides of the pan. This is like cream-puff dough. Remove from the heat and beat in the eggs, one at a time, then add the cream and ⅓ cup of cheese. Grease a 10-inch pie dish, spread the batter in it, and sprinkle the top with the diced cheese. Put it in a 375° oven. Bake for 5 minutes, then turn down to 350° and bake another 10 minutes, then to 325° for 20 minutes. Do not open the oven while the pastry is baking. This is a fine puffed-cheese pastry from Burgundy to serve for lunch or supper with perhaps a creamed shrimp dish. Serve it hot with butter. Serves 4 to 6.

PAIN PERDU

8 slices good white bread,
½ inch thick
2 eggs, beaten
⅓ cup milk
⅓ cup sour cream
1 teaspoon cinnamon or anise

2 or 3 tablespoons honey
¼ cup brandy, Madeira, or rum
Sweet butter
Garnish: Powdered sugar, honey,
or syrup

Beat the eggs until light and add all the other ingredients except the butter. Soak the bread in the mixture on both sides until it is well saturated but not until it breaks. If the bread absorbs a lot of the mixture, another egg beaten with some sour cream may be needed. Fry the bread on both sides in a generous amount of hot butter. A little of the mixture spooned over the bread while it is frying may be a good idea. Serve hot.

SOUR CREAM CORNBREAD

1 cup cornmeal
¾ cup white flour
2½ teaspoons baking powder
1 teaspoon salt
3 tablespoons light brown sugar

¼ cup milk
2 tablespoons melted butter
2 eggs, beaten
1 cup heavy sour cream

Mix the dry ingredients and combine with the liquids. Bake in a greased 7½- by 11-inch pan 10 minutes at 375°, then turn heat down to 325° and bake 12 minutes more.

OAT PONES

1 cup oatmeal flour
¾ teaspoon salt
1½ teaspoons baking powder
¼ teaspoon soda

3 tablespoons melted butter
1 egg, beaten
¼ cup buttermilk, more or less
Butter or ham fat

Mix the dry ingredients together. Beat the butter and egg together and stir into the dry mixture with the buttermilk. This should be a light batter but thick enough not to spread. Make 4 large cakes of the batter. Put a good quantity of butter or good fat in a big skillet, cover tightly, and fry slowly 12 minutes. Turn the cakes over and in less than a minute they will be done. Serve with butter. They are very light.

CORNMEAL MUNKS

1 cup waterground cornmeal
½ cup boiling water
¾ teaspoon salt
1 teaspoon baking powder

1 teaspoon brown sugar or honey
2 eggs, beaten
⅓ cup sour cream (about)
Butter or oil for frying

Put the cornmeal in a bowl, pour the boiling water over it, and mix. Mix the salt, baking powder, sugar or honey with the eggs and beat until light, then combine with the cornmeal. Mix in enough sour cream to make a thick but light batter. Put 2 teaspoons of butter in each munk mold and fill with batter to the top. Fry over a medium flame, turn once, using two pointed knives, and cook until the underside is brown. They are delicious served hot with butter. Makes 10 or 11 munks.

RICE DUMPLINGS
(for Chicken or Lamb Stew)

1¼ cups cooked brown rice
⅔ cup brown rice flour
2 teaspoons baking powder
1 tablespoon brown sugar
¾ teaspoon salt

1 egg, beaten
¼ cup milk
1 tablespoon melted butter or oil
Chopped dill or mint (for lamb;
optional)

Mix all the ingredients together to make quite a solid but not heavy dough. For lamb stew 1 or 2 tablespoons of chopped fresh mint or dill may be stirred into the dough. Form into balls and roll in a little rice flour, then drop on top of the simmering stew, cover it tightly, and simmer for 12 minutes. Lift the dumplings onto a hot platter and surround with stew. Serves 4 to 6.

GREEN CORN PANCAKES

2 cups corn cut from ears
1 cup milk
2 tablespoons melted butter
2 egg yolks, beaten

½ cup flour
1 teaspoon baking powder
1 teaspoon salt
2 egg whites, beaten

You will need about 3 ears of corn. Bring them to the boil and remove from the water. Score the kernels and cut from the ears. Add the milk, melted butter, and egg yolks. Sift the dry ingredients and add to the corn mixture. Fold in the stiffly beaten whites last. Fry on a well-buttered griddle. Serve with maple syrup.

BROWN RICE PANCAKES

1 cup cooked brown rice
2 cups milk
1 cup wholewheat flour
1½ teaspoons baking powder
½ teaspoon salt
3 tablespoons light brown sugar

¼ cup sour cream or 2 tablespoons
   melted butter
2 egg yolks
2 egg whites, beaten
Butter and oil

Soak the cooked rice in the milk about 2 hours. Mix all the dry ingredients and add them to the rice and milk, then add the sour cream or melted butter and the egg yolks. Fold in the beaten whites last. Fry in mixed butter and oil on a hot griddle. This makes 18 or 20 wonderful pancakes. The recipe may be cut in half. If the batter is too thick for your taste, thin it with a little milk. Serve with maple syrup, honey, or thinned damson or apricot jam.

POTATO SCONES

1¼ cups seasoned mashed potatoes
½ cup flour
½ teaspoon salt

1½ teaspoons baking powder
1 egg, beaten
¼ cup buttermilk

Mix the potatoes with the sifted dry ingredients. Beat the egg and add the buttermilk to it. Blend the two mixtures together and pat the batter ¾ inch thick in a greased and floured pie plate. If the mashed potatoes (which may be leftover) are very thick, a little more buttermilk may have to be added. Cut almost through in 6 pie-shaped pieces. Bake at 400° for 8 minutes, then turn down the heat to 350° for 4 minutes more. Serve hot with butter. This serves 3 or 4.

SKILLET BREAD

1¼ cups mixed flours: wholewheat, oat flour, rye,
semolina, cornmeal, buck-
wheat
¾ teaspoon salt
3 teaspoons baking powder

2 eggs, beaten
½ cup heavy sour cream
2¼ cups milk
1 tablespoon brown sugar
½ teaspoon cinnamon and 1
teaspoon anise seeds

You may use any mixture of flours you like. Using ½ cup of buckwheat with a mixture of the others is very good, especially with the specified seasonings. You may use other seasonings you may prefer. Put the unsifted flours in a mixing bowl and stir in the salt and baking powder. In another bowl beat the eggs until light, then beat in the sour cream, milk, sugar, and seasonings. Stir into the flours and empty into a 10-inch well-greased iron skillet. Bake at 375° 15 minutes, then at 325° 15 minutes more. Serve hot with plenty of butter. This should be a little custardy inside.

SOUR CREAM PANCAKES

1 cup flour
½ teaspoon salt
½ teaspoon baking powder
1 teaspoon sugar
4 egg yolks, beaten

1 cup heavy sour cream
4 egg whites, beaten
Garnish: Fresh raspberries and
cream

These are very light and delicate, and must not be piled in stacks after they are fried. Combine the dry ingredients. Beat the egg yolks and add the sour cream. Mix into the dry ingredients and fold in the stiffly beaten whites last. Fry the cakes in a little butter. They may be served as dessert with fruit sauce or with honey or syrup.

COTTAGE CHEESE PANCAKES

½ cup cottage cheese
½ cup sour cream
2 large egg yolks
1 tablespoon honey or light brown
sugar
½ cup flour

1 teaspoon baking powder
½ teaspoon salt
¼ teaspoon nutmeg
2 egg whites, beaten
Fat for frying

Mix the cheese, cream, egg yolks, honey or sugar in a bowl. Sift all the dry ingredients and add them to the cheese mixture. Beat the egg whites until stiff and fold them in. Fry in quite a quantity of fat on a hot griddle—unless plenty of fat is used they will stick. This makes 11 or 12 very delicate pancakes. They may be served with maple syrup. This serves 2 or 3 depending on the rest of the menu.

Desserts

FRUIT for dessert is popular and is becoming more so. But care must be taken in serving it, so that all your guests, even those with a sweet tooth, will be satisfied. Fruit compôtes, well made and rich, are not the only way to serve fruit. When fruit is served fresh, it must be at the height of the season and it must be paired with the proper wine, and sometimes with cheese. I have given a molded dessert cheese for this purpose, which is a change from the seasoned creamy Brie or other fine cheeses from home and abroad. Cheese must always be removed from a cold place at least 2 hours before serving. The English have a fine traditional winter dessert of nuts and good port or Madeira, which might be augmented with dates, figs, or raisins. Fresh grapes go with most dessert wines. Raspberries and other berries may be served with a flowery white Anjou. For special occasions (since it is always expensive), serve Château Yquem with peaches, apricots, and nectarines. If really good apples and Comice or Anjou pears are obtainable, serve them with cheese, sherry, or port. Cheese spread on a slice of apple or pear outshines the same cheese on a cracker. Reserve the citrus fruits for breakfast or lunch; or for cooked desserts. When serving fresh pineapple, you might even omit wine; you will find it delicious well moistened with Marasquin.

Because our land provides such bounty we have become creatures of change; thus we want on occasion something other than fruit for dessert; something rich and baked, hot or cold, or molded. Sometimes we crave ice cream. In June we must have cherry pie at least once or twice. The birds like cherries too, so the season is apt to be short.

Hot puddings or beautiful puffed soufflés are always a compliment to the guest, and the family appreciates them too. I've never met anyone who felt he had to "sell" homemade ice cream. Rapture is a word for it, but we can't have heaven every day, nor can we wish for it or deserve it. There is a time and place for everything—as becomes quite evident in a section on desserts.

Les Soufflés

SOUFFLÉ AU COCKTAIL DE LIQUEURS
Maurice Cazalis, Chartres

This lovely soufflé to serve 8 was another dish demonstrated for The Friends of Chartres in Chichester, England, by M. Cazalis.

Crème Patissière:

2 cups milk, or half milk and half light cream
1 vanilla bean
¾ cup sifted flour
1 cup sugar
6 egg yolks, beaten
1 cocktail glass (½ cup) mixed: cognac, gin, Chartreuse, Grand Marnier, cherry brandy, Benedictine, etc.

1 cup diced glacé fruits: cherries, pineapple, angelica, etc.
8 egg whites, beaten
Few grains salt
Butter
Sugar
Powdered sugar

For the *Crème Patissière*, bring the milk or half milk and half light cream to the boil with the vanilla bean, cut in half. Sift the flour and sugar together and mix with the thickly beaten egg yolks. Remove the vanilla bean and slowly pour the boiling milk into the egg mixture. When it is mixed, simmer over boiling water, stirring continuously until thickened. Pour into a bowl. Butter 8 individual soufflé molds, and sprinkle the sides and bottom with sugar, turn upside down and tap to remove excess sugar. Beat the egg whites stiff with the few grains of salt. Mix the liqueurs and diced fruits into the crème patissière. Twenty-five minutes before serving mix one-fourth of the egg whites into the crème, then lightly fold in the rest of the whites. Fill the molds to within 1 inch of the top and put in a 375° oven for 10 minutes, then turn down the heat to 325° and bake about 10 minutes more. Sprinkle the tops liberally with powdered sugar and serve immediately.

DIANA'S MOCHA SOUFFLÉ

When we visit London we usually visit Cambridge and our friends there give us a gay luncheon party. Usually I manage to persuade the girls to part with a special dish or two. This is one of the loveliest soufflées imaginable and very easy to make.

6 egg whites	Sauce:
1⅛ cups of sugar	1 cup heavy cream
1½ teaspoons powdered coffee	4 egg yolks, beaten
1 teaspoon cocoa	1 teaspoon vanilla
4 or 5 drops mocha extract	No sugar

Use large eggs. Make the sauce first so it may be served at room temperature. Scald the heavy cream and pour it over the beaten egg yolks; return to the flame a moment, then let cool. Add the vanilla. Serve in a sauceboat with the hot soufflé. The soufflé is sweet and needs no sugar in the sauce. For the soufflé, beat the egg whites until stiff. Sift the sugar with the coffee and cocoa. Add it very slowly to the whites and beat to a stiff meringue. Add the mocha extract. Butter and sugar a 7½-inch soufflé dish, pour in the egg-white mixture and set the dish in a pan with a little hot water. Bake 15 minutes at 375°, then 10 or 15 minutes more at 325°. Serves 6.

SOUFFLÉ AU RHUM

3 tablespoons dark rum	8 egg yolks, beaten
⅓ cup mixed glacé fruits	¼ cup finely crushed macaroons
3 teaspoons cornstarch	2 teaspoons vanilla extract
½ cup sugar	8 egg whites, beaten
1 cup light cream	

Soak the rum and sliced fruits an hour before making the soufflé. Put the cornstarch in the top of the double boiler, mix with the sugar, and slowly blend in the cream until the mixture is smooth. Cook over simmering water until it thickens, then pour it slowly over the beaten egg yolks. Return to the simmering water and cook until it is thick. Let it cool a little. Before baking the soufflé, add the fruits and rum, macaroons, and vanilla. Beat the egg whites until stiff and stir one-fourth of them into the custard, then lightly fold in the rest of the whites. Empty into a buttered and sugared 7½-inch soufflé dish, set the dish in a pan of hot water, and bake 10 minutes at 375°, then reduce the heat to 325° and bake 18 to 20 minutes more. Serves 6 or 7. The fruits used may be citron, currants, angelica, pineapple, cherries, in any combination.

COLD CARAMEL SOUFFLÉ

1 cup sugar
⅓ cup boiling water
6 egg whites, beaten

Garnish:
Fresh peach halves, or guava shells in syrup, or mangos marinated in rum

Caramelize the sugar in an iron skillet. Cook it over a good flame until it is very dark brown, then turn off the flame and add ⅓ cup of boiling water. Stir over a low flame until it is a very heavy syrup. Have the egg whites beaten very stiff and pour the boiling syrup over them. Beat until well blended, then pour into an 8-inch melon mold to chill. To unmold put a platter over the mold and give it a quick flip; caramel syrup collects at the bottom of the mold and is served around it on the platter. Garnish the platter with skinned peach halves, or drained guava shells which come canned in heavy syrup, or canned mangos. If mangos are used, drain them and marinate them 2 hours in 2 or 3 tablespoons of dark **rum**. Put the mangos around the mold and the rum juice over the top. Serves 6. To serve 8, use 1¼ cups of sugar and 8 egg whites.

LIQUEUR SOUFFLÉ
(GRAND MARNIER, CURAÇAO, OR ANISETTE)

3 tablespoons butter
3 teaspoons flour
4 tablespoons sugar
1 cup light cream

6 egg yolks, beaten
¼ cup liqueur
6 egg whites, beaten

Melt the butter in the top of the double boiler and blend in the flour, then the sugar, and add the light cream. Cook over simmering water until the mixture is thick and smooth, then pour it slowly over the beaten egg yolks. Then cook over the simmering water again and cook until the custard is thick. Let it cool a little, then add the liqueur. This may be done an hour before baking the soufflé. Beat the egg whites until stiff and stir one-fourth of them, into the custard, then lightly fold in the rest. Empty into a buttered, sugared 7½-inch soufflé dish set in a pan of hot water. Bake 10 minutes at 375°, then turn down the heat to 325° and bake about 18 minutes more. Serves 4 or 5. Serve with *Liqueur Sauce* (recipe follows).

LIQUEUR SAUCE

⅓ cup water
¼ cup sugar
1 tablespoon grated orange rind
1 tablespoon cornstarch

1 cup light cream
3 tablespoons Grand Marnier,
    Curaçao, or Anisette

Simmer the water, sugar, and orange rind very gently for 10 minutes. It should be reduced to half. Blend in the cornstarch and mix with the cream. Cook until it thickens, then let it cool. When ready to serve add the liqueur; if it is too thick, use a little more liqueur. Pass the sauce in a sauceboat.

ROSE'S DOLCI AMARETTI

1 cup sugar
⅓ cup boiling water
4 ounces macaroons, crumbed
6 egg whites, beaten
1 teaspoon almond extract

Sauce:
1 cup heavy cream
2 tablespoons light brown
    sugar
4 egg yolks
1 teaspoon almond extract
1 teaspoon vanilla extract

Caramelize 1 cup of sugar in a heavy skillet by cooking it until it is very dark brown. Turn off the flame and add ⅓ cup boiling water. Cook a moment, then empty the caramel into an 8-inch aluminum baking dish. Tip it so the syrup runs over the sides and bottom. If it doesn't stick to the sides let it cook a moment over the flame. Let it chill and harden. Crumble the macaroons very fine. Beat the egg whites until stiff, then add the crumbs and almond extract. Fill the caramelized pan with the mixture. Set the pan in a pan of hot water and bake at 375° for 10 minutes, then turn down to 350° for 10 minutes and to 325° for 70 minutes more. To make the sauce, scald the cream with the sugar and pour it over the beaten egg yolks. Cook over a gentle flame just a moment. It thickens as it cools. When cool add the extracts. When the pudding is done, let it stand a minute, loosen the sides a little, cover with a round serving plate and quickly invert it. It will be covered with caramel. Serve the sauce in a sauceboat. Serves 6.

SOUFFLÉ GRAND MARNIER
(or Marasquin, Benedictine, or Curaçao)

5 egg yolks, beaten
6 tablespoons sugar
⅓ cup liqueur

7 egg whites, beaten
⅛ teaspoon cream of tartar

Use large eggs. Put the egg yolks in the top of a double boiler and beat them until thick. Gradually add the sugar and when the mixture is creamy put it over simmering water and continue beating until it begins to cook, then slowly add the liqueur and cook to a custard almost as thick as zabaione. Empty the hot water from the lower part of the boiler, fill it with cold water, and beat the mixture until it cools a little. Heat the oven to 400°. Beat the egg whites with the cream of tartar until they stand in peaks. Stir into the custard one-fourth of the egg whites, then lightly fold in the rest. Butter a 7-inch soufflé dish (sides and bottom) and sprinkle with sugar. Pour the mixture into it and set it in a pan of hot water. Bake the soufflé at 400° for 4 minutes, then turn down the heat to 350° and bake about 7 minutes more. It will puff up 3 inches above the top of the dish. This is gossamer light compared to soufflés made with a milk and flour base. It serves 4. To serve 6, use 8 yolks, ⅔ cup of sugar, ½ cup of liqueur, a pinch more cream of tartar, and 10 egg whites. Bake 5 minutes at 400° and 10 to 12 minutes at 350°.

COCONUT SOUFFLÉ

1 cup fresh grated coconut, or 1
    3½-ounce can moist coconut
3 teaspoons cornstarch
1 cup light cream
¼ cup light brown sugar

¼ cup sweet butter
5 egg yolks, beaten
1 teaspoon each vanilla and
    almond extract
5 egg whites, beaten

Blend the cornstarch gradually with the cream and add the sugar. Cook until it thickens, then turn off the heat and add the butter. Add the beaten egg yolks and let it cook a moment. Stir in the coconut and the extracts. Beat the egg whites until stiff and stir in one-fourth of them, then lightly fold the rest into the custard. Pour into a greased 8½-inch soufflé dish and put it into a 375° oven. Bake 8 minutes, then turn down the heat to 325° and bake 10 minutes more. It must be moist inside. Serves 4. If you use canned coconut, which is inclined to dryness, a fruit sauce is recommended. A little thinned jam or marmalade (¼ cup) mixed with ½ cup of whipped cream makes a good one. If you are using fresh coconut, stir a little of it into the sauce.

FRUIT EGG-WHITE SOUFFLÉ

½ cup glacé fruits: cherries, pine-
    apple, angelica, citron, dates,
    etc.
½ cup imported sherry
1 tablespoon sieved apricot jam

6 egg whites (¾ cup)
6 tablespoons sugar
½ cup chopped browned almonds
1 teaspoon almond extract

Slice the fruit and soak it in the sherry 2 or 3 hours. When you are ready
to make the soufflé, mix the fruits and sherry with the jam. Beat the egg
whites until they are stiff and then add the sugar gradually. Mix one-fourth
of the meringue with the fruits and sherry and add the nuts and extract.
Lightly fold the rest of the meringue into the mixture. Butter and sugar
a 7½-inch soufflé dish, put in the mixture, and set the dish in a pan with
a little hot water. Bake 15 minutes at 375° and another 15 minutes at 325°.
Serve with cream for those who want it. Serves 4. This is a chance to use
those accumulated egg whites.

LEMON SOUFFLÉ

Grated rind of 2 large lemons
2 teaspoons cornstarch
Juice of the lemons plus water to
    make 1 cup liquid

1 cup sugar
1 tablespoon sweet butter
6 egg yolks, beaten
6 egg whites, beaten

Grate the lemon rind into the top of a double boiler over simmering water.
Add the cornstarch and the liquid slowly, blending it smooth with a rubber spatula. Do not sieve the juice but remove the seeds with a teaspoon.
Add the sugar and butter and cook until the mixture thickens. Pour it
slowly over the beaten egg yolks. Return the pan to the simmering water
and cook until the sauce thickens, stirring continuously. This may be made
an hour or so before baking. Butter and sugar a 7½-inch soufflé dish. Beat
the egg whites until stiff and stir one-fourth of them into the custard sauce,
then lightly fold in the rest of the whites. Empty into the soufflé dish, set
it in a pan with 1 cup of hot water, and put it into a 375° oven. Bake 10
minutes, then reduce the heat to 325° and bake 20 to 25 minutes more,
until the soufflé has puffed above the dish. Serves 4 or 5. Individual soufflés are always popular. To fill six 4½-inch soufflé dishes use 3 lemons, 1½
cups liquid (lemon juice and water), 3 teaspoons cornstarch, 2 tablespoons
butter, and 9 eggs. Bake the soufflés 5 minutes at 375° and 18 or 20 minutes at 325°. This may be broken down to one-third to serve two, allowing
3 eggs, etc.

ORANGE SOUFFLÉ

Grated rind 2 large navel oranges
2 teaspoons cornstarch
Juice of 1 lemon plus orange
    juice to make 1 cup

¾ cup sugar
2 tablespoons sweet butter
6 egg yolks, beaten
6 egg whites, beaten

Follow the directions for *Lemon Soufflé*. Serves 4 or 5. This too is fine for individual soufflés. Pass around a bottle of one of the orange liqueurs; a teaspoon or two is a marvelous addition to the soufflé.

RASPBERRY OR STRAWBERRY SOUFFLÉ

1 10-ounce package of frozen
    berries
2 or 3 tablespoons lime juice
½ cup heavy cream
2½ tablespoons cornstarch
¼ cup instant superfine sugar
4 large egg yolks, beaten

1½ teaspoons almond extract
1 teaspoon rose extract
6 large egg whites, beaten
Garnish:
    Powdered sugar
    Maraschino liqueur

Thaw the berries and purée them in an electric blender or mash them through a sieve. Raspberries require an extra fine sieving to remove their seeds. Add the lime juice (which is necessary, as the berries have been sweetened). There should be 1 full cup of purée. Blend the cream and cornstarch in the top of the double boiler, add the sugar, and cook over simmering water until the mixture begins to thicken, then add the egg yolks. When it is thick add the purée and cook about 2 minutes until it thickens again. Let it cool and add the extracts. Grease and sugar a 7½-inch soufflé dish. When ready to bake the soufflé, beat the egg whites until stiff and mix one-fourth of them into the berry custard, then fold in the rest. Empty into the soufflé dish, set it in a pan of hot water, and bake at 400° for 5 minutes, then turn down the heat to 325° and bake 25 to 28 minutes more. The soufflé will be puffed above the dish. Sprinkle the top with powdered sugar and serve immediately. Pass a bottle of Maraschino liqueur so each guest may spoon a little over this fragrant soufflé. Serves 6. If you wish to use fresh berries, mash 2 cups of them (or enough to make a cup of purée) through a sieve. Use only 1 tablespoon of lime juice, and increase the sugar to ½ cup.

SOUFFLÉ GLACÉ AU KIRSCH
Maxim's, Paris

12 egg yolks, beaten thick
1⅓ cups sugar
¼ cup water
½ cup fine old Kirsch

1 tablespoon vanilla
1¾ to 2 cups heavy cream, whipped
3 tablespoons *Praliné Powder* (optional)

This elegant dish is served at Maxim's in grand style. The soufflé dish has a buttered collar fastened around it, for the mixture more than fills the dish. Before serving, the collar is removed and the "hot" puffed soufflé is brought to the table set on a bowl of ice. Beat the egg yolks in the top of the double boiler until thick. Boil the sugar and water until it threads from the spoon. Pour this heavy syrup little by little into the egg yolks, beating continuously over simmering water. When it thickens, expands in volume and ribbons like a genoise, remove from the heat and beat it until it is cool. Add the Kirsch, vanilla, and thickly whipped cream. Empty into the prepared soufflé dish and refrigerate at least 4 hours. Before serving, remove the collar. Sprinkle the top with the praliné powder if you like. This will serve 10. Maxim's uses 16 egg yolks, nearly 3 cups of cream, and other ingredients in proportion to serve 16.

Puddings, Molds & Crêpes

BLACKBERRY FLUMMERY

1 quart blackberries
¼ cup light corn syrup
¼ cup honey
¼ cup red wine
2 tablespoons cornstarch

3 tablespoons Kirsch
1 cup heavy cream, whipped
1 jigger blackberry brandy or Cherry Heering
2 tablespoons powdered sugar

Put the blackberries in a saucepan with the syrup, honey, and wine. Simmer gently 8 minutes. Blend the cornstarch with the Kirsch, add to the blackberries, and cook until thickened. Chill in a shallow bowl. Whip the cream and add the brandy or cherry liqueur and the sugar. Pile on top of the blackberry sauce just in the center. Serves 6.

FRUIT BREAD PUDDING

8 ounces homemade-type bread
　　or soft egg rolls
1 cup milk
1 cup light cream
4 large eggs
⅓ cup light brown sugar
3 tablespoons dark rum

Caramel:
　　1 cup white sugar
　　⅓ cup boiling water
Choice of fruit:
　　1¼ cups fresh pitted cherries
　　　　or berries
　　or ¾ cup mixed glacé fruits
　　or 1 cup sliced stewed dried
　　　　apricots
3 tablespoons whisky

This pudding may be made with many different kinds of fruit; you may experiment with your own favorite. It is one of the loveliest of party desserts. The bread mixture must stand in the pan at least 3 hours before baking. Caramelize an 8-inch, 3-inch-deep aluminum baking pan. Cook 1 cup white sugar in a heavy skillet until dark brown. Turn off the heat. Add the boiling water, then cook it until it is a heavy syrup. Pour it into the baking pan and tip it in all directions so it is well covered. If the syrup is too thin to stay on the sides, put the pan over the flame a moment. When the caramel is hard, fill with the bread mixture. Only the best firm bread is suitable for this. Remove the crust from 8 or 9 slices of bread and cut in the tiniest cubes, almost crumbs (or crumble the rolls), then put one-fourth of it in the mold and cover with one-fourth of the chosen fruit. Repeat this until all fruit and bread are used, ending with a layer of bread. Beat the milk, cream, eggs, sugar, and rum together and pour over the bread. The liquid should come almost to the top; add ¼ cup of light cream if necessary. Let this stand 3 hours. An hour before serving, set the mold in a pan with a little hot water and bake at 325° 1 hour. Turn upside down on a serving plate. Put the whisky in the pan and melt the caramel over the flame, then scrape it over the pudding.

VARIATION. Orange bread pudding. Use 1 cup of orange juice instead of the milk, ⅔ cup of sliced sugared orange peel for the fruit, and add 2 tablespoons of grated orange rind. Serves 8.

STEAMED ALMOND PUDDING

½ cup sugar
1 cup hot milk
3 tablespoons sweet butter
1 tablespoon flour
4 egg yolks
¾ cup (4 ounces) almonds, ground

1 teaspoon vanilla extract
1 teaspoon almond extract
5 egg whites, beaten
Garnish:
    Caramel Sauce, or *Chocolate Sauce*, or *Sabayon Sauce*

This light almond dessert deserves a good sauce. The first part may be made ahead of time and put together with the beaten egg whites a little over an hour before serving. Put the sugar in an iron skillet over a good flame and when it is a medium dark brown and all melted, turn off the flame and add the boiling milk. Cook until the caramel is well mixed with the milk. Add the butter. Sift the flour and beat a scant measuring tablespoon of it with the egg yolks. Four ounces of almonds equals ¾ cup and when ground measures 1 cup. Brown the almonds a little before grinding to get a richer flavor. Combine the hot milk mixture with the egg yolks and ground almonds. When it is cool add the extracts. Grease and sugar an 8-inch melon mold, including the cover. Beat the egg whites until stiff and mix one-fourth of them into the custard, then lightly fold the rest in and empty the custard into the mold. It should come within an inch of the top of the mold to allow for expansion. Cover tightly, put the mold into a big kettle, and pour in boiling water halfway up the mold. Cover the kettle and boil over a medium flame for 1 hour. Unmold on a platter and serve with one of the sauces suggested. Hazelnuts, pecans, or black walnuts may be used instead of almonds. Serves 8.

APPLE CHARLOTTE

5 pounds tart apples
2 tablespoons sweet butter
3 tablespoons lime or lemon
    juice
6 slices homemade-type bread
    Melted sweet butter
½ cup brown sugar
½ cup sieved damson or apricot
    jam

3 tablespoons rum or Kirsch or
    2 tablespoons vanilla
Sauce:
    1 cup heavy cream, whipped
    ½ cup sieved apricot or
        damson jam
    3 tablespoons dark rum

Peel, core and shred the apples and put them in an iron roaster. Dot with
butter and sprinkle with the juice. Cover and bake at 375° for 35 to 40
minutes. Meanwhile remove the crusts from the bread and cut the slices
in 2-inch strips. Dip the strips in melted butter and line sides and bottom
of a 4-inch-deep, 7-inch-across charlotte mold. When the apples are done,
mash them with the sugar, jam, and the rum, Kirsch, or vanilla. Pour the
mixture into the bread-lined mold and bake it at 400° for 10 minutes, then
at 350° 30 minutes more. If the center seems soft, bake it 15 minutes more.
When it comes from the oven let it stand 20 minutes before unmolding.
Run a knife around the sides of the mold to loosen it, put a serving dish
over it, and reverse it. Blend the ingredients for the sauce and spread it
on the top and sides of the mold. It may be served either partially warm or
cold. In either case spread the sauce on the charlotte just before serving.
Serves 8.

SOUFFLÉ PUFF CAKE

⅓ cup butter
1 cup milk
⅔ cup sifted flour
3 egg yolks

⅓ cup sugar
1 teaspoon vanilla
6 egg whites, beaten
Sauce: *Lemon Sauce* or *Fruit Sauce*

Make a pâte choux (cream-puff paste) by heating the butter and milk in
a sauce pan until the butter melts. Dump in the flour all at once and beat
hard until the paste is smooth and leaves the sides of the pan. Over very
low heat beat in the egg yolks, one at a time, turn off the heat, and beat
in the sugar and vanilla. This may be mixed beforehand. Beat the egg
whites until stiff, mix in one-fourth of them, stir until the mixture is
smooth and light, then lightly fold in the rest of the whites. Butter and
sugar the sides and bottom of an 8-inch ring mold and put in the batter.
Set the mold in a pan of hot water and put it in a 375° oven. Bake 8
minutes, then turn down to 350° and bake 22 to 25 minutes more. Let
stand a minute, then unmold on a larger round serving plate. Serve hot
with a sauce served in a sauceboat. Serves 6 or 8. This is feathery light with
an unusual texture.

LEMON SAUCE

2 large lemons
2 cups water
2 tablespoons cornstarch
3 tablespoons orange or grapefruit
    juice

1½ cups white sugar
2 tablespoons butter

Grate the rind of the lemons into a saucepan. Remove the ends of the lemons and discard. Slice the lemons paper thin with a very sharp knife, removing the seeds. Add the slices and 2 cups water to the rind and simmer over low heat for 20 minutes. Mix the cornstarch with the juice (or with water if juice is not at hand). Mix with the hot sauce. Add the sugar and butter and cook until it thickens and is clear. This is a fine sauce for hot cakes or cottage puddings.

APPLE SOUFFLÉ PUDDING

1 cup apple sauce
  Brown sugar and lemon juice
1 tablespoon cornstarch
3 egg yolks
4 egg whites
¼ cup light brown sugar

Sauce:
¼ cup raisins or chopped
    candied fruit
3 tablespoons dark rum
⅓ cup light brown sugar
⅓ cup water
1 tablespoon cornstarch
⅓ cup heavy cream

Marinate the rum and fruit an hour before making the pudding. Make a full cup of apple sauce, sweetening it with brown sugar and adding lemon juice if the apples aren't tart enough. Cool the applesauce, blend in the cornstarch, and mix in the beaten egg yolks. Put in 1 tablespoon of the rum marinade. Beat the egg whites until stiff, then add ¼ cup brown sugar and beat again. Mix one-fourth of the meringue with the apple mixture, then lightly fold in the rest of the meringue. Butter and sugar a 7½-inch soufflé dish and pour in the mixture. Set the dish in a pan with some hot water and bake 10 minutes at 375°, then about 25 minutes more at 350°. Meanwhile make the sauce. Simmer the brown sugar and water 5 minutes in a saucepan, blend the cornstarch with the cream, add it to the syrup, and cook until it thickens, then add the fruit and marinade. When the pudding is done, serve it immediately, accompanied by the sauce in a sauceboat. Serves 4 or 5. This sauce is good over cold rice pudding.

CHERRY PUDDING

⅓ cup butter
½ cup light brown sugar
2 tablespoons flour
1 cup light breadcrumbs
3 egg yolks
2 tablespoons Kirsch or cherry
   brandy
1 pound pitted cherries

½ teaspoon almond extract
5 egg whites, beaten
Sauce:
¾ cup cherry juice or syrup
1 tablespoon cornstarch
Brown sugar
1 teaspoon butter
1 jigger rum or Kirsch

If fresh cherries are used, pit them and boil for just 1 minute in ½ cup of water and ⅓ cup light brown sugar. Let stand until cool, drain, and use the syrup for the sauce. In the off season use a 1-pound can of good dark or red pitted cherries. Drain and add a little light brown sugar (to taste) to the juice. In either case add the Kirsch or cherry brandy to the drained cherries. For the pudding cream the butter with the sugar, add the flour, crumbs, and egg yolks. Lightly mix in the liqueur, cherries, and extract. Beat the egg whites until stiff and mix in one-fourth of them, then lightly fold in the rest. Put the mixture in an 8-inch greased pudding dish, set it in a pan of hot water, and bake at 375° for 10 minutes and at 325° about 25 minutes more. For the sauce, blend the cornstarch with the syrup, sweeten to taste, add the butter, and cook until it thickens. Add the rum or Kirsch and serve in a sauceboat. The pudding is served hot. Serves 5 or 6.

SOUR-CHERRY COBBLER

1 quart fresh sour cherries
1 cup light brown sugar
2½ tablespoons sifted flour
2 tablespoons butter

Dough:
1 cup sifted flour
¼ teaspoon salt
¾ teaspoon baking powder
¼ cup butter
¼ cup shortening
½ cup milk (or more)

Pit the cherries. Mix the sugar and flour together and toss through the cherries. Grease a shallow (2½-inch-deep) baking dish and put the cherries on the bottom. Put bits of butter over the top of cherries. To make the dough, sift the flour with the salt and baking powder, then cut in the butter and shortening with a pastry cutter. Add ½ cup of milk, or more if needed, to make a soft dough that may be dropped in tablespoons over the cherries. Bake in a 400° oven for 10 minutes, then reduce the heat to 325° for 10 or more minutes, until the crust is golden. Serves 4 or 5. Other berries and fruits in season may be used instead of cherries: strawberries, blackberries, raspberries, sliced peaches, or apricots, etc. Pass a pitcher of heavy cream or *Crème Fraîche*.

STEAMED CHERRY OR BLACKBERRY PUDDING

1½ cups sour pitted cherries
½ cup sweet butter
⅞ cup sugar
½ cup milk
2 cups cake flour, sifted, with 2
   teaspoons baking powder
4 large egg whites, beaten
3 tablespoons light brown sugar

Sauce:
1 cup sour pitted cherries
⅔ cup red or white wine
⅔ cup light corn syrup
⅓ cup light brown sugar
2 tablespoons sweet butter
¼ cup Kirsch or rum
2 tablespoons cornstarch

Grease an 8-inch melon mold and put ½ cup of the pitted cherries in the bottom of it. Cream the butter until soft, then add the sugar and mix until smooth and fluffy. Add the milk alternately with the flour sifted with the baking powder. Stir in 1 cup of cherries. Beat the egg whites until stiff, stir one-fourth of them into the batter, then lightly fold in the rest. Put 3 tablespoons brown sugar over the cherries in the mold, then add the batter. Grease the lid, cover the mold, set it in a big kettle, and add boiling water halfway up the mold. Cover the kettle and boil for 1½ hours. Loosen the sides of the pudding and turn it onto a platter. For the sauce, put 1 cup cherries in a saucepan with the wine, syrup, sugar, and butter and bring to a simmer. Blend the Kirsch or rum with the cornstarch and add to the cherry mixture. Boil until clear and serve the warm sauce in a tureen or sauceboat with the hot pudding. Serves 10. The quantities are the same for blackberries.

FRESH BLUE-PLUM PUDDING

22 small blue plums
¼ cup red wine
¼ cup light corn syrup
⅓ cup light brown sugar

Batter:
¼ cup butter
½ cup light brown sugar
1 egg, beaten
½ cup milk
2½ teaspoons baking powder
1½ cups sifted flour
1 teaspoon almond or
   vanilla extract

This is a pudding for late summer and fall, when blue plums are in the market. Clean and dry the plums; halve and pit them. Put them in a heavy pot with the wine, syrup, and brown sugar. Cook uncovered 3 or 4 minutes over a good flame. Butter a good-sized baking dish and put the plums and syrup on the bottom. For the batter, cream the butter and sugar until smooth. Beat the egg and add the milk. Sift the baking powder with the flour. Add the egg and milk alternately with the flour to the butter-sugar mixture. Add the extract. Cover the plums with the batter and bake at 350° about 35 minutes or until the cake part is done. Serve hot with cream. Serves 4 to 6.

RASPBERRY PUDDING

Cake:
 ½ cup light brown sugar
 2 tablespoons butter
 ½ cup milk
 1 cup sifted flour
 2 teaspoons baking powder

1 package frozen raspberries
Raspberry syrup and water to
 make a cup
Juice of 1 lime, or 3 or 4 tablespoons lemon juice
1 tablespoon butter

Put the raspberries in a sieve and let them thoroughly defrost. Drain and save the syrup. For the cake, cream the sugar and butter. Sift the flour with the baking powder, and add alternately with the milk. Grease a 7-inch baking dish, put in the batter, and distribute the berries over it. Measure the syrup from the berries and add enough water to make 1 cup. Add the juice, lime if possible; it gives a fragrance to the raspberries that lemon does not. Boil up the syrup, juice, and 1 tablespoon butter and pour it over the batter. Bake at 350° for 35 to 40 minutes. This is a most delicious pudding and is nice for winter when fresh berries are not in season. In summer 1½ cups of fresh raspberries may be used. Put them in a saucepan with ⅓ cup of light corn syrup, ¼ cup light brown sugar, and water (scant ½ cup) to fill 1 cup, and 1 tablespoon of butter. Boil up and pour over the batter. Strawberries, peaches and cherries and blackberries may be used instead of raspberries. More or less sugar is used depending on the sweetness of the fruit. Pass heavy cream or *Crème Fraîche*. Serves 4.

COTTAGE PUDDING WITH MARMALADE SAUCE

Pudding:
 ½ cup butter
 ¾ cup light brown sugar
 2 eggs, beaten
 ½ cup milk
 1½ cups flour
 2 teaspoons baking powder
 1 teaspoon vanilla
Powdered sugar

Marmalade Sauce:
 2 cups orange juice
 2 tablespoons cornstarch
 2 tablespoons butter
 ½ cup orange marmalade or
  grapefruit marmalade
 1 jigger Curaçao or Cointreau

Make the pudding by creaming the butter and sugar until very light. Add alternately the beaten eggs, milk, and flour that has been sifted with the baking powder. Add the vanilla. Grease and flour a fluted, tube gugelhupf pan, pour in the batter and bake at 350° for 25 minutes. When it is done, turn it out on a round chop plate, sprinkle with powdered sugar, and serve hot. Meanwhile make the sauce. Blend the cornstarch with a little of the orange juice, then add the rest of the juice and cook until it is translucent and thickens. Stir in the butter and marmalade. Just before serving, heat the sauce and add the liqueur. Serve separately in a bowl. Serves 6 or 8. It is a lovely dessert for a winter dinner.

STEAMED DATE PUDDING

This recipe and the next are two delicious steamed puddings, light enough to serve from the late fall through the holidays to early spring, because they are not loaded with suet. If this date pudding has a familiar ring, it is because I think it is too good to leave out of any book I write. The second one is fig with a lemon tang.

1 cup chopped dates
1 cup shredded raw carrots or
    peeled and shredded raw
    tart apple
1 cup shredded raw potato
1 cup light brown sugar
1 cup flour
1 teaspoon cinnamon
½ teaspoon clove

1 teaspoon vanilla
1 teaspoon soda mixed with 2
    tablespoons hot water
1 egg, plus 2 whites, beaten
2 tablespoons butter, melted
Jigger of whisky or rum for
    blazing

Put the dates in a large mixing bowl and add the carrots or apple and the potato. These are shredded on a disk shredder, not grated; it makes all the difference in the texture. Mix in the sugar. Sift the flour with the spices and add it and the vanilla and soda mixed with hot water. Beat the whole egg with the extra whites and stir them in. Grease an 8-inch melon mold and put in the batter. Melt the butter and pour it over the top. Cover the mold tightly and put it in a big kettle. Add boiling water halfway up the side of the mold, cover the kettle, and boil gently 2½ hours. Good timing is to put the pudding on to boil ½ hour before the guests are due—drinks, two courses, and then dessert. When ready to serve the pudding, uncover it and loosen the sides, then cover with an oval platter and turn it over and it will unmold. A jigger of whisky or rum may be poured over the top and the pudding brought to the table blazing. It will serve 10 or 12. Serve *Brandy Cream Sauce* in a sauceboat.

STEAMED FIG PUDDING

1 cup sliced soft figs
1 cup nuts (hazelnuts, almonds,
    pecans, black walnuts, or
    Brazil nuts), ground
1 cup soft breadcrumbs
4 ounces moist glacé lemon peel
    (or grapefruit peel), diced

¾ cup light brown sugar
1 teaspoon vanilla
3 tablespoons butter, melted
4 eggs, well beaten
Jigger of whisky or rum for
    blazing

Slice the figs quite fine into a large mixing bowl. Any of the specified nuts may be used or a mixture of nuts. Add them to the figs, with the breadcrumbs, the diced lemon peel (which comes in 4-ounce glass jars), the sugar, vanilla, melted butter, and well-beaten eggs. The cooking procedure is the same as for date pudding. Serve *Brandy Cream Sauce* in a sauceboat.

BRANDY CREAM SAUCE FOR STEAMED PUDDINGS

1 cup heavy cream	4 egg yolks
2 tablespoons flour	1 cup light brown sugar
⅓ cup sweet butter	1 jigger whisky or brandy

Put a little of the cream with the flour in the top of the double boiler over simmering water, blend with a rubber spatula until it is smooth, then stir in the rest of the cream. Cook until it thickens, then add the butter. Remove from heat. Beat the egg yolks, add the sugar, and beat until thick, then add the cream slowly. Put back over the simmering water for a moment, then turn off the heat and keep the sauce warm. When ready to serve add the whisky or brandy, reheat for a minute, and serve in a sauceboat with the hot pudding. If the sauce is too thick, add a little cream and brandy. The consistency should be like very heavy cream.

LE TURINOISE

2 pounds chestnuts, or 1 10-ounce tin chestnut purée	1 teaspoon vanilla
4 to 6 ounces sweet butter	½ cup browned almonds
½ to ⅔ cup sugar	1½ cups heavy cream, whipped
4 to 6 ounces bitter chocolate	1 jigger liqueur, or 2 tablespoons rum (optional)

If two pounds of fresh chestnuts are cooked, use the larger quantities of the other ingredients. Boil the chestnuts 1½ minutes, drain, peel, and skin them while they are warm. Then cook them in boiling water with a vanilla bean until they are tender; drain and mash through a sieve (or use canned purée). Cream the butter and sugar until smooth. Shave the chocolate, melt it in 2 tablespoons of hot water, and add it to the butter-sugar mixture. Lightly mix with the puréed chestnuts and add the vanilla. Put in a greased mold and refrigerate until the following day. When ready to serve, unmold on a fancy serving plate and stick halved or whole browned almonds over the surface. Serve with whipped cream, either plain or with the liqueur or rum added. Serves 8. Use any left over for *Prunes Monique*.

CHESTNUT CREAM

2 pounds chestnuts	1½ cups heavy cream, whipped
¼ cup honey	Garnish: Browned almonds
¼ cup rum	

Boil the chestnuts 1½ minutes; peel and skin them. Boil them in water until they are soft, then mash through a sieve. Mix lightly with the honey and rum and fold in the whipped cream. Chill in a fancy bowl. Instead of rum you may use a favorite liqueur: Curaçao, Strega, or Maraschino would be good. Pass a bowl of browned almonds. Serves 8.

CHESTNUT CREAM FOR
PUDDING, SOUFFLÉ, MOLD, AND ICE CREAM

After chestnuts are prepared, puréed, and mixed with custard, you can do a variety of things with them.

1 pound fresh chestnuts	2 tablespoons dark rum
1½ cups light cream	1 tablespoon water
1½ tablespoons cornstarch	1 teaspoon vanilla
3 egg yolks	1 or 2 more tablespoons dark
½ cup light brown sugar	rum (to taste)
1 tablespoon gelatin	

Make a slit in each chestnut with a sharp pointed knife. Cover them with cold water and bring to the boil for 1½ minutes. Shell and skin them while they are still warm. Cover them again with water and cook them 15 to 18 minutes, or until they are soft enough to mash through rather a coarse sieve. Mash them with ¼ cup of the water they boiled in. Cool this purée. For the custard blend the cream with the cornstarch and cook it in the top of a double boiler over simmering water until it thickens. Meanwhile soak the gelatin in 2 tablespoons rum mixed with 1 tablespoon of water. Mix the egg yolks and brown sugar together and pour the hot milk over them, then return to the double boiler and cook until thickened, stirring with a rubber spatula. Add the gelatin and rum to the custard and stir it until the gelatin is melted. Let it cool and add the vanilla and the rest of the rum. Blend the custard with the chestnut purée until it is a smooth cream.

CHESTNUT PUDDING. Pour the chestnut cream into an 8-inch fireproof pudding dish and cover with a meringue made of 3 egg whites beaten stiff. Beat in ½ cup sugar gradually and flavor with 1 teaspoon of vanilla. Pile onto the cold cream and bake in a 375° oven until it puffs and browns. Serve hot or cold. If you prefer, the cream may be put in 8 custard cups, covered with the meringue, and baked.

CHESTNUT SOUFFLÉ.

1½ cups of the chestnut cream	½ cup instant superfine sugar
6 egg whites, beaten	

Omit the gelatin and the 2 tablespoons of rum and water. Beat the egg whites until stiff, then add the sugar gradually and beat to a thick meringue. Stir one-fourth of it into the chestnut cream, then fold in the rest of the meringue. Butter and sugar a 7½-inch soufflé dish, pour in the mixture, set the dish in a pan with a little hot water, and bake 5 minutes at 400°, then turn the heat to 350° and bake 25 to 30 minutes more. Serve with a thin chocolate sauce made of bitter chocolate. Serves 6.

MOLDED CHESTNUT CREAM. Make the chestnut cream with 3 teaspoons of gelatin. Fold in ½ cup of whipped heavy cream and pour into a fancy mold. Chill until set. Unmold and decorate with ½ cup of whipped cream mixed with ⅓ cup of glacé fruits.

CHESTNUT ICE CREAM. Make the chestnut cream, omitting the gelatin. Fold in 1 or 2 cups of whipped heavy cream, depending on how much ice cream you require. Freeze. Each serving may be sprinkled with shaved bitter chocolate.

CRÈME BRULÉE

2 cups heavy cream
3 tablespoons light brown sugar

4 large egg yolks
More light brown sugar

Put the cream and 3 tablespoons of brown sugar in the top of the double boiler over simmering water. When it is hot let it boil up once over the flame so it will surely be scalded. Beat the egg yolks until thick, then pour the hot cream over them. Put the mixture back over the simmering water for a few seconds, stirring it continuously with a rubber spatula. Remove and pour into 6 custard cups and let become thoroughly cooled outside the refrigerator. Cover with ½ inch of brown sugar. Run the cups under a hot flame until the top becomes bubbly and a very little burned. Remove and chill. This is a well-known and delicious sweet to end an important lunch or dinner. Every cup of cream calls for 2 large yolks and serves 3; ⅓ cup cream being allowed for each custard cup.

POTS DE CRÈME AU CHOCOLAT

4 ounces semisweet chocolate
¼ cup light brown sugar
2 cups heavy cream

6 egg yolks, beaten
1 teaspoon vanilla
1 tablespoon dark rum (optional)

Put the chocolate in the top of a double boiler with the sugar and cream. Cook over simmering water until the chocolate is melted. Add a little to the beaten egg yolks, then blend all together and cook a moment over the water. When the mixture coats the spoon remove from heat and add the flavorings. Pour into 8 small pots de crème or custard cups and chill. Serve plain, or garnish the tops with ground almonds or *Praliné Powder* or a small dab of whipped cream.

CRÈME DE MENTHE MOUSSE

½ pound white peppermint
   creams
½ cup light cream
2 teaspoons gelatin
1 tablespoon cold water
1½ cups heavy cream, whipped

3 or 4 drops green vegetable color-
   ing
Garnish:
   Sprigs fresh mint
   Crème de Menthe

Crumble the candy into the top of the double boiler, add the cream, and cook over boiling water until the candy is dissolved. Meanwhile soak the gelatin in the cold water and then melt it in the hot cream mixture. Let it cool, then mix it with the whipped cream and tint with the green coloring. Oil an 8-inch melon mold and pour in the mixture. Let chill and set several hours until firm. When ready to serve unmold on a silver platter and decorate with the mint. Serve at the table, pouring 1 tablespoon of the liqueur over each serving. This is a very delicate crème and should not stand after it is unmolded. To add more gelatin would destroy its melting texture. Serves 8.

CRÈME RENVERSÉE AU CARAMEL

1 cup white sugar
⅓ cup boiling water
1 cup light cream
1 cup heavy cream
2 cups milk

6 tablespoons light brown sugar
7 eggs, plus 2 egg yolks, beaten
2 teaspoons vanilla extract
2 teaspoons almond extract
2 tablespoons whisky

Caramelize a charlotte mold or 8-inch aluminum baking dish. Put 1 cup white sugar in an iron skillet and cook it over a good flame until it is dark brown. Turn off the heat and add the boiling water. Cook it down to a heavy syrup and put it in the mold or baking pan and tip in all directions so the syrup covers the sides and bottom. If the syrup is too thin to stick put the mold over the fire a moment. Mix all the liquids with the brown sugar and scald. Beat the eggs and yolks together and add the liquid slowly. Blend well and add the extracts. Pour this into the caramelized mold and set it in a pan filled with boiling water halfway up the mold. Bake at 325° until a silver knife comes out clean—this may take nearly an hour. The water must never boil but must be kept at a simmer. When the crème is cool, put it in the refrigerator to become cold and set. After it is thoroughly cold, cover and let stand until the next day. When ready to serve, cover the mold with a serving dish and turn it upside down. Put the whisky in the mold over a flame to melt the residue of caramel. Scrape it over the mold. Serves 10. I have tried many formulas for this and consider this one to have the finest texture of any I have ever made.

MILK-CHOCOLATE MOUSSE WITH CHERRIES

½ pound sweet milk chocolate   6 egg whites, beaten
2 tablespoons hot coffee   Pinch of salt
6 egg yolks, beaten   32 preserved or black pitted cherries
⅓ cup sweet butter

Lindt Swiss milk chocolate is good for this. Break up the chocolate and put it in the top of a double boiler with the coffee. Melt it over simmering water. Add the beaten egg yolks; cut the butter in pieces and add them, and stir the mixture until smooth and thick. The butter is added for richness and thickening when the mousse is chilled. Let the chocolate mixture cool somewhat. Beat the egg whites with the salt until very stiff. Mix a third of the whites into the chocolate mixture, then fold in the rest. Put 4 cherries in the bottom of each of 8 ramekins and fill with the chocolate mixture. Chill 8 or 10 hours. If you prefer, pile the mousse in a fancy bowl to chill and set, and garnish with cherries.

CHOCOLATE MOUSSE (OR FROSTING FOR CAKE)

2 cups heavy cream   Garnish: Coarsely chopped nuts:
4 tablespoons sugar   almonds, macadamias, or
5 tablespoons bitter cocoa   pecans
2 teaspoons vanilla or almond
    extract

This is a light, delicious dessert, either a mousse, or a frosting for a white or chocolate cake. Put the cream in a bowl and sprinkle it with the sugar and cocoa and let it stand outside the refrigerator 1½ hours. Then whip it until it is thick and flavor it with 2 teaspoons vanilla or almond, or 1 teaspoon of each. Refrigerate until ready to serve. Serve in 6 parfait glasses. Sprinkle the top with nuts. You may experiment with the flavoring. If mocha is desired sprinkle with 2 teaspoons of powdered coffee with the cocoa and sugar. After it has been beaten add a teaspoon of mocha extract. For mousse, every cup of cream makes 3 servings; for frosting, the amount needed is determined by the size of the cake.

PEARS WITH COCONUT CREAM SAUCE

Coconut Cream Pudding (without   ⅓ cup light corn syrup
    the sugar glaze)   1 jigger Maraschino or Curaçao
3 large fine pears

Make the coconut cream and let it cool. Peel, core, and halve the pears. Poach them in the syrup 4 or 5 minutes until they are tender. Chill and add the liqueur. When ready to serve put 1 pear in each of 6 serving dishes, divide the syrup over them and cover with coconut cream. Serves 6.

COCONUT CREAM PUDDING

1 cup coconut, closely packed
3 cups milk
Heavy cream
1½ tablespoons cornstarch

3 tablespoons light brown sugar
6 egg yolks, beaten
More light brown sugar

Use packaged coconut. Put the coconut in a saucepan with 1½ cups of the milk, let come to a boil, and cool. Mash it through a sieve. Repeat this process with the same coconut and the rest of the milk. Discard the coconut. Measure the coconut milk and add enough heavy cream to make 3 cups. Blend the cornstarch with the liquid, add 3 tablespoons light brown sugar, and put it in the top of the double boiler. Cook over boiling water until it thickens. Remove and let it boil up over the flame so that the custard is scalded, then slowly add to the beaten egg yolks. Cook a minute so that it thickens. Empty into a shallow oval baking dish and let become thoroughly cold. Cover the custard ½ inch thick with light brown sugar and run it under a hot flame until it bubbles and burns a little. Chill in the refrigerator. Serves 6.

PRUNE CHARLOTTE

1 pound large sweet prunes
1½ cups water
1½ cups red wine
1 envelope gelatin
⅓ cup light brown sugar

1 teaspoon almond extract
½ cup heavy cream, whipped
Garnish: Whipped cream, honey, and rum

Wash the prunes and soak them overnight with the water and wine. Next day simmer them until they are tender, about 20 minutes. Drain the juice. Soak the gelatin in 2 tablespoons cold water, add to the prune juice and stir until it is dissolved. Pit the prunes and mash them through a sieve or purée them in a blender with some of the juice. Combine the prunes with all the juice, add the sugar and extract and let cool. When it is cold fold in the cream. Oil a charlotte mold, put in the mixture, and let it set and chill. Unmold and serve with whipped cream flavored with rum and honey. Serves 6.

TRIFLE

Hot Milk Cake (see Almond Cream Cake)
2 cups Crème Patissière
Grape Jelly, grapefruit marmalade, or apricot jam
or 2 cups fresh raspberries or strawberries
½ cup glacé fruits: cherries, pineapple, citron
¼ cup port wine
1 cup heavy cream, whipped
5 tablespoons browned slivered almonds

Trifle doesn't have to be deadly if the wine-marinated fruits are mixed with the cold Crème Patissière and whipped cream and the whole thing put together 15 minutes before it is served. It is the wine-soaked cake that makes trifles heavy. Make the cake in two 9-inch layers and let it cool. Make the Crème Patissière and let it cool. Soak the glacé fruits in the wine 1 hour. Put one layer of cake in a wide shallow serving bowl and spread it with one of the jams (or the fresh fruit if you prefer). Mix the Crème Patissière with the wine and fruits and fold in the whipped cream. Spread half of it over the jam or fruit, then put the second layer of cake on top and cover that with the rest of the cream mixture. Sprinkle the top with the almonds. Serves 8 to 10.

COURTHOUSE TRIFLE

What an irresistible name for a trifle!—an old favorite of an English friend. No cake in this, so serve it to 6 in individual goblets.

The 1st layer, a dollop of apricot jam; the 2nd, divide a pint of Crème Patissière; the 3rd, a thick sprinkle of grated bitter chocolate; the 4th, divide 1½ cups of whipped cream flavored with sugar and sherry.

RICE CREAM WITH LEMON SAUCE

½ cup patna rice
1 cup light cream
2 cups milk
2 eggs, beaten
½ cup light brown sugar
2 tablespoons vanilla or 1 tablespoon vanilla and 1 teaspoon almond extract
1 cup heavy cream, whipped
Lemon Sauce

Wash rice and put it in the top of the double boiler with the light cream and the milk. Cover and cook over simmering water for an hour, stirring occasionally. Beat the eggs with the sugar, add to the rice, and remove from the fire. The mixture thickens more when it cools. When it is cool add the flavoring and the whipped cream. Turn the mixture into a serving bowl. Serve with the lemon sauce either at room temperature or chilled. Serves 6.

RICE CREAM TRIFLE. A remarkable trifle may be made with this rice cream as the foundation. Omit the lemon sauce. Spread the rice cream in a wide shallow serving dish and follow the recipe for *Courthouse Trifle*. A wonderful dish for 10 or 12. No cake in this.

CARAMEL RICE PUDDING

1 cup patna rice
2 cups milk
½ cup glacé fruits: cherries, pineapple, citron, currants
3 tablespoons dark rum
¼ cup butter
¾ cup light cream
1 tablespoon cornstarch
⅓ cup light brown sugar

3 large egg yolks
1 tablespoon vanilla
Caramel:
   ¾ cup white sugar
   ¼ cup boiling water
Sauce:
   3 tablespoons dark rum
   ¼ cup heavy cream

Cook the rice with the milk in the top of a double boiler for 45 minutes, covered. Let it boil up once over the flame. It will have absorbed the milk. While it is cooking, soak the fruits in the rum. When the rice is done stir in the butter. Blend the cream with the cornstarch and cook it over a low flame until it thickens. Beat the sugar and egg yolks together and add to the cream. Cook the mixture over a low flame a moment. Mix the custard with the rice; stir in the rum and fruits and vanilla. Caramelize an 8-inch aluminum baking dish. Cook the white sugar in an iron skillet until it is dark brown. Turn off the flame and add the boiling water. Return to the fire and cook to a heavy syrup. Pour the syrup into the baking dish and tip the dish until the bottom and sides are covered with caramel. In a minute it will harden, then pour in the rice mixture. Set the dish in a pan of hot water which comes halfway up the sides of the dish. Bake at 375° for 30 minutes. Turn the heat to 350° if it bakes too fast. To serve, cover the baking dish with a serving dish and turn it upside down. For the sauce, rinse the pan out with the rum over a low flame until the caramel melts, then scrape it into a sauceboat. Then boil up the cream in the baking dish to get all the syrup and mix it with the rum syrup. The pudding may not hold its shape but nobody cares, it has such a delicious flavor. Serves 6.

COCONUT RICE PUDDING

2½ cups milk
  1 cup finely grated coconut
  ½ cup patna rice
Custard:
  2 cups milk
  3 egg yolks
  3 tablespoons light brown
    sugar
  1 teaspoon vanilla
  1 teaspoon almond

Meringue:
  3 egg whites, beaten
  3 tablespoons light brown
    sugar
  1 teaspoon vanilla extract
  1 teaspoon almond extract
  ⅓ cup finely grated coconut

Blend the milk and coconut in a blender, then boil it up and let stand until it cools. If you have no blender the infusion will do as well by simply boiling it and letting it cool. Mash it through a sieve. Cook the washed rice in the coconut milk covered tightly, over a very low flame, about 25 minutes. If it becomes too thick add a little milk. With the mashed coconut make another infusion, using the 2 cups milk for the custard; boil together and let cool. Mix the egg yolks with the brown sugar. Sieve out the coconut, and discard. Add the coconut infusion to the egg yolks, and cook over a low flame until it thickens, then mix with the cooked rice. Add the flavorings. For the meringue, beat the egg whites until thick, add the sugar, and beat again. Add the flavorings. Put the rice mixture into a 7½- or 8-inch baking dish and cover with the meringue, then sprinkle the top with the coconut. Put the pudding in the oven until it browns. Let it become thoroughly cooled. It may be refrigerated before serving. Serves 6.

ITALIAN ORANGE RICE PUDDING

  ½ cup rice
1⅓ cups milk
  Few grains salt
  ⅓ cup sweet butter
  ½ cup light brown sugar
  ⅓ cup slivered orange peel
  3 eggs, separated

Orange Sauce:
1¼ cups orange juice
  1 tablespoon grated orange rind
  ¼ cup lemon juice
  ¼ cup sugar
  3 teaspoons cornstarch
  1 tablespoon butter
  Jigger Curaçao

Cook the rice in the milk, covered, over a low flame, until the milk is absorbed. Add the salt, butter, sugar, candied orange peel, and egg yolks. Beat the egg whites until stiff, mix in one-fourth of them, then fold in the rest very lightly. Grease and sugar a soufflé dish, put in the rice mixture, put the dish in a pan of hot water, and bake at 350° about 25 minutes or until set. Serve hot or cold with orange sauce. Cook the orange juice with the rind 2 minutes. Blend the lemon juice, sugar, and cornstarch, and add to the orange juice. When it has thickened, add the butter and let it cool. Add the liqueur. Serve in a sauceboat. Serves 6.

MOLDED RICE PUDDING

¾ cup brown or patna rice
1⅓ cups skim milk
1 cup light cream
¼ cup Kirsch or dark rum
1 cup glacé fruits: cherries, pineapple, currants, citron, etc.,
sliced
3 tablespoons apricot preserves,
sieved

1 cup milk
5 egg yolks, beaten
⅓ cup light brown sugar
1 tablespoon cornstarch
1⅓ tablespoons gelatin
2 tablespoons cold water
1 tablespoon vanilla extract
1 teaspoon almond extract
1 cup heavy cream, whipped

Pour the Kirsch over the sliced fruits and marinate for 1 hour, then add the sieved apricot preserves or jam. Wash the rice and cook it in the skim milk, tightly covered, over a low flame for 45 minutes. Add ½ cup light cream and let the rice absorb it. Scald the milk and the remaining ½ cup light cream. Beat the egg yolks and add the sugar and cornstarch. Soak the gelatin in 2 tablespoons water. Combine the scalded cream and milk with the egg yolk mixture and cook until it thickens, stirring continuously, then add the gelatin to the hot custard to melt. When it cools stir in the fruits, vanilla and almond extracts, combine with the rice; and fold in the whipped cream. Empty into a greased fancy mold to chill and set. Unmold. It may be served with a thinned *Crème Patissière* sauce or puréed frozen raspberries poured over it. This will serve 10 or 12.

SEMOLINA PUDDING

⅓ cup semolina (or Cream of
Wheat)
1½ cups milk
⅓ cup sugar
2 tablespoons butter

Grated rind 1 lemon
¼ cup diced citron
3 eggs, separated
Sugar or cookie crumbs

Mix the semolina with the cold milk so it won't be lumpy, add the sugar and butter, and bring to a boil, stirring continuously until it thickens. Remove from the fire and add the lemon rind, citron, and 1 whole egg beaten with the other two yolks. Beat the remaining two whites until stiff and fold them in. Grease a pudding dish and sprinkle sides and bottom with sugar or crushed cookie crumbs. Pour in the batter. Put the dish in a pan of hot water and bake about 35 or 40 minutes at 350°. This Italian pudding is good served with cream, or a light orange sauce. The citron must be fresh and of perfect quality. Serves 4 to 6. This would make an excellent substitute for rice or potatoes with a meat course, if you omit the sugar and citron, stir in ⅔ cup grated cheese while the semolina is hot, and bake as described.

ITALIAN FRUIT CREAM

2 cups milk and 2 cups heavy
    cream, or 4 cups light cream
½ cup light brown sugar
2 tablespoons flour
4 egg yolks, beaten
1 tablespoon vanilla

1 cup candied fruits:
    ¼ cup slivered angelica or
    citron
    ¼ cup currants soaked 2
    hours in 3 tablespoons
    rum
    ½ cup sliced candied cher-
    ries, pineapple, apricots

The candied fruits in Italy are a great specialty. They candy to an amazing translucency fruits of all kinds: peaches, cantaloupe, even bananas and pineapples, skins, spines and all. It is strange to munch a banana with its skin and find it very good. Sift the flour with the sugar. Scald the milk and cream or all light cream and mix with the sugar and flour. Cook until it thickens, then pour it over the beaten egg yolks. Cook over simmering water a minute to thicken a little more, then let it cool thoroughly. Add the vanilla. Mix with the fruits and add the rum with the currants. Divide in 8 or 10 parfait glasses and chill.

SAINT HONORÉ, SABATINI
Sabatini, Florence

This spectacular dessert is not hard to make, but anything this good takes a little time.

9- or 10-inch circle *Pie Pastry*
12 tiny chocolate cream puffs
Caramel syrup:
    ½ cup sugar
    ¼ cup water
Powdered chocolate
Flaked pistachio nuts

Crème Saint-Honoré:
    2 cups rich milk
    ¼ cup flour
    ½ cup sugar
    3 egg yolks, beaten
    1 tablespoon vanilla
    1½ cups heavy cream,
        whipped
    3 egg whites, beaten

Make a circle of *Pie Pastry*, bake, and cool it. If you do not wish to make the cream puffs, buy them at a good pastry shop. For the caramel syrup, cook the sugar and water to a pale gold and cool a little. Dip each puff in the syrup to secure them and place them around the edge of the pastry. A teaspoon of cooled caramel may be put on each puff. For the crème, scald the milk. Sift the flour with the sugar and beat with the egg yolks until stiff. Pour the scalded milk over it slowly and cook a moment until it thickens. Cool thoroughly. Add the vanilla and fold in the cream beaten stiff and the egg whites, also beaten stiff. Chill. Before serving pile the cream in the center of the pastry and puffs. Sprinkle powdered chocolate lightly over the top and then sprinkle with the nuts. Serves 8 or 10 or 12.

SEMIFREDDO ALLO ZABAIONE
Hotel Della Rocca, Bazzano

Friends in Bologna drove us to Bazzano, an ancient Roman town thirteen miles west into the Po Valley, on the "road of the castles." We had dinner and spent the evening at Hotel Della Rocca, a delightful eighteenth-century inn, all newly refurbished with good taste in keeping with its period. The inn has been in the present family since 1796 and is run by Signore Rosvaldo Rocchi and his young son Vittorio and his wife. Vittorio showed us a "book of documents" containing letters and autographs from people (some quite famous names) over the last hundred years. What a lovely two weeks one could spend in this hotel, roaming over the countryside, along the via Claudia, a road laid in 196 B.C. by the Roman consul M. Claudius Marcellus, and visiting the old castles in the neighborhood. As would be expected, the food is not the customary hotel fare but includes unusual dishes, many from old family recipes handed down over the years. This molded sweet is one of these.

Cake or ladyfingers
1 jigger Maraschino or Strega (or more)
Zabaione:
    4 egg yolks
    4 teaspoons sugar
    4 tablespoons Marsala
1 cup heavy cream, whipped

¼ cup powdered sugar
Caramel syrup:
    ⅔ cup sugar
    ¼ cup water
1 cup sweet butter
3 tablespoons cocoa
Chocolate sauce (optional)

Soften the butter at room temperature at least 1 hour. Dip thin slices of cake, or ladyfingers, in the liqueur and line a greased mold. If you use pound cake, a tin 11-inch-long log pan is very good for this. For the zabaione, beat the egg yolks in the top of the double boiler until thick, gradually adding the sugar and then the wine. Put over simmering water and beat and scrape from the sides until it thickens. This takes only a minute. Let it cool. Whip the cream and mix with the powdered sugar. Make a caramel by boiling the sugar and water until pale golden. If you cook it too long you will have to add a little water and melt it again. It should make ½ cup of cool dark brown caramel syrup. Let cool. Beat the butter and caramel syrup together. Now lightly mix the zabaione, the whipped cream, and the caramel mixture together. Put half of it in the cake-lined mold, then mix the cocoa into the remaining half of the mixture and add it to the mold. Refrigerate. When it is cold, wrap it in wax paper and leave 3 days in the refrigerator. The directions say to chill serving glasses and roll a little chocolate sauce around in them so that it clings to the sides, then add a small serving of this cake. I prefer it without this additional rich touch. Serves 12.

SFORMATO DE BANANE
3-G Ristorante, Bologna

6 bananas
1½ tablespoons butter
⅔ cup sugar
Cream sauce:
    1 tablespoon cornstarch
    ¾ cup light cream
    6 egg yolks
    1 teaspoon each vanilla extract and almond extract

6 egg whites, beaten
Sauce:
    1 cup light cream
    1 tablespoon cornstarch
    1 tablespoon sugar
    3 tablespoons Curaçao

Cut the bananas in very thin slices and put them in a heavy pot with the butter and sugar; cover and cook until the bananas are soft. Stir occasionally so that they do not burn. Mash the bananas. Make the cream sauce in the top of a double boiler. Blend the cornstarch with the cream, cook a moment until it begins to thicken, and pour it over the egg yolks. Put over simmering water and cook a moment. It will become quite thick. Cool it a little, then add the extracts. Mix it with the bananas. Beat the egg whites until stiff, then mix one-fourth of them into the banana mixture and lightly fold in the rest. Grease an 8½-inch soufflé dish and sprinkle the bottom and sides with sugar. Put in the mixture and set the dish in a pan of hot water. Bake at 375° for 10 minutes, then reduce the temperature to 350° and bake about 20 minutes more. This may be served with a light custard cream sauce containing only a little sugar. Blend the cream with the cornstarch, cook it until it thickens, add the sugar, and let it cool. Add the liqueur and serve from a sauceboat. Serves 7 or 8.

RICOTTA PUDDING

2 cups ricotta or sieved creamed cottage cheese
2 tablespoons sifted flour
3 egg yolks
½ cup sugar

⅓ cup slivered citron
½ teaspoon cinnamon
3 tablespoons rum
Grated rind 1 large lemon
Few grains salt
3 egg whites, beaten

Mix the cheese with the flour, egg yolks, and sugar and stir until light and smooth. Two cups of cheese weigh 1 pound. The ricotta is worth trying to get. Add the citron, cinnamon, rum, and grated rind. Beat egg whites with the salt until stiff. Mix in one-fourth of the whites with the cheese mixture, then fold in the rest. Empty into a buttered and sugared 8-inch pudding dish and bake 35 to 40 minutes at 350° in a water bath. This is a lovely Italian-style cheese cake which is served hot, with or without cream. It should be quite moist. It may also be served cold. Serves 4 to 6.

DOLCE SAMPIERI
Sampieri, Bologna

At number 3 via Sampieri there is a very popular old-fashioned restaurant with paintings, four deep lining the walls. It is a comfortable and Victorian setting for delicious food. This molded sweet is an example of the rich fare. The pastry shops in Bologna have such beautiful displays it is impossible to choose among them, so to simplify matters you let Sampieri settle it for you. The helpful maitre d'hotel gave me a bottle of their red liqueur to take with me because the mold is spectacularly lined with strips of red cake. This is not necessary; your favorite liqueur will do, as long as it is not Crème de Menthe.

Praliné Powder:
- ⅔ cup sugar
- ¼ cup water
- ½ cup lightly browned almonds
- 1 cup heavy cream, whipped
- ¼ cup powdered sugar
- 2 teaspoons vanilla
- 1 cup sweet butter

¼ cup shaved chocolate
Thin strips of sponge cake or pound cake
1 jigger liqueur (or more)
Thin chocolate sauce:
- ¾ cup light cream
- 2 or 3 squares bitter chocolate

Make the *Praliné Powder* ahead of time. Put the sugar and water in a heavy saucepan and cook until it is golden; add the nuts and cook a moment longer. Empty onto a greased slab or into an iron skillet to harden. When it is hard, break it in pieces and grind it to a powder. Whip the cream until stiff and add the powdered sugar and vanilla. Have the butter softened to room temperature. Never use whipped butter for molded cakes, as it is too moist to stiffen the mixture when it is chilled. Mix the butter with the *Praliné Powder,* then fold in the whipped cream. Grease the mold. A tin 11-inch-long log-shape is excellent for this. Dip ½-inch-thick strips of cake in a plate holding a jigger or more of liqueur and line the mold with them. Put half the cream mixture in the cake-lined mold, sprinkle with the shaved chocolate, then add the rest of the mixture. Chill in the refrigerator, then wrap in wax paper and let stand in the refrigerator 24 hours. When ready to serve, unmold and serve in slices ½-inch thick. Make thin bitter chocolate sauce by melting the grated chocolate in the hot cream. Let it cool and serve in a sauceboat. Serves 12.

DOLCE VASCO
Da Vasco, Bologna

Thin slices of cake
1 jigger Strega (or more)
1 cup heavy cream, whipped
3 eggs, beaten
⅓ cup sugar
4 ounces macaroons, crushed

1 cup sweet butter, softened
Sauce:
 6 egg yolks, beaten
 ½ cup sugar
 6 tablespoons Marsala

Let the butter soften at room temperature for at least 1 hour. Pound cake is good for lining molds. Cut it thin, dip it in the Strega, and line a buttered mold. You may also use your favorite liqueur, as long as it isn't Crème de Menthe. Whip the cream. Beat the eggs until thick, then gradually add the sugar and beat until it ribbons. Crush the macaroons very fine and mix with the softened butter. Combine with the cream and the egg mixture. Empty into the cake-lined mold and refrigerate for 24 hours. After it has thoroughly chilled wrap it in wax paper. Vasco calls the sauce "uncooked zabaione sauce." Beat the egg yolks until very thick, add the sugar gradually, and beat until it ribbons, then add the wine, a little at a time. An electric mixer would be good for this. Serve sauce in a sauceboat. Serves 12.

ZABAIONE

Egg yolks
Sugar

Marsala or sherry
Nutmeg

Use 3 large egg yolks for each 2 servings. For every yolk use 1 teaspoon sugar and 1 tablespoon wine. Put the yolks in the top of the double boiler, and beat with a rotary beater until thick, then add the sugar and beat until heavy. Add the wine slowly and continue beating. Put over simmering water and continue beating. When it begins to thicken, remove the pan from the heat and scrape the bottom and sides with a rubber spatula to cook evenly. Put the pan back over the water and continue cooking until the mixture is fluffy and thick. This only takes about 2 minutes for enough for 4. Serve in tumblers or goblets with a dash of nutmeg on top. If desired it may be chilled in the glasses, but it is better warm.

COQUILLETTES AUX NOIX
Capucin Gourmand, Nancy

6 ounces egg noodle shells
2 tablespoons sweet butter
½ cup nuts

½ cup powdered sugar
Powdered sugar
Garnish: Cup of sugared nuts

Cook the noodles in boiling salted water until they are done, then rinse them quickly in a little cold water so they won't stick. Put them in a saucepan with the butter and heat quickly. Mix with the nuts and sugar and put them in a shallow baking dish. Sprinkle with powdered sugar and caramelize in a 425° oven a few minutes. Serve accompanied by a bowl of mixed sugared nuts as a dessert for 4.

CRÊPES SUZETTE

Crêpes:
1½ cups milk
1½ cups sifted flour
1 teaspoon grated orange
   rind
¼ cup melted sweet butter
¼ cup orange liqueur
4 eggs, beaten
Butter for frying

Sauce:
1 tablespoon grated orange
   rind
⅓ cup orange juice
¾ cup sweet butter
½ cup sugar
¾ cup orange liqueur: Grand
   Marnier, Cointreau, or
   Curaçao
½ cup cognac
Powdered sugar

As this batter must be refrigerated 2 hours before frying, mix it well ahead of time. After the crêpes are fried, they may be set aside another 2 hours before serving. Put the milk, flour, orange rind, melted butter, and liqueur in an electric blender until well mixed. Beat the eggs until very light, then stir in the flour mixture. Refrigerate. In a 7-inch crêpe pan melt a teaspoon of butter for each crêpe and when it is quite hot put in a big serving spoon (scant ¼ cup) of batter and tip the pan so that the bottom is covered. Time it 60 seconds before turning, as they are so delicate that they will break if not cooked through. Turn with a narrow spatula and with the aid of your fingers and fry about 20 seconds on the other side. Remove them to a platter and cover lightly with wax paper until ready to add the sauce. This makes about 18 to 20 crêpes to serve 6.

When you are ready to serve the crêpes, put the rind, orange juice, butter, and sugar in a wide shallow chafing dish over a medium flame. Stir until the butter is melted and the sauce mixed, then add the liqueur. Put the crêpes into the sauce, one at a time, covering each well with sauce, fold twice, and remove to the side of the pan. When all are folded, put them back in the pan, sprinkle with sugar, add the cognac, and light it. Spoon it over the crêpes until the flames die. Sprinkle again with powdered sugar and serve 3 to a person.

CHERRY CRÊPES

16 *Crêpes*
1 pound big black cherries
½ cup red wine
¼ cup light brown sugar
1 tablespoon cornstarch

Cream:
1½ cups light cream
1½ tablespoons cornstarch·
3 tablespoons light brown
   sugar
1 teaspoon vanilla
½ cup *Praliné Powder*

Make 5-inch crêpes and cool them. Pit the cherries, bring them to a boil with the wine and sugar for 1 minute, and drain them. Thicken the syrup with 1 tablespoon cornstarch. This preparation may be done in advance. For the cream, blend 1½ tablespoons cornstarch with the cream, add the sugar, and cook in a saucepan until it thickens. Cool and add the vanilla. Shortly before serving, put 4 or 5 cherries and a tablespoon of the cherry syrup in each crêpe. Roll them and lay them close together in the bottom of a long baking dish. Put a big tablespoonful of cream sauce on each crêpe and sprinkle with praliné powder. Put in a 400° oven and cook 4 minutes, or until they are hot. Serve immediately. Serves 8.

CRÊPES AU KIRSCH, SURPRISE
Valentin-Sorg, Strasbourg

12 6-inch *Crêpes*
1 cup sweet butter

1 cup powdered sugar
1 cup old Kirsch d'Alsace

Make the crêpes and have them at room temperature. Make the mousse: lightly cream the butter and sugar, whisk in the Kirsch, and chill so that it is firm. Just before serving, put a big spoonful of mousse in each crêpe, roll, and fold under the ends so that the filling is sealed in airtight. Sprinkle the tops with powdered sugar. Pass the pan under a hot flame to heat quickly and lightly glaze the crêpes. When they are served the crêpe is hot and the mousse inside has become a delicious sauce. Serve 2 to a person. Mme. Gaby Sorg imparted her "secret" to me. You'll agree women shouldn't keep secrets.

CARAMEL SAUCE

1 cup light brown sugar
⅔ cup light corn syrup
2 tablespoons sweet butter

1 cup light cream
1 tablespoon dark rum, or 1 teaspoon vanilla

Put the sugar and syrup in a heavy saucepan over low heat and stir until it is blended, then add the butter and cream. Simmer until it has the consistency of heavy cream. This should be served warm. Just before serving add either the rum or vanilla. Serve in a sauceboat. Suitable with *Almond Pudding,* and with cottage, chocolate, or rice puddings.

CHOCOLATE SAUCE

3 or 4 squares bitter chocolate
⅔ cup strong black hot coffee
½ cup light brown sugar
2 tablespoons sweet butter
½ cup light corn syrup

3 or 4 drops mocha extract (optional)
2 tablespoons dark rum, or 1 teaspoon vanilla
Light cream

Break up the chocolate, put it in the top of a double boiler over simmering water, and add the coffee, sugar, butter, and corn syrup. Stir until the chocolate is melted and the mixture is smooth. Add the flavorings. Thin with light cream to the consistency of heavy cream. This is served over puddings, hot or cold. If it becomes too thick when it is cold, stir in either cold coffee or light cream, to suit your taste.

SABAYON SAUCE

4 egg yolks
1 cup powdered sugar

1 cup fine sherry or Madeira

Beat the egg yolks with the sugar until light and creamy. Add the wine, a little at a time, beating continuously. Cook over gently simmering water beating with a whisk until thick and double in bulk. It is served warm over pudding. It may also be served cold, with whipped cream added, over a shallow bowl of berries or sliced fruit.

Fruit Desserts

BAKED FRUITS, BLAZED

1 pound fresh cherries, or 1 large
 can Bing cherries
1 pound fresh apricots, or 1 large
 can peeled apricots
2 firm bananas
3 fine fresh peaches, skinned and
 quartered, or 1 can peeled
 peaches

Fresh pineapple
Brown sugar
½ cup orange juice or syrup
Bits of sweet butter
⅓ cup dark rum
1 cup fresh strawberries or raspberries (optional)
Garnish: *Crème Fraîche*

Of course any fruit dish is better made with fresh fruit but in the winter good brands of canned fruit may be used. Omit pineapple if fresh is not available. Pit the canned or fresh cherries. Pit the apricots. Cut the bananas in slant-wise slices. Allow ¾ cup to 1 cup of fruit for each serving. Arrange the fruit on the bottom of a shallow baking dish that may be brought to the table. If canned fruit is used, drain out the fruit, boil down the syrup with 3 tablespoons of brown sugar until it is quite thick, and use ½ cup of it. Use the orange juice if fresh fruit is used. Pour either over the fruit and put bits of butter over the top. Sprinkle a little brown sugar over it only if the fruit needs it. This may be prepared ahead of time. Fifteen minutes before serving, put it in a 375° oven. Remove from the oven, pour the rum over the top, and bring to the table blazing. A cup of fresh berries may be put over the top just before adding the rum. *Crème Fraîche* may be served for those who want it. For a party this may be used to serve over ice cream.

BAKED BANANAS, FLAMBÉ

6 large medium-firm bananas
3 tablespoons butter
Juice of 1 lime
Grated rind and juice of 1 large
 navel orange

½ cup light brown sugar, or ⅓
 cup honey
⅓ cup Jamaica rum
Garnish:
 Crème Fraîche, or heavy cream

Butter lavishly a baking dish that can be brought to the table. Put the skinned bananas on the bottom of the dish and cover with bits of butter and the grated rind of the orange. Mix the lime and orange juice and pour it over the bananas. Sprinkle the sugar or honey over the bananas. Bake uncovered in a 375° oven for 20 minutes or until the bananas are puffy and tender. Bring to the table and pour the rum over the bananas and blaze. This may be made at the table in a chafing dish. Serves 6.

ALDO'S BLAZED FRUITS
Buca di San Rufillo, Florence

Choice of fruits:
    Peaches, skinned, and halved
    Pears, peeled, halved, and cored
    Bananas, skinned and halved
        lengthwise
2 tablespoons water
2 tablespoons sweet butter

Anisette
Brown sugar
Jigger rum or brandy
Ice cream (optional)

Choose and prepare the fruit. If you like, use two kinds. Put the water and butter in a chafing dish, add the fruit, put 1 teaspoon of anisette on each piece, and cook over a low flame. While it is cooking, sprinkle with brown sugar. Turn the fruit once. When the fruit is done add the liquor and blaze. Serve it on plates with or without vanilla ice cream

COMPOTE OF CANNED FRUIT

1 large can of Bing cherries,
    apricots, or green gage plums
⅓ cup light brown sugar
    Juice of ½ lime
1 teaspoon almond extract (or
    vanilla for plums)

3 tablespoons red currant jelly
1 jigger Maraschino or an orange
    liqueur
Garnish:
    Slivered browned almonds
    (optional)

Pit the chosen fruit and drain for 5 minutes through a coarse sieve. Add the sugar and lime juice to the syrup and boil it down for about 20 minutes or until it is quite thick, then add the extract and the jelly and stir until the jelly is melted. Add the fruit to the syrup, empty into a fancy serving dish, and chill. Do not cover it or the syrup will become thin. When ready to serve pour the liqueur over the fruit. A few browned slivered almonds may be sprinkled over the top. Serve plain, or over vanilla or coffee ice cream. Cherries may be served over chocolate ice cream. This is an elegant dessert but demands the best brands of fruit. The canned apricots should be skinned. Serves 6, or as a garnish for ice cream, 8 or 10.

COMPOTE OF PEACHES AND CHERRIES

6 peaches
1 large can Bing cherries
1 tablespoon honey
1 jigger Kirsch

1 teaspoon almond extract
¼ to ⅓ cup chopped browned
    almonds
1 cup heavy cream, whipped

Peel the peaches and put them in the bottom of a big saucepan. Drain the juice from the can of cherries over the peaches and poach them until they are tender. Gently remove them without breaking them. Boil down the juice until it is reduced to ½ cup. Add the pitted cherries, Kirsch, and extract. Let the fruit become cold. When ready to serve whip the cream and flavor and color it with some of the juice of the cherries. Pile the cream in the center of a large shallow serving dish and surround the cream with the peaches. Add the cherries and liquid on and around the peaches. Sprinkle the top with chopped almonds. Serves 6.

FRUIT AND CHAMPAGNE

Peaches or nectarines
Raspberries or strawberries
Orange, lemon, or raspberry ice

Chilled Champagne
Curaçao or Cointreau
Honey

When you have a bottle of champagne that you want to serve with dessert for 4 people, this is a good time to have it. Prepare the fruit you choose, dribbling it with a little honey and liqueur. Make or buy a very good ice and put some in each goblet. Fill the goblet with the fruit and flood with Champagne. There should be enough Champagne left for 4 glasses.

MÉLANGE OF FRUITS

2 or 3 cups fresh red currants
⅓ to ½ cup light brown sugar
¼ cup honey
4 or 5 skinned halved peaches

2 cups strawberries
2 cups raspberries
2 jiggers Maraschino liqueur

Stem and clean the currants and put in layers in a bowl with the sugar; dribble the honey over the top and let them marinate 2 or 3 hours. If the currants are very tart, add more honey and sugar. An hour before serving prepare the other fruit and mix it lightly in a serving bowl and chill. A half hour before serving pour the currants and syrup over the bowl of fruit. This will be as much sweetening as needed. Just before serving add the liqueur. Other liqueurs may be used if desired. Serves 8. For a greater number this may be served over vanilla ice cream.

ALDO'S FRUIT MACÉDOINE
Buca di San Rufillo, Florence

Pears	Sugar or honey
Peaches	Marsala or lemon juice
Cherries	
Grapes	

Aldo, one of the captains at this popular restaurant in Florence, likes to serve this fruit mixture, which is just the right dessert to follow a dinner of rich pasta. The pears and peaches are peeled and sliced and the cherries pitted and mixed with the stemmed grapes. A couple of hours before dinner it is sweetened to taste and lightly mixed with a jigger or two of Marsala or the juice of 1 lemon. It is served cold.

MELON WITH PORT

Fine port	Honey (optional)
Half a cantaloupe or honey ball, or	
honeydew balls	

There is no better fruit dessert than a fine, sweet, juicy, almost overripe melon with a jigger of good port added to each half. Or balls may be cut from a honeydew to fill a goblet and the port poured over them. If the melon lacks the proper sweetness, a drop of honey added is a great help. The melon does not need to be marinated with the wine. A fine pungent cheese goes well with this.

ICED MELON WITH WINE

Large honeydew or Persian melon	Fine sherry or port or Grand
Honey	Marnier

Use only the sweetest ripest melon for this. Remove a very small slice from the base so the melon will stand without tipping, then a thick slice from the top so that all the seeds may be removed. With a ball cutter remove all the ripe pulp from the inside. Season the balls with dribbles of honey and 1 or 2 jiggers of the chosen wine or liqueur. Return the balls and wine to the melon, replace the top and chill several hours before serving. Remove the top, drain the syrup into a pitcher and serve the melon balls in goblets, passing the syrup to pour over them. Another jigger of liquor may be added to the pitcher if required. A big melon should serve 6 or 8. This may be a first course or served for dessert with fancy cakes or cheese. Serve the melon on a silver plate or dish with its cap on.

PINK PEACHES WITH RASPBERRY SAUCE

6 fine ripe peaches
   Juice of 2 limes
⅓ cup white wine
⅔ cup light corn syrup
3 drops red vegetable coloring

1 package frozen raspberries
⅓ cup heavy cream, whipped
¼ to ⅓ cup browned chopped
   almonds (optional)

Make a syrup with the juice of 1 lime, wine, corn syrup, and vegetable coloring. Skin the peaches, put them with the syrup in the bottom of a large saucepan, and cook them gently until they are tender, rolling them constantly until they are cooked and colored. Lift them out and boil the syrup down until it is thick and pour it over the peaches. Chill. When ready to serve put the cold peaches in 6 goblets. Purée the raspberries in a blender with the juice of the other lime, then sieve to remove the seeds. Fold in the cream with the purée and divide over the peaches. Sprinkle the chopped browned almonds over the top.

PEACHES WITH STRAWBERRY SAUCE

Sauce:
   ½ cup orange juice
   Juice of 1 lemon
   ½ cup light corn syrup
   ¼ cup sugar

1 quart fresh strawberries, halved
8 fine peaches, skinned and halved
Garnish:
   Slivered browned almonds

Put the orange and lemon juices, syrup, and sugar in a saucepan and cook until thickened. Pour the syrup over the prepared strawberries and let stand 1 hour. Skin and halve the peaches and put them in a serving dish. Pour the strawberry sauce over them and let them chill 1 hour before serving. Prepare about ¼ to ⅓ cup of almonds and sprinkle them over the top just before serving. Serves 8.

BING CHERRY COMPOTE

1½ pounds fine cherries, stemmed
1½ cups good red wine
   1 stick cinnamon

1 cup light brown sugar
3 tablespoons currant jelly
⅓ cup slivered browned almonds

Stem the cherries but do not pit them. Simmer them 5 minutes with the wine, cinnamon, and sugar. Drain them and the cinnamon out and boil down the syrup until it is syrupy, then add the jelly and cook until it melts. Put the cherries in a shallow glass serving dish and when the syrup is cool enough pour it over the cherries and chill. When ready to serve sprinkle the top with almonds. Serves 6, or, with little cookies, 8.

PEELED BAKED APPLES OR PEARS

McIntosh apples or Comice pears   Sweet butter
Cooked prunes or dates   Light corn syrup
Cinnamon   Cream
Light brown sugar

Choose juicy fruit, peel, and core. Stuff each pear or apple with a date or a pitted prune. This is a time when those prunes in port that you keep in the refrigerator come in handy. Roll the fruit in plenty of cinnamon and sugar in a bowl, then put it on the bottom of a buttered baking dish. Put ⅓ cup of corn syrup in the bowl and scrape it over the fruit. Put a piece of butter in each piece of fruit and a few bits in the dish. Add no water. Cover with a tight lid. Bake 25 minutes, half the time at 375° and half at 350°. Remove the fruit to separate serving dishes or a big serving dish. Put ¼ to ⅓ cup of cream in the baking dish and thoroughly mix with the syrup in the dish and pour it over the fruit. A fine dessert for guests.

BLAZED BAKED APPLES

Fine tart apples   ⅔ cup light corn syrup (for 6
Brown sugar   apples)
Cinnamon   ½ cup water
Chopped browned almonds or   Jigger of brandy
    pecans   ½ cup heavy cream, whipped

Core the apples and peel halfway down. Fill the apples with sugar, cinnamon, and nuts. Pat cinnamon and sugar on the outside of the peeled part. Put them in a baking pan and pour the syrup and water over them. Bake at 325° until they are tender, basting twice with the pan syrup. When they are done, blaze with brandy. Remove them to serving dishes. Put the whipped cream in the baking pan and mix it with the pan syrup and divide it over the apples. They may be served hot or at room temperature.

BREAKFAST PRUNES
Le Beurre Fondu, London

Chef Ross-Muir practices French cuisine sprinkled with Scots dishes.

1 pound dried prunes, washed   Juice 1 lemon
1 quart strong hot tea   ½ teaspoon cinnamon
1 cup brown sugar

Brew the tea and strain it over the washed prunes and let them soak 24 hours. Add the sugar, lemon, and cinnamon and cook over low heat for 1½ hours, never allowing them actually to boil. Serve cold.

PRUNES MONIQUE
Le Beurre Fondu, London

This is a dessert specialty of Robert Ross-Muir, the chef of Le Beurre Fondu.

1 pound large sweet prunes   Whipped cream
1 pint cider   Brandy
  Marron purée

Wash the prunes and soak them in the cider for 24 hours. The prunes are not cooked so they must be soft and of the finest quality. Remove them from the cider and put 3 or 4 in each small serving dish. Put a dessert spoon of puréed chestnuts on top of the prunes and top with a blob of whipped cream, flavored with brandy.

PRUNES IN PORT

Large soft sweet prunes   Port
Honey

If the prunes are of fine quality, they need no presoaking or cooking. Put them in a jar, dribble in 3 tablespoons of honey for 1 pound of fruit, completely cover with port wine, and screw on the lid. Forget them for 2 weeks. They are good as a dessert, as a garnish for ham, duck, or goose, for stuffing baked pears or apples, and other uses you may think of.

ORANGE, PASSETTO

This is a Passetto specialty and very good because, as everyone knows, comparatively small countries allow their fruit to ripen before picking it. So the fruit in Italy and France is wonderful.

For each serving:
    A ring of fresh pineapple
    A whole orange, skinned
    A half-peach, skinned
    A pitted cherry and a toothpick
    Strega, Aurum, or Maraschino

This is built from the bottom up. Put the pineapple on a dessert plate. Place on it an orange free of all white pith. Cap the orange with the half-peach and put on top a cherry fastened through the peach into the orange with a toothpick. A liqueur is poured over all. Using a knife and fork you may dip each piece of fruit into one of Italy's popular liqueurs.

POIRES AU CASSIS
Hotel du Chapeau Rouge, Dijon

Whole peeled Anjou or Comice
  pears
2 cups water
2 cups sugar

2 teaspoons vanilla (or vanilla
  bean
Cassis de Dijon

Robert Mornand, the host of this best of all Dijon restaurants, gave me several recipes using the specialties of Dijon. Here is the delicious Cassis. Select fine juicy pears, peel them, and leave them whole with stem attached. Make a syrup of the water, sugar, and either vanilla bean or extract. Boil it for 10 minutes, then poach the pears in the syrup until just tender, testing with a cake tester. Replace the syrup with Cassis de Dijon and let the pears marinate overnight before serving.

While we are on the subject of Cassis, here is a dividend: a very delicious aperitif is a goblet of chilled white Macon Burgundy with 2 tablespoons of Cassis de Dijon added.

FRESH FIG COMPOTE

12 fresh figs
  Grated rind 2 navel oranges
⅔ cup light corn syrup
¼ cup light brown sugar or honey

3 tablespoons Kirsch
Garnish: Whipped cream or
  Crème Fraîche

Wash the figs and dry them. Simmer the orange rind and syrup very gently for 15 minutes, then add the sugar or honey and the Kirsch. Put the figs in the syrup and simmer for 6 or 8 minutes. Do not let them cook until they break. Serve warm or cold with cream. Serve 2 or 3 figs to each person. If desired sprinkle with chopped almonds or black walnuts.

MACEDONIA AL MARASCHINO
Nerina, Bologna

Macedonia is not exclusive with Nerina but hers is very good because it is marinated in a liqueur that is one of the best with fruit—Maraschino.

Pineapple
Cherries
Bananas
Peaches

Pears
Melon
Maraschino, Strega, or Aurum

The fresh fruits are cubed or sliced and little or no sugar is added. Marinate the fruit 2 hours in the chosen liqueur. This is a popular dessert in Italy and is particularly appreciated after a rich pasta.

CHEESE MOLD TO SERVE WITH FRUIT

½ pound creamy Gorgonzola
4 ounces cream cheese
1 teaspoon gelatin

2 tablespoons water
⅓ cup Curaçao or Cointreau
1 cup heavy cream, whipped

Let the cheeses remain at room temperature until they may be blended together to a smooth cream. I say creamy Gorgonzola because the too old yellow cheese is strong and won't do. Soak the gelatin in the water, melt it over hot water, and mix it thoroughly with the cheese. Stir in either liqueur, then mix in the cream very lightly. Put the mixture in an oiled fancy mold and chill several hours before unmolding on a serving plate. This will serve 10 or 12 with beautiful fruit. If you prefer, use Madeira or port instead of the liqueur.

WINE JELLY

2 cups good claret or Burgundy
2 cups grape juice
¾ cup blackberry jelly
¼ cup fruit brandy (optional)

Grated rind 1 lemon
Juice 1 lemon
5 teaspoons gelatin

This is a very old recipe which calls for a cup of brandy. I found it too strong. The better the wine the better the jelly and this is a very nice dessert to serve with a fine cheese. Dilute a can of frozen grape concentrate with enough water to make 2 cups of juice—about 1¼ cups water. Let the gelatin soak in the lemon juice, add the jelly, and melt over hot water, then mix all the ingredients together and pour into a fancy oiled 5- or 6-cup mold and chill until it is set. Serves 6. If brandy is used, choose a plum brandy (Mirabelle) or one of the orange liqueurs.

ORANGE JELLY

2 tablespoons grated orange rind
½ cup light corn syrup
3 cups fresh, strained orange juice
4 teaspoons gelatin
Juice 1 lime

⅓ cup Curaçao or Cointreau
Garnish:
   Orange segments
   Ground almonds

Gently simmer the orange rind with the corn syrup for 8 or 10 minutes. Squeeze fresh orange juice and strain it. Soak the gelatin in the lime juice, add it to the hot syrup to melt, and mix it with the orange juice and liqueur. Oil a fancy mold and pour in the liquid; chill until set. Unmold on a round plate and serve this refreshing aspic with or without cheese after a rich dinner. To be fancy, dip orange segments in ground almonds to decorate the mold. Serves 6.

Pastry, Pies & Tarts

PIE (OR TART) PASTRY

2 cups sifted flour
1 teaspoon salt
½ teaspoon sugar
⅓ cup butter

⅓ cup vegetable shortening or lard
¼ cup ice water
2 tablespoons soft butter

Sift and measure the flour, then sift with the salt and sugar. Cut in ⅓ cup butter and ⅓ cup shortening or lard with a pastry cutter and, to insure that the ingredients are cold, refrigerate 1 hour before finishing the crust. I grew up with rich lard pie crust, but I know that tastes change as well as styles, and as we are influenced so much by French cuisine which never calls for lard in pastry, it is a matter of personal taste whether one uses it. Lard pastry may be used in apple pies, but for the more delicate *Cream Pie* I suggest butter and vegetable shortening. Add the ice water a little at a time and moisten the dough just enough to handle without its becoming sticky or too wet. Put it on a floured board, half of it at a time if a 2-crust pie is made. One cup of flour is sufficient for a 1-crust 8- or 9-inch pie. Roll the dough a little larger than the pie pan, fold it in half and lay it over half the pan, then unfold to cover it. Fold over the edges and pinch them to make a rim. After the filling is added the same procedure is followed with the rest of the dough. When it is rolled out spread the soft butter on the dough, fold, and roll again. This makes for added flakiness. Make 6 or 8 incisions in the top crust for the steam to escape. A little flour may be sprinkled on the bottom crust if juicy berry pies are being baked. A 1-crust pastry shell for *Quiche* is baked 8 minutes at 400° before it is filled and baked again. This insures a flakier crust. Prebaked crust for cream pies is pricked with a sharp pointed knife before it goes into the oven and may be pricked again halfway through the baking. Bake at 400° for 15 to 17 minutes until the crust is a golden brown.

CREAM CHEESE CRUST

1 cup flour
¼ teaspoon salt
4 ounces cream cheese

½ cup butter
Cream

Sift the flour and salt. Mix the cheese and butter together with a wire pastry cutter, then mix with the flour. It may not be necessary to use any cream to form into a ball and roll out; but if it is, 1 tablespoon should be enough. This may be used as a bottom crust for pies or cut in 2-inch rounds for filling and folding for turnovers. These may be filled with creamed crab or lobster meat, shrimp or tuna; also with sausage or hashed chicken or beef. For sweet turnovers, fill them with jam or sweetened berries, or cherries. Bake at 375° for 12 or 15 minutes.

PUFF PASTE

1 cup sweet butter
2 cups flour

½ teaspoon salt
½ to ⅔ cup ice water

Reserve 2 tablespoons of the butter and form the rest into a cake ¼-inch thick. Have all utensils cold. Sift the flour with the salt and cut the 2 tablespoons of butter into it. Make a well in the flour and add ½ cup of ice water and mix to a soft dough. Use a tablespoon or so more water if needed, not more. Chill the dough for 10 minutes. Knead the dough a moment on a very lightly floured board, then roll it into an oblong strip ¼-inch thick. Put the cake of butter on one half of the dough, fold over the other half, pressing the edges a little, then fold one side over the top and the other side beneath. Roll out without letting the butter break through, fold twice, incorporating as much air as possible, then chill for 15 minutes. Roll out, fold over twice like a handkerchief, and chill. Repeat until it has been rolled and chilled 6 times. The more air incorporated the higher and lighter the paste will be when baked. The dough must be very cold before it is rolled and cut into shapes. For turnovers the dough is rolled ¼-inch thick and cut into 5-inch squares. For patty shells it is rolled ½-inch thick and cut with a cookie cutter. The tops are cut with a doughnut cutter the same size. The solid round is brushed with ice water and the round with a hole in it is placed on top. The small rounds left by the doughnut cutter are baked separately. If the dough isn't cold after cutting, chill before baking. Cover a cookie sheet with buttered brown paper, put the pastry on it, and put it in a 450° oven. Bake 10 minutes, then turn the heat down to 375° for 25 or 30 minutes, more. The tiny rounds take less time to bake so put them on a separate sheet.

SUGAR CRUST

1 cup flour
⅛ teaspoon salt
1 to 3 tablespoons sugar

3 tablespoons butter
3 tablespoons vegetable shortening
Ice water

One cup of flour will line an 8- or 9-inch tart pan. The French sometimes use an egg as part of the liquid. With the egg, this is somewhat like a cookie dough. They use more butter, but with our flour part vegetable shortening makes a more tender and flaky crust. The mixing procedure is the same as for *Pie Pastry*. A crust baked without filling must be well pricked before it is baked and may be pricked again half through the baking to prevent shrinkage and blistering.

ALSATIAN APPLE TART

8- or 9-inch *Pie Pastry* shell
4 or 5 tart apples
2 or 3 tablespoons lemon juice
(if needed)
1 cup light brown sugar

⅔ cup water
Garnishes (optional):
Chopped browned almonds
Heavy cream or whipped
cream

Line the tart pan with rich pastry, making a high fluted rim. Bake it 8 minutes at 400°. Have the apples ready for it. Peel and core the apples and cut them in eighths. If they aren't very tart sprinkle with the lemon juice. Boil ¾ cup of the sugar with the water for 4 or 5 minutes, then poach the apples in the syrup until they are almost tender. Put them in the hot pie shell, then pour the syrup over them. Sprinkle the remaining ¼ cup sugar over the top. Put the tart in the oven, turning the heat down to 375°, and bake until the crust is a good brown. Let the tart cool to room temperature, unless you prefer to serve it hot. You may put a few slivered almonds on top, or decorate with a few rosettes of whipped cream, or serve heavy cream in a pitcher.

APPLE OR PEACH TART

6 fine peaches or tart apples
½ cup light wine
¾ cup light corn syrup
½ cup light brown sugar
1 tablespoon cornstarch
1 prebaked, cooled, 8- or 9-inch
    pastry shell

4½ ounces cream cheese
3 tablespoons heavy cream
Garnish:
    ¼ cup chopped almonds, or
    rosettes of whipped cream

Skin the peaches or peel the apples. Cut them in eighths. Cook the wine, syrup, and sugar, and poach the fruit until it is tender but still holds its shape. Carefully skim out the fruit and let it cool to room temperature. If apples need it, add 2 tablespoons of lemon juice to the syrup. Boil the syrup down to 1⅓ cups. Blend in the cornstarch and cook until it thickens and is clear. Make the tart crust and when it is cool spread the cheese softened with the cream over the bottom of it. Arrange the fruit on the cheese and pour the syrup over it. The top may be sprinkled with chopped browned nuts or decorated with whipped-cream rosettes.

CHESTNUT TARTS

1 cup chestnut purée
1 square bitter chocolate
1 teaspoon vanilla
2 tablespoons rum

1 cup Crème Pâtissière
Pastry for 8 tart shells
Garnish: Glacé chestnuts, or
    chestnuts in syrup

Use 1 pound of chestnuts. Gash them with a sharp pointed knife. Put them in a saucepan, cover with water, and after they come to the boil, cook 1½ minutes. Remove from heat and peel them while they are still warm. Put the peeled chestnuts in a saucepan with ¾ cup of water and simmer until they are tender, then drain and mash through a sieve. Melt the chocolate over hot water and add it to the purée with the vanilla and rum. Make 1 cup of Crème Pâtissière, using 1 tablespoon of cornstarch blended with a cup of light cream and ¼ cup of light brown sugar; cook until it thickens, then stir in 2 egg yolks and cook a second. Stir into the chestnut purée very lightly and let it cool. Line muffin tins with tart pastry and bake in a 400° oven to a golden brown. Cool them. Divide the purée into the tart shells and top with a glacé chestnut, or use chestnuts in syrup, first draining them. The filling may be lightened if desired by folding in ⅓ to ½ cup of whipped cream. Serves 8. This filling may also fill tiny fluted tart shells for dessert or tea.

FRESH BERRY TART

1 9-inch pie shell, prebaked and
    cooled
1 quart fresh berries: strawberries,
    blackberries, or blueberries
½ cup water
1 cup light brown sugar
2 tablespoons cornstarch
2 tablespoons Kirsch
Garnish:
    Slivered browned almonds
    Heavy cream

Make the crust and let it cool. The berries must be clean and dry. Put the water and sugar in a saucepan and when it is heated put in the fruit. Blend the cornstarch with 3 tablespoons of water, add, and bring to a boil. Do not cook more than 1 minute. Let cool. Stir in the Kirsch. Put the filling into the crust and sprinkle some almonds over the top if desired. Pass the cream, or serve with *Crème Fraîche*.

LORRAINE CHERRY TART
(Clafoutis)

8- or 9-inch *Pie Pastry* shell
1 pound fresh tart cherries
½ cup light brown sugar
⅓ cup red wine
½ cup heavy cream
2 tablespoons cornstarch
¼ cup light brown sugar
3 large egg yolks
1 teaspoon almond extract
¼ cup Kirsch or rum
Garnish: ⅓ cup slivered browned
    almonds (optional)

Pit the cherries. Line a tart pan with rich pastry and bake it at 400° for 8 minutes before putting in the filling. Bring the cherries, brown sugar, and wine to a boil and cook for 2 minutes, then drain out the cherries. Cook the syrup down to ⅔ cup. Blend the cream with the cornstarch and cook it until it begins to thicken. Mix the sugar with the egg yolks and add them and the syrup to the cream. Add the extract and Kirsch or rum. Remove the crust from the oven and fill with the cherries, pour the liquid over them, and return the tart to the oven for 20 minutes, reducing the heat to 325°. Cool a little before serving. Sprinkle the top with the almonds if you like. Serves 6.

STRAWBERRY, BLACKBERRY, OR RASPBERRY CREAM TART

1 8- or 9-inch *Pie Pastry* shell or *Cream Cheese Crust*, prebaked and cooled
4½ ounces cream cheese
⅓ cup heavy cream
Filling: 1 quart berries

1 10-ounce package frozen berries
Juice ½ lime
1 tablespoon cornstarch
Garnish:
Rosettes of whipped cream

Prebake the crust and let it become entirely cool. Soften the cheese at room temperature and mix with the cream. This pie is best assembled an hour before dinner. Clean and hull the berries and reserve 3 cups of them. Put the fourth cup in a blender with the frozen berries and purée them, or they may be mashed through a sieve. Add the lime juice and blend the purée with the cornstarch. Simmer the purée until it thickens and then let it cool. If the whole berries are very tart they may be marinated in a dribble of honey. Spread the cream cheese mixture over the crust and put the 3 cups of berries over the cream. Then cover with the berry sauce. Rosettes of whipped cream may decorate the top. A 9-inch tart will serve 8.

If frozen blackberries aren't available get 3 pints of fresh blackberries and purée 2½ cups of them for the sauce. The sauce may be flavored with blackberry brandy.

TARTE AU CITRON
Capucin Gourmand, Nancy

1 *Sugar Crust*, 8 or 9 inches
Filling:
⅔ cup sugar
⅓ cup sweet butter
1 teaspoon cornstarch

2 eggs, beaten
Grated rind and juice of 2 large lemons

Make pastry of 1 cup of sifted flour, ½ teaspoon salt, and ⅓ cup of shortening. Roll it very thin and line a tart pan 9 or 10 inches in diameter. Bake it 10 minutes at 400°. For the filling, cream the sugar and butter until fluffy, then stir in the cornstarch. Add the beaten eggs, lemon rind and juice. Put the filling in the pastry and bake at 400° 10 minutes more. Georges Romain says an orange tart may be made the same way. The lemon tart is lemony and delicious. Let it cool to room temperature to serve. Little tart pans may be lined with pastry, baked 6 minutes, filled, and baked 6 minutes more. This makes 2 dozen small tarts. A delicious addition is a sprinkle of shaved almonds over the top.

ITALIAN MARZIPAN TORTA

Pie Pastry

Filling:
  1¼ cups almonds
  ¼ cup candied orange peel
  ¾ cup sugar
  2 tablespoons butter
  2 eggs, beaten
  ¼ cup "Cin" aperitif
  ¼ cup water

Make pastry for a 2-crust 8-inch pie. Roll half of it thin and line a pie pan. Lightly brown the almonds and grind them. Toss the almonds with the sliced orange peel. Cream the sugar and butter. Mix all the ingredients together. "Cin" made by Cinzano is a little sweeter than dry vermouth and perfect for this. Put the filling into pie shell. Roll the rest of the dough thin and cut it in ½-inch strips and lay it crisscross over the filling to make a lattice crust. Bake 10 minutes at 400°, then turn down the heat to 325° and bake until it is a golden color, about 15 to 18 minutes more. Let cool a little before serving. Serves 6 or 8.

ITALIAN APRICOT TORTA

8-inch *Pie Pastry* shell
Cream filling:
  1 cup milk
  1 cup light cream
  ⅓ cup sugar
  ⅓ cup sifted flour
  3 egg yolks
  Grated rind 1 large lemon

Powdered sugar
1 pound can apricots

Line an 8-inch pie pan with rich pie pastry and bake it 10 minutes at 400°. Have the filling ready. Scald the milk and cream and pour it over the rest of the ingredients beaten together in the top of a double boiler. Stir over simmering water until it is quite thick. Remove the pastry from the oven and fill the pan, sprinkle with powdered sugar and bake at 375° for 8 minutes. Remove and place the apricots on top, cut side down, sprinkle well with powdered sugar and run under the flame until it glazes. Be careful not to let it burn. Serve at room temperature. This is a delicious tart and may be made with peaches or mangos. The best peeled canned apricots should be used. A pound can usually contains 7 whole apricots; 14 halves just covers an 8-inch tart.

OLD-FASHIONED COCONUT TARTS

2 cups sugar
1½ cups dessicated coconut
1½ cups boiling water

7 large egg yolks, beaten
2 tablespoons sweet butter
Garnish: Whipped cream

Line 12 muffin tins with rich pastry and bake 6 minutes in a 400° oven. Have the filling ready. Boil the sugar, coconut, and water for 10 minutes at a gentle simmer, then pour over the beaten egg yolks and stir in the butter. Put the filling in the hot pastry shells and bake at 375° 10 or 12 minutes, or until the filling thickens a little and the crust is a rich brown. These are best moist inside. Serve at room temperature. They thicken more as they cool. They may be eaten plain or with a small dab of whipped cream.

CREAM PIE

1 cup light cream
1 cup heavy cream
2 tablespoons cornstarch
¼ cup light brown sugar
4 egg yolks, beaten
1 teaspoon vanilla
1 teaspoon almond
2 tablespoons Kirsch or sherry

Meringue:
4 egg whites, beaten
4 tablespoons light brown
    sugar
1 teaspoon each almond and
    vanilla
1 9-inch prebaked, cooled pie shell

This is rich but one of the most delicious of confections. Make the crust ahead and let cool. Put the creams in the top of a double boiler. Blend the cornstarch with a little of the cream, then add it to the rest. Cook over simmering water until it thickens. Beat the sugar and egg yolks until thick. When the cream mixture is thickened add some gradually to the egg yolks, then scrape the egg mixture into the rest of the custard and cook until it thickens, but not too long as it will curdle. (If it does curdle it may be saved by putting it in a blender or beating it smooth with a rotary beater.) Let it cool thoroughly, then add the flavorings. Pour it into a thoroughly cooled crust. If both custard and crust aren't cooled, the steam will thin the custard when the meringue is put on top. Beat the egg whites stiff, then add the sugar and beat until thick. Add the extracts. Pile the meringue on the custard and bake the pie in a 375° oven until it puffs and browns. This is best made several hours before serving and served at room temperature. Serves 6 or 8. If a less rich filling is desired a cup of milk may replace the light cream but the heavy cream should be used in any case to give it the delicious creamy quality.

CHOCOLATE CREAM PIE

Filling for *Cream Pie*   2 or 3 squares bitter chocolate,
                                                melted

Melt the chocolate over hot water and add it to the hot custard. When cold, cover with the meringue.

CHOCOLATE RUM PIE

5 ounces bitter chocolate, grated
4 ounces semisweet chocolate,
    grated
¼ cup milk or black coffee
¼ cup brown sugar
5 egg yolks, beaten

2 teaspoons vanilla
¼ cup dark rum
5 egg whites, beaten
9- or 10-inch rich *Pie Pastry* shell,
    or *Meringue Shell*, prebaked
    and cooled

Put the chocolate, the coffee or milk, and the brown sugar in the top of a double boiler and cook over boiling water until melted and smooth. Remove from the fire and add the beaten egg yolks. When it is cool add the vanilla and rum. Fold in the stiffly beaten egg whites and pour the mixture into either a cooled *Pie Pastry* shell or *Meringue Shell*. If a pie shell is used, cool several hours but do not refrigerate. If the meringue shell is used, wrap in wax paper and refrigerate 12 hours; remove from refrigerator 2 hours before serving. Serves 8. This filling may be piled in a fancy dish and served as a mousse. The top may be decorated with chopped almonds or whipped cream.

MERINGUE SHELL. Beat 4 egg whites until frothy, add ¼ teaspoon cream of tartar, and beat until stiff. Slowly add 1 cup of sugar, beating continuously. Pour into a greased glass 9- or 10-inch pie plate and bake 50 minutes at 275°. Let cool.

OLD-FASHIONED COCONUT PIE

2 cups sugar
1½ cups shredded coconut
1½ cups boiling water
7 egg yolks, beaten

2 tablespoons butter
1 9-inch pie shell
Whipped cream (optional)

Boil the sugar, coconut, and water gently for 10 minutes. Pour slowly into the thickly beaten egg yolks and add the butter. Bake the crust in a 400° oven for 7 minutes, then pour in the slightly cooled custard and bake at 350° until it sets, about 15 minutes. Let cool thoroughly but do not chill. Serve whipped cream for those who want it. Serves 7 or 8. This filling may also be baked in pastry-lined muffin tins.

OLD-FASHIONED CUSTARD PIE

1 cup heavy cream
1 cup milk
½ cup light brown sugar
4 eggs, beaten

2 teaspoons vanilla
1 8-inch tart crust
Nutmeg, or *Praliné Powder*

Scald the cream and milk. Beat the eggs and sugar until thick and add the milk and cream gradually. Add the vanilla. Bake the crust at 400° for 8 minutes, then add the hot custard, if desired sprinkle with nutmeg, and bake at 350° until it is set, 22 to 25 minutes. Test with a silver knife and when the knife comes out clean it is done. Cool and serve. If you prefer to use praliné powder instead of the nutmeg, sprinkle it on top when the pie is cool.

COCONUT CREAM PIE

Filling for *Cream Pie*

1¼ cups grated fresh coconut or dessicated coconut

When the filling is thoroughly cooled add ⅔ cup of coconut. Fill the cool pastry shell, cover with meringue and put it in a 375° oven; when the meringue is ivory color and puffed up, sprinkle the top with the rest of the coconut. Return to the oven to brown. Coconut browns very quickly.

MACAROON PIE

Filling for *Cream Pie*
⅔ cup finely crumbled macaroons

2 tablespoons rum or Kirsch
Whipped cream or meringue

When the custard has cooled, stir in the macaroon crumbs and the rum or Kirsch, instead of the liquor specified in *Cream Pie*. Cover with either flavored whipped cream or the meringue.

RASPBERRY CREAM PIE

Filling for *Cream Pie*
2 cups fresh raspberries

2 tablespoons honey
1¼ cups heavy cream, whipped

Make the filling and let it cool. Marinate the raspberries in the honey an hour. A half-hour before serving, put the custard in the baked cooled crust. Drain the raspberries and spread them over the custard. Put the marinade in the whipped cream and spread the pink cream over the top.

FRENCH CUSTARD PIE

The little pâtisserie across the street from Madame de Sévigné's one-time abode, the fascinating Musée Carnavalet, is the inspiration for this pastry.

8-inch pie shell   3 tablespoons slivered angelica
Filling:
    1 cup light corn syrup
    3 eggs
    3 tablespoons light brown sugar
    3 tablespoons sweet butter
    1 teaspoon each vanilla and
        rose extract

Line a pie pan with rich pie crust and bake it 8 minutes in a 400° oven. Get the filling ready. Beat the eggs. Cream the sugar and butter together. Mix the corn syrup with the eggs, then blend with the sugar and butter. Add the extracts. Remove the pie shell from the oven, pour in the filling, and return it to the oven for 15 or 20 minutes, reducing the heat to 325°. When it is cool it will thicken more. Decorate with slivers of angelica. This should be creamy of texture and is served at room temperature. Serves 6.

ITALIAN RICOTTA PIE

Pastry: Filling:
    2½ cups sifted flour   3 cups sieved ricotta
    ½ teaspoon salt   ¼ cup chopped almonds
    ¼ cup sugar   ¼ cup diced candied cherries
    ¼ cup butter   ¼ cup diced orange peel
    ¼ cup vegetable shortening   ½ cup sugar
    1 egg, beaten   2 tablespoons cocoa
    3 tablespoons light rum   (optional)
    Ice water   4 eggs, beaten

For the pastry sift the flour, then sift again with the salt and sugar. Cut in the butter and shortening with a pastry cutter and put the mixture in the refrigerator to chill 1 hour. Beat the egg and mix with the rum and 1 or 2 tablespoons of ice water. Mix it with the flour mixture just enough so the mixture can be handled. Use no more ice water than is necessary. Roll out a little more than half the dough and line a 10-inch tart pan. For the filling add all the ingredients to the sieved cheese adding the beaten eggs last. The cocoa may be omitted and vanilla or a teaspoon of almond extract substituted. Put the filling in the dough and cover with lattice strips of the pastry. Put the pie in a 400° oven for 5 minutes, reduce the heat to 350° for 20 minutes, then reduce again to 325° for 15 or 20 minutes, or until the filling is set.

ALMOND OR PECAN PIE

¾ cup lightly browned almonds
   or pecans
5 or 6 bitter almonds and 2
   teaspoons almond extract
   (for almonds), or 2 teaspoons
   vanilla (for pecans)

2 eggs
2 tablespoons soft sweet butter
1 cup light corn syrup
1 cup light brown sugar
1 8-inch *Pie Pastry* crust

Brown the nuts in the oven a little to improve their flavor. Grind ½ cup of them (with the bitter almonds if almonds are used). Sliver the remaining ¼ cup of nuts and mix them together. With a rotary beater beat the eggs, butter, syrup, and sugar together and add the extract and nuts. Line an 8-inch pie plate with the crust and bake it 7 minutes at 400°. Warm the filling slightly, put it in the crust, and bake at 350° about 30 minutes or until the filling is set and still soft. It thickens as it cools. It is rich and will serve 7 or 8.

LIME PIE

5 egg yolks, beaten
1 cup sugar
½ cup fresh lime juice
   Grated rind 2 limes
2 tablespoons cornstarch
½ cup boiling water
3 drops green vegetable coloring

2 egg whites, beaten
1 9-inch prebaked pie shell
Meringue:
   4 egg whites, beaten
   ½ cup light brown sugar
   1 teaspoon vanilla

Make the crust and let it cool. Beat the egg yolks until light, add the sugar gradually, and beat until thick. Blend the cornstarch with the lime juice and rind, add the boiling water and the egg-yolk mixture. Cook in the top of a double boiler until thick. Let cool thoroughly. Tint with green coloring and fold in the 2 stiffly beaten egg whites. For the meringue, beat 4 egg whites until stiff and beat in the sugar and vanilla. Put the filling in the cooled crust, pile the meringue on top, and bake in a 350° oven for about 8 minutes, until it is puffed and brown. Serves 7 or 8.

RUM SQUASH PIE

1¼ cups acorn or Hubbard squash
1 cup light brown sugar
1 teaspoon cinnamon
½ teaspoon nutmeg
½ teaspoon clove
¼ teaspoon mace or ginger

3 eggs, beaten
½ cup heavy cream
⅓ cup dark rum
8- or 9-inch pie shell
Garnish: *Crème Fraîche*

Make the crust and line a pie pan with it. Boil 2 acorn squash in a kettle of water until tender. Test with a cake tester. Peel, seed, and mash the squash. Beat the eggs, and mix with the squash and all the other ingredients. Bake the pie shell at 400° 8 minutes, then fill it with the squash mixture. Bake 10 minutes at 375°, then turn down to 325° and bake until the filling is set, about 25 minutes more. This is served at room temperature or warmer if you like, with or without *Crème Fraîche*.

Cakes & Cookies

FOUR-EGG-WHITE CAKE

½ cup sweet butter
1 cup instant superfine sugar
½ cup milk
1½ cups cake flour

1½ teaspoons baking powder
1 teaspoon vanilla
4 egg whites, beaten

Preheat the oven to 350°. All ingredients must be brought to room temperature before beginning the cake. Cream the butter with ¾ cup of the sugar until light and fluffy. Sift the flour, measure it, and sift it 3 or 4 times with the baking powder. Stir in the milk and flour alternately, beating well after each addition. Add the vanilla. Beat the egg whites until stiff, then slowly add the ¼ cup of sugar to the egg whites. Stir one-fourth of the egg whites into the batter, then fold in the rest. Do not beat again. Divide the batter in two 8-inch greased floured cake pans and bake about 25 minutes. After 5 minutes remove the layers to a cake rack to cool. Caramel Frosting (see *Pecan* or *Black Walnut Cake*) is very good on white cake.

FIVE-EGG-WHITE CAKE

1½ cups instant superfine sugar	1 teaspoon vanilla
⅔ cup sweet butter	¾ cup milk
2 cups sifted cake flour	5 egg whites, beaten
1 teaspoon baking powder	

Follow the directions for the *Four-Egg-White Cake*, creaming the butter and 1 cup of the sugar. Add the ½ cup of sugar to the stiffly beaten egg whites, adding them last. Bake in two 9-inch pans about 30 minutes at 350°.

ANNIVERSARY CAKE

This wonderful white butter cake is suitable for weddings, birthdays, or any occasion when the best is required. Or make it for the family and a few friends—it makes any dinner festive. For a wedding the recipe may be made twice for a tiered cake. Several frostings and fillings are included in this section (see index). Everyone has his favorite; perhaps mine is lemon jelly filling and frosting because my favorite grandmother always made it for me when I visited her.

½ cup sweet butter	8 egg whites (1 full cup)
1 cup instant superfine sugar	½ cup more sugar
½ cup milk	2 of these extracts:
½ cup warm water	1 teaspoon vanilla
2½ cups sifted cake flour	1 teaspoon rose
2½ teaspoons baking powder	1 teaspoon almond

At least an hour before you begin the cake remove the butter and egg whites from the refrigerator. The butter must be soft and the egg whites at room temperature. Preheat the oven to 350°. Cream the butter and 1 cup sugar (instant superfine) until fluffy and smooth. Warm the milk by combining the milk and water. Grease and flour two 9-inch cake pans. Use unprepared cake flour (Swansdown), sift and measure it, then sift it with the baking powder several times. Add the milk and water mixture alternately with the flour to the butter and sugar, beating very hard for about 4 minutes. Add the extracts. Beat the egg whites until stiff, then add the ½ cup of instant sugar very gradually. Stir one-fourth of the egg-white mixture into the batter, stir until it is light, then gently fold in the rest of the whites. Do not beat again. Divide the batter into the cake pans and bake about 30 to 35 minutes at 350°. The cake will be firm to the touch of the finger and will shrink from the sides of the pans. Let it stand 4 minutes, then loosen the edges with a sharp pointed knife and turn it onto wire racks to cool. The layers should be filled and frosted as soon as they are entirely cool. It may be baked in three 8-inch layers.

BUTTER SPONGE CAKE

This delicate cake has many uses. It may be baked in shallow pans and cut in small squares to frost for *Petits Fours*, as the French use *Genoise*. It may be baked in a tube pan, left plain or frosted any way you choose, or cut across in three layers, and filled and iced for *Cassata alla Siciliana*.

¾ cup instant superfine sugar
8 or 9 egg yolks
½ cup sweet butter, melted
   Grated rind 1 Sunkist orange
2 tablespoons orange juice

1¼ cups sifted cake flour
½ teaspoon cream of tartar
½ cup instant superfine sugar
8 or 9 egg whites

Put the ¾ cup sugar in the top of a double boiler over simmering water while you prepare the other ingredients. If the eggs are not large, use 9. Separate the eggs. Melt the butter in a saucepan (do not let it become oily), grate the orange rind into it, and add the juice. One teaspoon of grated lemon rind and 1 tablespoon of lemon juice may be used instead of orange if you prefer. Sift the flour twice then measure it. Mix the cream of tartar with the ½ cup of sugar. Preheat the oven to 350°. Put the egg yolks in the double boiler with the sugar, turn off the heat, and beat hard with a rotary beater or electric hand-beater. The sugar and yolks are to become warm but not cook. When they are thick and have increased in volume, empty the hot water from the double boiler and replace it with cold water. Continue beating until the mixture is cool. Then add slowly and alternately the butter-orange mixture and the flour, beating continuously. Beat the egg whites until stiff, then gradually add the mixed sugar and cream of tartar. Mix one-third of the egg whites into the flour mixture until it has a fluffy texture, then lightly fold in the rest of the whites and do not beat again. Empty into the pan or pans and put it in the oven on the center shelf. A 9-inch tube pan takes about 45 minutes. Nine-inch square pans take about 22 minutes, or until the cake is firm to the touch. Let the cake stand 5 minutes when it comes from the oven then turn it out onto a cake plate. Cake baked in a tube pan is put upside down on a cake plate and when it cools it will fall to the plate. If it sticks, loosen it with a narrow sharp knife and give it a gentle shake. This cake does not fall but it shrinks a little as it cools.

YELLOW BUTTER CAKE

1 cup sweet butter
2 cups instant superfine sugar
4 egg yolks
1 cup milk

3 cups sifted cake flour
3 teaspoons baking powder
2 teaspoons vanilla
4 egg whites, beaten

Always measure the butter and let it become soft outside the refrigerator an hour or so before you begin the cake; have the milk and eggs at room temperature also. Preheat the oven to 350°. Cream the butter and sugar until fluffy and smooth. (Always use instant superfine sugar for cakes.) Stir in the egg yolks, one at a time and beat very well. Sift and measure the flour, then sift it 2 or 3 times with the baking powder. Add the milk and flour alternately to the egg-butter mixture and beat well. Add the vanilla. Beat the egg whites until stiff and stir one-fourth of them into the batter, then lightly fold in the rest. Do not beat again. This cake may be baked in three greased floured 8-inch layer pans or in two 9-inch pans. The layers are baked 25 to 30 minutes at 350°. When the cake is done it springs back to the gentle touch of a finger and shrinks from the side of the pan. This cake may be baked in one large pan and used for *Baked Alaska*, or baked in square pans and cut in squares for *Petits Fours* which are iced with tinted icing and decorated with sliced glacé fruits.

ORANGE CAKE

Yellow Butter Cake
Grated rind of 1 Sunkist orange
Filling:
  2½ tablespoons cornstarch
  ½ cup sugar
  1 egg yolk
  1 cup orange juice
  1 tablespoon lemon juice
  1 tablespoon grated orange rind

Frosting:
  1½ cups sugar
  1 tablespoon grated orange rind
  ¼ cup orange juice
  1 teaspoon lemon juice
  ¼ teaspoon cream of tartar
  2 egg whites, unbeaten

Make *Yellow Butter Cake* according to directions, but omit the vanilla and add the grated orange rind. Deep-colored oranges without artificial coloring must always be used in cooking. Bake the cake in two 9-inch layers and let it cool. For the filling, mix the cornstarch and sugar together, stir in the egg yolk, juices, and rind. Cook the mixture in a double boiler over simmering water until it is thick. Cool and spread on one layer of the cake. For the frosting, put all the ingredients in the top of the double boiler and cook over simmering water, beating with a rotary or electric beater until it stands in peaks. Remove from fire and beat until it cools a little. Spread on the sides of the cake and pile thickly over the top. This will also make three 8-inch layers if you prefer; double the quantity of filling.

ORANGE EGG-YOLK CAKE

1 cup instant superfine sugar
6 egg yolks (½ cup)
  Grated rind of 1 Sunkist orange
¼ cup orange juice

3 tablespoons melted sweet butter
1 cup sifted cake flour
½ teaspoon baking powder

This incredible, melting cake really doesn't need frosting, but a thin spread of butter icing sprinkled with chopped pecans makes it an amazing confection. Put the sugar in the top of a double boiler over simmering water while you prepare the cake. Grate the orange and add the juice. Grease and flour a 9-inch cake pan. Turn the heat to 350°. Sift and measure Swansdown cake flour, then sift three times with the baking powder. Beat the egg yolks and mix with the warmed sugar, then turn off the fire and beat with an electric beater or a rotary beater for 7 or 8 minutes. Empty the hot water from the lower part of the double boiler and fill with cold water. Continue to beat the batter another 5 minutes, then slowly add the orange juice, rind, and melted butter, beating continuously. Add the flour, folding it in a little at a time without beating it. When all is mixed, put the batter into the pan and bake the cake 30 minutes. This cake may be mixed entirely in the top of the double boiler. Make it when you have collected some egg yolks; they keep well in the refrigerator in a glass jar with a tight screw top. Never hesitate collecting egg whites either. They may be used for meringues, cheese egg-white soufflé, white cake, and dessert soufflés that use only whites.

ALMOND CREAM CAKE

Hot Milk Cake:
  ½ cup butter
  1 cup milk
  4 eggs, beaten
  2 cups sugar
  1 teaspoon vanilla
  2 cups flour
  2 teaspoons baking powder

2 cups almonds, browned and
  ground
4 bitter almonds, ground
2 cups heavy cream, whipped
2 teaspoons almond extract
¼ cup powdered sugar

Put the butter and milk in a saucepan over a low fire just long enough to melt the butter; do not let it boil. Beat the eggs until thick, then slowly add the sugar. Continue beating until the mixture is thick and light and add the vanilla. Sift the flour, measure, and sift with the baking powder. To the egg mixture alternately add the milk and butter and the flour. Bake in two 9-inch or three 8-inch greased, floured cake pans at 350° 25 to 30 minutes. Let stand 4 minutes, then remove from the pans and cool on wire racks. Fill when cool. Spread the almonds on a big pan and dry out in the oven until they color a very little. Grind the almonds and the bitter almonds (if available). Whip the cream until stiff, add the extract and sugar, and lightly fold in the almonds. Spread between the layers and all over the cake.

ORANGE-LEMON CREAM CAKE

Hot Milk Cake

Filling and frosting:
2 tablespoons cornstarch
⅔ cup orange juice
½ cup lemon juice
Grated rinds of 1 lemon
and 1 navel orange
1 cup sugar
3 egg yolks, beaten
1 cup heavy cream, whipped

Blend the cornstarch with a little of the juice, add the juices, rinds, and sugar and cook in a saucepan until thickened, stirring constantly with a rubber spatula. Pour over the beaten egg yolks and return the mixture to the fire a moment until it thickens. Let cool thoroughly. Bake the hot milk cake in two 9-inch greased floured cake pans and let it cool. Put half the custard on the bottom layer. Mix the rest of the custard with the whipped cream and cover the top and sides of the cake.

GRAPE CREAM CAKE

Hot Milk Cake, or *Yellow Butter Cake*

Grape jelly
Crème Fraîche

This is a delicious dessert and very handsome. To serve 6 or 8 halve the cake recipe you choose and bake it in a 9-inch cake pan. (You may use your own favorite small 3-egg sponge cake.) The cake must be freshly made. When it is cool spread it with a moderately thick layer of grape jelly. Bring it to the table and over each piece pour a nice thick layer of *Crème Fraîche*.

GINGERBREAD

½ cup sweet butter
½ cup light brown sugar
½ cup molasses
1 egg, beaten
Grated rind and juice of 1
Sunkist orange

½ cup cold tea
1¾ cups pastry flour
¾ teaspoon soda
1 teaspoon ginger

Cream the butter and sugar until smooth, then add the molasses, egg, rind and juice. Beat well, then stir in the tea. Sift and measure the flour, then sift twice with the soda and ginger. Stir in the flour and bake at 350° in an 8-by-11-inch pan which has been greased and floured. Bake about 28 to 30 minutes. Serve warm and pass sweet butter for those who like it.

SUSANNE'S POPPY SEED CAKE
(Hungarian)

½ cup sweet butter
1 cup light brown sugar
7 egg yolks
 Grated rind ½ lemon

Juice ½ lemon (3½ tablespoons)
¼ cup raisins
½ pound poppy seeds, ground
7 egg whites, beaten

Cream the butter with the sugar until it is light and smooth. Add 1 egg yolk at a time and beat well. Use large eggs. Add the rind and juice and the raisins. Beat the egg whites until stiff and add two-thirds of them alternately with the poppy seeds to the butter mixture. Last, fold in the remaining one-third of the whites lightly. Grease and flour an 8-inch spring cake pan, 2¼ inches deep. Pour in the batter and bake at 350° 40 to 45 minutes. When it is done the cake shrinks from the sides of the pan. Loosen it from the sides of the pan after 5 minutes and remove the outside ring. The cake may remain on the bottom of the pan. This cake improves with age; keeps well wrapped in wax paper. It is a solid dark cake, not too sweet but with a delicious poppy-seed flavor. It will serve 10 or 12.

FRUITCAKE

1 cup soft figs, chopped
2 cups dates, chopped
1 cup seeded raisins
½ cup dried currants
⅓ cup each citron, lemon peel,
 and orange peel, diced
1½ cups candied cherries and
 pineapple, sliced
½ cup mashed apricot or damson
 jam
½ cup brandy or rum

1 cup almonds, finely chopped
¾ cup butter
1½ cups light brown sugar
1 tablespoon vanilla extract
1 teaspoon almond extract
½ cup sour cream
5 eggs, beaten
2¼ cups sifted cake flour
½ teaspoon soda
2 teaspoons cinnamon
1 teaspoon each clove and mace

Eight hours before mixing the cake to bake, prepare the fruit in a large mixing bowl, mix in the jam, and pour the liquor over it. Cover and let it stand. When ready to mix the cake, stir in the nuts. Cream the butter and sugar until fluffy and smooth, then add the extracts, cream and well-beaten eggs. Sift and measure the flour, then sift twice with the soda and spices. Combine with the butter-egg mixture and mix well. Mix in the fruit with the hands. Grease breadpans as needed and line them with greased wax paper. Put in the mixture and tie foil over the pans. Bake 2 hours at a scant 300°. Remove the foil for the last 20 minutes to brown the cakes. When cool empty from the pans. As fruitcake is to last through the holidays and winter it must be kept moist with brandy sprinkled over it from time to time and kept in covered earthenware jars. When serving, slice very thin.

WHITE FRUITCAKE

If you wish to make a fruitcake as a bridegroom's cake this is a fine one.
For a wedding, bake it in a 9-inch tube pan and ice with *Kirsch Icing*.

1 pound sultanas	6 egg yolks
1 cup sliced soft figs	¼ cup milk
1 cup candied cherries	3 cups sifted cake flour
½ cup candied pineapple	2 teaspoons baking powder
½ cup green candied pineapple	6 egg whites
⅓ cup light rum	1 cup instant sugar
1 cup sweet butter	1 tablespoon each vanilla and
1 cup instant sugar	rose extracts

Several hours before mixing the cake prepare the fruit. Thinly slice the
cherries and pineapple. Mix them together and marinate with the rum,
covered. When ready to mix the cake, cream the butter and sugar until
fluffy and light. Add 1 egg yolk at a time and beat very hard. Add the milk.
Sift the flour, measure, and sift it 3 times with the baking powder, and
add it to the butter-egg mixture. Beat the egg whites until stiff, then gradually add the sugar and then the extracts. Mix the fruits into the butter-
flour mixture. Mix in one-fourth of the egg whites, then lightly fold the
rest in. Bake 2 hours at a scant 300°. Put a pan of water in the oven while
the cake is baking. This may be kept a long time in a covered jar.

ITALIAN NUT AND CITRON CAKE

5 egg yolks, beaten	Garnish:
⅔ cup sugar	1½ cups heavy cream,
1 teaspoon almond extract	whipped
1 teaspoon rose or vanilla extract	3 tablespoons powdered
1 cup nuts: unsalted cashews,	sugar
pecans, almonds, or walnuts,	2 tablespoons dark rum
browned and ground	¼ cup sliced citron
⅓ cup citron, sliced	
5 egg whites, beaten	

Beat the egg yolks a minute, then gradually add the sugar and beat until
very thick and creamy. Add the extracts. Almond and rose are a very fragrant combination. After you have ground the nuts there will be 1¼ cups.
Add them and the citron, finely sliced. Beat the egg whites until stiff and
mix one-third of them with the nut mixture then fold in the rest. Bake in
a greased, floured 8-inch spring tort pan at 350° 30 minutes and at 325°
20 more minutes. After it comes from the oven let it stand for 5 minutes,
then carefully loosen the sides of the cake, unclamp the pan, and let the
cake cool on the bottom of the pan on a cake plate. Whip the cream, add
the other ingredients, and cover the top and sides of the cooled cake.

PECAN OR BLACK WALNUT CAKE WITH
CARAMEL FROSTING

Cake:
- 1 cup sweet butter
- 2 cups light brown sugar
- 1 teaspoon almond extract
- 1 teaspoon vanilla extract
- 3 egg yolks
- 1 cup buttermilk
- 2 cups sifted cake flour
- 2 teaspoons baking powder
- 1 cup chopped pecans or
  black walnuts
- 3 egg whites

Frosting:
- ⅔ cup white sugar
- ½ cup boiling water
- ¾ cup light brown sugar
- 2 egg whites, beaten

Preheat the oven to 350°. Have all the ingredients at room temperature, especially the butter and eggs. Use very large eggs. Cream the butter until soft and mix with the sugar until light and fluffy. I find a hard rubber spatula excellent for mixing cakes. Add the extracts and the egg yolks, one at a time, beating well. Sift the cake flour, measure, and sift with the baking powder. Do not grind the nuts but chop them quite fine in a wooden bowl, then mix them with the flour. Add to the batter alternately the buttermilk and the flour-nut mixture, beating well. Beat the egg whites until stiff. Stir one-fourth of them into the batter and then lightly fold in the rest. Divide the batter in two greased, floured 9-inch cake pans and bake a good 25 minutes. Let the cakes stand 3 or 4 minutes, then loosen the edges and carefully turn them out onto wire racks to cool. For the frosting, put the white sugar in an iron skillet over a hot flame and let it become quite dark brown. Turn off the flame and add the boiling water. When the white sugar is melted add the light brown sugar, turn on the heat, and stir until it is melted and a heavy syrup is formed. Beat the egg whites until stiff, then gradually pour in the syrup, beating continuously with a rotary beater. It will almost immediately become stiff enough to spread. Spread it between the cooled layers and over the top and sides of the cake. This is a delicate nut cake and has a marvelous flavor, especially with black walnuts if you like them. It is also fine made with chopped almonds. It will serve 12.

CHOCOLATE LOG

Cake:
    5 egg yolks, beaten
    ¾ cup powdered sugar
    5 tablespoons cocoa
    1 teaspoon vanilla
    5 egg whites, beaten
Filling:
    1½ cups heavy cream, whipped
    ¼ cup *Chocolate Butter
        Cream*

Chocolate Butter Cream:
    4 squares chocolate, grated
    ¼ cup cream
    4 egg yolks, beaten
    1 teaspoon powdered coffee
    ⅓ cup powdered sugar
    1 cup sweet butter
    3 drops mocha extract
    ¼ cup chopped pistachio nuts
        or almonds

Preheat the oven to 375°. For the cake, beat the egg yolks 2 or 3 minutes, then gradually add the sugar and beat until thick; add the cocoa and vanilla. Beat the egg whites until stiff, then fold them into the cocoa mixture. Grease a jelly-roll pan and line it with heavy waxed paper, greased. Spread the batter in a rectangle and bake 12 minutes at 375°. Empty the cake onto a damp tea towel, roll it up, and let it stand until it is cool. Unroll to fill. Make the Chocolate Butter Cream first because you will need ¼ cup of it for the filling. Put the grated chocolate and cream in the top of a double boiler and cook until the chocolate is melted. Stir in the beaten egg yolks and coffee and cook until it thickens. Let it cool a little. Cream the sugar and butter until fluffy and smooth. Add the mocha extract. Stir this into the chocolate mixture. For the filling, whip the cream until it is stiff, then stir in ¼ cup of the Chocolate Butter Cream. Unroll the cake and trim the edges and spread it with the filling. Roll it the long way so the log is long. Cover the outside entirely with Chocolate Butter Cream. Score the surface unevenly with the back of a teaspoon, so it will look like tree bark. Sprinkle the nuts down the center of the roll. Serves 8.

CHOCOLATE MOCHA CREAM

    4 squares bitter chocolate
    4 egg yolks
    ½ cup white or light brown sugar
    ¼ cup heavy cream

    ¼ cup strong coffee
    ⅓ cup powdered sugar
    1 cup sweet butter
    3 drops mocha extract

Grate the chocolate and melt it in the top of a double boiler over simmering water, then add the egg yolks, sugar, cream, and coffee. Stir until thick and smooth, remove from the fire, and cool a little. Cream the powdered sugar and sweet butter until smooth and add the extract. One teaspoon of vanilla may be added if desired. Work into the first mixture a little at a time and mix well. Chill until it is the right consistency to spread. This will fill a many-layered Dobos. To fill two layers of cake cut the recipe in half.

CHOCOLATE CAKE

¾ cup boiling coffee
½ cup cocoa
½ cup sweet butter
1 cup light brown sugar
1 teaspoon vanilla
½ teaspoon soda
½ cup sour cream
2 cups sifted pastry flour

3 egg whites, beaten
1 cup sugar
Dark rum
Icing:
   4 tablespoons cocoa
   4 tablespoons hot coffee
   4 tablespoons sweet butter
   2 cups powdered sugar

Mix the coffee and cocoa and let it cool. Cream the butter and sugar until fluffy and smooth and add the vanilla. Mix the soda and sour cream and add them, then add the cocoa mixture. Add the flour a little at a time. Beat the egg whites until stiff, then beat to a meringue with the sugar and fold it into the batter. Grease and flour three 8-inch or two 9-inch cake pans. Bake at 350° about 25 minutes, or until the cake shrinks from the sides of the pans. Cool the layers on cake racks and then sprinkle each layer with rum. Put the layers together. For the icing melt the cocoa in the hot coffee and let it cool a little, then mix it with the softened butter and blend with the powdered sugar until it is stiff enough to spread. Fill and ice the top and sides of the cake.

ALMOND OR PECAN BUTTER FROSTING

⅔ cup sweet butter
1¼ cups powdered sugar
3 teaspoons heavy cream
1 teaspoon vanilla or almond
   extract

½ teaspoon rose extract (optional)
⅔ cup nuts (or more), browned
   and sliced
3 or 4 tablespoons olive oil

The cake is frosted and sprinkled with the nuts which have been lightly browned in olive oil and cooled. Cream the butter and sugar until light and smooth and blend with the cream. Add the flavoring. Either vanilla or almond and the rose give an exquisite flavor. Spread the frosting on thoroughly cool cake, and sprinkle thickly with nuts.

ALMOND CREAM FILLING AND FROSTING

1 cup heavy cream, whipped
¾ cup almonds, ground
1 teaspoon almond extract

1 teaspoon vanilla extract
½ cup powdered sugar, or more

Whip the cream until stiff and add the rest of the ingredients. If necessary, add more sugar to make the mixture stiff enough to spread. This amount will cover the sides and top of an 8-inch cake. If filling is desired, double the recipe.

LEMON-JELLY FILLING AND FROSTING

½ cup sweet butter
1 cup sugar
2½ tablespoons flour

Grated rind and juice of 2 large
lemons
3 egg yolks, beaten
1 cup boiling water

Cream the butter and sugar until smooth, then stir in the flour. Add the rind and lemon juice and the beaten eggs. Add the boiling water and cook in the top of a double boiler over boiling water until thickened. Let cool thoroughly before filling and frosting a cake. This is delicious on white butter cakes, sunshine cakes, and yellow butter cakes. To use for filling only cut the recipe in half. Use between layers of a white layer cake and frost the top and sides with white icing.

LIQUEUR ICING

1½ tablespoons sweet butter
2 tablespoons Kirsch or Curaçao,
   or 2 tablespoons orange or
   lemon juice with 1 teaspoon
   grated orange or lemon rind

½ cup powdered sugar (and more)

Have the butter at room temperature and work in the liqueur or the juice and rind, then blend in ½ cup of powdered sugar so that it is very smooth. Add more sugar, a little at a time, until it is the right consistency to spread on a cool cake. To cover the top and sides of a very large cake, double the recipe. It may be tinted for anniversary occasions.

WHITE BOILED FROSTING
(Plain or with Coconut)

1 cup sugar
¼ cup water
¾ teaspoon cream of tartar

½ cup white corn syrup
4 egg whites (½ cup)
1 teaspoon vanilla

Cook the sugar, water, cream of tartar, and syrup together until the mixture drops heavily from a spoon. Pour it slowly over the stiffly beaten egg whites and beat until it is thick enough to spread. This is a most dependable white frosting. This quantity will fill and cover a good-sized cake. Use half the recipe for a small one. This is very good for coconut cake. Put the frosting on the bottom layer, sprinkle with coconut, cover with the top layer, and spread frosting all over the sides and top of the cake and sprinkle all over with coconut. Use freshly grated coconut or packaged fine moist coconut.

BUTTER CUSTARD CREAM FOR FILLING

1½ tablespoons cornstarch
1 cup light cream
4 egg yolks

⅔ cup light brown or white sugar
¾ cup sweet butter
¼ cup powdered sugar

Blend the cornstarch with the cream in the top of a double boiler and cook until it thickens. Beat the yolks with the sugar until thick, then add the cream mixture slowly. Return to the top of the double boiler and cook a minute, until it thickens. Let the custard cool thoroughly. Cream the butter with the powdered sugar and beat it into the cold custard. Spread between layers of cooled cake. If necessary, chill before spreading.

KIRSCH BUTTER CREAM

½ cup sweet butter
2 tablespoons Kirsch

1 egg yolk
1 to 1½ cups powdered sugar

Soften the butter and blend with the Kirsch, beat in the egg yolk, add ¼ cup of sugar, and beat until light and smooth. Continue to add sugar until it is light, fluffy and smooth and thick enough to spread. This is a nice filling for the *Gâteau aux Fraises* that one sees in French pastry shops. Make cake in two layers, one 8-inch and one 9-inch. Completely cover the larger layer with *Kirsch Butter Cream*, cover with the smaller layer, and cover that with *Italian Meringue* or *Liqueur Icing*. Press fresh strawberries into the filling along the top edge of the lower layer. Put a few berries on top of the cake, 3 groups of 3, or make some sprays with slivered angelica, ending in berries.

CAKE GLAZE

Melt ¾ cup sugar until it is light brown and quickly spread it over the top of a thoroughly cooled cake. This will become stiff. When it is cool cover the sides of the cake with frosting. This is for Dobos.

ITALIAN MERINGUE

½ cup sugar
¼ cup water

2 egg whites, beaten
1 tablespoon Kirsch or vanilla

Boil the sugar and water until the syrup drips heavily from the spoon, about 3½ to 4 minutes, or to 238°. Beat the egg whites until stiff, add the syrup gradually, and beat until stiff enough to spread. Add the flavoring. This will cover the top of an 8- or 9-inch cake. Double the recipe to cover the sides.

CASSATA ALLA SICILIANA

When we were in Rome, my friend Licia gave me her native cake, insisting that nowhere else do they make it the way they do in Sicily. I promised to go there. This is a party cake and serves 10 or 12.

Butter Sponge Cake
Filling:
  2⅔ cups ricotta cheese
  ¾ cup sifted powdered sugar
  1 teaspoon vanilla
  3 tablespoons Maraschino
     or Strega
  2 ounces bitter chocolate,
     melted
  ⅓ cup finely sliced candied
     fruits

Icing:
  1 egg white
  1½ tablespoons light corn
     syrup
  ¾ cup sifted powdered
     sugar (and more)
  1 teaspoon vanilla extract
  1 teaspoon almond extract
Garnish:
  ½ cup slivered candied fruit:
     angelica, cherries, citron,
     pineapple

Bake the sponge cake in a 9-inch tube pan and when it is thoroughly cool and ready to fill, cut it in 3 parts, horizontally with a very sharp knife. Care must be taken not to break the cake as it is tender. If it breaks, build it up. For the filling, melt the chocolate over hot water, sieve the cheese, and lightly mix all the ingredients. Spread half on the bottom layer, cover with the middle layer, and cover it with the rest of the filling. Put on the top layer. For the icing, mix the unbeaten egg white with the corn syrup, ¾ cup of sifted powdered sugar, and the extracts. Beat very hard until it is creamy and smooth. Add more sifted sugar until it is the right consistency to spread. Cover the top and sides of the cake. This icing may be tinted for a festive cake. If this doesn't cover a large cake, make another batch. Use your ingenuity in decorating the top with the fruit. Or you may mix the fruit with icing left after covering the sides of the cake and cover the top with icing and fruit.

CREAM CHEESE CAKE

Crust:
  6 Holland rusks
  3 tablespoons melted sweet
      butter
  2 tablespoons sugar
  1 teaspoon cinnamon
Filling:
  12 ounces cream cheese,
      softened
  ½ cup sugar
  2 eggs, beaten
  1 teaspoon vanilla

Top:
  1 cup sour cream
  1 tablespoon sugar
  1 teaspoon vanilla
Garnish:
    Fresh strawberries or rasp-
      berries (optional)

Grind or blender the rusks and mix with the melted butter, sugar, and cinnamon. Pat the mixture on the bottom and sides of an 8-inch straight-sided Pyrex cake pan in which the cake can be served. Preheat the oven to 350°. Have the cream cheese softened at room temperature. Beat the sugar into the eggs until thick, add the vanilla, and beat with the cheese. Pour this into the lined cake pan and bake 20 minutes, half the time at 350° and half the time at 325°. Remove from the oven. Mix the sour cream mixed with the sugar and vanilla and cover the cake. Turn the oven up to 375° and bake for 5 minutes, no longer. This is best made several hours before it is served. Cool it at room temperature; do not refrigerate as the texture changes. It should be delicate and not stiffened by the cold. This may not be new but it is the best cheese cake I know. Serves 8.

CHOCOLATE BOUCHÉES

⅓ cup sweet butter
½ cup sugar
  4 squares bitter chocolate
      (4 ounces)
  1 teaspoon almond extract
  2 tablespoons flour
  3 egg yolks
  3 egg whites, beaten

Icing:
  ½ cup semi-sweet chocolate
      bits
  1 teaspoon sweet butter
  1 tablespoon Kirsch, rum, or
      Cointreau

Cream the butter and sugar. Melt the chocolate in the top of a double boiler over hot water. Set aside a minute or two, then mix with the creamed mixture, extract, flour, and egg yolks. Fold in the stiffly beaten egg whites. Butter tiny muffin tins, 1½ inches in diameter and fill them two-thirds full. Be sure to use butter so the cakes won't stick. Bake them at 325° for 11 minutes. Let them cool 2 minutes, then empty them onto a cake rack. This makes 3 dozen very delicate, soft cakes or "bites." For the icing, melt the chocolate and stir in the butter and liqueur. When the cakes are entirely cold, put a teaspoon of icing on each.

BABA AU RHUM

1 envelope yeast
⅓ cup lukewarm water
2 tablespoons sugar
¼ teaspoon salt
2 cups sifted flour
4 eggs, beaten
½ cup sweet butter

Rhum Syrup:
   1 cup water
   1½ cups sugar
   ½ cup Jamaica rum
   ⅔ cup glacé fruits: pineapple,
      cherries, citron, angelica

Have the eggs and butter at room temperature. Melt the yeast in the luke-warm water with the sugar until it is foamy. Sift the salt and flour and make a well in the center of the flour and add the yeast. Beat very hard, then stir in the eggs and beat well. Stir in the softened butter and beat with a wooden spoon until the dough is elastic. Set the mixing bowl in a large pan of quite warm water and cover with a tea towel; let rise an hour or more until it doubles in bulk. Meanwhile begin the syrup by boiling the water and sugar 2 minutes, so it may cool. Butter a cake ring or tube pan, or 12 baba molds or cylindrical custard cups. Fill with dough two-thirds full, spooning out the dough with a wooden spoon. Let rise until they reach the top of the mold—45 minutes to 1 hour. They must not be allowed to overrise or they will fall. Put them in a 375° oven; the small babas take 15 minutes, the large one takes about 25 minutes. When they are done remove them to a cake rack. When they are lukewarm, put them on a deep platter. Warm the syrup to lukewarm and add the rum. Make 3 incisions with a needle on each baba and spoon the syrup over them. After 15 minutes spoon syrup over them again. Put the glacé fruits around them in the syrup. When ready to serve, put the baba or babas on serving plates, decorate with the fruit, and spoon more syrup over them. If 1 large baba is served, blaze with a jigger of rum at the table. Serves 8 to 12.

SAVARIN

Baba paste
Ring mold
Rhum syrup
½ cup sieved apricot jam
½ cup glacé fruits: pineapple,
   cherries, citron, angelica

Center filling:
   1 cup *Crème Patissière*
   1 cup heavy cream, whipped
   ⅓ cup pulverized macaroons
   1 teaspoon almond extract

Make the dough and bake in a buttered ring mold 9 inches in diameter. Bake it 25 minutes at 375°. Make the rhum syrup and soak the baba in it, according to directions for *Baba au Rhum*. Sieve the jam and mix in 1 or 2 tablespoons of orange juice if it is too thick. Glaze the baba with the jam and decorate it with sliced glacé fruits. Make a cup of *Crème Patissière*, and when it is cold, fold in the whipped cream, pulverized macaroons, and almond extract. Pile the cream filling in the center of the Savarin. Serves 8 or 10.

ROLLA CAKE

Meringue layers:
    4 egg whites
    ⅛ teaspoon cream of tartar
    1 cup sugar
    ⅓ cup *Praliné Powder*
    Few drops almond extract

Chocolate filling:
    2 egg whites, half beaten
    ½ cup light brown sugar
    4 ounces bitter chocolate, melted
    ¾ cup sweet butter
    1 cup chopped brown almonds
    Powdered sugar

Beat the egg whites with the cream of tartar until they stand in peaks. Gradually beat in the sugar, then fold in the *Praliné Powder* and extract. Butter four 8-inch circles of wax paper and put them on cookie sheets. Divide the batter and spread it on the circles. Bake in a 250° oven until it is pale ivory, about 25 minutes. Let cool. For the filling, put the half-beaten egg whites in the top of a double boiler and gradually beat in the sugar over simmering water. Then add the melted chocolate and butter and cook until the mixture thickens, stirring constantly. Let cool. Spread the filling on the meringue layers and pile them up. Spread filling on the sides. Sprinkle the nuts over the top. Put several 2-inch strips of paper diagonally over the top and sprinkle with powdered sugar. Remove the paper strips. Wrap in wax paper and refrigerate until the next day. Serves 8.

CHOCOLATE MACAROONS

⅓ cup semi-sweet chocolate chips
1 large egg white
⅓ cup sugar

2½ tablespoons fine coconut, or ground nuts, or fine macaroon crumbs
¾ teaspoon almond or vanilla extract

Put the chocolate chips in a small saucepan over boiling water and stir with a rubber spatula until they are melted. Remove from heat and let cool. Meanwhile beat the egg white until it is stiff, then gradually add the sugar and beat until smooth. Add the coconut, nuts, or macaroon crumbs and the extract. Stir in the chocolate. Grease a cookie sheet with butter or lard (so they won't stick). Drop the mixture by teaspoons, level or rounded, onto the sheet and bake 15 minutes at 350°. Level teaspoonfuls make 3 dozen cookies; rounded 2 dozen. These whiffs are fragile, so be careful when you remove them from the cookie sheet, which should be done when they come out of the oven.

PAUL'S OLD WHALER RUM COOKIES

¼ cup sweet butter
½ cup brown sugar
½ teaspoon cinnamon
¼ teaspoon allspice
¼ teaspoon clove

¼ teaspoon nutmeg
¼ cup dark rum
½ cup molasses
1¾ cups sifted flour
1 teaspoon soda

Cream the butter with the sugar; add the spices, rum, and molasses. Sift the flour with the soda and stir it into the butter mixture. Grease and flour a cookie sheet and drop teaspoons of the batter the size of a small walnut onto the sheet. Bake 10 minutes at 350°. They are soft when they come out of the oven but stiffen as they cool. Makes 50 cookies. Keep them in a tin box.

CALCIONETTI FOR CHRISTMAS EVE

These exquisite little cakes are made for the Italian Christmas and would be a nice present any time.

Sugar pastry
Deep oil for frying
Powdered sugar

Filling:
½ pound chestnuts
3 tablespoons honey
2 tablespoons grated chocolate
½ teaspoon cinnamon
¼ cup ground almonds
2 tablespoons candied citron
2 tablespoons orange rind
1 teaspoon powdered coffee
1 or 2 tablespoons rum

Make the filling first. Canned chestnut purée may be used, or fresh chestnuts. Score the fresh chestnuts with a sharp pointed knife, boil them 1½ minutes, and shell them while they are warm. Cook them in water or milk for 20 minutes or until they are tender, then mash through a sieve. Mix the purée with all the other ingredients to a soft paste. The citron is cut in small pieces. Make the pastry with 2 cups of flour, roll it thin, and cut it in small rounds. Put a little mound of filling on 1 round and cover with another pastry round, pressing the edges together. Fry in deep oil at 375° until golden. Drain on brown paper and when cool sprinkle with powdered sugar. This filling may also be used for filled baked cookies. The quantity of filling is enough for 3 dozen small cookies.

CHESTNUT TRUFFLES

20 chestnuts
¼ cup sugar
1 cup almonds, ground

1 tablespoon butter
Chocolate grains

Boil the chestnuts 1½ minutes; peel and skin while warm. Boil them in water until they are soft, drain, and mash through a sieve. Make a paste of the chestnuts, sugar, almonds, and butter. Chill, then roll into small balls and roll these in chocolate grains. This is a nice confection for the tea table.

CINNAMON NUT COOKIES

1 cup butter
1 cup light brown sugar
4 teaspoons cinnamon
¼ teaspoon nutmeg
2 cups sifted flour

1 egg yolk
1 egg white
¾ cup chopped nuts: pecans, English walnuts, or black walnuts

Cream the butter and sugar and stir in the spices. Add the egg yolk and the flour. Pat this mixture into an ungreased 9- by 12-inch pan. Brush with egg white and sprinkle with the nuts, pressing them in a little. Bake 25 minutes at 325°. Cool a little then cut in squares.

Frozen Desserts

FRENCH ICE CREAM

7 large egg yolks, beaten
1¼ cups powdered sugar

3 cups heavy cream
2 tablespoons best vanilla

Beat the egg yolks until thick, then slowly add the sugar and beat until pale yellow. Whip the cream until it is half thick then beat it into the sugar-egg mixture with a rotary beater. Add the vanilla. Put the mixture in a tightly sealed mold and pack in layers of ice and ice cream salt for 6 hours. Other flavors may be added to this velvet ice cream either before freezing or as a dressing when served.

GELATI VANIGLIA
(Vanilla Ice Cream)
Sampieri, Bologna

This restaurant makes its own ice cream. For most of us old-fashioned homemade crank-freezer vanilla ice cream is only a pleasant memory.

Custard: 1 quart heavy cream
  2¼ cups rich milk
  1 vanilla bean
  1 tablespoon flour
  1 cup sugar
  4 egg yolks, beaten

Put the milk in the top of a double boiler with the vanilla bean broken into 3 or 4 pieces. Cook over boiling water 15 minutes. Mix the flour and sugar and beat into the egg yolks until thick. Remove the vanilla bean and slowly pour the hot milk over the sugar-egg mixture. Put it back over simmering water and cook until it thickens, stirring continuously. Let the custard cool thoroughly. Taste it and if it is not flavored enough add 1 tablespoon of vanilla extract; the cream will dilute it further. Whip the cream until stiff and combine it with the custard and freeze. Makes 2 quarts.

CHOCOLATE ICE CREAM. Add 3 squares of melted bitter chocolate or milk chocolate to *Vanilla Ice Cream* before freezing.

PEPPERMINT ICE CREAM. Add ¼ to ⅓ cup of Crème de Menthe to *Vanilla Ice Cream* before freezing.

RASPBERRY ICE CREAM. Mash 2 packages of frozen berries through a sieve or purée in an electric blender, and add to *Vanilla Ice Cream* before freezing.

BROWN SUGAR ICE CREAM

2 cups rich milk   2 tablespoons vanilla
6 egg yolks   2 cups heavy cream
¾ cup light brown sugar

If you have a sweet tooth, use 1 cup of sugar. This has a rich and delicious flavor and not as sweet a taste as ice cream made with white sugar. Beat the egg yolks with the sugar until thick. Scald the milk and pour it over the yolks. Cool a little and add the vanilla; when thoroughly cool add the cream. Turn the freezer unit quite high. Freeze in trays for 30 minutes, then stir and continue freezing until it is solid but not hard. Turn the unit back to normal. May be used as foundation for *Chocolate Ice Cream.*

CARAMEL ICE CREAM

1 cup white sugar
½ cup boiling water
1½ cups milk, scalded
3 egg yolks
¼ cup light brown sugar
1 teaspoon vanilla

1½ cups heavy cream
Garnish:
    Black walnuts, or browned
    almonds, pecans, or maca-
    damia nuts

Caramelize the white sugar in an iron skillet by cooking it until it is almost black. Turn off the heat, add the boiling water, and stir until it is a syrup. Beat the egg yolks with the brown sugar. Scald the milk and pour it over the yolks. Put this custard in the top of a double boiler over simmering water, add the caramel, and cook it until it is blended, stirring continuously. Let it cool and add the vanilla and heavy cream. Pour it into a refrigerator tray and turn the unit to very cold. Stir 2 or 3 times while it is freezing. When it has frozen, turn the unit to normal temperature. It may be served plain or each serving may be sprinkled with a few nuts.

LEMON ICE CREAM

2 cups milk
1 cup sugar
½ cup lemon juice

1 teaspoon grated lemon rind
1½ cups heavy cream

Scald the milk. Mix the sugar, lemon juice, and rind. Pour the hot milk over the lemon mixture. When it is cool add the cream. Put it in refrigerator trays and stir 2 or 3 times while it is freezing. Makes a full quart.

FRUIT JUICE ICE CREAMS

Frozen juice concentrates: lemonade, orange, limeade, pineapple, grape

Whipped cream
Garnish:
    Fresh berries, sliced fruit, or
    liqueurs

For every can of undiluted frozen concentrate mix in 1 cup of whipped heavy cream and freeze. These ice creams are quick and delicious and are convenient for filling cakes and for *Baked Alaska*. Various ice creams may be frozen in layers in melon molds or long deep refrigerator trays. When turned out on a platter they may be covered with a cup of raspberry or strawberry purée, or with Cassis or Grenadine. The dressings make a handsome combination of colors.

CRÈME DE MENTHE ICE CREAM

¾ cup Crème de Menthe
1 teaspoon vanilla
1 quart heavy cream

Garnish:
    Crystallized mint leaves **or**
    grated chocolate

Mix the liqueur, vanilla, and cream and freeze in trays or in a freezer. Serve in parfait glasses, decorating the top with 2 or 3 sugared mint leaves **or** some grated bitter chocolate. Makes a full quart.

RASPBERRY ICE

2 or 3 packages frozen raspberries
    Juice of 2 limes or 1 large lemon

1½ cups water
½ cup sugar

Purée the fruit. If it is puréed in a blender give it an extra sieving to remove the seeds. Mix it with the lime or lemon juice. The frozen raspberries are sweetened so use more juice if they need it. Boil the water and sugar together for 5 minutes, mix with the puréed berries, and freeze. This may easily be doubled.

GLACE AUX CASSIS

4 egg yolks
⅔ cup sugar
2½ cups rich milk
⅓ cup black currant jam

1 teaspoon vanilla
⅓ cup Cassis de Dijon
1½ cups heavy cream, whipped

Beat the egg yolks and sugar until thick. Scald the milk and slowly pour some of it over the egg mixture, then add the rest and cook over simmering water until the mixture thickens a little and coats the spoon. Stir in the jam. Cool thoroughly and add the vanilla and liqueur. Whip the cream until stiff and fold into the custard. Freeze, stirring once when it is half frozen. This delicious black-currant liqueur ice cream comes from Burgundy. Serves 6 or 8, depending on the size of the parfait glasses.

RUM AND COFFEE ICE CREAM

¼ cup dried currants
3 tablespoons rum
⅓ cup light brown sugar

3 cups hot strong black coffee
3 drops mocha extract
1 cup heavy cream, whipped

Soak the currants in the rum for several hours. Mix the sugar with a little warm coffee and let all the coffee cool. When ready to freeze the cream, mix all the ingredients together and freeze in trays.

SOUR CREAM ICE CREAM

4 ripe bananas, sieved
4 ripe skinned peaches, sieved
⅓ cup lemon juice

1⅓ cups sugar
1⅓ cups heavy sour cream

Use peaches that are fine, ripe, and full of flavor and this ice cream will be most subtle in flavor and the ingredients very hard to guess if one has not had it before. All ice creams are best made in the churn freezer but most people must make do with the ice box tray. Mix all the ingredients in the order given and freeze. This makes over a quart.

SPUMONI

1 quart vanilla ice cream

Filling:
⅔ cup slivered glacé fruits
3 tablespoons rum
¼ cup coarsely chopped pistachio nuts
1½ cups heavy cream, whipped

First soak the glacé fruits in rum an hour. Use a mixture of cherries, pineapple, citron, angelica, and orange rind. If you make the ice cream, flavor it with vanilla and 1 teaspoon of anise or almond extract. Mix all the ingredients for the filling with the fruits and rum. Line a large melon mold with ice cream and put the filling in the center. If there is any ice cream left, spread it over the top. Cover and put the mold in the freezing compartment of your refrigerator for 6 hours or until the center is firm. Unmold on a fancy platter and cut in slices to serve. Serves 10. Instead of vanilla ice cream, *Chocolate, Brown Sugar,* or *Caramel Ice Cream* may be used to line the mold. Any one of them make an elegant confection.

ORANGE SHERBET WITH FRUIT AND KIRSCH

Orange sherbet:
¾ cup sugar
1 cup water
1 teaspoon lemon rind
Grated rind 1 orange
Juice of 2 lemons
3 cups orange juice

Garnish:
Black pitted cherries, sliced strawberries, raspberries, or sliced fresh pineapple
Honey
Kirsch

To make the sherbet boil the sugar, water, and grated rinds for 10 minutes, very gently. Add the juices and freeze. An hour before serving, dribble the chosen fruit with honey. Prepare 3 tablespoons of fruit for each serving. Put a scoop of ice in each goblet, add the fruit, and pass a bottle of Kirsch so each person may help himself to a tablespoon or two to pour over the fruit and sherbet.

STRAWBERRY OR RASPBERRY DRESSING
FOR VANILLA ICE CREAM

1 10-ounce package of frozen
   berries
Crème:
   2 cups heavy cream
   4 egg yolks, beaten
   3 tablespoons light brown
     sugar
   1 teaspoon vanilla

1½ quarts vanilla ice cream
Garnish: 1½ cups whole fresh
   berries

Fine fresh berries may be used if preferred; use 2½ cups. For the frozen, either press them through a sieve or purée them in an electric blender. Raspberries need additional sieving to remove the seeds. For the crème, beat the yolks and sugar well together, scald the cream, and pour it over them. Cook a moment, stirring continuously, then let thoroughly cool. Add the vanilla and the berry purée. When ready to serve, coarsely cut up the ice cream (which should be homemade if possible), put it in a wide shallow serving bowl, and pour the sauce over it. Serves 8 or 10. Additional fresh berries sprinkled on top make it a little handsomer, but in the winter this is not necessary.

MANGOS WITH VANILLA ICE CREAM

1 large can of mangos
⅓ cup dark rum

1 quart vanilla ice cream (homemade)

This is quite a fine dessert to serve 8. Several hours before serving, drain the mangos and boil down the syrup until it is quite thick, then pour it over the mangos and when it cools a little add the rum. To serve put a big scoop of ice cream in each goblet, and add to each a slice of mango and 2 tablespoons of the rum syrup.

GINGER SAUCE FOR ICE CREAM

1 cup light corn syrup
1 teaspoon grated lemon rind

2 tablespoons lemon juice
¼ cup minced preserved ginger

Boil the syrup and rind with the lemon juice very slowly, 1 minute just so it blends. Add the ginger and serve warm over vanilla ice cream.

Menus

Menus

In CONSIDERING why dining on the continent is so interesting, attractive, and completely satisfying, one reaches the conclusion that not only the quality of the food, the novelty of some of it, and the imagination and capacities of the trained cooks and chefs are responsible—but also the arrangement of the menus. The diner is given a list of very tempting hors d'œuvre, soups or (in Italy) pastas; then comes fish, meat or poultry and vegetables; then assorted cheeses followed by fruit or a sweet. Wine is served which aids digestion, not to mention the fact that it is the best complement to a good meal. Bread is always eaten, but often a green vegetable replaces the potato. Too often our fussy American tables are laden with jams, jellies, relishes, hot breads, 2 or 3 vegetables accompanying the meat, cake with ice cream. This sort of imbalance may account for the obesity prevalent on this continent.

When planning menus for your family or friends, serve no more than three courses. Make each dish perfect and appropriate in relation to the others, and you will have interesting, well-balanced, and more sophisticated meals. For elaborate entertaining you need not increase the number of courses, but you may want to serve a complicated dish calling for a special sauce. This may require care and time, but what achievement in any field doesn't! Occasionally, and especially in winter, a rich sweet for dessert may be just the thing to follow a light fish or meat course.

Many of the following menus we enjoyed in Europe. One night in Beaune we entertained friends at a farewell dinner party. M. Marc Chevillot and I planned the menu, *Dinner in Beaune*, but I must say that my part was mainly approval of his suggestions. The lobsters were small so one was served to each person. We were detained a full hour past the scheduled time set for dinner, but any expert cook or French chef allows for these contingencies, which is to say that the baby lamb was roasted to perfection—pink inside as it should be.

In these menus I have attempted to alternate rich with lean dishes to achieve balance and texture. The menus are not elaborate but will, I hope, prove satisfying to family and friends.

Dinners

Crevettes au Pierre   *Pouilly-Fuissé*
(Skewered Shrimp)
Steak au Poivre Flambé à la Normande   *Grands-*
Rissolée Potatoes   *Echézeaux*
Fresh Peaches with Raspberry Purée
Café Noir

Antipasto   *Chianti*
Stufatino de Manzo con Pepperoni Romano   *or Barola*
(Roman Beef Stew)
Potatoes or Rice
Formaggio
Italian Fruit Cream   *Asti Spumanti*
Espresso

Liver Pâté   Okra à la Turc   *Beaujolais*
Lamb Stew with Mint or Dill Dumplings
Fromage
Alsatian Cherry Tart
Café Noir

Carrot and Orange Soup
Roast Boned Shoulder of Pork   *Châteauneuf*
and   *du Pape*
Curried Onions
Glacé Fruit Soufflé
Café Noir

Onion Soup
Braised Fresh Brisket of Beef   *Vosne-Romanée*
and
Mashed Potatoes
Fromage
Bing Cherry Compôte
Café Noir

Tomato-Cheese-Egg Hors d'Oeuvre
Indian Chicken Curry *Muscadet*
and
Sambals
Molded Orange Jelly
Café Noir

Pâté de Campagne *Volnay*
French Bread with Butter
Pheasant Casserole with Mushrooms
Fromage
Raspberry Soufflé *Champagne*
Café Noir

Watercress Soup
Fillets of Turkey *Meursault*
and
Green Beans
Fromage
Raspberry Pudding
Café Noir

Spinach Soup
Duck à la Robert *Chambolle-*
Cheese Mold to Serve with Fruit *Musigny*
and
Pears and Grapes
Café Noir

Melon with Prosciutto
Shad Roe à l'Oseille *Chablis*
and
Potatoes with Cream and Cheese
Fresh Blue Plum Pudding
Café Noir

DINNER IN BEAUNE

Steamed Lobster, Beurre Blanc *Pouilly-Fuissé*
Roast Young Lamb *Volnay-*
and *Clos des Chênes*
Green Beans
Fromages
Strawberry Soufflé *Moët Champagne*
Café Noir

Oeufs Pôches Bourguignon
La Volaille à la Crème   *Aloxe-Corton*
Fromages   *(white)*
Glace au Cassis
Café Noir

Jambon Persillé
Le Canard à l'Orange   *Chambertin*
and
Green Peas
Fromages
Melon and Port
Café Noir

Soupe au Poisson à la Rouille
(Lorraine Fish Soup)
Rognons de Veau, Bercy   *Haut Brion*
and
Rissolée Potatoes
Fresh Strawberries and Crème Fraîche
Café Noir

Caviar, Chopped Onions,   *Riesling*
and Sour Cream
Choucroute (Strasbourg)   *Beer or Wine*
Fromage
Prunes in Port
Café Noir

Cold Stuffed Peppers
Couscous Libanais   *Beaujolais*
Apricot Compote
Café Noir

Fresh Tomato Soup
Jarrets de Veau à l'Orange   *Muscadet*
and
Nouilles aux Pommes Gratinées
(Noodles and Potatoes)
Fresh Raspberries and Crème Fraîche
Café Noir

Two Holiday Dinners

Oysters Poulette	*Montrachet*
Roast Turkey with Mashed Potato Stuffing	
and	
Bananas Baked in Cranberry Purée	
Brussels Sprouts and Chestnuts	
Fromages	
Soufflé aux Cocktail de Liqueurs	*Champagne*
Café Noir	

Salmon Mousse	*Pouilly Fuissé*
Roast Goose	*Nuits-Saint-Georges*
and	
Apple Horseradish Sauce	
Baked Sweet Potatoes	
Fromages	
St. Honoré, Sabatini	
Café Noir	

Salade Niçoise	
Truite Lucullus	*Riesling*
Parsley Potatoes	
Fromage	
Crêpes au Kirsch, Surprise	
Café Noir	

Cheese Tarts	
Volaille Demi-Deuil	*Chassagne-*
and	*Montrachet*
Mushrooms in Cream	
Fromage	
Poires au Cassis	
Café Noir	

Tomato, Cheese and Egg Hors d'Oeuvre	
Suprême de Barbue Bordelaise	*Haut Brion*
Parsley Potatoes	
Diana's Mocha Soufflé	
Café Noir	

Hot or Cold Fresh Asparagus
Gratin de Crabes, Sauce Crevette   *Sancerre*
and
Egg Noodles
Fromage
Orange Soufflé
Café Noir

Artichokes or Endive à la Grècque
French Bread and Butter
Shrimps Flamingo   *Soave*
and
Pilau
Pineapple with Maraschino
Espresso

Champignons à la Grècque   *Sauvignon*
French Bread and Butter
La Bourride
(Fish Soup)
Cherry Crêpes
Café Noir

Sardines Hors d'Oeuvre
Filet de Veau Moutarde   *Beaujolais*
and
Green Beans
Fromage
Fruit Compôte
Café Noir

Pesto Sauce and Egg Noodles   *Valpolicella*
Piccata alla Pizzaiola
(Veal)
Macedonia alla Maraschino
Espresso

Consommé with Bowls of
Shredded Cheese and Croutons
Coquilles St. Jacques   *Meursault*
Artichoke and Lettuce Salad
Sformato de Banane
Café Noir

Oeufs Mayonnaise
Kolczavari Kaposzta   *Beaune du Château*
(Pork Goulash)
and
Boiled Potatoes
Fromage
Orange Soufflé
Café Noir

Smoked Salmon   *Chablis*
Cassoulet with Duck   *La Tâche*
Black Bread and Butter
Fromages
Orange, Passetto
Café Noir

Seafood Bisque
Chicken Marengo   *Puligny-Montrachet*
Fromage
Crème de Menthe Mousse
Café Noir

La Croûte Landaise   *Muscadet*
Dorade Grillée au Fenouil
(Sea Bass or Red Snapper)
and
French Fried Potatoes
Raspberry Tarts
Café Noir

DINNER AT MAXIM'S

Potage Germiny
Paillettes Parmesan
Sole Albert   *Montrachet 1934*
Noisette d'Agneau de Behague, Edward VII   *Haut Brion 1919*
Pommes Maxim's (Rissolée)
Soufflé Glace   *Champagne*
au Kirsch

Luncheons

Scampi Cocktail
Oeufs Cocotte Perigourdine   *Meursault*
Italian Citron Cake
Café Noir

Brioche de Brillat Savarin   *Charmes-Chambertin*
Soufflé Grand Marnier
Café Noir

Chinese Salad Platter   *Sancerre*
Gougère
Tarte au Citron
Café Noir

La Friandise du Petit Colombier   *Montrachet*
(Rolled Crêpes)
Endive with French Dressing
Prunes Monique
Café Noir

Salade Niçoise
Cheese Soufflé   *Bordeaux Blanc*
Paul's Old Whaler Rum Cookies
Coffee

Cold Roast Beef   *Claret*
Spinach Salad and Brie
Liqueur Soufflé
Coffee

Kitchen Equipment & Pantry Shelf

IF THE following lists seem a bit formidable, remember that you can collect the equipment gradually as everyone does. The more interested in cooking one becomes, the more one collects. If, for instance, a cake recipe specifies a certain size of pan, and a certain time to bake, the size of the pan must be right or the baking time will be different. An experienced cook knows this; the amateur has to learn it. I have a great many more utensils than I have listed because I have been cooking and experimenting so long. If some seem luxury items I can say that I find them all useful. An enamel-covered iron lasagne pan has many uses. It is idea for *Jambon à la Crème*, for rows of filled crêpes in sauce, etc. An electric blender pays for itself in no time as a food saver; it has infinite uses. I don't use the pressure cooker for meat stews because I prefer long slow cooking, and of course it is too violent for fish. But I like it for some fresh vegetables because, cooking but a matter of seconds, the vegetables have a marvelously fresh taste. I like to steam some vegetables. Most kitchens have mixing bowls, saucepans, and favorite knives, forks, and spoons, so I have listed a minimum of these.

A well-stocked pantry shelf is essential to fine cooking. It is not possible for the ordinary cook to keep stocks of basic sauces and soups such as are in the kitchens of the great chefs, but it *is* possible to have on hand the ingredients for making stocks and sauces that are very good indeed. The packing houses have provided us with the meat extract and glazes that are frequently called for in this book. Wine and liqueurs are often called for; the list may seem extensive, but a good supply lasts a long time unless it is consumed in other pleasant ways.

Basmati aromatic Indian rice and patna rice can be obtained from the Orient Expert (not export) Trading Corporation, 123 Lexington Avenue, New York. They will send wonderful ingredients for curry, curry powders, rice, and fruit chutneys anywhere in the United States and Canada. Write for their catalog. There is nothing finer than these rices for pilaus, risottos, plain boiled rice, and for desserts.

Equipment

For Frying and Broiling

iron skillets: 7-inch and 10-inch
2-piece grill for steaks and chops
omelette pan, 8½-inch

pancake griddle
munk pan
crêpe pan: 7-inch

For Boiling

saucepans with lids: 1- to 4-quart
pressure cooker: 4-quart
steamer
cuiseur de vapeur (adjustable
  steamer)

double boiler
soup kettle: 8-quart

For Roasting

iron roaster: 8 inches by 12½ inches

large turkey roaster

Miscellaneous

fancy molds for creams and aspics
pastry cutter
funnels, large and small
mixing bowls: 4 graduated
sieves: large, small, fine, coarse
colander
chafing dish
wire salad basket
garlic press
onion press
mortar and pestle
meat grinder
electric blender
graters: coarse, medium, fine

disk shredders: coarse, medium, fine
wooden cutting board
rubber spatulas (important)
flour sifters, large and small
measuring cups, 4 graduated
measuring spoons, 4 graduated
kitchen shears
egg poachers
wooden chopping bowl
twin-bladed chopping knife
egg slicer
rotary beater
wire whisks
steel spatula

For Baking

oblong aluminum pans: 10½ inches by 16 inches

lasagne pan: 8½ inches by 16 inches

round baking dish: 8 inches by 3 inches deep

shallow oval baking dish: 11 inches long

round oven glass dish: 8½ inches by 1¾ inches deep

soufflé dishes:

7 inches by 2½ inches deep
7½ inches by 3¼ inches deep
8½ inches by 3 inches deep

medium-sized casserole: 9 inches across

large casserole: 12 inches across

long baking dish for fish

ramekins

iron popover forms

muffin tins, large and small

individual soufflé dishes: 4½ inches across

tort spring form: 8 inches by 2½ inches deep

Gugelhupf pan

tube pans: 8 inch and 9 inch

melon mold: 8 inches long

1 cake pan: 7 inches

2 cake pans: 8 inches

2 cake pans: 9 inches

1 cake pan: 10 inches

ring molds: 8-inch and 9½-inch

bread pans

pâté pan with cover

tart pan, movable bottom, 9-inch

charlotte mold: 7 inches by 4 inches deep

pie pans: 7-, 8-, 9-, 10-inch

Pantry Shelf

Herbs

anise
basil
bay leaves
caraway, seeds and powder
chervil
chives (fresh only)
coriander, seeds and powder
cumin powder
fennel seeds and powder
marjoram

mint (fresh only)
orégano
parsley
rosemary
sage
savory
sorrel (fresh only)
tarragon
thyme

Spices and Condiments

allspice, whole and powdered
Angostura Bitters

anise seeds and powder
aromatic pepper for the mill:

whole black and white pepper,
whole allspice
cardamom, berries and powder
catsup
cayenne pepper
chili powder
chili sauce
cinnamon, powder and stick
cloves, whole and powder
curry powder
ginger, root and powder
juniper berries and powder

Kitchen Bouquet
mustard, dry and prepared
nutmeg
orange bitters
paprika
poppy seeds
sesame seeds
tabasco sauce
tomato sauce
turmeric
Worcestershire sauce

Sweeteners

brown sugars
caramel
honey
light corn syrup

molasses
granulated sugar
powdered sugar
instant superfine sugar

Extracts

almond
anise
mocha

pistachio
rose
vanilla

Miscellaneous

beef and chicken consommé
beef and chicken powdered concentrate
BV meat extract
cornstarch
garlic

gelatin
freshly grated cheese
olive oil
tomato purée, juice, paste
vegetable juices
vegetable oil

Liquor Cabinet

applejack
Benedictine
Chartreuse
cognac
Cointreau
Crème de Cacao
Crème de Menthe
Curaçao
Grand Marnier

fruit brandies
Kirsch
maraschino liqueur
Madeira
Marsala
port
sherry
red and white wines
dry and sweet vermouths

Weights & Measures

3 teaspoons	1 tablespoon
4 tablespoons	¼ cup
16 tablespoons	1 cup
5 tablespoons plus 1 teaspoon	⅓ cup
1 cup minus 2 tablespoons	⅞ cup
1 cup	½ pint
2 cups	1 pint
4 cups	1 quart
4 quarts	1 gallon
¼ cup	1 jigger
3 tablespoons	1 pony
1 cup	8 fluid ounces (227 grams)
4 cups	32 fluid ounces (908 grams)
4⅓ cups fluid	1000 grams (1 kilogram or 1 liter)

Breadcrumbs

4½ cups soft	½ pound
2 cups dry sieved	½ pound

Butter

2 cups	1 pound
½ cup (1 stick; 8 tablespoons)	4 ounces

Chocolate

3 tablespoons grated	1 ounce
1 square	1 ounce

Cocoa

¼ cup	1 ounce

Cream, heavy, sweet, and sour

1 cup	8 ounces

Dates

2½ cups	1 pound

Eggs

1 medium large	2 ounces
8 whites	1 cup
12 yolks	1 cup

Figs
   3 cups   1 pound
Flour
      4 unsifted cups   1 pound (454 grams)
   4½ sifted cups   1 pound
    1 tablespoon   6 grams
Gelatin
   3 tablespoons   1 ounce
Milk
   1 cup   8 ounces
Mushrooms (fresh)
   2½ cups sliced   ½ pound
Nuts
   pecans, shelled 3½ cups   1 pound
   walnuts, shelled 4½ cups   1 pound
   almonds, shelled 3 cups   1 pound
   unshelled nuts 3 pounds   1 pound shelled
Oil
   2 cups   1 pound
Potato
   1 medium   4 ounces
Raisins
   2½ cups   1 pound
Rice
   2 cups   1 pound
Salt
   ½ cup   4 ounces
Sugar
   granulated, 2 cups   1 pound (454 grams)
   granulated, 1 tablespoon   12 grams
   instant superfine, 2⅓ cups   1 pound
   powdered, 2¾ cups   1 pound
   powdered sifted, 4½ cups   1 pound
   light-brown packed, 2½ cups 1 pound
Water
   1 cup   8 ounces

A

Acorn Squash Pie, 427
Acorn Squash Pudding, 320
Agnello dell'Accademico, 198–99
Agrodolce Sauce, 257
Aioli Dip, 15
Aioli Sauce, 340
  Blender, 347
Al Pappagallo (restaurant). *See* Pappagallo
"Al Teatro" Pizza Palace, 43
Aldo's Blazed Fruits, 407
Aldo's Fruit Macédoine, 409
Almond Butter Frosting, 437
  Coffee Cake, 362
  Cream Cake, 431
  Cream Filling and Frosting, 437
  Filling for Crescent Rolls, 364–65
  Pie, 426
  Pudding, Steamed, 381
  Sauce, 339
  Sauce, Dolci Amaretti, 375
Almonds, Measuring, 465
Alsatian Apple Tart, 417
Anchovy Garlic Spread, 14
Anchovy Potatoes, Swedish, 316
Anglaise, 183
Anguilles au Vert, 117
Anisette Soufflé, 374
Anniversary Cake, 429
Antipasto, Da Vasco's, 30
Antipasto, "Passetto," 29
Apéritif, Cassis-Burgundy, 413
Appetizers. *See* Hors d'Oeuvre and Entrées
Apples (and Apple Dishes),
  Blazed Baked, 411
  Charlotte, 382
  Peeled Baked, 411
  Pork Chops with Onions and, 217
  and Raisin Stuffing, 362
  Sauce, Horseradish, 348
  Soufflé Pudding, 382
  Tart, Alsatian, 417
Apricots (and Apricot Dishes). *See also*
  Fruit Desserts
  Bread Pudding, 380

Apricots (*Continued*)
  Cobbler, 384
  Mustard Sauce, 340
  Torta, Italian, 421
Artichokes, 276–77
  alla Crema, 276
  and Egg Hors d'Oeuvre, 36, 56
  al Forno, 329
  à la Grècque, 33
  Jerusalem, Creamed, 297
  with Mushroom Sauce, 277
  with Vinaigrette Sauce, 276
Asparagus, 277–78
  as an Entrée, 31
  French Style, 278
  on Toast, 277
  Variations, 277
Aspic. *See also* Jelly
  Beet, 338
  for Eggs Janine, Wine, 51
  for Eggs Surprise, 58
  Salads, 338
    Salmon, 122–23
    Tomato Ring, 338
Auberge de l'Empereur (restaurant), Champignons à la Grècque, 33
  Chicken in Cream with Chives, 235
Aubergines pour Hors d'Oeuvre Froid, 28

B

Baba au Rhum, 442
Babka, 362–63
Bacon, Eggplant Baked with, 293
Bacon, Potatoes Baked with, 311
Baeckenofe, Le, 270
Baking Equipment, 462
Ballotine de Canard Truffée et Pistachée, La, 27–28
Bananas (and Banana Dishes). *See also*
  Fruit Desserts
  Flambé, Baked, 406
  Peach-Sour-Cream Ice Cream, 449
  Sformato de Banane, 400
Barbecued Spareribs, 220

Barry's Pot Roast, 172
Basque Sauce, 127
Bass,
 for Baking, 119
 Burgundy Fish Stew, 107
 Chowder, 116–17
 Fish Stew, 112–13
 for Frying or Broiling, 120
 with Marinade, 131
 Soupe au Poisson à la Rouille, 110
Basting Sauce for Barbecued Spareribs, 220
Batters. See also Cakes; Pancakes; etc.
 for Butterfly Shrimp, 37
 for Chicken Liver Appetizers, 36
 for Fritto Misto, 272
 for Sweet-and-Sour Spareribs, 220–21
Bazzano, Hotel Della Rocca at, 65, 182–83,
  399
Beans (and Bean Dishes), 278–81. See also
  Kidney Beans; Lima Beans; etc.
 Baked, 280
 Baked, Big-Party, 279
 Baked, with Burgundy, 281
 Baked, with Ham, 230
 and Beef, Casserole of, 162
 Big-Party, 279
 Cassoulet, 266
 with Cheese, 278
 and Ham, Baked, 230
 and Ham, Casserole, 225
 Lamb with, 200–1
 with Peas and Cheese Sauce, 307
 with Peas and Onions, Casserole, 279
 Soups, 90–91
  with Roast Beef Bones, 90–91
 Succotash, 322
Béarnaise Sauce, 151, 341
Beaune,
 Dinner Menus from, 454
 Hôtel de la Poste at, 26, 51
Béchamel Sauces, 47, 62, 341–42. See also
  Cream Sauces
 Medium, 342
 Rich, 342
 Thick, 188, 342
 Thin, 341
Beef, 150–72
 for Baeckenofe, 270
 Barry's Pot Roast, 172
 and Beans, Casserole of, 162
 Boeuf Bourguignonne, 158–59
 Bolliti with Green Sauce, 271
 Bracioline alla Fiorentina, 160–61

Beef (Continued)
 Brisket, Braised Fresh, 155
 Chateaubriand Maison, 154
 Chili, 171
 Chinese Steak Flambé, 273
 Chipolata, 157
 Corned Beef Hash, 169
 Corned Beef with Vegetables, 164
 Filet Mignon, 154
 Goulash, 170–71
 Gravy Soup, 101
 Gypsy Goulash, 170–71
 Hash of Cooked Meat, 169
 with Horseradish Sauce, Boiled, 166
 Hungarian Goulash, 170
 Italian Meatballs, 163
 Kidneys. See Kidneys
 Liver. See Liver
 Marinade for Steak, 153
 Meatballs, Cocktail, 15–16
 Meatballs, Italian, 163
 Meat Loaf for Ten or Twelve, 164
 à la Mode, 159
 Oxtails, Braised, 167
 Pie, Steak and Kidney, 160
 Polpettine, 163
 Ribs of, Roast, 150
 Ribs, Short, Braised, 167
 Rognons de Boeuf, Vigneronne, 163
 Rump Roast, Braised, 168
 Sauerbraten, 156–57
 Short Ribs, Braised, 167
 Soup, Gravy, 101
 Steak, Braised Chuck, 169
 Steak, Broiled Porterhouse, Sirloin, or
  Club, 153
 Steak Flambé, Chinese, 273
 Steak Fondue, 156
 Steak and Kidney Pie, 160
 Steak, Marinade for, 153
 Steak au Poivre Flambé à la Normande,
  152
 Steak, Wine Sauce for, 153
 Stew, 165
 Stew with Dumplings, 165
 Stroganoff, Russian Style, 162
 Stufatino de Manzo con Peperoni alla
  Romana, 161
 Stuffed Fillet, Braised, 155
 Swiss Steak Fondue, 156
 Tongue, Boiled Fresh, 171
 Tournedos Belle Hélène, 151
 Tournedos aux Champignons, 150–51

Beef (Continued)
　Wine Sauce for Steak, 153
Beets (and Beet Dishes), 281–82
　Aspic, 338
　Mashed, 282
　Soufflé, 282
　Soup, Borscht, 91
　Soup with Fruit, 91
　and Sour Cream, 281
Benedictine Soufflé, 376
　Berry Bread Pudding, 380
　Berry Tart, 419
Beurre Blanc for Fish, 340
Beurre Fondu, Le (restaurant),
　Breakfast Prunes, 411
　Crevettes au Pierre, 39
　Duck à laRobert, 256
　Prunes Monique, 412
Beurre Manie, 134, 232
Beurre Noir, 341
Bibb Lettuce Salad, 331
Big-Party Beans, 279
Bisque, Seafood, 111
Bisque, Sweet Potato, 323
Black Bean Soup, 90–91
Black Radish Cakes, Chinese, 318
Black Walnut Cake with Caramel Frost-
　ing, 435
Blackberry Cream Tart, 420
Blackberry Flummery, 379
Blackberry Pudding. See also Raspberry
　Pudding
　Steamed, 385
Blackberry Tarts, 419
　Cream, 420
Blanquette d'Agneau, 199
Blanquette de Veau, 178
Blender Hollandaise or Aioli Sauce, 347
Blue-Plum Pudding, Fresh, 385
Blueberry Tart, 419
Boeuf Bourguignonne, 158–59
Boiling Equipment, 461
Bolliti with Green Sauce, 271
Bologna, Baked Sandwiches of, 19
Bologna restaurants,
　Da Vasco, 30, 402
　Freddy Martini, 250
　Hotel Majestic, 70
　Nerina, 71, 250
　Pappagallo, 64, 177, 248, 250
　Rosticceria Giuseppe, 271
　Sampieri, 69, 401, 446
　3 G Rosticceria-Ristorante, 198–99

Bordelaise Sauce, 157
Borscht, 91
Bouchées, Chocolate, 441
Bougival, Le Coq Hardi at, 24, 238, 253
Bouillabaisse Blanche (La Bourride), 109
Bouillabaisse à la Marseillaise, 108–9
Bouillon, Clear, 98–99
Bouillon, Court, 26
Bourride, La, 109
Bracioline alla Fiorentina, 160–61
Brains,
　Beurre Noir, 194
　Cervelle de Veau aux Pistaches, 193
　in Fritto Misto, 272
　with Ham, 193
　Pistaches, 193
Brandade avec Pommes de Terre, Proven-
　çal, 132
Brandy Cream Sauce for Steamed Pud-
　dings, 388
Bread Pudding, Fruit, 380
Breadcrumbs, Measuring, 464
Breads, 357–69 (Note: Asterisks denote
　breads which might be used as des-
　serts). See also Toast
Almond Coffee Cake, 362 *
Babka, 362–63 *
Brioche, 363
Coffee Cake, Almond, 362 *
Corn Pancakes, Green, 368
Cornbread, Pimento, 365
Cornbread, Sour-Cream, 366
Cornmeal Munks, 367
Cottage-Cheese Pancakes, 369
Crescent Rolls, Filled, 364–65 *
Croissants, 364
Delicate, 359
Dumplings. See Dumplings
English Muffins, 365
French, 358
Gougère, 366
Italian, 358
Limpa Bread, Swedish, 359
Maritozzi, 361 *
Muffins, English, 365
Munks, Cornmeal, 367
Oat Pones, 367
Pain Perdu, 366 *
Pane Misto, 358
Pancakes, Buckwheat, 368
Pancakes, Corn, 368
Pancakes, Cottage-Cheese, 369
Pancakes, Potato, 317

Breads (Continued)
  Pancakes, Rice, 368
  Pancakes, Sour-Cream, 369 *
  Pancakes, Turkey, 248
  Pimento Cornbread, 365
  Pones, Oat, 367
  Potato Scones, 368
  Pumpernickel, 360
  Rice Dumplings, 367
  Rice Pancakes, Brown, 368
  Rye and Wholewheat, 360
  Sally Lunn, 361 *
  Scones, Potato, 368
  Skillet, 369
  Sour-Cream Cornbread, 366
  Sour-Cream Pancakes, 369 *
  Swedish Limpa, 359
  Wholewheat and Rye, 360
Breakfast Prunes, 411
Brill, Suprème du Barbue Bordelaise, 134
Brioche, 363
Brioche de Brillat Savarin, 267
Broccoli, 282–83
  Italian Style, 283
  Steamed, 282–83
Broiling Equipment, 461
Broth,
  Chicken, 246
  Fish, ·07, 108, 109, 116
  Poultry, 230, 246
  Roast Beef Bones, 90
  Scotch, 100, 101
  Veal, 180–81
Broth Sauces,
  for Brioche de Brillat Savarin, 267
  for Crab Foo Yong, 137
  Mushroom, 353
  for Stuffed Veal, 181
Brown Sauce, 343
Brown Sugar Ice Cream, 446
Brussels, Grand Hotel in, 117, 141
Brussels Sprouts, 283–84
  with Chestnuts, 284
  Marie, 283
Buca di San Rufillo (restaurant),
  Aldo's Blazed Fruits, 407
  Aldo's Fruit Macédoine, 409
  Breast of Chicken, 248
  Cannelloni alla San Rufillo, 61
Buckwheat Pancakes with Caviar, 48
Buongustaia Nerina, 250
Burgundy Fish Stew, 107
Burgundy Sauce, for Eggs, 51

Bush Scallop Squash, 321
Butter and Butter Sauces,
  Beurre Blanc for Fish, 340
  Beurre Manie, 134, 230
  Beurre Noir, 341
  Cheese, 18
  Fish, 18
  Lemon, 349
  Lobster, 121
  Measuring, 464
  Meat-Flavored, 18
Butter Cake, Yellow, 430
Butter Cream,
  Chocolate, 436
  Chocolate Mocha, 436
  Kirsch, 439
Butter Custard Cream for Filling, 439
Butter Frosting, Almond, 437
Butter Omelette, 59
Butter Sauces. See Butter and Butter Sauces
Butter Sponge Cake, 429
Butterfish, for Baking, 119
Butterfly Shrimp, 37
Buttermilk Marinade, 206
Butternut Squash, 321
  Mashed, 321

C

Cabbage, 284–85. See also Sauerkraut
  Buttered, 284
  Creamed, 284
  and Pork Chops, Baked, 217
  Red, with Red Wine and Apples, 285
  Salad, 334
Café Procope, Le (restaurant),
  Canard aux Cerises, 254–55
  Escalope de Veau à la Crème, 184
Cakes, 427–43. See also Breads
  Almond Cream, 431
  Anniversary, 429
  Baba au Rhum, 442
  Black Walnut, 435
  for Blue-Plum Pudding, 385
  Bouchées, Chocolate, 441
  Butter, Sponge, 429
  Butter, Yellow, 430
  Cassata alla Siciliana, 440
  Cheese, 441
  Chocolate, 437

Cakes (Continued)
Chocolate Bouchées, 441
Chocolate Log, 436
Citron and Nut, 434
Cream Cake, Almond, 431
Cream Cake, Grape, 432
Cream Cake, Orange-Lemon, 432
Cream Cheese, 441
Fillings. See also specific cakes
Almond Cream, 437
Butter Custard Cream, 439
Lemon Jelly, 438
Five-Egg-White, 428
Four-Egg-White, 427
Frostings. See also Cakes: Icings
Almond Butter, 437
Almond Cream, 437
Butter, Almond, 437
Butter Cream, Chocolate, 436
Butter Cream, Chocolate Mocha, 436
Butter Cream, Kirsch, 439
Caramel, 435
for Cassata alla Siciliana, 440
Chocolate, 392
Chocolate Butter Cream, 436
Chocolate Mocha Cream, 436
Coconut Boiled, 438
Italian Meringue, 439
Kirsch Butter Cream, 439
Lemon Jelly, 438
Orange, 430
Orange-Lemon, 432
White Boiled, 438
Fruitcake, 433-34
Fruitcake, White, 434
Gâteau aux Fraises, 439
Gingerbread, 432
Glaze for, 439
Grape Cream, 432
Hot Milk, 431
Icings,
for Cassata alla Siciliana, 440
Chocolate-Liqueur, 441
Liqueur, 438
Nut and Citron, Italian, 434
Orange, 430
Orange Egg-Yolk, 431
Orange-Lemon Cream, 432
Pecan, 435
Poppy Seed, 433
for Raspberry Pudding, 386
Rolla, 443
Rum (Baba au Rhum), 442

Cakes (Continued)
Savarin, 442
Soufflé Puff, 383
Sponge, Butter, 429
Strawberry (Gâteau aux Fraises), 439
Susanne's Poppy Seed, 433
Walnut, Black, 435
White Fruitcake, 434
Yellow Butter, 430
Calcionetti for Christmas Eve, 444
Calf's Brains,
Beurre Noir, 194
Cervelle de Veau anx Pistaches, 19
in Fritto Misto, 272
with Ham, 193
Calf's Head, Bolliti with Green Sauce, 271
Calf's Liver. See Liver
Canapés,
Caviar, 16
Pimento, 15
Canard Braisé à l'Orange, 252-53
Canard Braisé aux Pêches, Maurice Cazalis, 251
Canard aux Cerises, 254-55,
Canard à l'Orange, Le, 253
Canepa, The (restaurant),
Eggs Andalusia, 53
Fried Rice Balls, 84
Scampi Canepa, 39
Veal Cutlet alla Canepa, 184
Cannelloni alla Nizzarda, 62
Cannelloni alla San Rufilio, 61
Cantaloupe,
with Port, 409
Soup, 92
as a Vegetable, Baked, 299
Caper Sauces, 100, 343
Caprice, 43
Capucin Gourmand (restaurant),
Coquillettes aux Noix, 403
Côtes de Mouton Champvallon, 201
Gratin de Crabes, Sauce Crevettes, 137
Jarrets de Veau à l'Orange, 176
Lièvre en Saupiquet, 270-71
Oeufs Pôches Bourguignonne, 52-53
Pojarsky aux Pommes Amandines, 183
Rognons de Boeuf, Vigneronne, 163
Soupe au Poisson à la Rouille, 110
Terrine de Lapin Lorraine, La, 19-20
Tournedos Belle Hélène, 151
Caramel, 252-53, 344
Crème Renversée, 391
Frosting, 435

Caramel (*Continued*)
Ice Cream, 447
Rice Pudding, 395
Sauce, 405
Soufflé, Cold, 374
Sweet Potato, 323
Syrup, 344
Cardinal Sauce, 121–22
Carrots (and Carrot Dishes), 286–88
Buttered New, 286
Consommé or Drink, 93
Curaçao, 286
Lemon Sauce for, 286
Mashed, 287
Orange Sauces for, 286, 353
Orange Soufflé, 286–87
with Peas, Shredded, 288
Ring, 287
Salad, 34
Soups, 92–93
Consommé, 93
Orange, 93
Tomato, 93
Tomato-Juice, 92
Cassata alla Siciliana, 440
Cassis,
Apéritif of, 413
Ice Cream, 448
Poires au, 413
Cassoulet with Duck, 266
Cauliflower, 288–89
with Curry Sauce, 288
Parmesan, 288
Variations, 289
Caverne Ali Baba (restaurant),
Couscous Libanais, 268
Caviar,
Buckwheat Pancakes with, 48
Canapés, 16
Fish Dip with Red, 14–15
Sauces for Roast Veal, 174, 343
"Caviar," Eggplant, 34
Celeriac,
Cèleri-rave, 35
Creamed, 289
Mashed with Potatoes, 289
Cèleri-rave, 35
Celery,
Braised, 289
in Broth, 289
and Tomato Soup, 102
Celery Root (Celeriac),
Cèleri-rave, 35

Celery Root (*Continued*)
Creamed, 289
Mashed with Potatoes, 289
Cervelle de Veau aux Pistaches, 193
Chailly-en-Bière, Auberge de l'Empereur
at, 32, 235
Champagne and Fruit, 408
Champagne, Poularde au, 240
Champignons à la Grècque, 33
Chantilly Sauce, 350–51
Chapeau Rouge. *See* Hôtel du Chapeau
Rouge
Chapon Fin (restaurant),
Ballotine de Canard Truffée et Pistachée,
La, 27–28
Crêpes Parmentier, 47–48
Filets de Brochets à la Crème, 134–35
Gâteau de Foies de Volaille à la Bressane,
26–27
Volaille à la Crème, La, 233
Charlotte, Apple, 382
Charlotte, Cheese, 81
Charlotte, Prune, 393
Chartres, Maurice Cazalis (restaurant) at,
127, 152, 193, 195, 313, 372
Chateaubriand. *See* Beef
Chateaubriand (restaurant),
Shad Roe à l'Oeille, 132
Chausson aux Queues de Homard, 141
Cheese Dishes, 78–82. *See also* Pastas; spe-
cific meat and vegetable dishes, etc.;
Cottage Cheese; Ricotta Cheese
Ball, Cocktail, 14
Balls for Consommé, 100
Butters, 18
Cake, 441
Caprice, 43
Charlotte, 81
-Egg-Tomato Hors d'Oeuvre, 36
Fondue, 80
Fonduta Lombardy, 82
in Fritto Misto, 272
Fromage à la Crème, 82
Garlic Toast, 81
Loaf, Cocktail or Supper, 18
Mold to Serve with Fruit, 414
and Mushroom Quiche, 41
Pastries, 45
Pastry, Gougère, 366
Pie, Parmesan, 45
Pie with Potato Crust, 79
Pizza, 44
Popovers, 16

Cheese Dishes (*Continued*)
  Pudding, 82
  Sandwiches, Baked, 19
  Sauces. *See also* Mornay Sauce; specific
    dishes
    with Ham, 187
    for Peas and Lima Beans, 307
    Tomato, 356
  Semolina Pudding with, 297
  Soufflé, Egg-White, 78–79
  Soufflé, Lazette's Famous, 80
  Soufflé, for Three or Four, 79
  Straws, 17
  Toast, 81
  Wafers, Cheddar, 17
  and Wine Paste, 16
Chef Salad, Elie's, 32
Cherries (and Cherry Dishes). *See also* Fruit
    Desserts
  Bread Pudding, 380
  Chocolate Mousse with, 392
  Cobbler, 384
  Compote, 410
  Compote with Peaches, 408
  Duck with (Canard aux Cerises), 254–55
  Ham with, 222
  Pudding, 384
  Pudding, Bread, 380
  Pudding, Steamed, 385
  Tart, Lorraine, 419
  Wine Sauce for Ham or Game, 346
Chestnuts (and Chestnut Dishes),
  Brussels Sprouts with, 284
  Cream, 388
    Molded, 390
    for Various Uses, 389
  Ice Cream, 390
  Pudding, 389
  Soufflé, 389
  Soup, 93–94
  Stuffing, 262
  Tarts, 418
  Truffles, 445
  Turinoise, Le, 388
Chez Pauline (restaurant),
  Poulet Sauté au Duc de Bourgogne, 236
  Quiche Lorraine, 40–41
Chick Peas, in Big-Party Beans, 279
Chicken, 230–48
  Almond Sauce for, 339
  Bolliti with Green Sauce, 271
  Breast of, 248
  Buongustaia Nerina, 250

Chicken (*Continued*)
  with Cheddar Cheese, Baked Broilers,
    242
  Coq au Riesling, 233
  Coq au Vin, Bourguignon, 240
  in Cream with Chives, 235
  Creamed, 245
  in Creole Gumbo, 113
  Curry, 242
  Demi-Deuil, 234
  Egg Soup, 102–3
  Florida, Breast of, 239
  Fricassée de Volaille aux Morilles, 232
  Fried, 241
  Gallina Faraona, 258–59
  with Garden Greens, 274
  Glazed Baked, 247
  Gravy Soup, 101
  with Ham, Smothered, 237
  Indian Curry, 242
  Jellied, 246–47
  -Lamb Stew for Couscous, 268
  Livers, Appetizers of, 36
  Livers, Cake of, 26–27
  Livers, in Desir des Gourmets, 265
  Livers, in Fritto Misto, 272
  Livers, and Lamb Kidneys, 208
  Livers, and Mushrooms with Rice, 87
  Livers, with Noodles, 65, 68, 76
  Livers, Pasta Sauce of, 73
  Livers, Pâtés of, 22–23
  Marengo, 239
  in Onions and Cream, 236
  in Paella, 269
  Paprika, 246
  Paupiettes de Poulet aux Morilles à la
    Crème, 234–35
  Peeti de Pollo alla Sabatini, 249
  Pie, 244–45
  Pies, Coq Hardi, 238
  Potato Stuffing for, 262
  Poularde au Champagne, 210
  Poulet à l'Angevine, 231
  Poulet Sauté au Duc de Bourgogne, 236
  Rice Dumplings for Stewed, 267
  Roast, 230–31
  Salads, 30, 334
  Soup, 103
  Soup, Egg, 102–3
  Soup, Gravy, 101
  Steamed, Stuffed, 243
  Steamed in Wine, 243–44
  Steamed in Wine, Capon, 237

Chicken (*Continued*)
  with Vegetables, Casserole of, 241
  Volaille à la Crème, La, 233
Chicory Salad with Croutons, 332
Chili Beef, 171
Chili Sauce with Sour Cream, 345
Chinese Black Radish Cakes, 318
  Eggplant, 295
  Glazed Spareribs, 221
  Noodles, 66
  Rice-Stick Noodles, 272
  Salad Platter, 32
  Sea Bass with Marinade, 131
  Steak Flambé, 273
  Sweet-and-Sour Spareribs, 220–21
Chipolata, 157
Chocolate Bouchées, 441
  Butter Cream, 436
  Cake, 437
  Cream Pie, 423
  Filling for Rolla Cake, 443
  Ice Cream, 446
  Log, 436
  Macaroons, 443
  Measuring, 464
  Mocha Cream, 436
  Mousse with Cherries, 392
  Pies, 423
  Pots de Crème, 390
  Rum Pie, 423
  Sauce, 405
  Sauce, Thin, 401
Choucroute, 223
Chowders,
  Clam, 111, 112
  Corn and Chicken, 94
  Red Snapper or Sea Bass, 116–17
Cinnamon Nut Cookies, 445
Citron and Nut Cake, Italian, 434
Clafoutis, 419
Clams (and Clam Dishes),
  Chowders, 111, 112
  Creamed, 143
  in Fritto Misto, 272
  and Mussel Soup, 112
  Pie, 142
  Sauce, 65
Clear Bouillon, 98–99
Cobbler, Sour-Cherry, 384
Cocktail Accessories, 14–19
  Aioli Dip, 15
  Anchovy Garlic Spread, 14
  Canapés, Caviar, 16

Cocktail Accessories (*Continued*)
  Canapés, Pimento, 15
  Caviar Canapés, 16
  Cheese Ball, 14
  Cheese Popovers, 16
  Cheese Straws, 17
  Cheese Wafers, 17
  Cheese and Wine Paste, 16
  Cocktail Loaf, 18
  Dips,
    Aioli, 15
    for Meatballs, 15–16
    Salmon, Red Caviar, 14–15
    Tuna Fish, Red Caviar, 14–15
  Garlic Spread, Anchovy, 15
  Meatballs with Dip, 15–16
  Mushroom Sandwiches, 17
  Paillettes Parmesan, 17
  Paste, Cheese and Wine, 16
  Pimento Canapés, 15
  Popovers, Cheese, 16
  Salmon Dip, Red Caviar, 14–15
  Sandwiches, 15ff., 17–19
    Baked, 19
    Caviar Canapés, 16
    Pimento Canapés, 15
    Cocktail or Supper Loaf, 18
    Mushroom, 17
    Striped, 18
  Spread, Anchovy Garlic, 15
  Striped Sandwich, 18
  Supper Loaf, 18
  Tarama, 15
  Tuna Fish Dip, Red Caviar, 14–15
  Vegetables with Aioli Dip, 15
  Wafers, Cheddar Cheese, 17
  Wine and Cheese Paste, 16
Cocktail Loaf, 18
Cocktails, Seafood,
  Crab, 39
  Lobster, 39
  Shrimp, 39, 40
Cocoa, Measuring, 464
Coconut Cream Pie, 424
  Cream Pudding, 393
  Cream Sauce, 392
  Frosting (Boiled Frosting), 438
  Milk, 324
  Pie, 423
  Pie, Cream, 324
  Pudding, Cream, 393
  Pudding, Rice, 396
  Pudding, Sweet Potato, 324

Coconut (*Continued*)
Rice Pudding, 396
Soufflé, 376
Tarts, 422
Codfish,
Baked, 133
Baked, Sour-Cream Tomato Sauce, 355
Brandade avec Pommes de Terre, Provençal, 132
Cakes, 136
for Quenelles, 124–25
Stew, 112–13
Coffee Cake, Almond, 362
Coffee and Rum Ice Cream, 448
Compotes,
Canned Fruit, 407
Cherry, 410
Cherry and Peach, 408
Fig, 413
Condiments, Basic, 463
Connaught Hotel (restaurant),
Moussclines de Saumon, Adam, 120
Consommé, Carrot, 93
Consommé, Cheese Balls for, 100
Consommé, with Noodles (Tagliarini), 99
Consommé, Turtle, with Madeira, 117
Cookies, 443–45
Calcionetti for Christmas Eve, 444
Chestnut Truffles, 445
Chocolate Macaroons, 443
Cinnamon Nut, 445
Macaroons, Chocolate, 443
Nut Cinnamon, 445
Rum, Old Whaler, 444
Coq Hardi, Le (restaurant),
Canard à l'Orange, Le, 253
Chicken Pies, 238
Croûte Landaise, La, 24
Coq au Riesling, 233
Coq au Vin, Bourguignon, 240
Coquilles St. Jacques, 144
Coquillettes aux Moix, 403
Corn, 290–92
Cakes, 290–91
Cakes, Early Days, 290
and Chicken Chowder, 94
on the Cob, 290
Mexican, 292
with Onions and Pepper, Sautéed, 292
Pancakes, Green, 368
Pudding, 291
Succotash, 322

Cornbread,
Pimento, 365
Sour-Cream, 366
Corned Beef Hash, 169
Corned Beef with Vegetables, 164
Cornish Game Hen, 259
Cornmeal Dumplings, 179
Cornmeal Munks, 367
Cornmeal Polentas, 77–78
Côtes de Mouton Champvallon, 201
Cottage-Cheese Pancakes, 369
Cottage-Cheese Pudding, 400
Cottage Pudding with Marmalade Sauce, 386
Court Bouillon, 26
Courthouse Trifle, 394
Couscous Libanais, 268
Crab,
Bisque, 111
Butter, 18
Buttered Fresh Cooked, 139
Cakes, 138
Casserole, 125
Casserole, Noodle, 76
Cocktail, 39
Creamed, 138–39
Foo Yong, 137
Gratin de Crabes, Sauce Crevettes, 137
in Gratin aux Fruits de Mer, 142
Mayonnaise Cream Sauce for, 350
Mousse, 38
for Noodle Casserole, 76
Quiche, 41–42
Salad, 335
Salad, with Rice, 336
Stuffed Eggs, Creamed, 60
Cranberry Jelly, 345
Cranberry Sauce, 345
with Red Wine, 344
Crappie, for Frying or Broiling, 120
Cream. See also Sour Cream
Measuring, 464
Cream Cakes,
Almond, 431
Grape, 432
Orange-Lemon, 432
Cream Cheese. See also Cheese Dishes; Cocktail Accessories; specific desserts
Cake, 441
Cream Filling and Frosting, Almond, 437
Cream Filling for Torta, 421

Cream Pies, 422
  Chocolate, 423
  Coconut, 424
  Raspberry, 424
Cream Sauces, 24, 64, 146. *See also* Béchamel Sauces; Coconut Cream Sauce; Mayonnaise Cream Sauce; Mushroom Cream Sauce; etc.
  for Dessert Crêpes, 404
  for Dessert Soufflé, 373
  for Egg Sauce, 345
  for Lobster, 140
  for Lobster Sauce, 352
  for Noodle Casserole, 76
  for Seafood Casserole, 125
  Shrimp-Flavored, 60
  for Soubise Sauce, 352
Cream Vegetable Soup, 105
Cream of Wheat Pudding, 397
Crème Brulée, 390
Crème Fraîche, 342
Crème de Menthe Ice Cream, 448
Crème de Menthe Mousse, 391
Crème Patissière, 372
Crème Renversée au Caramel, 391
Crème Saint-Honoré, 398
Creole Oyster Gumbo, 113
Creole Sauce, 192
  for Fish or Omelettes, 345
Crêpes, 46–48
  Cherry, 404
  Dessert, 403–4
  Friandise du Petit Colombier, La, 46–47
  Ham-Filled, 226
  au Kirsch, Surprise, 404
  Panzerotti alla Romana, 47
  Parmentier, 47–48
  Suzette, 403
Crescent Rolls, Filled, 364–65
Crevettes au Pierre, 39
Croissants, 364
Crookneck Squash, 321
Croquettes, Potato, 312
Croûte Landaise, La, 24
Croutons, 332
Crusts. *See also* Pies
  Potato, 79, 318
  Rusk, 441
Cucumber Sauce, 131–32
Cucumbers with Dill, Braised, 292
Cumin Sauce, 204
Curaçao, Carrots with, 286
Curaçao Icing, 438

Curaçao Sauce for Bananas, 400
Curaçao Soufflés, 374, 376
Currants, in Fruit Mélange, 408
Curries and Curry Sauces,
  Cauliflower with, 288
  Chicken, Indian, 242
  Lamb, Cooked, 205
  Lamb, Indian Style, 211
  Lentils, Indian Style, 298–99
  Onions, 305
  Pork, Western Style, 204
  Quick Curry Sauce, 346
  Shrimp, 148
  Veal, Cooked, 205
Custard, 396. *See also* Desserts: Puddings, Molds, and Custards
  Fillings, 364–65, 439
  for Ice Cream, 446
  Pie, French, 425
  Pie, Old-Fashioned, 424

D

Da Vasco (restaurant),
  Antipasto, 30
  Dolce Vasco, 402
Dad's Best Noodles, 67
Danieli. *See* Hotel Danieli
Date Pudding, Steamed, 387
Dates, Measuring, 464
Deer Steak, 168
Delicate Bread, 359
Désir des Gourmets, 265
Dessert Sauces,
  Almond, for Dolci Amaretti, 375
  Blackberry Pudding, 385
  Brandy Cream, for Steamed Puddings, 388
  Caramel, 344, 405
  Cherry Pudding, 384, 385
  Chocolate, 405
  Chocolate, Thin, 401
  Coconut Cream, 392
  Cream. *See also* specific flavors
  Cream, for Crêpes, 404
  Cream, for Soufflé, 373
  Crème Fraîche, 342
  Curaçao, for Bananas, 400
  Ginger, for Ice Cream, 450
  Jam-Rum, for Apple Charlotte, 382

Dessert Sauces (*Continued*)
Lemon, 383
Liqueur, 375, 403
Marmalade, 386
Marsala, for Dolce Vasco, 402
Orange, 396
Praliné Powder, 356
Raisin-Rum, for Apple Pudding, 383
Raspberry, 410
Raspberry, for Ice Cream, 450
Rum-Jam, for Apple Charlotte, 382
Rum-Raisin, for Apple Pudding, 383
Strawberry, 410
Strawberry, for Ice Cream, 450
Desserts, 371–450. *See also* Cakes; Cookies;
    Pies; Tarts; etc.
Crêpes, 403–4
    Cherry, 404
    au Kirsch, Surprise, 404
    Suzette, 403
Frozen, 445–50
    Brown Sugar Ice Cream, 446
    Caramel Ice Cream, 447
    Cassis Ice Cream, 448
    Chestnut Ice Cream, 390
    Chocolate Ice Cream, 446
    Coffee and Rum Ice Cream, 448
    Crème de Menthe Ice Cream, 448
    French Ice Cream, 445
    Fruit Juice Ice Cream, 447
    Gelati Vaniglia, 446
    Glace aux Cassis, 448
    Lemon Ice Cream, 447
    Mangos with Ice Cream, 450
    Orange Sherbet with Fruit and Kirsch,
        449
    Peppermint Ice Cream, 446
    Raspberry Ice, 448
    Raspberry Ice Cream, 446
    Rum and Coffee Ice Cream, 448
    Sour-Cream Ice Cream, 449
    Spumoni, 449
    Vanilla Ice Cream, 446
    Vanilla Ice Cream, French, 445
    Vanilla Ice Cream, Mangos with, 450
    Vanilla Ice Cream, Sauces for, 450
Fruit Desserts, 406–14. *See also* specific
    fruits
    Aldo's Blazed, 407
    Aldo's Macédoine, 409
    Baked Blazed, 406
    Bread Pudding, 380
    and Champagne, 408

Desserts (*Continued*)
    Cheese Mold to Serve with, 414
    Compote of Canned, 407
    Egg-White Soufflé, 377
    Italian Cream, 398
    Juice Ice Creams, 447
    Macedonia al Maraschino, 413
    Mélange of, 408
Puddings, Molds, and Custards, 379–403
    Almond Pudding, Steamed, 381
    Apple Charlotte, 382
    Apple Soufflé, 383
    Apricot Bread Pudding, 380
    Apricot Cobbler, 384
    Berry Bread Pudding, 380
    Blackberry Flummery, 379
    Blackberry Pudding, Steamed, 385
    Blue-Plum, Fresh, 385
    Bread Puddings, Fruit, 380
    Caramel Crème Renversée, 391
    Caramel Rice Pudding, 395
    Charlotte, Apple, 382
    Charlotte, Prune, 393
    Cherry Bread Pudding, 380
    Cherry Cobbler, 384
    Cherry Pudding, 384
    Cherry Pudding, Steamed, 385
    Chestnut Cream, 388–89
    Chestnut Cream, Molded, 390
    Chestnut Pudding, 389
    Chestnut Pudding (Le Turinoise), 388
    Chocolate Mousse with Cherries, 392
    Chocolate Pots de Crème, 390
    Cobbler, Sour-Cherry, 384
    Coconut Cream Pudding, 393
    Coconut Rice Pudding, 396
    Coquilettes aux Noix, 403
    Cottage-Cheese Pudding, 400
    Cottage Pudding, 386
    Courthouse Trifle, 394
    Cream of Wheat Pudding, 397
    Crème Brulée, 390
    Crème de Menthe Mousse, 391
    Crème Renversée au Caramel, 391
    Crème Saint-Honoré, 398
    Date Pudding, Steamed, 387
    Dolce Sampieri, 401
    Dolce Vasco, 402
    Fig Pudding, Steamed, 387
    Flummery, Blackberry, 379
    Fruit Bread Puddings, 380
    Fruit Cream, Italian, 398
    Italian Fruit Cream, 398

Desserts (*Continued*)
Italian Orange Rice Pudding, 396
Milk-Chocolate Mousse with Cherries, 392
Mousse, Chocolate, 392
Mousse, Chocolate, with Cherries, 392
Mousse, Crème de Menthe, 391
Nut Pudding, Steamed, 381
Orange Bread Pudding, 380
Orange Rice Pudding, 396
Peach Cobbler, 384
Plum Pudding, Fresh Blue-, 385
Pots de Crème au Chocolat, 390
Prune Charlotte, 393
Raspberry Cobbler, 384
Raspberry Pudding, 386
Raspberry Trifle, 394
Rice Cream with Lemon Sauce, 394
Rice Cream Trifle, 395
Rice Pudding, 395–97
Rice Pudding, Caramel, 395
Rice Pudding, Coconut, 396
Rice Pudding, Molded, 397
Rice Pudding, Orange, 396
Saint Honoré, Sabatini, 398
Semifreddo allo Zabaione, 399
Semolina Pudding, 397
Sformato de Banane, 400
Soufflé Pudding, Apple, 383
Soufflé Puff Cake, 382
Sour-Cherry Cobbler, 384
Steamed Pudding, Blackberry, 385
Steamed Pudding, Brandy Cream Sauce for, 388
Steamed Pudding, Cherry, 385
Steamed Pudding, Date, 387
Steamed Pudding, Fig, 387
Strawberry Cobbler, 384
Strawberry Trifle, 394
Trifle, 394
Trifle, Courthouse, 394
Trifle, Rice Cream, 395
Turinoise, Le, 388
Zabaione, 399, 402
Sauces for. *See* Dessert Sauces
Soufflés, 372–79
Anisette, 374
Benedictine, 376
Caramel, Cold, 374
Chestnut, 289
au Cocktail de Liqueurs, 372
Coconut, 376
Curaçao, 374, 376

Desserts (*Continued*)
Diana's Mocha, 373
Dolci Amaretti, 375
Fruit Egg-White, 377
Glacé au Kirsch, 379
Grand Marnier, 374, 376
Kirsch, 379
Lemon, 377
Liqueur, 372, 374. *See also* specific liqueurs
Marasquin, 376
Mocha, 373
Orange, 378
Raspberry, 378
au Rhum, 373
Rice, 88
Rose's Dolci Amaretti, 375
Rum, 373
Strawberry, 378
Diamantaires (restaurant),
Tarama, 15
Diana's Mocha Soufflé, 373
Dijon, Hôtel du Chapeau Rouge at, 28, 172–73, 413
Dill Dumplings, 203
Potato, 317
with Tomato Sauce, 327
Dill Sauce, for Squash, 321
Dinner Menus, 453–58
in Beaune, 454
Holiday, 456–58
at Maxim's, 458
Dipping Sauce, for Butterfly Shrimp, 37
Dips, Cocktail,
Aioli, 15
for Meatballs, 15–16
Salmon, Red Caviar, 14–15
Tuna Fish, Red Caviar, 14–15
Dolce Sampieri, 401
Dolce Vasco, 402
Dolci Amaretti, 375
Dorade Grillée au Fenouil, 132–33
Doughs. *See also* Breads; Cakes; Pies; etc.
Cobbler, 384
Pizza, 44–45
Dressings. *See* Salad Dressings
Drinks,
Carrot, 93
Cassis-Burgundy Apéritif, 413
Drouant, Le (restaurant),
Bouillabaisse à la Marseillaise, 108–9
Paupiettes de Poulet aux Morilles à la Crème, 234–35

Duck, 251–55
  with Agrodolce Sauce, 257
  Apple and Raisin Stuffing for, 263
  "Bundle" of, 27–28
  Canard Braisé à l'Orange, 252–53
  Canard Braisé aux Pêches, 251
  Canard aux Cerises, 254–55
  Canard à l'Orange, Le, 253
  Cassoulet with, 266
  Fruit Stuffing for, 263
  Pâtés. See Pâtés and Terrines
  Port Wine Jelly for, 356
  à la Robert, 256
  with Vegetables, Roast, 251
  Wild, Roast, 254
Dumplings, 165
  Cornmeal, 179
  Dill, 203
  Dill, Potato, 317
  Dill, with Tomato Sauce, 327
  Mint, 203
  Parsley, Potato, 317
  Potato, with Fresh Dill or Parsley, 317
  Rice, 367

𝓔

Early Days Corncakes, 290
Eels, au Vert, 117
Eggplant, 293–96
  with Bacon and Cheese, Baked Whole, 293
  "Caviar," 34
  with Cheese and Bacon, Baked Whole, 293
  with Cheese and Cream, Baked, 293
  Chinese, 295
  al Forno, 329
  with Ham and Tomato Sauce, Baked, 295
  with Herbs, Baked Fried, 293
  Hors d'Oeuvre, 28
  Lamb with, Braised, 207
  Moussaka, 294
  Ratatouille, 294–95
  Stuffed, 29
  in Tomato Sauce and Cream, Baked, 296
  with Tomato Sauce and Ham, Baked, 295
Eggs (and Egg Dishes), 49–61. See also
    Mousses; Soufflés; etc.

Eggs (Continued)
  Andalusia, 53
  Artichoke and Egg Hors d'Oeuvre, 36, 56
  Avocado and Egg Hors d'Oeuvre, 36, 56
  Boiled, 55
  Butter Omelette, 59
  Caprice, 43
  Coddled, 55
  Crab Foo Yong, 137
  Creamed Stuffed, 60
  Creole Sauce, 345
  Eve's Spanish, 56
  Foo Yong, Crab, 137
  Fried Stuffed, 57
  Frittata al Verde, 53
  Hors d'Oeuvre, Avocado or Artichoke, 36, 56
  Hors d'Oeuvre, Tomato-Cheese, 36
  Measuring, 464
  Oeufs Bourguignons, 51
  Oeufs Cocotte Perigourdine, 49
  Oeufs Janine, 51
  Oeufs Mayonnaise, 51
  Oeufs Mollets, 56
  Oeufs Pôchés Bourguignonne, 52–53
  Omelette, Butter, 59
  Omelette, Creole Sauce for, 345
  Omelette Mousseline, 58
  Pea Roulade, 54
  Pipérade, 309
  Poached, 55
  Poached in Potato Soup, 57
  Potato and Egg Salad, Hot, 337
  Roulade, Spinach or Pea, 54
  Sauce for Boiled Fish, 345
  Soup, 102
  Spanish, Eve's, 56
  Spinach Roulade, 54
  Stuffed, 54–55
  Stuffed, Creamed, 60
  Stuffed, Fried, 57
  Surprise, 58
  Tomato-Cheese Hors d'Oeuvre, 36
  Zucchini al Forno, 328–29
Egg-White Cheese Soufflé, 78–79
Egg-White Fruit Soufflé, 377
Elie's Chef Salad, 32
Emily's Creamed Onions, 304
Endive,
  Braised, with Cheese Sauce, 296
  Braised, with Prosciutto, 296
  à la Grècque, 33

Endive (*Continued*)
Salad, 333
English Muffins, 365
Entrées. *See* Hors d'Oeuvre and Entrées
Equipment, Kitchen, 460–62
Escalope de Veau à la Crème, 184
Escargot Montorgueil, L' (restaurant),
Rognons de Veau, Bercy, 195
Suprème de Barbue Bordelaise, 134
Eve's Spanish Eggs, 56
Extracts, Basic, 463

F

Fagiano al Vino Rosso, 255
Fair Aurora's Pillow, 24–25
Fegatello con Rete, 218–19
Fettuccine,
all'Alfredo, 62
Bianche e Verdi, 63
with Clam Sauce, 65
with Grated Chicken Livers, 65
Paris Style, 63
Field Salad, 332
Figs (and Fig Dishes),
Compote, 413
Measuring, 465
Prosciutto with, 30
Pudding, Steamed, 387
Filet au Poivre à Ma Façon, 152
Filet de Veau à la Moutarde, 172–73
Filets de Brochets à la Crème, 134–35
Finnan Haddie, 133
Fish and Shellfish, 119–48. *See also* specific kinds
Almond Sauce for, 339
with Anchovy Butter, Fillets, 126
for Baking, 119
Beurre Blanc Sauce for, 340
for Broiling, 120
Butters, 18
Creole Sauce for, 345
Egg Sauce for Boiled, 345
Entrées, 37–40
Fritto Misto, 272
for Frying, 120
Gratin aux Fruits de Mer, 142
in Parchment, 127
for Poaching, 120
Seafood Pie, 135
Soufflé, 136

Fish and Shellfish (*Continued*)
Soups, 107–17
Anguilles au Vert, 117
Bass Chowder, 116–17
Bisque, Seafood, 111
Broth, 107, 108, 109, 116
Bouillabaisse Blanche (La Bourride),
109
Bouillabaisse à la Marseillaise, 108–9
Bourride, La, 109
Burgundy Fish Stew, 107
Chowder, Clam, 111, 112
Chowder, Red Snapper or Sea Bass,
116–17
Clam Chowder, 111, 112
Clam and Mussel, 112
Consommé, Turtle, with Madeira, 117
Crab Bisque, 111
Creole Oyster Gumbo, 113
Eels au Vert, 117
Gumbo, Creole Oyster, 113
Italian Clam and Mussel, 112
Lobster Bisque, 111
Lobster Stew, 114
Mussel, 114
Mussel and Clam, 112
Myron's Clam Chowder, 112
Oyster Gumbo, 113
Oyster Stew, 115
Red Snapper Chowder, 116–17
Rose's Tuna Fish, 115
à la Rouille, 110
Salmon and Shrimp, 116
Sea Bass Chowder, 116–17
Seafood Bisque, 111
Shrimp Bisque, 111
Shrimp and Salmon, 116
Snapper Chowder, 116–17
Stew, 112–13
Stew, Burgundy, 107
Stew, Lobster, 114
Stew, Oyster, 115
Stock, 115
Toast for, 110
Tuna Fish, 115
Turtle Consommé with Madeira, 117
Turtle and Pea, 105
Sour-Cream Tomato Sauce for Baking,
355
Stew, 112–13
Stew, Burgundy, 107
Stock, 127, 134
in Wine or Cream, Fillets, 128

Five-Egg-White Cake, 428
Flageolets, Lamb with, 200–1
Florence restaurants,
  Buca de San Rufillo, 61, 248, 407, 409
  Sabatini, 47, 62, 83, 160–61, 398
Flounder,
  Fillets with Anchovy Butter, 126
  for Frying or Broiling, 120
Flour, Measuring, 465
Flummery, Blackberry, 379
Foie Gras,
  for Croûte Landoise, La, 24
  Frais Truffée et Poche au Porto, 22
Fondue, Cheese, 80
Fondue, Swiss Steak, 156
Fonduta Lombardy, 82
Four-Egg-White Cake, 427
Fowl. See Poultry
Frank's Macaroni Genovese, 71
Frank's Sciué Sciué, 67
Freddy Martini (restaurant),
  Turkey Fillets alla Freddy, 250
Freddy's Cheese Toast, 81
French Bread, 358
French Custard Pie, 425
French Dressing, 333
French Ice Cream, 445
Friandise du Petit Colombier, La, 46–47
Fricassée de Volaille aux Morilles, 232
Frittata al Verde, 53
Fritto Misto, 272
Fromage à la Crème, 82
Frostings, Cake. See under Cakes
Frozen Desserts, 445–50
  Brown Sugar Ice Cream, 446
  Caramel Ice Cream, 447
  Cassis Ice Cream, 448
  Chestnut Ice Cream, 390
  Chocolate Ice Cream, 446
  Coffee and Rum Ice Cream, 448
  Crème de Menthe Ice Cream, 448
  French Ice Cream, 445
  Fruit Juice Ice Cream, 447
  Gelati Vaniglia, 446
  Glace aux Cassis, 448
  Lemon Ice Cream, 447
  Mangos with Ice Cream, 450
  Orange Sherbet with Fruit and Kirsch, 449
  Peppermint Ice Cream, 446
  Raspberry Ice, 448
  Raspberry Ice Cream, 446
  Rum and Coffee Ice Cream, 448

Frozen Desserts (Continued)
  Sour-Cream Ice Cream, 449
  Spumoni, 449
  Vanilla Ice Cream, 446
    French, 445
    Ginger Sauce for, 450
    Mangos with, 450
    Raspberry or Strawberry Dressing for, 450
Fruit and Beet Soup, 91
Fruit Desserts, 406–14. See also specific Fruits
  Aldo's Blazed, 407
  Aldo's Macédoine, 409
  Baked Blazed, 406
  Bread Pudding, 380
  and Champagne, 408
  Cheese Mold to Serve with, 414
  Compote of Canned, 407
  Egg-White Soufflé, 377
  Italian Cream, 398
  Juice Ice Creams, 447
  Macedonia al Maraschino, 413
  Mélange of, 408
Fruit Stuffing, 263
Fruitcake, 433–34
  White, 434
Frying Equipment, 461

G

Gallina Faraona, 258–59
Game, 254–61. See also specific game
  Cherry Wine Sauce for, 346
  Jelly Sauce for, 348
  Port Wine Jelly for, 356
Garlic Mayonnaise. See Aioli Sauce
Garlic Spread, Anchovy, 15
Garlic Toast, Cheese, 81
Gâteau de Foies de Volaille à la Bressane, 26–27
Gâteau aux Fraises, 439
Gazpacho, 104
Gelati Vaniglia, 446
Gelatin, Measuring, 465
Gin-Cream Sauce for Venison, 168
Ginger Sauce for Vanilla Ice Cream, 450
Gingerbread, 432
Glace aux Cassis, 448
Glaze, Cake, 439
Gnocchi, 77

Goose,
  Apple and Raisin Stuffing for, 263
  in Cassoulet, 266
  Chestnut Stuffing for, 262
  Fruit Stuffing for, 203
  Liver (Foie Gras), for Croûte Landais,
    24
  Liver Pâté, 22
  Lyonnaise, Braised, 249
  Port Wine Jelly for, 356
  Roast, 230-31
Gougère, 366
Goulash, 170-71
  Pork, with Sauerkraut and Sour Cream,
    215
Goulash Sauce for Leftover Meats, 346
Grand Hotel (restaurant),
  Anguilles au Vert, 117
  Chaussons aux Queues de Homard, 141
Grand Marnier Soufflé, 374, 376
Grand Veneur Sauce, 198
Grape Cream Cake, 432
Grape Ice Cream, 447
Grapefruit Salad with Greens, 335
Grapes. See Fruit Desserts
Gratin de Crabes, Sauce Crevettes, 137
Gravy,
  for Fried Chicken, 241
  Soup of, 100
Green Beans, 278-79
  with Cheese, 278
Green Mayonnaise, 349
Green Peppers. See Peppers
Green Sauce, 271
  for Egg Noodles, 71
Gremolata, 175
Grouse Smitane, 259-60
Grouse Stew, 260-61
Guinea Hen,
  Gallina Faraona, 258-59
  Stew, 260-61
Gumbo, Creole Oyster, 113
Gypsy Goulash, 70-71

ℋ

Haddock, for Frying or Broiling, 120
Halibut,
  for Baking, 119
    Sour-Cream Tomato Sauce, 355

Halibut (Continued)
  for Frying or Broiling, 120
  for Quenelles, 124-25
Ham. See also Prosciutto
  in Big-Party Beans, 279
  Butter, 18
  and Cheese Sauce, 187
  with Cherries, Boiled, 222
  Cherry Wine Sauce for, 346
  Chicken with, Smothered, 237
  Creamed Potatoes with, 315
  in Creole Gumbo, 113
  Crêpes Filled with, 226
  Jambon à la Crème, 228-29
  Jambon Persillé à la Bourguignonne, 26
  and Kidney Beans, Casserole of, 225
  Kraut and Knackwurst Casserole, 225
  with Lima Beans, Baked, 230
  Loaf, 227
  Mousse, Cold, 227
  New England Boiled Dinner, 222
  Noodles and Sour Cream with, 67
  with Orange Raisin Sauce, 229
  and Potato Hash, 228
  Potatoes Stuffed with, 311
  Quiche, 41
  Roast Marinated Fresh, 214
  Sandwiches, Baked, 19
  Sauce, 249
  Sauce with Cheese, 187
  Sharp Sauce for, 271
  Soufflé, 229
  and Sweet Potatoes, 228
  Sweetbreads with, 193
  Tetrazzini, 225-26
  Tomatoes Stuffed with, 326
  Veal with, 185
Hanstown Club (restaurant),
  Baked Lobster, 140-41
Hare. See also Rabbit
  Lièvre en Saupiquet, 270-71
Hash, Cooked Meat, 169
Hash, Ham and Potato, 228
Helen di Georgio (restaurant),
  Zucchini al Forno, 328-29
Henri's (restaurant),
  Lobster Américaine, 139
Herbs, Basic, 462
Herring,
  for Frying or Broiling, 120
  in Sour Cream with Onions, 40
Hollandaise Sauce, 347
  Blender, 347

Hollandaise Sauce (*Continued*)
  Simple, 347
  Variation, for Brussels Sprouts, 283
Honeydew,
  with Port, 409
  as a Vegetable, Baked, 299
  with Wine, 409
Hors d'Oeuvre and Entrées, 13–88
  Aioli Dip, 15
  Anchovy Garlic Spread, 14
  Antipastos, 29, 30
  Artichoke and Egg Hors d'Oeuvre, 36, 56
  Artichokes à la Grècque, 33
  Asparagus as an Entrée, 31
  Aubergines pour Hors d'Oeuvre Froid, 28
  Avocado Egg Hors d'Oeuvre, 36, 56
  Ballotine de Canard Truffée et Pistachée, 27–28
  Buckwheat Pancakes with Caviar, 48
  Butter Omelette, 59
  Butterfly Shrimp, 37
  Canapés, Caviar, 16
  Canapés, Pimento, 15
  Cannelloni alla Nizzarda, 62
  Cannelloni alla San Rufillo, 61
  Caprice, 43
  Carrot Salad, 34
  Caviar Canapés, 16
  "Caviar," Eggplant, 34
  Cèleri-rave, 35
  Champignons à la Grècque, 33
  Charlotte, Cheese, 81
  Cheese, 78–82
  Cheese Ball, Cocktail, 14
  Cheese Charlotte, 81
  Cheese-Egg-Tomato Hors d'Oeuvre, 36
  Cheese Fondue, 80
  Cheese Fonduta Lombardy, 82
  Cheese, Fromage à la Crème, 82
  Cheese Garlic Toast, 81
  Cheese and Mushroom Quiche, 41
  Cheese Pastries, 45
  Cheese Pie, Parmesan, 45
  Cheese Pie with Potato Crust, 79
  Cheese Popovers, 16
  Cheese Pudding, 82
  Cheese Soufflé, Egg-White, 78–79
  Cheese Soufflé, Lazette's Famous, 80
  Cheese Soufflé, for Three or Four, 79
  Cheese Straws, 17
  Cheese Toast, 81
  Cheese Wafers, Cheddar, 17

Hors d'Oeuvre and Entrées (*Continued*)
  Cheese and Wine Paste, 16
  Chef Salad, 32
  Chicken Liver Appetizers, 36
  Chicken Liver Cake, 26–27
  Chicken Liver Noodles, 68
  Chicken Liver Pasta Sauce, 73
  Chicken Liver Pâtés, 22–23
  Chicken Livers and Mushrooms with Rice, 87
  Chicken Salad, 30
  Chinese Noodles, 66
  Chinese Salad Platter, 32
  Cocktail Accessories, 14–19
  Cocktail Loaf, 18
  Cocktails, Seafood, 39, 40
  Crab Cocktail, 39
  Crab Mousse, 38
  Crab Quiche, 41–42
  Crêpes, 46–48
  Crevettes au Pierre, 39
  Croûte Landaise, La, 24
  Dad's Best Noodles, 67
  Dip, Aioli, 15
  Dip, for Meatballs, 15–16
  Dip, Salmon or Tuna with Caviar, 14–15
  Egg-White Cheese Soufflé, 78–79
  Eggplant "Caviar," 34
  Eggplant Hors d'Oeuvre, 28
  Eggplant, Stuffed, 29
  Eggs and Egg Dishes, 49–61
    Andalusia, 53
    Artichoke and Egg Hors d'Oeuvre, 36, 56
    Avocado and Egg Hors d'Oeuvre, 36, 56
    Creamed Stuffed, 60
    Fried Stuffed, 57
    Frittata al Verde, 53
    Mousse, Hot Egg, 57
    Mushroom Soufflé, 60
    Oeufs Bourguignons, 51
    Oeufs Cocotte Perigourdine, 49
    Oeufs Janine, 51
    Oeufs Mayonnaise, 51
    Oeufs Mollets, 56
    Oeufs Pôches Bourguignonne, 52–53
    Omelette, Butter, 59
    Omelette Mousseline, 58
    Pea Roulade, 54
    Poached in Potato Soup, 57
    Soufflé, Mushroom, 60
    Soufflé Surprise, 60

Hors d'Oeuvre and Entrées (*Continued*)
Spanish, 56
Spinach Roulade, 54
Stuffed, Creamed, 60
Stuffed, Fried, 57
Surprise, 58
-Tomato-Cheese Hors d'Oeuvre, 36
Elie's Chef Salad, 32
Endive à la Grècque, 33
Eve's Spanish Eggs, 56
Fair Aurora's Pillow, 24–25
Fettuccine all'Alfredo, 62
Fettuccine Bianche e Verdi, 63
Fettuccine with Clam Sauce, 65
Fettuccine with Grated Chicken Livers, 65
Fettuccine Paris Style, 63
Figs, Prosciutto with, 30
Fish, 37–40
Foie Gras Frais Truffée et Poche au Porto, 22
Fondue, Cheese, 80
Fonduta Lombardy, 82
Frank's Macaroni Genovese, 71
Frank's Sciué Sciué, 67
Freddy's Cheese Toast, 81
Friandise du Petit Colombier, 46–47
Frittata al Verde, 53
Fromage à la Crème, 82
Garlic Spread, Anchovy, 15
Garlic Toast, Cheese, 81
Gâteau de Foies de Volaille à la Bressane, 26–27
Gnocchi, 77
Goose Liver Pâté, 22
Ham, Jambon Persillé a la Bourguignonne, 26
Ham Quiche, 41
Herring in Sour Cream with Onions, 40
Italian Pâté of Cooked Meats, 23
Jack's Chicken Liver Noodles, 68
Jambon Persillé à la Bourguignonne, 26
Lasagne with Ricotta, 65
Lasagne Verdi al Forno, 64
Lazette's Famous Cheese Soufflé, 80
Lentil and Rice Casserole, 87
Lobster Cocktail, 39
Lobster Mousse, 38
Lobster Quiche, 41–42
Macaroni Genovese, 71
Macaroni de Luxe, Vaucresson, 75
"Maestosissime Fettuccine all'Alfredo," 62

Hors d'Oeuvre and Entrées (*Continued*)
Meatballs with Dip, 15–16
Melon with Prosciutto, 30
Mousse, Hot Egg, 57
Mousse, Seafood, 38
Mushroom and Cheese Quiche, 41
Mushroom Sandwiches, 17
Mushroom Soufflé, 60
Mushrooms à la Grècque, 33
Mushrooms, Stuffed, 34
My Polenta, 77
Noodles. *See also* Fettuccine; Lasagne; etc.
Casserole for Twelve, 76
Chinese, 66
with Clam Sauce, 65
Dad's Best, 67
Danieli, 66
Frank's Sciué Sciué, 67
with Grated Chicken Livers, 65
Green Sauce for, 71
with Ham and Sour Cream, 67
Jack's Chicken Liver, 68
Pesto alla Genovese, 72
Pesto Sauce for, 72, 73
Ring of, 75
Sicilian Sauce for, 72
Soufflé of, 74
Oeufs Bourguignons, 51
Oeufs Cocotte Perigourdine, 49
Oeufs Janine, 51
Oeufs Mayonnaise, 50
Oeufs Mollets, 56
Oeufs Pôches Bourguignonne, 52–53
Okra à la Turc, 35
Omelette, Butter, 59
Omelette Mousseline, 58
Onion Tart, 43
Oreiller de La Belle Aurore, 24–25
Oriental Pilau, 85
Pailettes Parmesan, 17
Pancakes. *See also* Crêpes
Buckwheat, with Caviar, 48
Panzerotti alla Romana, 47
Parmesan Pie, 45
Pastas, 61–78
Pâtés and Terrines, 19–28
Pea Roulade, 54
Peppers, Stuffed, 29, 35
Persimmons, Prosciutto with, 30
Pies, Cheese, 45, 79
Pilau, Oriental, 85
Pimento Canapés, 15

Hors d'Oeuvre and Entrées (*Continued*)
Pissaladière Provençal, 42
Pizza Napoli, 44
Polentas, 77–78
Popovers, Cheese, 16
Pork Liver Pâté, 21
Prosciutto with Melon, Figs, or Persimmons, 30
Pudding, Cheese, 82
Quiche Lorraine, 40–41
Quiches, 40–42
Rice, 83–88
    Baked Wild, 86
    Balls, Fried, 84
    Boiled Brown, 85–86
    with Chicken Livers and Mushrooms, 87
    and Lentil Casserole, 87
    Oriental Pilau, 85
    Ring, 86
    Risottos, 83, 84
    Salad, Salmon, 37
    with Sausages, 84–85
    Soufflé, 88
    Wild, 86
Risotto with Patna Rice, 83
Risotto alla Principe da Napoli, 83
Risotto, Shrimp, 84
Rose's Italian Pâté of Cooked Meats, 23
Russian Salad, 30
Salade Niçoise, 31
Salads, 28ff.
Salmon,
    Dip, Red Caviar, 14–15
    Mousse, 38
    Quiche, 42
    Rice Salad, 37
    Smoked, 38
Sandwiches, 15ff., 17–19
    Baked, 19
    Canapés, 15, 16
    Cocktail or Supper Loaf, 18
    Mushroom, 17
    Striped, 18
Sardine Hors d'Oeuvre, 37
Scampi Canepa, 39
Scampi Cocktail, 40
Sciué Sciué, Frank's, 67
Shrimp, Butterfly, 37
Shrimp Cocktail, 39
Shrimp au Pierre, Broiled, 39
Shrimp Risotto, 84
Shrimp, Scampi Canepa, 39

Hors d'Oeuvre and Entrées (*Continued*)
Shrimp, Scampi Cocktail, 40
Soufflés,
    Cheese Egg-White, 78–79
    Cheese, Lazette's Famous, 80
    Cheese, for Three or Four, 79
    Mushroom, 60
    Noodle, 74
    Rice, 88
    Surprise, 50
Spaghetti Napolitana, 69
Spaghetti alla Tonnara, 68
Spanish Eggs, Eve's, 66
Spinach Pasta, 70
Spinach Roulade, 54
Striped Sandwich, 18
Supper Loaf, 18
Swedish Salad, 31
Tarama, 15
Tart, Onion, 43
Terrine de Lapin Lorraine, 19–20
Toast, Cheese, 81
Tomato-Cheese-Egg Hors d'Oeuvre, 36
Tortellini alla Bolognese, 70
Tortellini alla Panna, 71
Tortelloni, 69
Tuna Fish Dip, Red Caviar, 14–15
Vegetables, 28–36
Vegetables with Aioli Dip, Raw, 15
Wafers, Cheddar Cheese, 17
Wild Rice, Baked, 86
Wine and Cheese Paste, 16
Zucchini, Stuffed, 29
Horseradish Sauce,
    with Apple, 348
    Hot, 348
    with Sour Cream, 348
Hosteria Romano (restaurant),
    Stufatino de Manzo con Peperoni alla Romana, 161
Hot Milk Cake, 431
Hôtel du Chapeau Rouge (restaurant),
    Aubergines pour Hors d'Oeuvre Froid, 28
    Filet de Veau à la Moutarde, 172–73
    Poires au Cassis, 413
Hôtel de la Côte d'Or (restaurant),
    Oeufs Cocotte Perigourdine, 49
    Omelette Mousseline, 58
Hotel Danieli. *See also* Royal Danieli Roof
    Scaloppine San Giorgio, 184
    Shrimp Flamingo, 147
Hotel Della Rocca (restaurant),
    Noodles with Grated Chicken Livers, 65

Hotel Della Rocca (*Continued*)
  Semifreddo allo Zabaione, 399
  Vitello Castellana, 182–83
Hotel Majestic (restaurant),
  Tortellini alla Bolognese, 70
Hôtel de la Poste (restaurant),
  Jambon Persillé a la Bourguignonne, 26
  Oeufs Bourguignons, 51
Hubbard Squash Pie, 427
Hubbard Squash Pudding, 320
Hungarian Goulash, 170
Hungarian Mushroom Soup, 105

I

Ice, Raspberry, 448
Ice Cream, 445–50
  Banana-Peach Sour Cream, 449
  Brown Sugar, 446
  Caramel, 447
  Cassis, 448
  Chestnut, 390
  Chocolate, 446
  Coffee and Rum, 448
  Crème de Menthe, 448
  French, 445
  Fruit Juice, 447
  Ginger Sauce for, 450
  Grape, 447
  Lemon, 447
  Lemonade, 447
  Limeade, 447
  Mangos with, 450
  Orange, 447
  Peppermint, 446
  Pineapple, 447
  Raspberry, 446
  Raspberry Dressing for, 450
  Rum and Coffee, 448
  Sour Cream, 449
  Spumoni, 449
  Strawberry Dressing for, 450
  Vanilla, 446
    French, 445
    Ginger Sauce for, 450
    Mangos with, 450
    Raspberry or Strawberry Dressing for,
      450
Icings. *See under* Cakes
Indian Chicken Curry, 242

Indian Shrimp Curry, 148
Italian Apricot Torta, 421
  Bread, 358
  Cheese Balls for Consommé, 100
  Clam and Mussel Soup, 112
  Fruit Cream, 398
  Marzipan Torta, 421
  Meatballs, 163
  Meringue, 439
  Nut and Citron Cake, 434
  Orange Rice Pudding, 396
  Pâté of Cooked Meats, 23
  Ricotta Pie, 425
  Roast Veal, 177
  Stuffed Tomatoes, 325

J

Jack's Chicken Liver Noodles, 68
Jam-Rum Sauce for Apple Charlotte, 382
Jambon à la Crème, 228–29
Jambon Persillé a la Bourguignonne, 26
Jarrets de Veau à l'Orange, 176
Jellied Chicken, 246–47
Jelly. *See also* Aspic
  Cranberry, 344
  Duck, 27
  Lemon, Filling and Frosting, 438
  Orange, 414
  Sauce, 348
  Wine, 414
  Wine, Port, 356
Jerusalem Artichokes, Creamed, 297
Juice, Fruit, Ice Cream of, 447

K

Kebab, Shish, 211
Kebabs, Turkish, 203
Kidney Beans,
  Baked, 280
  Baked, Big-Party Beans, 279
  Baked with Burgundy, 281
  and Beef, Casserole of, 162–63
  and Ham Casserole, 225
  Soups, 90–91

Kidneys (and Kidney Dishes),
  Beefsteak and Kidney Pie, 160
  in Boeuf Bourguignonne, 158
  Broiled Veal, 194
  Broiled Lamb, 194
  and Chicken Livers, Lamb, 208
  in Chipolata, 157
  Désir des Gourmets, 265
  Flambée, 194
  Lamb Chops with, 210
  Rognon de Veau Grillé en Paupiette avec
      Sauce Bérnaise, 195
  Rognons de Boeuf, Vigneronne, 163
  Rognons Fricadelles, 209
  Rognons de Veau, Bercy, 195
  Stew, Lamb, 208
  Stew with Red Wine, 166
Kingfish, for Frying or Broiling, 120
Kirsch Butter Cream, 439
Kirsch with Crêpes, 404
Kirsch Icing, 438
Kirsch with Orange Sherbet, 449
Kirsch Soufflé, 379
Kitchen Equipment, 460–62
Knackwurst, Sauerkraut with, 285
  with Ham, 225
Kolozsvari Kaposzta, 215

L

Lamb, 196–212
  Agnello dell'Academico, 198–99
  Baby Spring, 196
  with Beans, French Style, 200–1
  Blanquette d'Agneau, 199
  Breast of, Casserole of, 207
  with Buttermilk Marinade, Roast, 206
  Casserole of Breast of, 207
  in Cassoulet, 266
  Chops, Baked Boned, 201
  Chops with Kidneys, Broiled, 210
  Chops and Lentils, Shoulder, 212
  Cooking Note on, 196
  Côtes de Mouton Champvallon, 201
  Crown Roast of, 200
  with Cumin Sauce, Cooked, 204
  Curried, Western Style, 204
  Curry, Indian Style, 211
  Curry Sauce for Cooked, 205
  with Dry Vermouth, Roast, 198

Lamb (Continued)
  with Eggplant, Braised, 207
  Eggplant Stuffed with (Moussaka), 294
  with Juniper, Loin of, 205
  Kebab, Shish, 211
  Kebabs, Turkish, 203
  Kidney Stew, 208
  Kidneys, Broiled, 194
  Kidneys and Chicken Livers, 208
  Kidneys, Désir des Gourmets, 265
  Kidneys, Rognons Fricadelles, 209
  Leg of, Br···, 206
  Loin of, with Juniper, 205
  Mint Sauce for, 349
  Noisette d'Agneau de Behague, Edward
      VII, 209
  Patties, Minced, 202
  Pie, 210
  Rack of, Roast, 197
  Rognons Fricadelles, 209
  Scotch Broth, 100, 101
  Shanks, Braised, 202
  with Sherry, Roast, 197
  Shish Kebab, 211
  Shoulder of, Stuffed, 181
  Stew of Cooked Meat with Dumplings,
      165
  Stew, for Couscous Libanais, 268
  Stew, with Dill or Mint Dumplings, 203
  Stew, with Leeks, 211
  Stew, Rice Dumplings for, 367
  Turkish Kebabs, 203
Lapérouse (restaurant),
  Désir des Gourmets, 265
Lasagne with Ricotta, 65
Lasagne Verdi al Forno, 64
Lazette's Famous Cheese Soufflé, 80
Leeks,
  Braised in Broth, 297
  with Cheese, Creamed, 297
  Lamb and Veal Stew with, 211
  Potatoes Stuffed with, 311
  Soup with Potatoes, 94
Lemon Butter Sauce, 349
  Ice Cream, 447
  Icing (or Liqueur Icing), 438
  Jelly Filling and Frosting, 438
  Sauce, 383
  Sauce, Butter, 349
  Sauce, Carrots with, 286
  Soufflé, 377
  Tart (au Citron), 420
Lemonade Ice Cream, 447

Lentils (and Lentil Dishes),
  Curried, 298–99
  Lamb Chops and, 212
  Pork Chops with, 221
  Purée, 298
  and Rice Casserole, 87
  Soup, 95
Lettuce,
  Bibb, 331
  Romaine or Chicory with Croutons, 332
  Wilted, 298
Licia Grego (restaurant),
  Spaghetti Napolitana, 69
  Spaghetti alla Tonnara, 68
Lièvre en Saupiquet, 270–71
Lima Beans, 280
  Ham with, Baked, 230
  and Peas with Cheese Sauce, 307
  Peas and Onions, Casserole of, 279
  Soup of, 90–91
  Succotash, 322
Lime Pie, 426
Limeade Ice Cream, 447
Limpa Bread, Swedish, 359
Linda Bocconi (restaurant),
  Artichokes alla Crema, 276
Liqueur Icing, 438
Liqueur Sauces, 375, 403
Liqueur Soufflés, 372, 374. See also specific
      liqueurs
Liquor Supplies, 463
Liver. See also Chicken: Livers; Pâtés and
      Terrines
  Baked Whole Calf's, 189
  Fegatello con Rete, 218–19
  French Style, 188–89
  in Fritto Misto, 272
  for Meatballs, Cocktail, 15–16
  Meatballs, Veal and, 180
  in Meat Loaf, 164
  in Meat Loaf, with Veal, 190
  in Meat Loaf, with Vegetables, 215
  and Onions, 190
  and Veal Loaf, 190
Lobster,
  Américaine, 139
  Baked, 140–41
  Butter, 18, 121
  Bisque, 111
  Chaussons aux Queues de Homard, 141
  Cocktail, 39
  Creamed, 122, 140
  Creamed Stuffed Eggs, 60

Lobster (Continued)
  in Gratin aux Fruits de Mer, 142
  Mayonnaise Cream Sauce for, 350
  Mousse, 38
  for Noodle Casserole, 76
  for Paella, 269
  Puffs (Chaussons aux Queues de Ho-
      mard), 141
  Quiche, 41–42
  Salad, 335
  Sauces, 124, 141, 352
    Cardinal, 121–22
  in Seafood Pie, 135
  Stew, 114
London restaurants,
  Beurre Fondu, Le, 39, 256, 411, 412
  Connaught Hotel, The, 120
  Hanstown Club, 140–41
  Hosteria Romano, 161
Lorraine Cherry Tart, 419
Lotus d'Or (restaurant),
  Chinese Salad Platter, 32
Louise Junior (restaurant),
  Breast of Chicken, Florida, 239
  Grouse Smitane, 259–60
Lyon, La Mère Guy at, 22, 24–25

M

Macaroni Genovese, 71
Macaroni de Luxe, Vaucresson, 75
Macaroon Pie, 424
Macaroons, Chocolate, 443
Macédoine, Aldo's Fruit, 409
Macedonia al Maraschino, 413
Mackerel for Baking, 119
Madeira,
  Cream Sauce for Pojarsky, 183
  Sauce with Sweetbreads, 190–91
  Turtle Consommé with, 117
"Maestosissime Fettuccine all'Alfredo," 62
Maison Kammerzell (restaurant),
  Baeckenofe, Le, 270
  Choucroute, 223
  Coq au Riesling, 233
  Veal Chop Surprise, Alsacienne, 188
Mangos with Vanilla Ice Cream, 450
Maraschino, Macedonia al, 413
Marasquin Soufflé, 376

Marinades,
  for Baeckenofe, 270
  for Lamb Roast, Buttermilk, 198
  for Lamb Shish Kebab, 211
  for Sauerbraten, 156
  for Scallops and Mushrooms, 144–45
  for Sea Bass, Chinese, 131
  for Spareribs, 220
  for Steaks, 153
  for Veal with Rosemary, 174
  for Venison, 168
Maritozzi, 361
Marmalade Sauce, 386
Marsala Sauce for Dolce Vasco, 402
Marzipan Torta, Italian, 421
Maurice Cazalis (restaurant),
  Cervelle de Veau aux Pistaches, 193
  Filet au Poivre à Ma Façon, 152
  Pommes Soufflés, 313
  Rognon de Veau Grillé en Paupiette avec
    Sauce Béarnaise, 195
  Soufflé au Cocktail de Liqueurs, 372
  Steak au Poivre Flambé a la Normande,
    152
  Truites Farcies Basquaise, 127
Maxim's (restaurant),
  Dinner Menu, 458
  Noisette d'Agneau de Behague, Edward
    VII, 209
  Potage Germiny, 97
  Sole Albert, 130
  Soufflé Glacé au Kirsch, 379
Maya's Roast Suckling Pig, 224
Mayonnaise, 349–50
  Cream Sauce for Lobster or Crab, 350
  Garlic. See Aioli Sauce
  Green, 349
  Mustard, 350
  Sour-Cream, 349
Measures and Weights, 464–65
Meat, 149–230. See also Pâtés and Ter-
    rines; Special Dishes; specific meats
  Butters, 18
  Filling for Noodle Casserole, 76
  Goulash Sauce for Leftover, 346
  Hash of Cooked, 169
  Loaf, 164. See also specific kinds
  Polpettine, 163
  Sauces for Pastas, 74, 355
  Soups,
    Bouillon, Clear, 98–99
    Broth of Roast Beef Bones, 90
    Broth, Scotch, 100, 101

Meat (Continued)
  Chicken, 103
  Egg, 102
  Gravy, 100
  Scotch Broth, 101
  Scotch Broth with Neck of Lamb or
    Mutton, 100
  Turkey Wing, 103
  Wines for, 149–50
Meatballs,
  Cocktail, 15–16
  for Fritto Misto, 272
  Italian, 163
  Veal, and Liver, 180
  Veal, Tiny, 267
Medium White (Béchamel) Sauce, 342
Mélange of Fruits, 408
Melon. See also Cantaloupe; Fruit Desserts
  with Port, 409
  Prosciutto with, 30
  as a Vegetable, Baked, 299
  with Wine, 409
Menus, 452–58
  Dinners, 453–58
  Luncheons, 459
Mèrje Guy, La (restaurant),
  Foie Gras Frais Truffée et Poche au
    Porto, 22
  Oreiller de la Belle Aurore, L', 24–25
Meringue, 396
  for Cream Pie, 422
  Italian, 439
  Layers for Rolla Cake, 443
  Shell for Pie, 423
Mexican Corn, 292
Micheline's Rice Salad, 335
Milk, Measuring, 465
Milk-Chocolate Mousse with Cherries, 392
Minestrone, 104
Mint Dumplings, 203
Mint Sauce for Lamb, 349
Mocha Cream, Chocolate, 436
Mocha Soufflé, 373
Mont Blanc (restaurant),
  Toast for Fish Soup, 110
Mornay Sauce, 144, 173, 351
Moules Farcies de Tante Annette, Les, 145
Moules Marinière, 146
Moules Normande, 145
Moussaka, 294
Mousseline Sauce, 350–51
Mousselines de Saumon, Adam, 120

Mousses,
  Chocolate, 392
  Chocolate, with Cherries, 392
  Crab, 38
  Crème de Menthe, 391
  Dessert, 391, 392
  Ham, Cold, 227
  Hot Egg, 57
  Lobster, 38
  Salmon, 38
Muffins, English, 365
Munks, Cornmeal, 367
Mushrooms (and Mushroom Dishes), 299–302
  Cheese Quiche, 41
  Chinese Dried, to Prepare, 299
  Cream of, 41
  Creamed, 300–1
  à la Grècque, 33
  Grilled, Italian Style, 300
  Measuring, 465
  Potatoes Stuffed with, 311
  Provençal, 302
  Purée, 301
  Russian Style, 301
  Sandwiches, 17
  Sauces, 24, 277
    with Broth, 353
    for Chicken Demi-Deuil, 233
    for Chicken Pie, 238
    Cream, 353
  and Scallops, Broiled, 144–45
  Soufflé, 60
  Soup, 95
  Soup, Hungarian, 105
  Stuffed, 34, 302
Mussels (and Mussel Dishes),
  Creamed, 146
  Moules Farcies de Tante Annette, Les, 145
  Moules Marinière, 146
  Moules Normande, 145
  Soup, 144
  Soup with Clams, 112
Mustard Sauce, 173, 351
  Apricot, 340
  Mayonnaise, 350
  Wine, 351
Mutton,
  for Baeckenofe, Le, 270
  Boiled Leg of, 206
  Broiled Chops with Kidneys, 210
  in Cassoulet, 266

Mutton (*Continued*)
  Côtes de Mouton Champvallon, 201
  Scotch Broth, 100
My Polenta, 77
Myron's Clam Chowder, 112

N

Nancy, Capucin Gourmand at, 19–20, 52–53, 110, 137, 151, 163, 176, 183, 201, 270–71, 403
Navy Beans, Baked, 280
Nerina (restaurant),
  Buongustaia Nerina, 250
  Tortellini alla Panna, 71
New England Boiled Dinner, 222
New York restaurants,
  Chateaubriand, 132
  Henri's, 139
  Louise Junior, 239, 259–60
  Tom's Shangri-La, 272, 273, 274
Nicolas Flamel (restaurant),
  Pâté de Champagne, 20–21
Noisette d'Agneau de Behague, Edward VII, 209
Noodles,
  Casserole for Twelve, 76
  Chinese, 66
  Chinese Rice-Stick, 272
  with Clam Sauce, 65
  Coquillettes aux Noix, 403
  Creamed Mushrooms for Ring, 300–1
  Dad's Best, 67
  Danieli, 66
  Fettuccine all'Alfredo, 62
  Fettuccine, Bianche e Verdi, 63
  Fettuccine, Paris Style, 63
  Frank's Sciué Sciué, 67
  with Grated Chicken Livers, 65
  Green Sauce for, 72
  with Ham and Sour Cream, 67
  Jack's Chicken Liver, 68
  Lasagne with Ricotta, 65
  Lasagne Verdi al Forno, 64
  Pesto alla Genovese, 72
  Pesto Sauces for, 72, 73
  with Potatoes (Nouilles aux Pommes Gratinées), 176
  Pudding, with Peas, 308
  Ring, 75

Noodles (*Continued*)
  Ring, Creamed Mushrooms for, 300–1
  Sicilian Sauce for, 72
  Soufflé, 74
  Veal and Liver Meatballs and Sauce on, 180
Northern Bean Soup, 90–91
Northern Beans, Baked, 280
Nouilles aux Pommes Gratinées, 176
Nuts (and Nut Dishes). *See also* Almonds; etc.
  Citron Cake, Italian, 434
  Cookies, Cinnamon, 445
  Measuring, 465
  Praliné Powder, 356
  Pudding, Steamed, 381

O

Oat Pones, 367
Oeufs Bourguignons, 51
  Cocotte Perigourdine, 49
  Janine, 51
  Mayonnaise, 50
  Mollets, 56
  Pôches Bourguignonne, 52–53
Oil, Measuring, 465
Okra, 302–3
  Fried Creamed, 302
  and Onions, Casserole of Creamed, 302
  à la Turc, 35
  Uses for, 303
Old-Fashioned Coconut Pie, 423
Old-Fashioned Coconut Tarts, 442
Old-Fashioned Custard Pie, 424
Old Whaler Rum Cookies, 444
Omelettes (Note: Asterisks indicate sweet omelettes),
  Butter, 59
  au Citron, 58–59 *
  Creole Sauce for, 345
  Mousseline, 58 *
Onions, 303–6
  with Cream, Baked Bermuda, 304–5
  Creamed, 303
  Creamed, Emily's, 304
  Curried, 305
  "Fried," 305
  Glazed, 304
  Glazed, with Potatoes, 315

Onions (*Continued*)
  Lima Beans and Peas, Casserole of, 279
  Liver and, 190
  and Peppers, 305
  Pork Chops with Apples and, 217
  and Potatoes, Baked Glazed, 315
  Puréed, for Soubise Mustard Sauce, 173
  Sauce (Soubise), 352
  Sauce (Soubise Mustard), 173
Orange Bread Pudding, 380
  Cake, 430
  Cake, Egg-Yolk, 431
  Cake, Lemon Cream, 432
  Carrot Soufflé, 286–87
  and Carrot Soup, 93
  Egg-Yolk Cake, 431
  Ice Cream, 447
  Icing (or Liqueur Icing), 438
  Jelly, 414
  Lemon Cream Cake, 432
  Passetto, 412
  Raisin Sauce, 229
  Rice Pudding, 396
  Sauce, 396
  Sauce, Beets with, 281
  Sauce, for Carrots, 286, 353
  Sauce, Raisin-, 229
  Sherbet with Fruit and Kirsch, 449
  Soufflé, 278
  Soufflé, Carrot-, 286–87
  Sweet Potatoes, Blazed, 323
Oreiller de La Belle Aurore, L', 24–25
Oriental Pilau, 85
Osso Buco, 175
Oxtails, Braised, 167
Oyster Plant, Creamed, 297
Oysters (and Oyster Dishes),
  in Fritto Misto, 272
  Gumbo, 113
  Poulette, 143
  with Sauce Mornay, 144
  in Seafood Pie, 135
  Stew of, 115
  Stuffing, for Small Game Birds, 261

P

Paella, 269
Paillettes Parmesan, 17
Pain Perdu, 366

Pancakes. *See also* Crêpes
Buckwheat, with Caviar, 48
Corn, 368
Cottage-Cheese, 369
Potato, 317
Rice, Brown, 368
Richelieu, Turkey, 248
Sour-Cream, 369
Pane Misto, 358
Pantry Supplies, 462–63
Panzerotti alla Romana, 47
Pappagallo (restaurant),
Fillets of Turkey, 250
Lasagne Verdi al Forno, 64
Turkey Pancakes Richelieu, 248
Veal Cutlets Pappagallo, 177
Paris restaurants,
Café Procope, Le, 184, 254–55
Caverne Ali-Baba, 268
Chez Pauline, 40–41, 236
Diamantaires, 15
Drouant, Le, 108–9, 234–35
Escargot Montorgueil, L', 134, 195
Lapérouse, 265
Lotus d'Or, 32
Maxim's, 97, 130, 209, 379, 458
Mont Blanc, 110
Nicolas Flamel, 20–21
Petit Colombier, Le, 46–47, 145
Petit Navire, Le, 109
Restaurant Voltaire, 132–33
Parmesan Pie, 45
Parsley Dumplings, 317
Parsley Potatoes, 313
with Sour Cream, 316
Parsnips, Glazed, 306
Passetto's (restaurant),
Antipasto, 29
Veal Scaloppine Passetto, 182
Pastas, 61–78. *See also* Noodles
Cannelloni alla Nizzarda, 62
Cannelloni alla San Rufillo, 61
Chicken Liver Noodles, 68
Chicken Liver Pasta Sauce, 73
Chinese Noodles, 66
with Clam Sauce, 65
Dad's Best Noodles, 67
Fettuccine all'Alfredo, 62
Fettuccine Bianche e Verdi, 63
Fettuccine with Clam Sauce, 65
Fettuccine with Grated Chicken Livers, 65
Fettuccine Paris Style, 63

Pastas (*Continued*)
Frank's Macaroni Genovese, 71
Franks Sciué Sciué, 67
Gnocchi, 77
Green Sauce for, 71
Lasagne with Ricotta, 65
Lasagne Verdi al Forno, 64
Macaroni Genovese, 71
Macaroni de Luxe, Vaucresson, 75
"Meastosissime Fettuccine all'Alfredo," 62
Meat Sauces, 74, 355
My Polenta, 77
Pesto Sauces, 72, 73
Plain, 70
Polentas, 77–78
Sauces, 69
Chicken Liver, 73
Clam, 65
Green, 71
Meat, 74, 355
Pesto, 72, 73
Sicilian, 72
Tomato, 352, 354–55
Tuna Fish, 68, 177
Sciué Sciué, 67
Sicilian Sauce, 72
Soufflé, Noodle, 74
Spaghetti Napolitana, 69
Spaghetti alla Tonnara, 68
Spinach Pasta, 70
Tortellini alla Bolognese, 70
Tortellini alla Panna, 71
Tortelloni, 69
Pastry, 415–27. *See also* Crusts; Doughs; Pies; Quiches; Tarts; etc.
Cheese, 45
Cheese, Gougère, 366
Cream Cheese Crust, 416
Puff Paste, 416
Pâté Brisée, 40–41
Pâté à Choux, 124–25
Roll Dough, 44–45
Sugar Crust, 417
Pâté Brisée, 40–41
Pâté à Choux, 124–25
Pâtés and Terrines, 19–28
Ballotine de Canard Truffée et Pistachée, La, 27–28
de Campagne, 20–21
Chicken-Liver Cake, 26–27
Chicken-Liver Pâtés, 22–23
Croûte Landaise, La, 24

Pâtés and Terrines (*Continued*)
  Fair Aurora's Pillow, 24–25
  Foie Gras (La Croûte Landaise), 24
  Foie Gras Frais Truffée et Poche au
    Porto, 22
  Gâteau de Fois de Volaille à la Bres-
    sane, 26–27
  Goose Liver (Foie Gras), 22, 24
  Ham Persillé à la Bourguignonne, 26
  Italian Pâté of Cooked Meats, 23
  Jambon Persillé a la Bourguignonne, 26
  Oreiller de La Belle Aurore, L', 24–25
  Pork Liver, 21
  Rose's Italian, 23
  Terrine de Lapin Lorraine, La, 19–20
Paul's Old Whaler Rum Cookies, 444
Poupiettes de Poulet aux Morilles à la
    Crème, 234–35
Peaches (and Peach Dishes). *See also* Fruit
    Desserts
  Banana Sour-Cream Ice Cream, 449
  and Cherries, Compote of, 408
  Cobbler, 384
  with Meat. *See* specific meats
  Pudding. *See* Raspberry Pudding
  with Raspberry Sauce, 410
  with Strawberry Sauce, 410
  Tart, 418
Pears. *See also* Fruit Desserts
  au Cassis, 413
  with Coconut Cream Sauce, 392
  Peeled Baked, 411
Peas (and Pea Dishes), 307–9
  Buttered, 306
  with Carrots, Shredded, 288
  with Lima Beans and Cheese Sauce, 307
  Mashed Split, 308
  and Noodles Pudding, 308
  Onions and Lima Beans, Casserole of,
    279
  Pork Chops with Split, 221
  Purée of, 307
  Roulade of, 54
  Salad, Cold, 307
  Salad, Summer Vegetable, 333
  Soufflé, 309
  Soup, 96
  Soup, Fresh, 96
  Soup, Split-Pea, 96
  Soup, Turtle, 105
  Succotash, 322
  with Turkey Pancakes Richelieu, 248
Pecan Butter Frosting, 437

Pecan Cake with Caramel Frosting, 435
Pecan Pie, 426
Pecans, Measuring, 465
Peppermint Ice Cream, 446
Peppers, 309–10. *See also* Pimentos
  and Onions, 305
  Pipérade, 309
  Roasted, 309
  Stuffed, 29, 35, 310
Perch,
  for Baking, 119
  for Frying or Broiling, 120
  Soupe au Poisson à la Rouille, 110
Perigourdine Sauce, 25
Persimmons, Prosciutto with, 30
Pesto alla Genovese, 72
Pesto Sauces, 72, 73
Petit Colombier, Le (restaurant),
  Friandise du Petit Colombier, La, 46–47
  Moules Farcies de Tante Annette, Les,
    145
Petit Navire, Le (restaurant),
  Bourride, La, 109
Petti de Pollo alla Sabatini, 249
Pheasant,
  with Agrodolce Sauce, 257
  Casserole with Mushrooms, 258
  Fagiano al Vino Rosso, 255
  Piccata alla Pizzaiola, 185
Piccolo Mondo (restaurant),
  Fagiano al Vino Rosso, 255
  Fettuccine, Bianche e Verdi, 63
  Quaglia alla Diavola, 256
Piekerel,
  Burgundy Fish Stew, 107
  for Frying or Broiling, 120
Pies. *See also* Quiches
  Almond, 426
  Beefsteak and Kidney, 160
  Cheese, Parmesan, 45
  Cheese, Potato Crust, 79
  Cheese, Ricotta, 425
  Chicken, 244–45
  Chicken, Coq Hardi, 238
  Chocolate Cream, 423
  Chocolate Rum, 423
  Clam, 142
  Coconut, 423
  Coconut Cream, 424
  Cream, 422
  Cream, Chocolate, 423
  Cream, Coconut, 424
  Cream, Raspberry, 424

Pies (Continued)
  Custard, French, 425
  Custard, Old-Fashioned, 424
  Dessert, 422–27
  French Custard, 425
  Italian Ricotta, 425
  Lamb, 210
  Lime, 426
  Macaroon, 424
  Meringue for Cream, 422
  Meringue Shell for, 423
  Old-Fashioned Coconut, 423
  Old-Fashioned Custard, 424
  Onion, Green, 303
  Pastry for, 415–17. See also specific pies,
    types of pastry
  Pecan, 426
  Raspberry Cream, 424
  Ricotta, Italian, 425
  Rum Chocolate, 423
  Rum Squash, 427
  Seafood, 135
  Seafood, Clam, 142
  Squash Rum, 427
  Turkey, 244–45
  Veal, 210
Pike,
  for Baking, 119
  Burgundy Fish Stew, 107
  Filets de Brochets à la Crème, 134–35
  for Frying or Broiling, 120
  Quenelles de Brochet Lyonnaise, 124–25
Pilau, 147
  Oriental, 85
  Tomato, 327
Pimento Canapés, 15
Pimento Cornbread, 365
Pimento Forms, Sweet Potatoes in, 323
Pimentos, Sweet-Potato Stuffed, 324–25
Pineapple. See also Fruit Desserts
  Ice cream, 447
Pipérade, 309
Pissaladière Provençal, 42
Pistou Sauce, 106
Pizza Napoli, 44
Plums. See also Fruit Desserts
  Pudding, Fresh Blue, 385
Poires au Cassis, 413
Pojarsky aux Pommes Amandines, 183
Polentas, 77–78
Polpettine, 163
Pommes Amandines, 183

Pommes Soufflés, 313
Pommes de Terre à la Parisienne (Rissolée
    Potatoes), 195, 314
Pompano,
  for Baking, 119
  Fillets, Baked Stuffed, 126
  Fillets in Wine or Cream, 128
Pones, Oat, 367
Popovers, Cheese, 16
Poppy Seed Cake, Susanne's, 433
Pork, 213–30. See also Ham
  for Baeckenofe, Le, 270
  Barbecued Spareribs, 220
  in Cassoulet, 266
  Chinese Glazed Spareribs, 221
  Chinese Sweet-and-Sour Spareribs, 220–
    21
  Chops, 188
  Chops, with Apples and onions, 217
  Chops, Baked, 218
  Chops, and Cabbage, Baked, 217
  Chops, with Caramel, Shoulder, 217
  Chops, with Dried Split Peas or Lentils,
    Baked, 221
  Chops, Italian Style, 216
  Chops, with Rice, Baked, 218
  Choucroute, 223
  Curried, Western Style, 204
  Cutlets with Port and Cream, 216
  Fegatello con Rete, 218–19
  Goulash, with Sauerkraut and Sour
    Cream, 215
  and Ham Loaf, 227
  Kolozsvari Kaposzta, 215
  Liver, Fegatello con Rete, 218–19
  Liver Loaf with Vegetables, 215
  Loin of, Roast, 213
  Loin of, Roast, with Nut Butter, 213
  Maya's Roast Suckling Pig, 224
  Pâtés. See Pâtés and Terrines
  with Sauerkraut, 223
  Sausage, 219
  Sharp Sauce for, 271
  Shoulder, Roast Boned, 214–15
  Spareribs, Baked, 218
  Spareribs, Barbecued, 220
  Spareribs, Chinese Glazed, 221
  Spareribs, Chinese Sweet-and-Sour, 220–
    21
  Suckling Pig, Roast, 224
  Sweet-and-Sour Spareribs, 220–21
  with Vegetables, Roast, 215

Port Wine,
Jelly, 356
Melon with, 409
Prunes in, 412
Potage Germiny, 97
Potage Marron Suprême, Grebanier, 93–94
Potatoes (and Potato Dishes), 311–18
Anchovy, Swedish, 316
with Bacon, Baked, 311
Brandade avec Pommes de Terre, Provençal, 132
Cakes, 317
Cakes, Shredded Fried-, 314
Celeriac Mashed with, 289
with Cheese, Baked, 312
with Cheese, Double Boiler, 313
with Cheese, Gruyère Creamed, 315
Creamed, 315
Creamed, Dill, 315
Creamed, Gruyère, 315
Creamed, with Ham, 315
Crêpes Parmentier of, 47–48
Croquettes, 312
Crusts, 79, 318
Dauphinois, 312
Dill Creamed, 315
Double-Boiler Cheese, 313
Dumplings with Fresh Dill or Parsley, 317
Glazed, Baked with Onions, 315
with Ham, Creamed, 315
and Ham Hash, 228
Lyonnaise, Boiled, 315
Measuring, 465
with Noodles (Nouilles aux Pommes Gratinées), 176
and Onions, Baked Glazed, 315
Pancakes, 317
Parsley, 313
with Parsley and Sour Cream, New, 316
Pommes Amandines, 183
Pommes Gratinées, Nouilles aux, 176
Pommes Soufflés, 313
Rissolée, 195, 314
Salad, 337
Salad, Hot Egg, 337
Salad, Provençale, 337
Scones, 368
Soup, Eggs Poached in, 57
Soup, with Leeks, 94
Soup, Sweet-Potato Bisque, 107
Soup, Vichyssoise, 97

Potatoes (Continued)
with Sour Cream, Mashed, 314
with Sour Cream and Parsley, 316
Stuffed Baked, 311, 312
Stuffing of, 262
Swedish Anchovy, 316
Sweet. See Sweet Potatoes
Tart, 318
and Turnips, Puréed, 328
Pots de Crème au Chocolat, 390
Poularde au Champagne, 240
Poulet à l'Angevine, 231
Poulet Sauté au Duc de Bourgogne, 236
Poultry and Game, 230–63. See also Chicken; etc.
Butter, 18
Stew of Cooked Meat with Dumplings, 165
Stuffings, 261–63
Praliné Powder, 356, 401
Prosciutto,
Endive with, 296
with Melon, Figs, or Persimmons, 30
Prunes,
Breakfast, 411
Charlotte, 393
as Garnish, 214–15
Monique, 412
in Port, 412
Puddings,
Almond Steamed, 381
Apple Soufflé, 383
Apricot Bread, 380
Berry Bread, 380
Blackberry, Steamed, 385
Bread, Fruit, 380
Caramel Rice, 395
Cheese, 82
Cherry, 384
Cherry Bread, 380
Cherry Steamed, 385
Chestnut, 389
Coconut Cream, 393
Coconut Rice, 396
Coconut Sweet Potato, 324
Corn, 291
Cottage, with Marmalade Sauce, 386
Cream of Wheat, 397
Date, Steamed, 387
Dessert, 379–403. See also Desserts: Puddings, Molds, and Custards
Fig, Steamed, 387

Puddings (*Continued*)
　Fruit Bread, 380
　Italian Orange Rice, 396
　Noodles-and-Peas, 308
　Nut, Steamed, 381
　Orange Bread, 380
　Orange Rice, 396
　Peas-and-Noodles, 308
　Plum, Fresh Blue-, 385
　Raspberry, 386
　Rice, 395–97
　Rice, Caramel, 395
　Rice, Coconut, 396
　Rice, Molded, 397
　Rice, Orange, 396
　Semolina, 397
　Soufflé, Apple, 383
　Squash, 320
　Sweet Potato, 324
　Sweet Potato Coconut, 324
Puff Paste, 416
Pumpernickel, 360
Pumpkin Soup, 107
Purées,
　Lentil, 298
　Mushroom, 301
　Onion-Mustard (Soubise Moutarde), 173
　Pea, Fresh, 307
　Spinach, 319
　Turnips and Potatoes, 328

Q

Quaglia alla Diavola, 256
Quail,
　Quaglia alla Diavola, 256
　Sautéed, 261
Quenelles de Brochet Lyonnaise, 124–25
Quiches, 40–42
　Cheese and Mushroom, 41
　Crab, 41–42
　Ham, 41
　Lobster, 41–42
　Lorraine, 40–41
　Mushroom and Cheese, 41
　Salmon, 42
Quick Curry Sauce, 346
Quick Tomato Sauce, 355

R

Rabbit. *See also* Hare
　Pâté, 19–20
Radish Cakes, Chinese Black, 318
Ragout Sauce Pappagallo, 64
Raisin Orange Sauce, 229
Raisin Rum Sauce, for Apple Pudding, 383
Raisins, Measuring, 465
Raspberries (and Raspberry Dishes). *See also* Fruit Desserts
　Cobbler, 384
　Cream Pie, 424
　Cream Tart, 420
　Dressing for Vanilla Ice Cream, 450
　Ice, 448
　Ice Cream, 446
　Pie, Cream, 424
　Pudding, 386
　Sauce, 410
　Sauce, Dressing for Ice Cream, 450
　Soufflé, 378
　Trifle, 394
Ratatouille, 294–95
Ravigote Sauce, 354
Red Snapper,
　for Baking, 119
　Chowder, 116–17
　for Frying or Broiling, 120
　Grillée au Fenouil, 133
Remoulade Sauce, 353
Restaurant Voltaire,
　Dorade Grillée au Fenouil, 132–33
Restaurants. *See under names of cities or towns* Paris restaurants, Rome restaurants, etc.
Rice (and Rice Dishes), 83–88
　Balls, Fried, 84
　Boiled Brown, 85–86
　with Chicken Livers and Mushrooms, 87
　Cream with Lemon Sauce, 394
　Cream Trifle, 395
　Dumplings, 367
　Eggplant Stuffed with (Moussaka), 294
　and Lentil Casserole, 87
　Oriental Pilau, 85
　Paella, 269
　Pancakes, Brown, 368
　Peppers Stuffed with, 310
　Pilau, 147
　　Oriental, 85

Rice (*Continued*)
Tomato, 327
Pork Chops with, 218
Puddings, 395–97
Caramel, 395
Coconut, 396
Molded, 397
Orange, 396
Ring, 86
Ring, Creamed Mushrooms for, 300–1
Risotto with Patna Rice, 83
Risotto alla Principe da Napoli, 83
Risotto, Shrimp, 84
Salad, 335
Salad, with Salmon, 37
Salad, with Seafood, 336
Salad, Wild, 336
with Sausages, 84–85
Soufflé, 88
and Squabs or Game Hens, 259
-Stick Noodles, 272
Stuffing, Wild, 254
Tomato Pilau, 327
Tomatoes Stuffed with, 325
Wild, 86
Wild, Salad of, 336
Wild, Stuffing of, 254
Rich White (Béchamel) Sauce, 342
Ricotta Cheese,
Filling for Cassata alla Siciliana, 440
Pastas with. *See* Pastas
Pie, Italian, 425
Pudding, 400
Risottos,
with Patna Rice, 83
alla Principe da Napoli, 83
Shrimp, 84
Rissolée Potatoes, 195, 314
Roasting Equipment, 461
Roe à l'Ocille, Shad, 132
Rognon de Veau Grillé en Paupiette avec
Sauce Béarnaise, 195
Rognons de Boeuf, Vigneronne, 163
Rognons Fricadelles, 209
Rognons de Veau, Bercy, 195
Roll Dough, 44–45
Rolla Cake, 443
Romaine Salad with Croutons, 332
Rome restaurants,
Canepa, The, 39, 53, 84, 184
Licia Grego, 68, 69
Linda Bocconi, 276
Passetto's, 29, 182

Rome restaurants (*Continued*)
Piccolo Mondo, 63, 255, 256
Rose's Dolci Amaretti, 375
Rose's Italian Pâté of Cooked Meats, 23
Rose's Scaloppines, 186
Rose's Tuna Fish Soup, 115
Rosticceria Giuseppe (restaurant),
Bolliti with Green Sauce, 271
Rouille, 108, 109, 110
Roulade, Spinach or Pea, 54
Royal Danieli Roof (restaurant),
Noodles Danieli, 66
Rum Cake (Baba au Rhum), 442
Chocolate Pie, 423
and Coffee Ice Cream, 448
Cookies, Old Whaler, 444
-Jam Sauce for Apple Charlotte, 382
-Raisin Sauce, for Apple Soufflé Pudding,
383
Soufflé, 373
Squash Pie, 427
Syrup, 442
Rusk Crust, 441
Russian Salad, 30
Rye and Wholewheat Bread, 360

S

Sabatini (restaurant),
Bracioline alla Fiorentina, 160–61
Cannelloni alla Nizzarda, 62
Panzerotti alla Romana, 47
Risotto alla Principe da Napoli, 83
Saint Honoré, Sabatini, 398
Sabayon Sauce, 405
Saint Honoré, Sabatini, 398
Salad Dressings,
Chinese, 32
French, 333
Mayonnaise, 349
Mayonnaise, Green, 349
Mayonnaise, Sour-Cream, 349
Sour-Cream, for Cabbage Salad, 334
Sour-Cream Mayonnaise, 349
Salade Niçoise, 31
Salade Provençale, 337
Salads, 331–38
Aspic, 338
Aspic, Beet, 338
Aspic, Tomato Ring, 338

Salads (*Continued*)
  Beet Aspic, 338
  Bibb Lettuce, 331
  Cabbage, 334
  Carrot, 34
  Chef, 32
  Chicken, 30, 334
  Chicory, with Croutons, 332
  Chinese Platter, 32
  Crab, 335
  Crab and Rice, 336
  Dressings for. *See* Salad Dressings
  Egg and Potato, Hot, 337
  Endive, 333
  Entrées, 28ff.
  Field, 332
  Grapefruit, with Greens, 335
  Lettuce, Bibb, 331
  Lettuce, Romaine or Chicory with Croutons, 332
  Lettuce, Wilted, 298
  Lobster, 335
  Micheline's Rice, 335
  Niçoise, 31
  Pea, Cold, 307
  Pea, Summer Vegetable, 333
  Potato, 337
  Potato, Hot Egg and, 337
  Potato, Provençale, 337
  Rice, 335
  Rice, Salmon, 37
  Rice, and Seafood, 336
  Rice, Wild, 336
  Romaine, with Croutons, 332
  Russian, 30
  Salmon Rice, 37
  Shrimp, 335
  Shrimp and Rice, 336
  Spinach, 332
  Summer Vegetable, 333
  Swedish, 31
  Tomato Aspic Ring, 338
  Turkey, 334
  Wild Rice, 336
  Wilted Lettuce, 298
Sally Lunn, 361
Salmon,
  as Appetizer, Smoked, 38
  in Aspic, Cold Boiled, 122–23
  for Baking, 119
  Sour-Cream Tomato Sauce, 355
  Butter, 18
  Casscrole, 18

Salmon (*Continued*)
  Creamed, 122
  Dip, Red Caviar, 14–15
  with Lobster Sauce, Boiled, 124
  Mousse, 38
  Mousselines de Saumon, Adam, 120
  for Poaching, 120
  Quiche, 42
  Salad, Rice, 37
  in Seafood Pie, 135
  with Shrimp Sauce, Boiled, 123
  and Shrimp Soup, 116
Salmone Affumicato, 38
Salsify, Creamed, 297
Salt, Measuring, 465
Sampieri (restaurant),
  Dolce Sampieri, 401
  Gelati Vaniglia, 446
  Tortelloni, 69
Sandwiches, Cocktail, 15ff., 17–19
  Baked, 19
  Canapés, Caviar, 16
  Canapés, Pimento, 15
  Cocktail or Supper Loaf, 18
  Mushroom, 17
  Striped, 18
Sardine Hors d'Oeuvre, 37
Sauces, 339–56
  Agrodolce, 257
  Aioli, 340
  Aioli, Blender, 340
  Almond, 339
  Almond, for Dolci Amaretti (Dessert), 375
  Apple-Horseradish, 348
  Apricot-Mustard, 340
  Basque, 127
  Basting, for Spareribs, 220
  Béarnaise, 151, 341
  Béchamel, 47, 62, 341–42. *See also* Cream Sauces
    Medium, 342
    Rich, 342
    Thick, 188, 342
    Thin, 341
  Beet, for Soufflé, 282
  Bercy, 120–21
  Beurre Blanc for Fish, 340
  Beurre Noir, 341
  Blackberry Pudding, 385
  Blender Hollandaise or Aioli, 347
  Brandy Cream, for Steamed Puddings, 388

Sauces (*Continued*)

Broth, for Brioche de Brillat Savarin, 267
Broth, for Crab Foo Yong, 137
Broth, Mushroom, 353
Broth, for Stuffed Veal, 181
Brown, 343
Burgundy, for Oeufs Bourguignons, 51
Butter, Beurre Blanc, 340
Butter, Beurre Noir, 341
Butter, Lemon, 349
Caper, 100, 343
Caramel, 344, 405
Cardinal, 121–22
Caviar, for Veal, 174
Chantilly, 350–51
Cheese. *See also* Mornay Sauce; specific dishes
Cheese, with Ham, 187
Cheese, for Peas and Lima Beans, 307
Cheese, Tomato, 356
Cherry Pudding, 384–385
Cherry Wine, 346
Chicken Liver, 73
Chili, with Sour Cream, 345
Chinese, for Butterfly Shrimp, 37
Chinese for Chicken with Garden Greens, 274
Chinese, for Crab Foo Yong, 137
Chinese, for Eggplant, 295
Chinese, for Salad, 32
Chinese, for Shrimp in Egg White, 274
Chinese, for Steak Flambé, 273
Chocolate, 405
Chocolate, Thin, 401
Clam, 65
Coconut Cream, 392
Cranberry, 345
Cranberry Jelly, 345
Cranberry Red Wine, 344
Cream, 24, 64, 146. *See* also Béchamel Sauces; Coconut Cream Sauce; Mushroom Cream Sauce; etc.
 for Dessert Crêpes, 404
 for Dessert Soufflé, 373
 for Egg Sauce, 345
 for Lobster, 140
 for Lobster Sauce, 352
 for Noodle Casserole, 76
 for Seafood Casserole, 125
 Shrimp-Flavored, 60
 for Soubise Sauce, 352
Crème Fraîche, 342
Creole, 192

Sauces (*Continued*)

Creole, for Fish or Omelettes, 345
Crevettes, 137
Cucumber, 131–32
Cumin, 204
Curaçao, for Bananas, 400
Curry. *See* Curries and Curry Sauces
Dill, for Squash, 321
Dipping, for Shrimp, 37
Egg, for Boiled Fish, 345
Gin, for Venison, 168
Ginger, for Ice Cream, 450
Goulash, for Leftover Meats, 346
Grand Veneur, 198
Green, 271
Green, for Egg Noodles, 71
Green Mayonnaise, 349
Ham, 249
Ham and Cheese, 187
Hollandaise, 347
Hollandaise, Variation for Brussels Sprouts, 283
Horseradish Apple, 248
Horseradish, Hot, 348
Horseradish Sour Cream, 348
Jam-Rum, for Apple Charlotte, 382
Jelly, 348. *See also* Jelly
Lemon, 383
Lemon Butter, 349
Lemon, Carrots with, 286
Liqueur, 375, 403
Lobster, 124, 141, 352
Madeira Cream, for Pojarsky, 183
Marmalade, 386
Marsala, for Dolce Vasco (Dessert), 402
Mayonnaise, 349–50
Mayonnaise Cream, 350
Mayonnaise, Garlic. *See* Aioli Sauce
Mayonnaise, Green, 349
Mayonnaise, Mustard, 350
Mayonnaise, Sour-Cream, 349
Meat, for Pastas, 74, 355
Mint, 349
Mornay, 44, 173, 351
Mousseline, 350–51
Mushroom, 24, 277
Mushroom Broth, 353
Mushroom, for Chicken Demi-Deuil, 233
Mushroom, for Chicken Pie, 238
Mushroom Cream, 353
Mustard, 173, 351
Mustard Apricot, 340

Sauces (*Continued*)
Mustard Mayonnaise, 350
Mustard Wine, 351
Onion, 304–5
Onion (Soubise), 352
Onion-Mustard (Soubise Moutarde), 173
Orange, 396
Orange, Beets with, 281
Orange, for Carrots, 286, 353
Orange Raisin, 229
Pesto, 72, 73
Pistou, 106
Quick Curry, 346
Quick Tomato, 355
Pasta. *See under* Pastas
Perigourdine, 25
Port Wine Jelly, 356
Ragout, 64
Raisin-Orange, 229
Raisin-Rum, for Apple Pudding, 383
Raspberry, 410
Raspberry, for Ice Cream, 450
Ravigote, 354
Remoulade, 353
Rum-Jam, for Apple Charlotte, 382
Rum-Raisin, for Apple Pudding, 383
Saupiquet, 270–71
Shrimp, 123, 137, 354
Sicilian, 72
Simple Syrup, 356
Soubise, 352
Soubise Mustard, 173
Sour Cream Chili, 345
Sour Cream Horseradish, 348
Sour Cream Mayonnaise, 349
Sour Cream Tomato, 180, 355
Spaghetti, 69. *See also* Pastas: Sauces for
Spaghetti, Tuna Fish, 68
Spinach, 320
Steak. *See* Beef: Steak
Strawberry, 410
Strawberry, for Ice Cream, 450
Tartar, 350
Tomato, 87, 354–55
Tomato Cheese, 356
Tomato Cream, for Crêpes, 226
Tomato Cream, for Ham Tetrazzini, 225–26
Tomato, for Dill Dumplings, 327
Tomato, Fresh, 354
Tomato, Meat, 355
Tomato, for Pork Chops, 216
Tomato, Quick, 355

Sauces (*Continued*)
Tomato Sour Cream, 180, 355
Tongue, 249
Tuna, 68, 177
Veloute, 127, 342
Wine, 153
Wine, Cherry, 346
Wine, Cranberry, 344
Wine, Jelly, 356
Wine, Mustard, 351
Sauerbraten, 156–57
Sauerkraut,
Choucroute, 223
with Grapes, 285
with Knackwurst, 285
with Knackwurst and Ham in Casserole, 225
with Pork Goulash, 215
Saulieu, Hôtel de la Côte d'Or at, 49, 58
Saupiquet, 271
Sausage, 219
Butter, 18
in Cassoulet, 266
in Chipolata, 157
with Kidney Beans, Baked, 281
for Noodle Casserole, 76
Polenta, 77
Rice with, 84–85
Sauerkraut with Knackwurst, 285
Sauerkraut with Knackwurst and Ham, 225
Zucchini Stuffed with, 329
Savarin, 442
Scaloppine Passetto, 182
Scaloppine San Giorgio, 184
Scaloppines, Rose's, 186
Scallops,
Coquilles St. Jacques, 144
in Fritto Misto, 272
in Gratin aux Fruits de Mer, 142
and Mushrooms, Broiled, 144–45
for Noodle Casserole, 76
in Seafood Pie, 135
Scampi Canepa, 39
Scampi Cocktail, 40
Sciué Sciué, Frank's, 67
Scones, Potato, 368
Scotch Broth, 101
with Neck of Lamb or Mutton, 100
Sea Bass,
for Baking, 119
Chowder, 116–17
à la Crème, Fillets of, 134–35

Sea Bass (*Continued*)
  Grillée au Fenouil, 133
  with Marinade, Chinese, 131
Sea Trout, for Frying or Broiling, 120
Seafood. *See also* Fish and Shellfish; Lobster; Shrimp; etc.
  Bisque, 111
  Filling for Noodle Casserole, 76
  Gratin aux Fruits de Mer, 142
  Pie, 135
Semifreddo allo Zabaione, 399
Semolina Pudding, 397
Sformato de Banane, 400
Shad, for Baking, 119
Shad Roe à l'Oeille, 132
Sharp Sauce, 270–71
Shellfish. *See* Fish and Shellfish; Seafood; specific kinds
Sherbet, Orange, with Fruit and Kirsch, 449
Sherry, Roast Veal with, 197
Shish Kebab, 211
Shrimp,
  Bisque, 111
  Broiled, 147
  Broiled au Pierre, 39
  Butter, 18
  Butterfly, 37
  Cocktail, 39
  Creamed Stuffed Eggs, 60
  in Creole Gumbo, 113
  Curry, 148
  in Egg White, 274
  Flamingo, 147
  alla Freddy, 148
  in Fritto Misto, 272
  in Gratin aux Fruits de Mer, 142
  for Noodle Casserole, 76
  for Paella, 269
  au Pierre, Broiled, 39
  and Rice Salad, 336
  Risotto, 84
  Salad, 335
  Salad, Rice, 336
  and Salmon Soup, 116
  Sauce, 123, 137, 354
  Scampi Canepa, 39
  Scampi Cocktail, 40
  in Seafood Pie, 135
  Soup, Salmon with, 116
Sicilian Sauce for Egg Noodles, 72
Simple Syrup, 356
Skillet Bread, 369

Smelts, for Frying or Broiling, 120
Snapper. *See* Red Snapper
Sole,
  Albert, 130
  Fish Stew, 112–13
  for Frying or Broiling, 120
  Fillets with Anchovy Butter, 126
  Fillets in Wine or Cream, 128
  Normande, 129
  Soupe au Poisson à la Rouille, 110
  Turban of, 130
Sorrel Soup, 98
  Potage Germiny, 97
Soubise Sauce, 352
  Mustard, 173
Soufflé Pudding, Apple, 383
Soufflé Puff Cake, 382
Soufflés,
  Anisette, 374
  Beet, 282
  Benedictine, 376
  Caramel, Cold, 374
  Carrot-Orange, 286–87
  Cheese, Egg-White, 78–79
  Cheese, Lazette's Famous, 80
  Cheese, for Three or Four, 79
  Chestnut, 389
  Coconut, 376
  Curaçao, 374, 376
  Dessert, 372–79
  Dolci Amaretti, 377
  Fish, 136
  Fruit Egg-White, 377
  Grand Marnier, 374, 376
  Ham, 229
  Kirsch, 379
  Lemon, 377
  Liqueur, 372, 274. *See also* specific liqueurs
  Marasquin, 376
  Mocha, 373
  Mushroom, 60
  Noodle, 74
  Onion, 306
  Orange, 378
  Orange-Carrot, 286–87
  Pea, 309
  Raspberry, 378
  Rice, 88
  Rum, 373
  Spinach, 319
  Strawberry, 378
  Surprise, 50

Soufflés (Continued)
  Sweet Potato, 323
Soupe au Pistou, 106
Soupe au Poisson à la Rouille, 110
Soups, 89–117
  Anguilles au Vert, 117
  Bean, 90–91
  Beef Gravy, 101
  Beet, Borscht, 91
  Beet, and Fruit, 91
  Bisque, Seafood, 111
  Bisque, Sweet Potato, 323
  Borscht, 91
  Bouillabaisse, 108–9
  Bouillon, Clear, 98–99
  Bourride, La, 109
  Broths. See Broth
  Burgundy Fish Stew, 107
  Cantaloupe, 92
  Carrot, 92
  Carrot Consommé, 93
  Carrot and Orange, 93
  Carrot and Tomato, 93
  Carrot and Tomato Juice, 92
  Celery and Tomato, 102
  Chestnut, 93–94
  Chicken, 103
  Chicken and Corn Chowder, 94
  Chicken Egg, 102–3
  Chicken Gravy, 101
  Chowder, Clam, 111, 112
  Chowder, Corn and Chicken, 94
  Chowder, Red Snapper or Sea Bass,
    116–17
  Clam Chowder, 111, 112
  Clam and Mussel, 112
  Consommé, Carrot, 93
  Consommé, Cheese Balls for, 100
  Consommé with Noodles (Tagliarini),
    99
  Consommé, Turtle, with Madeira, 117
  Corn and Chicken Chowder, 94
  Crab Bisque, 111
  Cream Vegetable, 105
  Creole Oyster Gumbo, 113
  Eels au Vert, 117
  Egg, 102
  Eggs Poached in, 57
  Fish, 107–17
  Fruit and Beet, 91
  Gazpacho, 104
  Gravy, 100
  Gumbo, Oyster, 113

Soups (Continued)
  Hungarian Mushroom, 105
  Italian Clam and Mussel, 112
  Leek and Potato, 94
  Lentil, 95
  Lobster Bisque, 111
  Lobster Stew, 114
  Minestrone, 104
  Mushroom, Fresh, 95
  Mushroom, Hungarian, 105
  Mussel, 114
  Mussel and Clam, 112
  Myron's Clam Chowder, 112
  Onion, 99
  Orange and Carrot, 93
  Oyster Gumbo, 113
  Oyster Stew, 115
  Pea, 96
  Pea and Turtle, 105
  au Pistou, 106
  au Poisson à la Rouille, 110
  Potage Germiny, 97
  Potage Marron Suprème, Grebanier, 93–
    94
  Potato and Leek, 94
  Potato, Sweet, 107
  Potato, Sweet, Bisque of, 323
  Potato, Vichyssoise, 97
  Pumpkin, 107
  Red Snapper Chowder, 116–17
  Rose's Tuna Fish, 115
  Salmon and Shrimp, 116
  Scotch Broth, 100, 101
  Sea Bass Chowder, 116–17
  Seafood Bisque, 111
  Shrimp Bisque, 111
  Shrimp and Salmon, 116
  Sorrel, 98
  Sorrel, Potage Germiny, 97
  Spinach, 96–97
  Split-Pea, 96
  Squash, 107
  Sweet Potato, 107
  Sweet Potato Bisque, 323
  Tagliarini al Consommé, 99
  Tomato, 102
  Tomato and Carrot, 93
  Tomato and Celery, 102
  Tomato Juice and Carrot, 92
  Tuna Fish, 115
  Turkey Egg, 102
  Turkey Gravy, 101
  Turkey Wing, 103

Soups (*Continued*)
Turtle Consommé with Madeira, 117
Turtle and Pea, 105
Vegetable and Meat, 90–107
Vichyssoise, 97
Watercress, 98
Sour-Cherry Cobbler, 384
Sour Cream (and Sour-Cream Dishes),
with Chili Sauce, 345
Cornbread, 366
Dressing for Cabbage Salad, 33
Horseradish Sauce, 348
Ice Cream, 449
Mayonnaise, 349
Measuring, 464
in Meat Dishes. *See* specific meats
Pancakes, 369
Tomato Sauce, 180, 355
Tomatoes with, 326
Spaghetti Napolitana, 69
Spaghetti Sauce, 69. *See also* Pastas:
Sauces for
Tuna Fish, 68
Spaghetti alla Tonnara, 68
Spanish Eggs, Eve's, 56
Spareribs,
Baked, 218
Barbecued, 220
Chinese Glazed, 221
Chinese Sweet-and-Sour, 220–21
Special Dishes, 265–74
Baeckenofe, Le, 270
Bolliti with Green Sauce, 271
Brioche de Brillat Savarin, 267
Cassoulet with Duck, 266
Chicken with Garden Greens, 274
Chinese Rice-Stick Noodles, 272
Chinese Steak Flambé, 273
Couscous Libanais, 268
Désir des Gourmets, 265
Fritto Misto, 272
Lièvre en Saupiquet, 270–71
Paella, 269
Shrimp in Egg White, 274
Spices, Basic, 462–63
Spinach, 318–20
Bolognese, 320
Buttered, 318–19
Pasta, 70
Purée, 319
Ring, Creamed Mushrooms for, 300–1
Roulade, 54
Salad, 332

Spinach (*Continued*)
Soufflé, 319
Soup, 96–97
Spinaci Bolognese, 320
Split Peas,
Mashed, 308
Pork Chops with, 221
Soup of, 96
Sponge Cake, Butter, 429
Spotted Trout, for Frying or Broiling, 120
Spread, Anchovy Garlic, 15
Spumoni, 449
Squab, 259
Sautéed, 261
Smitane, 260
Squash, 320–21
Acorn, Pudding, 320
Acorn, Rum Pie, 427
Bush Scallop, 321
Butternut, 321
Butternut, Mashed, 321
Crookneck, 321
with Dill Sauce, Yellow Summer, 321
Hubbard, Pudding, 320
Hubbard, Rum Pie, 427
Mashed Butternut, 321
Pudding, 320
Rum Pie, 427
Soup, 107
Summer, with Dill Sauce, 321
Zucchini, 328–29
Baked, 329
al Forno, 328–29
Italian Style, 329
Stuffed, 29
Stuffed with Sausage, 329
Steak. *See under* Beef
Stock, Fish, 115, 127, 134
Stock, White, 252
Strasbourg restaurants,
Maison Kammerzell, 188, 223, 233, 270
Valentin-Sorg, 128–29, 404
Strawberries (and Strawberry Dishes). *See
also* Fruit Desserts
Cake (Gâteau aux Fraises), 439
Cobbler, 384
Cream Tart, 420
Dressing for Vanilla Ice Cream, 450
Pudding. *See* Raspberry Pudding
Sauce, 410
Sauce, Dressing for Ice Cream, 450
Soufflé, 378
Tart, 419

Strawberries (*Continued*)
  Tart, Cream, 420
  Trifle, 394
Strega, Macedonia al, 413
Striped Bass, for Baking, 119
Striped Sandwich, 18
Stufatino de Manzo con Peperoni alla Romana, 161
Stuffings, Poultry. *See also* specific fowl
  Apple and Raisin, 263
  Chestnut, 262
  Fruit, 263
  Oyster, for Small Birds, 261
  Potato, 262
  Wild Rice, 254
Succotash, 322
Suckling Pig, Roast, 224
Sugar, Measuring, 465
Sugar Crust, 417
Summer Squash with Dill Sauce, 321
Summer Vegetable Salad, 333
Supper Loaf, 18
Supplies, Pantry, 462–63
Suprême de Barbue Bordelaise, 134
Susanne's Poppy Seed Cake, 433
Swedish Anchovy Potatoes, 316
Swedish Limpa Bread, 359
Swedish Salad, 31
Sweet Potatoes, 322–25
  Bisque of, 323
  Cakes of, 323
  Caramel, 323
  Ham and, 228
  Mashed, 322
  Orange, Blazed, 323
  in Pimento Forms, 323
  Pimentos Stuffed with, 324–25
  Soufflé of, 323
  Soup of, 107
  Soup of, Bisque, 323
  Pudding, 324
  Pudding, Coconut, 324
Sweet-and-Sour Sauce, 220–21
Sweet-and-Sour Spareribs, 220–21
Sweetbreads,
  in Brioche de Brillat Savarin, 267
  in Cream, 191
  Creole, 192
  in Fritto Misto, 272
  with Ham, 193
  with Madeira Sauce, 190–91
  for Noodle Casserole, 76
  Sautéed, 192

Sweetbreads (*Continued*)
  Tetrazzini, 191
Sweeteners, Basic, 463
Swiss Steak Fondue, 156
Swordfish,
  with Cucumber Sauce, Broiled, 131
  for Frying or Broiling, 120
Syrups,
  Caramel, 344
  Rum, 442
  Simple, 356

T

Tagliarini al Consommé, 99
Tarama, 15
Tartar Sauce, 350
Tarte au Citron, 420
Tarts, 417–22
  Alsatian Apple, 417
  Apple, 418
  Apple, Alsatian, 417
  Apricot Torta, Italian, 421
  Berry, 419
  Blackberry, 419
  Blackberry Cream, 420
  Blueberry, 419
  Cherry, Lorraine, 419
  Chestnut, 418
  au Citron, 420
  Clafoutis, 419
  Coconut, 422
  Cream, 420
  Italian Apricot Torta, 421
  Italian Marzipan, 421
  Lemon (au Citron), 420
  Lorraine Cherry, 419
  Marzipan Torta, Italian, 421
  Old-Fashioned Coconut, 422
  Onion, 43
  Peach, 418
  Raspberry Cream, 420
  Strawberry, 419
  Strawberry Cream, 420
Taverna la Felice (restaurant),
  Pesto Sauce, 73
  Piccata alla Pizzaiola, 185
Terrapin, Creamed, 128
Terrine de Lapin Lorraine, La, 19–20

Terrines. *See* Pâtés and Terrines
Thick White (Béchamel) Sauce, 188, 342
Thin White (Béchamel) Sauce, 341
Thoissey, Chapon Fin at, 26–28, 47–48, 134–35, 233
3 G Rosticceria Ristorante (restaurant),
  Agnello dell'Accademico, 198–99
  Sformato de Banane, 400
Toast,
  Cheese, 81
  for Fish Soup, 110
Tomatoes (and Tomato Dishes), 325–27
  Aspic Ring, 338
  Baked, 325
  Cheese-Egg Hors d'Oeuvre, 36
  Creole, 326
  Ham-Stuffed, 326
  Italian Stuffed, 325
  Pilau, 327
  Sauces, 37, 354–55
    Cheese, 356
    Cream, for Crêpes, 226
    Cream, for Ham Tetrazzini, 225–26
    for Dill Dumplings, 327
    Fresh, 354
    Meat, 355
    for Pork Chops, 216
    Quick, 355
    Sour-Cream, 180, 355
  Soup, with Carrot, 92, 93
  Soup, with Celery, 102
  Soup, Fresh, 102
  with Sour Cream, 326
  Stuffed, 325, 326
Tom's Shangri-La (restaurant),
  Chicken with Garden Greens, 274
  Chinese Rice-Stick Noodles, 272
  Chinese Steak Flambé, 273
  Shrimp in Egg White, 274
Tongue, Boiled Fresh, 171
Tongue Sauce, 249
Torte, Italian Apricot, 421
Torte, Italian Marzipan, 421
Tortellini alla Bolognese, 70
Tortellini alla Panna, 71
Tortelloni, 69
Tournedos Belle Hélène, 151
Tournedos aux Champignons, 150–51
Trattoria alla Madonna (restaurant),
  Polenta, 78
Trifle, 394
  Courthouse, 394
  Rice Cream, 395

Trout,
  for Baking, 119
  Burgundy Fish Stew, 107
  for Frying or Broiling, 120
  Truite Lucullus, 128–29
  Truites Farcies Basquaise, 127
Truffles, 300. *See also* specific dishes
Truffles, Chestnut (confection), 445
Truite Lucullus, 128–29
Truites Farcies Basquaise, 127
Tuna Fish,
  Casserole, 125
  Dip, Red Caviar, 14–15
  Rice Salad, 335
  Sauces, 68, 177
  Soup, 115
Turinoise, Le, 388
Turkey,
  Buongustaia Nerina, 250
  Chestnut Stuffing for, 262
  Creamed, 245
  Fillets of, 250
  Fillets alla Freddy, 250
  Pancakes Richelieu, 248
  Pie, 244–45
  Potato Stuffing for, 262
  Roast, 230–31
  Salad, 334
  Soups, 101–3
    Egg, 102
    Gravy, 101
    Wing, 103
  Steamed in Wine, 243–44
Turkish Kebabs, 203
Turnips, 328
  and Cream, 328
  and Potatoes, Puréed, 328
Turtle Consommé with Madeira, 117
Turtle and Pea Soup, 105

Valentin-Sorg (restaurant),
  Crêpes au Kirsch, Surprise, 404
  Truite Lucullus, 128–29
Vanilla Filling for Crescent Rolls, 364–65
Vanilla Ice Cream, 446
  French, 445
  Ginger Sauce for, 450
  Mangos with, 450

Vanilla Ice Cream (Continued)
  Raspberry Dressing for, 450
  Strawberry Dressing for, 450
Veal, 172–95
  Blanquette de Veau, 178
  Bolliti with Green Sauce, 271
  Brains, Beurre Noir, 194
  Brains, Cervelle de Veau aux Pistaches, 193
  Brains, in Fritto Misto, 272
  Brains, with Ham, 193
  Broth, 180–81
  with Buttermilk Marinade, Roast, 206
  Calf's Brains Beurre Noir, 194
  Calf's Brains, Cervelle de Veau aux Pistaches, 193
  Calf's Brains, in Fritto Misto, 272
  Calf's Brains, with Ham, 193
  Calf's Liver. See Liver
  Cannelloni Stuffed with, 61, 62
  Caviar Sauces for Roast, 174, 343
  Cervelle de Veau aux Pistaches, 193
  with Cheese, Baked Chops, 242
  with Cheese and Ham Sauce, 187
  with Cheese and Port, Roast, 174–75
  Chops, 188
  Chops with Cheese, Baked, 242
  Chops Surprise, Alsacienne, 188
  with Cumin Sauce, Cooked, 204
  Curry Sauce for Cooked, 205
  Cutlet alla Canepa, 184
  Cutlet alla Freddy, 250
  Cutlets Pappagallo, 177
  Escalope de Veau à la Crème, 184
  Filets de Veau à la Moutarde, 172–73
  with Ham and Mozzarella, 185
  Italian Meatballs, 163
  Italian Roast, 177
  Jarrets de Veau à l'Orange, 176
  Kidneys. See Kidneys
  and Liver Loaf, 190
  and Liver Meatballs and Sauce, 180
  Marengo, 178–79
  Meatballs, Italian, 163
  Meatballs, with Liver, 180
  Meatballs, Tiny, 267
  Meat Loaf, with Liver, 190
  with Mushrooms and Cream, Breast of, 180–81
  Osso Buco, 175
  Pâtés. See Pâtés and Terrines
  Piccata alla Pizzaiola, 185
  Pie, 210

Veal (Continued)
  Pojarsky aux Pommes Amandines, 183
  Rognon de Veau Grillé en Paupiette avec Sauce Béarnaise, 195
  Rognons de Veau, Bercy, 195
  with Rosemary, Roast, 174
  Rose's Scaloppines, 186
  Scaloppine Passetto, 182
  Scaloppine San Giorgio, 184
  Scaloppines, Rose's, 186
  with Sour Cream and Mushrooms, 186
  Stew with Dumplings, 179
  Stew with Leeks, 211
  Stuffed Breast of, 181
  Stuffed Rolled Cutlet, 187
  Sweetbreads in Cream, 191
  Sweetbreads Creole, 192
  Sweetbreads with Ham, 193
  Sweetbreads with Madeira Sauce, 190–91
  Sweetbreads, Sautéed, 192
  Sweetbreads Tetrazzini, 191
  with Tuna Sauce (Vitello Tonnato), 177
  Vitello Castellana, 182–83
  Vitello Tonnato, 177
  Wiener Schnitzel, 186
Vegetable Entrées, 28–36
  Antipastos, 29–30
  Artichoke Egg Hors d'Oeuvre, 36
  Artichokes à la Grècque, 33
  Asparagus, 31
  Aubergines pour Hors d'Oeuvre Froid, 28
  Avocado Egg Hors d'Oeuvre, 36
  "Caviar," Eggplant, 34
  Cèleri-rave, 35
  Champignons à la Grècque, 33
  Cheese-Egg-Tomato Hors d'Oeuvre, 36
  Egg Hors d'Oeuvre, Avocado or Artichoke, 36
  Egg Hors d'Oeuvre, Tomato-Cheese, 36
  Eggplant "Caviar," 34
  Eggplant Hors d'Oeuvre, 28
  Eggplant, Stuffed, 29
  Endive à la Grècque, 33
  Mushrooms à la Grècque, 33
  Mushrooms, Stuffed, 34
  Okra à la Turc, 35
  Peppers, Stuffed, 29, 35
  Tomato-Cheese-Egg Hors d'Oeuvre, 36
  Zucchini, Stuffed, 29
Vegetable Soups, 90–99ff.
  Bean, 90–91

Vegetable Soups (*Continued*)
Beet, Borscht, 91
Beet and Fruit, 91
Borscht, 91
Cantaloupe, 92
Carrot, 92
Carrot Consommé, 93
Carrot and Orange, 93
Carrot and Tomato, 93
Carrot and Tomato Juice, 92
Celery and Tomato, 102
Chestnut, 93–94
Chowder, Corn and Chicken, 94
Consommé, Carrot, 93
Corn and Chicken Chowder, 94
Cream, 105
Fruit and Beet, 91
Gazpacho, 104
Hungarian Mushroom, 105
Leek and Potato, 94
Lentil, 95
Minestrone, 104
Mushroom, 95
Mushroom, Hungarian, 105
Onion, 99
Orange and Carrot, 93
Pea, 96
Pea and Turtle, 105
au Pistou, 106
Potage Germiny, 97
Potage Marron Suprème, 93–94
Potato, with Leeks, 94
Potato, Sweet, 107
Potato, Sweet, Bisque of, 323
Potato, Vichyssoise, 97
Pumpkin, 107
Sorrel, 98
Sorrel, Potage Germiny, 97
Spinach, 96–97
Split-Pea, 96
Squash, 107
Sweet Potato, 107
Sweet Potato Bisque, 323
Tomato, 102
Tomato and Carrot, 92, 93
Tomato and Celery, 102
Vichyssoise, 97
Watercress, 98
Vegetables, 275–329. *See also* Vegetable
Entrées; Vegetable Soups; specific
vegetables
with Aioli Dip, Raw, 15
in Fritto Misto, 272

Vegetables (*Continued*)
Pork Roast with, 215
Velouté Sauce, 127, 342
Venice restaurants,
"Al Teatro" Pizza Palace, 43
Hotel Danieli, 147, 184
Royal Danieli Roof, 66
Taverna la Fenice, 73, 185
Trattoria alla Madonna, 78
Venison,
Braised, 168
with Buttermilk Marinade, Roast, 206
Steak, 168
Vermouth, Roast Veal with, 198
Vichyssoise, 97
Vinaigrette Sauce, 276
Vitello Castellana, 182–83
Vitello Tonnato, 177
Volaille à la Crème, La, 233

W

Wafers, Cheddar Cheese, 17
Walnut Cake, Black, with Caramel Frost-
ing, 435
Walnuts, Measuring, 465
Water, Measuring, 465
Watercress Soup, 98
Wax Beans, 278–79
Weakfish, for Baking, 119
Weights and Measures, 464–65
White Beans,
Cassoulet, 266
Lamb with, 200–1
White Boiled Frosting, 438
White Fruitcake, 434
White Sauce. *See* Béchamel Sauces
White Stock, 252
Whitefish,
for Baking, 119
Fillets, Baked Stuffed, 126
Fillets in Wine or Cream, 128
for Frying or Broiling, 120
Wholewheat and Rye Bread, 360
Wiener Schnitzel, 186
Wild Rice,
Baked, 86
Salad, 336
Stuffing, 254
Wine. *See also* specific wines
and Cheese Paste, 16

Wine (*Continued*)
  Jelly, 356, 414
  Melon with, 409
  Sauce, Cherry, for Ham, 346
  Sauce, Cranberry, 344
  Sauce, Mustard, 351
  Sauces for Steak, 153

Y

Yellow Butter Cake, 430
Yellow Perch, for Frying or Broiling, 120
Yellow Pike, for Frying or Broiling, 120

Yellow Summer Squash with Dill Sauce,
  321
Yellow Wax Beans, 278–79

Z

Zabaione, 399, 402
Zucchini, 328–29
  Baked, 329
  al Forno, 328–29
  Italian Style, 329
  Stuffed, 29
  Stuffed with Sausage, 329